Social Problems

To B. D. S. and B. W. S.

Social Problems
Community, Policy, and Social Action

Anna Leon-Guerrero
Pacific Lutheran University

www sage pub . com

PINE FORGE PRESS
An Imprint of Sage Publications, Inc.
Thousand Oaks • London • New Delhi

For information:

Pine Forge Press
A Sage Publications Company
2455 Teller Road
Thousand Oaks, California 91320
E-mail: order@sagepub.com

Sage Publications Ltd.
1 Oliver's Yard
55 City Road
London EC1Y 1SP
United Kingdom

Sage Publications India Pvt. Ltd.
B-42, Panchsheel Enclave
Post Box 4109
New Delhi 110 017 India

Printed in the United States of America

Library of Congress Cataloging-in-Publication Data

Leon-Guerrero, Anna.
Social problems : community, policy, and social action / Anna Leon-Guerrero.
    p. cm.
Includes bibliographical references and index.
   ISBN 0-7619-8782-7 (pbk.)
1. Social problems—United States. 2. Social problems. 3. Critical thinking. I. Title.
HN59.2.L46 2005
361.1'0973—dc22

                                    2004023028

This book is printed on acid-free paper.

05   06   07   08   09   10   9   8   7   6   5   4   3   2   1

Acquisitions Editor:	Jerry Westby
Editorial Assistants:	Vonessa Vondera/Laura K. Shigemitsu
Production Editor:	Kristen Gibson
Copy Editor:	Jacqueline Tasch
Typesetter:	C&M Digitals (P) Ltd.
Cover Designer:	Glenn Vogel

Contents

gwb

Preface

During the 2004 presidential campaign, the majority of Americans identified the threat of terrorism, the U.S.-Iraq war, the economy, and health care as our most important social problems. When surveyed, individuals explained that they were voting for a particular candidate because of how well they thought he would handle these issues.

Although social problems are an important part of our lives, even determining the outcome of presidential elections, many people still do not understand the problems we face. Perhaps you are like the many students in my classroom who have never met a homeless person, never been a victim of a violent crime, or never experienced discrimination. How much do you really know about homelessness, violent crime, or discrimination?

I wrote this text with two goals in mind: to offer a better understanding of social problems and to begin working toward real solutions. In the pages that follow, I present three connections that you can use to increase your understanding. The first connection is the one between sociology and the study of social problems. Using your sociological imagination (which you'll learn more about in Chapter 1), you will be able to identify the social and structural forces that determine our social problems. I think you'll discover that this course will be interesting, challenging, and sometimes frustrating. After you review these different social problems you may ask, "What can be done about all this?" The second connection that will be made is between social problems and their solutions. In each chapter, we will review selected social policies along with innovative community programs that attempt to address or correct these problems. The final connection is the one that I ask you to make yourself: recognizing the social problems and identifying how you can be part of the solution in your community.

To assist your learning, this text includes a variety of special features.

A focus on the basis of social inequalities. Throughout the text, we will examine how race, gender, social class, sexual orientation, and age determine our life chances. Chapters 2 and 3 are special chapters that focus on why we are different and how our differences contribute to our experience of social problems.

A focus on social policy and social action. Each chapter includes a discussion on relevant social policies or programs. In addition, each chapter highlights how individuals or groups have made a difference in their community. The text concludes with a chapter, "Social Problems and Social Action," that identifies ways you can become more involved.

Voices in the community. The chapters include personal stories from people experiencing social problems or attempting to make a difference in their community. Some of these stories come from professionals in their field; others come from ordinary individuals who accomplish extraordinary things. For example, in Chapter 3, you'll be introduced to Bernice R. Sandler, the woman behind Title IX, and in Chapter 8, you'll meet Linda Elliot, a parent who decided to do something about unchaperoned teen parties in her community.

Putting it together and Internet and Community Exercises. Each chapter includes questions or activities that can be completed by small student groups or on your own. Some of the exercises ask you to reflect on the material in the chapter. But many of the exercises require you to collect data and information on what is going on in your own state, city, or campus. These exercises take you out of the classroom, away from the textbook, and into your community!

Taking a World View. In this boxed feature, social problems are examined from a global perspective. We will take a look at Canada's livable cities (Chapter 12), India's all female international news organization (Chapter 11), and Mexico's maquiladoras (Chapter 6).

Visual essays. Each chapter includes a visual essay, a collection of photos focusing on a particular social problem. Several of the essays focus on emerging solutions: Different housing programs for the poor and homeless are profiled in Chapter 12 and new systems of health care are identified in Chapter 7.

I wanted to write a book that captured the experiences that I've shared with students in my own social problems course. I sensed the frustration and futility that many felt by the end of the semester—imagine all those weeks of discussing nothing else but "problems"! I decided that my message about the importance of *understanding social problems* should be complemented with a message on the importance of *taking social action.*

Social action doesn't just happen in Washington, D.C., or in your state's capital, and political leaders aren't the only ones engaged in such efforts. Social action takes place on your campus, in your neighborhood, in your town, in whatever you define as your "community." I knew that there were stories to be told by ordinary people—community, church, business, or student leaders—who recognized that they had the power to make a difference in the community. Each semester, I brought these individuals into the classroom to share their stories, but also to illustrate that despite the persistence of many social problems, members of our community have not given up. Their stories inspired me and my students to find our own paths to social action.

I hope that by the time you reach the end of this text, with your newfound sociological imagination, you will find your own path to social action. Wherever it leads you, good luck.

Acknowledgments

My heartfelt appreciation goes to Jerry Westby and his team at Pine Forge Press. In particular, I would like to acknowledge the invaluable support and feedback provided throughout this project by Jerry and Denise Simon. Special thanks to Katja Werlich Fried, Vonessa Vondera, Kristen Gibson, and Karen Wiley for getting me through the production process. I am indebted to Becky Smith, for her contribution of the visual essays in each chapter; to Jacqueline Tasch, for her editing and patience with my many revisions; to Mark Guillette, for his work on the instructor's manual; and to Heather Feldhaus, for her work on the PowerPoint slides.

The following sociologists served as the first audience and reviewers for this text.

Arfa Aflatooni, *Linn-Benton Community College*

Joanne Ardovini, *Sam Houston State University*

Bernadette Barton, *Morehead State University*

Allison Camelot, *California State University, Fullerton*

Janine Dewitt-Heffner, *Marymount University*

Dan Dexheimer, *University of Florida*

Woody Doane, *University of Hartford*

Joe Dupris, *California State University, Humboldt*

Rachel Einwohner, *Purdue University*

Heather Smith Feldhaus, *Bloomsburg University*

Jim Fenelon, *California State University, San Bernardino*

Bobbie Fields, *Central Piedmont Community College*

Debbie Franzman, *Allan Hancock College*

Marcie Goodman, *University of Utah*

George Gross, *Northern Michigan University*

Mark J. Guillette, *Valencia Community College*

Julia Hall, *Drexel University*

Dan W. Hayden, *University of Southern Indiana*

Chuck Holm, *San Diego State University*

Leslie Houts, *University of Florida*

James R. Hunter, *Indiana University—Purdue University at Indianapolis*

K. Land, *Duke University*

Nick Larson, *Chapman University*

Stephen Light, *SUNY Plattsburgh*

Dennis Loo, *Cal Poly Pomona*

Scott Lukas, *Lake Tahoe Community College*

Kari Lerum, *Seattle University*

Christina Myers, *Oklahoma State University*

Paul Roof, *San Juan College*

Kim Saliba, *Portland Community College*

Norma K. Simmons, *Washington State University*

Deborah Sullivan, *Arizona State University*

Mary Texeira, *California State University, San Bernardino*

Linda A. Treiber, *North Carolina State University*

Gailynn White, *Citrus College*

Anthony W. Zumpetta, *West Chester University*

Thank you all for your encouragement and for your insightful critiques.

I am greatly indebted to my talented sociology students who provided research assistance for this text: Nova Schauss, Emily Brown, Heather Ottum, and Elizabeth Widmer.

I wish to express my appreciation to my family, friends, and colleagues, all of whom endured my never-ending stories about this text. Mahalo for supporting my work. And special thanks to Jacob and Molly.

I dedicate this book to the two people who have been there from the very beginning of this journey: to my mentor, Byron D. Steiger, and to my husband, Brian W. Sullivan. From Byron, I learned the importance of loving one's work. Thank you for showing me what an excellent teacher can and should be. From Brian, I learned the value of caring for one's community and the environment. Thank you for all that you do—this book would not have been possible without you.

Sociology and the Study of Social Problems

I f I asked everyone in your class what they believe is the most important social problem facing the United States, there would be many different answers. Terrorism. Poverty. Unemployment. AIDS. Crime. Drug abuse. Are all of these social problems? Most would agree that some or all of these social conditions are problems. But which is the most important, and how would we solve it? The answers to these questions may not be so straightforward. If you think about it, this is how we spend much of our public conversation—on the Senate floor, on afternoon talk shows, at work, or in the classroom—arguing, analyzing, and just trying to figure which problem is most serious and what needs to be done about it. In casual or sometimes heated conversations, we offer opinions on whether the United States should have invaded Iraq, explanations for increasing gas prices, or theories on how to reduce drug use. Often, these explanations are not based on firsthand data collection or on an exhaustive review of the literature. For the most part, they are based on our opinions and life experiences, or they are just good guesses.

What this text and your course offer is a sociological perspective on social problems. Unlike any other discipline, sociology provides us with a form of self-consciousness, an awareness that our personal experiences are often caused by structural or social forces. **Sociology** is the systematic study of individuals and social structures. A sociologist examines the relationship between individuals and society, which includes social institutions like the family, military, economy, and education. As a social science, sociology offers an objective and systematic approach to understanding the causes of social problems. From a sociological perspective, problems and their solutions don't just involve individuals, but also have a great deal to do with the social structures in our society. This perspective was first promoted by sociologist C. Wright Mills in his 1959 essay, "The Promise."

I

Using Our Sociological Imagination

According to Mills, the sociological imagination can help us distinguish between personal troubles and public issues. The **sociological imagination** links our personal lives and experiences with our social world. Mills (1959/2000) describes how personal troubles occur within the "character of the individual and within the range of his immediate relationships with others" (p. 8), whereas public issues are a "public matter: some value cherished by publics is felt to be threatened" (p. 8). As a result, the resolution of a trouble can be accomplished by the individual and/or those he or she is in contact with, but the resolution of an issue requires public debate about what values are being threatened and the source of such a threat.

In his essay, Mills (1959/2000) makes this connection in the case of unemployment. One man unemployed is his own personal trouble. Resolving his unemployment involves reviewing his current situation, reassessing his skills, considering his job opportunities, and submitting his résumés or job applications to employers. Once he has a new job, his personal trouble is over. However, what happens when your city or state experiences high levels of unemployment? What happens when there is a nation-wide problem of unemployment? This does not affect just one person, but thousands or millions. A personal trouble has been transformed into a public issue. This is the case not just because of how many people it affects; something becomes an issue because of the public values it threatens. Unemployment threatens our sense of economic security. It challenges our belief that everyone can work hard to succeed. Unemployment raises questions about society's obligations to help those without a job.

We can make the personal trouble-public issue connection with regard to another issue, the problem of increasing college tuition. Salvador Henriquez works three jobs, and his wife, Colleen, works two. But even with five jobs between them, they are unable to support their daughter, Ana, a sophomore at New York University. She graduated in the top 5 percent of her class and receives a $14,300 scholarship, but it does not cover all of her school expenses. Each year, the family takes out an additional $25,000 in loans for Ana's school expenses (Fresco 2004). Ana and her family may have found a way to support her education, but what will Salvador and Colleen Henriquez do when Ana's three younger siblings are ready for college? Is this a personal trouble facing only the Henriquez family? Or is this a public issue?

The cost of tuition is rising at a faster rate than family income or student financial aid. During the 1980s, the cost of attending college rose three times as fast as median family income. Between 1981 and 2003, the cost of a public four-year education increased by 202 percent, while the consumer price index (the change in the cost of living) increased 80 percent (Boehner and McKeon 2003). In the 2003–2004 academic year, the average total fees (tuition, room and board) at a four-year public institution were $10,636, while at four-year private institutions, the average cost was $26,854 (College Board 2003).

Although most Americans believe that all students have the opportunity to earn a college degree, a recent study concluded that the promise of a college education is an empty one for low- and moderate-income students. It is estimated that nearly one half of all college-qualified, low- and moderate-income high school graduates are unable to afford college. During the first decade of the twenty-first century, 4.4 million high school graduates will not attend a four-year college, and about 2 million will attend no college at all (Advisory Committee on Student Financial Assistance 2002). On average, poor families spent about 25 percent of their annual income for their children to attend public four-year colleges in 2000. In comparison, middle-income families spent 7 percent of their income, and the wealthiest families spent 2 percent of their annual income (National Center for Public Policy and Higher Education 2002). College cost has become a serious social problem, as the "barriers that make higher education unaffordable serve to erode our economic well being, our civic values, and our democratic ideals" (Callan and Finney 2002:10).

The sociological imagination challenges the claim that the problem is "natural" or based on individual failures, instead reminding us how the problem is rooted in society (Irwin 2001). We understand that we cannot resolve unemployment by changing one individual at a time. In the same way, we know that the Henriquez family is not to blame for the high cost of Ana's education. In both cases, the sociological imagination identifies the structural bases of social problems, making us aware of the economic, political, and social structures that govern employment and unemployment trends and the cost of higher education.

As Mills (1959/2000) explains, "To be aware of the ideal of social structure and to use it with sensibility is to be capable of tracing such linkages among a great variety of milieux. To be able to do that is to possess the sociological imagination" (pp. 10–11). Throughout this text, we will apply our sociological imagination to the study of social problems. Before we proceed, we need to understand what a social problem is.

What Is a Social Problem?

The Negative Consequences of Social Problems

First, a problem is a social condition that has negative consequences for individuals, our social world, or our physical world. If there were only positive consequences, there would be no problem. A social problem such as unemployment, alcoholism, or drug abuse may negatively impact a person's life and health, along with the well-being of that person's family and friends. Problems can threaten our social institutions, for example, the family (spousal abuse), education (the rising cost of college tuition), or the economy (unemployment and underemployment). Our physical and social worlds can be threatened by problems related to urbanization and the environment.

Objective and Subjective Realities of Social Problems

Second, a social problem has objective and subjective realities. A social condition does not have to be personally experienced by every individual in order to be considered a social problem. The **objective reality** of a social problem comes from acknowledging that a particular social condition does exist. For example, you or I do not have to be poor in order to recognize that some men, women, and children experience the consequences of living in poverty. We can confirm the realities of poverty

VISUAL ESSAY: SEEING PROBLEMS SOCIOLOGICALLY ❖

We often speculate about the causes for the moods and behaviors we observe in others. If we saw this unhappy little boy, we might assume that he's spoiled or tired or sick or perhaps even a temperamental, bratty type.

But if we think sociologically and expand our focus beyond this boy to include the social context in which he exists, we begin to notice a few things. The social context gives us additional information to explain the individual and his experiences. One thing we notice is that the boy is part of a family.

Another thing we might notice is that his family appears rather poor, at least judging from their clothing and their home and car, seen in the background. We could speculate on the causes of the family's poverty. We might conclude that their poverty is a result of laziness or a lack of ambition.

What we have done, however, is to identify personal shortcomings or failures as the source of problems and to define the family's poverty as a personal trouble, affecting just one boy and his family. The sociological imagination provides us with an awareness that personal troubles are often caused by institutional or structural forces. Take another look at the family, and this time note what is in the background.

The boy's father used to work in the lumber mill but lost his job when the factory closed. The sociological imagination reminds us that a social problem is not based simply on individual failures but rather is rooted in society. In this case, unemployment is not just experienced by one boy and his family but by all in the community.

Which makes more sense to you: Is it better to try to solve the problem of poverty by helping this boy and his family, and others like them, one family at a time? Or is it better to seek long-term solutions through structural changes?

❖

by observing conditions in our own community, at local clothing drives, food banks, or shelters. Objective realities of a social problem can be confirmed by the collection of data. For example, we know from the 2003 U.S. Census figures that 34.6 million people were poor, and among them, the number of children under the age of 18 was 12.1 million (Proctor and Dalaker 2003).

The **subjective reality** of a social problem addresses how a problem becomes defined as a problem. This idea is based on the concept of the **social construction of reality**. Coined by Peter Berger and Thomas Luckmann (1966), the term refers to how our world is a social creation, originating and evolving through our everyday thoughts and actions. Most of the time, we assume and act as though the world is a given, objectively predetermined outside of our existence. However, according to Berger and Luckmann, we also apply subjective meanings to our existence and experience. In other words, our experiences don't just happen to us. Good, bad, positive, or negative—we also attach meanings to our reality.

From this perspective, social problems are not objectively predetermined. They become real only when they are subjectively defined or perceived as problematic. This perspective is known as **social constructionism**. Recognizing the subjective aspects of social problems allows us to understand how a social condition may be defined as a problem by one segment of society but be completely ignored by another. For example, do you believe poverty is a social problem? Some may argue that it is a problem only if you are the one who is poor. Or poverty is your problem if you are "lazy" or a "welfare mother." However, others would argue that it qualifies as society's problem.

Sociologist Denise Loseke (2003) explains that "conditions might exist, people might be hurt by them, but conditions are not social problems until humans categorize them as troublesome and in need of repair" (p. 14). To frame their work, social constructionists ask a set of questions:

> What do people say or do to convince others that a troublesome condition exists that must be changed? What are the consequences of the typical ways that social problems attract concern? How do our subjective understandings of social problems change the objective characteristics of our world? How do these understandings change how we think about our own lives and the lives of those around us? (Loseke and Best 2003:3–4)

The social constructionist perspective focuses on how a problem becomes defined. In particular, it examines how powerful groups, like politicians, religious leaders, and the media, can influence our opinions and conceptions of what is a social problem. For example, in an effort to preserve their definition of the "traditional family," conservative political and religious groups encourage laws and practices that discriminate against parents with a gay or lesbian sexual orientation and the families they build. Such groups continue to offer support for the Defense of Marriage Act of 1996, which denies federal recognition of same-sex marriages and gives states the right to refuse to recognize same-sex marriages performed in other states. The act also created a federal definition of marriage: the legal union between one man and one woman as husband and wife. When the act passed, Senator Philip Gramm (R-Texas) explained, "The traditional family has stood for 5,000 years. Are we so wise today that we are ready to reject 5,000 years of recorded history? I don't think so" (CNN 1996). Although conservatives considered the act a victory, opponents expressed concern that the act created a social problem, specifically legislating discrimination against gay and lesbian couples and their families. According to Senator Carol Moseley-Braun (D-Illinois), the act was really about "the politics of fear and division and about inciting people in an area which is admittedly controversial" (CNN 1996). From the social constructionist perspective, problems are in the "eye of the beholder" (Konradi and Schmidt 2001).

Definitions of what is a social problem may even come from grassroots efforts. The national campaign against drunk driving began in 1980 with a group of California mothers. Their organization, Mothers Against Drunk Driving (MADD), has been credited with changing our definition of drunk driving and strengthening state and federal drunk-driving laws. The term *designated driver,* now part of our language and promoted by bars and restaurants, was originally popularized by MADD in the 1980s (Lord 2000). Currently, MADD boasts more than 600 chapters and 3 million members.

❖ PUTTING IT TOGETHER:

Apply the concepts of "objective" versus "subjective" reality to the social problem of homelessness. What are the objective realities of homelessness in your neighborhood? According to the National Law Center on Homelessness and Poverty (2002), more than 3 million women, men, and children were homeless in 2001. It is estimated that in any given year, more than 1.5 million youth between the ages of 12 and 17 spend at least one night in an emergency shelter or on the streets (U.S. Department of Housing and Urban Development 1999). Use the Internet (or local resources) to determine the number of homeless in your city or state. What are the subjective realities of homelessness?

The History of Social Problems

Problems don't appear overnight; rather, as Malcolm Spector and John Kituse (1987) argue, the identification of a social problem is part of a subjective process. Spector and Kituse identify four stages to the process. Stage 1 is defined as a transformation process: taking a private trouble and transforming it into a public issue. In this stage, an influential group, activists, or advocates call attention to and define an issue as a social problem. Stage 2 is the legitimization process: formalizing the manner in which the social problems or complaints generated by the problem are handled. For example, an organization or public policy could be created to respond to the condition. An existing organization, such as a federal or state agency, could also be charged with taking care of the situation. In either instance, these organizations begin to legitimize the problem by creating and implementing a formal response. Stage 3 is a conflict stage, when Stage 2 routines are unable to address the problem. During Stage 3, activists, advocates, and victims of the problem experience feelings of distrust and cynicism toward the formal response organizations. Stage 3 activities include readjusting the formal response system: renegotiating procedures, reforming practices, and engaging in administrative or organizational restructuring. Finally, Stage 4 begins when groups believe that they can no longer work within the established system. Advocates or activists are faced with two options, to radically change the existing system or to work outside of the system.

Understanding the Sociological Perspective

The way sociologists conduct sociology and study social problems begins first with their view on how the world works. Based on a **theory**—a set of assumptions and propositions used for explanation, prediction, and understanding—sociologists begin to define the relationship between society and individuals. Theories vary in their level of analysis, focusing on a **macro** (societal) or a **micro** (individual) level. Theories help inform the direction of sociological research and data analysis. In the following section, we will review four theoretical perspectives: functionalism, conflict, feminist, and interactionist. Research methods used by sociologists are summarized below.

❖ FOCUS ON: THE SCIENCE OF SOCIOLOGY

Sociology is not commonsense guessing about how the world works. In his book, *Investigating the Social World* (1999:10), Russell Schutt explains how the social sciences rely "on the use of scientific methods to investigate individuals, societies, and social process [and on] the knowledge produced by these investigations."

Research is divided into two areas: basic and applied. The knowledge we gain through **basic research** expands our understanding of the causes and consequences of a social problem, for example, homelessness among female-headed households or declining educational attainment among Latina students. On the other hand, **applied research** involves the pursuit of knowledge for program application or policy evaluation (Katzer, Cook, and Crouch 1998). Often, social programs are evaluated for their effectiveness in reducing a problem or in creating some desired change. The information gained through applied research can be incorporated into social programs serving homeless female-headed households or Latina high school students.

All research begins with a **theory**— identifying the phenomenon we're trying to explain and then offering an explanation for social patterns or causal relationships

❖ FOCUS ON (Continued)

between variables (Frankfort-Nachmias and Leon-Guerrero 2003). **Variables** are a property of people or objects that can take on two or more values. As we try to explain homelessness, we may have a specific explanation about the relationship between two variables, for example, educational attainment and homelessness among female-headed households. Education could be measured according to different categories: less than a high school degree, a high school degree, some college, or a bachelor's degree or higher. Homelessness could be measured according to whether a woman and her family experienced homelessness in the previous 10 years. The relationship between these variables can be stated in a **hypothesis**, a tentative statement about how the variables are related to each other. We could predict that higher educational attainment will decrease the likelihood that a woman and her family will experience homelessness. In this hypothesis statement, we've identified a **dependent variable** (the variable to be explained, homelessness among female-headed households) along with an **independent variable** (the variable expected to account for the cause of the dependent variable, educational attainment). Data may confirm or refute this hypothesis.

Research methods can include quantitative or qualitative approaches or a combination. Quantitative methods rely on the collection of statistical data. It requires the specification of variables and scales collected through surveys, interviews, or questionnaires. Qualitative methods are designed to capture social life as participants experience it. These methods involve field observation, depth interviews, or focus groups.

A brief description of research methods based on Schutt's text is presented in the following table.

Research Method	Description
Survey research	Collection of data based on responses to a series of questions. Surveys can be offered in several formats: a self-administered mailed survey, group surveys, in-person interviews, or telephone surveys.
Field observation	This category includes data collection conducted in the field, emphasizing the observations about natural behavior as experienced or witnessed by the researcher. Field observation can include participant observation, focus groups, and/or intensive interviewing techniques.
Historical and comparative methods	Research that focuses on one historical period or traces a sequence of events over a number of years. Comparative research involves multiple cases or data from more than one time period.
Secondary data analysis	Research that involves working with data that the researcher did not originally design or collect. Secondary data analysis usually involves the analysis of large public data sets, such as the U.S. Census, the General Social Survey, or the National Election Survey.

The Functionalist Perspective

Among the theorists most associated with the functionalist perspective is French sociologist Emile Durkheim. Borrowing from biology, Durkheim likened society to a human body. As the body has essential organs, each with a specific function in the body, he theorized that society has its own organs: the institutions of the family, economy, politics, education, and religion. These organs: or social structures have essential and unique functions. For example, the institution of the family maintains the health and socialization of our young and creates a basic economic unit. The institution of education provides knowledge and skills for women and men to work and live in society. No other institution can do what the family or education does.

Durkheim proposed that the function of society was to civilize or control individual actions. He wrote, "It is civilization that has made man what he is; it is what distinguishes him from the animal: man is man only because he is civilized" (Durkheim 1914/1973:149). The social order can be threatened during periods of rapid social change, such as industrialization or political upheaval, when social norms and values are likely to be in transition. During this state of normlessness or **anomie**, Durkheim believed society was particularly prone to social problems. As a result, social problems cannot be solved by changing the individual; rather the problem has to be solved at the societal level. The entire social structure or the affected part of the social structure needs to be repaired.

The functionalist perspective, as its name suggests, examines the functions or consequences of the structure of society. Functionalists use a macro perspective, focusing on how society creates and maintains social order. Social problems are not analyzed in terms of how "bad" it is for parts of society. Rather, a functionalist asks: How does the social problem emerge from the society? Does the social problem serve a function?

The systematic study of social problems began with the sociologists at the University of Chicago. Part of what has been called the Chicago School of Sociology, scholars such as Ernest W. Burgess, Homer Hoyt, Robert Park, Edward Ullman, and Louis Wirth used their city as an urban laboratory, pursuing field studies of poverty, crime, and drug abuse during the 1920s and 1930s. Through their research, they captured the real experiences of individuals experiencing social problems, noting the positive and negative consequences of urbanization and industrialization (Ritzer 2000). Taking it one step further, sociologists Jane Addams and Charlotte Gilman not only studied urban life in Chicago but also developed programs to assist the poor and lobbied for legislative and political reform (Adams and Sydie 2001).

According to Robert Merton (1957), social structures can have positive benefits as well as negative consequences, which he called **dysfunctions**. A social problem such as homelessness has a clear set of dysfunctions but can also have positive consequences or functions. One could argue that homelessness is clearly dysfunctional and unpleasant for the women, men, and children who experience it; and for a city or community, homelessness can serve as a public embarrassment. Yet, a functionalist would say that homelessness is beneficial for at least one part of society, or else it would cease to exist. Think of it, the population of the homeless supports an industry of social service agencies, religious organizations, and community groups and service workers. In addition, the homeless also serve to highlight problems in other parts of our social structure, namely the problems of the lack of a livable wage or affordable housing.

PUTTING IT TOGETHER: Merton (1957) separated functions into two categories: **manifest** and **latent**. Manifest functions are the consequences that are intended and recognized, whereas latent functions are the consequences that are unintended and often hidden. What are the manifest and latent functions of homelessness?

The Conflict Perspective

Like functionalism, conflict theories examine the macro level of our society, its structures and institutions. Whereas functionalists argue that society is held together by norms, values, and a common morality, conflict theorists consider how society is held together by power and coercion (Ritzer 2000) for the benefit of those in power. In this view, social problems emerge from the continuing conflict between groups in our society—based on social class, gender, ethnicity/race—and in the conflict, the powerful groups usually win. As a result, this perspective offers no easy solutions to social problems. There could be a total overhaul of the system, but that is unlikely to happen. We could reform parts of the structure, but those in power would retain their control. The biggest social problem from this perspective is the system itself and the inequality it creates.

The first to make this argument was German philosopher and activist Karl Marx. Conflict, according to Marx, emerged from the economic substructure of capitalism, which defined all other social structures and social relations. He focused on the conflict based on social class, created by the tension between the **proletariat** (workers) and the **bourgeoisie** (owners). Capitalism did more than separate the haves and have-nots. Unlike Durkheim, who believed that society created a civilized man, Marx argued that a capitalist society created a man alienated from his **species being**, from his true self. **Alienation** occurred on multiple levels: Man would become increasingly alienated from his work, the product of his work, other workers and finally, his own human potential. For example, a salesperson could be so involved in the process of her work that she doesn't spend quality time with her coworkers, talk with her customers, or stop and appreciate the merchandise. Each sale transaction is the same; all customers and workers are treated alike. According to Marx, workers needed to achieve a **class consciousness**, an awareness of their social position and oppression, in order to unite and overthrow capitalism, replacing it with a more egalitarian socialist/communist structure.

Widening Marx's emphasis on the capitalist class structure, contemporary conflict theorists have argued that conflict emerges from other social bases, such as values, resources, and interests. C. Wright Mills (1959/2000) argued the existence of a "power elite," a small group of political, business, and military leaders who control our society.

Ralf Dahrendorf (1959) explained that conflict of interest is inherent in any relationship because those in powerful positions will always seek to maintain their dominance. Lewis Coser (1956), in *The Functions of Social Conflict*, focused on the functional aspects of conflict, arguing that conflict creates and maintains group solidarity by clarifying the positions and boundaries between groups. Conflict theorists may also take a social constructionist approach, examining how social problems are subjectively defined by powerful political, economic, and social interest groups.

The Feminist Perspective

Rosemarie Tong (1989) explains that "feminist theory is not one, but many, theories or perspectives and that each feminist theory or perspective attempts to describe women's oppression, to explain its causes and consequences, and to prescribe strategies for women's liberation" (p. 1). By analyzing the situations and lives of women in society, feminist theory defines gender (and sometimes race or social class) as a source of social inequality, group conflict, and social problems. For feminists, the patriarchal society is the basis of social problems. **Patriarchy** refers to a society in which men dominate women and justify their domination through devaluation; however, the definition of patriarchy has been broadened to include societies in which powerful groups dominate and devalue the powerless (Kaplan 1994).

Patricia Madoo Lengermann and Jill Niebrugge-Brantley (2004) explain that feminist theory was established as a new sociological perspective in the 1970s, due in large part to the growing presence of women in the discipline and the strength of the women's movement. Feminist theory treats the experiences of women as the starting point in all sociological investigations, seeing the world from the vantage point of women in the social world and seeking to promote a better world for women and for humankind.

Although the study of social problems is not the center of feminist theory, throughout its history, feminist theory has been critical of existing social arrangements and has focused on such concepts as social change, power, and social inequality (Madoo Lengermann and Niebrugge-Brantley 2004). Research in the field has included Jessie Bernard's (1972/1982) study of gender inequality in marriage, Patricia Hill Collins's (1990) development of Black feminist thought, Dorothy Smith's (1987) sociology from the standpoint of women, and Nancy Chodorow's (1978) psychoanalytic feminism and the reproduction of mothering. Although sociologists in this perspective may adopt a conflict, functionalist, or interactionist perspective, their focus remains on how men and women are situated in society, not just differently but also unequally (Madoo Lengermann and Niebrugge-Brantley 2004).

The Interactionist Perspective

An interactionist focuses on how we use language, words, and symbols to create and maintain our social reality. This perspective highlights what we take for granted: the expectations, rules, and norms that we learn and practice without even noticing. In our interaction with others, we become the products and creators of our social reality. Through our interaction, social problems are created and defined.

The foundation of this microlevel perspective was provided by the work of George Herbert Mead. Also a member of the Chicago School of Sociology, Mead (1934/1962) argued that society was the organized and patterned interactions among individuals. As Mead defined it, the self is a mental and social process. It is the reflective ability to see others in relation to ourselves and to see ourselves in relation to others. The term *symbolic interactionism* was coined by Herbert Blumer in 1937. Building on Mead's work, Blumer emphasized how the existence of mind and self emerges from interaction and the use of symbols (Turner 1998).

How does the self emerge from interaction? Consider the roles that you and I play. As a university professor, I am aware of what is expected of me; as university students, you are aware of what the student role means. There are no posted guides in the classroom that instruct us where to stand, how to dress, or what to bring into class. Even before we enter the classroom, we know how we are supposed to behave. We act based on our past experiences and based on what we have come to accept as definitions of each role. But we need each other to create this reality; our interaction in the classroom reaffirms each of our roles and the larger educational institution. Imagine what it takes to maintain this reality: consensus not just between a single professor and her students but between every professor and every student on campus, on every university campus, ultimately reaffirming the structure of a university classroom and higher education.

So, how do social problems emerge from interaction? First, for social problems such as alcoholism or juvenile delinquency, an interactionist would argue that the problem behavior is learned from others. According to this perspective, no one is born a juvenile delinquent. Like any other role we play, people learn how to become juvenile delinquents. Although the perspective does not answer the question of where or from whom the first delinquent child learned this behavior, it attempts to explain how deviant behavior is learned through interaction with others.

Second, social problems emerge from the definitions themselves. Objective social problems do not exist; they become real only in how they are defined or labeled. A sociologist using this perspective would examine who or what group is defining the problem and who or what is being defined as deviant or a social problem. We'll examine this more closely in Chapter 10, Crime, when we review labeling theory, an interactionist approach to the study of deviance.

❖ PUTTING IT TOGETHER:

A summary of these sociological perspectives is presented in Table 1.1. These sociological perspectives will be reintroduced in each chapter as we examine a new social problem or set of problems. As you review each perspective, do not attempt to classify one as the definitive explanation. Consider how each perspective focuses on different aspects of society and its social problems. Which perspective(s) best fits with your understanding of society? your understanding of social problems?

❖ Table 1.1   Summary of Sociological Perspectives: A General Approach to Examining Social Problems

Level of analysis	Functional Macro	Conflict/Feminist Macro	Interactionist Micro
Assumptions about society	Order. Society is held together by a set of social institutions, each of which has a specific function in society.	Conflict. Society is held together by power and coercion. Conflict and inequality are inherent in the social structure.	Interaction. Society is created through social interaction.
Questions asked about social problems	How does the problem originate from the social structure? How does the problem reflect changes among social institutions and structures? What are the functions and dysfunctions of the problem?	How does the problem originate from the competition between groups and from the social structure itself? What groups are in competition and why?	How is the problem socially constructed and defined? How is problem behavior learned through interaction? How is the problem labeled by those concerned about it?

The Transformation from Problem to Solution

Although C. Wright Mills identified the relationship between a personal trouble and a public issue more than 50 years ago, less has been said about the transformation of issue to solution. Mills leads us in the right direction by identifying the relationship between public issues and social institutions. By continuing to use our sociological imagination and recognizing the role of larger social, cultural, and structural forces, we can identify appropriate measures to address these social problems.

Let's consider homelessness. It does not arise out of mysterious or special circumstances; it emerges out of familiar life experiences. The loss of a job, the illness of a family member, domestic violence, or divorce could make a family more susceptible to

❖ TAKING A WORLD VIEW

SOCIAL PROBLEMS AND HOMELESSNESS IN JAPAN

The study of social problems in Japan is different than it is in the United States (Ayukawa 2000). In Japan, there are few courses called "Social Problems"; instead, courses are simply titled "Sociology" or "The Introduction to Sociology." However, within each course, social problems are discussed. Japan has two main academic societies in the field of the sociological study of social problems: the Japan Society of Social Pathology (or the Japan Society of Social Problems) and the Japan Society of Sociological Criminology (Ayukawa 2000).

One social problem that Japanese sociologists have attempted to address is homelessness. The number of homeless has risen sharply since Japan's economic recession in the mid-1990s. It is estimated that there are more than 20,000 homeless men and women in Japan. The homeless are primarily single men in their late fifties who are former or active laborers. These men are too young to receive social security and too old to work in construction. Recently, a new population of homeless has emerged, youths and unemployed white-collar laborers and women (Aoki 2000).

The experience of homelessness is linked closely to the availability of work for day laborers. Large groups of day laborers live in Japan's cities; more than 20,000 day workers live in a one quarter-square mile radius in Japan's second-largest city, Osaka, and the second-largest group of day workers, approximately 8,000, lives in Tokyo. The male workers rely on skilled or unskilled construction jobs to survive. When employed and earning money, the day workers live in cheap hotels called *yosebas*. It costs more than $20 U.S. a night to sleep in an approximately 60-square foot room with a tatami mat, a shared bath, boiler, and kitchen (Ayukawa 2000).

However, as Japan's economy worsens and construction work has steadily declined, more day laborers who are unable to find jobs are becoming homeless (Aoki 2000). The number of homeless people who sleep in building entrances, next to windows, or in small self-made cardboard houses in parks in the middle of the largest cities has increased. In Tokyo's parks, several tent communities have been erected. Homes are often marked with real addresses, with painted wooden markers that read "3-29," row 3, tent 29 (Prusher 2001). Clashes between Japan's homeless and the police have been covered by the print and television media. The largest incident occurred in 1996, between 400 homeless men and 1,000 police officers in the Shinjuku Station in Tokyo. Media coverage has been credited with increasing public awareness of homelessness as a problem in Japan (Aoki 2000).

Japan's poor do not ask for money on the street; most consider this a degrading act. Still, most do not receive regular public assistance. In 2001, the city of Tokyo had two homeless shelters, with a third one being planned. Smaller towns and cities set their own policies on how to deal with the homeless. Many, but not all, offer a small daily or weekly handout of goods or foods. A voucher to bathe at a public bathhouse may also be offered (Prusher 2001). Many of Japan's homeless refuse to apply for public aid.

homelessness. Without informal social support, a savings account, or suitable and adequate employment—and with the increasing cost of health care and the lack of affordable housing—a family's economic and emotional resources can quickly be tapped out. What would it take to prevent homelessness in these situations? The answers are not based in each individual or each family; rather, the long-term solutions are structural solutions such as affordable health care, livable wages, and affordable low-income housing.

Modern history reveals that Americans do not like to stand by and do nothing about social problems. In fact, most Americans support current efforts to reduce homelessness, curb violence, or improve the quality of education. In some cases, there are no limits to our efforts. Helping our nation's poor has been a major social project of many U.S. presidents. President Franklin Roosevelt proposed sweeping social reforms during his New Deal in 1935, and President Johnson declared the War on Poverty in 1964. President Clinton offered to "change welfare as we know it" with sweeping reforms outlined in the Personal Responsibility and Work Opportunity Reconciliation Act of 1996. And in 2003, President George W. Bush supported the reauthorization of the 1996 welfare reform bill. No president or Congress has ever promised to eliminate poverty; instead, each promised only to improve the system serving the poor or to reduce the number of poor in our society.

Solutions require social action—in the form of social policy, advocacy, and innovation—to address problems at their structural or individual levels. **Social policy** is the enactment of a course of action through a formal law or program. Policy-making usually begins with identification of a problem that should be addressed; then, specific guidelines are developed on what should be done to address the problem. Policy directly changes the social structure, particularly how our government, an organization, or community responds to a social problem. In addition, policy governs the behavior and interaction of individuals, controlling who has access to benefits and aid (Ellis 2003). An example of homeless social policy occurred in July 2002, when the Senate Appropriation Committee approved the use of a portion of $8 million from the Social Security Administration research budget to support innovative local programs to assist homeless people in gaining eligibility for Supplemental Security Income (SSI) benefits. At a community level, there are eligibility guidelines to determine which individuals and families can be served at a homeless shelter. Rules govern how long individuals may receive aid and the type of aid they may receive (Ellis 2003).

Social advocates use their resources to support, educate, and empower individuals and their communities. Advocates work to improve social services, change social policies, and mobilize individuals. National organizations such as the National Coalition for the Homeless or local organizations such as Project H.O.M.E. in Philadelphia provide service, outreach, education, and legal support for the homeless. **Social innovation** may take the form of a policy, a program, or advocacy that features an untested or unique approach. Innovation usually starts at the community level, but it can grow into national and international programming. The concept of "partnership housing" was developed by Millard and Linda Fuller in 1965, partnering those in need of adequate shelter with community volunteers to build simple interest-free houses. In 1976, the Fullers' concept became Habitat for Humanity International, a nonprofit, ecumenical Christian housing program responsible for building more than 125,000 houses worldwide. When Millard Fuller was awarded the Presidential Medal of Freedom, the nation's highest civilian honor, President Bill Clinton described Habitat as "the most successful continuous community service project in the history of the United States" (Habitat for Humanity 2004). We will consider the impact of social action in the last chapter of this text.

❖ PUTTING IT TOGETHER:
On your campus.

Are there any campus groups or organizations that address the problem of homelessness? What activities does the campus group sponsor? How does it provide assistance to the homeless population in your area? How does the group educate students and faculty about the problem of homelessness?

Making Sociological Connections

In his book, *Social Things: An Introduction to the Sociological Life*, Charles Lemert (1997) tells us that sociology is often presented as a thing to be studied instead of lived. However, Lemert argues that sociology is also a thing "lived." He says:

> To use one's sociological imagination, whether to practical or professional end, is to look at the events in one's life, to see them for what they truly are, then to figure out how the structures of the wider world make social things the way they are. No one is a sociologist until she does this the best she can. (P. 105)

Throughout this text, we will explore three connections. The first connection is the one between personal troubles and public issues. Each sociological perspective—functionalism, conflict, feminist, and interactionist—highlights how social problems emerge out of our social structure or social interaction.

The sociological imagination will also help us make a second connection: the one between social problems and social solutions. C. Wright Mills believed that the most important value of sociology was in its potential to enrich and encourage the lives of all individuals (Lemert 1997). In each chapter, we will review selected social policies, advocacy programs, and innovative approaches that attempt to address or solve these problems.

Textbooks on this subject present neat compact chapters on a social problem, reviewing the sociological issues and sometimes providing some suggestions on how it can and should be addressed. This book follows the same outline but instead takes a closer look at community-based approaches. This text will not identify perfect solutions. We do not live in a perfect world. There may even be some solutions that work but are no longer operating because of lack of funds or public support. Social policies

VISUAL ESSAY: WORKING TOGETHER TO LIGHTEN THE LOAD ❖

Although many of the social problems we see in our communities seem insurmountable, it is hard to stand by and do nothing about them. Individuals and groups have made an effort to improve the quality of life for their neighbors and ultimately have made a difference in their communities.

Here, Habitat for Humanity volunteers pitch in to build a house for a family in their community.

Every community, even your own, has opportunities for those who want to help. Volunteering allows you to contribute to an important cause and provides opportunities to work with others who share your interests or concerns.

These volunteers are cleaning up an empty lot in Philadelphia. Work goes faster, and might even be fun, when others help.

You can volunteer anywhere. These volunteers are helping out at an oil cleanup in Orange County, California.

Age is not a barrier to volunteering. These Atlanta teens are packing food for distribution to the homeless.

Why do you suppose community efforts to address social problems are so popular? Do these efforts make a real difference? Why or why not?

and programs have been effective in helping individuals, families, or groups improve their lives and in reducing the prevalence of particular problems. In the end, I hope you agree that it is important that we continue to do something about the social problems we face.

Each chapter will include a Voices in the Community feature, focusing on individuals or groups who are experiencing, but mostly doing, something about some of these problems. They are women, men, and children, common citizens or professionals, from different backgrounds and experiences. Whether they are working within the system or working to change the system, these individuals are part of their community's solution to a problem. They have decided to be part of the solution and not part of the problem. The point is: People are making a difference.

In addition, I will ask you to make the final connection to social problems and solutions in your community. For this quarter or semester, instead of focusing only on problems reported in your local newspaper or the morning news program, start paying attention to the solutions offered by professionals, leaders, and advocates. Through the Internet or through local programs and agencies, take this opportunity to investigate what social action is taking place in your community. Your community may include your campus, your residential neighborhood, or the city where your university is located. Consider what other avenues of change can also be taken and whether you can be part of that effort.

I often tell my students that the problem with being a sociologist is that my sociological imagination has no "off" switch. In almost everything I read, see, or do, there is some sociological application, a link between my personal experiences and the broader social experience that I share with everyone else, including you. As you progress through this text and your course, I hope that you will begin to use your own sociological imagination and see connections that you never saw before.

MAIN POINTS

- **Sociology** is the systematic study of individuals and social structures. A sociologist examines the relationship between individuals and our society, which includes institutions (the family), organizations (the military), and systems (our economy). As a social science, sociology offers an objective and systematic approach to understanding the causes of social problems.

- The **sociological imagination** is a way of recognizing the links between our personal lives and experiences and our social world.

- A social problem is a social condition that has negative consequences for individuals, our social world, or physical world.

- A social problem has objective and subjective realities. The **objective reality** of a social problem comes from acknowledging that a particular social condition does negatively impact human lives. The **subjective reality** of a social problem addresses how a problem becomes defined as a problem. Social problems are not objectively predetermined. They become real only when they are subjectively defined or perceived as problematic. This perspective is known as **social constructionism**.

• Problems don't just appear overnight; rather, as Malcolm Spector and John Kituse (1987) argue, the identification of a social problem is a process.

• Four theoretical perspectives are used by sociologists: functionalist perspective, conflict perspective, feminist perspective, and interactionist perspective. The functionalist perspective examines the functions or consequences of the structure of society. Functionalists use a macro perspective, focusing on how society creates and maintains social order. A social problem is not analyzed in terms of how "bad" it is for parts of society. Rather, a functionalist asks how the social problem emerges from the society. What function does the social problem serve?

• Conflict, according to Marx, emerged from the economic substructure of capitalism, which defined all other social structures and social relations. He focused on the conflict based on social class, created by the tension between the **proletariat** (workers) and the **bourgeoisie** (owners). Marx argued that a capitalist society created a man alienated from his **species being**, from his true self. **Alienation** occurred on multiple levels: Man would become increasingly alienated from his work, from the product of his work, from other workers, and finally, from his own human potential.

• By analyzing the situations and lives of women in society, feminist theory defines gender (and sometimes race or social class) as a source of social inequality, group conflict, and social problems. For feminists, the patriarchal society is the basis of social problems.

• An interactionist focuses on how we use language, words, and symbols to create and maintain our social reality. This perspective highlights what we take for granted: the expectations, rules, and norms that we learn and practice without even noticing. In our interaction with others, we become the products and creators of our social reality. Through our interaction, social problems are created and defined.

• Solutions require social action—in the form of social policy, advocacy, and innovation—to address problems at their structural or individual levels. **Social policy** is the enactment of a course of action through a formal law or program. **Social advocates** use their resources to support, educate, and empower individuals and their communities. **Social innovation** may take the form of a policy, a program, or advocacy that features an untested or unique approach. Innovation usually starts at the community level, but it can grow into national and international programming.

INTERNET AND COMMUNITY EXERCISES

1. Review issues of your local newspaper from the past 90 days. Based on the front page or local section, what issues are important for your community? Crime? Job layoffs? Transportation? Pollution? Examine how the issue is defined and by whom. Is input from community leaders and neighborhood groups being included? Why or why not? Do the issues you have identified include the three elements of a social problem?

2. Social actions or responses are also linked to how we define the problem. If we believe the problem is structural, we'll find ways to change the structure. If the problem is defined at the individual level, a solution will attempt to change the person. Investigate the programs and resources that are available for the homeless in your community or state. Select three local programs and assess how each defines and responds to the homeless problem in your community.

3. What do you think is the most important social problem? Investigate what federal and state policies govern or regulate this problem and those it affects. What is the position of the main political parties—Democrats and Republicans—on this problem?

On your own. Log on to *Study Site—Community and Policy Guide* for more information about the social problems, social policies, and community responses discussed in this chapter.

References

Adams, B. and R. A. Sydie. 2001. *Sociological Theory.* Thousand Oaks, CA: Pine Forge.

Advisory Committee on Student Financial Assistance. 2002. "Empty Promises: The Myth of College Access in America." Retrieved May 15, 2004 (www.ed.gov/about/bdscomm/list/acsfa/emptypromises.pdf).

Aoki, Hideo. 2000. "The Underclass in Japan: A Case Study of Homeless Men in Kamagasaki and Their Winter Struggle." *The International Scope* 2(4):1–20.

Ayukawa, Jun. 2000. "The Sociology of Social Problems in Japan." *American Sociologist* 31(3):15–27.

Berger, Peter and Thomas Luckmann. 1966. *The Social Construction of Reality.* Garden City, NY: Anchor.

Bernard, Jessie. 1982. *The Future of Marriage,* 2ed. New Haven, CT: Yale University Press. (Original work published 1972)

Boehner, J. and H. McKeon. 2003. "The College Cost Crisis." Retrieved May 15, 2004 (http://edworkforce.house.gov/issues/108th/education/highereducation/CollegeCostCrisisReport.pdf).

Callan, Patrick and Joni Finney. 2002. "State Policies for Affordable Higher Education." Pp. 10–11, 13 in *Losing Ground: A National Status Report on the Affordability of American Higher Education.* San Jose, CA: National Center for Public Policy and Higher Education.

Chodorow, Nancy. 1978. *The Reproduction of Mothering: Psychoanalysis and the Sociology of Gender.* Berkeley: University of California.

CNN. 1996. "Anti Gay Marriage Act Clears Congress." Retrieved September 27, 2003 (www.cnn.com/US9609/10/gay.marriage/).

College Board. 2003. "Tuition Levels Rise but Many Students Pay Significantly Less Than Published Rates." Retrieved May 15, 2004 (www.collegeboard.com/press/article/0,3183,29541,00.html).

Collins, Patricia Hill. 1990. *Black Feminist Thought: Knowledge, Consciousness, and Empowerment.* Boston: Unwin Hyman.

Coser, L. 1956. *The Functions of Social Conflict.* New York: Free Press.

Dahrendorf, Ralf. 1959. *Class and Class Conflict in Industrial Society.* Stanford, CA: Stanford University Press.

Durkheim, Emile. 1973. "The Dualism of Human Nature and Its Moral Condition." Pp. 149–163 in *Emile Durkheim on Morality and Society,* edited by R. Bellah. Chicago, IL: University of Chicago Press. (Original work published 1914)

Ellis, R. A. 2003. *Impacting Social Policy: A Practitioner's Guide to Analysis and Action.* Pacific Grove, CA: Thomson Brooks/Cole.

Frankfort-Nachmias, C. and A. Leon-Guerrero. 2003. *Social Statistics for a Diverse Society.* Thousand Oaks, CA: Pine Forge.

Fresco, Robert. 2004. "A High Price to Pay." *Newsday,* March 21, 2004. Retrieved March 30, 2004 (www.newsday.com/business.local/longisland/nyepcoll0321,0,740823,printstory).

Habitat for Humanity. 2004. "Millard Fuller." Retrieved June 9, 2004 (www.habitat.org/how/millard.html).

Irwin, Alan. 2001. *Sociology and the Environment.* Cambridge, UK: Polity Press.

Kaplan, Laura Duhan. 1994. "Women as Caretaker: An Archetype That Supports Patriarchal Militarism." *Hypatia* 9(2):123–133.

Katzer, Jeffrey, Kenneth Cook, and Wayne Crouch. 1998. *Evaluating Information: A Guide for Users of Social Science Research* (4th ed). Boston: McGraw-Hill.

Konradi, Amanda and Martha Schmidt. 2001. *Reading Between the Lines: Toward an Understanding of Current Social Problems.* Mountain View, CA: Mayfield.

Lemert, Charles. 1997. *Social Things: An Introduction to the Sociological Life.* Lanham, MD: Rowan and Littlefield.

Lord, Janice. 2000. "Really MADD: Looking Back at 20 years." Retrieved December 31, 2002 (www.madd.org/aboutus/0,1056,1686,00.html).

Loseke, Denise. 2003. *Thinking about Social Problems.* New York: Aldine de Gruyter.

Loseke, Denise and J. Best 2003. *Social Problems: Constructionist Readings.* New York: Aldine De Gruyter.

Madoo Lengermann, Patricia and Jill Niebrugge-Brantley. 2004. "Contemporary Feminist Theory." Pp. 436–480 in *Sociological Theory,* edited by G. Ritzer and D. Goodman. Boston: McGraw-Hill.

Mead, George Herbert. 1962. *Mind, Self, and Society: From the Standpoint of a Social Behaviorist.* Chicago, IL: University of Chicago Press. (Original work published 1934)

Merton, Robert. 1957. *Social Theory and Social Structure.* New York: Free Press.

Mills, C. Wright. 2000. *The Sociological Imagination.* New York: Oxford University Press. (Original work published 1959)

National Center for Public Policy and Higher Education. 2002. *Losing Ground: A National Status Report on the Affordability of American Higher Education.* San Jose, CA: Author.

National Law Center on Homelessness and Poverty. 2002. "Overview." Retrieved January 12, 2004 (www.nlchp.org/FA_HAPIA).

Proctor, Bernadette and Joseph Dalaker. 2003. *Poverty in the United States: 2002* (Current Population Reports P50-222). Washington, DC: U.S. Census Bureau.

Prusher, Ilene. 2001. "Well-Ordered Homelessness: Life on Japan's Fringe." Retrieved September 12, 2003 (http://search.csmonitor.com/durable/2001/05/14/pls3.htm).

Ritzer, George. 2000. *Sociological Theory.* Boston: McGraw-Hill.

Schutt, R. (1999). *Investigating the Social World: The Process and Practice of Research.* Thousand Oaks, CA: Pine Forge.

Smith, Dorothy. 1987. *The Everyday World as Problematic: A Feminist Sociology.* Boston: Northeastern University Press.

Spector, Malcolm and John Kituse. 1987. *Constructing Social Problems.* New York: Aldine de Gruyter.

Tong, Rosemarie. 1989. *Feminist Thought: A Comprehensive Introduction.* Boulder, CO: Westview Press.

Turner, Jonathan. 1998. *The Structure of Sociological Theory,* 6th ed. Belmont, CA: Wadsworth.

U.S. Department of Housing and Urban Development. 1999. "Homeless Teens." Retrieved April 1, 2004 (www.huduser.org/periodicals/urm/1299/urm2.html).

2

The Bases of Inequality

Social Class, Ethnicity, and Race

❝ **L** ike trees in a vast forest, humans come in a variety of sizes, shapes, and colors.❞ Marilyn Loden and Judy Rosener (1991) wrote these words to describe human **diversity** or what the women call "**otherness** or those human qualities that are different from our own and outside the groups to which we belong" (p. 18). They created the Diversity Wheel (see Figure 2.1) to represent our primary and secondary characteristics.

Our primary characteristics are presented in the center of the wheel. These dimensions—age, ethnicity, gender, physical abilities, race, and sexual orientation—serve as our basic self-image and affect our lives from birth. As Loden and Rosener (1991) tell us, "there is no escaping the life-long impact of these six core elements" (p. 19). Secondary characteristics are less salient than primary characteristics. We can change these characteristics, such as our educational attainment, geographic location, income, marital status, military experience, parental status, religious beliefs, and work experience.

Each characteristic serves as a social boundary, letting us know who should be included in or excluded from our particular social group (Sernau 2001), defining the "otherness" each of us possesses. Sociologists use the term **social stratification** to refer to the ranking of individuals into social strata or groups. Not only are we divided into groups such as women versus men or African Americans versus Asian Americans. Our lives are also transformed because of our group membership. In U.S. society, being different has also come to mean that we are unequal.

The differences between social strata become more apparent when we recognize how some individuals are more likely to experience social problems than others. Attached to each social position are **life chances**, a term Max Weber used to describe the consequences of social stratification, how each social position provides access to goods and services such as wealth, food, clothing, shelter, education, and health care. Sociologists refer to the unequal distribution of resources, services, and positions as

❖ Figure 2.1   Diversity Wheel

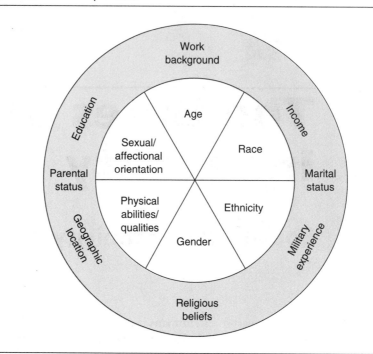

Source: Loden and Rosener 1991.

social inequality. Certain social positions are subject to **prejudice** (a negative attitude based on the attributes of an individual) and **discrimination** (acts based on prejudiced beliefs against a specific individual or group) not experienced by others. And sadly, some social positions are also targets of violence.

In this chapter and Chapter 3, we will explore two basic sociological questions: Why does social inequality exist and how are we different from one another? First, we will review sociological theories that attempt to explain social inequality. Second, we will examine the bases of social inequality in the United States. If this is your first sociology course, this chapter will provide you with an overview of several basic sociological concepts. If you have already had a sociology course, welcome back; this chapter should provide a good review.

❖ PUTTING IT TOGETHER:

Based on some of the primary and secondary characteristics identified in the Diversity Wheel, I'd describe myself as a married, college educated, Asian Pacific Islander, heterosexual female. What social characteristics would you use to describe yourself? Which social characteristics are essential to your identity?

Why Does Social Inequality Exist?

Many would attribute inequality to the fact that we are different: fast versus slow, strong versus weak, smart versus not as smart. You could think that inequality is inevitable and irreversible. But is there something "natural" to dividing and treating groups differently on the basis of ethnicity/race, sexual orientation, or social class? Our sociological imagination, as C. Wright Mills suggests, allows us to understand the larger social forces that affect the bases of social inequality. Four sociological perspectives offer explanations on how social structures serve to create social stratification and social inequality.

Functionalist Explanations for Inequality

Functionalists assume that not everyone in society can and should be equal. From this perspective, inequality is necessary for the social order. Some individuals are more important to society because of their function to society. For example, society values the life-saving work of a medical surgeon more than the retail function of a grocery store cashier. Based on the value of one's work or talent, society rewards individuals at the top of the social structure (surgeons) with more wealth, income, or power than those lower down in the social structure (grocery cashiers).

Functionalists argue that certain individuals are better suited for their positions in society than others. According to this perspective, individuals are sorted according to their abilities or characteristics—their age, strength, intelligence, physical ability, or even sex—in order to play their particular role for society. Our social institutions, especially education, sort everyone into their proper place and reward them accordingly. Because not all of us can become surgeons, the system ensures that only the most talented and qualified become surgeons. In many ways, the functionalist argument reinforces the belief that we are naturally different.

 ❖ PUTTING IT TOGETHER:

The functionalist perspective is often criticized for its "value" argument. For example, the argument is not supported when comparing elementary school teachers with professional athletes. What is the social function of an elementary school teacher? What is the function of a professional football player? Does one position have more "value" than another? The average salary for first-year elementary teachers is $30,719, whereas the average salary of an NFL player is more than $1 million. Why does our society reward the football player more than the school teacher?

Conflict and Feminist Explanations for Inequality

Conflict and feminist perspectives address how inequality is created and maintained by those in power. Like the functionalist perspective, these perspectives argue

VISUAL ESSAY: "INVISIBLE" DIVIDING LINES ❖

It is difficult to escape from our social differences and the system of stratification that separates us. However, society has attempted to eliminate some of the barriers between groups. In schools and workplaces in particular (where laws have been most stringent), we've had some success in overcoming stratification based on gender, race, and ethnicity.

Americans generally value diversity but remain committed to some dividing lines. For example, many forms of sex-based discrimination and segregation are rigidly enforced by mores, even among the most liberal Americans.

Class distinctions also persist and can be compounded by differences based on ethnicity, race, and gender. About 45 percent of the U.S. poor are non-Hispanic Whites, with African Americans having the highest poverty rate among minority groups.

What "invisible" dividing lines (that is, discriminatory practices) can you think of that people may be taking for granted?

that inequality is inevitable, but for different reasons. For a functionalist, inequality is necessary because of the different positions and roles needed in society. From a conflict perspective, inequality is systematically created and maintained by those trying to maintain their advantage over the system. Advantage can be based on many characteristics: class (the domination of upper classes over working classes), ethnicity/race (the domination of Whites over all other groups), or age (the domination of the young over the old). From a feminist perspective, gender inequality is the product of the patriarchal system perpetuated through social structures like the family, the workplace, and education.

Interactionist Explanations for Inequality

Is inequality real? According to this micro perspective, inequality is a social creation. Interactionists address how inequality is the result of human interaction, the meanings and values we attach to individuals and their social positions. Our own social identity, as well as how we perceive others, comes from our everyday interactions. In his book, *Privilege, Power, and Difference*, Allan G. Johnson (2001) says it best:

> We think the way our culture defines race or gender or sexual orientation is simply the way things are in an objective sense. We think there really is such as thing as "race" and that the words we use simply name an objective reality that is "out there." The truth is, however, that once human beings give something a name—whether it be skin color or whom you want to sleep with—that thing acquires a significance it otherwise would not have. More important, the name quickly takes on a life of its own as we forget the social process that created it and start treating it as "real" in and of itself. (Pp. 22–23)

Johnson makes an important point. Humans bestow great power on the name. Whether it is *poor, gay, disabled,* or *Latina*—attached to each of these names is a set of stereotypes, beliefs, and attitudes that shape our behavior and produce the inequality we believe is real. We make these categories of inequality real by acting upon them. Language not only reinforces our expectations of inequality at the individual level; it also defines inequality at the institutional level.

How Are We Different?

Otherness is as natural as taking a breath. We seem to automatically separate "us" from "them" without giving much thought to our criteria or the process.

Voices in the Community:
Sherri Muzher

In this chapter's Voices in the Community feature, Sherri Muzher (2001) writes about her experiences as an Arab American, particularly after September 11, 2001.

In an era where political correctness is the norm, there are few groups that are still legitimate targets for harassment and popular stereotyping—except for Arab Americans.

With the recent abominable tragedies in New York, Pennsylvania and Washington D.C., many in the Arab-American community fear retribution from fellow Americans, should the perpetrators be Arab. Already, violence has been reported on university campuses, and death threats have been called in to numerous Arab organizations.

When I was little, I remember being puzzled by all of the stereotypes of my culture. Whether it was watching Bugs Bunny or Charlie's Angels, the Arabs were always the bad guys. In elementary and junior high school, there were the ignorant classmates who had an obsession with the words, "camel jockey."

"Why are we such bad people?" I once asked an Arab adult. He was horrified by my question, and yet saddened that the images perpetrated by the media and pop culture could make me question a proud heritage that was once the cradle of the world's civilization. Add to the recipe that I was of Palestinian descent.

I knew better, of course. I had heard enough personal testimonies from loved ones and Palestinian acquaintances to know that a huge injustice had been done to our people. Even now, every Palestinian group has condemned this tragedy, and yet some analysts are determined to make some sort of link to the Palestinians. . . .

The memories of anti-Arab discrimination during the Gulf War are still vivid. I was a senior at Michigan State University. There were reports that the MSU Department of Public Safety had submitted the names of all Arab-sounding names to the FBI. Comments such as "We should nuke all Ay-rabs in Dearborn" and "Kill the sand n——s" were heard in the cafeteria at my residence hall. Fist fights were common. Uncomfortable stares followed us much of the time.

In 1995, the Oklahoma City bombing occurred. From Jerusalem, where I was then, I watched CNN and was dumbfounded to hear reporters' attempts to link the bombings to Arabs, even though American antigovernment militias and Timothy McVeigh were already nailed as perpetrators.

The usual racial profiling awaited us at the various airports. I don't think I have ever been on an international flight where I wasn't separated at the Detroit Metropolitan Airport without having my suitcase searched and asked a number of questions. Days later, the vandalism of Arab-owned property and death threats became known to us. . . .

And now, it's starting all over again. There is good and bad in every culture, and every community has its radicals and extremists. Let's not forget our own Michigan militia.

It is so important that we not hold entire communities responsible for the acts of a few. Even if the perpetrators of the latest outrage turn out to be Arabs, that is hardly a reason to vilify a community. The Arab community has worked hard to be contributing and productive members of the great American tapestry. Whether they are doctors saving lives, small business owners, engineers or human rights activists, they make a difference as Americans. The horrors of the latest tragedy affect us as fellow Americans and human beings.

It has always been difficult being an Arab American, especially at a time when people are understandably angry and need to take it out on someone. The dehumanization of Arabs in pop culture has made it easier to place Arab Americans, as well as Muslim Americans, as targets.

We understand that there is nothing worse than feeing helpless. A lot of our relatives in the Middle East feel this helplessness every day.

As Americans, we are outraged that innocent people were taken into this barbaric and uncivilized manner. Let's be careful not to place our anger among those who are also innocent.

In the rest of this chapter, we will examine two social characteristics which serve as the bases of social inequality—social class and ethnicity/race—and explore how each characteristic affects our life chances. Sex/gender, sexual orientation, and age will be reviewed in Chapter 3. Although each characteristic is presented separately, keep in mind that we do not occupy one characteristic at a time. At this moment, I am not just a female; I am also a heterosexual, an Asian Pacific Islander and a university professor. My social position is the product of *all* my characteristics, as is yours.

Which characteristic really makes the difference? Is it ethnicity/race, sexual orientation, gender, or something else? Social scientists have long debated this question. Some sociologists examine inequalities based on ethnicity/race whereas others focus exclusively on inequalities based on gender. Research has documented that these inequalities do exist, but the debate continues on which characteristic is more important in determining inequality. We begin first by examining the effects of social class.

Inequalities Based on Social Class

For Karl Marx, one's social class is solely determined by one's position in the economic system: You are either a worker or an owner of the means of production. But social class, according to Max Weber, is multidimensional. Economic factors include **income**, the money earned for one's work, and **wealth**, the value of one's personal assets such as savings and property. A person's social class is also influenced by **prestige**, the amount of social respect or standing given to an individual based on occupation. We assign higher prestige to occupations that require specialized education or training, that provide some social good to society, or that make more money. A final component of class is **power**. Weber defined power as the ability to achieve one's goals in spite of the opposition of others. Power is the ability to do whatever you want because no one can stop you.

Power is not limited to individuals. People with similar interests (or with similar income, wealth, and prestige backgrounds) often collaborate to increase their advantage in society. C. Wright Mills (1959/2000) argued that the United States is ruled by what he called a **power elite**. According to Mills, this elite group is composed of business, political, and military leaders. The power elite has true power because of its ability to withhold resources and prevent others from realizing their interests. Refer to the Focus On feature opposite for an in-depth look at the modern power elite.

Economic inequality is one of the most important and visible of America's social problems (McCall 2002). Martin Marger (2002) writes, "Measured in various ways, the gap between rich and poor in the United States is wider than [in] any other society with comparable economic institutions and standards of living" (p. 48). The overall

❖ FOCUS ON: WHO HAS THE REAL POWER

G. William Domhoff (2002) argues that real power is **distributive power**, the power individuals or groups have over other individuals or groups. Power matters when a group has the ability to control strategic resources and opportunities to obtain such resources. Money, land, information, and skills are strategic resources when they are needed by individuals to do what they want to do (Hachen 2001). Domhoff argues that distributive power is limited to an elite group of individuals whose economic, political, and social relationships are closely interrelated.

He writes about an elite power group composed of "members of the upper class who have taken on leadership roles in the corporate community and the policy network, along with high-level employees in corporations and policy-network organizations" (p. 9). Despite affirmative action policies and society's affirmation of the value of social equity, and although women and minorities are increasing their representation on corporate boards, presidential Cabinets, and leadership groups, the power elite is still composed of White male Christians.

Power elites are members of various policy planning groups, corporate boards, advisory councils, and leadership forums. These individuals frequently exchange positions, moving back and forth between private and public spheres as advisers, lobbyists, or Cabinet officials (Marger, 2000). U.S. presidents rely on a small network of influential corporate and policy leaders. A study of presidential Cabinet appointees from 1934 to 1980 (ending with the Carter administration) found that 64% of appointees were top wealth holders or were on the corporate boards of the largest companies in their area of expertise.

The pattern of influence among the wealthy and the influent is evident in the selection of President George W. Bush's first-term Cabinet appointees. Domhoff (2002) reports on the following Cabinet members:

Before his term as President George W. Bush's vice president Dick Cheney spent eight years as president of Halliburton, an oil drilling company. During the U.S.-Iraq war, Halliburton received over $8.2 billion in contracts, more than any other firm (Waxman 2004). He was also a member of the board of directors of Electronic Data Systems, Procter & Gamble, and Union Pacific. Cheney also served on the board of the American Enterprise Institute, a pro-business think tank.

Secretary of State, retired army general Colin Powell, served as a director of Gulfstream Aerospace until it merged with General Dynamics in 1999. Powell earned $1.49 million in stock options in exchange for helping the company sell corporate jets to Kuwait and Saudi Arabia. He was director of America Online at the time he was appointed. It is estimated that since retiring from the military, his net worth in 2001 was over $28 million.

Donald Rumsfeld, Secretary of Defense, previously served as chief executive officer of G. D. Searle & Co. and at General Instruments. In 1998 he was a member of four corporate boards: Kellogg, Sears Roebuck, The Tribune Publishing Co., and Gulfstream Aerospace (like Powell, Rumsfeld made over $1 million in stock options in exchange for helping sell corporate jets). He served as a trustee of two think tanks, the American Enterprise Institute and the Rand Corporation.

Former Secretary of Treasury, Paul H. O'Neill was retired chair of Alcoa, the world's largest aluminum manufacturer (holding more than $50 million in stock) and director of Lucent Technologies. He was chair of the board of trustees at the Rand Corporation and was a trustee at the American Enterprise Institute, along with Cheney and Rumsfeld. O'Neill was forced to resign from office in 2002 after he publicly voiced his disapproval of tax cuts and increasing budget deficits.

Log on to *Study Site Chapter 2* for more information.

distribution of wages and earnings has become more unequal, or to state it simply: The rich are getting richer and the poor are getting poorer (Duncan and Smeeding 1992). Richard Caputo (2003) describes a condition of **econosclerosis**, the hardening of economic arteries, where increasing proportions of young adults are unable to exceed their parents' economic status. Based on his research, Caputo finds that, between 1979 and 1993, increasing proportions of young adults from poor and affluent families experienced no net gains or losses in economic mobility from year to year. He reports that affluent families were more likely than poor families to hold their economic ground. On the other hand, increasing percentages of middle-class families experienced downward mobility. Caputo (2003) writes, "The 'econosclerotic' nature of economic mobility among poor and affluent youth in this study and, to a lesser degree, the downward mobility among poor youth portend a class structure that may exacerbate social tensions for decades to come" (p. 59).

The U.S. Census examines income distribution by dividing the U.S. household population into fifths or quintiles. If all U.S. income were equally divided, each quintile would receive one fifth of the total income. Based on U.S. Census 2001 data, about 50 percent of the total U.S. income was earned by households in the highest quintile or among households making more than $83,500 year. The richest 5 percent of households (earning over $150,499 per year) received 22 percent of total national income. The lowest 20 percent of households (earning $17,970 per year or less) had 3.5 percent of the total income (DeNavas-Walt and Cleveland 2002). (See Table 2.1.) Inequality grew during the period between 1973 and 1999, when the top fifth of the distribution began to increase their share of aggregate income, while the bottom four fifths began to lose their share (Jones and Weinberg 2000).

However, wealth, not income, may be more important in determining one's access to life chances. Wealth is more stable within families and across generations than income, occupation, or education (Conley 1999). As Melvin Oliver and Thomas Shapiro (1995) explain:

> Wealth is a particularly important indicator of individual and family access to life chances. Wealth is a special form of money not used to purchase milk and shoes and other life necessities. More often it is used to create opportunities, secure a desired stature and standard of living, or pass class status along to a one's children. . . . [T]he command over resources that wealth entails is more encompassing than income or education, and closer in meaning and theoretical significance to our traditional notions of economic well-being and access to life chances. (P. 2)

Wealth is more unequally distributed than income. Since the early 1920s, the top 1 percent of wealth holders has owned an average of 30 percent of household wealth. During the late 1980s and 1990s, the top 1 percent of wealth owners owned nearly 40 percent of all net worth and nearly 50 percent of all financial assets (Keister and Moller 2000). Wealth preserves the division between the wealthy and the nonwealthy. Scott Sernau (2001) tells us:

❖ Table 2.1   Share of Aggregate Income Received by Each Fifth and Top 5% of Households, 2001

Fifth	Income	Share
Top 5 Percent	$150,499 or higher	22.4
Top Fifth	$83,501 or higher	50.1
Second Fifth	$53,001–83,500	23.0
Third Fifth	$33,315–53,000	14.6
Fourth Fifth	$17,971–33,314	8.7
Lowest Fifth	Less than $17,970	3.5

Source: DeNavas-Walt and Cleveland 2002.

Wealth begets wealth. . . . It ensures that those near the bottom will be called on to spend almost all of their incomes and that what wealth they might acquire, such as an aging automobile or an aging house in a vulnerable neighborhood, will more likely depreciate than increase in value, and the poor will get nowhere. (P. 69)

Inequalities Based on Ethnicity or Race

From a biological perspective, **a race** can be defined as a group or population that shares a set of genetic characteristics and physical features. The term has been applied broadly to groups with similar physical features (the White race), religion (the Jewish race), or the entire human species (the human race) (Marger 2002). However, generations of migration, intermarriage, and adaptations to different physical environments have produced a mixture of races. There is no such thing as a "pure" race.

Social scientists reject the biological notions of race, instead favoring an approach that treats race as a social construct. In *Racial Formations in the United States: From the 1960s to the 1980s*, Michael Omi and Howard Winant (2003) explain how race is a "concept which signifies and symbolizes social conflicts and interests by referring to different types of human bodies" (p. 20). Instead of thinking of race as something "objective," the authors argue that we can imagine race as an "illusion," a subjective social, political, and cultural construct. According to the authors, "The meaning of race is defined and contested throughout society, in both collective action and personal practice. In the process, racial categories themselves are formed, transformed, destroyed, and reformed" (p. 21). Omi and Winant argue that although particular stereotypes and meanings can change, "the presence of a system of racial

CASTE DISCRIMINATION

It is estimated that over 250 million people worldwide suffer from caste segregation. A caste system segregates or excludes individuals on the basis of their descent. Caste communities exist in Asia and parts of Africa and include groups such as the Dalits (or untouchables) of Nepal, Bangladesh, India and Sri Lanka; the Buraku people of Japan; and the Osu of Nigeria. Despite formal legislation to abolish or combat abuses based on caste systems, the Human Rights Watch (2001) reports that "discriminatory treatment remains endemic and discriminatory societal norms continue to be reinforced by government and private structures and practices." The inequalities suffered by these groups affect every level of their lives—social, physical, economic and political.

The world's longest surviving social hierarchy is India's caste system. The caste is justified by the religious doctrine of "karma," a belief that an individual's place in life is determined by deeds in a previous life. The Dalit are the lowest members of the caste system, representing one-sixth of India's population or approximately 160–240 million. The status of the Dalits is reinforced by state allocation of resources and facilities—separate facilities are provided for different castes. For example, electricity, running water, or sanitation facilities may be installed for the upper caste section of town, but not for the Dalits and other lower castes. Dalits are prohibited from crossing from their side of the village. They cannot use the same water wells or visit the same temples as members of upper castes.

Children face discriminatory and abusive treatment at school by their teachers and their fellow students. Dalit children are often forced to sit in the back of the classroom. It is reported that most of the Indian schools with Dalit students are deficient in classrooms, teachers, and teaching aids. It should not come as a surprise that Dalit children also have the highest drop out rates among Indian children—49.3 percent at the primary level, 67.8 percent for middle school, and 77.6 percent for secondary school.

Dalits are prohibited from performing marriage or funeral rites in public areas or from speaking directly to members of upper castes. Intermarriage among castes is still condemned in India, punishable by social ostracism or violence. The Dalits are usually employed as the removers of human waste and dead animals, leather workers, street cleaners, and cobblers. Dalit children are often sold into slavery to pay off debts to creditors. It is estimated that about 15 million children are working as slaves in order to pay off family debts.

Source: Adapted from Human Rights Watch 2001.

meaning and stereotypes, of racial ideology, seems to be a permanent feature of U.S. culture" (p. 22).

Ethnic groups are groups that are set off to some degree from other groups by displaying a unique set of cultural traits, such as their language, religion, or diet. Members of an ethnic group perceive themselves as members of an ethnic community, sharing common historical roots and experiences. Marger (2002) explains how ethnicity serves as a basis of social ranking, ranking a person according to the status of his or her ethnic group. He states that although class and ethnicity are separate dimensions of stratification, they are closely related. "In virtually all multiethnic societies, people's ethnic classification becomes an important factor in the distribution of societal rewards and hence, their economic and political class positions. . . . The ethnic and class hierarchies are largely parallel and interwoven" (p. 286).

Income is one indicator that we could use to assess the level of inequality among ethnic groups. In 2001, the median income for White families was $44,517, whereas the median income for Black families was $29,470 and for Hispanic families, $33,565 (DeNavas-Walt and Cleveland 2002) (see Figure 2.2). The income gap seems even wider when looking at median incomes for men and women. The median income for White non-Hispanic males is $31,213 compared with $21,659 for Black males and $19,829 for Hispanic males. Among women, White non-Hispanic females have a median income of $16,804, Black females $16,084, and Hispanic females, $12,249 (U.S. Census Bureau 2002).

Due to years of discrimination, low educational attainment, high unemployment or underemployment, African Americans have not been able to achieve the same earnings or level of wealth as White Americans. Studies indicate that for every dollar earned by White households, Black households earned 62 cents (Oliver and Shapiro 1995). Blacks have between $8 and $19 of wealth for every $100 possessed by Whites. Whites have nearly 12 times as much median net worth as Blacks, $43,000 compared with $3,700 (Oliver and Shapiro 1995).

As of 2002, Hispanic Americans were the nation's largest minority group. (The U.S. Census treats Hispanic origin and race as separate and distinct concepts; as a result, Hispanics may be of any race.) The U.S. Census Bureau includes in this category women and men who are Mexican, Central and South American, Puerto Rican, Cuban, and other Hispanic. The growth in the number of Hispanic Americans has been attributed to increased international immigration and higher birthrates. The ethnic and racial composition of the United States is presented in Table 2.2.[1]

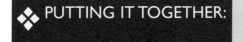

❖ PUTTING IT TOGETHER:

You may not be able to tell from my last name (Leon-Guerrero), but I consider my ethnic identity to be Japanese. My middle name is Yuri, a Japanese name that means "Lily." I am Japanese not only because of my middle name or because of my Japanese mother, but also because of the Japanese traditions that I practice, the Japanese words that I use, and even the Japanese foods that I like to eat. Do you have an ethnic identity? If you do, how do you maintain it?

❖ Figure 2.2   Median Household Income by Race and Hispanic Origin: 1967 to 2001

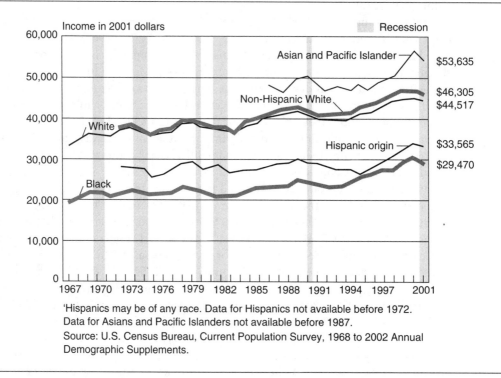

'Hispanics may be of any race. Data for Hispanics not available before 1972.
Data for Asians and Pacific Islanders not available before 1987.
Source: U.S. Census Bureau, Current Population Survey, 1968 to 2002 Annual
Demographic Supplements.

Source: DeNavas-Walt & Cleveland 2002, Figure 1, page 5.

Sociologists explain that **ethnocentrism** is the belief that one's own group values and behaviors are right, in fact, better than all others. Feeling positive about one's group is important for group solidarity and loyalty. However, it can lead groups to believe that certain racial or ethnic groups are inferior and that discriminatory practices against them are justified. This is called **racism**.

While not all ethnic/racial inequality can be attributed to racism, our nation's history reveals how ethnic/racial groups have been singled out and subject to unfair treatment. Certain ethnic/racial groups have been subject to **institutional discrimination**, discrimination practiced by the government, social institutions, and organizations. Institutional discrimination may include segregation, exclusion, or expulsion. **Segregation** refers to the physical and social separation of ethnic or racial groups. Although we consider explicit segregation to be illegal and a thing of the past, ethnic and racial segregation still occurs in neighborhoods, schools, and personal relationships. According to Van Ausdale and Feagin (2001):

> Racial discrimination and segregation are still central organizing factors in contemporary U.S. society.... For the most part, Whites and Blacks do not live in the same

❖ Table 2.2   Number of U.S. Adults by Hispanic Origin and Race, 2000

Hispanic Origin and Race	Number	Percentage of Population
Hispanic or Latino (of any race)	35,305,818	12.5
Non-Hispanic or -Latino	246,116,088	87.5
White	216,930,975	77.1
Black or African American	36,419,434	12.3
American Indian and Alaska Native	4,119,301	1.5
Asian	11,898,828	4.2
Native Hawaiian or Other Pacific Islander	874,414	.3
Some other race	18,521,486	6.6

Source: U.S. Census Bureau, 2000.

neighborhoods, attend the same schools at all educational levels, enter into close friendships or other intimate relationships with one another, or share comparable opinions on a wide variety of political matters. The same is true, though sometimes to a lesser extent, for Whites and other Americans of color, such as most Latino, Native and Asian American groups. Despite progress since the 1960s, U.S. society remains intensely segregated across color lines. Generally speaking, Whites and people of color do not occupy the same social space or social status. (P. 29)

Exclusion refers to the practice of prohibiting or restricting the entry or participation of groups in society. For example, from 1882 to 1943, the United States prohibited Chinese immigration because of concerns that Chinese laborers would compete with American workers. The Personal Responsibility and Work Opportunity Reconciliation Act of 1996, also known as the welfare reform law, restricted legal immigrants' access to assistance programs such as Medicaid, food stamps, and welfare. Finally, **expulsion** is the removal of a group by direct force or intimidation. After the Japanese attack on Pearl Harbor in 1941, President Roosevelt signed Executive Order 9066, which authorized the military to detain anyone perceived as a threat to national security. As a result, 120,000 people of Japanese ancestry were interned in desert camps located in Arizona, California, Utah, Idaho, Colorado, and Wyoming. The camps operated from 1942 through 1945. After the terrorist attacks of September 11, 2001, Arab Americans and American Muslims were victims of a severe wave of backlash violence. Latinos and Indian Americans were singled out because of their physical similarities to Arabs. Arab and Muslim groups reported more than 2,000 incidents related to the events of September 11. Since then, the U.S. government has detained more than 1,200 Middle Eastern and South Asians because of possible links to terrorism (Human Rights Watch 2002).

Policy Focus—Affirmative Action in the Workplace

Affirmative action is a policy that has attempted to improve minority access to occupational and educational opportunities (Woodhouse 2002). Since its inception nearly 40 years ago, it has been a "contentious issue on national, state, and local levels" (Yee 2001:135). No federal initiatives enforced affirmative action until 1961, when President John Kennedy signed Executive Order 10925. The order created the Committee on Equal Employment Opportunity and forbade employers with federal contracts from discriminating on the basis of race, color, national origin, or religion in their hiring practices. In 1964, President Lyndon Johnson signed into law the Civil Rights Act, which prohibits discrimination based on race, color, religion, or national origin by private employers, agencies, and educational institutions receiving federal funds (Swink 2003).

In June 1965, during a graduation speech at Howard University, President Johnson spoke for the first time about the importance of providing opportunities to minority groups, an important objective of affirmative action. According to Johnson (1965):

> You do not take a person who, for years, has been hobbled by chains and liberate him, bring him to the starting line of a race and then say, "You are free to compete with all others" and still justly believe you have been completely fair. Thus it is not enough just to open the gates of opportunity. All our citizens must have the ability to walk through those gates. This is the next and the more profound stage of the battle for civil rights. We seek not just freedom but opportunity.

In September 1965, Johnson signed Executive Order 11246, which required government contractors to "take affirmative action" toward prospective minority employees in all aspects of hiring and employment. Contractors are required to take specific proactive measures to ensure equality in hiring without regard to race, religion, and national origin. The order also established the Equal Employment Opportunities Commission (EEOC), charged with enforcing and monitoring compliance among federal contractors. In 1967, Johnson amended the order to include discrimination based on gender (Swink 2003). In 1969, President Richard Nixon initiated the Philadelphia Plan, which required federal contractors to develop affirmative action plans by setting minimum levels of minority participation on federal construction projects in Philadelphia and three other cities (Idelson 1995). This was the first order that endorsed the use of specific goals for desegregating the workplace (Kotlowski 1998), but it did not include fixed quotas (Woodhouse 2002). In 1970, the order was extended to all federal contractors (Idelson 1995).

According to Swink (2003), "While the initial efforts of affirmative action were directed primarily at federal government employment and private industry, affirmative action gradually extended into other areas, including admissions programs in higher education" (pp. 214–215). State and local governments followed the lead of the federal government and took formal steps to encourage employers to diversify their workforces.

Opponents of affirmative action believe that such policies encourage preferential treatment for minorities (Woodhouse 2002), giving women and ethnic minorities an unfair advantage over White males (Yee 2001). Affirmative action, say its critics, promotes "reverse discrimination," the hiring of unqualified minorities and women at the expense of qualified White males. Some believe affirmative action has not worked and ultimately results in the stigmatization of those who benefit from the policies (Herring and Collins 1995; Heilman, Block, and Stahatos 1997).

Proponents argue that only through affirmative action policies can we address the historical societal discrimination that minorities experienced in the past (Kaplan and Lee 1995). Although these policies have not created true equality, there have been important accomplishments (Tsang and Dietz 2001). As a result of affirmative action, women and people of color have gained increased access to forms of public employment and education that were once closed to them (Yee 2001). Yet, research indicates that ethnic minorities and women do not have an unfair advantage over White men. Women and ethnic minorities are not receiving equal compensation in comparison to White males with similar education and background (Tsang and Dietz 2001). Although it may not be perfect, affirmative action has been the "only comprehensive set of policies that has given women and people of color opportunities for better paying jobs and access to higher education that did not exist before" (Yee 2001:137).

Woodhouse (2002, 1999) argues that the differences in individual perceptions of affirmative action policy may be related to the differences of racial group histories and socialization experiences. She writes:

> Based upon these rationalizations, it is implicit that individuals interpret affirmative action through an ethnic specific lens. In other words, most individuals will assess their group condition when considering contentious legislation such as affirmative action because after all, a group's history impacts its view of American society. (Woodhouse 2002:158)

MAIN POINTS

- Sociologists use the term **social stratification** to refer to the ranking of individuals into social strata or groups. Attached to each social position are **life chances**, a term Max Weber used to describe the consequences of social stratification or how each social position provides access to resources such as wealth, food, clothing, shelter, education, and health care. Sociologists refer to the unequal distribution of resources as **social inequality**. Certain social positions are subject to **prejudice** (a negative attitude toward individuals based on attributes ascribed to a group) and **discrimination** (acts based on prejudiced beliefs against a specific individual or group) not experienced by others. And sadly, some social positions are also targets of violence.

- Why does social inequality exist? Functionalists assume that not everyone in society can and should be equal. From this perspective, inequality is necessary for the social order.

- From a conflict perspective, inequality is systematically created and maintained by those trying to maintain their advantage over the system. From a feminist perspective, gender inequality is the product of the patriarchal system and is perpetuated through social structures like the family, the workplace, and education.

- Interactionists view inequality as the result of human interaction, the meanings and values we attach to individuals and their social positions.

- For Karl Marx, one's social class is solely determined by one's position in the economic system: You are either a worker or an owner of the means of production. According to Max Weber, however, social class is multidimensional. Economic factors include **income**, the money earned for one's work, and **wealth,** the value of one's personal assets such as savings and property. A person's social class is also influenced by **prestige**, the amount of social respect or standing given to an individual based on occupation. A final component of class is power. Weber defined **power** as the ability to achieve one's goals in spite of the opposition of others.

- From a biological perspective, a race can be defined as a group or population that shares a set of genetic characteristics and physical features. Social scientists reject the biological notion of race, instead treating race as a social construct.

- **Ethnic groups** are groups that are set off to some degree from other groups by displaying a unique set of cultural traits, such as their language, religion, or diet. Members of an ethnic group perceive themselves as members of an ethnic community, sharing common historical roots and experiences.

- Sociologists explain that **ethnocentrism** is the belief that the values and behaviors of one's own group are right and, in fact, better than all others. Although feeling positive about one's group is important for group solidarity and loyalty, it can lead groups to believe that certain racial or ethnic groups are inferior and that discriminatory practices against them are justified. This is called **racism.**

- Certain ethnic/racial groups have been subject to **institutional discrimination**, discrimination practiced by the government, social institutions, and organizations. Institutional discrimination may include segregation, exclusion, or expulsion. **Segregation** refers to the physical and social separation of ethnic or racial groups. **Exclusion** refers to the practice of prohibiting or restricting the entry or participation of groups in society. **Expulsion** is the removal of a group by using direct force or intimidation.

- Affirmative action is a policy that has attempted to improve minority access to occupational and educational opportunities. Since its inception nearly 40 years ago, it has been a controversial issue on federal, state, and local levels.

❖

INTERNET AND COMMUNITY EXERCISES

1. Are categories of "otherness" supported on your campus? Investigate whether your campus has a student diversity center or office. What student populations does it serve? Is participation open to everyone on campus or just members of particular groups? (If your campus does not have a diversity office, do you believe it would benefit from one? Why or why not?)

2. What is the median income for your state? The median income is the exact point where 50 percent of all incomes are above and 50 percent of all incomes are below. Log on to *Study Site Chapter 2* to access the U.S. Census Bureau Web site.

3. To learn more about the internment of Japanese Americans during World War II, visit the Web sites for the Manzanar War Relocation Center and internment camps located in Tule Lake, California, and Topaz, Utah. These Web sites feature virtual tours, photographs, and testimony from those interned. Masumi Hayashi, photography professor from Cleveland State University, supports a Web site that chronicles the Japanese internment through amateur and professional photographs taken by internees. Log on to *Study Site Chapter 2* for links.

On your own. Log on to *Study Site—Community and Policy Guide* for more information about the social problems, social policies, and community responses discussed in this chapter.

Note

1. Tracy Ore (2003) acknowledges that externally created labels for some groups may not always be accepted by those viewed as belonging to a particular group. For example, those of Latin American descent may not consider themselves to be "Hispanic." In this text, I've adopted Ore's practice regarding which racial and ethnic terms are used. In my own material, I will use *Latina/o* to refer to those of Latin American descent and will use *Black* and *African American* interchangeably. However, original terms used by authors or researchers (e.g., use of the term Hispanic by the U.S. Census Bureau) will not be altered.

References

Caputo, Richard K. 2003. "Assets and Economic Mobility in a Youth Cohort, 1985–1997." *Families in Society: The Journal of Contemporary Human Service* 84(1):51–62.

Conley, D. 1999. *Being Black, Living in the Red: Race, Wealth, and Social Policy in America.* Berkeley: University of California Press.

DeNavas-Walt, Carmen and Robert Cleveland. 2002. *Money Income in the United States: 2001* (Current Population Reports, P. 60–218). Washington, DC: Government Printing Office.

Domhoff, G. William. 2002. *Who Rules America? Power and Politics.* Boston: McGraw-Hill.

Duncan, G. and T. Smeeding. 1992. "The Incredible Shrinking Middle Class." *American Demographics* 14(5):34–39.

Hachen, D. 2001. *Sociology in Action.* Thousand Oaks, CA: Pine Forge.

Heilman, M. E., C. J. Block, and P. Stathatos. 1997. The Affirmative Action Stigma of Incompetence: Effects of Performance Information Ambiguity. *Academy of Management Journal* 40:603–625.

Herring, Cedric and Sharon Collins. 1995. "Retreat from Equal Opportunity? The Case of Affirmative Action." Pp. 163–181 in *The Bubbling Cauldron: Race, Ethnicity, and the Urban Crisis,* edited by Michael Smith and Joe Feagin. Minneapolis: University of Minnesota Press.

Human Rights Watch. 2001. *Caste Discrimination: A Global Concern.* New York: Author.

———. 2002. *We Are Not the Enemy: Hate Crimes Against Arabs, Muslims, and Those Perceived to Be Arab or Muslim after September 11.* New York: Human Rights Watch.

Idelson, Holly. (1995). "A 30-Year Experiment." *Congressional Quarterly Weekly Report* 53(22):1579.

Johnson, Allan G. 2001. *Privilege, Power, and Difference.* Boston: McGraw Hill.

Johnson, Lyndon. 1965. *Public Papers of the Presidents of the United States: Lyndon B. Johnson, 1965* (Vol. 2, entry 301, pp. 635–640). Washington, DC: Government Printing Office.

Jones, Arthur and Daniel Weinberg. 2000. *The Changing Shape of the Nation's Income Distribution 1947–1998* (Current Population Reports P. 60–204). Washington, DC: Government Printing Office.

Kaplan, W. and B. Lee. 1995. *The Law of Higher Education: A Comprehensive Guide to Legal Implications of Administrative Decision Making.* San Francisco: Jossey-Bass.

Keister, Lisa and Stephanie Moller. 2000. "Wealth Inequality in the United States." *Annual Review of Sociology* 26:63–81.

Kotlowski, Dean. 1998. "Richard Nixon and the Origins of Affirmative Action." *Historian* 60(3):523–542.

Loden, Marilyn and Judy Rosener. 1991. *Workforce America! Managing Employee Diversity as a Vital Resource.* New York: McGraw-Hill.

Marger, Martin. 2002. *Social Inequality: Patterns and Processes.* Boston: McGraw-Hill.

McCall, Leslie. 2002. *Complex Inequality: Gender, Class, and Race in the New Economy.* New York: Routledge.

Mills, C. Wright. 2000. *The Sociological Imagination.* New York: Oxford University Press. (Original work published 1959)

Muzher, Sherri. 2001. "It's Not Easy Being an Arab-American: One Person's Experience." Retrieved June 3, 2004 (www.mediamonitors.net/sherri22.html).

Oliver, M. and T. Shapiro 1995. *Black Wealth/White Wealth.* New York: Routledge.

Omi, Michael and Howard Winant. 2003. "Racial Formation." Pp. 18–27 in *The Social Construction of Difference and Inequality: Race, Class, Gender, and Sexuality,* edited by T. Ore. Boston: McGraw-Hill.

Ore, Tracy, ed. 2003. *The Social Construction of Difference and Inequality: Race, Class, Gender, and Sexual Orientation.* Boston: McGraw-Hill.

Sernau, Scott. (2001). *Worlds Apart: Social Inequalities in a New Century.* Thousand Oaks, CA: Pine Forge.

Swink, Dawn. 2003. "Back to Bakke: Affirmative Action Revisited in Educational Diversity." *BYU Education and Law Journal* 1:211–257.

Tsang, Chiu-Wai Rita and Tracy Dietz. 2001. "The Unrelenting Significance of Minority Statuses: Gender, Ethnicity, and Economic Attainment Since Affirmative Action." *Sociological Spectrum* 21:61–80.

U.S. Census Bureau. (2000). "Census 2000 Summary File 1 (SF1) 100-Percent Data." Retrieved June 30, 2004 (http://factfinder.census.gov)

———. 2002. *Historical Income Tables—People* (Table P-2, Race and Hispanic Origin of People by Median Income and Sex: 1947–2000). Washington, DC: Government Printing Office.

Van Ausdale, D. and J. R. Feagin. 2001. *The First R: How Children Learn Race and Racism.* Lanham, MA: Rowan & Littlefield.

Waxman, H. 2004. "Correspondence to Committee on Government Reform," June 14. Retrieved June 30, 2004 (www.house.gov/reform).

Woodhouse, Shawn. 1999. "Faculty Perceptions of the Impact of Affirmative Action on Employment Practices in the University of Missouri System." PhD dissertation, University of Missouri.

———. 2002. "The Historical Development of Affirmative Action: An Aggregated Analysis." *Western Journal of Black Studies* 26(3):155–59.

Yee, Shirley. 2001. "The Past, Present, and Future of Affirmative Action: AHA Roundtable, January 1998—Introduction." *NWSA Journal* 10(3):135–41.

B

The Bases of Inequality

Sex and Gender, Sexual Orientation, and Age

In this chapter, we will review three additional bases of inequality: sex and gender, sexual orientation, and age. Each inequality is the basis for a form of prejudice and or discrimination. **Sexism** refers to prejudice or discrimination based solely on someone's sex. Although sexism has come to refer to negative beliefs and actions directed toward women, men can also be subject to sexism. **Heterosexism** is the privileging of heterosexuality over homosexuality in society. Heterosexism includes individual attitudes (nearly 60 percent of U.S. adults would support a constitutional amendment that would define marriage as occurring only between a man and a woman; CBS News/New York Times 2004) and institutional forms of discrimination (gay or lesbian partners are routinely excluded from health insurance policies). Age also serves as a basis of prejudice or discrimination. **Ageism** is defined by Robert Butler (1969) as the "systematic stereotyping of and discrimination against people because they are old, just as racism and sexism accomplish this with skin color and gender" (p. 243). We begin first with a look at inequalities based on gender.

Inequalities Based on Gender

What is the basis of gender inequality? Some may argue that there are fundamental differences between males and females, based on fixed physiological differences or our **sex**. Yes, there are biological differences—our sexual organs, our hormones, and other physiological aspects—that are relatively fixed at birth (Marger 2002), but more than that makes us unequal. Sociologists focus on the differences determined by our society and our culture, our **gender**. Although we are born male and female, we must understand and learn masculine or feminine behaviors (Marger 2002). Gender serves to legitimate certain activities and ways of thinking over others; it grants privilege to one group over another (Tickner 2002). Many sociological theories have been offered to explain the differences between women and men, focusing primarily on the inequalities evident in educational attainment, income, and employment. In each area, research and data confirm how women are subordinated to men (for more discussion, refer to Chapter 5, Education, and Chapter 6, The Workplace).

Let's consider the history of women in the U.S. Senate. In the 214-year history of the U.S. Senate, only 33 women have been elected or appointed as members. The first woman senator was Rebecca Latimer Felton, sworn into office on November 21, 1922. The Georgia senator was appointed to fill a vacancy and served only for two days. In the early 1990s, there were only two women senators. In 1992, Patty Murray, from my home state of Washington, was the first elected female senator to have young children at home during her term (Stolberg 2003). But by 2002, there were 14 women senators. Four senators were working moms with young or school-age children.

There is nothing automatic at birth that makes men more suited to become senators than women. Sociologists have examined how girls and boys are subject to differential gender socialization from birth. Traditional gender role stereotypes are reinforced through the family, school, peers, and the media with images of what is appropriate behavior for girls and boys. This includes defining appropriate occupations for women versus men.

Boys are exposed to images and models of "masculine" occupations such as firefighters, attorneys, and even politicians. Our educational system directs and encourages boys to pursue studies in math, science, and engineering. In contrast, girls are directed to "feminine" service or helping professions, such as nursing or teaching. Despite educational and occupational gains made by women, women continue to dominate traditional female occupations: secretaries (96.3 percent are women), receptionists (93.2 percent), registered nurses (90.2 percent) and preschool teachers (98.3 percent) (U.S. Department of Labor, Women's Bureau, 2003). Fourteen women senators out of 100 U.S. senators make only 14 percent. (In contrast, Iraq's temporary constitution adopted in 2004 required that 25 percent of the seats in the national assembly must be filled by women. Yet, equal rights for Iraqi women regarding marriage and inheritance were not guaranteed by the constitution.) Although women have been in the labor force for many years, women and men still work at different jobs.

Functionalists may argue that it is appropriate for men, not women, to pursue political office because it is more practical or natural for men to be in leadership positions. It must be the correct arrangement because it is how it has always been done. In fact, women may contemplate certain occupations believing that the type of work is compatible with their gender. However, conflict and feminist theorists identify how our social and political structures are created to maintain the dominance of men. Sexism or discrimination may be an individual act, but it can also become institutionalized in our organizations or through laws and common practices. Sociologist Rosabeth Moss Kanter (1977) identified how business corporations have a hidden gender structure: functioning, but unwritten rules about what positions can be occupied by women and how many women should be employed in the corporation.

Organizations implicitly or explicitly withhold support from their female employees in the form of training, promotion, or wages. Even if men and women have similar jobs within a company, men usually have more income and authority than women (Beeghley 2005).

One could argue that the U.S. Senate is a patriarchal system, dominated and maintained by men. Something that we take for granted, such as a bathroom, can be considered as evidence of subordination or exclusion. For example, for many years, there was no women's restroom in the Senate Chambers. The nearest available restroom was on the first floor, along with the public restrooms. Women senators had to "schlep downstairs and stand in line with the tourists" (Collins 1993:93). It was not until 1993 that female senators had their own bathroom located outside the Senate Chamber, next to the restroom for male senators. To make room for the facility, the existing men's restroom was remodeled into two separate restrooms. When the restroom was built, Eleanor Smeal, president of the Fund of the Feminist Majority, declared, "[This] signifies the end of one of the last all-male bastions in the country that has real power" (Picker 1993).

As interactionists explain, many social values and meanings are expressed in our language. As more women are elected to public office, our language has changed. The state legislatures in New York, Rhode Island, and Utah are revising their constitutions to gender-neutral language, eliminating the exclusive use of *he* or *him*. Such sexist language only accentuates the dominance of men in political affairs; however, the usage of *she* or *they* may reinforce and encourage the increasing participation of women in politics. Sandy Galef, an assemblywoman who led the drive to revise New York's state constitution, explained, "These constitutions were written about men because that was the history of our country. But that's not the history anymore" ("Some States" 2003:A28).

Policy Focus—Title IX

Title IX of the Educational Amendments of 1972 prohibits the exclusion of any person from participation in an educational program or the denial of benefits based on one's sex (Woodhouse 2002). The preamble to Title IX states, "No person in the United States shall, on the basis of sex, be excluded from participation in, be denied the benefits of, or be subject to discrimination under any educational programs or activity receiving federal financial assistance." In particular, the law requires that members of both sexes have equal opportunities to participate in sports and enjoy the benefits of competitive athletics (National Women's Law Center 2002b).

❖ ─────────────────

Voices in the Community:
Bernice R. Sandler

In this feature, Bernice Sandler (1997), the woman behind Title IX, explains how she was transformed into a voice of change.

The year was 1969. I had been teaching part-time at the University of Maryland for several years during the time that I worked on my doctorate and shortly after I finished it. There were seven openings in the department, and I have just asked a fellow faculty member and friend why I was not considered for any of the openings. My qualifications were excellent, "But let's face it," he said, "You come on too strong for a woman." . . . I had no idea that this rejection would not only change my life but would ultimately change the lives of millions of women and girls because it triggered a series of events that would lead to the passage of Title IX. . . .

Although sex discrimination was illegal in certain circumstances, I quickly discovered that none of the laws prohibiting discrimination covered sex discrimination in education. I turned to the civil rights movement to see what African Americans had done to break down segregated school systems and employment discrimination, with the hope of learning what might be applicable to women's issues. I discovered a presidential Executive Order prohibiting federal contractors from discrimination in employment on the basis of race, color, religion and national origin that had been amended by President Johnson, effective October 13, 1968, to include discrimination based on sex. This discovery meant that there was a legal route to combat sex discrimination on campuses that held federal contracts.

The Director of the Office of Federal Contract Compliance at the Department of Labor, Vincent Macaluso, had been waiting for someone to use the Executive Order in regard to sex discrimination. Together we planned the first complaint against universities and colleges, and the strategies to bring about enforcement of the Executive Order.

Two months later under the auspices of the Women's Equity Action League (WEAL), I began what quickly became a national campaign to end discrimination in education and eventually culminated in the passage of Title IX. One January 31, 1970, WEAL filed a historic class action complaint against all universities and colleges in the country with specific charges against the University of Maryland. . . . During the next two years, I filed charges against approximately 250 institutions. Another 100 or so were filed by other individuals and organizations such as the National Organization for Women (NOW); in tandem with these administrative charges, we began a massive letter-writing campaign to members of Congress. . . .

Rep. Edith Green (OR), . . . chair of the subcommittee that dealt with higher education, agreed to hold Congressional hearings in June and July of 1970 on education and employment of women. It was a time when there were virtually no books and only a few articles that addressed the issue of discrimination against women in education. There was little research or data, and barely a handful of unnoticed women's studies courses. There were no campus commissions on the status of women and only a few institutions had even begun to examine the status of women on their campus. . . .

In the spring of 1972, two years after the hearings, a portion of Rep. Green's original bill became law when Title VII of the Civil Rights Act was amended by Congress to cover all employees in educational institutions. Initially, Rep. Green had also sought to amend Title VI of the Civil Rights Act to include sex discrimination. However, at the urging of African-American leaders and others, who were worried that opening Title VI for amendment could weaken its coverage, she proposed a separate and new title, which became Title IX. . . . On June 23, 1972, Title IX of the Education Amendments of 1972, was passed by Congress and on July 1, was signed into law by President Richard Nixon. . . .

The words "too strong for a woman" turned me into a feminist. At that time, I had no legal, political or organizing experience. I was also extraordinarily naïve; I believed that if we passed Title IX, it would only take a year or two for the all the inequalities based on sex to be eliminated. Eventually, I realized that the women's movement was trying not simply to pass a piece of legislation, but to alter strongly embedded gender patterns of behavior and belief. To change all that would take masses of strong women and more than my lifetime to accomplish.

—————————————— ❖·❖ ——————————————

According to Title IX, schools are required to offer women and men equal opportunities to participate in athletics. This can be done in one of three ways: Schools demonstrate that the percentage of male and female athletes is about the same as the percentage of male and female students enrolled (also referred to as the "proportionality rule"), or the school has a history and a continuing practice of expanding opportunities for female students, or the school is fully and effectively meeting its female students' interests and abilities to participate in sports. In addition, schools must equitably allocate athletic scholarships. The overall share of financial aid going to female athletes should be the same as the percentage of female athletes participating in their athletic program. Finally, schools must treat men and women equally in all aspects of sports programming. This requirement applies to supplies and equipment, the scheduling of games and practices, financial support for travel, and the assignment and compensation of coaches (National Women's Law Center 2002a).

The law has been widely credited with increasing women's participation in high school and collegiate sports and also for women's achievement in education. In 1997, data released by the U.S. Department of Education revealed the successes of Title IX after 25 years. In 1995, 37 percent of collegiate athletes were women, compared to 15 percent in 1972. In 1996, girls represented 39 percent of all high school athletes compared with only 7.5 percent in 1971 (U.S. Department of Education 1997). Today more than 150,000 women participate in college sports, and about 3 million girls participate in high school sports (Garber 2002). In 1994, 63 percent of female high school graduates were enrolled in college, an increase from 43 percent in 1973. About 18 percent of women and 26 percent of men had completed four or more years of college in 1971 (U.S. Department of Education 1997). In 2002, 24.1 percent of men and 21.9 percent of women had completed a bachelor's degree or higher (U.S. Census Bureau 2002).

After more than 30 years, the controversy over Title IX continues. Many blame Title IX for the demise of some 400 collegiate men's programs. To achieve proportionality between the number of male and female athletes, schools have reduced the number of male athletes in minor sport programs such as wrestling, gymnastics, golf, and tennis (Garber 2002). In 2002, the National Wrestling Coaches Association filed a lawsuit against the U.S. Department of Education, claiming that by enforcing Title IX, the department was practicing sexual discrimination against men. In June 2003, a federal judge threw out the lawsuit, ruling that the coaches did not have standing to bring the lawsuit.

There is also evidence that not all colleges and universities are complying with the law. Although women in Division I colleges represent more than half the student body, women's sports receive only 43 percent of athletic scholarships, 32 percent of recruiting funds, and 36 percent of operating budgets (National Women's Law Center 2002a). Most surveyed Americans, about 70 percent, think Title IX should be strengthened or left alone (Brady 2003).

In June 2002, Secretary of Education Rod Paige announced the formation of the Commission on Opportunity in Athletics. Paige directed the 14-member commission to identify improvements in how Title IX is implemented. In January 2003, the Commission on Opportunity in Athletics reviewed Title IX and recommended several changes. In general, the Commission endorsed recommendations that would give schools more latitude in identifying athletic opportunities and scholarships. The Commission deadlocked on a proposal to allow schools to allocate 43 percent of slots on varsity sports teams for women, although women make up 55.5 percent of college enrollments (Fletcher and Sandoval 2003). Department of Education officials confirm that they will retain Title IX enforcement, keeping the proportionality rule, but they will also begin emphasizing the other ways schools can meet the law through demonstrating a pattern of expanding opportunities for women or by proving the sports interests of women have been met (Associated Press 2003).

❖ **PUTTING IT TOGETHER:**
On your campus.

Investigate how Title IX is administered in your college or university. How many male and female athletes are at your university? How many programs for each? Have any programs been cut as a result of Title IX requirements? Interview coaches, athletes, and administrators on their view of Title IX: Has it made a difference for students and athletes at your school?

Inequalities Based on Sexual Orientation

One's sexual orientation also serves as a basis of inequality. **Sexual orientation** is defined as the classification of individuals according to their preference for emotional-sexual relationships and lifestyle with persons of the same sex (**homosexuality**) or persons of the opposite sex (**heterosexuality**). **Bisexuality** refers to emotional and sexual attractions to persons of either sex.

There is no definitive study on the number of individuals who identify themselves as homosexual or bisexual. The study that is most often cited is one conducted in 1994 by Robert Michael and his colleagues (1994). Based on a random survey of 3,432 U.S. adults age 18 to 59 years, Michael et al. found that 2.8 percent of males and 1.4 percent of females thought of themselves as homosexual or bisexual. About 5 percent of surveyed males and 4 percent of females said they had had sex with someone of the same gender after they turned 18. About 6 percent of males and 4 percent of females reported that they were sexually attracted to someone of the same gender.

In our society, no one gets "outed" for being straight. There is little controversy in identifying someone as heterosexual. Socially, culturally, and legally, the heterosexual life style is promoted and praised. Although homosexuality has existed in most societies, it has usually been attached to a negative label—abnormal, sinful, or inappropriate. A socially determined prejudice, **homophobia**, is an irrational fear or intolerance of homosexuals (Lehne 1995). Homophobia is particularly directed at gay men. Bisexual or homosexual men, women, and their families are subject to social inequalities through practices of discrimination and prejudice, many of them surprisingly institutionalized in formal law.

Sodomy laws criminalize oral and anal sex between two adults. Although the laws may apply to homosexuals and heterosexuals, sodomy laws are more vigorously applied against same-sex partners. Thirteen states still had state sodomy laws in 2003 (in 1960, sodomy was outlawed in every state). In 1986, the U.S. Supreme Court ruled that Georgia's sodomy law did not violate privacy rights.

In 1998, John Lawrence and Tyron Garner were fined $200 and spent a night in jail for violating a Texas statute that prohibits "deviate sexual intercourse" between two people of the same sex. The Texas statute does not apply to heterosexual couples. Their case was heard before the U. S. Supreme Court in March 2003. Attorneys for Lawrence and Garner argued that the Texas law was an invasion of their privacy and violated the equal protection clause of the 14th Amendment because the law unfairly targets same-sex couples. Attorneys for the state argued that Texas has the right to set moral standards for its residents. In June 2003, the Court voted 6 to 3 to overrule the Texas law and all other remaining sodomy laws. Writing for the decision, Justice Anthony Kennedy said, "The state cannot demean their [homosexuals'] existence or control their destiny by making their private sexual conduct a crime" (Greenhouse 2003: A17). According to Kevin Cathcart, executive director of Lambda Legal, "This ruling starts an entirely new chapter in our fight for equality for lesbian, gay, bisexual, and transgendered people" (Lambda Legal 2003b).

Gay and lesbian couples are denied the same legal and social support given heterosexual couples. Their families are denied common legal protections that non-gay families take for granted such as adoption, custody, guardianship, social security, and inheritance (Lambda Legal 2003a). Due to the "don't ask, don't tell" policy for homosexuals in the U.S. military, many gay and lesbian couples must keep their relationships secret. During the U.S.-Iraq war, Christopher Marquis (2003) wrote about the secrecy, paranoia, and frustration that was common among homosexual couples and their families. Homosexual couples were forced to lie about their relationship and were not able to access supportive services provided to heterosexual married partners. Although their partners were deployed in the Middle East, the stateside gay or lesbian partners were not eligible to use the base store or have access to support groups or status reports on the troops' whereabouts.

Reacting to what he called the "divisiveness" of President George W. Bush's 2004 State of the Union Address on the issue of gay marriage, San Francisco Mayor Gavin Newsom secretly began planning to marry gay and lesbian couples and convinced longtime lesbian rights activists Del Martin, 83, and Phyllis Lyon, 79, to be the first to get married (Quittner 2004). Said Newsom, "We wanted to put a human face on this, and Phyllis and Del were critical. . . . To deny them the same protections as married couples would be to deny them as human beings, not as theory" (Quittner 2004). Between February 12 and March 10, 2004, more than 4,000 same-sex marriage licenses were issued in San Francisco. Although the majority of couples were from California, couples from 45 other states and 8 countries also applied for marriage licenses in the city (Leff 2004).

The California Supreme Court ordered San Francisco to stop issuing same-sex marriage licenses on March 11, 2004. In August 2004, the California Supreme Court ruled that San Francisco Mayor Newsom did not have the authority to issue marriage licenses to same-sex couples and declared the marriage licenses invalid. At the time of the decision, Phyllis Lyon said, "it is a terrible blow to have the rights and protections of marriage taken away from us. At our age, we do not have the luxury of time" (Lambda Legal 2004).

In response to the same-sex marriages in California, President Bush endorsed a constitutional amendment that would restrict marriage to two people of opposite sexes but left open the possibility that states could allow civil unions in same-sex relationships. However, in July 2004, the U.S. Senate failed to pass a constitutional amendment that would have declared marriage as a union only between a man and a woman. Democratic presidential and vice presidential candidates, Senators John Kerry and John Edwards, were opposed to the measure. Vice President Dick Cheney also opposed the measure, stating that he believes that states should have the right to decide what constitutes a marriage. (We will examine gay and lesbian families further in Chapter 4, Families. Employment discrimination against gays and lesbians will be discussed in Chapter 6, Work.)

❖ **PUTTING IT TOGETHER:**
In your community.

Lambda Legal is a national organization committed to achieving full recognition of the civil rights of lesbians, gay men, the transgendered, and people with HIV or AIDS. The organization identifies each state that prohibits sexual orientation discrimination in employment. Investigate whether your state has discrimination laws by logging on to Lambda Legal's Web site (log on to *Study Site Chapter 3*). If your state does include such laws, a brief summary of the legislation is included.

Inequalities Based on Age

We have socially and culturally defined expectations about the meaning of age, our understanding of it, and our responses to it (Calasanti and Slevin 2001). Age serves to distinguish acceptable behavior for different social groups. Voting rights, the legal age to consume alcohol, or the ability to hold certain elected offices (you can't be president of the United States until you are at least 35 years old) are examples of formal age norms. Informal age norms also demonstrate how a society defines what is considered appropriate by age (Calasanti and Slevin 2001). We make a fuss over the 78-year-old weight lifter or the 13-year-old college student, noting their accomplishments simply because they are unexpected or deemed "unusual" for people of their age.

Dependency is one of the most negative attributes of being identified as "old" in our society (Calasanti and Slevin 2001). Stereotypes about the capacities, activities, and interests of older people reinforce the view that they are incapable of caring for themselves (Pampel 1998). There is widespread acceptance of negative stereotypes about the elderly regarding their intellectual decline, conservatism, sexual decline, and lack of productivity (Levin and Levin 1980).

Research suggests that ageist attitudes may affect a physician's therapeutic decisions toward older patients (Peppin 1995). Physicians perform fewer examinations and tests on older patients in comparison with younger patients. Older patients are denied life-saving treatments and access to new experimental treatments. A study reviewing the treatment of women with breast cancer found that women older than 50 are 6 to 62 times more likely not to receive chemotherapy treatments. Researchers hypothesized that the physicians felt the risk of drug toxicity outweighed the benefits of treatment for their older female patients ("Age Bias" 2003). However, what if the older patient has the same life expectancy as a younger patient? Another study examined the records of prostate cancer patients and found that older men who were healthier and expected to live at least for another 10 years were more likely to receive inadequate cancer treatment than younger patients with shorter life expectancy. Studies reveal that healthy older men, those in their 70s, who have aggressive prostate cancer can benefit from surgery or radiation therapy. Yet, it appears that doctors are using age, not life expectancy, to determine whether prostate cancer patients receive appropriate treatment ("Older Patients" 2004).

Although much attention has been given to the marginalization of Black, Hispanic, or female workers, another labor force group—older workers—have experienced their own set of unique problems. Older workers, those 45 years or older, may find it increasingly difficult to do their work, keep their job, or find another position (Swuwade 1996). In the workplace, older workers have been discriminated against in favor of younger, cheaper, less experienced workers. It used to be that seniority mattered in the workplace, but in *The Incidence of Job Loss: The Shift from Younger to Older Workers, 1981-1996*, researchers Michele Siegel, Charlotte Muller, and Marjorie Honig (2000) state how especially vulnerable older workers are in our new economy. The authors explain that during the recession of the early 1980s, men age 45 to 59 were less likely to lose their jobs than men age 25 to 39. The job loss rate for younger men was 60 percent higher than men age 45 to 59. It was normal practice that younger, less tenured employees were laid off, maintaining employment for older, more experienced workers. But during the recession of the early 1990s, older men were just as likely to be laid off as younger men. From 1991 to 1992, the rate of job loss among older workers was identical to the rate for younger workers, and the job loss rate among older college graduates was higher than among younger college graduates (Siegel et al. 2000).

When older workers are laid off, they are more likely to find jobs that are lower paying, temporary, and low skill in comparison to the jobs they left. Many equate older workers with more experience but also with higher salaries, which discourages potential employers (Fountain 2002). There is also the belief that older workers cannot be (re)trained, hindering their ability to find or retain a new job (Swuwade 1996). Yet, older workers are protected under the Age Discrimination in Employment Act of 1967. The Act prohibits employers from discriminating based on age against people 40 to 64 years old.

VISUAL ESSAY: TWO VIEWS OF THE TWILIGHT YEARS ❖

Most Americans picture retirement as a time when they can pursue leisure activities, help raise their grandchildren, and perhaps do some meaningful volunteer work in their community.

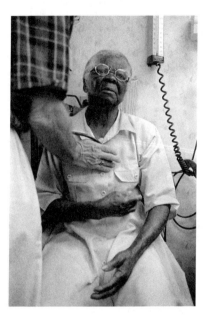

In reality, many of the elderly are not able to pursue this dream. They do not have ample wealth, good health, or the support of families and friends around them. Some of these problems might be worsened because of their social class, ethnicity, or gender.

Is society obligated to help the disadvantaged elderly? What types of assistance might be beneficial?

Operation ABLE (Ability Based on Long Experience) is based in Chicago, Illinois. In 1977, this nonprofit agency began reaching out to older workers, but it has recently revised its mission statement to serve people of all ages (Operation ABLE 2003a). The program has been honored locally and nationally for its service to employers and job seekers. In addition to its general employment assistance programs, Operation ABLE operates programs targeting older workers. Experience Works for 55+ is an information and referral program for retired men and women 55 years or older. The Senior Community Services Employment Program (SCSEP) was designed to help job seekers (55 years of age or older) on a limited income reenter the job market. The program, sponsored by the Illinois Department on Aging, places job seekers in temporary positions at nonprofit or community service agencies where they can enhance their jobs skills and return to full-time work (Operation ABLE 2003b). Chicago's Operation ABLE is part of the National ABLE Network, a network of agencies that focus on serving mid-career or older workers and job seekers. Other Operation ABLE locations are in Boston, Los Angeles, Michigan, Nebraska, Vermont, and Washington, D.C. (National ABLE Network 2003).

What Are Your Life Chances?

Our discussion on inequality does not end here. In the remaining chapters of this text, I will highlight how certain problems differentially affect particular social groups. Here is a preview:

In 1996, there were 450,000 reports of elder abuse in domestic settings. Female elderly were more likely to be abused than male elderly; men and women 80 years or older are at higher risk for maltreatment; and in almost 90 percent of the reported incidents with a known perpetrator, the perpetrator was a family member. (Chapter 4, Families)

As reported in the 1999 Massachusetts Youth Risk Behavior Survey, lesbian, gay, bisexual, and transgendered (GLBT) youth are three times as likely to be assaulted or involved in at least one physical fight in school, three times more likely to have been threatened with a weapon in school, and nearly four times more likely to skip school because they felt unsafe than their heterosexual peers. (Chapter 5, Education)

The highest rates of poverty are among Black and Hispanic Americans. Individuals under 18 years of age have the highest poverty rate for any age group. (Chapter 9, Poverty)

Men and women with lower socioeconomic status, lower educational attainment, and lower occupational status have higher rates of mortality and disease than those higher on each dimension. (Chapter 7, Health and Medicine)

People of color and people with low income are disproportionately exposed to substandard housing. (Chapter 12, Cities and Suburbs)

This short list reflects how some groups—people of color, GLBT students, the elderly, or lower socioeconomic men and women—are at greater risk to experience social problems than other social groups. This should not be taken as an indictment against particular social groups or as evidence about their inherent weakness.

At first, you may believe that some are less prone to social problems because of their innate abilities or strong work ethic. But what should your sociological imagination tell you? Social problems may impact individuals, but social problems emerge out of the larger social structure. Throughout this text, you will learn how particular social characteristics contribute to advantages for some and disadvantages for others (Pampel 1998). Your life experience may have less to do with your ability or your hard work and more to do with how (well) you are positioned in society. We need to recognize how each social characteristic (class, gender, sexual orientation, ethnicity/race, or age) serves to shape the history, experiences, and opportunities of men, women, and children in the United States (Shapiro 2001). Ultimately, this includes one's experience of social problems.

❖ PUTTING IT TOGETHER: Which characteristic contributes most to social inequality? Class? Ethnicity or race? Gender? Sexual orientation? Age? Or something else?

MAIN POINTS

- Three additional bases of inequality have been discussed in this chapter: sex and gender, sexual orientation, and age. Each inequality is the basis for a form of prejudice or discrimination.

- Whereas **sex** refers to our biological differences (those set at birth), **gender** refers to our masculine and feminine behaviors (those set by our society or culture). Gender serves to legitimate certain activities and ways of thinking over others; it grants privilege to one group over another.

- Title IX of the Educational Amendments of 1972 prohibits the exclusion of any person from participation in an educational program or the denial of benefits based on one's sex. As one of the provisions of Title IX, schools are required to offer women and men equal opportunities to participate in athletics. The law has been widely credited with increasing women's participation in high school and collegiate sports and also for supporting women's achievement in education. However, some feel Title IX has been harmful to collegiate men's programs. Out

of concern that not all colleges and universities were complying with Title IX, the U.S. Department of Education formed a commission in 2002 to make recommendations. In January 2003, the commission recommended several changes.

- **Sexism** refers to prejudice or discrimination based solely on someone's sex. Sexism may be an individual act, but it can also become institutionalized in our organizations or through laws and common practices.

- **Heterosexism** is the privileging of heterosexuality over homosexuality in society. **Sexual orientation** is defined as the classification of individuals according to their preference for emotional-sexual relationships and lifestyle with people of the same sex (homosexuality) or people of the opposite sex (heterosexuality). Bisexuality refers to a condition of emotional and sexual attraction to people of either sex.

- A socially determined prejudice, **homophobia**, is an irrational fear or intolerance of homosexuals. Homophobia is particularly directed at gay men. Bisexual or homosexual men, women, and their families are subject to social inequalities through practices of discrimination and prejudice, surprisingly many of them institutionalized in formal law.

• Age also serves as a basis for prejudice or discrimination. **Ageism** is defined by Robert Butler (1969) as the "systematic stereotyping of and discrimination against people because they are old, just as racism and sexism accomplish this with skin color and gender" (p. 243). Age serves to distinguish acceptable behavior for different social groups. Research suggests that ageist attitudes may affect a physician's therapeutic decisions toward older patients.

• Social problems may impact individuals, but social problems emerge out of the larger social structure.

• The discussion of inequality will continue throughout the text.

❖

INTERNET AND COMMUNITY EXERCISES

1. The United Nations Human Development Report began in 1990 with the goal of monitoring people's long-term well-being. Data collected in more than 120 nations track demographic trends, access to health services and resources, literacy and school enrollment, technology, and women's political participation, among many other characteristics. You can go to the Human Development Report site to compare the level of women's political participation in the United States with other nations. Go to *Study Site Chapter 3* for the link.

2. Human Rights Campaign monitors several legal issues that impact the rights of lesbians, gay men, bisexuals, the transgendered, and people with HIV or AIDS. Explore your state laws and pending legislation on privacy issues, workplace discrimination, marriage, and HIV/AIDS. Log on to *Study Site Chapter 3* for a link to the Human Rights Campaign.

3. The Center for American Women and Politics (CAWP) at Rutgers University was founded in 1971. CAWP provides informational materials on women in federal and state political offices, convenes national forums for women public officials, and organizes educational programs to prepare young women for public leadership. To find out the history of women public officials in your state, go to the Center's Web site (log on to *Study Site Chapter 3*). The site also provides current fact sheets on women in the U.S. Senate and House of Representatives. The site also provides links to other political women's groups such as Emily's List ("Early Money Is Like Yeast"), a political organization for pro-choice Democratic women, and the National Federation of Republican Women, a political organization for women in the Republican Party.

4. The Grey Panthers is a national advocacy organization for older and retired adults. Organized in 1970 by Maggie Kuhn and five of her friends, the Grey Panthers' first goal was to combat ageism. The Grey Panthers have also taken a stand on other important social issues: economic justice, medical care, education, and peace. Recent efforts have been directed toward policies assuring affordable prescription drugs for seniors, children, cancer, and HIV patients. Grey Panthers have more than 50 local chapters. To see if there is a chapter in your state, log on to *Study Site Chapter 3*. Contact the chapter for information about what activities are supported in your area.

On your own. Log on to *Study Site–Community and Policy Guide* for more information about the social problems, social policies, and community responses discussed in this chapter.

References

"Age Bias Undermines the Treatment of Older Women." 2003. *Cancer Weekly*, August 6, pp. 20–21.

Associated Press. 2003. "Title IX Cornerstone Remains Intact, but Schools Will Be Educated." *The News Tribune*, July 12, p. C10.

Beeghley, L. 2005. *The Structure of Social Stratification in the United States*. Boston: Pearson.

Brady, Erik. 2003. "Poll: Most Adults Want Title IX Left Alone." Retrieved June 12, 2003 (www.usatoday.com/sports/college/others/2003-01-07-title-ix_x.htm).

Butler, Robert. 1969. "Ageism: Another form of bigotry." *The Gerontologist* 9(3):243–246.

Calasanti, Toni and Kathleen Slevin. 2001. *Gender, Social Inequalities, and Aging*. Walnut Creek, CA: AltaMira Press.

CBS News/New York Times. 2004. "Poll: Few Favor Same-Sex Marriage." Retrieved March 23, 2004 (www.cbsnews.com/stories/2004/03/15/opinion/polls/main606453.shtml).

Collins, Gail. 1993. "Potty Politics: The Gender Gap." *Working Woman* 18(3):12.

Fletcher, Michael and Greg Sandoval. 2003. "Proposals would relax law promoting women's sports." *The News Tribune*, January 31, p. A4.

Fountain, John. 2002. "Age Counts in Hiring, the Older Jobless Find." *The New York Times*, November 13, p. A16.

Garber, Greg. 2002. "Landmark Law Faces New Challenges Even Now." Retrieved June 12, 2003 (www.espn.go.com/gen/womenandsprots/020619title9.html).

Greenhouse, L. 2003. "Texas Sodomy Law Held Unconstitutional—Scathing Dissent." *The New York Times*, June 27, pp. A1, A17.

Kanter, Rosabeth Moss. 1977. *Men and Women of the Corporation*. New York: Basic Books.

Lambda Legal. 2003a. "Family." Retrieved July 8, 2003 (www.lambdalegal.org/cgi-bin/iowa/issues/record?record=5).

———. 2003b. "Landmark Victory." Retrieved July 8, 2003 (http://cache.lambdalegal.org/cgi-bin/iowa/splash.html).

———. 2004. "California Supreme Court Invalidates Marriages from San Francisco, Without Resolving Whether Same-Sex Couples Have the Right to Marry." Retrieved August 27, 2004 (http://www.lambdalegal.org/cgi-bin/iowa/documents/record?record=1525).

Leff, Lisa. 2004. "Bay City Licensed 4,037 Couples." Retrieved March 24, 2004 (www.dailynews.com/eda/article/print/0,1674,200%7E20954%7E2024613,00.html).

Lehne, Gregory K. 1995. "Homophobia among Men: Supporting and Defining the Male Role." Pp. 325–336 in *Men's Lives*, edited by M. Kimmel and M. Messner. Boston: Allyn & Bacon.

Levin, Jack and William Levin. 1980. *Ageism: Prejudice and Discrimination against the Elderly*. Belmont, CA: Wadsworth.

Marger, Martin. 2002. *Social Inequality: Patterns and Processes*. Boston: McGraw-Hill.

Marquis, C. 2003. "Gay Partners Too Are Separated by War, and by Their Need for Secrecy." *The New York Times*, April 18, p. B9.

Michael, Robert, John Gagnon, Edward Laumann, and Gina Kolata. 1994. *Sex in America: A Definitive Survey*. Boston: Little, Brown.

National ABLE Network. 2003. "The National ABLE Network." Retrieved May 17, 2003 (www.operationable.org/network.html).

National Women's Law Center. 2002a. *The Battle for Gender Equity in Athletics: Title IX at Thirty*. Washington, DC: National Women's Law Center.

———. 2002b. "Quick Facts on Women and Girls in Athletics." Retrieved June 12, 2003 (www.nwlc.org/pdf/quickfacts_June2002.pdf).

"Older Patients May Face Age Bias." 2004. *Health & Medicine Week*, January 5, pp. 666–667.

Operaton ABLE. 2003a. "Mission Statement." Retrieved May 17, 2003 (www.operationablechicago.org/pages/529493/index.htm).

———. 2003b. "Programs and Services." Retrieved May 17, 2003 (www.operationablechicago.org/pages/571820/index.htm).

Pampel, Fred C. 1998. *Aging, Social Inequality, and Public Policy*. Thousand Oaks, CA: Pine Forge.

Peppin, John. 1995. "Physician Neutrality and Patient Autonomy in Advance Directive Decisions." *Issues in Law and Medicine* 11(1):13–28.

Picker, Lauren. 1993. "The Women's Room." *The New York Times,* January 8, page unknown.

Quittner, Jeremy. 2004. "Newsom to Bush: "Keep Your Hands off the Constitution." Retrieved March 24, 2004 (www.advocate.com/html/stories/911/911_newsom.asp).

Sandler, Bernice. 1997. "'Too Strong for a Woman'—The Five Words That Created Title IX." Retrieved March 24, 2004 (http://bernicesandler.com/id44.htm).

Shapiro, Thomas M. 2001. "Introduction." Pp. 1–6 in *Great Divides: Readings in Social Inequality in the United States,* edited by T. Shapiro. Mountain View, CA: Mayfield.

Siegel, Michele, Charlotte Muller, and Marjorie Honig. 2000. *The Incidence of Job Loss: The Shift from Younger to Older Workers, 1981–1996.* New York: International Longevity Center–USA.

"Some States' Constitutions Are Going Gender-Neutral." 2003. *The New York Times,* May 22, p. A28.

Stolberg, Sheryl Gay. 2003. "Working Mothers Swaying Senate Debate, as Senators." *The New York Times,* June 7, pp. A1, A11.

Swuwade, Philip. 1996. "U.S. Older Workers: Their Employment and Occupational Problems in the Labor Market." *Social Behavior and Personality* 24(3):235–238.

Tickner, J. A. 2002. "Gendering World Politics: Issues and Approaches in the Post-Cold War Era." *Political Science Quarterly* 117(2):336–337.

U.S. Census Bureau. 2002. *Current Population Survey, March 2002* (Table 1a). Washington, DC: Author.

U.S. Department of Education. 1997. *Title IX: 25 Years of Progress.* Washington, DC: Office of Educational Research and Improvement.

U.S. Department of Labor, Women's Bureau. 2003. "20 Leading Occupations of Employed Women: Full Time Wage and Salaried Workers, 2003." Retrieved August 27, 2004 (http://www.dol.gov/wb/factsheets/20lead 2003.htm).

Woodhouse, Shawn. 2002. "The Historical Development of Affirmative Action: An Aggregated Analysis." *Western Journal of Black Studies* 26(3):155–159.

4

Families ❖

Do you recall the first "crew" you ever hung out with? You know the type—all of its members know each other, speak the same language, laugh at the same jokes, dress alike, and maybe even look alike. Sound familiar? These are the people that you slept, ate, and lived with in your own home: your family.

You may not always think of it this way, but your family is part of the larger social institution of "the family." Consider for a moment that your family was among the 76 million family groups counted by the U.S. Census in 2000 (Fields and Casper 2001). What does your family have in common with the other family groups? Your first response might be that your family has nothing in common with the others. No other family has the unique arrangement or history of individuals related through blood or by choice. From this position, any problem experienced by your family, such as a divorce, would be defined as a personal trouble. The divorce is a private family matter kept among immediate family members. It would be none of our business.

However, if we use our sociological imagination, we can uncover the links between our personal family experiences and our social world. Divorce is not just a family matter but also a public issue. Looking at the recent divorce rate of four divorces per 1,000 people, divorce doesn't occur in just one household, but in millions of U.S. households. It impacts the economic and social well-being of millions of women, men, and children. Divorce challenges the fundamental values of home and love and the value of the family itself. Divorce could be everyone's business.

In this chapter, our goal is to explore this private, yet public world of the family. For our discussion, we'll define the **family** as a construct of meaning and relationships both emotional and economic. It is a social unit based on kinship relations, not only relations based on blood, but also those created by choice, marriage, partnership, or adoption. A **household** is defined as an economic and residential unit. These definitions will allow for the diversity of families that we'll discuss in this chapter, while not presenting one configuration as the standard. As you'll see, the family as we think we know it may not exist at all.

Myths of the Family

The image of the nuclear family—a father, a mother, and biological or adopted children living together—is exalted as the ideal family. Television families like the 1960s Cleavers

VISUAL ESSAY: WHAT IS A FAMILY?   ❖

We have all grown up with an understanding of what a family is. If asked to describe a "typical" family, most Americans would first think of something like the nuclear family shown in this image: a woman and a man and their children.

And yet our description could be broader, encompassing grandparents, aunts, uncles, and cousins—in other words, an extended family.

What is it about the two groups of people shown in these images that makes them seem like a "family"?

Now think about your own experience: the family you grew up in and the family you are a part of now. Is your family consistent with the previous images? Does your own family fit the traditional definition of "family"? Or does your family more closely resemble these other images?

The social reality of what a family is has changed considerably in the past few decades. But our social definition of what constitutes a "typical" family is changing more slowly.

What social problems might be caused by the conflict between our mythology—the notion that most families are "traditional" families—and the reality of the growing diversity in family form?

❖

and the 1980s Huxtables reinforce this ideal image of families. Millions of faithful viewers tuned in each week to see how the family handled (and always resolved at the end of the half hour) the current family crisis. Our image of the nuclear family has been transformed over the years; in the beginning, that image featured a stay–at-home mom like June Cleaver; but due to economic realities, we've modified the image to include a working mother like Claire Huxtable. We may admire and idolize them, but these television families are not representative of the majority of U.S. families.

Fields and Casper (2001) identify several changes in family composition between 1970 and 2000. First, the percentage of families composed of married couples with children declined from 40.3 percent in 1970 to 24.1 percent in 2000. Take note of this—the nuclear family form fits less than one quarter of all 2000 U.S. households. Second, the only increase in family groups over that time period came in the category of "other family households." Other family households include families whose house-holder has no spouse present, but such families may include other relatives, as well as children. These family groups made up 16 percent of all U.S. households, increasing from 10.6 percent in 1970. Included in this 2000 category are 12 million single-parent families, 10 million headed by mothers and 2 million headed by fathers. Finally, there has been an increase in the percentage of non-family households, individuals living alone or with nonrelatives. (See Table 4.1.)

PUTTING IT TOGETHER: On the Web.

Using data from the U.S. Census, identify the number of family and nonfamily households in your college's state. If possible, compare census data from 1970 and 2000. Have there been any changes in household composition over the past 30 years? Log on to *Study Site Chapter 4.*

In addition to the false image of the nuclear family, we also embrace other myths about the family. We tend to believe that the families of the past were better and happier than modern families. We believe that families should be safe havens, protecting their members from harm and danger. And a final myth relates to the topic of this book: We also assume that the family and its failings lead to many of our social problems.

There is a persistent belief that nontraditional families, such as divorced, father-less, or working-mother families, threaten and erode the integrity of the family as an institution. These "pathological" family forms are blamed for drug abuse, delinquency, illiteracy, and crime. As a group, female-headed households were condemned in the Personal Responsibility and Work Opportunity Act of 1996, also known as the Welfare Reform Act, for their dependency on the public welfare system. During his presi-dency, George W. Bush advanced several program initiatives intended to strengthen American families. As presented in this chapter's Taking a World View feature, family blaming also goes on in Israel, dividing the attention of family researchers. It's a fine line, but although we respect the sanctity of the family, classifying most of its problems as personal troubles, we also blame families for many social problems, turning family troubles into very public issues.

❖ Table 4.1   Households by Type: 1970 and 2000 (percent distribution)

	1970	2000
Total number of households	63 million	105 million
Nonfamily households		
Women living alone	11.5	14.8
Men living alone	5.6	10.7
Other nonfamily households	1.7	5.7
Family households		
Married couples without children	30.3	28.7
Married couples with children	40.3	24.1
Other family households	10.6	16.0

Source: Fields and Casper 2001, Figure 1.

 **❖ PUTTING IT TOGETHER:** Despite the fact that the nuclear family is not the statistical majority in our society, its image as the "perfect" family persists. Why do you think this is the case? How could a different image of the family be accepted by society?

Sociological Perspectives on the Family

Functionalist Perspective

From a functionalist perspective, the family serves many important functions in society. Some functionalists claim that the family is the most vital social institution. The family serves as a child's primary group, the first group membership we claim. We inherit not only the color of our hair or eyes but also our family's social position. The family serves to confer social status and class. The family helps define who we are and how we find our place in society. And, without the family, who would provide for the essential needs of the child: affection, socialization, and protection?

Social problems emerge as the family struggles to adapt to a modern society. Functionalists have noted how many of the family's original functions have been taken

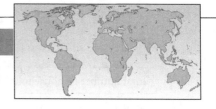

THE STUDY OF FAMILIES IN ISRAEL

The basis of much of sociological work in Israel, including that on the family, can be traced to the Israeli common-sense understanding about how their society is put together. Two grand images of this common-sensical understanding of Israeli society are relevant here: (1) Israel is a land of exotica waiting to be revealed and (2) Israel is a land of social problems waiting to be solved.

In their extreme forms, these images take the following shapes. According to the image of Israel as a land of exotica, the country encompasses a variety of different ethnic groups and social categories whose members are settled in planned and unplanned urban and rural communities, each with its own specific, unique family form and pattern. These are all in place, waiting to be studied. The social scientist simply has to choose the subject and the population, to set border around it and call it "my people" or "my community." In such cases, the study is primarily confined to the chosen community, and every detail of family life is studied within the pre-set boundaries. . . . Rarely is it asked what impact patterns of family life in one's researched community have upon family life styles in Israel in general.

The image of Israel as a land of social problems is shared by social scientists and policymakers and is, to a large extent, at the root of the early cooperation between them. Research carried out with this image in mind tends to be directed toward social problems rather than social phenomena. Much of this research was commissioned either by government ministries or by public organizations, e.g. the Jewish Agency. As noted, little attention was given to the family in the early stages of this cooperation, and family sociologists joined in (if at all) only later.

The image of Israel as the land of exotica is most prominent in the study of "kibbutz family." . . . [T]he study of kibbutz families is varied and extensive, ranging from the most general of questions to the specific details of this very distinctive family form. However, the search for exotica leads scholars, more often than not, to treat a kibbutz as a closed community, almost in the way functionalist anthropologists used to treat "their" tribes, thus ignoring the relation between the kibbutz and the wider society.

. . . . At the other extreme of the continuum are those studies aimed at solving "social problems." The meaning of "social problem" is often the product of ideological definitions—political, bureaucratic or professional—and these keep changing in keeping with special interests and historical conditions. So, too, is the degree of importance attached to the family as an active agency, either in creating problems or in solving them. Harboring this image of Israeli society, scholars draw their subject of study sometimes from Israeli understandings of social difficulties, and sometimes from what is considered elsewhere to be a social problem.

. . . .Those who seek the exotic in Israeli society are preaching the conservation of what they perceive as unique ethnic culture and its family patterns. This position advocates cultural pluralism, in which each group retains its ethnic identity. Those holding this view conceive a society composed of ethnic groups that are different from but equal to one another. Those that are concerned with solving social problems are looking for ways to "absorb" immigrants, "blend the exiles," and consequently clear the way for the emergence of the "Israeli family."

Both political positions expect the family to take an active part in either retaining or eliminating ethnic cultural differences. In this way, for the first time, families in Israel are assigned an active, if contradictory, role in shaping society.

Source: Shamgar-Handelman 1996:403–407.

over by organized religion, education, work, and the government in modern society (Lenski and Lenski 1987); but still the family is expected to provide its remaining functions of raising children and providing affection and companionship for its members (Popenoe 1993). From a functionalist perspective, the family is inextricably linked to the rest of society. The family does not work alone; rather it functions in concert with the other institutions. Changes in other institutions, such as the economy, politics, or law, contribute to changes and problems in the family. Consider the education of children. Before the establishment of mandatory public school systems, the family educated its own children. As a formal system, education has become its own institution, taking primary responsibility for educating everyone's children. Functionalists examine how the institutions of the family and education effectively work together. To what extent should parents participate in their children's education, and to what extent is the educational system responsible for raising our children?

Because of this perspective's emphasis on the family and its social and emotional functions, when the family fails—as in the case of divorce or domestic violence—functionalists take these problems seriously. These problems afflict not only the family but, according to functionalists, can also lead to problems in the society, such as crime, poverty, or delinquency.

Conflict and Feminist Perspectives

For the conflict theorist, the family is a system of inequality where conflict is normal. Conflict can derive from economic or power inequalities between spouses or family members. From a feminist perspective, inequality emerges from the patriarchal family system, where men control decision making in the family. The persistent social ideals that view the woman as homemaker and the man as breadwinner are problematic from both perspectives. Men's social and economic status increases as their work outside of the home is more visible and rewarded, whereas women's work inside the home remains invisible and uncompensated. The family structure, as our society has come to define it, upholds a system of male social and economic domination.

Families are also subject to powerful economic and political interest groups that control social programs and policies. Conflict arises when the needs of particular family forms are promoted while others are ignored. For example, heterosexual marriages are recognized by formal law and social policies while homosexual marriages and families are ignored. To resolve social problems in the family, both perspectives suggest the need for structural change.

Interactionist Perspective

Through social interaction, we create and maintain our definition of a family. As we do this, it affects our larger social definition of what everyone's family should be like and how we envision the family that we create for ourselves.

Within our own families, our interaction through words, symbols, and meanings defines our expectation of what the family should be like. How many children in the family? Who does the house cleaning? Who gets to carve the holiday turkey? As a family, we collectively create and maintain a family definition on which members agree. Problems arise when there is conflict about how the family is defined. A couple starting their own family must negotiate their own way of doing things. Two partners may carry definitions and expectations from their families of origin, but together, they create a new family reality.

Problems may also occur when partners' expectations of family or marriage do not match their real life. In our culture, romantic love is idealized, misleading individuals to believe that they are destined for a fulfilling emotional partnership with one perfect mate. Then after the realities of life set in, including the first fight, the notion of romantic love is shattered. Couples recognize that it may take more than romantic love to make a relationship work.

Putting all our separate definitions of the family together, we create a portrait of what all families should be like. But as political and religious forces uphold and encourage a patriarchal nuclear family as the norm, by default, other family forms are considered deviant or against some set of moral codes. Blended families, gay or lesbian families, or single-parent families become social problems based only on how they deviate from the definition of a "normal" family. Refer to Table 4.2 for a summary of all sociological perspectives on the family.

Problems in the American Family

Divorce

If you do an Internet search on divorce, you might be surprised at your search results. In addition to divorce facts and access to support groups, you'll also find handy guides to complete your own divorce paperwork. Looking to save time, money, and pain? Please try our services. Looking for a divorce lawyer, why not search for one online? And if you'd like to send a divorce greeting card that says, "Happy to be without you," you can find one of those online, too.

Divorce was a rare occurrence until the 1970s. In the 1950s and 1960s, the divorce rate was around 2.2 to 2.6 per 1,000 individuals (U.S. Census Bureau 1999). With the

❖ Table 4.2   Summary of Sociological Perspectives: Families

	Functional	Conflict/Feminist	Interactionist
Explanation of the family and its social problems	Functionalists examine how the family interacts with other social institutions. Functionalists believe that social problems emerge as the family struggles to adapt to a modern society. Functionalists also examine the manifest and latent functions of the family.	Problems emerge from conflict inherent in the family structure. Conflict can derive from economic or power inequalities between family members. From a feminist perspective, the family is a patriarchal system, where men dominate social and economic spheres.	An interactionist focuses on the social meaning and expectations of the "family." Interactionists will also focus on how family members define their own family.
Questions asked about the family	What functions does the family serve? How is the family affected by other social institutions? How does the problem reflect changes between the family and other social institutions?	What is the basis of conflict within the family? How does conflict affect family members and their relationships?	How do we define the "family"? What social forces influence our definition of the family? What are the consequences of these definitions?

introduction of no-fault divorce laws in the 1970s, the divorce rate began to climb in the 1970s, reaching a high of 5.3 in 1979 and 1981 (U.S. Census Bureau 1999). The increase in divorce rates has been attributed to other factors: the increasing economic independence of women, the transition from extended to nuclear family forms, and the increasing geographic and occupational mobility of families. Furthermore, as our societal and cultural norms about divorce have changed, the stigma attached to divorce has decreased.

In recent years, the divorce rate has remained stable at around 4.0 divorces per 1,000 individuals in the total U.S. population. The rate was 4.1 in 1999, 4.2 in 2000, and 4.1 in 2001 (Centers for Disease Control 2002). (The marital rate has also remained stable for the same time period: 8.5 per 1,000 for 1999, 8.7 for 2000, and 8.5 for 2001; Centers for Disease Control 2002.)

Recent census data on divorce indicate that certain groups are more susceptible to divorce than others. Based on 1996 Census data, Kreider and Fields (2002) concluded that divorce continues to be more likely among those who marry when they are younger than 20 years of age. The majority of separated and divorced men and women were between 25 and 44 years of age. The median age of divorce from first marriage was 29 years for women and 30.5 years for men. Divorce rates were higher for those living at 200 percent of the poverty level, higher among those with a high school degree or some college, and higher among those working full-time (Kreider and Fields 2002).

Sociologists have paid particular attention to the effects of divorce on children and their families. In general, the research indicates that children with divorced parents have moderately poorer life and educational outcomes (emotional well-being, academic achievement, labor force participation, divorce, and teenage childbearing) than children living with both parents (Amato and Keith 1991). For example, boys living with a divorced mother are four times more likely to display severe delinquency or to engage in early sexual intercourse than those living in two-parent households (Simons 1996). Some of these effects carry into adolescence and young adulthood (Cherlin, Kiernan, and Chase-Lansdale 1995; Amato and Keith 1991), with more negative outcomes for adult females than for adult males due primarily to paternal absence (van Schaick and Stolberg 2001).

However, research also suggests that marital separation is beneficial to the well-being of children (Videon 2002). Research indicates that parent-child relations are important influences on children's well-being, even mediating the effects of marital dissolution (Videon 2002). Divorce is less disruptive if both parents maintain a positive relationship with the child, if parental conflict decreases after separation or divorce, and if the level of socioeconomic resources for the child is not reduced (Amato and Keith 1991).

Violence and Neglect in the Family

Intimate Partner Violence

One of the myths mentioned at the beginning of this chapter was how the family was a safe place for its members. This myth ignores the incidence of violence and abuse in families. Current data suggests that 21 percent to 34 percent of women will be assaulted by an intimate partner during their lifetime (Browne 1993). In 2001, 671,710 violent crimes were committed by an intimate partner: current or former spouses, boyfriends, or girlfriends. In about 85 percent of these crimes, the victims were women (Rennison 2003). Research has consistently linked the following social factors to family violence: low socioeconomic status, social and structural stress, and social isolation (Gelles and Maynard 1987). Feminist researchers argue that domestic violence is rooted in gender and represents men's attempts to maintain dominance and control over women (Anderson 1997).

In their study of victims of domestic violence, Levendosky, Lynch, and Graham-Bermann (2000) found that female victims reported both positive and negative impacts on their parenting due to domestic violence. The women reported their emotional feelings or concerns made parenting difficult. Women noted the reduced amount of quality time or emotional energy they could devote to their children. Battered women also reported how they had increased empathy and caring toward their children. The researchers suggested that battered women were actively working to protect their children from the effects of violence in their household.

Child Abuse and Neglect

Some children are subject to abuse and neglect in their families. In 2000, 879,000 children were victims of child maltreatment. The majority of child victims, about 63 percent, suffered from neglect. Tragically, about 1,200 children died as a result of abuse or neglect in 2000 (Children's Bureau 2002).

According to McKay (1994), child abuse is 15 times more likely to occur when spousal abuse occurs. Children are three times more likely to be abused by their fathers than by their mothers. Poverty is consistently identified as a risk factor for child abuse. It is not clear whether the relationship exists because of the stresses associated with poverty or if reporting is higher due to the constant scrutiny of poor families by social agencies. Poor health care, lack of social and familial support, along with fragmented social services have been linked with both poverty and child abuse (Bethea 1999).

While physical, sexual, and emotional abuses are often identified, cases of neglect often go unnoticed. **Neglect** is characterized by a failure to provide for a child's basic needs, and it can be physical (inflicting physical injury), educational (failure to enroll a school-age child in school, allowing chronic truancy), or emotional in nature (spousal abuse in the child's presence, permission for drug or alcohol use by the child, inattention to a child's needs for affection) (National Clearing House on Child Abuse and Neglect Information 2002).

Elder Abuse and Neglect

Also victims of abuse are the elderly, usually in the care of their older children and their families. Elder abuse can also occur within a nursing home or hospital setting. Federal definitions of elder abuse, neglect, and exploitation first appeared in the 1987 Amendments to the Older Americans Act (National Center on Elder Abuse 2002a). Elder abuse can consist of physical, sexual, or psychological abuse, neglect/abandonment, or financial exploitation. **Domestic elder abuse** refers to any form of maltreatment of an older person by someone who has a special relationship with the elder (a spouse, child, friend, or caregiver); **institutional elder abuse** refers to forms of abuse that occur in residential facilities for older people.

The abuse and mistreatment of the elderly has increased as a result of significant demographic changes. The number of U.S. adults age 60 years or older increased 12 percent from 1990 to 2000. In 2000, 35.0 million adults were 60 years or older compared with 31.2 million in 1990 (Hetzel and Smith 2001). As the population ages, there has been an increased need for long-term care of the elderly, with spouses and adult children assuming the role of caretaker. It is estimated that 15 million individuals provide informal care to relatives and friends (Navaie-Waliser et al. 2002). Although caregiving can positively affect the physical and psychological well-being of the care recipients, the added burden of elder care may strain the family's and the caregiver's emotional and financial resources.

There were 450,000 reports of elder abuse in domestic settings in 1996 (National Center on Elder Abuse 1998). Men and women 80 years or older are at higher risk for maltreatment; and in almost 90 percent of the reported incidents with a known perpetrator, the perpetrator was a family member. The majority of victims were women (80 percent of all reported cases of physical abuse, more than 90 percent of financial abuse, and more than 70 percent of emotional abuse), despite the fact that they accounted for only 58 percent of the total elderly population in 1996 (National Center on Elder Abuse 1998). Elder abuse, particularly with family perpetrators, has been attributed to social isolation, personal problems such as mental illness, alcohol, or drug abuse, and domestic violence (spouses make up a large percentage of elder abusers) (National Center on Elder Abuse 2002a). A major risk factor is dependency: Abusers tend to be more dependent on the elderly person for housing, money, and transportation than relatives who do not abuse (Lang 1993).

Teen Pregnancies and Newborn Abandonment

The U.S. has the highest teen birthrate in the developed world (Card 1999). But teenage birthrates declined significantly in each state between 1991 and 2000. The birthrate for teenagers (age 15 to 19 years) declined throughout the 1990s, falling from 62.1 births per 1,000 teenagers in 1991 to 48.5 in 2000 (Ventura, Matthews, and Hamilton 2002). The state of Mississippi had the highest teen birthrate for 1991 and 2000, 85.6 and 72.0, respectively. Birthrates were consistently lowest for New Hampshire: 33.3 in 1991 and 23.4 in 2000 (Ventura et al. 2002). Despite the decline in the overall birthrate, birthrates for Black and Hispanic teens remain higher than for any other ethnic-racial group (U.S. Department of Health and Human Services 1998). Our high teenage birthrate has been attributed to a range of factors from inadequate sexuality education to declining morals (Somers and Fahlman 2001). Research suggests that earlier or more frequent sexual activity among U.S. teens is not the cause of the higher birthrates; rather, it is that sexually active American teens are less likely to use contraceptives than their European peers (Card 1999).

Teen mothers, in comparison with their childless peers, are likely to be poorer and less educated, less likely to be married, and more likely to come from families with lower income (Hoffman 1998). Their children often lag behind in standards of early development (Hoffman 1998); are less likely to receive proper nutrition, health care, and cognitive stimulation (Annie E. Casey Foundation 1998); and are at greater risk of social behavioral problems and lower intellectual and academic achievement (Maynard 1997). Early childbearing also has its effects on teen fathers. Teen fathers are more likely to engage in delinquent behaviors such as alcohol abuse or drug dealing. In addition, they complete fewer years of school and earn less per year (Annie E. Casey Foundation 1998).

While teenage childbirth has always been considered a social problem, there has been another phenomenon that has captured the public's attention. Reports of abandoned babies found in trash bins, restrooms, parks, and public buildings have become more frequent since the late 1990s. The first case that caught national attention was "Prom Mom" Melissa Drexler. While attending her senior prom in 1997, Drexler gave birth to a full-term baby boy in a bathroom stall. She wrapped her baby in several plastic bags, left him in a garbage can, and returned to her prom. She pleaded guilty to manslaughter. Although there is no comprehensive national reporting system for abandoned babies, data collected by the U.S. Department of Health and Human Services (HHS) indicate increases in the rate of abandonment (D'Agostino 2000). Between 1991 and 1998, the number of infants abandoned in public places rose from 65 to 105 cases. HHS also reports that the number of children abandoned in hospitals grew from 22,000 in 1991 to 31,000 in 1998.

The Problems of Time and Money

In a survey conducted by the Radcliffe Public Policy Center (2000), 79 percent of respondents reported that having a work schedule that enabled them to spend time with their family was a top priority. Nearly everyone reported feeling pressed for more time in their lives, wanting to spend more time with their families, to have more flexible work options and even just more time to sleep (Radcliffe Public Policy Center 2000).

According to Lillian Rubin (1995), economic realities make it especially difficult for working-class parents to maintain their juggling act. In her book, *Families on the Fault Line,* Rubin documented how structural changes in the economy undermine the quality of life among working-class families. This is a functional argument: Because the family is part of our larger social system, what happens at an economic level will inevitably impact the family. The reality of long workdays and weeks does take its toll on families: The loss of intimacy between couples, the lack of time for couples and their children, tense renegotiations over household work, and juggling child care arrangements are just some of the issues that working families face.

Despite their hard work, there seems never to be enough money. As Mike Fillman, a White, 49-year-old machinist describes it (Rubin 1995):

> Dammit, I don't get it. Between me and the wife we make $38,000 a year, and we're always behind. I remember when I thought that was a fortune. If anybody'd ever told me I wouldn't be rich on that kind of money, I'd have told him he was nuts. Back when I was making twelve or thirteen grand a year, I used to think if I could just get up to twenty I'd have it made. Now thirty-eight doesn't make it. How do you figure it? (P. 138)

Rubin's study shed some light on the condition of working-class families, but often overlooked is the plight of lower income families—too rich to be classified as living in poverty, but still too poor to be working class. In their two-year study, Lisa Dodson, Tiffany Manuel, and Ellen Bravo (2002) studied lower income families in Milwaukee, Wisconsin; Denver, Colorado; and Boston, Massachusetts. The researchers concluded that lower income families deal with problems of the most basic kind on a daily basis: managing the safety, health, and education of their children while staying employed. Lower income parents are not "bad" parents; it's just that their parenting may require more time and resources than they have. Among low-income families, there is a higher prevalence of children with chronic health issues or special learning needs; at least two thirds of the families in the Dodson et al. study reported having a child with special needs. These children require much more time and patience from their parents, sometimes jeopardizing parents' ability to maintain employment and earnings. To support lower-income parents, the authors recommend comprehensive and flexible child care, along with workplace flexibility (taking time off work, adjusting their work schedule) (Dodson et al. 2002).

Family Policy, Advocacy, and Innovation

Family Medical Leave Act of 1993

The Family Medical Leave Act (FMLA) of 1993 was envisioned as a way to help employees balance the demands of the workplace with the needs of their families. The Act provides employees with up to 12 weeks of unpaid, job-protected leave per year. It also provides for group health benefits during the employee's leave. The FMLA applies to all public agencies and all private employers with 50 or more workers. Some states have enacted their own family and medical leave laws, extending the coverage provided by the FMLA or extending coverage to those not eligible under FMLA guidelines. For example, the State of Oregon passed its own Family and Medical Leave Act in 1995, extending benefits to employers with 25 or more employees.

Although there is strong support for the FMLA and its stated goals, the act has also been criticized since its enactment. Almost 41 million workers are not covered by the FMLA because they work for private employers not covered under the law (AFL-CIO 2002). Although an estimated 20 million Americans have used the FMLA, nearly two thirds of eligible workers have not taken advantage of the FMLA because they could not afford the lost wages (AFL-CIO 2002; National Partnership for Women and Families 2002).

Community Responses to Domestic Violence and Neglect

Responses to domestic violence can be characterized as having a distinct community approach. In the area of child abuse, the U.S. Office of Juvenile Justice and Delinquency Prevention established community-based children's advocacy centers to provide coordinated support for victims in the investigation, treatment, prosecution, and prevention of child abuse. Programs at each children's advocacy center are uniquely designed by community professionals and volunteers to best meet their community's needs. One such center is Project Harmony, based in Omaha, Nebraska. Project Harmony provides medical exams, assessment, and referrals. By co-housing representatives from child protective services, law enforcement, and project staff, Project Harmony attempts to improve communication and coordination between all professionals involved in a case.

Since its inception in 1995, the Violence Against Women Office (VAW) has handled the U.S. Department of Justice's legal and policy issues regarding violence against women. The Office offers a series of program and policy technical papers for individuals, leaders, and communities to support their efforts to end violence against women. These papers highlight some of the best program models and practices and were produced by the Promising Practices Initiative of the STOP Violence Against Women Grants Technical Assistance Project (Little, Malefyt, and Walker 1998). Two featured programs are:

The Duluth Minnesota Domestic Abuse Intervention Project (DAIP) was developed in 1980 and serves as a national and international program model. It was the first program of its kind to coordinate the intervention activities of each criminal justice agency in one city. The goals of the program include victim safety, offender accountability, and changes in the climate of tolerance toward violence in the Duluth community. The program also offers a men's nonviolence education program, an advocacy and support group for the men's partners, a class for women who have used violence, and a victim advocacy program for Native Americans through the Mending the Sacred Hoop project.

The Women's Center and Shelter (WC&S) of Greater Pittsburgh was founded in 1974. WC&S coordinates its program efforts with the medical community, criminal justice agencies, and other organizations. The programs focus on the ability of women to take control of their own lives. WC&S provides comprehensive victim services, which also includes parenting education and employment readiness. It also provides a follow-up program for former shelter residents and child care services for residents, nonresidents, and follow-up participants. In 1997, the Pittsburgh School District contracted with WC&S to provide crisis response and assessment for students who may have witnessed domestic violence or are violent themselves. WC&S has also created a school-based curriculum called Hands Are Not for Hurting. The curriculum uses age-appropriate lessons that encourage nonviolent conflict resolution and teach youth that they are responsible for the choices they make.

The National Center on Elder Abuse (NCEA) believes that community education and outreach are important in combating the problem of elder abuse and neglect. The NCEA supports community "sentinel" programs, which train and educate professionals and volunteers to identify and refer potential victims of abuse, neglect, or exploitation. In 1999, the NCEA established partnerships with the Human Society of the United States (HSUS), Meals on Wheels Association of America (MOWAA), and the National Association of Retired Senior Volunteer Program Directors. These organizations were selected because of their unique access to isolated elders in their homes. NCEA funded six coalition projects in Arizona, California, New York, North Carolina, and Utah. As a result of the sentinel programs, there was an increase in the number of abuse referrals. In addition, administrators noticed an increase in the level of satisfaction among volunteers, who as a result of the project were able to assist individuals who they believed might be victims or potential victims (National Center on Elder Abuse 2002b).

❖ **PUTTING IT TOGETHER:**
On the Web.

On its Web site, the NCEA features on online locator for program models and information resources throughout the United States. From the NCEA's homepage, click on "Promising Practices" and select your state to find more information about local programs. Log on to *Study Site Chapter 4.*

Teen Pregnancy and Infant Abandonment

In the 1980s, social and human service programmers defined prevention as an effective way to address the problems of teen pregnancy and parenthood (Card 1999).

In the 1990s, several new prevention approaches emerged, particularly after the passage of the Welfare Reform Act of 1996. Under Section 905 of the Act, the U.S. Department of Health and Human Services (DHHS) was mandated to assure that at least 25 percent of all U.S. communities had teen pregnancy prevention programs in place. The majority of states identified target goals related to teen birthrates. For example, New Hampshire's goal is to reduce the nonmarital teen rate to 21.0 per 1,000 by 2005; in North Dakota, the goal is to reduce its teen birthrate by 2 percent per year.

Along with funding national educational programs such as the Girl Neighborhood Power: Building Bright Futures for Success program, DHHS also funded comprehensive state- and community-wide initiatives through the Abstinence Only Education Program and the Adolescent Family Life Program (administered through the Office of Population Affairs). An example of this approach is School-Linked Reproductive Health Services (The Self Center), a school-neighborhood clinic partnership in Baltimore, Maryland. The program offers education, counseling, and reproductive services to teens. Students at participating schools reported reduced levels of sexual activity, and among those already sexually active, there was more effective contraceptive use. Also reported was a delay in the onset of sexual activity among abstinent youth (Card 1999).

Under welfare reform, two primary provisions affected teen parents and their access to welfare assistance. First, teen parents must stay in school; financial assistance cannot be provided to unmarried, minor, custodial parents who do not have a high school degree or equivalent. Early data on the educational provision indicate that programs offering a range of options—GED programs designed for public assistance recipients, educational activities, and life skills training—proved helpful for teen parents. Second, teen parents must live in an adult-supervised setting (U.S. Department of Health and Human Services 1998).

Kalil and Danzinger (2000) studied the effects of these welfare reform rules on low-income teen mothers living in Michigan, most of whom were complying with the new welfare requirements and satisfied with their living arrangements. Many were still experiencing child care problems, depression, and domestic violence. Living with the baby's grandmother reduced teen mothers' economic strain; however, it was also related to poorer educational outcomes. Although the teen mothers expressed high educational goals, researchers were uncertain whether the attendance requirement under welfare reform would actually increase overall educational attainment of these young mothers.

❖ **PUTTING IT TOGETHER:**
❖ **In your community.**

What teen pregnancy programs exist in your community? On your college campus? Do any of these programs include abstinence strategies?

In response to newborn and infant abandonment, 39 states have passed laws since 1999 that offer safe and confidential means to relinquish unwanted newborns without the threat of prosecution for child abandonment. State laws vary according to child's age (72 hours to one year old) and the personnel or places authorized to accept the infant (hospital personnel, emergency rooms, church, and police).

In Illinois, the Newborn Abandoned Infant Protection Act was spearheaded by a coalition of community women's groups (Collier 2001). Dawn Geras, a Northbrook businesswoman, started her volunteer group, Save Abandoned Babies, after being moved by several newspaper articles on the issue. A second group of women (from Melrose Park) were inspired to act after watching an "Oprah" show on the topic. A third group of women (from the Rockford area) completed the coalition. One of the Rockford women was Sue Moye, whose daughter, Kelli, abandoned her newborn baby when she was 15. Over a two-year period, the coalition encouraged and lobbied legislators to draft a protection bill. The Act became law in 2001 (Collier 2001).

It is unclear how effective these safe-surrender or safe-haven laws have been in reducing infant abandonment or death. New Jersey, home of the first infant abandonment case that gained national attention, passed a safe-haven law in August 2000 (Gould 2001). Since then, 10 babies have been abandoned, and 7 were brought to safe havens (Gould 2001). In Illinois, eight babies have been relinquished since the passage of the 2001 bill. However, the safety of abandoned infants is still a concern; 12 babies have also been found dead (Illinois Hospital Association 2004).

❖ **PUTTING IT TOGETHER:** In your community.

Investigate whether your state has a safe-haven law. What are the features of the law? What protections does it offer the mother? How many children have been protected under the law?

Supporting Different Family Forms

According to sociologist David Popenoe (1993), there has been a serious decline in the structure and function of the family since the 1960s. Families are not meeting society's needs as they once did and have lost most of their "functions, social power and authority over their members" (Popenoe 1993:527–528), he says. He attributes the weakening of family function to high divorce rates, declining family size, and the growing absence of fathers and mothers in their children's lives. Data that we reviewed at the beginning of this chapter—the declining percentage of nuclear families, along with the increase in single-parent families and nonfamily households—lend support to his observation.

But critics of Popenoe's position argue that the "family in decline" hypothesis relies too heavily on the definition of family in its nuclear form (Bengston 2001). Sociologist Judith Stacey (1996) agrees that the "family" as defined by a nuclear form of mom, dad, and children is in decline. This family system has been replaced by what Stacey calls a "postmodern family condition," one characterized by diverse family patterns and forms, where no single family form is dominant. It is undeniable that there have been significant changes in the traditional family's structure and functions (Bengston 2001); modern families are best characterized by their diversity (Hanson and Lynch 1992).

The proportion of nuclear families is decreasing, replaced with family structures that include single-parent, blended, adoptive, foster, grandparent, and same-sex partner households (Copeland and White 1991). The increasing diversity of American families requires that we broaden our research and policy agendas beyond traditional family forms (Demo 1992). Perhaps one solution to the "problem" of families is to appreciate and embrace other family forms. Let's discuss two emerging family forms: grandparents as primary caregivers to grandchildren and gay or lesbian families.

Grandparents as Parents

Fifty–nine-year-old Pat and Ken Owens of Lewiston, Maryland, are the primary caretakers of their grandchildren, Michael and Brandi (Armas 2002). Michael and Brandi are among 3.7 million children living in households where the grandparent is the primary householder (Fields 2003), an increase from 2.2 million grandchildren in 1970 (Casper and Bryson 1998). In 2002, about 1.3 million children lived with their grandparents alone, with neither parent present. The areas with the highest percentage of these households are in the South and rural counties across the Midwest and West. Wyoming and Oklahoma led the country in the percentage of grandparents who are primary caregivers. (See U.S. Data Map 4.1 for the number of grandparents who are primary caregivers for each state.) According to the Census 2002, Black children were more likely than children from other ethnic/racial groups to live in a grandparent's household (Fields 2003).

Grandparents may assume caretaking responsibilities when parents are unable to live with or care for their children due to death, illness, divorce, incarceration, substance abuse, or child abuse or neglect. The Owenses have not heard from Michael's mother in the past two years and only recently began receiving financial support from Michael's father. The alternative for the Owenses' grandchildren would have been foster care, something that Pat Owens did not want to happen. "I don't want to make it sound like it's easy because there are some tough, tense times. But I'm very proud of the fact that all the grandchildren still play together and go to school together," said Mrs. Owens (Armas 2002:A6).

Regardless of the circumstances, the sudden responsibility for children leaves many grandparents on fixed incomes with unexpected financial burdens. In one study, children living in a grandparent's household without a parent present were twice as likely to be living below the poverty level as children living with both grandparents and a parent. In addition, children who lived with just their grandparents were also at risk of not being covered by health insurance (Fields 2003). If eligible, grandparents can get assistance through DHHS Temporary Assistance for Needy Families (TANF) benefits. Some states offer guardianship or kinship care subsidy programs for grandparents.

Emotional and social support is available for grandparent-headed households. Local grandparent support groups are listed by organizations such as the American Association for Retired Persons (AARP), Generations United, or GrandsPlace. These organizations also provide fact sheets, community links, and suggestions for clothing and school supplies, recipes, and travel and activity guides for grandparents and their grandchildren. AARP (2002) recognized several model support programs such as the Kinship Support Network in San Francisco, California, Project Healthy Grandparents in Atlanta, Georgia, and Grandma's Kids in Philadelphia, Pennsylvania.

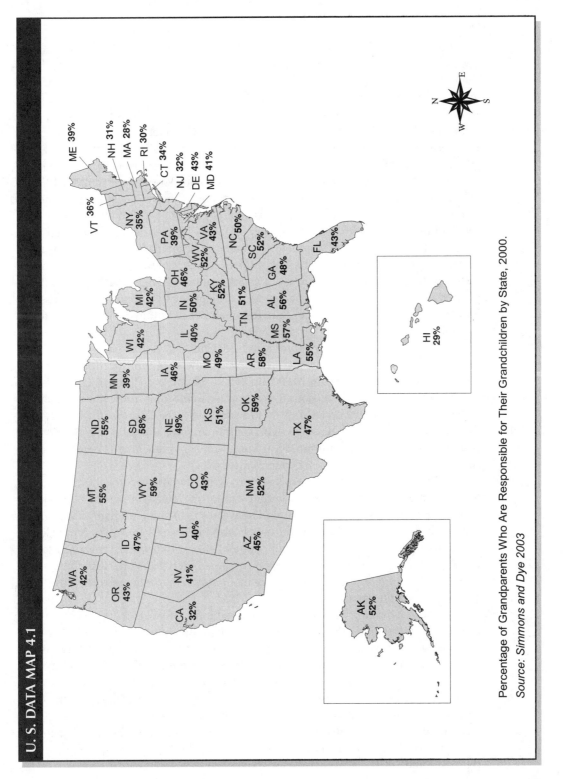

ME 39%
NH 31%
MA 28%
RI 30%
CT 34%
NJ 32%
DE 43%
MD 41%

VT 36%
NY 35%
PA 39%
WV 52%
VA 43%
NC 50%
SC 52%
FL 43%

OH 46%
KY 52%
GA 48%
AL 56%
MI 42%
IN 50%
TN 51%
MS 57%
WI 42%
IL 40%
MO 49%
AR 58%
LA 55%

MN 39%
IA 46%
OK 59%
ND 55%
SD 58%
NE 49%
KS 51%
TX 47%

MT 55%
WY 59%
CO 43%
NM 52%

ID 47%
UT 40%
AZ 45%

WA 42%
OR 43%
NV 41%
CA 32%

HI 29%

AK 52%

Percentage of Grandparents Who Are Responsible for Their Grandchildren by State, 2000.

Source: Simmons and Dye 2003

Gay and Lesbian Families

The Defense of Marriage Act of 1996 permits states to ban all recognition of same-sex marriages, and now more than 35 states have such bans in place. According to the Defense of Marriage Act, the federal government will not accept marriage licenses granted to same-sex couples, regardless of whether a state provides equal license privileges to all types of partnerships. However, in June 2002, President George W. Bush signed into law the Mychal Judge Act, which allows for federal death benefits to be paid to the same-sex partners of firefighters and police officers who die in the line of duty (Bumiller 2002). The bill was named after the Reverend Mychal Judge, the New York City Fire Department Chaplain who died in the collapse of the World Trade Center. Although White House officials say that President Bush did not consider the bill a gay issue, gay rights organizations consider its signing as a milestone for gays (Bumiller 2002).

California, Delaware, Hawaii, Maine, and New Jersey offer a very limited form of partnership to same-sex couples. The State of Vermont has created civil union partnerships, extending full and equal protection accorded to married couples under state law to lesbian and gay couples. On September 1, 2002, *The New York Times* printed the first same-sex marriage announcement for two men, Daniel Gross and Steven Goldstein. The couple was married in a civil ceremony in Vermont and in a commitment ceremony with Jewish vows.

In 2003, the Massachusetts Supreme Judicial Court ruled that same- and opposite-sex couples must be given equal civil rights under the state's constitution. The ruling will allow same-sex couples in Massachusetts to obtain a civil marriage license, to make health and financial decisions for each other, to file joint state tax returns, and to receive other protections under state law. In early 2004, the Court reaffirmed its decision, adding that only full marriage rights for gay couples, not just civil unions, would conform to the state's constitution. As of May 17, 2004, Massachusetts became the first state in the nation to let same-sex couples marry.

In February 2004, San Francisco's Mayor Gavin Newsom ordered the county clerk to issue same-sex marriage licenses, despite California voters' support of a 2000 ballot measure that defines marriage as a union between a man and a woman, an action that a state court later declared unconstitutional. Also in February 2004, President George W. Bush endorsed a constitutional amendment that would restrict marriage to two people of the opposite sex, leaving open the possibility that states could allow civil unions. Later, in November 2004, voters in 11 states supported state constitutional amendments banning same-sex unions.

The laws governing the rights and responsibilities of gay parents vary from state to state. It is estimated that there are more than 1.5 million lesbian mothers and 1 million gay fathers in the United States (Gottman 1990). The overwhelming trend has been to recognize the rights of gay parents, although four states—Arkansas, Florida, Mississippi, and Utah—do not allow same-sex couples to adopt children or serve as foster parents. In cases where one partner is the biological parent, the other parent may apply for second-parent adoption. Second-parent adoption has been recognized in more than 20 states but was rejected in Colorado, Ohio, and Wisconsin. When gay or straight partners adopt a child jointly, both partners have full parental rights (Leland 2000).

Academic research has consistently indicated that gay parents and their children do not differ significantly from heterosexual parents and their children (McLeod and Crawford 1998). There is little or no evidence that the children of gay or lesbian parents are disadvantaged in any important way in comparison to children of heterosexual parents (Patterson and Redding 1996). For their 2001 research, Judith Stacey and Timothy Biblarz examined the findings of 21 studies that explored how parental sexual orientation affected children. Based on the evidence, they concluded that there are no significant differences between children of lesbian mothers and children of heterosexual mothers in measures of social and psychological adjustment, such as self-esteem, anxiety, and depression. Across studies, there was no relationship between parental sexual orientation and measures of children's cognitive ability. Also, levels of closeness and the quality of parent-child relationships did not vary significantly by parental sexual orientation. Stacey and Biblarz (2001) concluded:

> We propose that homophobia and discrimination are the chief reasons why parental sexual orientation matters at all. Because lesbigay parents do not enjoy the same rights, respect and recognition as heterosexual parents, their children contend with the burdens of vicarious sexual stigma. (P. 177)

Voices in the Community:
Megan McGuire

Megan McGuire (1996) talks about growing up in her two Mom family.

High school was the hardest. I was into all kinds of clubs, but I was afraid everything I had gained socially would disappear if anyone ever found out that while they went home after volleyball practice to their Brady Bunch dinners with Mom and Dad, I went home to two moms. My brother and I would never allow Mom and Barb to walk together or sit next to each other in a restaurant. We wouldn't have people spend the night; if we did have friends over, we would hide the gay literature and family pictures. When a friend asked about the pink triangle on our car, our brother told him it was a used car and we hadn't had time to take the sticker off. We lived like this for three years, until we moved to a house with a basement apartment. We told our friends Barb lived there. It was really a guest room.

Ironically, our home life then was really the same as a straight family's. We had family meetings, fights, trips and dinners. My brother and I came to accept Barb (our mother's partner) as a parent. There were things she could never have with us the way our mother did. But she helped support us while my mother got her PhD in public health. And she pushed my brother and I to succeed in school, just like a mom.

With the help of a really great counselor and a friend who had a "it's not a big deal and I knew anyway" attitude, I started to become more comfortable with my two-mom family. The spring of my junior year, a local paper interviewed me for an article on gay families. I was relieved, but also afraid. The day the article appeared was incredibly tense. I felt like everyone was looking at me and taking about me. One kid said to my brother, "I saw the article, you fag." My brother told him to get lost. Some people avoided me, but most kids were curious about my family. People asked me if I was gay. I chose not to answer, as teenagers, most of us can't explain the feelings in our minds and bodies.

Last year, in my final year of high school, I decided to speak at our school's National Coming Out Day. Sitting up front were my best friend, my mother, my brother, and my counselor, Al. That day was the best. I no longer had to laugh at the jokes or keep a secret. I hoped I was making a path for others like me: a kid with a gay parent, scared and feeling alone. After my speech, I lost some friends and people made some remarks that hurt. But that only made me stronger. The hardest thing to deal with is other people's ignorance, not the family part. That's just like any other family.

Advocates, policy analysts, and family organizations have been actively engaged in promoting and advocating the rights of gay, lesbian, bisexual, and transgendered (GLBT) individuals and their families. The National Gay and Lesbian Task Force, based in Washington, D.C., is an organization committed to building a progressive GLBT political infrastructure. The organization embodies many of the elements of an advocacy organization: educating, training, organizing, and empowering GLBT people and community leaders. Support groups have also been formed to provide aid to families and friends of GLBT individuals.

Parents, Families and Friends of Lesbians and Gays (PFLAG) was started by Jeanne Manford after her son, Morton, was attacked at a gay rights protest demonstration in New York. Later, as Ms. Manford marched with her son at New York's Pride Day parade, she was approached by many gay and lesbian people, asking her to speak with their parents. Ms. Manford decided to begin a support group, and in 1973, 20 people attended the first meeting. The national PFLAG organization was established in 1981. PFLAG is a national nonprofit organization with more than 80,000 members and more than 460 affiliate organizations throughout the United States (PFLAG 2002).

MAIN POINTS

- The **family** is defined as a construct of meaning and relationships both emotional and economic. It is a social unit based on kinship relations—not only relations based on blood, but also those created by choice, marriage, partnership, or adoption.

- A household is defined as an economic and residential unit.

- From a functionalist perspective, social problems emerge as the family struggles to adapt to a modern society. Functionalists have noted how many of the original family functions have been taken over by organized religion, education, work, and the government in modern society, but still, the family is expected to provide its remaining functions of raising children and providing affection and companionship for its members.

- For the conflict theorist, the family is a system of inequality where conflict is normal. Conflict can derive from economic or power inequalities between spouses or family members. From a feminist perspective, inequality emerges from the patriarchal family system, where men control decision making in the family.

- According to an interactionist, through social interaction, we create and maintain our definition of a family. As we do this, it affects our larger social definition of what everyone's family should be like and the kind of family that we create for ourselves.

- We reviewed several problems based on the family in this chapter.

- **Divorce.** The U.S. divorce rate has remained stable at around 4.0 divorces per 1,000 in the total U.S. population. The rate was 4.1 in 1999, 4.2 in 2000 and 4.1 in 2001. Recent census data on divorce indicate that certain groups are more susceptible to divorce than others.

- **Domestic violence.** Current data suggest that 21 percent to 34 percent of women will be assaulted by an intimate partner during their lifetime. Research has consistently linked the following social factors to family violence: low socioeconomic status, social and structural stress, and social isolation. Feminist researchers argue that domestic violence is rooted in gender and represents men's attempts to maintain dominance and control over women.

- **Child abuse and neglect.** In 2000, 879,000 children were victims of child maltreatment. Neglect is characterized by a failure to provide for a child's basic needs. It can be physical, educational or emotional in nature.

- Responses to domestic violence can be characterized as having a distinct community approach. In the area of child abuse, the U.S. Office of Juvenile Justice and Delinquency Prevention established community-based children's advocacy centers to provide coordinated support for victims in the investigation, treatment, prosecution, and prevention of child abuse.

- **Elder abuse and neglect.** Elder abuse can occur in the care of their older children and their families or within a nursing home or hospital setting. Domestic elder abuse refers to any form of maltreatment of an older person by someone who has a special relationship with the elder (a spouse, child, friend, or caregiver); institutional elder abuse refers to forms of abuse that occur in residential facilities for older people. The National Center on Elder Abuse (NCEA) believes that community education and outreach are important in combating the problem of elder abuse and neglect. The NCEA supports community "sentinel" programs, which train and educate professionals.

- **Teen pregnancy.** The United States has the highest teen birthrate in the developed world. But teenage birthrates have declined significantly in each state between 1991 and 2000. The birthrate for teenagers (age 15 to 19 years) declined throughout the 1990s, falling from 62.1 births per 1,000 teenagers in 1991 to 48.5 per 1,000 in 2000.

- **The problems of time and money.** Economic realities make it especially difficult for working-class parents to maintain their juggling act. The Family Medical Leave Act (FMLA) of 1993 was envisioned as a way to help employees balance the demands of the workplace with the needs of their families. Although there is strong support for the FMLA, the act has also been criticized since its enactment.

- The proportion of nuclear families is decreasing, replaced with family structures that include single-parent, blended, adoptive, foster, grandparent, and same-sex partner households. The increasing diversity of American families requires that we broaden our research and policy agendas beyond traditional family forms. Perhaps one solution to the "problem" of families is to appreciate and embrace other family forms.

INTERNET AND COMMUNITY EXERCISES

1. Contact your local PFLAG (Parents and Friends of Lesbians and Gays) chapter. If one does not exist in your community, visit the Web site to find the chapter nearest you. What services or activities do they offer parents and families? Do they offer any educational programs or materials for communities? *Log on to Study Site Chapter 4.*

2. Interview a student who is also a parent. The student can be from your social problems class or any of your other classes. What challenges do student-parents face? How are their challenges different from those of students who are not parents? Does your school support programs or services for parents? Please check with your professor about campus policies regarding research involving human subjects.

3. Contact two domestic violence shelters in your community. What is the mission of each organization? Do different shelters serve different groups? If so, how are services tailored to various groups? Does each program promote violence prevention? Domestic shelters often support student internships for a quarter or semester. If you're interested in learning more about a shelter, ask about its internship program.

4. Identify the "family friendly" practices of your school. Does your school provide child care on site? Has your school provided leaves under the Family and Medical Leave Act? You may have to contact the human resources department in your school for more information.

On your own. Log on to *Study Site—Community and Policy Guide* for more information about the social problems, social policies, and community responses discussed in this chapter.

References

AFL-CIO. 2002. "Fact Sheet: Bargaining for Family Leave." Retrieved August 28, 2002 (www.aflcio.org/women/f_fam).

Amato, E. R. and B. Keith. 1991. "Parental Divorce and the Well-Being of Children: A Meta-analysis." *Journal of Marriage and the Family* 53:895–915.

American Association of Retired Persons (AARP). 2002. "Facts about Grandparents Raising Children." Retrieved August 28, 2002 (http://www.aarp.org/congacts/grandparents/grandfacts).

Anderson, Kristin. 1997. "Gender, Status, and Domestic Violence: An Integration of Feminist and Family Violence Approaches." *Journal of Marriage and the Family* 59(3):655–679.

Annie E. Casey Foundation. 1998. *Kids Count Special Report: When Teens Have Sex: Issues and Trends.* Baltimore, MD: Author.

Armas, Genaro. 2002. "Census Shows More Grandparents Are Raising Their Grandchildren." *The News Tribune,* July 8, pp. A1, A6.

Bengston, V. L. 2001. "Beyond the Nuclear Family: The Increasing Importance of Multigenerational Bonds." *Journal of Marriage and the Family* 63(1):1–17.

Bethea, L. 1999. "Primary Prevention of Child Abuse." *American Family Physician* 59(6):1577–1586.

Browne, A. 1993. "Violence Against Women by Male Partners: Prevalence, Outcomes, and Policy Implications." *American Psychologist* 48:1077–1087.

Bumiller, E. 2002. "The Most Unlikely Story Behind a Gay Rights Victory." *New York Times,* June 27, p. A19.

Card, J. 1999. "Teen Pregnancy Prevention: Do Any Programs Work?" *Annual Review of Public Health* 20:257–285.

Casper, L. and K. Bryson. 1998. "Co-resident Grandparents and Their Grandchildren: Grandparent Maintained Families" (Population Division Working Paper No. 26). Washington, DC: U.S. Bureau of the Census.

Centers for Disease Control and Prevention. 2002. *Births, Marriages, Divorces, and Deaths: Provisional Data for October 2001* (National Vital Statistics Reports Vol. 50, No. 11, June 26, 2002). Atlanta, GA: Author.

Cherlin, A., K. Kiernan, and P. Chase-Lansdale. 1995. "Parental Divorce in Childhood and Demographic Outcomes in Young Adulthood." *Demography* 32:299–318.

Children's Bureau. 2002. *National Child Abuse and Neglect Data System: Summary of Key Findings from Calendar Year 2000.* Washington, DC: U.S. Department of Health and Human Services, Administration for Children and Families.

Collier, L. 2001. "Havens for Abandoned Babies Occupy Tricky Terrain." *Chicago Tribune,* February 18, 2001, C1. Retrieved August 30, 2002 from www.adoptionnation.com/chicago_trib_02-18-01.

Copeland, A. P. and K. M. White. 1991. *Studying Families.* Newbury Park, CA: Sage.

D'Agostino, J. 2000. "Infant Abandonment Has Become an Epidemic." *Human Events* 56(12):4.

Demo, D. H. (1992). "Parent-Child Relations: Assessing Recent Changes." *Journal of Marriage and the Family* 54:104–117.

Dodson, Lisa, Tiffany Manuel, and Ellen Bravo. 2002. *Keeping Jobs and Raising Families in Low-Income America: It Just Doesn't Work.* Cambridge, MA: Radcliffe Public Policy Center and 9 to 5 National Association of Working Women.

Fields, Jason. 2003. *Children's Living Arrangements and Characteristics: March 2002* (Current Population Reports, P20–547). Washington, DC: U. S. Census Bureau.

Fields, Jason and Lynne M. Casper. 2001. *America's Families and Living Arrangements: Population Characteristics: March 2000* (Current Population Reports, P20-537). Washington, DC: U.S. Census Bureau.

Gelles , Richard and Peter Maynard. 1987. "A Structural Family Systems Approach to Intervention in Cases of Family Violence." *Family Relations* 33(2):270–276.

Gottman, J. S. 1990. "Children of Gay and Lesbian Parents." Pp. 177–196) in *Homosexuality and Family Relations,* edited by F. W. Bozett and M. B. Sussman. New York: Harrington Park.

Gould, Joe. 2001. "Local 'Safe Haven' Law Seldom Used." *The News Times.* Retrieved August 28, 2002 (http://www.cwealf.org/articles/safehaven12_2_01).

Hanson, Marci and Eleanor Lynch. 1992. "Family Diversity: Implications for Policy and Practice." *Topics in Early Childhood Special Education,* 12(3):283–305.

Hetzel, Lisa and Annetta Smith. 2001. *The 65 Years and Over Population: 2000* (Current Population Reports, C2KBR/01-10). Washington, DC: U.S. Census Bureau.

Hoffman, Saul. 1998. "Teenage Childbearing Is Not So Bad After All . . . Or Is It? A Review of the New Literature." *Family Planning Perspectives* 30(5):236–239, 243.

Illinois Hospital Association. 2004. "UPDATE—Abandoned Newborn Infant Protection Act." Retrieved August 29, 2004 (http://www.ihatoday.org/public/legal/abandonedact.htm).

Kalil, Ariel and Sandra Danzinger. 2000. "How Teen Mothers Are Faring Under Welfare Reform." *Journal of Social Issues* 56(4):775–798.

Kreider, Rose and J. Fields. 2002. *Number, Timing, and Duration of Marriages and Divorces: Fall 1996* (Current Population Reports, P70–80). Washington, DC: U.S. Census Bureau.

Lang, Susan. 1993. "Findings Refute Traditional Views on Elder Abuse." *Human Ecology* 21(3):30.

Leland, John. 2000. "State Laws Vary, but a Broad Trend Is Clear." *The New York Times,* December 21, p. F4.

Lenski, G. and G. Lenski 1987. *Human Societies.* New York: McGraw-Hill.

Levendosky, A., S. Lynch, and S. Graham-Bermann. 2000. "Mothers' Perceptions of the Impact of Woman Abuse on Their Parenting." *Violence Against Women* 6(3):247–271.

Little, Kristin, Mary Malefyt, and Alexander Walker. 1998. "A Tool for Communities to Develop Coordinated Responses." In *Promising Practices Initiative of the STOP Violence Against Women Grants Technical Assistance Project.* Retrieved August 29, 2002 (www.vaw.umn.edu/Promise/PP3).

Maynard, Rebecca, ed. 1997. *Kids Having Kids: Economic Costs and Social Consequences of Teen Pregnancy.* Washington, DC: The Urban Institute Press.

McGuire, Megan. 1996. "Growing Up with Two Moms." *Newsweek,* November 4, p. 53.

McKay, M. 1994. "The Link between Domestic Violence and Child Abuse: Assessment and Treatment Considerations." *Child Welfare* 73(1):29–39.

McLeod, A. and I. Crawford. 1998. "The Postmodern Family: An Examination of the Psychosocial and Legal Perspectives of Gay and Lesbian Parenting." Pp. 211–223 in *Stigma and Sexual Orientation: Understanding Prejudice Against Lesbians, Gay Men, and Bisexuals,* edited by G. Herek. Thousand Oaks, CA: Sage.

National Center on Elder Abuse. 1998. *The National Elder Abuse Incidence Study—Final Report.* Washington, DC: Author.

———. 2002a. "The Basics: What Is Elder Abuse?" Retrieved August 29, 2002 (www.elderabusecenter.org/basic/).

———. 2002b. *Sentinels: Reaching Hidden Victims—Final Report, May 2002.* Washington, DC: Author.

National Clearing House on Child Abuse and Neglect Information. 2002. "What Is Child Maltreatment?" Retrieved August 27, 2002 (www.calib.com/nccanch/pubs/factsheets/childmal.cfm).

National Partnership for Women and Families. 2002. "What It Took to Pass the Family and Medical Leave Act: A Nine-Year Campaign Pays Off." Retrieved August 28, 2002. (http://www.nationalpartnership.org/content.cfm?L1=202&DBT=Documents&NewsItemID=275).

Navaie-Waliser, Maryam, P. Feldman, D. Gould, C. Levine, A. Kuebris, and Karen Donelan. 2002. "When the Caregiver Needs Care: The Plight of Vulnerable Caregivers." *American Journal of Public Health* 92(3):409–413.

Parents, Families and Friends of Lesbians and Gays (PFLAG). 2002. "The History Behind PFLAG." Retrieved September 18, 2002 (www.pflag.org/about/history.html).

Patterson, Charlotte and Richard Redding. 1996. "Lesbian and Gay Families with Children: Implications of Social Science Research for Policy." *Journal of Social Issues* 52(3):29–50.

Popenoe, David. 1993. "American Family Decline, 1960–1990: A Review and Appraisal." *Journal of Marriage and the Family* 55:527–555.

Radcliffe Public Policy Center. 2000. *Life's Work: Generational Attitudes Toward Work and Life Integration.* Cambridge, MA: Author.

Rennison, Callie Marie. 2003. *Intimate Partner Violence, 1993–2001* (NCJ 197838). Washington, DC: U.S. Department of Justice, Office of Justice Programs.

Rubin, Lillian. 1995. *Families on the Fault Line: America's Working Class Speaks About the Family, the Economy and Ethnicity.* New York: Harper Perennial.

Shamgar-Handelman, Lea. 1996. "Family Sociology in a Small Academic Community: Family Research and Theory in Israel." Pp. 377–416 in *Intercultural Variation in Family Research and Theory: Implications for Cross-National Studies,* edited by M. Sussman and R. Hanks. New York: Haworth Press.

Simmons, T. and J. L. Dye. 2003. *Grandparents Living with Grandchildren: 2000* (Current Population Reports, C2KBR-31). Washington, DC: U.S. Census Bureau.

Simons, R. L. 1996. *Understanding Differences between Divorced and Intact Families: Stress, Interaction, and Child Outcomes.* Thousand Oaks, CA: Sage.

Somers, Cheryl and Mariane Fahlman. 2001. "Effectiveness of the 'Baby Think It Over' Teen Pregnancy Prevention Program." *Journal of School Health* 71(5):188–207.

Stacey, Judith. 1996. *In the Name of the Family: Rethinking Family Values in the Post-Modern Age.* Boston: Beacon Press.

Stacey, Judith and Timothy Biblarz. 2001. "(How) Does the Sexual Orientation of Parents Matter?" *American Sociological Review* 66:159–183.

U.S. Census Bureau. 1999. *Statistical Abstract of the United States: 1999* (Table No. 91). Washington, DC: Author.

U.S. Department of Health and Human Services. 1998. *A National Strategy to Prevent Teen Pregnancy: Annual Report 1997–1998.* Washington, DC: Author.

Van Schaick, Kelly and Arnold Stolberg. 2001. "The Impact of Paternal Involvement and Parental Divorce on Young Adults' Intimate Relationships." *Journal of Divorce and Remarriage* 36(1–2):99–123.

Ventura, Stephanie, T. J. Matthews, and Brady Hamilton. 2002. *Teenage Births in the United States: State Trends, 1991–2000, an Update* (National Vital Statistics Reports, Vol. 50, No. 9). Hyattsville, MD: National Center for Health Statistics.

Videon, Tami. 2002. "The Effects of Parent-Adolescent Relationships and Parental Separation on Adolescent Well-Being." *Journal of Marriage and Family* 64(2):489–504.

Education

E ducation is assumed to be the great equalizer in our society. There are inspirational stories of women and men who, after a tough childhood or adulthood, complete their education and become successful members of society, held up as role models. Education is presented as an essential part of their success, serving as a cure for personal or situational shortcomings. If you are poor, education can make you rich. If your childhood was less than perfect, a college degree can make up for it. On the occasion of launching the Head Start program in 1965, President Lyndon Johnson is quoted as saying, "If it weren't for education, I'd still be looking at the southern end of a northbound mule" (Zigler and Muenchow 1992).

Yet, along with these images of success, we are also bombarded with images of failure. Media coverage and political rhetoric highlight problems with our educational system, in particular with our public schools. In recent state and national political campaigns, the quality of teaching and preparation of teachers were scrutinized, school districts with low scores on standardized exams were criticized, and school vouchers and standardized testing were promoted as the means to effective education reform.

So which is it: Is education a key to individual success or an institutional failure? In this chapter, we'll first examine this question by reviewing our educational system from different sociological perspectives. Then we'll explore current social problems in education, along with policy and program responses.

The New Educational Standard

We tend to define a high school degree as the educational standard of the past, now replaced with a bachelor's degree. In fact, data from the U.S. Census Bureau confirm that the United States has an increasingly more educated population (see Table 5.1 and U.S. Data Map 5.1).

For 2003, the U.S. Census Bureau (Stoops 2004) reported that an all time high of 85 percent of adults (25 years and older) completed at least a high school degree and more than 27 percent of all adults had attained at least a bachelor's degree. Younger Americans are more educated than older Americans. Approximately 67 percent of all Americans 75 years or older attained a high school degree or more

❖ Table 5.1   Educational Attainment of the Population, 25 years and Older, 2003

Characteristics	Percentage with		
	High school graduate or more	Some college or more	Bachelor's degree or more
Population aged 25 years and over	84.6	52.5	27.2
By age group:			
25-29 years old	86.5	57.4	28.4
30-34 years old	87.6	58.6	31.5
35-39 years old	87.6	56.5	29.8
40-44 years old	88.4	56.5	29.1
45-49 years old	89.3	57.4	29.9
50-54 years old	88.7	58.9	31.1
55-59 years old	86.9	55.1	29.0
60-64 years old	83.0	47.3	24.5
65-69 years old	76.9	39.1	19.6
70-74 years old	72.8	36.4	18.5
75 years or older	67.5	32.4	15.4

Source: Stoops 2004.

compared with 86 percent of those 25 to 29 years old. Educational attainment level of adults will continue to rise, as younger more educated age groups replace older less educated ones.

❖ PUTTING IT TOGETHER:

Compare the educational attainment of three generations of your family: yourself, your parents, and your grandparents. Does your family reflect the same educational attainment pattern as the census data indicate? Are younger generations more educated than older generations in your family? Why or why not?

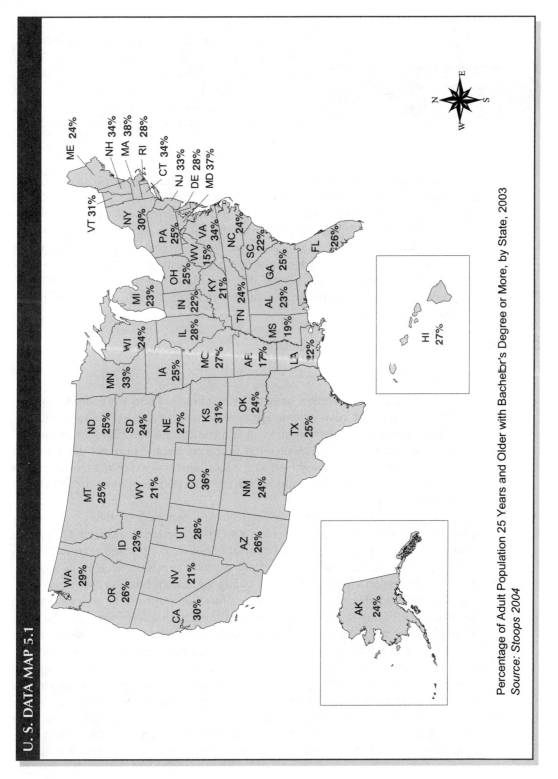

Percentage of Adult Population 25 Years and Older with Bachelor's Degree or More, by State, 2003
Source: Stoops 2004

Based on data from the U.S. Census, compare the percentage of high school graduates and college graduates among males and females in your home and college state. If data are available for several years, how would you characterize the state trend in educational attainment? Log on to *Study Site* *Chapter 5*.

Why should we be concerned about educational attainment? We are concerned about our education because we assume that it will lead to something. You and others in your class are likely to answer that you are reading this textbook to obtain a degree and, ultimately, a job. It has become harder and harder to get a job with substantial income and benefits without a college degree. We know that educational attainment is correlated with your potential job placement and earnings. In 2003, those 25 years or older who completed high school only had mean annual earnings of $30,084 (U.S. Census Bureau 2004). In contrast, those with a bachelor's degree reported higher average earnings of $53,356.

Sociological Perspectives on Education

Functionalist Perspective

The institution of education has a set of **manifest** and **latent functions**. Manifest functions are intended goals or consequences of the activities within an institution. Education's primary manifest function should come as no surprise: It is to educate! Along with educating, the other manifest functions include personal development, proper socialization, and employment. Our educational system ensures that each of us will be appropriately socialized and adequately educated to become a contributing member of society.

Education's latent or unintended consequences may be less obvious. One unintended function that education serves is as a public babysitter. No other institution can claim such a monopoly over the total number of hours, months, and years of a child's life. From kindergarten through high school, parents can rely on teachers, administrators, and counselors not only for their child's education, but also for supervision, socialization, and discipline. In addition, education controls the entry of young women and men into the labor force and the timing of that entry. Consider the surge in employment rates after high school and college graduation. There is always a rush to get a job each summer; employers rely on the temporary labor of high school and college students during busy summer months. Finally, education serves to establish and protect social networks by ensuring that individuals with similar backgrounds, education, and interests are able to form friendships, partnerships, or romantic bonds.

Functionalists argue that education has been assigned so many additional tasks that it struggles in its primary task to educate the young. In addition to its own main functions, our educational system has taken over functions of other institutions.

For example, the educational system provides services to students with family problems, emotional needs, or physical challenges. Schools also provide services for parents in the form of adult education or parenting classes.

Conflict Perspective

Conflict theorists would not see education as an equalizer; rather, they would consider education a "divider"—dividing the haves from the have-nots in our society. From this perspective, conflict theorists would focus on the social and economic inequalities inherent in our educational system and how the system perpetuates these inequalities.

Conflict theorists highlight the socialization function of education as part of the indoctrination of Western bureaucratic ideology. The popular posters and books on "What I learned in kindergarten" could serve as the official list of adult life rules: Share everything, play fair, put things back where you found them. Never mind kindergarten—the indoctrination can begin as early as nursery school. Rosabeth Moss Kanter (1972) describes a child's experience in nursery school as an "organizational experience" creating an **organizational child**. Carefully instructed and supervised by their teachers, students are guided through their day in ordered agendas; they are rewarded for conformity, and any signs of individuality are discouraged. The organizational child is sufficiently prepared for the demands and constraints of a bureaucratic adult world.

The educational system can also perpetuate racial and economic inequalities, according to Jonathan Kozol in his 1991 book, *Savage Inequalities*. As he documents the conditions of inner-city schools in Illinois, New York, Washington, D.C., New Jersey, and Texas, Kozol presents a dark portrait of student learning in schools that are understaffed, undersupplied, and in disrepair. From his description, the gap between the haves and have-nots is so wide it seems impossible to attain educational equity. As Kozol (1991) observes,

> Children in one set of schools are educated to be governors; children in another set of schools are trained to be governed. The former are given the imaginative range to mobilize ideas for economic growth; the latter are provided with the discipline to do the narrow tasks the first group will prescribe. (P. 176)

Kozol asks: Even if we can't provide immediate assistance for the problems of racial segregation or toxic pollution, why can't we invest more money and talent in these public schools?

Feminist Perspective

Inequalities are based not just on social class but also on gender. Research reveals the persistent replication of gender relations in schools, evidenced by the privileging of males, their voices, and activities in the classroom, playground, and hallways (Smith 2000).

One of my favorite illustrations of the privilege given to a male voice comes from my own discipline. In sociology, there is a concept called the "definition of the situation," which refers to the phrase: "If men define situations as real, they are real in their consequences" (Thomas and Thomas 1928:572). The concept is an important one to the symbolic interactionist perspective and is often attributed solely to sociologist W. I. Thomas. However, the correct acknowledgment is to Thomas and his wife, Dorothy Swaine Thomas. Smith (1995) investigated the citation in more than 244 introductory sociology textbooks and found that most attributed the concept solely to W. I. Thomas. One reason for the omission of Dorothy Swaine Thomas is that she may not have contributed to the phrase (although there is no documented evidence to support this), but Smith (1995) suggests that the omission is due to a professional and structural ideology that historically represented sociology as a "male" domain. Smith notes that the citations began to include Dorothy Swaine Thomas after the mid 1970s, a time when sociology and introductory texts began to respond to and reflect the changes brought about by a growing women's movement and increasing numbers of female sociologists.

Gender bias and gender stereotypes work to exclude and alienate girls early in their educational experience (AAUW 1992; Sadker and Sadker 1994). Males have favored status in education, particularly in their interactions with their teachers. In the classroom, girls are invisible, often treated as "second-class educational citizens." This is how Myra and David Sadker (1994) explained the subtle yet consequential gender bias in the classrooms they visited. After observing teachers and their interactions with girls and boys in more than 100 classrooms, the Sadkers found that teachers were more responsive to boys and were more likely to teach them more actively. Overall, girls received less attention while boys got a double dose, both negative and positive. Boys received more praise, corrections, and feedback, whereas girls received a cursory "OK" response from their teachers. Sadker and Sadker concluded that over time, the unequal distribution of teacher time and attention may take its toll on girls' self-esteem, achievement rates, test scores, and ultimately careers.

Structural factors along with interpersonal dynamics also contribute to creation and maintenance of gender inequality on college and university campuses (Stombler and Yancey Martin 1994). Men and women experience college differently and have markedly different outcomes (Jacobs 1996). College women are subjected to male domination through their peer relations (Stombler and Yancey Martin 1994) in the classroom, in romantic involvements (Holland and Eisenhart 1990), and in organized activities. Even activities like fraternity "little sister" programs, which were studied by Stombler and Yancey Martin (1994), provide the structural and interpersonal dynamics necessary to create an atmosphere conducive to women's subordination.

Interactionist Perspective

In Sadker and Sadker's 1994 study, we identified the differential effects of teacher communication on female and male students. The interaction between teachers and students daily reinforces the structure and inequalities of the classroom and the educational system. From this micro perspective, sociologists focus on how classroom dynamics and practices educate the perfect student and at the same time create the not-so-perfect ones. In what ways does classroom interaction educate and create?

Assessment and testing are standard practices in education. Students are routinely graded and evaluated based on their work and ability. Interactionists would argue that along with assessment come unintended consequences. Based on test results, students may be placed in different ability or occupational tracks. In the practice called **tracking,** advanced learners are separated from regular learners; students are identified as college bound versus work bound. Advocates of tracking argue that the practice increases educational effectiveness by allowing teachers to target students at their ability level (Hallinan 1994). Yet, placing students in tracks has been controversial because of the presumed negative effects on some students. In addition to creating unequal learning opportunities (Hallinan 1994), tracking may encourage teachers, parents, and others to view students differently according to their track, and as a result, their true potential may be hindered (Adams and Evans 1996). Although tracking is intended to aid students, it may lead to a self-fulfilling prophecy: Students will fail because they are expected to do so.

Negative educational outcomes are found more often among male students. More grade school boys than girls are classified as needing special education. Beginning in the first grade, males have lower average levels of achievement in reading and writing than females (College Entrance Examination Board 1999). Achievement problems are more pronounced for underrepresented minority males and males at lower socio-economic levels (College Entrance Examination Board 1999). Although interactionists do not assess the appropriateness of the label, they would address how the label affects students' identity and educational outcomes. Issues of inequality must also be addressed if the data suggest that students of particular gender or ethnic/racial categories are targeted for tracking. A summary of all sociological perspectives on education is presented in Table 5.2.

❖ PUTTING IT TOGETHER:
On your campus.

Investigate how many female and male students have declared majors in math, engineering, English, nursing, and sociology in your university. Is there a difference in the number of female majors in engineering versus English? Math majors versus nursing majors? What sociological perspective(s) might best explain the gender gap in majors?

Problems and Challenges in American Education

The idea that there is a public education crisis is not a new one. A 1918 government report referred to the "erosion of family life, disappearing fathers, working mothers, the decline of religious institutions, changes in the workplace, and the millions of newly arrived immigrants" as potential sources of the public education crisis (Meier 1995:9). At the time, the government's response was the creation of the modern school system with two tracks, one for terminal high school degrees and the other for college-bound students (Meier 1995).

❖ Table 5.2 Summary of Sociological Perspectives: Education

	Functional	Conflict/Feminist	Interactionist
Explanation of education	Using a macro perspective, functionalists examine the functions of the educational system. The educational system is strained from performing multiple functions.	Conflict and feminist theorists address how the educational system serves to perpetuate economic, ethnic, and gender inequalities. Students, depending on their social backgrounds, are differentially treated by the educational system.	Using a micro perspective, an interactionist focuses on how the educational experience is created through interaction and shared meanings in the classroom.
Questions asked about education and its social problems	What manifest or latent functions does education serve? How is education affected by other social institutions?	How does education perpetuate social inequalities? Is one group more disadvantaged than another?	How do classroom dynamics determine the educational success of a student? What is the relationship between teacher-student interaction and student success? How does student tracking or labeling impact student achievement?

The current call for educational reform was initiated during President Reagan's administration. In 1983, the National Commission on Excellence in Education released its report, *A Nation at Risk,* a scathing indictment of the education system. The Commission was created by Secretary of Education T. H. Bell to respond to what he called the "widespread public perception that something is seriously remiss in our educational system" (National Commission on Excellence in Education 1983). Based on

18 months of study, the Commission concluded that there were widespread failures in our educational system. Claiming that we are raising a scientifically and technologically illiterate generation, the Commission made note of the relatively poor performance of American students in comparison to their international peers, declining standardized test scores, the weaknesses of our school programs and educators, and the lack of a skilled American workforce (National Commission on Excellence in Education 1983).

The educational reform movement marches on, gaining momentum with each elected president. At one time or another, each president after Reagan has referred to himself as the "Education President," declaring an educational crisis and calling for change. Educators and reformers agree that this is an exciting time for American education (Ravitch and Viteritti 1997). Under George H. W. Bush's administration, Congress passed America 2000, which was followed by the Goals 2000: Educate America Act in 1994 during Bill Clinton's administration. Recently, under George W. Bush's administration, Congress passed the No Child Left Behind Act of 2001. All congressional acts call for coordinated improvements and sweeping reform of our educational system.

David Berliner and Bruce Biddle (1995) contend that the crisis in public education is a manufactured one, constructed by well-meaning or not so well-meaning politicians, educational experts, and business leaders. Berliner and Biddle don't believe that public schools are problem-free; rather, by focusing on the manufactured crisis, they believe we're not addressing the real problems facing our schools, those based in social and economic inequalities. What is the evidence regarding these problems and challenges to our educational system? Let's first examine the basis of education: literacy.

The Problem of Basic Literacy

According to the Literacy Volunteers of America (2002), very few U.S. adults are truly illiterate. What is of concern is the number of adults with low literacy skills who are unable to find and retain employment, support their children's education, and participate in their communities. Basic literacy skills, such as understanding and using information in texts (newspapers, books, a warranty form) or instructional documents (maps, job applications) or completing mathematical operations (filling out an order form, balancing a checkbook) are related to social, educational, and economic outcomes (Sum, Kirsch, and Taggart 2002).

The most detailed literacy study conducted in the United States was the 1992 National Adult Literacy Survey (ALS). Past studies of adult literacy have focused on the number of illiterates in our society, failing to acknowledge the complexity of the literacy problem (Kirsch et al. 1993). According to the ALS, 40 million to 44 million adults demonstrated skills in Level 1 (out of five levels), the lowest level of prose, document, and quantitative proficiency. About 50 million adults demonstrated skills in Level 2. Adults in both levels, almost 50 percent of the U.S. population, were likely to experience difficulty integrating or synthesizing information from texts or performing quantitative tasks that involve two of more sequential operations (Kirsch et al. 1993).

According to the U.S. Department of Education, individuals at higher levels of literacy are more likely to be employed, to work more weeks per year, and to earn higher wages than individuals with lower levels of literacy. Nearly half of all adults performing at Level 1 were living in poverty, compared with only 4 percent to 8 percent of those in the two highest proficiency levels (Kirsch et al. 1993). Education increases an individual's literacy skills, and these skills also determine educational success. Basic academic skills influence such educational outcomes as high school completion, college enrollment, persistence in college, field of study, and type of degrees obtained (Sum et al. 2002).

Although the United States spends more per capita on education than other high-income countries, our literacy scores are average in a world comparison. The literacy scores of native-born U.S. adults rank 10th among the 17 high-income nations. The nations that scored higher were Sweden, Norway, Denmark, Finland, the Netherlands, Germany, Canada, Belgium, and Australia. Moreover, the United States ranked first for the largest gap between highly and poorly educated adults, with immigrants and minorities among those poorly educated (Sum et al. 2002).

Inequality in Educational Access and Achievement

According to the figures we reviewed earlier from the U.S. Census Bureau, educational attainment is increasing, especially among younger Americans. We could stop here and declare that there is no educational crisis. A closer look at the data, however, reveals that educational attainment is still unevenly distributed among social groups. In the following section, we will review the impact of social class, gender, and ethnicity on educational opportunity and achievement.

Social Class and Education

Socioeconomic status is one of the most powerful predictors of student achievement (College Entrance Examination Board 1999). The likelihood of dropping out of high school is higher among students from lower income families. In the year ending October 1999, about 520,000 students dropped out of high school (U.S. Census Bureau 2001). Nine percent of high school students from families with incomes below $20,000 dropped out of school versus just 2 percent of students from families with incomes of $40,000 or more (U.S. Census Bureau 2001). Students from lower income homes or who have parents with little formal education are less likely to be high achievers compared with students from high-income families or students who have parents with a college education (College Entrance Examination Board 1999). A national study revealed that only 5 percent of eighth graders whose parents do not have a high school degree had achievement test scores in the upper quartile; by comparison, more than 50 percent of students who have at least one parent with a graduate degree scored in the top quartile (College Entrance Examination Board 1999).

Poor children are not just poor economically, but also poor educationally. Poor children begin school less prepared and struggle to keep up with their learning and with their classmates (Maruyama 2003). In their analysis of reading and mathematics achievement among kindergarten and first-grade students, Denton and West (2002) discovered that twice as many first graders from families that were not poor were proficient in understanding words in context and in performing multiplication and division, compared to first graders from poor families. Differences in early school achievement may be attributable to differences in preschool experiences (Maruyama 2003). Inequalities begin even before children begin their formal education: in preschool. In 1999, 58 percent of three- or four-year-olds from families earning $40,000 or more attended nursery school compared with 41 percent of children from families with incomes less than $20,000. Although nursery school enrollment has increased over the past few decades, the cost of such programs may prohibit some families from enrolling their children (U.S. Census Bureau 2001), which may negatively impact the children's early school preparation.

Gender and Education

Census data (Stoops 2004) indicate slight differences in educational attainment for men and women. Overall, whereas more than 80 percent of men and women completed high school, 29 percent of men report having a bachelor's degree or more compared to 26 percent of women. For the U.S. population ages 25 to 29, women exceed men in educational attainment—for high school and college completion. About 88 percent of women and 85 percent of men completed high school; 31 percent of women earned a college degree or more compared to 26 percent of men.

Although more women are being awarded bachelor's degrees, fewer women than men complete bachelor's degrees in mathematics, engineering, physics, and other quantitative fields (College Entrance Examination Board 1999). By the time they leave high school, males are three times more likely to pursue careers in science, mathematics, or engineering than females (Strand and Mayfield 2002). Is this due to natural ability? The answer is no, according to the American Association of University Women. Their 1992 study reported that at age nine, there were no differences in math performance between boys and girls, and only minimal differences at age 13. Boys have higher achievement scores in physics, chemistry, earth sciences, and space sciences than girls, and the differences are largest among 17-year-olds.

Differences in mathematical and scientific abilities favoring boys do not appear until the intermediate grades. A study by Silverman (1986) suggests that females will eventually achieve less than males because they are gradually conditioned by "powerful environmental influences" such as the educational system, peers, and parents to believe that they are less capable than males. A "hidden curriculum" perpetuates gender inequalities in math and science courses. This curriculum takes the form of differential treatment in the classroom, where boys tend to dominate class discussion and monopolize their instructor's time and attention, whereas girls are silenced and their insecurities reinforced (Linn and Kessel 1996). Research suggests that girls, especially gifted ones, fail to achieve their potential due to lower expectations of success, the attribution of any success to chance, and the belief that success will lead to negative social consequences (Silverman 1986).

Ethnicity/Race and Education

About 3.4 million students entered kindergarten in U.S. public schools last fall and already . . . researchers foresee widely different futures for them. Whether they are White, Black, Hispanic, Native American or Asian-American will, to a large extent, predict their success in school. (Johnson and Viadero 2000:1)

There are persistent academic achievement gaps between Black, Hispanic, and Native American students and their White and Asian peers. This was the conclusion made by the College Entrance Examination Board's (1999) National Task Force on Minority High Achievement. In the mid-1990s, underrepresented minorities received less than 13 percent of all the bachelor's degrees awarded. The College Entrance Examination Board noted that in the latter half of the 1990s, only small percentages of Black, Hispanic, and Native American high school seniors in the National Assessment Educational Progress test samples had scores "typical" of students who are well prepared for college. Few students in these groups had scores indicating academic skills required for the most selective colleges or universities.

The educational attainment of the young Hispanic population, ages 25 to 29, is lower than for other ethnic/racial groups. As indicated in Table 5.3, at least 87 percent of non-Hispanic Whites, Blacks, and Asians completed high school or more. In contrast, only 62 percent of Hispanics (of any race) completed high school or more. At the bachelor's degree level, Asians have the highest proportion of college graduates, 61.6 percent, followed by non-Hispanic Whites, 34.2 percent; Blacks, 17.2 percent; and Hispanics, 10.4 percent.

It is predicted that by 2015, there will be large increases in the number of Latino and Asian American youth, a substantial growth in the number of African American students, and a slight drop in the number of White students. The challenges to our educational system will only increase if demographic predictions hold true. The current educational gaps among racial and ethnic categories have the potential to grow into larger sources of inequality and social conflict (College Entrance Examination Board 1999).

According to the American Association of University Women (2001b), Latino/a students are at greater risk of not finishing school than any other ethnoracial group. The graduation rate is lower for Latina girls than girls in any other racial or ethnic group. Census data for 1995 indicated that 30 percent of Hispanic girls leave school without a high school diploma, compared with 12.9 percent of Black girls and 8.2 percent of White girls. The only other group with a similar dropout rate is Hispanic boys, a rate of 30 percent. According to Headden (1997), Latino children don't attend preschool, and their parents don't read to them or provide encouragement for academic success.

Ethnicity/race, along with poverty, defines major sources of disadvantage in educational outcomes (Maruyama 2003). Poverty among Latino families produces significant educational disadvantages: Parents may work multiple jobs, may not have the time to spend reading or going over homework with their children, and may not have the skills to read to their children. Economics also play a role in dropout decisions. To support their families, Latino/a teens may leave school for a paying job.

The power of parental and peer influence on Latino/a educational attainment has also been recognized. Parents may have expectations for their children that conflict with school expectations or requirements (AAUW 2001b). This may be true particularly for Latinas, who are under pressure to follow "traditional" sex roles (married with children). For some Latinas, the dream of going away to college may conflict with the family's desire for their daughter to stay close to home and accept traditional sex roles. Latino/a peers may not support academic achievement for Latinas (sometimes referring to successful Latinas as "Anglo" or "White"), preferring that they embrace more

❖ Table 5.3   Differences in Educational Attainment (in percent) by Race and
Hispanic Origin for Adults Age 25 to 29 years, 2003

	Non-Hispanic White Alone	Black Alone	Asian Alone	Hispanic (of any race)
High school graduate or more	93.7	87.6	97.1	61.7
Some college or more	65.5	50.2	81.2	31.1
Bachelor's degree or more	34.2	17.2	61.6	10.4

Source: Stoops 2004.

traditional, less academic personas (AAUW 2001b). Research indicates that among academically successful Latinas, there are low levels of sex role traditionalism (Thorne 1995); Latinas who adhere to traditional sex roles were not attending or persisting in college as compared with nontraditional Latinas (Cardoza 1991).

According to Claude Steele and Joshua Aronson (1995), the pressure to conform to an image or a stereotype is so strong that it can actually impair intellectual performance. Steele and his colleagues tested the effects of a **stereotype threat** among African American (Steele and Aronson 1995; Steele 1997) and female college students (Spencer, Steele, and Quinn 1999). The stereotype threat is the risk of confirming in oneself a characteristic that is part of a negative stereotype about one's group. The threat is situational, present only when a person can be judged, treated in terms of, or self-fulfill negative stereotypes about group (and self) (Spencer et al. 1999). In their studies, Steele and his colleagues investigated the effect of the stereotype that African Americans and women have lower academic abilities than White or male students.

It doesn't matter if the individual actually believes the stereotype; if the stereotype demeans something of importance, like one's intellectual ability, the threat can be disrupting enough to impair intellectual performance (Steele and Aronson 1995). Subjects were compared in test-taking situations using GRE, SAT, or ACT sample questions. In all study conditions where the tests were represented as affected by gender or race, African American and female students underperformed their comparison group. In situations where the stereotype threat was moderated (where subjects were not told that the tests produced gender differences or where subjects were not asked to report their race on the examination form), African American and female students performed as well as White or male students.

Violence and Harassment in Schools

Since a series of deadly school shootings in the late 1990s, part of the focus on education has revolved around safety in schools. School violence can be characterized on a continuum that includes aggressive behavior, harassment, property crimes, threats, and physical assault (Flannery 1997). From July 1992 to June 2000, 390 people died in school-related violent incidents. Of these deaths, 234 were homicides and 43 were homicides in which victims were school-age youth (ages 5 to 19). During the same period, 24,406 children ages 5 to 19 were victims of homicide while away from school. In each school year, youth were 70 times more likely to be killed away from school than at school (DeVoe et al. 2003).

Although there were fewer school-associated violent death events in recent years, there were more deaths per event (Anderson et al. 2001). The deadliest incident took place in 1999 at Colorado's Columbine High School, where 14 students and a teacher were killed (Bowman 2001b). Nevertheless, schools remain a safe place for students, with the risk of a violent death less than one in a million (Bowman 2001a) and declining rates of violent and nonfatal student crime (DeVoe et al. 2003). Still, schools have been characterized as "battlegrounds" where both teachers and students fear for their safety (Kingery et al. 1993). It is estimated that we spend $200 million annually for school violence prevention and response (Flannery 1997).

The 2001 National School Based Youth Risk Behavior Survey conducted by the Centers for Disease Control indicated that nationwide about 7 percent of students had missed more than one day of school because they felt unsafe at school or on their way to or from school (Grunbaum et al. 2002). Hispanic and Black students were more likely than White students to have missed school because they felt unsafe. Among all students, 7 percent said they carried a weapon (a gun, knife, or club) on the school campus, with more male students (10.2 percent) than female students (2.9 percent) doing so. About 9 percent of all students reported being threatened or injured with a weapon on school property, and about 13 percent of students had been in a physical fight on school property. (Grunbaum et al. 2002). Based on a 2001 national study, it was reported that 75 percent of students said that they were concerned about a shooting happening in their schools (Bowman 2001b). About 87 percent of students believed that shooters want "to get back at those who have hurt them," and 13 percent believed that "nothing could be done to stop school shootings" (Bowman 2001b).

Lesbian, gay, bisexual, and transgendered (LGBT) youth are subject to verbal and physical harassment in high schools and middle schools. As reported in the 1999 Massachusetts Youth Risk Behavior Survey, LGBT youth are three times as likely as their heterosexual peers to be assaulted or involved in at least one physical fight in school, three times more likely to have been threatened with a weapon in school, and nearly four times more likely to skip school because they felt unsafe (Human Rights Watch 2001). In a separate study of sexual minority youth, 80 percent experienced some form of harassment, and 42 percent reported a past suicide attempt (D'Augelli and Hershberger 1995). Nearly all of the youth interviewed for the Human Rights Watch 2001 report, *Hatred in the Hallways,* experienced verbal or nonphysical harassment in school. The harassment was characterized as part of their normal daily routine. Harassment occurred in many forms: name calling in the hallways, written notes or graffiti on walls or lockers, whisper campaigns, or obscene telephone calls. Harassment creates a hostile environment for students, and it undermines their school performance and well-being (Human Rights Watch 2001).

The extent of sexual harassment in schools has been documented by the American Association of University Women's Educational Foundation (2001a). According to its 2001 report, 81 percent of students experience some form of sexual harassment during their school lives. Girls are more likely than boys to experience sexual harassment. How is sexual harassment defined in schools? The definition offered by the Equal Employment Opportunity Commission (2001) under Title VII of the Civil Rights Act of 1964 stands:

> Unwanted sexual advances, requests for sexual favors, and other verbal or physical conduct of a sexual nature constitutes sexual harassment when submission or rejection of this conduct explicitly or implicitly affects an individual's employment, unreasonably interferes with an individual's work performance or creates an intimidating, hostile or offensive work environment.

In schools, sexual harassment can include such behaviors as sexual messages on walls or locker rooms, sexual rumors, being flashed or mooned, being brushed up against in a sexual way, or being shown sexual pictures or material of sexual content (Fineran 2002). Sexual harassment of students has serious consequences, including mental health symptoms (such as loss of appetite, disturbances in sleep, feelings of isolation and sadness) and school performance difficulties (Fineran 2002).

Education Policy, Advocacy, and Innovation

As a nation we support the principle of educational excellence and, along with it, the assumption of educational opportunity for all; but in reality, we have an educational system that embraces these ideas, yet fails to achieve them (Ravitch 1997). The educational experiences of poor and/or minority students fundamentally conflict with the principles of public education, namely that public schools should provide these children with opportunities so that all children can succeed as a result of hard work and talent (Maruyama 2003). Reformers would argue that school choice, standardized testing, and school vouchers are improving our educational system. Critics argue that these strategies threaten to erode an already weak public school structure. There is a deepening chasm between what the American public deems as important in education (safety, skills, discipline) and the goals of the reform movement (access, standardization, multiculturalism) (Finn 1997). Although we have not completely abandoned our public educational system, we still have not found a way to agree on what is appropriate or essential to save it.

Policy Responses—The Basis for Educational Reform

Educate America Act of 1994 and No Child Left Behind Act of 2001

Providing fuel to the reform movement have been congressional acts passed in 1994 and 2001. Although they were adopted under presidents from different political parties, both congressional acts provide strong support for school reform and, along with it, changes to our educational system.

The Goals 2000 Educate America Act introduced the notion of "standards-based reform" at state and community levels. This 1994 Act, signed into law by President Bill Clinton, provided the grounds for sweeping reform at all levels and from all angles: curriculum and instruction, professional development, assessment and accountability, school and leadership organization, and parental and community involvement. However, school reform hinged on the use of student performance standards and the creation of a National Education Standards and Improvement Council. In a summary of the Act, it was reported that "performance standards clearly define what student work should look like [at] different stages of academic progress and for diverse learners" (Goals 2000 1998:14). The Act established performance and content standards in math, English, science, and social studies, and it encouraged participation from the entire community—local officials, educators, parents, and community leaders—in raising academic standards and achievement.

The No Child Left Behind Act (NCLB) of 2001 endorsed the mounting interest in school choice. Some of the major provisions of the bill include new reading and math standard assessments for Grades 3 to 8, more flexibility for states and local school officials with regard to budget spending and program development, the creation of a teaching quality program, consolidation of bilingual and immigrant education programs, and increases in federal funding for President Bush's Reading First plan.

The more controversial elements of the Act signed by President George W. Bush include the provision for public school choice and charter schools. The Act provides support to permit children in chronically failing public schools to transfer to other schools with better academic records. The bill also provides for annual testing of students in reading and math in the third to eighth grades, which would establish academic records for comparison. If there were no improvement in test results in two years, parents would have the option to move their children to another school. In such an event, the school district must pay for the child's transportation to a better school, and the failing school loses the per-pupil payment. Critics have argued that such school choice provisions will only work if there are schools to choose from within a district and if there is any room in these schools. The law does not provide school leaders with the means to create new slots for students (Schemo 2002). Refer to the Focus On feature, opposite, for more about standardized testing.

Promoting Educational Opportunities—Head Start

Called the most popular and most romantic of the War on Poverty efforts (Traub 2000), Head Start remains the largest early childhood program. More than 20 million poor and at-risk preschoolers have been served under Head Start since 1965. Head Start began with a simple model of service: organized preschool centers. At these centers, programs focused on the "whole child," examining and encouraging physical and mental health. Integrating strong parental involvement, Head Start provided a unique program targeting child development and school preparedness. Over the years, the Head Start program expanded to serve school-age children, high school students,

❖ FOCUS ON: STANDARDIZED TESTING—DOES IT WORK?

These reforms express my deep belief in our public schools and their mission to build the mind and character of every child, from every background, in every part of America.

—George W. Bush, January 2001

When he signed the No Child Left Behind (NCLB) Act, President Bush approved a plan that increased federal pressure on states to pursue a standards-based reform agenda. Under the NCLB, states are required to institute a system of standardized testing for all public school students in Grades 3 to 8 and high school. All students must be tested in reading and math by 2005 and in science by 2007. Each state must have a plan for annual yearly progress toward the goal of academic proficiency for all students (regardless of economic status, ethnicity/race, gender, and/or disability) by 2014.

Supporters of the Act point to the need for increasing accountability of our public schools through standardized testing. The Act is based on the premise that test score results are the product of schooling. The idea is that we can give all students the same test, review their test scores, and discover what is "wrong" in their schools. Schools that fail to make annual progress are labeled as "needing improvement" and are likely to face penalties and corrective action, including withdrawal of federal funding.

But NCLB has been called the "most intrusive federal intervention in local schools" (Dillon 2004:A13). According to James Popham (2003), standardized achievement tests measure little of what is taught in school.

But, by and large, they measure what children bring to school, not what they learn there. They measure the kinds of native smarts that kids walk through the door with. They measure the kinds of experiences the kids have had with their parents.

Education professor David Marshak (2003) argues that NCLB supporters did not envision the full impact of the law:

It (NCLB) puts a standardized test gun to the head of every child, every educator, and every parent in the nation. It guarantees pain and suffering for millions of children and teens whose cognitive and learning styles don't readily fit the narrow structure of standardized testing. It places enormous new demands on most states to pay for the development and administration of new tests. Finally, it seems that the standard for yearly improvement set by the No Child Left Behind Act will be impossible for many schools to meet—certainly many bad schools but also many schools that serve middle-class and upper-middle-class children and are currently held in high esteem by the parents whose children attend them. (P. 230)

While expressing commitment to the basic intent of NCLB, many state leaders and educators have expressed frustration in implementing the Act's requirements and achieving its goals. In particular, school administrators and educators have been critical of a key feature of NCLB: the "one size fits all" accountability standard that assumes that all schools, districts, and groups of students will demonstrate progress according to the standardized measures. The standards, say critics, seriously

❖ FOCUS ON (Continued)

compromise the abilities of schools to address the unique educational needs of special education students, low-income and minority students, and students with limited English proficiency.

A 2003 study of 3,000 California schools that were labeled as "needing improvement" under NCLB revealed that many of these schools were designated in that way not because of their overall achievement levels, but because a single student group—for example, disabled learners or Asian students—had fallen short of a target. The study concluded that "the chance that a school would be designated as failing increased in proportion to the number of demographic groups served by the school" (Dillon 2003:A17). In February 2004, the Bush administration announced new NCLB state regulations granting a one-year transition period for English language learners in their first year in U.S. public schools. As a result, test scores from first-year English learners will be excluded from their schools' test results.

Several states and educational organizations have charged the federal government with failing to provide adequate funding to implement NCLB. The National Education Association claimed that NCLB was underfunded by $7.5 billion in 2003. This is a particular issue for school districts that serve low-income and minority students. According to Kevin Carey (2003) of the Education Trust, in most states, school districts that educate the greatest number of low-income and minority students currently receive substantially less state and local money per student than districts with the fewest low-income and minority students. The costs of standardized tests, teacher training, and educational materials have fallen primarily to local school districts, which are concurrently dealing with teacher shortages, state budget crises, increasing operating costs, and chronic underfunding of existing programs.

Beginning in 2003, standardized achievement testing was established in Head Start programs throughout the country. Four-year-olds were given tests asking them to identify and point to the pictures of a "swamp" and the expression "horrified." The applicability of the test was immediately criticized. Head Start teachers reported that *horrified* is not a word they teach; they were more likely to use the word *scared* with their students. As with the NCLB, Head Start administrators report that the test results will not be used to evaluate the children; rather test results will be used to assess the effectiveness of the program.

pregnant women, and Head Start parents. In 1994, amendments to the Head Start Act established Early Head Start (EHS) services targeting economically disadvantaged families with children three years old or younger. EHS serves both children and their families through a comprehensive service plan that promotes child development and family self-sufficiency (Wall et al. 2000).

The effectiveness of Head Start programming, particularly the educational component, has been the focus of public and government debate (Washington and

Oyemade Bailey 1995). Early program research and evaluation efforts were spotty, with the major findings pointing to short-term or "fade out" gains in student learning and testing (Washington and Oyemade Bailey 1995).

Recent research efforts have been more systematic, including longitudinal studies with larger cohorts of Head Start children. Evaluation data have identified a positive relationship between early childhood program enrollment and high school graduation, home ownership, school attendance, and motivation. For example, Slaughter-Defoe and Rubin (2001) noted that among African American middle school students and adolescents, Head Start graduates perceived themselves as more achievement oriented and motivated than their non-Head Start peers. Head Start parents, teachers, and the family environment were important in sustaining the educational aspirations and expectations of Head Start graduates. Studies consistently indicate the effectiveness of strong parental involvement with the Head Start program. Head Start parents are more likely to remain involved in their children's education once they begin elementary school, and children whose parents have high participation rates perform better on achievement and development tests (Washington and Oyemade Bailey 1995).

However, a 2003 report released by the U.S. Department of Health and Human Services concluded:

> While making some progress, Head Start is not doing enough to enhance the language, pre-reading, and pre-mathematics knowledge and skills that we know are important for school readiness. The knowledge and skill levels of young children entering Head Start are far below national averages. Children graduating from Head Start remain far behind the typical U.S. child. (P. 2)

The report is based on data collected from Head Start children enrolled in 1997 and 2000. The report concluded by calling for improving coordination between federally managed Head Start programs and other early childhood programs to ensure children are prepared to succeed in school.

Promoting Educational Opportunities—Affirmative Action

Based on Title VI of the 1964 Civil Rights Act, affirmative action policies have been applied to student recruitment, admissions, and financial aid programs. Title VI permits the consideration of race, national origin, sex, or disability to provide opportunities to a class of disqualified people, such as minorities and women, who have been denied educational opportunities. Affirmative action policies have been supported as remedies for past discrimination and as means to encourage diversity in higher education. Affirmative action practices were affirmed in the 1978 Supreme Court decision in the Regents of California v. Bakke, suggesting that race-sensitive policies were necessary to create diverse campus environments (American Council on Education and American Association of University Professors 2000; Springer 2002).

Although affirmative action has been practiced since the Bakke decision, affirmative action has recently become vulnerable, particularly to challenges of the diversity argument in the Supreme Court's decision. The first challenge occurred in one of our

VISUAL ESSAY: INSIDE HEAD START

Head Start is best known as a comprehensive early childhood education program. Recently, it has become controversial because of the new nationwide mandates for improving learning standards. Head Start is placing renewed emphasis on teaching young children readiness skills for reading, writing, and arithmetic.

In addition to serving children, Head Start's programs also involve parents in their children's learning activities and enlist them as volunteers at child care and learning centers.

Many Head Start programs are also committed to helping parents and children achieve better nutrition and better overall health. For example, the Head Start program of Lane County in Oregon serves about 20,000 meals a year to eligible children and their families. The Paterson, New Jersey, program provides medical checkups to make sure children have no physical or mental barriers to learning.

What is perhaps less known is that Head Start programs involve both staff and parents in building strong communities. The Web site for the National Head Start Association (go to *Study Site Chapter 5* for more information) lists programs that foster children's physical, social, and emotional health, encourage further education, bridge the generations, promote environmental health, and encourage parents to become school and community leaders.

Can one program effectively serve all these needs? Or would Head Start serve its community best by narrowly focusing on a few things? What do you believe is the best element of Head Start?

most diverse states, California. In 1995, the California Board of Regents banned the use of affirmative action guidelines in admissions. In 1996, California voters followed and passed Proposition 209, the California Civil Rights Initiative, which effectively dismantled the state's affirmative action programs in education and employment. Also in 1996, a federal appeals court ruling struck down affirmative action in Texas. Called the Hopwood decision, the ruling referred to affirmative action policies as a form of discrimination against White students. State of Washington voters passed an initiative in 1998 that banned the use of race-conscious affirmative action in schools. In 1999, Florida Governor Jeb Bush banned the use of affirmative action in admission to state schools.

The Texas ruling led to a decline in the number of minority students enrolling in Texas A&M and the University of Texas (Yardley 2002). A similar drop in minority student applications and enrollment was experienced by California's state universities after the Board of Regents decision and the California Civil Rights Initiative. In response, states have instituted other practices with the goal of increasing minority student recruitment. For example, California and Texas have initiated percentage solutions. In Texas, the top 10 percent of all graduating seniors are automatically admitted into the University of Texas system. California initiated a similar plan, covering only the top 4 percent of students, and recently, Florida announced the One Florida Initiative, allowing the top 20 percent of graduating high school seniors into the state's public colleges and universities. The University of Georgia increased its recruitment efforts among minority students, hoping to enlarge the pool of applications from minorities (Schemo 2001).

In 2000, a federal judge upheld the University of Michigan's affirmative action program, ruling that "a racially and ethnically diverse student body produces significant educational benefits such that diversity, in the context of higher education, constitutes a compelling governmental interest" (Wilgoren 2000). In 2003, the case was considered by the U.S. Supreme Court, and in a 5 to 4 vote, the Court upheld the University of Michigan's consideration of race for admission into its law school. Writing for the majority, Justice Sandra Day O'Conner stated, "In order to cultivate a set of leaders with legitimacy in the eyes of the citizenry, it is necessary that the path to leadership be visibly open to talent and qualified individuals of every race and ethnicity" (Greenhouse 2003:A1). In a separate decision, the U.S. Supreme Court voted 6 to 1, invalidating the university's affirmative action program for admission into its undergraduate program. Unlike the law school program, the undergraduate program uses a point system based on race. Twenty points on a scale of 150 are awarded for membership in an underrepresented minority group; 100 points are necessary to gain admission into the university (Greenhouse 2003).

A new basis of affirmative action has emerged, considering family income rather than ethnic-racial or gender classifications (Yardley 2002). Texas universities have refocused recruiting efforts to large student minority populations in low-income high schools. The University of Texas created a $20,000 Longhorn grant aimed at specific low-income high schools. The University of California system expanded its application review policy for Fall 2003's freshman class, adding subjective factors like overcoming economic hardship. In a recent study, the James Irvine Foundation reported that among the nation's 40 top-rated colleges and universities, six institutions were purposely reaching out to low-income college applicants (Yardley 2002).

Mentoring, Supporting, and Valuing Networks

Women and Girls

In their 1992 report, the American Association of University Women called on local communities and schools to promote programs that encourage and support girls studying mathematics and science. Studies indicate that most girls and women learn best in cooperative, not competitive learning activities. With seed money from the W. K. Kellogg Foundation, the AAUW Educational Foundation initiated the Girls Can! Community Coalitions Project in 1996. The project supported 10 innovative programs in diverse communities that promoted gender equity and girls' self-esteem in collaborative settings. Lessons learned from the Girls Can! project led to the AAUW's community action grants for community-based programs or research projects that promote education and equity for women and girls.

One such community action grant was awarded to Linda Hensel and Hope McIllwain of Mercer University in Georgia (Jobe 2001). Hensel, a molecular biologist, and McIllwain, a mathematician, developed a summer camp called Mercer MESSAGE (Math, Engineering, and Science, Summer All Girl Experience) for fifth- and sixth-grade girls of color in Macon, Georgia. In addition to participating in a science fair, girls are introduced to mentors studying math or science in college. The girls also meet professional women in the field. MESSAGE was made possible through support from Mercer University and teachers and school principals from the Bibb County Public School District. Backed by strong community support and involvement, MESSAGE was also awarded a $100,000 grant from the American Honda Foundation to continue and expand the project. In addition to the girls' summer camp, a co-ed camp, Mercer TECH was implemented.

A program doesn't have to take up a whole summer—it can even involve a single day at work. The "Take Our Daughters to Work Day," an annual event begun by the Ms. Foundation in 1993, has attempted to expand girls' understanding of career opportunities and nontraditional careers. Over the past decade, the Ms. Foundation estimates that more than 71 million Americans or a member of their household participated in the event. In 2002, the Ms. Foundation renamed the event "Take Our Daughters and Sons to Work Day" to "bring the boys to work alongside the girls and take on the issues that they will both confront in the workplace," according to Marie C. Wilson, President of the Ms. Foundation for Women (Ms. Foundation for Women 2002).

❖ ─────────────

Voices in the Community:
Dr. Sima Samar

In 2001, Dr. Sima Samar was appointed deputy prime minister and the first minister responsible for women's affairs in Afghanistan. Samar was surprised by her appointment because for more than two decades, she defied Afghan laws that deny women their basic right to education and medical care. Since 1989, her Shuhada (Martyrs) Organization has brought education and health care to thousands of Afghani children and women.

Samar is a member of the Hazara tribe, one of the most persecuted of Afghanistan's ethnic minorities. She obtained her degree in medicine from Kabul University in 1982, becoming the first Hazara woman to do so. After the Soviet invasion, she was in the resistance movement until her husband, a professor at Kabul University, disappeared in 1984. Samar then fled with her young son to Quetta, Pakistan, where she worked as the sole female physician in a hospital and at a refugee camp. According to Samar, camp women lived in abject misery, forbidden to visit male doctors or to leave their homes to work or attend school (Sibbald 2001).

Samar and other women established Quetta's first hospital for women in 1987, treating more than 400 patients a day. After observing how women in camps had seven to nine children, Samar established her first outreach program to educate women about family planning. In 1989, she established the Shuhada Organization, a nonprofit group dedicated to the reconstruction and development of Afghanistan but with special emphasis on the empowerment of women and children. She and her medical staff operate four hospitals and 10 clinics in Afghanistan and another hospital in Quetta. More than 20,000 children attend one of her 48 Afghan schools. In addition, she runs a girls' school in Quetta.

During a 2001 speaking tour, Samar explained, "I want rights for women on all levels, in the political and social sectors, in everything—right to vote, right to be elected, right to work everywhere" (Day 2001). Her work is described in this interview by Sibbald (2001):

> When its [Taliban] leaders decided that schooling had to end at Grade 6, [Samar] changed the classroom signs, but the education continued. "Today girls say that they won't marry until they get their education," says Samar. . . . But there is still a long way to go. "Just because some women have removed their burqas this does not mean that there is respect for human rights." Only a democratic process in which women are actively involved can guarantee these rights, she maintains. (P. 368)

Six months after Dr. Sima Samar began her work as Afghan's deputy prime minister of women's affairs, Islamic fundamentalists launched a fierce attack, accusing her of blasphemy. Although a formal charge was dismissed in a Kabul court, after numerous death threats for supposedly saying she didn't agree with sharia law, Samar resigned from her position in 2002. Samar continues her work with the Shuhada Organization and began serving as chair of the Independent Afghanistan Human Rights Commission, conducting human rights and women's rights education programs while monitoring and investigating human rights abuses in Afghanistan.

❖ ❖

❖ PUTTING IT TOGETHER:
On the Web.

For more information about the Shuhada Organization, log on to *Study Site Chapter 5*. The organization's site includes updates on community health and education programs.

LGBT Students

The best estimate of the number of LGBT students is about 5 to 6 percent of the total student population (Human Rights Watch 2001). LGBT youth have been a driving force behind creating change in their schools and communities. Support groups and organized student activities have emerged in states such as California, Illinois, and Washington, providing valuable support to LGBT teens and their friends and families (Bohan and Russell 1999; Human Rights Watch 2001).

One such student group is the Gay Straight Alliance (GSA) in East High School in Salt Lake City, Utah. As chronicled by Bohan and Russell (1999), in October 1995, a group of students proposed to create a student alliance to provide a support network for LGBT students and their heterosexual friends. In response to the students' proposal, the school board and the state legislature banned all noncurricular clubs rather than allow the Gay Straight Alliance. The club continued to meet, paying rental and insurance fees for the use of school facilities. According to Bohan and Russell, students indicated how the club had a positive impact on their lives. The Alliance served as a safe refuge, decreasing their feelings of isolation and vulnerability, students said, and they reported decreases in substance abuse, depression, suicidal impulses, truancy, and conflict with parents. Positive effects were also reported by the straight student members. In September 2000, Utah's Salt Lake City School Board voted to permit noncurricular student groups to meet on school grounds, reversing its 1995 decision against the Gay Straight Alliance (Human Rights Watch 2001). Such groups are not unique to Utah. According to the Gay, Lesbian, and Straight Education Network, more than 900 clubs for GLBT students and their friends are registered throughout the United States.

Voices in the Community:
Alix M.

Alix M. (in Human Rights Watch 2001) talks about how her student group has helped her.

Beginning in middle school, I became really depressed. At first I didn't know why. Didn't have a clue. But I knew it wasn't okay to be gay. No one was out at my middle school, but I heard lots of slurs all the time. Lots of homophobic comments. I was scared. Scared to be a lesbian. Scared to be out at school. Scared of being alone. My grades started to fall. A counselor talked to me about my grades. I had always been a good student. But she didn't give me any opening to talk about sexuality. I needed to get information.

Now I am a senior in high school. It's better now for me. But public spaces are the worst. I hear things all the time. The halls have a very male macho feeling—very sexist. I also had one teacher who would say "that's so gay" instead of saying "that's so stupid."

I had read about [gay-straight alliances] and wanted to start one. I began thinking about it my sophomore year. I did research on the Internet. I knew I needed to find a teacher to support the club. I was a little nervous. There were no out teachers. I asked 15 teachers if they would be the faculty sponsor. They all said no. One really cool teacher just told me she couldn't deal with people's reaction. Finally, this one teacher said she would be the sponsor.

The Gay Straight Alliance [GSA] began through word of mouth. We meet once a week, read books, watch videos, talk about the coming out process. I feel support now for the first time. And I know other kids like me have somewhere to go for support. It's no longer just me.

. . . . There has been some negative response. When we introduced the GSA to the faculty, one teacher went off, saying we were all sinning, but other teachers defended us. Someone put graffiti on my car. Every once in a while I wonder what people are going to do to me, but mostly I just deal with it.

I'm doing a lot better. I've become a strong individual. I've conquered my fears. I don't fear anything.

❖ PUTTING IT TOGETHER:
On your campus.

Is there a Gay Straight Alliance organization at your school? If yes, investigate its history. What are its mission, student membership, and activities? If your school does not have an Alliance, would your school community support one? Why or why not?

Antiviolence Programs in Schools

As awareness of school violence has increased, so have the calls for effective means of prevention (Aber, Brown, and Henrich 1999). The current focus is less on reacting to school violence and more on promoting school safety through prevention, planning, and preparation (Shaw 2001). The largest and longest running school program focusing on conflict resolution and intergroup relations is the Resolving Conflict Creatively Program (RCCP). Initiated in 1985 in New York City by the local chapter of Educators for Social Responsibility, the program is a research based K–12 school program in social and emotional learning. Since its inception, the program has served more than 60,000 students in more than 150 schools (Flannery 1997). RCCP is in more than 60 New York City schools and in 12 other school systems throughout the country.

RCCP begins with the assumption that aggression and violent behavior are learned and therefore can be reduced through education. The program teaches children conflict resolution skills, promotes intercultural understanding, and provides models and opportunities for positive ways of dealing with conflict and differences. For kindergarten students, puppets and other objects are used to illustrate how conflict can be resolved by talking rather than hitting. RCCP includes training for teachers, parents, administrators, and school staff.

An evaluation of the New York City programs indicated that students who received RCCP instruction developed more positively than students without any RCCP exposure. RCCP students were more prosocial, perceived their world in a less hostile way, saw violence as unacceptable, and chose nonviolent ways to resolve conflict. An additional finding of the evaluation revealed that reading and math scores were higher for RCCP students, especially those who had 25 RCCP lessons over the school year. Evaluators concluded that the RCCP-intensive children were more able to focus on academics when there was less conflict with peers.

With the increase in school violence, more attention has been given to school safety through security screening or police-school liaison projects. Schools are more aware of the links between safety and violence and other student behaviors such as dropout rates, academic failures, bullying, and suicide (Shaw 2001). Violence prevention programs have become common throughout the country with the primary focus on early education. In addition to the RCCP, other national initiatives include the Safe and Drug Free Schools Initiative and the Safe Schools/Healthy Students Initiative. Regional initiatives include the PeaceBuilders elementary program operating in Arizona, California, Utah, and Ohio; the BrainPower Program in Southern California; Healthy Schools Bullying Prevention Program in South Carolina; and Positive Adolescent Choices Training (PACT) based in Ohio. U.S. and international approaches focus on school safety and less on school violence, use programs to serve students and the entire school population, develop school-community partnerships, and utilize evaluated program models (Shaw 2001). The most effective school-based violence prevention programs are those that included parental involvement and support, with parents backing school limits and consequences at home (Flannery 1997). Antiviolence programs have also begun on college and university campuses.

Does Having a Choice Improve Education?

There is a new term now, *public school choice*. Data issued by the National Center for Education Statistics reveal that more parents are turning away from local public schools to private schools or charter schools (Zernike 2000). The number of students enrolled in public schools of choice increased by 2.5 million from 1993 to 1999, reflecting a 50 percent increase. Today, at least one in four children attends a school other than one nearest their home (Wilgoren 2001). Parents and children have two additional options within the public education system: magnet schools and charter school.

Magnet schools offer specialized educational programs from elementary school through high school. These schools are organized around a theme such as performing arts, science, technology, or business or around different instructional designs such as free (where students can direct their own education) or open schools (with informal classroom designs). Often, magnet schools are placed in racially isolated schools or neighborhoods to encourage students of other races to enroll. Magnet schools have been criticized for creating a two-tier system of education (Kahlenberg 2002).

Charter schools are nonsectarian public schools of choice that operate free from most state laws and local school board policies that apply to traditional public schools. A charter contract establishes the school's operation, usually limited to three to five years, detailing the school's mission and instructional goals, student population, educational outcomes, and assessment methods, along with a management and financial plan. These schools have grown in popularity since 1991, when Minnesota became the first state to pass an "outcome-based" school law. As of 1999, about 1,400 charter schools were operating in 27 states (Good and Braden 2000). Charter schools are characterized by innovative teaching practices and accountability to students and families. If a school fails to meet its goals, it cannot be renewed under its charter.

School choice has become an even hotter topic with the idea of school vouchers. Simply stated, school vouchers allow for the transfer of public school funds to support a student's transfer to a private school, which may include religious institutions. Supporters of school vouchers argue that the system would give parents more choice and freedom in school selection and would create incentives for school improvement (Good and Braden 2000; Kennedy 2001).

Opponents argue that vouchers would siphon money away from public schools, removing any ability to resolve the schools' problems, thus only increasing problems. Others argue that schooling is a public good and must be provided by the government to all children (Good and Braden 2000) equally and fairly. In June 2002, the U.S. Supreme Court ruled that school voucher programs did not violate any church versus state separation and upheld the constitutionality of using public funds to support private school systems (Bumiller 2002).

On the effectiveness of voucher programs and charter or magnet schools, the research remains mixed and ultimately divided according to party lines. The same issues concerning charter schools and voucher systems continue to be the subject of inquiry and debate: defining clear systems of accountability, establishing comparable performance standards, and ensuring the racial and economic integration of students.

In 2002, the American Federation of Teachers released a report on charter schools, revealing that the majority of charter schools have not worked. According to the report, most operating charter schools fail to raise student achievement compared to traditional public schools in the area, tend to sort students by socioeconomic status, fall short of integrating innovations in the classroom, and spend more money on administration rather than instruction. The report also stated that 206 of the 2,327 charter schools opened since 1992 have closed. The primary reason for school closure was financial mismanagement.

In response, the Center for Education Reform (2002), along with five other national education organizations, dismissed the AFT report, claiming that the teachers union's bias against charter schools "colors all that they say and do in this area." The Center argued that dozens of studies document the effectiveness of charter schools in academic achievement, enrollment of minority or special needs students, academic accountability, and parent-teacher satisfaction. In addition, the Center claimed that only 120 charter schools have closed for financial reasons related to lack of facilities, proper funding, and, in few instances, accountability.

In 2004, data analysis based on the 2003 National Assessment of Educational Progress by the American Federation of Teachers revealed that children in charter schools were performing worse than their peers in public schools. Only 25 percent of fourth-grade charter school students were proficient in reading and math. Among public school fourth-graders, 30 percent were proficient in reading and 32 percent in math (Schemo 2004). The report's results were contested by charter school advocates, including Secretary of Education Ron Paige.

According to researchers Saporito and Lareau (1999), if there is one consistent finding on school choice, it is that students from poorer families or with less educated parents are less likely to apply to or participate in public choice programs than middle-class families. In addition, the researchers raise questions about the school selection process for White and African American families. Although school choice advocates suggest that promoting racial equality is one of the by-products of school choice, Saporito and Lareau (1999) found that White families as a group are more likely to avoid schools with higher percentages of Black students, whereas African American families show no such sensitivity to race. African American families in their study were likely to select schools with lower poverty rates. The researchers concluded that race was a persistent factor in the choice process.

MAIN POINTS

- For 2003, the U.S. Census Bureau reported that an all-time high of 85 percent of adults (people 25 years and older) had completed at least a high school degree, and more than 27 percent of all adults had attained at least a bachelor's degree. Younger Americans are more educated than older Americans. About 67 percent of all Americans 75 years or older attained a high school degree or more, compared with 86 percent of those 25 to 29 years old. The educational attainment level of adults will continue to rise, as younger, more educated age groups replace older, less educated ones.

- The institution of education has a set of **manifest** and **latent functions.** Manifest functions are intended goals or consequences of the activities within an institution. Education's primary manifest function is to educate. Along with educating, the other manifest functions include personal development, proper socialization, and employment. Education's latent or unintended consequences may be less obvious.

- Conflict theorists would not see education as an equalizer; rather, they would consider education a divider: dividing the haves from the have-nots in our society. From this perspective, conflict theorists would focus on the social and economic inequalities inherent in our educational system and how the system perpetuates these inequalities. Inequalities are based not just on social class but also on gender. Research reveals the persistent replication of gender relations in schools, evidenced by the privileging of males, their voices, and their activities in the classroom, playground, and hallways.

- From an interactionist perspective, the interaction between teachers and students reinforces the structure and inequalities of the classroom and the educational system. Sociologists focus on how classroom dynamics and practices educate the perfect student and at the same time create the not-so-perfect ones.

- Although educational attainment is increasing, it is still unevenly distributed among social groups. Socioeconomic status is one of the most powerful predictors of student achievement. The likelihood of dropping out of high school is higher among students from lower income families.

• Census data indicate slight differences in educational attainment for men and women. A "hidden curriculum" perpetuates gender inequalities in math and science courses. This curriculum takes the form of differential treatment in the classroom, where boys tend to dominate class discussion and monopolize their instructor's time and attention while girls are silenced and their insecurities reinforced.

• There are persistent academic achievement gaps between Black, Hispanic, and Native American students and their White and Asian peers. In the mid-1990s, underrepresented minorities received less than 13 percent of all the bachelor's degrees awarded. The College Entrance Examination Board noted that in the latter half of the 1990s, only small percentages of Black, Hispanic, and Native American high school seniors in the National Assessment Educational Progress test samples had scores typical of students who are well prepared for college. Latino/a students are at greater risk of not finishing school than any other ethnic-racial group.

• Part of the focus on education has revolved around safety in schools. School violence can be characterized on a continuum that includes aggressive behavior, harassment, threats, property crimes, and physical assault.

• Recent acts and initiatives to reform education include the Educate America Act of 1994 and the No Child Left Behind Act of 2001. Several education programs promote educational opportunities. Probably the most well-known early childhood program is Head Start.

• Based on Title VI of the 1964 Civil Rights Act, affirmative action policies have been applied to student recruitment, admissions, and financial aid programs. Although affirmative action has been practiced since the Bakke decision, affirmative action has recently become vulnerable, particularly to challenges of the diversity argument in the U.S. Supreme Court's decision.

• Programs such as Girls Can! encourage and support girls studying mathematics and science. Lesbian, gay, bisexual, and transgendered (LGBT) youth have been a driving force behind creating change in their schools and communities. Support groups and organized student activities have emerged in states such as California, Illinois, and Washington, providing valuable support to LGBT teens and their friends and families.

• There is a new term now: public school choice. School vouchers allow for the use of public school funds to support student transfers to private schools, which may include religious institutions. Supporters of school vouchers argue that the system would give parents more choice and freedom in school selection and would create incentives for school improvement. Opponents argue that vouchers would siphon money away from public schools, removing any ability to resolve the schools' problems, thus only increasing problems.

INTERNET AND COMMUNITY EXERCISES

1. Contact your local ProLiteracy Worldwide volunteer program (formerly known as Literacy Volunteers of America) or search their national Web site (log on to *Study Site Chapter 5*). Click on "find a program" and select your state. If a program does not exist in your community, find the one nearest you (your local library may have information on literacy programs). What services or activities do they provide students? Does the program have data regarding the number and types of students they have served? On the effectiveness of their program? What skills are necessary to become a literacy tutor?

2. Interview a student who is a first-generation college student. The student can be from your social problems class or any of your other classes. What challenges do

first-generation college students face? Do you believe their challenges are different from those of students who are second- or third-generation college students? Does your college provide programs for first-generation students? If not, what type of services or support might be valuable for this group of students?

3. Investigate whether your local school district supports educational outreach programs for girls or minority students. Select one program and answer the following: What group does the program serve? What educational "gaps" does the program address and how? How effective is the program? You could also investigate whether a "Girls Can" program is based in your community. Contact the local school district, the YWCA, or the American Association of University Women (log on to *Study Site Chapter 5*) for more information.

4. In addition to public school choice, home-schooling has become an option for many families. It was estimated that 850,000 children were home-schooled in Spring 1999, about 1.7 percent of all students age 5 to 17 years (Bielick and Chandler 2001). This figure includes students who were home-schooled only and students who were home-schooled and enrolled in school for 25 hours or less per week. Parents offered a variety of reasons for home-schooling their children: belief that they can give their child a better education at home, religious reasons, the poor learning environment at school, and family reasons. Home-schooled children were more likely to be White and non-Hispanic and to come from families with three or more children (Bielick and Chandler 2001). Home-schoolers are more likely to be located in rural and suburban areas of the Western United States (Bauman 2001). Home School World provides a listing of all national and state home school organizations. Log on to *Study Site Chapter 5*.

On your own. Log on to *Study Site—Community and Policy Guide* for more information about the social problems, social policies, and community responses discussed in this chapter.

References

Aber, J. L., J. Brown, and C. C. Henrich. 1999. *Teaching Conflict Resolution: An Effective School-Based Approach to Violence Prevention.* Washington, DC: National Center for Children in Poverty.

Adams, M. S. and T. D. Evans. 1996. "Teacher Disapproval, Delinquent Peers, and Self-Reported Delinquency: A Longitudinal Test of Labeling Theory." *The Urban Review* 28(3):199–211.

American Association of University Women. 1992. *How Schools Shortchange Girls: The AAUW Report.* New York: Author.

———. 2001a. *Hostile Hallways: Bullying, Teasing, and Sexual Harassment in School.* Washington, DC: Author.

———. 2001b. *Si, Se Puede! Yes, We Can: Latinas in School.* New York: Author.

American Council on Education and American Association of University Professors. 2000. *Does Diversity Make a Difference? Three Research Studies on Diversity in College Classrooms, Executive Summary.* Washington, DC: Authors.

American Federation of Teachers. 2002. "AFT Study Reveals Charter Schools Not Meeting Expectations" (AFT Press Release, July 17). Retrieved January 15, 2004 (www.aft.org/press/2002/071702).

Anderson, M., J. Kaufman, T. Simon, L. Barrios, L. Paulozzi, G. Ryan, R. Hammond, W. Modzeleski, T. Feucht, L. Potter, and the School-Associated Violent Deaths Study Group. 2001. "School Associated Violent Deaths in the United States, 1994–1999." *Journal of the American Medical Association* 286(21):2695–2702.

Bauman, Kurt J. 2001. "Home Schooling in the United States: Trends and Characteristics" (Working Paper No. 530). Washington, DC: U.S. Bureau of the Census.

Berliner, D. and B. Biddle. 1995. *The Manufactured Crisis: Myths, Frauds, and the Attack on America's Public Schools.* Reading, MA: Addison-Wesley.

Bielick, S. and K. Chandler. 2001. *Homeschooling in the United States: 1999* (NCES 2001-033). Washington, DC: National Center for Education Statistics.

Bohan, J. and G. M. Russell. 1999. "Support Networks for Lesbian, Gay and Bisexual Students." Pp. 279–94 in *Coming into Her Own: Educational Successes in Girls and Women,* edited by S. N. Davis, M. Crawford, and J. Sebrechts. San Francisco: Jossey-Bass.

Bowman, D. H. 2001a. "Federal Study Stresses Warning Signs of School Violence." *Education Week* 21(15):12.

———. 2001b. "Student Survey Sees 1 in 10 Peers as Potentially Violent." *Education Week* 21(1):9–10.

Bumiller, Elisabeth. 2002. "Bush Calls Ruling About Vouchers a 'Historic' Move." *The New York Times,* July 2, pp. A1, A15.

Carey, Kevin. 2003. *The Funding Gap.* Washington, DC: The Education Trust.

Cardoza, D. 1991. "College Attendance and Persistence Among Hispanic Women: An Examination of Some Contributing Factors." *Sex Roles* 7(3/4):147–165.

Center for Education Reform. 2002. "Charter Leaders Dismiss AFT Report: Data Deliberately Skewed for AFT Gain" (CER News Alert, July 16). Retrieved September 10, 2003 (www.edreform.com/press/2002/aft_charter_report).

College Entrance Examination Board. 1999. *Reaching the Top: A Report of the National Task Force on Minority High Achievement.* New York: Author.

D'Augelli, A, and S. Hershberger, S. 1995. "The Impact of Victimization on the Mental Health and Suicidiality of Lesbian, Gay, and Bisexual Youth." *Developmental Psychology* 31:65–74.

Day, Julie Finnin. 2001. "Turning Back the Afghan Clock." Retrieved January 26, 2004 (www.csmonitor.com/atcsmonitor/specials/women/world/world121901c.html).

Denton, K. and J. West. 2002. "Children's Reading and Mathematics Achievement in Kindergarten and First Grade." *Educational Statistics Quarterly.* Retrieved January 18, 2004 (http://nces.ed.gov/pubs2002/2002125.pdf).

DeVoe, J., K. Peter, P. Kaufman, S. Ruddy, A. Miller, M. Planty, T. Snyder, and M. Rand 2003. *Indicators of School Crime and Safety: 2003* (NCES 2004-004/NCJ 201257). Washington, DC: U.S. Departments of Education and Justice.

Dillon, Sam. 2003. "Diverse Schools More Likely to Be Labeled Failing, Study Says." *The New York Times,* December 25, p. A19.

———. 2004. "Some School Districts Challenge Bush's Signature Education Law." *The New York Times,* January 2, pp. A1, A13.

Equal Employment Opportunity Commission. 2001. "Facts about Sexual Harassment." Retrieved October 10, 2002 (www.eeoc.gov/facts/fs-sex.html).

Finn, Chester. 1997. "The Politics of Change" Pp. 226–50 in *New Schools for a New Century: The Redesign of Urban Education,* edited by D. Ravitch and J. Viteritti. New Haven, CT: Yale University Press.

Fineran, Susan. 2002. "Sexual Harassment between Same-Sex Peers: Intersection of Mental Health, Homophobia, and Sexual Violence in Schools." *Social Work* 47(1):65–74.

Flannery, Daniel. 1997. *School Violence: Risk, Preventive Intervention, and Policy.* (ERIC Clearing House on Urban Education, Publication Number RR93002016)

"Goals 2000: Reforming Education to Improve Student Achievement." 1998. Retrieved October 1, 2002 (www.ed.gov/pubs/G2KReforming/index.html).

Good, T. L. and J. S. Braden. 2000. *The Great School Debate: Choice, Vouchers, and Charters.* Mahwah, NJ: Lawrence Erlbaum.

Greenhouse, Linda. 2003. "Justices Back Affirmative Action by 5 to 4, but Wider Vote Bans a Racial Point System." *The New York Times,* June 24, pp. A1, A25.

Grunbaum, J. A., L. Kann, S. Kinchen, B. Williams, J. Ross, R. Lowry, and L. Kolbe. 2002. *Youth Risk Behavior Surveillance—United States, 2001* (Report 51[SS04]). Atlanta, GA: Centers for Disease Control.

Hallinan, Maureen. 1994. "Tracking: From Theory to P." *Sociology of Education* 67(2):79–91.

Headden, Susan. 1997. "The Hispanic Dropout Mystery." *U.S. News and World Report* 123(15):64–65.

Holland, D. C. and M. A. Eisenhart. 1990. *Educated in Romance: Women, Involvement, and College Culture.* Chicago, IL: University of Chicago Press.

Human Rights Watch. 2001. *Hatred in the Hallways: Violence and Discrimination Against Lesbian, Gay, Bisexual, and Transgender Students in U.S. Schools.* New York: Author.

Jacobs, Jerry A. 1996. "Gender Inequality and Higher Education." *Annual Review of Sociology* 22:153–185.

Jobe, Denise. 2001. "Coalitions Advance Educational Equity for Girls." *ENC Focus,* 8(1):30–31.

Johnson, R. C. and D. Viadero. 2000. "Unmet Promise: Raising Minority Achievement." *Education Week* 17(43):1.

Kahlenberg, Richard. 2002. "Socioeconomic Integration." Speech given at 20th Annual Magnet Schools of America Conference. Retrieved January 15, 2004 (www.magnet.edu/choice.html).

Kanter, Rosabeth Moss. 1972. "The Organization Child: Experience Management in a Nursery School." *Sociology of Education* 45:186–211.

Kennedy, S. 2001. "Privatizing Education." *Phi Delta Kappan* 82(6):450–457.

Kingery, P. M., B. E. Pruitt, G. Heuberger, and J. A. Brizzolara. 1993. *School Violence Reported by Adolescents in Rural Central Texas.* Unpublished manuscript, Texas A&M University, College Station, TX.

Kirsch, I. S., A. Jungeblut, L. Jenkins, and A. Kolstad. 1993. "Executive Summary of Adult Literacy in America: A First Look at the Results of the National Adult Literacy Survey." Retrieved September 5, 2003 (www.Nces.ed.gov/naal/resources/execsumm.asp).

Kozol, Jonathan. 1991. *Savage Inequalities: Children in America's Schools.* New York: Harper Perennial.

Linn, M. and C. Kessel. 1996. "Success in Mathematics: Increasing Talent and Gender Diversity Among College Majors." Pp. 83–100 in *Issues in Mathematics Education, Conference of the Mathematical Sciences: Vol. 6. Research in Collegiate Mathematics Education II,* edited by J. Kaput, A. H. Schoenfeld, and E. Dubinsky. Providence, RI: American Mathematical Society.

Literacy Volunteers of America. 2002. "Facts on Literacy in America." Retrieved September 5, 2003 (www.literacyvolunteers.org/about/faqs/facts.html).

Marshak, D. 2003. "No Child Left Behind: A Foolish Race into the Past." *Phi Delta Kappan* 85(3):229–231.

Maruyama, G. 2003. "Disparities in Educational Opportunities and Outcomes: What Do You Know and What Can We Do?" *Journal of Social Issues* 59(3):653–676.

Meier, D. 1995. *The Power of Their Ideas.* Boston: Beacon Press.

Ms. Foundation for Women. 2002. "Ms. Foundation for Women Announces Expanded New Program for 2003 Take Our Daughters and Sons to Work Day" (Press Release, April 23). Retrieved August 27, 2002 (www.takeourdaughterstowork.org).

National Commission on Excellence in Education. 1983. *A Nation at Risk: The Imperatives for Educational Reform.* Washington, DC: U.S. Department of Education.

Popham, J. 2003. Interview with *Frontline.* Retrieved January 23, 2004 (http://www.pbs.org/wgbh/pages/frontline/shows/schools/nochild/bush.html).

Ravitch, D. 1997. "Somebody's Children: Educational Opportunity for All American Children." Pp. 251–273 in *New Schools for a New Century: The Redesign of Urban Education,* edited by D. Ravitch and J. Viteritti. New Haven, CT: Yale University Press.

Ravitch, Diane and J. Viteritti, J. 1997. "Introduction." Pp. 1–16 in *New Schools for a New Century: The Redesign of Urban Education,* edited by D. Ravitch and J. Viteritti. New Haven, CT: Yale University Press.

Sadker, M. and D. Sadker, D. 1994. *Failing at Fairness: How Our Schools Cheat Girls.* New York: Simon & Schuster.

Saporito, S. and A. Lareau. 1999. "School Selection as a Process: The Multiple Dimensions of Race in Framing Educational Choice." *Social Problems* 46:418–439.

Schemo, Diana Jean. 2001. "U. of Georgia Won't Contest Ruling on Admissions Policy." *The New York Times,* November 10, p. A8.

———. 2002. "Few Exercise New Right to Leave Failing Schools." *The New York Times,* August 28, pp. A1, A14.

———. 2004. "Education Study Finds Weakened Charter Results: Public School Students Often Do Better—Data Bode Ill For Bush's Philosophy." *San Francisco Chronicle,* August 17, pp. A4.

Shaw, Margaret. 2001. *Promoting Safety in Schools: International Experience and Action* (Bureau of Justice Assistance Monograph, NCJ186937). Washington, DC: U.S. Department of Justice.

Sibbald, Barbara. 2001. "Beyond the Burqa." *Canadian Medical Association Journal* 166(3):368.

Silverman, L. K. 1986. "What Happens to the Gifted Girl?" Pp. 43–89 in *Critical Issues in Gifted Education: Defensible Programs for the Gifted* (Vol. 1), edited by C. J. Maker. Rockville, MD: Aspen.

Slaughter-Defoe, Diana and Henry Rubin. 2001. "A Longitudinal Case Study of Head Start Eligible Children: Implications for Urban Education." *Educational Psychologist* 36(1):31–44.

Smith, D. 2000. "Schooling for Inequality." *Signs* 25(4):1147–1151.

Smith, R. S. 1995. "Giving Credit Where Credit Is Due: Dorothy Swaine Thomas and the "Thomas Theorem." *American Sociologist* 26(4): 9–29.

Spencer, S., C. Steele, and D. Quinn. 1999. "Stereotype Threat and Women's Math Performance." *Journal of Experimental Social Psychology,* 35:4–28.

Springer, A. D. 2002. "Update on Affirmative Action in Higher Education: A Current Legal Overview, June 2002." Retrieved March 3, 2003 (www.aaup.org/Issues/AffirmativeAction/aalegal.htm).

Steele, C. 1997. "A Threat in the Air: How Stereotypes Shape Intellectual Identity and Performance." *American Psychologist* 52:613–629.

Steele, C. and J. Aronson. 1995. "Stereotype Threat and the Intellectual Test Performance of African Americans." *Journal of Personality and Social Psychology* 69(5):797–811.

Stombler, M. and P. Yancey Martin. 1994. "Bringing Women in, Keeping Women Down." *Journal of Contemporary Ethnography* 23(2):150–184.

Stoops, N. 2004. *Educational Attainment in the United States: 2003* (Current Population Report, P20-550). Washington, DC: U.S. Census Bureau.

Strand, K. and M. E. Mayfield. 2002. "Pedagogical Reform and College Women's Persistence in Mathematics." *Journal of Women and Minorities in Science and Engineering* 8:67–83.

Sum, A., T. Kirsch, and R. Taggart. 2002. *The Twin Challenges of Mediocrity and Inequality: Literacy in the U.S. from an International Perspective.* Princeton, NJ: Educational Testing Service.

Thomas, W. I. and D. Thomas. 1928. *The Child in America: Behavior Problems and Programs.* New York: Knopf.

Thorne, Y. M. 1995. "Achievement Motivation in High Achieving Latina Women." *Roeper Review* 18:44–49.

Traub, J. 2000. "What No School Can Do." *The New York Times Magazine,* January 16, pp. 52–57, 68, 81, 90–91.

U.S. Census Bureau. 2001. *School Enrollment in the United States—Social and Economic Characteristics of Students: October 1999* (Current Population Reports, P20-533, March 2001). Washington, DC: Author.

———. 2004. *Current Population Survey, 2004 Annual Social and Economic Supplement.* Washington, DC: Author.

U.S. Department of Health and Human Services. 2003. *Strengthening Head Start: What the Evidence Shows, June 2003.* Washington, DC: Author.

Wall, S., E. Timberlake, M. Farber, C. Sabatino, H. Liebow, N. Smith, and N. Taylor. 2000. "Needs and Aspirations of the Working Poor: Early Head Start Program Applicants." *Families in Society* 81(4):412–421.

Washington, V. and U. J. Oyemade Bailey. 1995. *Project Head Start: Models and Strategies for the Twenty First Century.* New York: Garland.

Wilgoren, J. 2000. "Affirmative Action Plan Is Upheld in Michigan." *The New York Times,* December 14, p. A32.

———. 2001. "Schools Are Now Marketers Where Choice Is Taking Hold." *The New York Times,* April 20, pp. A1, A12.

Yardley, J. 2002. "The Ten Percent Solution." *The New York Times Magazine,* April 14, pp. 28–31.

Zernike, K. 2000. "American Education Gets an A for Effort." *The New York Times,* June 2, p. A16.

Zigler, E. and S. Muenchow. 1992. *Head Start: The Inside Story of America's Most Successful Educational Experiment.* New York: Basic Books.

6

The Workplace ❖

In August 2004, more than 139 million women and men were employed in the United States, about 62 percent of the population 16 years or older (U.S. Bureau of Labor Statistics 2004a). Work isn't just what we do; work is a basic and important social institution. It fuels our economy and provides economic support for individuals and families. But work is also important for our social and psychological well-being. Individuals find a sense of fulfillment and happiness; and for most, work provides a self-identity. Much of our social status is conferred through our occupation or the type of work we do. Because of the importance of work, problems related to work become categorized as social problems, as everyone's problem.

When C. Wright Mills first wrote about the "sociological imagination" in 1959, he identified unemployment is a public issue. Public issues, like social problems, are matters that transcend the individual and have much more to do with the social organization of our lives. Mills writes (1959/2000):

> When, in a city of 100,000, only one man is unemployed, that is his personal trouble, and for its relief we properly look to the character of the man, his skills and his immediate opportunities. But when in a nation of 50 million employees, 15 million are unemployed, that is an issue, and we may not hope to find its solution within the range of opportunities open to any one individual. The very structure of opportunities has collapsed. (P. 14)

According to the U.S. Bureau of Labor Statistics (2004a), 8 million women and men were unemployed in August 2004, an overall rate of 5.4 percent. Almost 50 years after Mills wrote these words, unemployment remains a public issue. But it isn't the only problem facing U.S. workers. For some, work is a dangerous place, leading to injury or death. Others are victims of discrimination or harassment at the workplace. And for many working men and women, their paychecks do not provide a livable wage. In this chapter, we will examine the work that we do, the social organization of work itself, and the social problems associated with work. We will begin first with a review of the changing nature of work and society.

The Changing Nature of Work

During the late 18th century and early 19th century, the means of production shifted from agricultural to industrial. In agrarian societies, economic production was very simple, based primarily on family agriculture and hunting or gathering activities. Each family provided for its own food, shelter, and clothing. This changed during the **Industrial Revolution**, an economic shift in how people worked and how they earned a living. Family production was replaced with market production, in which capitalist owners paid workers wages to produce goods (Reskin and Padavic 1994).

As a whole, we don't produce goods anymore, we provide services. Since the late 1960s, the U.S. economy has shifted from a manufacturing to service-based economy (Brady and Wallace 2001). The **service revolution** is an economy dominated by service and information occupations. In 1950, manufacturing accounted for 33.7 percent of all nonfarm jobs; by 2000, manufacturing's share had dropped to 14 percent (Pollina 2003). Take a look at Table 6.1, a list of the fastest-growing occupations in 2000 and 2012. Notice that no occupations on the list involve manufacturing; instead, jobs in retail, food, and customer service dominate the list.

This shift has been referred to as **deindustrialization**, a widespread, systematic disinvestment in our nation's manufacturing and production capacities (Bluestone and Harrison 1982). Less manufacturing takes place in the United States as most jobs and plants have been transferred to other countries. Local U.S. factories have closed as a result of mergers or acquisitions as well as poor business. And thanks to technological advances, it takes fewer people to produce the same amount of goods.

Job losses in manufacturing have been particularly acute since early 2000: U.S. manufacturers lost a total of 2.7 million jobs since July 2000. Affected areas have experienced devastating social and economic losses, turning some into ghost towns (Brady and Wallace 2001) or leading cities to the brink of bankruptcy—the plight of Cleveland, Ohio, and Detroit, Michigan, in the mid 1980s and early 1990s. Lost manufacturing jobs are often replaced with unstable, low-paying service jobs, or no jobs at all. As a result, cities may experience a significant loss of revenue to support basic public services such as police, fire protection, and schools (Bluestone and Harrison 1982).

In addition to the transformation in the type of work we do, there has also been a transformation in who is doing the work. The first significant workforce change began in World War II with the entry of record numbers of women into the workplace. In 1940, the majority of 11.5 million employed women were working as blue-collar, domestic, or service workers out of economic necessity (Gluck 1987). White and Black women's entry into defense jobs signaled a major breakthrough. One fourth of all White women and nearly 40 percent of Black women were wage earners who previously worked in lower paid clerical, service, or manufacturing jobs. By 1944, 16 percent of working women held jobs in war industries. At the height of wartime production, the number of married women in the workplace outnumbered single

❖ Table 6.1 Occupations with the largest projected job growth (in thousands), 2000–2012

Industry Description	2000	2012
Registered nurses	2,284	2,908
Postsecondary teachers	1,581	2,184
Retail salespersons	4,076	4,672
Customer service representatives	1,894	2,354
Cashiers, except gaming	3,432	3,886
Janitors and cleaners	2,267	2,681
General and operations managers	2,049	2,425
Waiters and waitresses	2,097	2,464
Nursing aides, orderlies, and attendants	1,375	1,718
Truck drivers, heavy and tractor-trailer	1,767	2,104

Source: U.S. Bureau of Labor Statistics 2004b.

working women for the first time in U.S. labor history. Almost one in three women defense workers were former full-time homemakers. In Los Angeles, women made up 40 percent of the aircraft production workforce.

These heavy industry jobs may have paid better, but the jobs held an important symbolic value: These jobs were men's jobs. After the war, although the proportion of women workers in durable manufacturing increased in many cities, many women were forced back into low-paying, female-dominated occupations (Gluck 1987) or back to their homes.

Labor force participation rates have steadily increased for White, Black, and Hispanic women since World War II (see Table 6.2). In 2002, 63,582,000 women 16 years or older were employed in the U.S. labor force (U.S. Department of Labor Women's Bureau 2003). Women accounted for more than 40 percent of the 2002 U.S. labor force, dominating secretarial, receptionist, nursing, and bookkeeping occupations (U.S. Department of Labor Women's Bureau 2003).

❖ Table 6.2   Civilian Labor Force Participation Rates for White, Black, and
Hispanic Women, 1930–2010 (Projected)

	All Women	White Women	Black Women	Hispanic Women
1930	24.3	n.a	n.a	n.a
1940	25.4	n.a	n.a	n.a
1950	31.4	n.a	n.a	n.a
1960	37.1	36.2	n.a	n.a
1970	41.6	42.6	49.5	n.a
1980	51.5	51.2	53.1	47.4
1990	57.5	57.4	58.3	53.1
2000	60.2	59.8	63.2	56.9
2010 Projected	62.2	61.6	66.2	59.4

Source: U.S. Census Bureau 1951, 1960, 1966; U.S. Bureau of Labor Statistics 2003d, 2004a.

❖❖ PUTTING IT TOGETHER:
On the Web.

Just for one week, count the number of times you hand cash, a credit card, or a check to someone for payment. How many times do you hand it to a woman? For most of her paid work life, my mother worked as a cashier in a neighborhood grocery store. She fit the description of the typical woman worker offered by Fox and Hesse-Biber (1984): a working mother who attended high school but had little or no college experience, working in retail, clerical, or service occupations. For the current list of the 20 Leading Occupations for Employed Women, go to the U.S. Department of Labor's Women's Bureau (log on to *Study Site Chapter 6*). Has "women's work" has changed? Why or why not?

The second workforce change has been the record numbers of elderly Americans returning to work. According to the U.S. Labor Department, about 4.2 million people age 65 years or older were working in 2000, an increase from 3.5 million seniors in 1990 (Hollingsworth 2002). Elderly employment is predicted to grow to 5.4 million in 2010. Although Americans are working longer in part because they are living longer, there are additional factors contributing to the increase in 65-plus employment. At a time when most elderly Americans are considering retirement, some cannot afford to live on their retirement income, forcing them back to the workplace. Seniors are a valuable commodity in the workplace: Employers are grateful for their skills and work ethic. And the fact is that many seniors are working because they want to do so.

The final workforce shift began with the latest immigration boom in the period between 1996 and 2000 from Latin America and Asia (Mosisa 2002). The foreign-born U.S. population rose from a low of 9.6 million in 1970 to 14.1 million in 1980, 19.8 million in 1990 (Gibson and Lennon 1999), and 28.4 million in 2000 (Lollock 2001). In 1960, 1 out of 17 U.S. workers was foreign born, compared to one out of eight today. More than 80 percent of the labor force increase among workers between 35 and 44 years old can be attributed to the increase in foreign-born workers.

The last workforce change has been in the increasing number of foreign-born workers. Foreign-born workers account for half or more of the increase in the job categories of administrative support, services, precision production, craft and repair, operators, fabricators, and laborers. Foreign-born workers are overrepresented in low-paying occupations that do not require high school degrees. During 2000, about 60 percent of all foreign-born workers were living in four states—California, New York, Florida, and Texas. Immigrants settle in regions with perceived economic opportunities, seeking established ethnic enclaves providing interpersonal and job support (Mosisa 2002). In 1950, immigration accounted for only 6 percent of our annual population growth, but by 2003, it accounted for 40 percent. Pollina (2003) predicts that, as our native population continues to age, the U.S. workforce will become increasingly dependent on foreign-born workers.

Sociological Perspectives on Work

Functionalist Perspective

According to the functionalist perspective, work serves specific functions in society. Our work provides us with some predictability about our life experiences. We can expect to begin paid employment around the age of 18 or after high school graduation (or we could delay it for four or five more years by attending college and graduate school). Your work may determine when you get married, when you have your first child, and when you purchase your home. Work serves as an important social structure as we become stratified according to our occupations and our income. Finally, even for the most independent among us, the way we live is dependent on the work of thousands—for our food, clothing, safety, education, and health. Our lives are bound to the products and activities of the labor force (Hall 1994).

Recall that from this perspective, work can also produce a set of dysfunctions that can lead to social problems (or that may be problems themselves). Employers encourage workers to become involved with their work, hoping to increase their productivity as well as their quality of work (a function). However, getting too involved in one's work may lead to job stress, overwork, and job dissatisfaction for workers (all are dysfunctional). Although technology improves the speed and quality of work for some (a function), as machines replace human laborers, technology can also lead to job and wage losses (dysfunctions).

As some researchers have focused on the functions and dysfunctions of work, others have tried to understand the nature of work itself. Frederick W. Taylor, a mechanical engineer, offered an analysis that would revolutionize 19th- and 20th-century industrial work. Using what he called **scientific management**, Taylor broke down the functional elements of work, identifying the most efficient, fastest, best way to complete a task. In one of his first research projects, Taylor determined the best shovel design for shoveling coal. Taylor believed that with the right tools and the perfect system, any worker could improve his or her work productivity, all for the benefit of the company. In his book, *The Principles of Scientific Management*, Taylor (1911) wrote, "In the past the man has been first; in the future the system must be first" (p. 5)

Although scientific management in its pure form has rarely been implemented, Taylor's principles continue to serve as the foundation for modern management ideology and technologies of work organization (Bahnisch 2000). Beyond simply changing how work was organized, Taylor also offered his ideas about the organization of work: the need for defining a clear authority structure, separating planning from operational groups, providing bonuses for workers, and insisting on task specialization. Taylor's model shifted power to management, forcing skilled workers to give up control over their own work (Hirschhorn 1984), which was a cause for concern expressed by theorists from the next theoretical perspective.

Conflict Perspective

Power, explained Karl Marx, is determined according to one's relationship to the means of production. Owners of the means of production possess all the power in the system, he believed, with little (probably nothing) left for workers. As workers labor only to make products and profits for owners, workers' energies are consumed in the production of things over which they have no real power, control, or ownership (Zeitlin 1997). According to Marx, man's labor becomes a means to an end; we work only to earn money. Marx predicted that eventually, we would become alienated or separated from our labor, from what we produce, from our fellow workers, and from our human potential. Instead of work providing a transformation and fulfillment of our human potential, work would become the place where we felt least human (Ritzer 2000).

Modern systems of work continue to erode workers' power over their labor. **Deskilling** refers to the systematic reconstruction of jobs so that they require fewer skills, and ultimately, management can have more control over workers (Hall 1994). Although Taylor (1911) proposed scientific management as a means to improve production, sociologist Harry Braverman (1974) argues that by altering production systems, capitalists and management increase their control over workers. Workers become powerless when their skilled work is taken away, and they are eventually replaced by machines.

Although Marx predicted that capitalism would disappear, capitalism has grown stronger, and at the same time, the social and economic inequalities in U.S. society have increased. Capitalism has become more than just an economic system; it is an entire political, cultural, and social order (Parenti 1988). Modern capitalism includes the rise and domination of corporations, large business enterprises with U.S. and multinational interests. Conflict theorists argue that capitalist and corporate leaders maintain their power and economic advantage at the expense of their workers and the general public.

Before its demise in 2002, energy trader Enron was the epitome of corporate power and success. The company bought and sold natural gas, power facilities, telecommunications, and other energy-related businesses. In 2000, Enron operated in 30 countries, employing 18,000 women and men (Enron Corporation 2000). It was named by *Fortune* magazine as the "Most Innovative Company in America" for six consecutive years (Enron Corporation 2001) and was reportedly worth $70 billion at its peak (National Public Radio 2003a). A great company to work for, a powerful and successful company, Enron was unstoppable—or was it?

Through a complex web of tax-sheltering partnerships, Enron hid millions of dollars in debts and company losses. Enron's accounting firm, Arthur Andersen, was a partner in the deception and was later convicted of obstruction of justice in the government's investigation. The company's losses were first made public in October 2001, when the Securities and Exchange Commission launched a formal investigation into the company's dealings (Fowler 2001). On December 2, 2001, Enron declared bankruptcy, the largest in U.S. history.

Enron executives, including Chairman Kenneth Lay, left the company in disgrace. It is estimated that Enron's employees lost not only their jobs but more than $1 billion in pension holdings (National Public Radio 2003b). Several class action lawsuits have been filed against Enron executives, directors, and consultants, alleging that they knew about Enron's financial troubles but chose not to inform its employees or stockholders. As of February 2004, 29 Enron traders, accountants, finance officials, and executives had been indicted for conspiracy, fraud, and money laundering. Enron was not the only company involved in erroneous claims. In the 1990s, more than 700 companies were forced to correct misleading financial statements as a result of accounting failures or fraud (Frontline 2002). According to Lynn Turner, chief accountant of the Securities and Exchange Commission from 1998 to 2001 (Frontline 2002), Enron's demise is a symptom of something larger in our economic system.

> It's beyond Enron, it's beyond Andersen. It's embedded in the system at this time. . . . There's been a change in culture that arose out of the go-go times of the 1990s. Some people call it greed. But I think it is an issue where we got a lot of financial conflicts built into the system, and people forgot, quite frankly, about the investors.

Feminist Perspective

From a feminist perspective, work is a gendered institution. Through the actions, beliefs, and interactions of workers and their employers, as well as the policies and practices of the workplace (Reskin and Padavic 1994), men's and women's identities as workers are created, reproduced, then solidified in the everyday routines of informal work groups and formal workers' organizations (Brenner 1998). We already discussed the importance of World War II for women's employment; but recall that after the war, there was pressure on women to resume their roles as housewives or to assume more appropriate occupations. As a gendered institution, work defined the roles appropriate for World War II women and for women today. Simply stated, the workplace does not treat women and men equally. Women are concentrated in different—and lower ranking—occupations than men, and women are paid less than men (Reskin and Padavic 1994).

A fundamental feature of work is the **sexual division of labor:** the assignment of different tasks and work to men and women. This division of labor leads to a devaluing of female workers and their work, providing some justification for the differential compensation between men and women (Reskin and Padavic 1994). In the United States as in most other countries, women earn less than men (England and Browne 1992). For every dollar a man earns, a woman makes 76 cents (U.S. Department of Labor Women's Bureau 2003). (Refer to Table 6.3 for a comparison of average income for men and women with bachelor's degrees.) In the early 1960s, women earned about 59 cents for every dollar earned by men, or a ratio of 59 (Armas 2004). Pay equity is greater for men and women working as elementary school teachers (a ratio of 94.9), accountants (93.7) or general office clerks (96), but there is no single occupation where women make the same amount of money as men (U.S. Department of Labor Women's Bureau 2003). In terms of pay, compared with men, women are disadvantaged because they are in lower paying feminized jobs or because they are paid less for the same work (Budig 2002). Sociologists and feminists have offered several explanations for the differences: differential effort (men work harder than women), differential socialization (women are socialized to pursue careers that traditionally pay less or are lower in status), differential training (men are better educated, so should be rewarded with higher pay), and workplace discrimination (Reskin and Padavic 1994).

One workplace problem that feminist advocates and scholars have focused on is the exclusionary policies in toxic workplaces. Donna Randall (1985) explains that to ensure the reproductive health of female employees and their unborn children, some companies and industries have enacted policies that bar female employees of child-bearing age from positions that would expose them to lead and other toxic materials. These policies reflect stereotypical assumptions; for example, women are always potentially pregnant, women are unable to prevent pregnancy, and women are solely responsible for the health of their children. In fact, these policies ignore the threat of damage to unborn children of male workers. Women's advocates claim that these policies attempt to deny equal opportunities for women. If widely adopted, these practices would limit women's opportunities in traditionally male-dominated industries.

Interactionist Perspective

The sociologies of work and symbolic interaction were developed side by side in the 1920s and 1930s at the University of Chicago. There are strong similarities between

❖ Table 6.3   Mean Income for Persons 25 Years or Older Who Worked Full Time, Year Round With a Bachelor's Degree, 2001

	Men	Women
All races	$71,361	$45,896
White, Non-Hispanic	$74,247	$46,488
Black	$49,403	$40,556
Hispanic	$52,477	$42,429

Source: U.S. Census Bureau 2002.

the two sociological perspectives: In the same way that symbolic interactionists are interested in how individuals negotiate their social order, the sociologists of work are interested in the negotiated order of work (Ritzer 1989).

If you meet a fellow student for the first time, one of the first questions you may ask is, "What's your major?" Why ask about a major? Think of it as a shortcut for who you are. Based simply on whether you are a sociology major or a physics major, people make assumptions about how much you study or your academic quality. According to symbolic interactionists, we attach labels and meanings to an individual's work (and major). These social constructs create an order to our work and our lives, but they can also create social problems.

❖ PUTTING IT TOGETHER: On your campus.

What assumptions are made about majors on your campus? Which major is the "party" major? Which major is the "serious" major? Where do these assumptions come from? Are they true? How could they be changed?

These social constructs can also influence our behavior at work. Problems arise when these constructs serve as the basis of job discrimination. A recent study by researchers from the University of Chicago and Massachusetts Institute of Technology revealed discrimination in the recruiting process based only on what was perceived about someone's first name (Bertrand and Mullainathan 2003). It may help to have a "White sounding" first name when applying for a job. Researchers sent 5,000 resumes in response to job advertisements in the *Boston Globe* and *Chicago Tribune*. First names were selected, based on a review of local birth certificates. Fictional applicants with "White" first names—Neil, Brett, Emily, and Jill—received one callback for every 10 resumes mailed out. In contrast, equivalent "Black" applicants—with names such as Aisha, Rasheed, Kareem, and Tamika—received one response for every 15 resumes sent.

❖ Table 6.4   Summary of Sociological Perspectives: The Workplace

	Functional	Conflict/Feminist	Interactionist
Explanation of work and its social problems	Sociologists using this perspective examine the functions and dysfunctions of work and employment. Functionalists also analyze the functional elements of work itself.	Conflict or feminist theorists focus on how economic, ethnic, and gender inequalities are perpetuated in the economy and the workplace.	From this perspective, sociologists investigate how our work experiences are created through interaction and shared meanings. Social problems emerge from the meanings we associate with our work.
Questions asked about work	How does the institution of work help preserve the social order? How is economic and social stability maintained by the institution of work? How do other institutions affect our work?	What social inequalities are present in the institution of work? How do we become alienated from our work?	How is our work and workplace socially defined? How do we behave based on our meaning of work? Are there positive and negative meanings of work?

Other aspects of discrimination were revealed in the study. If the resume indicated that the applicant lived in wealthier, more educated, or more-White neighborhoods, the rate of callbacks increased. This effect did not vary by race. See Table 6.4 for a summary of all perspectives.

Problems in the Workplace

Unemployment and Underemployment

According to the U.S. Bureau of Labor Statistics (2004a), about 139.7 million Americans were employed in August 2004. The proportion of the population 16 years or older who were either working or looking for work was 62.4 percent. For August 2004, the unemployment rate was 5.4 percent or 8.0 million Americans. Nearly

1.6 million individuals were unemployed for 27 weeks or more. Compared to the unemployment rate of Whites, 4.7 percent, the rate was 10 percent for African Americans and 6.9 percent for Hispanics or Latinos (U.S. Bureau of Labor Statistics 2004b).

In addition to unemployment, there is another rate we should be aware of, **underemployment**. Underemployment is defined as the number of employed individuals who are working in a job that underpays them, is not equal to their skill level, or involves fewer working hours than they would prefer (taking a part-time job when a full-time job is not available). In February 2003, the number of people working part-time due to cutbacks or because they were unable to find a full-time job was 4.8 million (U.S. Bureau of Labor Statistics 2003b).

There is significant variation in unemployment and underemployment rates. People who are young, non-college educated, and ethnic/racial minorities have higher underemployment rates (Bernstein 1997). Minority group underemployment has been demonstrated to be significantly higher than underemployment among non-Hispanic Whites. Zhou (1993) reports at least 40 percent of the members of each minority group he analyzed (Puerto Ricans, Blacks, Mexicans, Cubans, Chinese, and Japanese) were underemployed. In particular, Blacks and Puerto Ricans have the highest rates of labor force nonparticipation (were not in the labor force and had not worked in the last two years) and joblessness. Joblessness includes subemployment (individuals who were not in the labor force but worked within the last two years) and underemployment rates (either based on low wage or occupational mismatch). Recent immigrants, a large portion of the Asian and Hispanic minority groups, may have difficulty in securing employment due to lack of job skills or language proficiency and as a result are more likely underemployed than native-born and non-Hispanic White workers (DeJong and Madamba 2001).

Scholars have documented the destructive effects of joblessness on overall health (Rodriguez 2001) and emotional well-being (Darity 2003). Unemployment has been consistently linked with higher levels of alienation, anxiety, and depression (Rodriguez 2001) and a lower sense of overall health (Darity 2003). Periods of unemployment are related to increased rates of suicide and spousal abuse. Among Blacks and non-Hispanic Whites, long-term exposure to unemployment produces a "scarred worker effect." The experience of unemployment undermines the worker's will to perform, leading that person to become less productive and less employable in the future (Rodriguez 2001).

Contingent or Temporary Workers

Contributing to the increase in unemployment and underemployment is the use of **contingent workers**. A contingent workforce is composed of full-time or part-time temporary workers. There were an estimated 2.9 million temporary workers in 1998, with a projected 53 percent increase in temporary workers by 2006 (Davidson 1999). Temporary workers have been around since 1946, beginning with the establishment of the Kelly Girls temp service (Saftner 1998). Kelly Girls were clerical and secretarial workers hired to provide temporary assistance to companies.

The image of temporary workers as low-skilled people who are brought in for a brief period of time has been replaced by educated and technically skilled professionals managing the most critical and complex job projects for months (Davidson 1999), transforming temporary workers into "permatemps" (Eisenberg 1999). Companies rely on temporary workers to handle temporary projects and work overloads or to fill in for employees who are vacationing, sick, or on family leave (Saftner 1998). Companies have also used temporary workers to eliminate positions and to reduce costs (Davidson 1999). Overall, temp workers are less likely to have health insurance or pension coverage. In addition, they are not covered by health and safety regulations and may not be qualified for workers' compensation if injured on the job (Davidson 1999). Many temps feel like second-class corporate citizens (Eisenberg 1999).

The term **outsourcing** refers to a practice by businesses of hiring external contractors to do the jobs that regular work staff once completed. One common task that is outsourced is accounting. In the past, businesses would have an in-house accountant, someone who did the books and took care of accounts receivable or payable. But businesses began to contract with external accountants or accounting firms to handle their accounts. By paying accountants as contract workers, companies avoid paying them employee or medical benefits.

U.S. companies also outsource internationally, a strategy referred to as *offshore outsourcing*. It is estimated that by 2015, more than 3.3 million U.S. jobs will be sent overseas, about 2.5 percent of the total U.S. employment. India, with its large number of English-speaking college graduates, is expected to receive 70 percent of these jobs. In 2004, the Internet travel company Travelocity.com announced it would outsource more than 300 call center jobs from Texas and Virginia to India. Indian labor is also used to conduct research and development, prepare tax returns, process health insurance claims, and transcribe medical notes (Waldman 2003), usually at wages substantially lower than their U.S. counterparts.

But offshore outsourcing isn't the perfect solution. Employees in India work 10- to 12-hour night shifts in order to be at their desks at the same time as colleagues in the United States (India is 10.5 hours ahead of U.S. Eastern Standard Time). Doctors in India report high levels of substance abuse and relationship breakups among its outsourcing workers. India's outsourcing industry has a rate of 60 percent employee turnover per year (Thottam 2004).

A Livable Wage

A hallmark of the Clinton administration was the more than 8.5 million new jobs created between 1993 and 1996 (Reich 1996). Despite record increases in employment, some Americans still needed two jobs or more to make a decent living. In 1990, the federal minimum wage was $3.80 per hour; in 1997, the minimum wage was increased to $5.15 per hour. Individuals earning poverty-level wages, about $8.47 per hour in 2000, are characterized as low-wage workers (AFL-CIO 2003). Data indicate that low-wage workers are likely to be minority, female, non-college educated, and non-union, working in low-end sales and service occupations (Bernstein 1997; Bernstein, Hartmann, and Schmitt 1999; U.S. Bureau of Labor Statistics, 2002). (See U.S. Data Map 6.1 for a state-by-state rundown of mean hourly wages.)

❖ TAKING A WORLD VIEW

MEXICO'S MAQUILADORAS

Maquiladoras are textile, electronics, furniture, chemical, processed food, or machinery assembly factories where workers assemble imported materials for export (Abell 1999; Lindquist 2001). The maquiladoras program allows imported U.S. materials to enter Mexico without tariffs; and when the finished goods are sent back to the United States, the shipper pays duties only on the value added by the manufacturer in Mexico (Abell 1999; Gruben 2001). The program began in 1965 as an employment alternative for Mexican agricultural workers. Drawn to Mexico because of its proximity to U.S. borders and by low labor costs, nearly every large U.S. manufacturer has a maquiladora location. Several Asian and European companies like Sony, Sanyo, Samsung, Hitachi, and Phillips also have maquiladora locations (Lindquist 2001). There are an estimated 4,000 export manufacturers along Mexico's border with the United States (Abell 1999), employing more than one million people (Sowinski 2000).

The maquiladora program became controversial as soon as it appeared (Gruben 2001). Supporters of the maquiladora program argue that if these plants had not located in Mexico, they would have gone to other low-wage countries. In fact, the maquiladora generate about $40 billion in Mexican exports, proving to be a vital part of Mexico's economy. Opponents argue that the program helped U.S. firms and others take advantage of the low-wage Mexican labor force. The maquiladoras have been criticized for their treatment of female workers, dangerous work conditions, and impact on the physical and social environment of border towns.

The majority of maquiladora workers are women. Yolanda is a worker from Piedras Negras.

> As the sun rises, Yolanda is already awake and working—carrying water from a nearby well, cooking breakfast over an open fire, and cleaning the one-room home that she and her husband built out of cardboard, wood, and tin. She puts on her blue company jacket and boards the school bus that will take her and her neighbors across Piedras Negras to a large assembly plant. Yolanda and 800 co-workers each earn US$25–35 a week for 48 hours' work, sewing clothing for a New York-based corporation that sub-contracts for Eddie Bauer, Joe Boxer, and other U.S. brands. These wages will buy less than half of their families' basic needs. (Abell 1999:595).

Yolanda's job provides a wage, but not a livable one to support herself or her family. According to Fussell (2000), early maquiladora factories attracted the "elite" of the Mexican female labor force: young, childless, educated women. But recently, maquiladora laborers have become the least skilled Mexican women: slightly older, poorly educated women with young children (Fussell 2000). Abell (1999) explains that sexual harassment is often used as a method of intimidation in the maquiladora. Supervisors taunt female workers and proposition them by offering lighter workloads in exchange for dates and sexual favors. In the worst cases, supervisors have raped female workers.

When forced to choose between a livelihood and safety, Yolanda and other workers submit themselves to dangerous work conditions (Abell 1999). Workers are routinely exposed to toxic chemicals, unsafe equipment, poor ventilation and lighting, high noise levels, and dangerously high production quotas. Many of the factories use toxic substances as part of their production work without providing adequate warning to employees. A 1993 study conducted by the U.S. General Accounting Office revealed that four out of eight maquiladoras studied had toxic warning signs posted only in English, and one factory did not provide any information for its workers. Both acute and chronic health problems have been observed among maquiladora workers. Workers experience serious health conditions such as sterility, seizures, organ failures, and cancer (Abell 1999).

Yolanda's town of Piedras Negras is no different from other maquiladora towns like Tijuana and Matamoros. Once-quaint border towns have been transformed by maquiladora activity. In Tijuana, the number of maquiladora workers grew from 2,000 in 1973 to more than 50,000 in 1990 (Abell 1999). Despite their profits, companies do not invest in the physical and social infrastructure of these border towns. As a result, most factory neighborhoods lack basic health and public services such as clean drinking water or sewage systems, electricity, schools, health facilities, and adequate housing (Abell 1999).

Under the 1994 North American Free Trade Agreement (NAFTA), tariff breaks formerly limited to all imported parts, supplies, and equipment used by Mexican maquiladoras now also apply to manufacturers in Canada and the United States (Lindquist 2001). Adding to their operation expenses, maquiladoras must document and prove the origin of all imported materials in order to receive tariff breaks. Although there has been a rapid growth in the number of maquiladoras and their workers, the program has been strained due to recent cost increases (added taxes, NAFTA administration, and rising wages) and labor problems (high turnover and worker shortages). Some manufacturers have left their maquiladora operations, while other companies are being lured to other countries with better deals (Lindquist 2001).

Since NAFTA took effect in 2000, all 50 states and the District of Columbia have experienced a net job loss. It is estimated that NAFTA is directly responsible for the loss of 766,030 actual and potential U.S. jobs between 1994 and 2000 (Scott 2001).

In her 2001 book, *Nickled and Dimed: On (Not) Getting By in America*, Barbara Ehrenreich explored life and work on minimum wage in three states: Florida, Maine, and Minnesota. Working as a hotel maid, a nursing home aide, a sales clerk, a waitress, and a cleaning woman, Ehrenreich rated her work performance as a B or maybe even a B+. In each new job, Ehrenreich had to master new terms, new skills, and new tools (and not as quickly as she thought she would be able to master them). How did Ehrenreich survive on minimum wage? She discovered that she needed to work two jobs or seven days a week to achieve a "decent fit" between her income and her

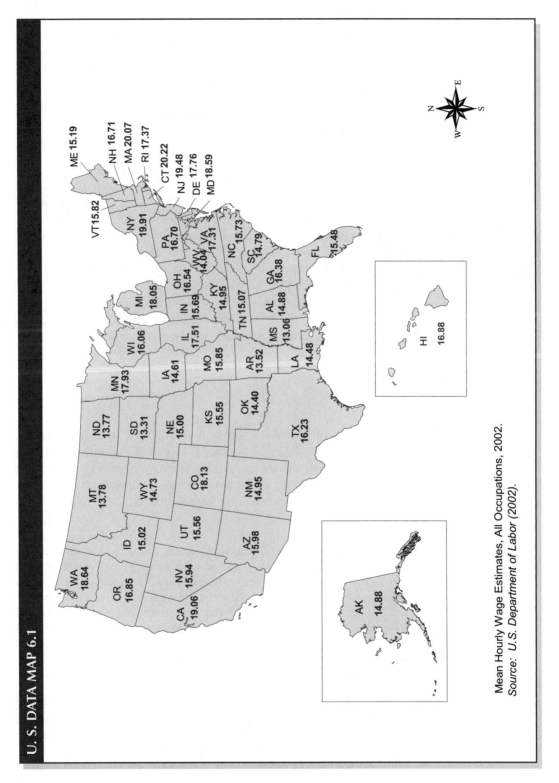

ME 15.19
NH 16.71
MA 20.07
RI 17.37
CT 20.22
NJ 19.48
DE 17.76
MD 18.59

VT 15.82

NY 19.91
PA 16.70
WV 14.04
VA 17.31
NC 15.73
SC 14.79
FL 15.48

MI 18.05
OH 16.54
IN 15.69
KY 14.95
TN 15.07
GA 16.38
AL 14.88
MS 13.06
LA 14.48

WI 16.06
IL 17.51
MO 15.85
AR 13.52

MN 17.93
IA 14.61
KS 15.55
OK 14.40
TX 16.23

ND 13.77
SD 13.31
NE 15.00

MT 13.78
WY 14.73
CO 18.13
NM 14.95

ID 15.02
UT 15.56
AZ 15.98

WA 18.64
OR 16.85
NV 15.94
CA 19.06

HI 16.88

AK 14.88

Mean Hourly Wage Estimates, All Occupations, 2002.
Source: U.S. Department of Labor (2002).

expenses. She describes getting her meals down to a "science": chopped meat, beans, cheese, and noodles when she had a kitchen in which to cook; if not, fast food at about $9 per day. For housing, she shuffled between motel rooms and apartments, moving to a trailer park at one point. Ehrenreich concluded:

> Something is wrong, very wrong, when a single person in good health, a person who in addition possesses a working car, can barely support herself by the sweat of her brow. You don't need a degree in economics to see that wages are too low and rents too high. (P. 199)

❖ PUTTING IT TOGETHER:

According to the U.S. Census, the median income for 2002 was $42,409 (DeNavas-Walt, Cleveland, and Webster 2003). The median is the exact point where 50 percent of all incomes are above and 50 percent are below. If this is the middle—or "average"—household income, could you raise a family of four on this income? Determine a monthly budget for your family, including rent/mortgage, food, entertainment, car expenses (gas/maintenance/insurance), clothing expenses, and savings account.

❖

Voices in the Community:
Barbara Ehrenreich

"How does anyone live on wages available to the unskilled?" With this question, Barbara Ehrenreich (2001:26–28) began her journey from best-selling author/journalist to waitress, hotel maid, cleaning woman, nursing home aide, and sales clerk. Her first job was as a waitress at the Hearthside Restaurant, where she worked from 2 to 10 p.m. for $2.43 an hour plus tips. Ehrenreich quickly learned how difficult it was to live a "low wage life."

> When Gail [server assigned to train Ehrenreich] and I are wrapping silverware in napkins—the only task for which we are permitted to sit—she tells me she is thinking of escaping from her roommate by moving into a Days Inn herself. I am astounded. How can she even think of paying between $40 and $60 a day? But if I was afraid of sounding like a social worker, I come out just sounding like a fool. She squints at me in disbelief, "And where am I supposed to get a month's rent and a month's deposit for an apartment?" I'd been feeling pretty smug about my $500 efficiency, but of course it was made possible only by the $1,300 I had allotted myself for start-up costs when I began my low wage life: $1,000 for the first month's rent and deposit; $100 for the initial groceries and cash in my pocket, $200 stuffed away for emergencies.
>
> There are no secret economics that nourish the poor; on the contrary, there are a host of special costs. If you can't put up the two months' rent you need to secure an apartment, you end up paying through the nose for a room by the week. If you have only a room, with a hot plate at best, you can't save by cooking up huge lentil stews that can be frozen for the week ahead. You eat fast food, or the hot dogs and Styrofoam cups of soup that can be

microwaved in a convenience store. If you have no money for health insurance—and the Hearthside's niggardly plan kicks in only after three months—you go without routine care or prescription drugs and end up paying the price. Gail, for example, was fine until she ran out of money for estrogen pills. She is supposed to be on the company plan now, but they claim to have lost her application form and need to begin the paperwork all over again. So she spends $9 per migraine pill to control the headaches she wouldn't have, she insists, if her estrogen supplements were covered. Similarly, Marianne's [a breakfast server] boyfriend lost his job as a roofer because he missed so much time after getting a cut on his foot for which he couldn't afford the prescribed antibiotic.

My own situation, when I sit down to assess it after two weeks of work, would not be much better if this were my actual life. The seductive thing about waitressing is that you don't have to wait to feel a few bills in your pocket, and my tips usually cover my meals and gas, plus something left over to stuff into the kitchen drawer I use as a bank. But as the tourist business slows in the summer heat, I sometimes leave work with only $20 in tips (the gross is higher, but servers share about 15 percent of their tips with the busboys and bartenders). With wages included, this amounts to about the minimum wage of $5.15 an hour. Although the sum in the drawer is piling up, at the present rate of accumulation it will be more than a hundred dollars short of my rent when the end of the month comes around. Nor can I see any expenses to cut. True, I haven't gone the lentil-stew route yet, but that's because I don't have a large cooking pot, pot holders, or a ladle to stir with (which costs about $30 at Kmart, less at thrift stores), not to mention the onions, carrots, and the indispensable bay leaf. I do make my lunch almost every day—usually some slow burning, high protein combo like frozen chicken patties with melted cheese on top and canned pinto beans on the side. Dinner is at the Hearthside, which offers its employees a choice of BLT, fish sandwich, or hamburger for only $2. The burger lasts longest, especially if it's heaped with gut-puckering jalapenos, but by midnight my stomach is growling again.

A Hazardous and Stressful Workplace

According to the U.S. Bureau of Labor Statistics (2003a), there were 5,524 fatal work injuries in 2002. The majority of fatalities occurred to men, due mostly to the type of work they do. Operators, fabricators, and laborers accounted for more than one out of every three fatalities. The most fatalities, about one quarter of all fatal incidents, occurred from highway accidents. Workplace violence—including assaults and suicides—accounted for 15 percent of all work-related fatal occupational injuries in 2002.

In the same year, a total of 4.7 million nonfatal injuries and illnesses were reported in private industry workplaces, a rate of about 5.3 cases per 100 full-time workers. The service and trade industries had the largest share of injury cases, about 27 percent each, followed by manufacturing with more than 23 percent. The U.S. Department of Labor monitors illnesses such as skin diseases, respiratory conditions, and poisonings. For 2002, manufacturing accounted for 45 percent of illness cases. New reported workplace illnesses were related directly to work activity, such as contact dermatitis or carpal tunnel syndrome. Some conditions, such as long-term illnesses related to exposure to carcinogens, are usually underreported and not adequately recognized (U.S. Bureau of Labor Statistics 2003e).

The National Institute for Occupational Safety and Health (NIOSH) (2003) defines job stress as the harmful emotional or physical response that occurs when a job's characteristics do not match the capabilities, resources, or needs of the worker. Certain job conditions are likely to lead to job stress: a heavy workload, little sense of worker control, a poor social environment, uncertain job expectations, or job insecurity. Eventually, job stress can lead to illness, injury, or job failure. Studies have analyzed the impact of stress on our physical health, noting the relationship of stress with sleep disturbances, ulcers, headaches, or strained relationships with family or friends. Recent evidence suggests that stress also plays a role in chronic diseases such as a cardiovascular disease, musculoskeletal disorders, and psychological disorders (NIOSH 2003).

Discrimination at the Workplace

The Equal Employment Opportunity Commission (EEOC) was established in 1964 by Title VII of the Civil Rights Act. The EEOC monitors and enforces several federal statues regarding employment discrimination. Under Title VII of the Civil Rights Act of 1964, employment discrimination based on race, religion, sex, or national origin is prohibited. Discrimination based on age was added to the prohibited activities in 1967 with the passage of the Age Discrimination in Employment Act, and employment discrimination against individuals with disabilities was prohibited in Title I and Title V of the Americans with Disabilities Act of 1990. The EEOC has received between 72,000 and 88,000 charges annually since 1992 (EEOC 2003).

Of the 84,000 cases that were filed during 2002, about 11 percent were based on national origin discrimination. Cases in this category and those involving religious discrimination increased after September 11, 2001, whereas discrimination charges based on race and sex declined. Complaints of discrimination based on national origin have increased 20 percent over the last eight years (McDonough 2003). According to EEOC spokesman David Grinberg, "Most people think about race and gender discrimination—national origin discrimination doesn't come to mind, but it's having a greater impact on the workplace" (McDonough 2003). Many incidents of national origin discrimination may still be unreported because of fear of retaliation or lack of awareness about EEOC laws.

Research indicates that more than one third of gay, lesbian, or bisexual (GLB) African Americans and more than one half of GLB Whites have experienced discrimination based on sexual orientation (Krieger and Sidney 1997). Protections against workplace discrimination in this area exist in only 10 states. In the other 40 states, employees fired for being gay have no legal recourse, unless they work in a community with its own antidiscrimination ordinance (Lambda Legal 2003). A review of existing studies on workplace discrimination reveals that somewhere between one quarter and two thirds of GLB people report losing their jobs or missing promotions because of their sexual orientation. In addition, studies that compared gay and heterosexual workers with similar backgrounds and qualifications found that gay workers earn less than heterosexual workers (Badgett 1997). Under current federal law, discrimination based on sexual orientation is not prohibited. However, 13 states, the District of

Columbia, and several hundred U.S. cities and counties provide legal protections for public and private employees. Among all Fortune 500 companies, 318 have antidiscrimination policies protecting gay employees (Kershaw 2003).

U.S. Garment Industry and Sweatshop Labor

Take a look at the labels on your shirts and jeans. Where were they made? We know that our clothing is often manufactured in countries like China, Hong Kong, India, Thailand, or Vietnam. But an estimated 23,000 apparel or textile businesses operated in the United States in 2000, employing about 633,000 garment workers. The majority of workers are production workers or sewing machine operators. Two thirds of these jobs are located in nine states: Alabama, California, Georgia, New Jersey, New York, North Carolina, Pennsylvania, Tennessee, and Texas (U.S. Bureau of Labor Statistics, 2003c).

All manufacturers must follow the Fair Labor Standards Act (FLSA), which establishes federal minimum wage, overtime, child labor, and industrial homework standards. The Department of Labor's Wage and Hour Division makes routine enforcement sweeps in major garment centers, fining businesses that are in violation of the FLSA. In its 1994 report, the General Accounting Office (GAO) concluded that "sweatshop working conditions" remain a major problem in the U.S. garment industry. In fact, "the description of today's sweatshop differs little from that at the turn of the century" (GAO 1994:1).

According to Sweatshop Watch (2003), there is no legal definition of a "sweatshop." The GAO (1994) defines a sweatshop as a workplace that violates more than one federal or state labor law. The term has come to include exploitation of workers, for example, with no livable wages or benefits, poor and hazardous working conditions, and possible verbal or physical abuse (Sweatshop Watch 2003); employers who fail to treat workers with dignity and violate basic human rights (Co-Op America 2003); and businesses that violate wage or child labor laws and safety or health regulations (Foo 1994). The term *sweatshop* was first used in the 19th century to describe a subcontracting system in which the middlemen (contractors) earned profits from the margin between the amount they received for a contract and the amount paid to their workers. The margin was "sweated" from the workers because they received minimal wages for long hours in unsafe working conditions (Sweatshop Watch 2003).

A random sample of apparel manufacturers in Southern California in 1996 revealed that 43 percent failed to pay their workers the minimum wage, 55 percent had overtime liabilities, and one third were not registered with the state (U.S. Department of Labor 1996). According to their October 2000–December 2000 Garment Enforcement Report, the Department of Labor recovered $519,666 in back wages for 712 garment workers. During the quarter, the department's Wage and Hour Division investigated 67 employers nationwide and found 48 percent (28 cases) in violation (U.S. Department of Labor 2000). In December 2002, the U.S. Department of Labor announced that $175 million in back wages was collected for 263,593 workers in 2000, the largest amount collected by the department in 10 years. Out of this, $6 million was collected for garment workers (U.S. Department of Labor 2003).

❖ Table 6.5   Where Do Your Dollars Go?

According to the organization, Sweatshop Watch (2003), the following is a rough description of where your dollars go when you buy a $100 piece of clothing.

Total Retail Price	$100.00		
Retailer	50.00		
Manufacturer	50.00		
Of that $50:	Expenses and profit	12.50	
	Textiles and materials	22.50	
	Production contractor (employer of garment workers)	15.00	
	Of that $15:	Expenses and profit	9.00
		Workers	6.00

It has been argued that sweatshops continue to exist because of unscrupulous manufacturers and increased competition from low-wage workers (U.S. Department of Labor 1996). Because garment production is labor intensive, manufacturers will subcontract to decrease their overhead, primarily saving on labor costs. (See Table 6.5 for a breakdown of where your dollars go for a $100 item of clothing.) Through the use of sweatshop labor, manufacturers shift much of their costs, risks, and responsibilities onto subcontractors (Foo 1994).

Workplace Policy, Advocacy, and Innovation

Federal Policies

When President William Howard Taft signed Public Law 426–62 in March 1913, he created the U.S. Department of Labor. From the beginning, the Department was intended to foster and promote the welfare of U.S. wage earners, to improve working conditions, and to advance opportunities for profitable employment. In its 2003 mission statement, the Department included improving working conditions, advancing opportunities for profitable employment, protecting retirement and health care benefits, helping employers find workers, and strengthening fee collective bargaining as part of its charge. The Department administers and enforces more than 180 federal laws that regulate workplace activities for about 10 million employers and 125 million workers.

In addition to the Fair Labor Standards Act (FLSA), the Department of Labor enforces several statutes applicable to most workplaces. It regulates the Employee Retirement Income Security Act (pension and welfare benefit plans), the Occupational

Safety and Health Act (ensuring work and a workplace free from serious hazards), the Family and Medical Leave Act (granting eligible employees up to 12 weeks of unpaid leave for family care or medical leave), and several Acts that cover workers' compensation for illness, disability, or death resulting from work performance.

Two labor issues continue to be debated in Congress. The first is raising the minimum wage. In 2000, Congress and President Bill Clinton failed to pass legislation that would have increased the minimum wage from $5.15 to $6.15. In 2001, Senator Ted Kennedy of Massachusetts and Representative David Bonior of Michigan, both Democrats, introduced legislation that proposed a $1.50 raise in the minimum wage over three years. Efforts to increase the minimum wage are supported by unions and poverty organizations who argue that doing so will help the nation's working poor and low-income families. Opponents, who include members of the business community and the U.S. Chamber of Commerce, argue that increasing the minimum wage would put an unnecessary stress on medium-size or small businesses and, in fact, would not decrease poverty. Some predict that businesses would be forced to eliminate jobs, reduce work hours, or be put out of business. Results from policy analyses and academic research have not provided conclusive evidence for either argument (Information for Decision Making 2000). In 2001, President George W. Bush expressed support for a minimum wage increase only if states were allowed to choose whether they would comply with the new law (Almanac of Policy Issues 2002).

❖ **PUTTING IT TOGETHER:**
On the Web.

The Association of Community Organizations for Reform Now (ACORN) is the nation's oldest and largest grassroots organization. ACORN organizes low- and moderate-income people in more than 600 chapters in 45 cities under a campaign for livable wages. A livable wage is defined as a wage that would allow a full-time primary worker with three dependents to earn just above the poverty line. Go to *Study Site Chapter 6* to determine the living wage for your state or area.

Several congressional actions provide protection against forms of discrimination: Title VII of the Civil Rights Act of 1964 (race, color, gender, national origin, or religion), Age Discrimination in Employment (1967), Vocational Rehabilitation Act (1973), and the Americans with Disabilities Act (1973). However, protection against workplace discrimination based on sexual orientation has yet to be enacted. The Employment Non Discrimination Act, which prohibits employment discrimination based on sexual orientation, has been introduced in Congress since 1994 but has not received enough votes to pass (Kovach and Millspaugh 1996; Human Rights Campaign 2003). Only 13 states—California, Connecticut, Hawaii, Maryland, Massachusetts, Minnesota, Nevada, New Hampshire, New Jersey, New York, Rhode Island, Vermont, and Wisconsin—and the District of Columbia have passed laws prohibiting sexual orientation discrimination (Human Rights Campaign 2003).

VISUAL ESSAY: WORKING THE MARGINS ❖

The Ortiz family experiences the whole gamut of problems present in the U.S. workplace. Janet Jarman, in her photo collection titled *Crossings*, shows how poverty, lack of education, and illegal status have conspired to push this family into migrant agricultural labor and threaten to keep them there.

To find work and a better life, the Ortiz family made the decision to emigrate from Mexico to the United States. The family has nine children. While the parents and the older children work in the fields, Marisol and her two younger siblings enjoy some of the benefits that the family seeks. Marisol was born here and has a chance of someday getting a more stable, better-paid job—if only she can stay in school despite her family's precarious situation.

The experiences of the Ortiz family may seem far removed from our comfortable lives. But think of the benefits we reap from the availability of cheaply produced food and other goods and services provided by marginal workers.

The Ortizes' private troubles are shared by other migrant workers and illegal immigrant workers in the United States. Their labor is important to society and sustains our way of life, but these men, women, and children are not rewarded for their work. Instead, they are trapped in a cycle of poverty and poor health.

Because of the "outsider" status of Marisol and her family, they are isolated even from those who live and work beside them.

It is estimated that more than eight million illegal immigrants reside in the United States today. Much of the emigration from Mexico is attributed to better employment opportunities on the U.S. side of the border. What do you think about illegal immigration to the United States? How do you think illegal immigration impacts the U.S. workforce?

Expanding Employment Opportunities for Women

In 1992, Congress passed the Nontraditional Employment for Women (NEW) Act to broaden the range of Job Training Placement Administration (JTPA) efforts on behalf of women (U.S. Department of Labor Women's Bureau 2000). Also enacted in 1992 was the Women in Apprenticeship and Nontraditional Occupations (WANTO) Act, designed to provide technical assistance to employers and labor groups. Through both programs, the federal government has provided support to more than 20 state and 32 community-based initiatives to provide technical assistance to employers and labor organizations, to improve JTPA programs, to promote apprenticeships in non-traditional occupations, and to provide information through community workshops, seminars, and outreach. According to the Women's Bureau (U.S. Department of Labor Women's Bureau 2000), almost 5,000 women participated in training and/or job placement programs, 30,000 women were reached through community programs, and 3,000 employers and labor groups were provided technical assistance through NEW and WANTO initiatives.

Hard Hatted Women, based in Cleveland, Ohio, received a WANTO 2002–2003 grant to increase the employment of women in a variety of blue-collar jobs in building and manufacturing trades. The program has served about 80 women per year since 1979 (Kucinich 2000). With WANTO funding, the program provides technical assistance to employers and labor unions, on-site counseling for women, a job search networking club, and training (U.S. Department of Labor 2002). The program also conducts outreach to elementary schools in Cleveland, promoting acceptance and awareness of females in blue-collar and nontraditional jobs (Hard Hatted Women 2000).

❖ PUTTING IT TOGETHER: On the Web.

To locate a WANTO program near you, go to *Study Site Chapter 6*. Investigate a program in your state. What services are provided under the grant? Determine whether the program is still in operation. If a program is not located in your state, select the nearest program.

Worker-Friendly Businesses—Conducting Business a Different Way

Each year *Fortune* magazine releases a list of the "100 Best Companies to Work For." For 2002, the magazine wrote, "In a tough year, these companies tried to do right by their employees" (Levering et al. 2002:72). No surprise, Enron did not make the list. No. 1 on Fortune's list was Edward Jones, described as a stock broker with small-town values. This No. 1-ranked company did not lay off any employees during a difficult year, and bonuses were handed out a week early to help brokers hurt by trading declines. About 97 percent of employees say that Edward Jones's management is "honest." The Container Store based in Dallas, Texas, was ranked No. 2 on this best-company list for its good pay, great benefits, and respect for employees. No. 3 was software developer the SAS Institute. The company was recognized for its employee perks, including on-site child care centers and fitness centers. SAS's health center offers free annual mammograms and lab tests.

There is no big secret to creating worker-friendly organizations, although some organizations are slow to learn their values. Beyond the standard employee benefit package of vacations, health care, retirement plans, and life insurance, innovative employers have used dependent care, flexibility work options, expanded leave time, and enhanced traditional benefits to attract and retain employees. As a result, these employers have reduced employee turnover, increased employee satisfaction, and improved worker productivity (Schmidt and Duenas 2002).

Even during tough economic times, several U.S. businesses have been holding firm to a no-layoff policy. Nucor is the nation's most profitable steelmaker and hasn't laid off an employee in 33 years (Clark 2002). Southwest Airlines is the most consistently profitable airline and hasn't had a single layoff in its 31-year history. And that AFLAC duck has something else to quack about: His company hasn't laid off a full-time worker in 47 years. Employers avoid layoffs by asking staff to put in overtime during busy periods and cutting hours during the slow ones. Temporary workers are also part of the equation. Companies like SC Johnson protect their full-time workforce by using and cutting temporary positions. Some companies keep their employees at work during slow periods—just doing other things. At Nucor, when there isn't enough business to support their $25-per-hour welding duties, workers are put on a factory maintenance detail at $10 per hour. In turn, these companies have been rewarded with loyal and productive employees (Clark 2002).

Voices in the Community: *Judy Wicks*

Businesses have also found a way to give back to their community, to combine their work with their social activism. Judy Wicks has been leading the way as the owner of Philadelphia's White Dog Cafe. In an interview with Maryann Gorman (2002), Wicks examines how her business and activist philosophies have merged at the White Dog.

> A person could go to The White Dog Café just to eat. Many customers do—at least for the first time. . . . But many of the diners who come just for the food end up staying for the activism. Wicks tells of a salesman who sold the restaurant its insurance, then attended a Table Talk on the School of the Americas and became a regular at the annual protests held at the School. Wicks jokes, "I use food to lure innocent customers into social activism."
>
> The Dog offers diners an array of learning experiences in lecture or hands-on formats as well as field trips to other countries. There are Table Talks on a variety of topics: the American war on drugs, the Supreme Court's decision in the 2000 election, racism. And the White Dog often organizes rides to rallies and marches, like the demonstrations against Clinton's impeachment that Jesse Jackson called for, the Million Mom March, Stand for Children and more. . . .
>
> Wicks' White Dog venture began when she sensed the dissonance between her profession and her activism. Her energies drained by splitting her values into the commercial and nonprofit worlds, she sought a simpler solution, which first led her to managing someone

else's restaurant. "I realized with the nonprofit and the for-profit that in order to really be effective, I needed to focus on one organization," Wicks says, "So I eventually abandoned the publishing work and focused on the restaurant. But it wasn't all my restaurant, and when I started experimenting with bringing my values to work, like having a breakfast for Salvadoran refugees, I had to part ways with my partner there. This idea of compartmentalizing your life, and having certain values in one area and other values in another, has never worked for me."

The first step, Wicks says, was simply to change her life so that she lived where she worked. "I think that society teach[es] us, 'Separate work from home; don't mix them together. That'll be too stressful.' And I've always worked against that." So the White Dog, located in a block of row houses near the University of Pennsylvania, became both her home and her business. "I'm kind of a holistic person," she says, "I live where I work. I live 'above the shop,' in the old-fashioned way of doing business." . . .

Not only does she not have to commute, . . . but she doesn't have to go food shopping or do the dishes. "But it's more than that," she says, "It's about energy and focus. And relationships. Being able to foster all these relationships."

The relationships she speaks of are those with her staff. One of the White Dog's missions is "Service to Each Other," an in-house goal of creating a tolerant and fair workplace. . . . Moving past standard business boundaries in this way has informed Wicks' creative development of the White Dog's missions. From encouraging her employees to re-create their job descriptions to fostering a sense of community among other Philadelphia restaurants, Wicks has shown that profitable businesses don't have to be stark-raving competitive.

In 1990, Wicks began the Sister Restaurant program, promoting small minority owned restaurants in Philadelphia. Currently, the program includes five such restaurants. The White Dog Web site features information about the cafe and also updated schedules for the Table Talks, community events, films, and special events. Log on to *Study Site Chapter 6* for more information.

Organized and Fighting Back

Labor unions have served as bargaining agents for workers, fighting for fair wages, safe work environments, and benefits from employers. Many of the worker benefits advocated by early labor unions are now mandated through federal, state, or local labor laws. In our changing and global economy, unions cannot sustain themselves by simply negotiating pay, benefits, and working rights. To remain vital and relevant, unions need to develop multilevel strategies and make use of new skills (Lazes and Savage 2000). Unions are still important for worker rights, as John Buell (1997) states, "The only strength most workers have lies in their numbers. To the extent that workers can build solidarities, not only within but also across firms and industries, the more likely is workplace reform, distributional justice and stable growth" (p. 42).

One example of union innovation is UNITE, the Union of Needletrades, Industrial, and Textile Employees. In 1996, it launched a "Stop Sweatshops" campaign linking union, consumer, student, civil rights, and women's groups in the fight against sweatshops. UNITE helped form United Students Against Sweatshops in 1998, bringing together a coalition of student groups to raise awareness about the problem of sweatshop labor in the manufacturing of collegiate clothing (caps, shirts, and sweatshirts sold in campus stores). In March 1998, Duke University adopted the nation's first Code of Conduct for University Trademark Licensees. Under the code, any clothing with the Duke logo would be subject to labor and human rights standards. The student group, Duke Students Against Sweatshops, played a key role in shaping the anti-sweatshop code (Sweatshop Watch 2000).

After September 11, 2001, UNITE began the "Proudly Made in New York" campaign, partnering with New York retailers and designers as a way for consumers to support the city's unionized garment industry. UNITE continues its work on behalf of its labor membership but also continues its educational and advocacy efforts in promoting sweatshop awareness (UNITE 2003). In 2004, UNITE announced that it was merging with the Hotel Employees and Restaurant Employees International Union. The new union, called UNITE HERE, will represent 440,000 active members and more than 400,000 retirees (UNITE 2004).

Unions continue their fight for basic worker rights, including rights for temporary workers. A group of Microsoft permatemps formed a collective bargaining group called the Washington Alliance of Technical Workers (WashTech) in 1998 (Eisenberg 1999). Founded by a former Microsoft permatemp, Marcus Courtney, WashTech describes itself as an "organization of high-tech workers and allies joining together to provide an effective voice in the legislative and corporate arenas, and to advocate for improved benefits and workplace rights" (WashTech 2003).

Fed up with their permatemp status, workers filed a lawsuit against Microsoft and threatened to unionize, eventually forming WashTech. The temporary employees won their suit against Microsoft. The U.S. Court of Appeals for the Ninth Circuit, in its 1997 ruling against Microsoft, redefined the way companies treat temporary employees (Bernstein 1999). The judges ruled that temporary workers were common-law employees and were entitled to the same benefits given permanent staff members. In addition to receiving the same benefits given any regular employee in the same position, the ruling opens the door for temps to sue employees under most employment laws (such as discrimination or family leave). For Microsoft, the ruling meant that their "temporary" labor force, more than 6,000, was entitled to participate in its stock-purchase plan (Bernstein 1999). Additional class action suits have also been filed against corporations Atlantic Richfield, Time Warner, and McGraw-Hill (Eisenberg 1999). In all cases, workers claim that they were misclassified as temporary workers, denying workers health or retirement benefits.

❖

MAIN POINTS

- In August 2004, about 62 percent of the population 16 years of age or older were employed. Work isn't just what we do; work is a basic and important social institution. Because of the importance of work, problems related to work quickly become categorized as social problems—as everyone's problem.

- During the late 18th century and early 19th century, the means of production shifted from agricultural to industrial. In agrarian societies, economic production was very simple, based primarily on family agriculture and hunting or gathering activities. During the Industrial Revolution, an economic shift occurred in how people worked and how they earned a living. Family production was replaced with market production, in which capitalist owners paid workers wages to produce goods.

- Since the 1960s, there has been another shift, referred to as deindustrialization, a widespread, systematic disinvestment in our nation's manufacturing and production capacities. Most manufacturing jobs and plants have been transferred to other countries. Local U.S. factories have closed as a result of mergers or acquisitions and poor business.

- At the same time, more women are working, and more elderly people are returning to work. A very recent shift includes an immigration boom and the presence of more foreign-born workers, often working in low-paying jobs.

- According to the functionalist perspective, work serves specific functions in society. Our work provides us with some predictability about our life experiences.

- Conflict theorists argue that capitalist and corporate leaders maintain their power and economic advantage at the expense of their workers and the general public.

- From a feminist perspective, work is a gendered institution. Through the actions, beliefs, and interactions of workers and their employers, as well as the policies and practices of the workplace, men's and women's identities as workers are created, reproduced, then solidified in the everyday routines of informal work groups and formal workers' organizations.

- According to symbolic interactionists, we attach labels and meanings to an individual's work. These social constructs create an order to our work and our lives but can also create social problems.

- Problems related to work include unemployment and underemployment (the number of employed individuals who are working in a job that underpays them, is not equal to their skill level, or involves fewer working hours than they would prefer), contingent (temporary) work, outsourcing (including offshore outsourcing), sweatshop labor, discrimination in the workplace, and hazardous work.

- Several federal policies and institutions have been created with regard to the workforce. This includes the U.S. Department of Labor, which oversees several laws and organizations relevant to the workforce. Two labor issues continue to be debated in Congress: raising the minimum wage and workplace discrimination.

- In addition to government efforts, some companies have independently tried to make the atmosphere at work more worker-friendly through such areas as enhanced traditional benefits, flexible time, and expanded leave. Others try to follow a no-layoff policy.

- Labor unions, which historically have attempted to defend worker rights and whose efforts have led to many federal laws, still attempt to help workers, often in innovative ways.

INTERNET AND COMMUNITY EXERCISES

1. Explore the Occupational Outlook Handbook, published by the U.S. Bureau of Labor Statistics (log on to *Study Site Chapter 6*). The on-line handbook provides career descriptions, earning information, and job prospects for a range of occupational groups. For information about what sociologists and other social scientists do, click on "Professional and related occupations" on the Handbook's main page, then find and click on "Social Scientists, other." Research other occupations that might be of interest to you.

2. Do you know what the fourth Thursday in April is? It is "Take Our Daughters and Sons to Work Day." The program is sponsored by the Ms. Foundation for Women, which first created the "Take Our Daughters to Work Day" in 1993. "Take Our Daughters and Sons to Work" is a program that explores career opportunities and work/life issues with girls and boys. To find out more about the national program and related activities, log on to *Study Site Chapter 6*. Does your school or workplace support this program? Why or why not? Do you believe that these or similar activities are effective in changing girls' and boys' definitions of work and family life? Why or why not?

3. The Kneel Center at the Cornell University Library presents an on-site historical exhibit of the Triangle Factory Fire. On March 25, 1911, a fire at the Triangle Waist Company in New York City killed 146 immigrant workers. In 2003, the site was recognized as an official landmark by New York's Landmarks Preservation Commission. This tragedy led to the creation of local and federal policies prohibiting sweatshop conditions and ensuring worker health and safety. Log on to *Study Site Chapter 6* for more information. The Web site provides a history of early industrial sweatshops, along with a detailed narrative of how the community, workers, and unions responded to the tragedy. The Web site includes photographs, interviews, and documents from the period.

4. The Employment and Training Administration (ETA) of the U.S. Department of Labor is charged with the training and placement of workers through comprehensive employment and training services. The ETA serves businesses, workers (youths, adults, and dislocated workers), and workforce professionals. Each state has its own ETA office and Web site. You can contact your local office by using the government pages of your local phone book or accessing the ETA Web site (log on to *Study Site Chapter 6*). The site includes a link to regional Web sites. Click on the name of your state, then click on your state on the state map (or follow other links to your state). Your state's ETA may have its own name. For example, Nevada's office is called Nevada Job Connect and Rhode Island's is called Rhode Island Department of Labor and Training. Identify the specific programs offered to workers, especially for youth, in your state. What state programs are available for employers?

5. The United Nation's Human Development Report 2003 tracks unemployment rates for more than 100 nations. Log on to *Study Site Chapter 6* to compare unemployment rates for the United States and other nations.

On your own. Log on to *Study Site—Community and Policy Guide* for more information about the social problems, social policies, and community responses discussed in this chapter.

References

Abell, Hilary. 1999. "Endangering Women's Health for Profit: Health and Safety in Mexico's Maquiladoras." *Development in Practice* 9(5):595–601.

AFL-CIO. 2003. "Who Are Low Wage Workers?" Retrieved April 13, 2003 (www.aflcio.org/issuespolitics/minimumwage/whoarelowwage.cfm).

Almanac of Policy Issues. 2002. "Minimum Wage." Retrieved April 27, 2003 (www.policyalmanac.org/economic/minimum_wage).

Armas, G. 2004. "Outearning Men Women's Toughest Job." *The News Tribune*, June 4, p. 7.

Badgett, M. and V. Lee. 1997. "Vulnerability in the Workplace: Evidence of Anti-Gay Discrimination." *Angles* 2(1):1–4.

Bahnisch, Mark. 2000. "Embodied Work, Divided Labour: Subjectivity and the Scientific Management of the Body in Frederick W. Taylor's 1907 'Lecture on Management.'" *Body & Society* 6(1):51–68.

Bernstein, Aaron. 1999. "Now, Temp Workers Are a Full-Time Headache." *Business Week,* May 31, p. 46.

Bernstein, Jared. 1997. "Low-Wage Labor Market Indicators by City and State: The Constraints Facing Welfare Reform" (EPI Working Paper No. 118). Washington, DC: Economic Policy Institute.

Bernstein, J., H. Hartmann, and J. Schmitt. 1999. *The Minimum Wage Increase: A Working Woman's Issue* (EPI Issue Brief No. 133). Washington, DC: Economic Policy Institute.

Bertrand, M. and S. Mullainathan. 2003. "Are Emily and Greg More Employable Than Lakisha and Jamal? A Field Experiment in Market Discrimination" (NBER Working Paper No. 9873). Cambridge, MA: National Bureau of Economic Research.

Bluestone, B. and B. Harrison. 1982. *The Deindustrialization of America.* New York: Basic Books.

Brady, D. and M. Wallace. 2001. "Deindustrialization and Poverty: Manufacturing Decline and AFDC Recipiency in Lake County, Indiana 1964–93." *Sociological Forum* 16(2):321–358.

Braverman, Harry. 1974. *Labor and Monopoly Capital: The Degradation of Work in the Twentieth Century.* New York: Monthly Press Review.

Brenner, Joanna. 1998. "On Gender and Class in U.S. Labor History." *Monthly Review: An independent socialist magazine* 50(6):1–15.

Budig, Michelle. 2002. "Male Advantage and the Gender Composition of Jobs: Who Rides the Glass Escalator?" *Social Problems* 49(2):258–277.

Buell, John. 1997. "The Future of Unions." *Humanist* 57(5):41–42.

Clark, Kim. 2002. "No Pink Slips at This Plant." *U.S. News and World Report* 132(4):40.

Co-Op America. 2003. "What Is a Sweatshop." Retrieved April 26, 2003 (www.sweatshops.org/educated/issue.html).

Darity, William A. 2003. "Employment Discrimination, Segregation and Health." *American Journal of Public Health* 93(2):226–232.

Davidson, Linda. 1999. "Temp Workers Want a Better Deal." *Workforce* 78(10):44–49.

DeJong, G. F. and A. Madamba. 2001. "A Double Disadvantage? Minority Group, Immigrant Status, and Underemployment in the United States." *Social Science Quarterly* 82(1):117–130.

DeNavas-Walt, C., R. Cleveland, and B. H. Webster, Jr. 2003. *Income in the United States: 2002* (Current Population Reports, P60–221). Washington, DC: Government Printing Office.

Ehrenreich, Barbara. 2001. *Nickled and Dimed: On (Not) Getting By in America.* New York: Metropolitan Book/Henry Holt.

Eisenberg, Daniel. 1999. "Rise of Permatemp." *Time* 153(2):48.

England, P. and I. Browne. 1992. "Trends in Women's Economic Status." *Sociological Perspectives* 35(1):17–51.

Enron Corporation. 2000. "Enron Milestones." Retrieved May 1, 2003 From www.enron.com/corp/pressroom/milestones.

———. 2001. "Enron Named Most Innovative for Sixth Year." Retrieved September 3, 2004 (www.enron.com/corp/pressroom/releases/2001/ene/15-MostInnovative-02-06-01-LTR.html).

Equal Employment Opportunity Commission (EEOC). 2003. "Charge Statistics FY 1992 Through FY 2002." Retrieved March 22, 2003 (www.eeoc.gov/stats/charges).

Foo, Lora Jo. 1994. "The Vulnerable and Exploitable Immigrant Workforce and the Need for Strengthening Worker Protection Legislation." *Yale Law Review* 103(8): 2179–2212.

Fowler, Tom. 2001. "Formal Upgrade of Enron Investigation Gives Subpoena Power to SEC." Retrieved September 3, 2004 (www.chron.com/cs/CDA/ssistory.mpl/special/enron/oct01/1114532).

Fox, M. F. and S. Hesse-Biber 1984. *Women at Work.* Palo Alto, CA: Mayfield.

Frontline. 2002. "Accounting Lessons." Retrieved May 1, 2003 (www.pbs.org/wgph/pages/frontline/shows/regulations/lessons).

Fussell, Elizabeth. 2000. "Making Labor Flexible: The Recomposition of Tijuana's Maquiladora Female Labor Force." *Feminist Economics* 6(3):59–79.

General Accounting Office (GAO). 1994. "Garment Industry: Efforts to Address the Prevalence and Conditions of Sweatshops" (GAO/HEHS-95–29, November). Retrieved April 26, 2003 (http://frwebfate.access.gpo.gov/).

Gibson, C. and E. Lennon. 1999. "Historical Census Statistics on the Foreign-Born Population of the United States: 1850–1999" (Population Division Working Paper No. 29). Washington, DC: U.S. Bureau of the Census.

Gluck, Sherna Berger. 1987. *Rosie the Riveter Revisited: Women, the War, and Social Change.* Boston: Twayne.

Gorman, Maryann. 2002. "The White Dog's Tale" *YES! Magazine,* Spring 2001. Retrieved August 25, 2004 (http://63.135.115.58/other/pop_print_article.asp?ID=425).

Gruben, William C. 2001. "Was NAFTA Behind Mexico's High Maquiladora Growth?" *CATO Journal* 18(2):263–275.

Hall, Richard. 1994. *Sociology of Work: Perspectives, Analyses, and Issues.* Thousand Oaks, CA: Pine Forge.

Hard Hatted Women. 2000. "Show and Tell." Retrieved May 1, 2003 (www.hardhattedwomen.org/ShowTell.htm).

Hirschhorn, L. 1984. *Beyond Mechanization: Work and Technology in a Post-Industrial Age.* Cambridge, MA: MIT Press.

Hollingsworth, Barbara. 2002. "Number of Working People 65 and Up Is Expected to Grow." *The News Tribune,* September 29, pp. D1–D2.

Human Rights Campaign. 2003. "ENDA Quickfacts: The Right Solution for a Real Need." Retrieved March 22, 2003 (www.hrc.org/issues/federal_leg/enda).

Information for Decision Making. 2000. "Minimum Wage Legislation and Living Wage Campaigns." Retrieved April 20, 2003 (www.financeprojectinfo.org/MWW/minimum.asp#effects).

Kershaw, Sarah. 2003. "Wal-Mart Sets a New Policy That Protects Gay Workers." *The New York Times,* July 2, pp. A1, A16.

Kovach, K. and P. Millspaugh. 1996. "Employment NonDiscrimination Act: On the Cutting Edge of Public Policy." *Business Horizons* 39(4):65–74.

Krieger, N. and S. Sidney. 1997. "Prevalence and Health Implications of Anti-Gay Discrimination: A Study of Black and White Women and Men in the CARDIA Cohort." *Journal of Health Services* 27(1):156–176.

Kucinich. D. 2000. "Cleveland Job Training Program Awarded $77,727 Federal Grant" (Press Release, September 22). Retrieved March 22, 2003 (www.house.gov/kucinich/press/laborss.html).

Lambda Legal. 2003. "Issues: Employment." Retrieved June 11, 2003 (www.lambdalegal.org/cbi-bin/iowa/issues/record?record=4/).

Lazes, P. and J. Savage. 2000. "Embracing the Future: Union Strategies for the 21st Century." *Journal for Quality and Participation* 23(4):18–24.

Levering, R., M. Moskowitz, L. Munoz, P. Hjelt, and A. Wheat. 2002. "The 100 Best Companies to Work For." *Fortune* 145(3):72–84.

Lindquist, Diane. 2001. "Rules Change for Maquiladoras." *Industry Week* 250(1):23–26.

Lollock, Lisa. 2001. *The Foreign Born Population in the United States: March 2000.* (Current Population Reports, P20–534). Washington, DC: U.S. Census Bureau.

McDonough, Sioban. 2003. "EEOC: Job Discrimination Up Since 9/11." Retrieved March 22, 2003 (www.softcom.net/webnews/wed/ch/Adiscrimination.RNTX_CD3).

Mills, C. W. 2000. *The Sociological Imagination.* New York: Oxford University Press. (Original work published 1959)

Mosisa, Abraham. 2002. "The Role of Foreign-Born Workers in the U.S. Economy." *Monthly Labor Review* 125(5):3–15.

National Institute for Occupational Safety and Health (NIOSH). 2003. "Stress at Work." Retrieved May 3, 2003 (www.cdc.gov/niosh/stresswk.html).

National Public Radio. 2003a. "The Fall of Enron." Retrieved May 2, 2003 (www.npr.org/news/specials/enron/).

———. 2003b. "What Enron Employees Have Lost." Retrieved May 2, 2003 (www.npr.org/news/specials/enron/employees).

Parenti, Michael. 1988. *Democracy for the Few* (5th ed.). New York: St. Martin's Press.

Pollina, Ronald. 2003. "Can We Maintain the American Dream?" *Economic Development Journal* 2(3):54–58.

Randall, Donna M. 1985. "Women in Toxic Work Environments: A Case Study and Examination of Policy Impact." Pp. 259–281 in *Women and Work: An Annual Review,* edited by L. Larwood, A. Stromberg, and B. Gutek. Beverly Hills, CA: Sage.

Reich, Robert. 1996. Testimony before the Subcommittee on Labor, HHS, Education and Related Agencies, Committee on Appropriations, U.S. House of Representatives. May 7, 1996. Retrieved March 22, 2003 (www.dol.gov/asp/programs/history/reich/congress).

Reskin, Barbara and Irene Padavic. 1994. *Women and Men at Work.* Thousand Oaks, CA: Pine Forge.

Ritzer, George. 1989. "Sociology of Work: A Metatheoretical Analysis." *Social Forces* 67(3):593–604.

———. 2000. *Sociological Theory.* Boston: McGraw-Hill.

Rodriguez, Eunice. 2001. "Keeping the Unemployed Healthy." *American Journal of Public Health* 91(9):1403–1412.

Saftner, T. J. 1998. "Temps for Hire." *Career World* 27(3):18–22.

Schmidt, D. and G. Duenas. 2002. "Incentives to Encourage Worker-Friendly Organizations." *Public Personnel Management* 31(3):293–309.

Scott, Robert E. 2001. "NAFTA's Hidden Costs: Trade Agreement Results in Job Losses, Growing Inequality, and Wage Suppression for the United States." *Economic Policy Institute Briefing Paper,* April, pp. 3–10.

Sowinski, Lara. 2000. "Maquiladoras." *World Trade* 13(9):88–92.

Sweatshop Watch. 2000. "Student Organizing." Retrieved September 5, 2004 (http://swatch.igc.org/swatch/codes/).

———. 2003. "Frequently Asked Questions." Retrieved April 15, 2003 (www.sweatshopwatch.org/swatch/questions).

Taylor, Frederick W. 1911. *The Principles of Scientific Management.* New York: Harper.

Thottam, Jyoti. 2004. "Is Your Job Going Abroad?" *Time* 163(9):26–36.

UNITE. 2003. "UNITE: A New Union With a Long History." Retrieved May 1, 2003 (www.uniteunion.org/research/history/unionisborn.html).

——— . 2004. "Labor Unions UNITE and HERE to Merge." Retrieved February 29, 2004 (we3ww.uniteunion.org/pressbox/merger.cfm).

U.S. Bureau of Labor Statistics. 2002. *Highlights of Women's Earnings in 2001* (Report 960). Washington, DC: U.S. Department of Labor.

U.S. Bureau of Labor Statistics. 2003a. "National Census of Fatal Occupational Injuries in 2002" (News Release). Retrieved February 27, 2004 (www.bls.gov/news.release/pdf/cfoi.pdf).

——— . 2003b. *News: The Employment Situation: February 2002* (Report USDL 03–99). Washington, DC: U.S. Department of Labor.

——— . 2003c. "Occupational Outlook Handbook: Apparel and Other Textile Products." Retrieved April 26, 2003 (www.bls.gov/oco/cg/text/cgs007.text).

——— . 2003d. Table 3. Retrieved February 1, 2004 (www.bls.gov/emp/emplab2000–03.pdf).

———. 2003e. "Workplace Injuries and Illnesses in 2002." Retrieved February 27, 2004 (www.bls.gov/newsrelease/osh.nr0.htm).

——— . 2004a. "The Employment Situation Summary." Retrieved September 3, 2004 (www.bls.gov/news.release/empsit.nr0.htm).

——— . 2004b. "Occupations with the Largest Projected Job Growth (in thousands), 2002–2012." Retrieved June 15, 2004 (www.bls.gov/emptab4.htm).

U.S. Census Bureau. 1951. *Statistical Abstract of the United States* (Table 203). Washington, DC: Author.

——— . 1960. *Statistical Abstract of the United States* (Table 274). Washington, DC: Author.

——— . 1966. *Statistical Abstract of the United States* (Table 319). Washington, DC: Author.

——— . 2002. *CPS: Annual Demographic Survey, March Supplement* (Table PINC-03). Retrieved April 15, 2003 from http://ferret.bls.census.gov/maro/032002/perinc/new03_076.htm h

U.S. Department of Labor. 1996. "Dynamic Change in the Garment Industry: How Firms and Workers Can Survive and Thrive." Retrieved April 26, 2003 (www.dol.gov/esa/forum/report.htm).

——— . 2000. "Garment Enforcement Report: October 2000–December 2000." Retrieved April 27, 2003 from www.dol.gov/esa/garment/garment21.htm.

——— . 2002. "Minimum Wage Laws in the States." Retrieved March 22, 2003 (www.dol.gov/esa/minwage/america.htm).

——— . 2003. "Labor Department Enforcement Reaches 10-year High" (Press Release, December 18, 2002). Retrieved March 22, 2003 (www.dol.gov/opa/media/press/esa/ESA2002694.htm).

U.S. Department of Labor Women's Bureau. 2000. "Facts of Working Women: Hot Jobs for the 21st Century." Retrieved March 22, 2003 (www.dol.gov/wb/wb_pubs/hotjobs02).

——— . 2003. "20 Leading Occupations of Employed Women: 2001 Annual Averages." Retrieved March 22, 2003 (www.dol.gov/wb/wb_pubs).

Waldman, Amy. 2003. "More 'Can I Help You?' Jobs Migrate from U.S. to India." *The New York Times,* May 11, p. 4.

WashTech. 2003. "About Us." Retrieved May 10, 2003 (www.washtech.org/wt/about/).

Williams, Kristian. 1999. "Reflections on the Georgetown Sit-In." Retrieved January 26, 2004 (www.zmag.org/ZMag/articles/may99williams.htm).

Zeitlin, Irving. 1997. *Ideology and the Development of Sociological Theory.* Englewood Cliffs, NJ: Prentice Hall.

Zhou, Min. 1993. "Underemployment and Economic Disparities Among Minority Groups." *Population Research and Policy Review* 12:139–157.

7

Health and Medicine

I n 2002, the Centers for Disease Control and Prevention released a report of health trends over the second half of the 20th century. In "Health, United States, 2002" (National Center for Health Statistics 2002), the Centers reported that life expectancy reached a record high of 76.9 years, with gaps between Blacks and Whites and men and women narrowing by 2002 (see Table 7.1). In addition, the Centers for Disease Control and Prevention reported improvements in many other aspects of our health:

- Death rates for heart disease have been cut by more than half. The decline was attributed to better medical care and a decrease in smoking rates.
- Death rates from injuries, in particular motor vehicle crashes, have fallen since 1970. The decline was attributed to safer cars on the road and more people wearing seat belts.
- Infant mortality dropped to a record low of 6.9 deaths per 1,000 live births in 2000.
- The rates of infectious disease have declined.

At the release of this report, Tommy Thompson, Secretary of Health and Human Services stated, "As we take better care of ourselves and medical treatments improve, the illnesses and behaviors that once cost us the lives of our grandparents will become even less threatening to the lives of our grandchildren" (U.S. Department of Health and Human Services 2002). Indeed, the report documents record lows and declines in many key areas of our nation's health. But despite the glowing report, Dr. Edward J. Sondik, director of the CDC's National Center for Health Statistics, warns that "the power of the [report] is that it shows what we're doing right, and where we still need to make improvements" (U.S. Department of Health and Human Services 2002).

Before we discuss where health improvements still need to be made, we'll use our sociological imagination to better understand the relationship between health, illness, and society.

Sociological Perspectives of Health, Illness, and Medicine

So if you're thinking that this is going to be a discussion about human physiology, theories about germs and viruses, full of a lot of medical terms, you'd be wrong. Although

❖ Table 7.1   Life Expectancy at Birth in Years According to Race and Sex in the
United States, Selected Years

	All Races		White		Black	
	Male	Female	Male	Female	Male	Female
1900	46.3	48.3	46.6	48.7	32.5	33.5
1950	65.6	71.1	66.5	72.2	59.1	62.9
1960	66.6	73.1	67.4	74.1	61.1	66.3
1970	67.1	74.7	70.7	78.1	60.0	68.3
1980	70.0	77.4	70.7	78.1	63.8	72.5
1990	71.8	78.8	72.7	79.4	64.5	73.6
2000	74.3	79.7	74.9	80.1	68.3	75.2

Source: National Center for Health Statistics 2003.

medicine can identify the biological pathways to disease (Wilkinson 1996), we will need
a sociological perspective to address the social determinants of health. Research continues to demonstrate the relationship between the individual and society and the structural
effects on health: about how our health is affected by our social position, our work, our
families, education, and wealth and poverty (Wilkinson 1996). According to sociologist
Peter Conrad (2001a), to make the connection between our social structure and health,
we must investigate how our political economy, our corporate structure, and the distribution of resources and social, political, and economic power influence health and illness.

The sociology of health and illness includes the field of epidemiology.
Epidemiology is the study of the patterns in the distribution and frequency of sickness, injury, and death and the social factors that shape them. Epidemiologists are like
detectives, investigating how and why groups of individuals become sick or injured
(Cockerman and Glasser 2001). They don't focus on individuals; rather, epidemiologists focus on communities and populations, addressing how health and illness experiences are based on social factors such as gender, age, race, social class, or behavior
(Cockerman and Glasser 2001). Epidemiology has successfully increased public awareness about the risk factors associated with disease and illness, leading many to quit
smoking, to participate in more physical exercise, and to eat healthier diets (Link and
Phelan 2001). For example, Type 2 diabetes, the most common form of the disease,
occurs when the body does not produce enough insulin or the cells ignore the insulin.
It is estimated that 16 million Americans have Type 2 diabetes. However, the disease
can be effectively managed with healthy behaviors like meal planning, exercise, and
weight management (American Diabetes Association 2003).

All of us practice healthy behaviors we believe or were told can prevent or cure illness or disease. Brushing our teeth is one practice that we routinely do without really remembering why we do it. What other healthy behaviors do you practice? Why do you do them? Where did you learn them?

Epidemiologists use three primary measures of health status: fertility, mortality, and morbidity. These data are routinely collected by the National Center for Health Statistics, Centers for Disease Control. **Fertility** is the level of childbearing for an individual or population. The basic measure of fertility is the crude birthrate, the number of live births per 1,000 women ages 15 to 44 in a population. The crude birthrate for 2000 was 65 births per 1,000 women (U.S. Census Bureau 2002). Related to this is the measure of **fecundity**, the maximum number of children that could be born (based on the number of women of childbearing age in the population).

In the early 1900s, a woman could expect to give birth to about four children, whereas a woman during the Great Depression of the 1930s could expect to have only two (U.S. Census Bureau 2002). The lowest number of births per woman was 1.8 children in the mid-1970s. Since then, the rate has averaged around two births per woman (U.S. Census Bureau 2002). Fertility is determined by a set of biological factors, such as the health and nutrition of childbearing women. But innovations in medicine, in the form of infertility treatments, have also made childbirth possible for women who once considered it impossible. Fertility is also determined by social factors, such as our social values and definitions of the role of women, the ideal family size, and the timing of childbirth.

Mortality is the incidence of death in a population. The basic measure of mortality is the crude death rate, the number of deaths per 100,000 people in a population in a given year. For 2000, the death rate was 873.1 deaths per 100,000 (National Center for Health Statistics 2002). In the United States, it is unlikely that we'll die from acute infectious diseases, such as an intestinal infection or measles. Rather, the leading causes of death are attributed to chronic conditions such as coronary heart disease, cancer, stroke, or chronic lower respiratory disease, all of which have been linked to heredity, diet, stress, and exercise. The leading causes of death vary considerably by age. The leading cause of death of college-age Americans is unintentional injuries, followed by homicide and suicide. Among the elderly, mortality due to chronic diseases is more prevalent. (See Table 7.2.)

Infant mortality is the rate of infant death per 1,000 live births. For 2000, the infant mortality rate was 6.9 per 1,000 (National Center for Health Statistics 2002). The three leading causes of death among infants were congenital birth defects, low birth weight, and sudden infant death syndrome. Matthews, McDorman, and Menacker (2002) report that 1999 rates were higher for young mothers who began prenatal care late or had none at all, who had 9 to 11 years of education, who were unmarried, or who smoked during pregnancy. According to the authors, there was wide variation in the infant morality rate by the race of the mother. The highest rate

❖ Table 7.2 The 10 Leading Causes of Death in Selected Age Groups for All Races, Both Sexes, United States, 2000

15 to 19 years	20 to 24 years	65 years and over
Accidents	Accidents	Diseases of the heart
Assault (e.g., homicide)	Assault (e.g., homicide)	Cancer
Intentional harm (e.g., suicide)	Intentional harm (e.g., suicide)	Cerebrovascular diseases (e.g., stroke)
Cancer	Cancer	Chronic lower respiratory diseases (e.g., chronic bronchitis and emphysema)
Diseases of heart	Diseases of heart	Influenza and pneumonia
Congenital malformations, deformations, and chromosomal abnormalities	Congenital malformations, deformations, and chromosomal abnormalities	Diabetes
Chronic lower respiratory diseases (e.g., chronic bronchitis and emphysema)	Chronic lower respiratory diseases (e.g., chronic bronchitis and emphysema)	Alzheimer's disease
Cerebrovasular diseases (e.g., stroke)	Cerebrovasular diseases (e.g., stroke)	Diseases of the kidney
Influenza and pneumonia	Influenza and pneumonia	Accidents
Diabetes	Diabetes	Septicemia (blood poisoning)

Source: Anderson 2002, Table 1.

was 14.0 for infants of Black mothers, more than four times higher than the lowest rate groups. In addition, infant mortality was higher in the South and lowest in the West and Northeast.

Morbidity is the study of illnesses and disease. Illness refers to the social experience and consequences of having a disease, whereas disease refers to a biological or physiological problem that affects the human body (Weitz 2001). Epidemiologists track the **incidence rate**, the number of new cases within a population during a specific time period, along with the **prevalence rate**, the total number of cases involving a specific health problem during a specific time period (Weitz 2001). For example, the 2000 incidence rate for diabetes was 1.0 million people age 20 years or older; the prevalence rate was 17.0 million or 6.2 percent of the population (Centers for Disease Control 2003). Incidence rates help measure the spread of **acute illnesses,** which strike suddenly and disappear quickly, like chicken pox or the flu. On the other hand, the prevalence rate measures the frequency of long-term or **chronic illnesses**, such as diabetes, asthma, or HIV (Weitz 2001). The National Center for Health Statistics publishes the *Morbidity and Mortality Weekly Report,* a weekly summary of surveillance information on reported diseases/deaths.

❖ PUTTING IT TOGETHER:
On the Web.

Based on data from the National Center for Health Statistics, determine the current rates of fertility and mortality (adult and infant) in your college state. Log on to *Study Site Chapter 7*. How do these rates compare with overall national figures (as reported in earlier paragraphs) or with neighboring states?

In addition to epidemiological analyses, sociologists have also applied theoretical perspectives to better explain the social problems of health and illness.

Functionalist Perspective

The stability of society is paramount from a functionalist's perspective. Consider for a moment what happens when you become sick. When are you sick enough not to attend class? How do others begin to treat you? According to the functionalist perspective, illness has a legitimate place in society. The first sociological theory of illness was offered by Talcott Parsons (1951), addressing how individuals are expected to act and to be treated while sick (Weitz 2001). This set of behaviors is part of Parsons' theory of the **sick role**.

The sick role has four parts. In the first, sick people are excused from fulfilling their normal social role. Illness allows them to be excused from work, from chores around the house, or even from attending class! Second, sick people are not held responsible for the illness. The flu that's going around is no one's fault, so you aren't personally blamed if you catch it. (Although your roommates may blame you if they catch what you have.) Third, sick people must try to get well. Illness is considered a temporary condition, and sick people are expected to take care of themselves with appropriate measures. In relation to this, Parsons offers the last part, that sick people are expected to visit medical authorities and to follow their advice.

Although Parsons legitimized the social role of illness, he also identified a critical source of the problem in health care today. In the fourth element, Parsons identified the authority and control of the physician. Even though you're the one who is sick, the doctor has the ultimate power to diagnose your condition and tell you that you're "really" sick. Doctors play a prominent role in managing our illnesses, but they don't do it alone. Doctors, along with nurses, pharmaceutical corporations, hospitals, and health insurers, form a powerful medical industry. The medical industry has served us well with its technological and scientific advances, offering a wider array of medical services and treatment options. However, this industry has also created a set of problems, or dysfunctions, as functionalists like to refer to them. Medicine has shifted from a general practitioner model (a family doctor who took care of all your needs) to a specialist model (where one doctor treats you for a specific ailment). You are receiving quality care, but at a price (and you are paying to be treated by many different doctors, instead of just one). As a result, health care costs have become less affordable, leaving many without adequate coverage and care. The system intended to heal us does not treat everyone fairly. We will explore this further in the next perspective.

Conflict Perspective

According to conflict theorists, patterns of health and illness are not accidental or due solely to an individual's actions. Conflict theorists identify how these patterns are related to systematic inequalities based not only on ethnicity/race or gender but also on differences in power, values, and interests.

Conflict theorists may take a traditional Marxist position and argue how our medical industry is based on a capitalist system, founded not on the value of human life, but on a pure profit motive. Studies consistently identify how those in upper social classes have better health, health insurance, and medical access than men and women of lower socioeconomic status. A conflict theorist can argue that instead of defining health care as a right, our capitalistic system treats health care as a valuable commodity dispensed to the highest bidder. The alternative would be a dramatic change in the medical system, ensuring that health care is provided to all regardless of their race, class, or gender.

What we continue to have is a medical system responsive to middle- or upper-class patients and their needs. According to Ken Silverstein (1999), 6.1 million people died worldwide of malaria or acute lower-respiratory infections because there were no drugs available to treat these illnesses. Silverstein notes that pharmaceutical companies have pursued drugs that maximize their profitability, focusing less on diseases of the poor or drugs that are commercially unviable. As he explains, the interest is in lifestyle drugs, "remedies that may one day free the world from the scourge of toenail fungus, obesity, baldness, face wrinkles, and impotence" (p. 14).

The medical system itself ensures that power is maintained by those already in charge. In health care, no other group has greater power than medical physicians and their professional organization, the American Medical Association, established in 1847. On its Web site, the AMA identifies itself as "the nation's most influential medical organization." In his book, *The Social Transformation of American Medicine,* Paul Starr (1982) explains how the AMA's authority over the medical profession and education was secured in the early 1900s, with a series of events that culminated with the Flexner Report. The 1910 report was written by Abraham Flexner and was commissioned by the Carnegie Foundation and supported by the AMA. Through the report, Flexner and the AMA were able to pass judgment on the quality of each medical school, based on an assessment of its curriculum, facilities, faculty, admission requirements, and state licensing record. This report led eventually to strict licensing criteria for all medical schools, leading to the closure of schools that could not meet the new standards. Starr (1982) reveals that although the increased standards and school closures may have improved the quality of medical training and care, they also increased the homogeneity and cohesiveness of the profession. From 162 schools in 1906, the number of medical schools dropped to 81 by 1922. Some of the closed schools were exclusively for African Americans and women. According to Rose Weitz (2001), with the increasing cost of education and higher educational prerequisites, fewer minorities, women, immigrants, or poor students could meet the requirements. As a result,

> fewer doctors were available who would practice in minority communities and who understood the special concerns of minority or female patients. At the same time, simply because doctors were now more homogenously White, male, and upper class, their status grew, encouraging more hierarchical relationships between doctors and patients. (Weitz 2001:327)

The AMA (2003) continues its lobbying and legislative efforts today, pursuing several legislative goals including medical liability reforms (asking for limits on punitive or noneconomic damages), preserving Medicare physician payments, expanding health insurance options, and obtaining regulatory relief from Medicare administration.

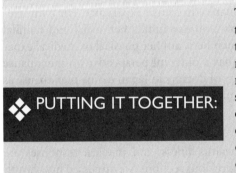

❖ PUTTING IT TOGETHER: The consumer movement has shifted some of the power in the doctor-patient relationship to the patient. For example, drug ads, previously reserved for professional journals, are now commonly found in popular magazines and on television. Pharmaceutical companies routinely take two or three full-page ads, featuring drug warnings, side effects, and precautions, along with a description of their drug and its benefits. It sometimes is difficult to figure out what the drug is for. How do you think this popular diffusion of pharmaceutical information has redefined the relationship between doctor and patient?

Feminist Perspective

According to Peter Conrad (2001b), illness and how we treat it can reflect cultural assumptions and biases about a particular group. Take, for example, the case of women and their medical care. Conrad explains that throughout history, there are examples of medical and scientific explanations for women's health and illnesses that reflect dominant and often negative conceptions of women. Since the 1930s, women's natural physical conditions and experiences, such as childbirth, menopause, and premenstrual syndrome, were medicalized. **Medicalization** refers to the process through which a condition or behavior becomes defined as a medical problem (Weitz 2001). Although the medicalization of these conditions may have been effective in treating women, various feminist theorists see it as an extension of medicine's control over women (Conrad 2001b), specifically normal female experiences linked with the female reproductive system (Markens 1996), inappropriately emphasizing the psychological, biomedical, or sociocultural origins (Hamilton 1994). Once a condition is defined as a medical problem, medicine, rather than the woman herself, gains control over its diagnosis and treatment.

Menopause, a natural physiological event for women, was defined in the medical community as a "deficiency disease" in the 1960s when commercial production of estrogen replacement therapy became available (Conrad 2001b; Lock 1993). Although a few medical writers refer to menopause as a natural process, many continue to describe it as a "hormonal imbalance" that leads to a "menopausal syndrome" (Lock 1993). Although estrogen replacement treatment was presented as a means for women to retain their femininity and to maintain good health, feminists argued that menopause was not an illness; in fact, estrogen therapy may not be necessary and may actually be dangerous (Conrad 2001b). A recent study indicated that although estrogen is an effective short-term treatment for hot flashes or night sweats, estrogen does little to improve the quality of older women's lives (Haney 2003).

Studies have suggested that the meanings and experiences of menopause may also be bound by cultural definitions. In North America, where women are defined by their youth and beauty, aging women are set up as a target for medicalization. In Japan, however, public attention focuses on a woman's life course experience. For a middle-aged Japanese woman, what matters is how well she fulfills her social and familial duties, especially the care of elderly family members, not her physical or medical experiences. The Japanese medical community has a different perspective on menopause than their American colleagues: The majority of doctors in Japan define menopause as natural and an inevitable part of the aging process (Lock 1993).

Interactionist Perspective

From the interactionist perspective, health, illness, and medical responses are socially constructed and maintained. In the previous sections, we discussed how health issues are defined by powerful interest or political groups. We just reviewed how the medicalization of women's conditions reflects our cultural assumptions or biases about women. Each example demonstrates how social, political, and cultural meanings affect our definition and response to health and illness.

A patient's experience with the medical system can be disempowering (Goffman 1961), but the experience can be mediated by social meaning and interpretations (Lambert et al. 1997). According to Peterson, Heesacker, and Schwartz (2001), when people contract a disease, they define their illness according to a socially constructed definition of the disease, which includes a set of images, beliefs, and perceptions. Patients use these definitions to create a personal meaning for their diagnosis and to determine their subsequent behavior. The authors argue that these social constructs have a greater influence on the patient's actions and decisions about his or her health than recommendations from health professionals.

Sociologists also examine how the relationship between doctors and their patients is created and maintained through interaction. In particular, sociologists focus on how medical professionals use their expertise and knowledge to maintain control over patients. Research indicates that doctors' power depends on their cultural authority, economic independence, cultural differences between patients and doctors, and doctors' assumed superiority to patients (Weitz 2001). Studies consistently demonstrate the systematic differences in the level of information provided by physicians to their patients. Although differences might be attributed to the doctor responding to a patient's particular communication style, researchers argue that information varies according to the doctor's impressions of a patient (e.g., intelligence) or according to subjective judgments about what information the patient needs (Street 1991). Educated and younger patients tend to receive more diagnostic information, as do patients who ask more questions and express more concerns; doctors are likely to communicate as equals with their educated, older male patients (Street 1991). African Americans, Asian Americans, and Hispanics are more likely than Whites to experience difficulties in communicating with their doctors. The difficulties include not understanding their doctor, not feeling that the doctor listened to them, or having questions for their doctor that they did not ask (Collins et al. 2002).

Interactionists and social constructionists also investigate how a disease is socially constructed. This doesn't mean that disease and illness do not exist. Rather, the focus is on how illness is created and sustained according to a set of shared social beliefs or definitions. In his essay, "The Myth of Mental Illness," Thomas Szasz (1960) argues that mental disorders are not actually illnesses. He considered mental illness a convenient myth to cover up the "everyday fact that life for most people is a continuous struggle" (p. 118). The disease of mental illness is constructed and maintained through a set of medical, legal, and social definitions. The social construction of disease has also been applied to anorexia nervosa (Brumberg 1988), black lung disease (Smith 1987), and chronic fatigue syndrome (Richman and Jason 2001).

❖ PUTTING IT TOGETHER: What social constructs or definitions exist for cancer? For AIDS? For diabetes? How would your social definitions of a disease affect your experience of the disease?

For a summary of sociological perspectives on disease and illness, see Table 7.3.

Inequalities in Mortality and Morbidity

Gender and Health

As noted in Table 7.1, women live about five years longer than men. The three leading causes of death for males and females are identical: heart disease, cancer, and stroke (see Table 7.4). Although women live longer than men, women experience higher rates of nonfatal chronic conditions (Waldron 2001; Weitz, 2001). Men experience higher

❖ Table 7.3 Summary of Sociological Perspectives: Health and Medicine

	Functional	Conflict/Feminist	Interactionist
Explanation of the social problems of health and medicine	Although illness may threaten the social order, it does have a legitimate place in society. This perspective also addresses the functions and dysfunctions of the medical industry.	Patterns of health and illness reflect systematic inequalities based on ethnicity/race or gender, and also differences in power, values, and interests. Conflict theorists examine the power of the medical industry and its consequences. Feminist theorists examine medicine's control over women, specifically over normal female experiences linked with the female reproductive system.	Acknowledges how illness is created and sustained according to a set of shared social beliefs or definitions. Theorists in this perspective address how social, political, and cultural meanings affect our definition and response to health and illness.
Questions asked about health and medicine	What is the role of illness in our society? What functions and dysfunctions does the medical industry provide?	How does the medical industry exert control over its patients? Is everyone treated fairly and equally by the medical system?	Who or what defines what it means to be "sick" in our society? How do our definitions of disease and illness shape our beliefs and behaviors?

rates of fatal illness, dying more quickly than women when illness occurs (Waldron 2001; Weitz 2001).

These differences in mortality have been attributed to three factors: genetics, risk taking, and health care (Waldron 2001). Biological differences seem to favor women; more females than males survive at every age (Weitz 2001). Due to differences in gender roles, men are more likely to engage in risk-taking behaviors or potentially dangerous activities: driving too fast or incautiously, using legal or illegal drugs, or participating in dangerous sports (Waldron 2001). The workplace offers more dangers for men. More men than women are employed, and men's jobs tend to be more hazardous

❖ **Table 7.4** Deaths and Percentage of Total Deaths for the 10 Leading Causes of Death by Sex: United States, 2000

	Males		Females	
	Rank	Percent of Death	Rank	Percent of Death
All causes	. . .	100.0	. . .	100.0
Diseases of heart	1	29.3	1	29.9
Cancer	2	24.3	2	21.8
Cerebrovascular diseases (e.g., stroke)	3	5.5	3	8.4
Accidents	4	5.4	8	2.8
Chronic lower respiratory diseases (e.g., chronic bronchitis and emphysema)	5	5.1	4	5.1
Diabetes	6	2.7	5	3.1
Influenza and pneumonia	7	2.4	6	3.0
Suicide	8	2.0	. . .	0.5
Diseases of the kidney	9	1.5	9	1.6
Chronic liver disease and cirrhosis	10	1.5	. . .	0.8
Alzheimer's disease	. . .	1.2	7	2.9
Septicemia (Blood poisoning)	. . .	1.1	10	1.4

Source: Anderson 2002.

(Waldron 2001); about 9 out of every 10 fatal workplace accidents occur to men (Men's Health Network 2002). Finally, because women obtain more routine health examinations than men do, their health problems are identified early enough for effective intervention (Weitz 2001).

According to the Men's Health Network (2002), "no effective program exists which is devoted to awareness and prevention of the leading killers of men." Although by the age of 75, men die of cancer at twice the rate of women, there is little education for men in cancer self-detection and prevention. Whereas there is a popular national campaign for breast cancer, there is no national educational campaign teaching men how to self-examine for testicular cancer, a leading killer of men from 15 to 40 years of age (Men's Health Network 2002). In addition, there are no quality educational programs regarding prostate cancer, a cancer that strikes one in five men (Men's Health Network 2002).

Women, Ethnicity/Race, and Health

Are all women healthier? As reported by the National Women's Health Information Center (NWHIC) (2002a), the health status of African American, Asian American, and Native American women is not as good as the health of White women. Diabetes is 60 percent more common in African American women than White women (NWHIC 2002a), with about one in four African American women over the age of 55 having the disease (NWHIC 2002c). Risk factors include obesity—more African American women between the ages of 24 and 74 are overweight, and by more pounds, compared to White women of the same age group—and genetic predisposition (NWHIC 2002c). Due to lack of effective follow-up care, African Americans experience higher rates of diabetes-related complications: blindness, amputation, and kidney failure. Moreover, African American women have higher death rates for both coronary heart disease and cardiovascular disease.

Although Asian American women have the highest life expectancy (85.8 years) of any racial or ethnic group in the United States, the NWHIC (2002b) reports wide disparities between Asian American subgroups: Samoan women (74.9 years), Native Hawaiian women (77.2), Japanese (84.5) and Chinese women (86.1 years). As a group, Asian American women are at risk for tuberculosis, hepatitis B (especially among women from Cambodia, China, Laos, Korea, India, Vietnam, and the Philippines), osteoporosis, and suicide. Asian American women have the highest suicide rate among women ages 15 to 24 and 65 years or older, due in part to the cultural barriers associated with seeking mental health support.

The status of Native American women's health is associated with cultural dislocation, poverty, and the historical neglect of Native American rights (NWHIC 2002d). Deaths due to accidents among Native American women are nearly three times the national average, with most deaths associated with lack of seat belt use and drunk driving. Native American women die due to alcoholism at a rate five to six times greater than the national average; drinking during pregnancy is three times the national average; and death due to tuberculosis is five times the national rate (NWHIC 2002d).

Among Latina women, diabetes is two or three times more common in Mexican American, Cuban American, and Puerto Rican women than in non-Hispanic women. Obesity is 1.5 times more common in Mexican American women than in the general female population. The rate of HIV infection is seven times higher in Latina women than in White women. Finally, there are more uninsured Latina women (30 percent) than any other race/ethnic group, even though many of them are employed or live with someone who is employed (NWHIC 2002e).

Social Class and Health

"It is the same cause that wears out our bodies and our clothes" (Brecht 1976). Data consistently indicate that those with higher education, income, or occupational prestige have lower rates of morbidity and mortality. Although no factor has been singled out as the primary link between socioeconomic position and health, scholars have offered many factors—standard of living, work conditions, housing conditions, and the social and psychological connections with others at work, home, or the community—to explain the relationship (Krieger, Williams, and Moss 1997).

The relationship between health and social class afflicts those most vulnerable: the young and the old. About 70 percent of children who live below the poverty line report being in excellent or good health in comparison to 85 percent of children who live at or above the poverty line (Federal Interagency Forum on Child and Family Statistics 2002). Children below the poverty line have lower rates of immunization and higher rates of activity limitation due to chronic illness than children who live above the poverty line (Federal Interagency Forum on Child and Family Statistics 2002). Although the majority of those over 65 years of age have health insurance through Medicare, the cost of health care jeopardizes the economic security of the elderly. Because Medicare coverage is inadequate for an elderly person's health needs, poor elderly report having to choose between buying food or medicine.

Rose Weitz (2001) offers several explanations for the unhealthy relationship between poverty and illness. First, the type of work available to poorly educated people can cause illness or death by exposing them to hazardous conditions. Second, poor and middle-class individuals who live in poor neighborhoods are exposed to air, noise, water, and chemical pollution that can increase rates of morbidity and mortality. Inadequate and unsafe housing increases the risk of injury, infections, and illnesses, including lead poisoning when children eat peeling paint. The diet of the poor increases the risk of illness. The poor have little time or opportunity to practice healthy activities like exercise, and due to life stresses, they may also be encouraged to adopt behaviors that might further endanger their health. Finally, poverty limits individual access to preventative and therapeutic health care.

Other Health Care Problems

Inequalities in Health Insurance

Access to health care is unevenly distributed across the U.S. population (Conrad and Leiter 2003). Data from the U.S. Census Bureau reveals that 45 million or 15.6 percent of Americans had no health insurance at anytime during 2003, an increase of 1.4 million from 2002 (DeNavas-Walt et al. 2004). (See U.S. Data Map 7.1.) A 2003 joint report released by the Robert Wood Johnson Foundation and Families USA estimated that 74.7 million nonelderly Americans were without insurance during 2001 or 2002. Although the majority of Americans receive health insurance through their employer, many uninsured individuals are either employed or are dependents of employed people (House Energy and Commerce Subcommittee on Health and Environment 1993). Nearly four in five of those without health insurance were in the labor force or had at least one parent who was employed (Families USA 2003). Most of the working poor are not eligible for public assistance medical programs (e.g., Medicaid) even though their employers do not provide health insurance (Seccombe and Amey 2001). Among households with incomes less than $25,000, only 75.8 percent received health insurance (DeNavas-Walt et al. 2004).

There are several social factors related to health coverage. In 2003, men accounted for two thirds of the increase in the number of uninsured because they were more likely to lose employer-sponsored health coverage than women. About 20.1 percent or 12.1 million children under the age of 18 did not have health insurance. When parents lose jobs, children lose health insurance coverage. Individuals 18 to 24 years of age were less likely than any other age group to have insurance coverage. Those with no high school diploma were more likely to be without health insurance than any other educational group (Mills and Bhandari 2003).

Among all minority groups, Hispanic Americans are most likely not to have insurance. Nearly half (45 percent) of Hispanics under age 65 and two thirds (65 percent) of working-age Hispanics with low incomes were uninsured for all or part of 2000 (Commonwealth Fund 2003a). Hispanic American women, compared with White women, are three times more likely to lack health insurance (NWHIC 2002e). Most Hispanic women obtain health insurance through their employer; however, lower income or part-time workers are less likely to be offered health coverage through their employment (NWHIC 2002e). According to Michelle Doty (Commonwealth Fund 2003a), "lack of insurance, unstable coverage, language barriers, and low income all contribute to the growing health care crisis among Hispanics."

However, losing health insurance is also becoming a middle-class issue, according to Drew E. Altman, president of the Henry J. Kaiser Family Foundation, which tracks health coverage trends. In 2001, about 800,000 people had incomes in excess of $75,000 but no health insurance (Broder, Pear, and Freudenheim 2002). They either lost their jobs in high-wage industries or were employed but unable to afford health insurance premiums. Altman predicts that the number of uninsured will grow as long as health insurance premiums rise faster than earnings. Advocates for the uninsured are hopeful that policymakers will respond to a more effective lobbying coalition of high-wage workers, the unemployed, the poor, and minorities (Broder et al. 2002).

Illegal Immigrants

According to the U.S. Immigration and Naturalization Service (2001), 5 million undocumented immigrants lived in the United States in 1996. The number of

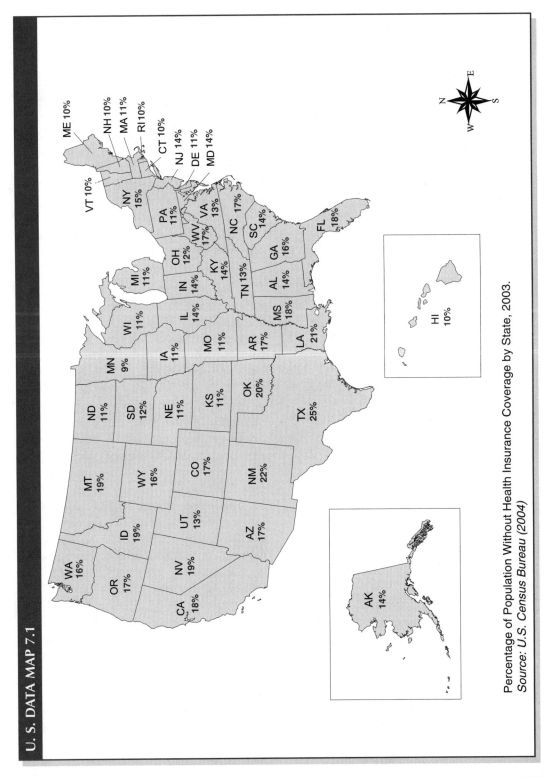

Percentage of Population Without Health Insurance Coverage by State, 2003.
Source: *U.S. Census Bureau (2004)*

❖ **FOCUS ON: HEALTH INSURANCE
AND HEALTH CARE DELIVERY SYSTEMS**

An estimated 62.6 percent of Americans receive health insurance from their employers (Mills and Bhandari 2003). This type of insurance is referred to as group insurance or as employment-based private insurance. Employers buy into a health insurance program, paying for part or all of the cost of the insurance premiums. A premium is a monthly fee to maintain your health coverage. Individual private insurance plans are also available, but only 9 percent of the U.S. population has this type of insurance coverage (Bodenheimer and Grumbach 2001).

Most college students are probably covered by their parents' insurance plan. That handy insurance card in your wallet identifies your insurance provider, the amount of your deductible (payment due at the time of service), and the amount of coverage for prescription drugs or emergency services. There are many different types of group insurance programs.

Fee for service plan. Under this plan, also known as an indemnity health plan, insurance companies pay fees for services provided to the people covered by the policy. This type of program emphasizes patient choice and immediate patient care.

Health maintenance organization (HMO). These organizations operate as prepaid health plans. For your premium, the HMO provides you and your family comprehensive care. This plan is also known as managed health care, a plan that controls costs by controlling access to care. You'll be assigned to a primary care provider who will provide most of your medical care, but if necessary, that doctor will refer you to specialists within the HMO practice or to providers contracted by the HMO. Under the plan, there is limited coverage for any treatment outside the HMO network.

Preferred provider organization (PPO). A PPO is a combination of the fee for service and HMO plan. With a PPO, you can manage your own health care needs by selecting your own doctors. These specialists will be on a preferred provider list supported by the PPO plan. If you use a provider outside of your plan, you may have to pay a larger percentage of your health care expenses.

In addition, two federal health plans are also available. Medicare is available to Americans 65 years or older or those with disabilities, while Medicaid pays for medical and long-term care for the poor; low-income children, pregnant women, and elderly; the medically needy; and people requiring institutional care. Both programs were enacted in 1965 under the Social Security Act and are currently administered by the Centers for Medicare and Medicaid Services (CMS) under the U.S. Department of Health and Human Services (DHHS).

undocumented immigrants is projected to grow 275,000 per year. Federal law requires hospitals to provide emergency care to critically ill or injured patients, regardless of their immigration status (Canedy 2002). But because illegal immigrants work in low-wage jobs or as day laborers with few or no medical benefits, they rely on emergency services as their primary source of routine and critical health care. Although counties and hospitals receive funds from the state and federal governments, the funding is not enough to cover the amount of unpaid medical services. It is estimated that U.S. hospitals are writing off as much as $2 billion a year in unpaid medical bills to treat illegal immigrants ineligible for Medicaid (Canedy 2002). The American Hospital Association reports that 24 of the southernmost counties from Texas to California amassed $832 million in unpaid medical care in 2000. Illegal immigrants accounted for a quarter of the expenses (Janofsky 2003).

Hardest hit have been medical facilities in states with a large population of undocumented immigrants, such as Florida, California, Arizona, and Texas (Canedy 2002). Hospitals in the Southwest report seeing more illegal immigrants each year (Janofsky 2003). In response, federal lawmakers introduced two bills in 2001. One bill, cosponsored by Senators Jon Kyle (R-Arizona), John McCain (R-Arizona), and Diane Feinstein (D-California), would have provided $200 million per year for four years to reimburse health care providers in border states. A second bill, the Border Hospital Survival and Illegal Immigrant Care Act, was introduced by Rep. Jim Kolbe (R-Arizona). The bill provided a $50 million reimbursement program for hospitals and ambulance services in Arizona. Both bills were stalled in committees (Canedy 2002).

The Rising Cost of Health Care

The United States spends about 14.1 percent of its gross domestic product (GDP) on health care—the largest expenditure in this category among industrialized countries. In 2002, total health care spending reached $1.6 trillion, with an average of $5,440 spent per person in health expenses (Sherman 2004). The rising cost of health care has been attributed to various factors: increases in the application of high technology for medical treatment and diagnosis, the aging population of the United States, the overall demand for health care, the amount of uncompensated care, and the cost of prescription drugs.

The fastest growing spending category in 2003 was prescription drugs (Sherman 2004), the cost of which rose more than 17 percent annually between 1998 and 2002 (Freudenheim 2002); in 2003, the cost increase declined to 15.3 percent (Sherman 2004). Increases in drug costs are expected to outstrip the overall growth in health care spending for the next 10 years. In all, consumers spent $154.5 billion for prescription drugs at pharmacies and $20.7 billion for mail-order drugs (Freudenheim 2002).

The cost of prescription drugs is a particular burden for elderly Americans. Because Medicare does not cover most prescription drugs, the elderly spent an average of $813 out of pocket on prescription drugs in 2000, $928 in 2001 and $1,051 in 2002 (Toner 2002). Our oldest Americans are the most vulnerable, with an estimated 45 percent of those 85 or older without any prescription drug coverage (Toner 2002). Federal agencies are able to negotiate discounts with pharmaceutical companies, but the government is prohibited from negotiating for Medicare recipients. It is estimated that uninsured Americans, including seniors without prescription drug coverage, pay an average of 72 percent more than the federal government pays for medications (Ishida 2003).

Costs are high not only for patients but also for their doctors. In recent years, doctors in Florida, Mississippi, Nevada, New Jersey, Ohio, and West Virginia have participated in strikes or walkouts to protest the rising cost of malpractice insurance premiums (Peterson 2002), which some say is a result of the increasing number of lawsuits and rising malpractice settlements. Throughout the country, physicians have reported 40 percent to 200 percent increases in their insurance payments. Premiums are highest for medical specialties such as internal medicine, general surgery, and obstetrics and gynecology (Oppel 2003). Some obstetricians in Miami, Florida, pay more than $200,000 per year for insurance, compared to the national average of $56,546 (Oppel 2003). During February 2003, about 70 percent of New Jersey's 22,000 physicians participated in coordinated walkouts. Doctors protested the way that excessive jury awards for patients' pain and suffering have led to the rising cost of insurance (Peterson 2002). Many explained that their colleagues are leaving New Jersey to practice in states with lower insurance premiums. In some states, doctors are retiring early or avoiding risky procedures to lower their premiums.

Health Care Policy, Advocacy, and Innovation

Health Care Reform

During his first administration, President Bill Clinton said problems connected with its health care system were the most pressing in the United States. In 1993, Clinton pushed for passage of the Health Security Act, an attempt at comprehensive health care reform. The Act would have required all employers to provide health insurance to their employees and gave small businesses and unemployed Americans subsidies to purchase insurance. After Clinton's health care plan was rejected, Americans looked to the private market to restrain health care costs and to enhance patient care and choice. U.S. medicine moved aggressively toward managed care arrangements, health maintenance organizations (HMOs), and for-profit health plans (Oberlander 2002).

According to Altman and Reinhardt (1996), although Americans in general are pleased with the quality of health care they receive, they are troubled by other aspects of health care. Americans are upset primarily about the cost of health care, both out-of-pocket costs and the cost of the health care system as a whole. Second, the structure of the health insurance system is viewed as having a number of shortcomings, foremost among them the lack of universal coverage. Finally, although the quality of health care is high, people believe it is not uniformly so.

The U.S. health care system is identified as a private health care system, but in reality, it is a mixed system of public and private insurance (Oberlander 2002). Since the failure of the Health Act of 1993, there have been no other proposals for universal health coverage. Instead, political attention has had a more limited scope and a slower pace (Begley et al. 2002), focused on improving the medical experiences of those already insured by regulating managed care and expanding existing programs (Oberlander 2002). Recent federal health care initiatives have included Medicare reform, the State Children's Health Insurance Program, and the Patient's Bill of Rights.

❖ TAKING A WORLD VIEW

HEALTH CARE IN CANADA

Imagine a world where you never see a doctor's bill, an insurance statement, or any other paperwork related to health care (Weitz 2001). That place exists: Canada. Canada has a publicly financed, privately delivered health care system known as Medicare. This national health insurance system provides all Canadians access to universal, comprehensive coverage for medically necessary hospital, inpatient, and outpatient care.

Although we tend to think of the Canadian insurance program as one program, there are actually 13 federally supported programs, each administered by one of its 10 provinces and three territories (Taylor 1990). The legislative foundation of Canada's national health insurance program comes from the 1957 Hospital Insurance Act and the 1966 Medical Care Insurance Act. In 1984, both Acts were consolidated into the Canada Health Act, which in addition outlawed extra billing by physicians and user fees by facilities and guaranteed a one-tier system of health insurance (Livingston 1998). Although the federal government is responsible for setting national standards of health care, each province or territory is responsible for the management and delivery of health care services and some aspects of prescription care and public health (Health Canada 2003). The federal government supports a province's health insurance program as long as it is universal (covering all citizens), comprehensive, accessible (with no limits on services), portable (each province must

recognize each other's coverage), and publicly administered (under the control of a public nonprofit organization) (Marmor and Mashaw 2001).

The insurance system is funded by a progressive federal tax: Those who earn more money pay a higher proportion of their income in taxes (Weitz 2001). In comparison to the United States, Canada spent less of its gross national product on health care, about $66 billion a year (Krauss 2003). The total budgets of hospitals and the level of physicians' fees are determined by annual negotiations between provinces and the health care providers (Marmor and Mashaw 2001). Budgets are adjusted each year, accounting for inflation, new programs, and changes in service volumes (Marmor and Mashaw 2001). The majority of Canadian physicians are paid according to a fee-for-service plan (Taylor 1990).

Administrative costs are much lower in Canada than in the United States. Because doctors and hospitals receive their payments from one source, they do not have to keep track of multiple insurance plans or file for insurance reimbursement (Marmor and Mashaw 2001). This benefit is also passed on to patients: Canadians do not have to file claim forms or pay out of pocket for uncovered expenses. In addition, Canadian doctors have lower malpractice insurance costs. The Canadian Medical Association formed the nonprofit Canadian Protective Association in 1912. All member physicians were first charged a flat fee for malpractice insurance; currently, there are six fee categories organized according to medical specialty (Taylor 1990).

According to Clifford Krauss (2003), growing complaints about health care services have begun to erode public confidence in Canada's health care system. Although Canadians continue to support their health system, many worry about its effectiveness, particularly its service delivery. Krauss cites many Canadian studies that indicate that the health system is overworked and understaffed and that patients wait impatiently for their health services. A recent Canadian government study reported 4.3 million Canadian adults or 18 percent of those who saw a doctor in 2001 had difficulty in seeing a doctor or getting a test completed in a timely fashion (Krauss 2003).

A report prepared by the Frasier Institute revealed that in 2000–2001, patients experienced an average waiting time of 16.5 weeks between receiving a general practitioner's referral and undergoing treatment, about 77 percent longer than in 1983. Wait times for MRIs, CT, and ultrasound scans have grown by 40 percent since 1984 (Krauss 2003). Esmail and Walter (2002), both from the Frasier Institute, concluded that:

> It [the Canadian health care model] produces inferior access to physicians and technology, produces longer waiting times, is less successful in preventing deaths from preventable causes, and costs more than any of the other systems that have comparable objectives. . . . The overwhelming evidence is that Canada has a comparatively underperforming system of health care delivery. (P. 6)

❖ FOCUS ON: UNFOUNDED FEARS—AIDS AND SARS

In March 2003, the World Health Organization (WHO) declared severe acute respiratory syndrome or SARS as the "new global health threat." SARS is a viral respiratory disease spread by close person-to-person contact. Patient symptoms begin with a high fever and chills, developing into a dry cough. Most patients develop pneumonia. The origin of the 2003 SARS outbreak was traced to Hong Kong and Vietnam, and from there the disease was carried throughout Southeast Asia, and then on to Europe, Canada, and the United States. According to the WHO, 8,098 people worldwide became sick with SARS and 774 died during 2003. In the United States, only eight cases were identified, and no one died from the disease. All U.S. cases were probably infected when they traveled to other countries (Centers for Disease Control 2004a). Outside of Asia, Canada was the country hardest hit by SARS. As of August 2003, there were 438 SARS cases in Canada, including 44 deaths (National Advisory Committee on SARS and Public Health 2003). Public health officials reacted quickly to this new threat, owing much to the lessons learned from the AIDS crisis 20 years earlier (Altman 2003).

AIDS or acquired immune deficiency syndrome was first reported in the United States in 1981. AIDS is caused by a virus called human immunodeficiency virus or HIV. Infection with HIV has been the only common factor shared by people with AIDS, including homosexual men, transfusion patients, hemophiliacs, sex partners of or children born to infected people, and health care workers infected with HIV while on the job. As of February 2004, more than 886,000 AIDS cases had been reported, along with 501,669 deaths in the United States. HIV is transmitted by the exchange of bodily fluids, especially during sexual contact, blood transfusion, pregnancy, birth, or breastfeeding. The AIDS epidemic is growing most rapidly among minority populations and is the leading killer of African American males ages 25 to 44 (Centers for Disease Control 2004b; National Institutes of Health 2003).

The first AIDS cases led to confusion about how the disease was transmitted. People believed that HIV could be spread by shaking hands, kissing, sharing food and water, using a toilet seat, or merely touching the phone. HIV/AIDS patients were routinely victimized, the subjects of discrimination and hate. Parents refused to allow their children to be in classes with students infected with HIV/AIDS. Health care workers and public health officials were unsure how to care for HIV/AIDS patients and protect themselves from infection. In the early days of AIDS, some hospital workers refused to enter the rooms of AIDS patients and even refused to deliver food to patients (Altman 2003). However, research and public health education significantly improved our understanding of HIV/AIDS and its transmission.

The established international network of AIDS doctors and scientists is credited with the swift epidemiological response necessary to understand how the new SARS virus worked. Learning from AIDS, the WHO reversed normal practice and quickly shared with the public scientific

information about SARS before it was sent to medical journals. Informing the public was considered an important public health strategy because poor communication was blamed for the irrational public behavior in the early days of AIDS. The WHO issued news releases and travel advisories for the first time in its 55-year history. The WHO was openly critical of Chinese authorities who attempted to keep their SARS cases secret (Altman 2003).

Despite the WHO's educational efforts, people still responded with unfounded fears (Altman 2003). Because the disease was linked to the Asian community, Asian women, men, and children were targeted for discrimination. In Toronto, Canada, there were reports of Asian Canadians being shunned in subways and streetcars, of real estate agents being told to not show houses to Asian clients, of public bus drivers using face masks on routes near Chinese communities, and of patrons avoiding Asian restaurants and markets. In fact, SARS in Canada was traced to a woman who died after traveling to Hong Kong. She infected her family, and they infected health care workers and other patients at a local hospital. As a result, public health officials suggested healthy people should avoid hospitals rather than Chinese restaurants (Schram 2003). The public perceived that SARS was contained to one group of people, identified by ethnicity, but the truth was/is that "pathogens know no race or creed" (Kinsella 2003).

As of December 2003, there have been no new confirmed cases of SARS in the United States and Canada. However, several new cases of SARS were confirmed in China in 2004.

Medicare Reform

The nation's largest health insurance program, Medicare, covers about 40 million elderly or disabled Americans (Centers for Medicare and Medicaid Services 2003). Medicare has two parts: Part A Hospital Insurance helps pay for care received as an inpatient in critical access hospitals or skilled nursing facilities, as well as some home health care; Part B Physician and Outpatient Coverage pays for medically necessary services and supplies that are not covered under Part A. Each part is financed under a different structure. Part A is offered as an automatic premium because most recipients (and/or their spouses) paid Medicare taxes while they were working. Part A is financed through a payroll tax paid equally by employers and workers. Three fourths of the financing for Medicare Plan B is received from general tax revenues, while the remaining quarter is financed through premiums: $58.70 per month for 2003 with a projected increase to $66 per month for 2004 (Pear 2003), paid directly by elderly patients (Centers for Medicare and Medicaid Services 2003). In 2004, it was announced that 2005 Medicare premiums would increase to $78.20 per month. In response to the 17 percent increase, the largest dollar increase in the program's history, Robert M. Hayes, president of the Medicare Rights Center of New York said, "Older Americans already are staggering under the relentless increases in the cost of prescription drugs. More older Americans will face harsh choices in meeting basic human needs—health, food and housing" (American Association of Retired Persons [AARP] 2004).

Since its inception, there has been concern that Medicare spending, especially for Part A, will outpace its revenue sources (Moon 1999). Medicare has been referred to as a "pay as you go" system; every payroll tax dollar that is contributed into the fund is immediately spent by those currently enrolled (Goodman 1998). Due to increases in health care costs, it is estimated that per capita expenditures for Medicare will increase from $5,943 in 1998 to $10,235 in 2025 (Moon 1999). Out-of-pocket expenses are also expected to increase, from $2,508 per beneficiary in 1998 to $4,855 in 2025. One additional projection casts more doubt on the stability of the system. The number of elderly beneficiaries is expected to continually increase. By 2025, the number of eligible elderly is projected to reach 69.3 million, about 20.6 percent of the U.S. population (Moon 1999).

Political rhetoric continues to swirl around how to preserve the system while trying to expand its services to an ever-increasing population of elderly. In 2003, the U.S. Congress passed the Medicare Reform Law, which included a prescription drug benefit for the first time in the program's history. The bill provides for a prescription drug benefit to older and disabled Americans, offered and managed by private insurers and health plans under contract with the federal government. Critics attacked the plan for its coverage gap, arguing that the bill failed to provide seniors with substantial relief for the cost of prescription drugs. The plan will cost about $420 per year and, once covered under the plan, seniors will have to pay a $250 deductible before the coverage begins. Medicare will pay 75 percent of annual drug costs between $251 and $2,250, but coverage then stops until the senior's annual drug cost reaches $5,100. Once at that point, the plan will cover 95 percent of all additional costs; but by then, seniors would have paid about $3,600 of their own money. Seniors with low incomes will qualify for extra assistance under the bill. Until the plan is implemented in 2006, seniors will have to pay up to $30 annually for a private drug discount card. It is estimated that the cost of the bill will be $534 billion over 10 years. Analysts predict that the reform bill will have little effect on slowing down the increasing costs of prescription drugs and medical services for the elderly.

State Children's Health Insurance Program

The State Children's Health Insurance Program (SCHIP) was adopted in 1997 as an amendment to the Social Security Act, Title XXI. The program is administered under the Centers for Medicare and Medicaid Services (CMS). SCHIP enables states to implement their own children's health insurance programs for uninsured low-income children 18 years old or younger. It targets the children of working parents or grandparents. For example, a family of four that earns up to $34,100 a year is eligible. The insurance plan would pay for regular checkups, immunizations, prescription medicines, and hospitalizations. SCHIP uses comprehensive outreach materials and educational programs to recruit eligible children and their families, especially through elementary and secondary schools. In many states, as SCHIP enrollments began, so did Medicaid enrollments. The State of Louisiana calls its program LACHIP, Louisiana Children's Health Insurance Program. As of August 2002, 75,749 Louisiana children had enrolled in LACHIP. At the same time, 153,872 children were added to the state's Medicaid program. Almost a quarter of a million more Louisiana children now have health insurance coverage.

Patient Bill of Rights

A patient protection law or patient bill of rights expands protections for patients and health care providers and is often enacted in response to the problems associated with managed care. Several states—Alaska, Arizona, Florida, Kentucky, Maine, New Hampshire, and Washington—have recently enacted comprehensive patient rights bills, and several hospitals, medical facilities, and organizations—for example, the American Hospital Association, Johns Hopkins Breast Center (Maryland), and Jersey Shore Medical Center (New Jersey)—have adopted their own statements. Typically, a patient bill of rights declares patients' rights and responsibilities, such as "receive the best care and treatment possible," "refuse treatment and be told what effect this may have on your health," or "receive an itemized bill and explanation of all charges."

In 2001, the U.S. House of Representatives and Senate passed separate versions of patient protection legislation, but a final compromise bill was stalled in negotiations between the Senate and the White House, which supported the House bill. Both House and Senate bills featured access to emergency care, specialists, pediatric care, continuity of care, and access to obstetrician/gynecologists. But the debate continues around the ability of HMO enrollees to file legal action against their health plans and health care providers. The Senate bill would have allowed patients to sue HMOs in state courts, limiting awarded damages in federal courts to $5 million but allowing state courts to make larger awards if allowed by the state's laws. The House bill would have allowed patients to sue health plans in state courts for noneconomic damages up to $1.5 million.

Health care reform did not die with the defeat of the Health Care Act. Pick up any newspaper or listen to the evening news and you'll hear stories about HMOs, insurance reform, prescription drugs, or quality care (how many news stories have you recently heard about medical mistakes, such as surgeons leaving instruments in their patients?). It appears that although Americans wanted health care reform, they didn't want more government regulation or to sacrifice quality of care or their access to it; instead, they simply wanted the bad parts of the current health system to work better (Altman and Reinhardt 1996). In the following section, we'll review state and community efforts to improve our health system.

State Health Care Reforms

As the federal government has failed to reach a compromise on comprehensive health coverage, the burden of health care reform falls to the states (Beatrice 1999). Several states have aggressively moved forward on health reform. Dennis Beatrice (1999) identifies six states—Florida, Hawaii, Massachusetts, Minnesota, Oregon, and Washington—committed to providing health coverage for all of their citizens. Summaries of two state plans are presented below.

Hawaii was one of the first states to act on health care reform. In 1974, the state passed the Hawaii Prepaid Health Care Act, requiring employers to provide health insurance for all employees working more than 20 hours per week and to pay at least 50 percent of the cost. Hawaii is the only state that requires employer payments to medical insurance under a congressional exemption of the Employee Retirement and Income Security Act (ERISA). ERISA bars states from requiring all employers to offer health insurance, from regulating or taxing self-insured plans, and from mandating the specific benefits to be covered by employer health plans (Beatrice 1999). Hawaii's plan also limits employees' share of the insurance premium expenses to no more than 1.5 percent of their income. Recently, there has been a call to repeal or at least revise the Prepaid Health Care Act due to increasing health care costs.

The MinnesotaCare Act became law in Minnesota in 1992. Also known as the HealthRight Act, the legislation included a variety of laws aimed at reducing costs and expanding access to health care for the uninsured (Beatrice 1999). MinnesotaCare is funded through a tax on health care providers and through enrollee premiums (based on family size, number of people covered, and income) (Sacks, Kutyla, and Silow-Carroll 2002). The Act set price controls for health care spending (repealed in 1997), set statewide managed care guidelines, initially mandated that all non-HMO physicians follow a state fee structure (repealed in 1995), placed all HMOs under the regulation of the Commission of Health, and mandated that HMOs be nonprofit (Citizens Council on Health Care 2003). The Act also subsidized health insurance to low- and middle-income uninsured families and individuals. Minnesota expanded Medicaid eligibility to 275 percent of the federal poverty guidelines (e.g., a family of four with $45,000 income would be eligible) and placed all MinnesotaCare recipients into HMOs (Beatrice 1999; Citizens Council on Health Care 2003). A small number of Minnesotans, about 5.4 percent, are uninsured (Sacks et al. 2002).

Does your state have a comprehensive health care policy? If the information is available, trace the history of the policy from legislation to implementation. What benefits and/or problems exist within the system? If your state does not have a comprehensive health policy, what roadblocks exist to adopting such a policy?

Prescription Drugs

In an effort to control drug costs for their residents, several states have offered innovative cost-control models. Pennsylvania is second to Florida in the proportion of its population that is 65 years or older (Pear 2002). About 12 percent of its elderly or 225,000 people are enrolled in Pharmaceutical Assistance Contract for the Elderly (PACE). Men and women 65 years or older can enroll in the program if they have annual incomes less than $14,000 for an individual or $17,200 per couple. The program costs patients a $6 copayment per filled prescription and is financed largely from state lottery proceeds. The program requires the use of low-cost generic drugs, which account for about 45 percent of all filled prescriptions. PACE was established in 1984 with strong bipartisan support, but with the rising cost of drugs and the increasing number of patients, lawmakers are looking for more cost-cutting strategies (Pear 2002).

In 2003, Pennsylvania joined with eight other states and the District of Columbia to form a nonprofit consortium to buy drugs in bulk, passing on their savings to their citizens (Freudenheim 2003). The consortium will include a drug benefit manager who will help states maximize their drug benefits by receiving full price discounts and rebates, determining the most cost-effective and appropriate drugs, and including coverage for mail order prescriptions and for importing drugs from Canada. The program is supported by the Heinz Family Philanthropies, a charitable organization (Freudenheim 2003).

In 2003, the city of Boston, Massachusetts, and the state of New Hampshire announced that they would begin buying prescription drugs from Canada. They aren't the first to defy U.S. laws, which forbid the reimportation of Canadian drugs unless their safety is certified by the U.S. Health and Human Services Department. Springfield, Massachusetts, was the first city to import Canadian drugs for city employees, beginning in March 2003. Boston plans to do the same for its city employees and retirees, estimating a savings of about $1 million annually. For example, 90 pills of Lipitor, a popular cholesterol drug, cost $183.97 in the United States, but the Canadian price is $136.70, a savings of $47.27 per prescription. New Hampshire will purchase the prescription drugs for prison inmates and Medicaid recipients, saving money on 9 of 10 drugs most commonly prescribed for inmates (Testa 2003).

Serving Patients at Risk—Preventative Health and Treatment for Minorities

Whether they are insured, minority Americans are more likely than Whites to be disconnected from the health care system and a regular doctor (Commonwealth Fund

VISUAL ESSAY: OVERCOMING HEALTH RISKS AMONG THE NEEDY ❖

Ethnic and racial minorities, the poor, the mentally ill, and the disabled tend to fall through the cracks of the health care system for a variety of reasons. Many of them have multiple intractable problems due to long-term poverty, poor health practices, and substance abuse. Such problems are compounded when health insurance and affordable health care are not readily available.

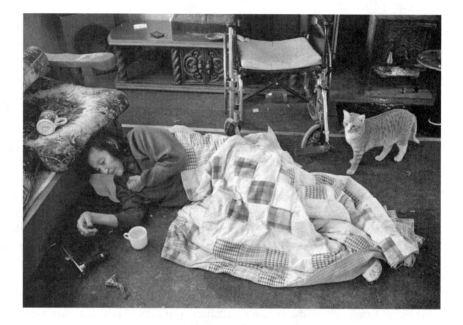

New systems of health care are now being designed to serve at-risk populations more effectively. Day care, respite care, mobile health facilities, and in-home health care help bring medical attention to those who need it most.

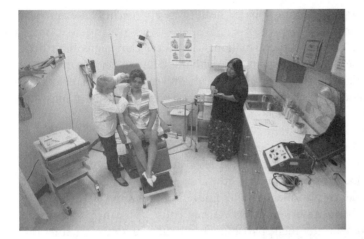

For example, community-based health clinics are being established in areas where the underserved live. In this photo, a Native American woman is being seen at a clinic based on the Viejas reservation in California.

Home-health-care workers provide both medical attention and invaluable social interaction for patients. Home health care is particularly beneficial for the elderly.

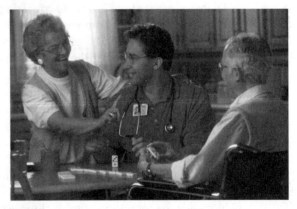

Health practitioners are also focusing on preventative care. In this photo, Wayne and his mother talk to a nutrition specialist about good eating habits.

In an era of increasing medical costs, how can we ensure that at-risk populations are able to access the health care system? Whose responsibility is it to provide health care to those who cannot afford it?

2003b). In response, unique community-based health care approaches have emerged to serve African Americans.

In the fight against diabetes, several national and local campaigns have been initiated. In fall 2002, the U.S. Department of Health and Human Services launched its first diabetes campaign, Small Steps, Big Rewards Prevent Type 2 Diabetes. The program encourages modest lifestyle changes—daily exercise (about 30 minutes of physical activity) and a healthier diet—to prevent the onset of Type 2 diabetes (National Diabetes Education Program 2003). The campaign targets its message to Hispanics and African Americans, who are at higher risk of the disease than Whites. National campaigns such as this one combine television and print public-service announcements with local promotion and educational materials for health care providers and local residents (National Diabetes Education Program 2003).

The American Diabetes Association (ADA) has enlisted the help of African American churches to educate their parishioners about the disease (American Diabetes Association 2003). Recognizing the importance of the African American church as a source of community support and vehicle for communication, "Diabetes Sunday" began in 1996. Diabetes Sunday is often held during Black History Month. Church pastors discuss diabetes and distribute education materials. Certified diabetes educators are on hand to answer questions after service.

The Project Brotherhood Black Men's Clinic, located on Chicago's South Side, was created to address the disproportionate disease burden and shorter life expectancy for Black men (Tanner 2003). Eric Whitaker, cofounder of the clinic, explained that many men avoid traditional health care providers because they never find doctors who look and talk like them. Focus groups indicated that Black men need a reason other than their health to go to the clinic, so program administrators latched on to a cornerstone of Black cultural life: the barbershop. Project Brotherhood opened a barbershop alongside the community health clinic, where men are able to get free haircuts and listen to informal presentations by the clinic staff on HIV, heart disease, and cancer. In addition, the clinic offers job search and resume writing information and parenting classes. As Whitaker describes it, "It's a place where information is exchanged, it's a place of familiarity. . . . We just transported that idea to the clinic setting" (Tanner 2003:A12). He explains, "We want to learn how to listen to our community and discover its own perception of needs and assets" (Phalen 2000).

Two additional community-based programs are featured in the following Voices of Change sections.

Voices in the Community:
Nina Agbayani

With funding from the Centers for Disease Control and Prevention, the BALANCE program for diabetes (Building Awareness Locally and Nationally through Community Empowerment) serves Asian Americans and Pacific Islanders (AAPIs) living with Type 2 diabetes and those at risk for diabetes and their families. While improving AAPI education, diagnosis, and treatment are part of the program, its ultimate goal is prevention of the disease, according to Nina Agbayani, director of programs for the Association of Asian Pacific Community Health Organizations. She explains, "The program was created because diabetes is a significant problem among Asians and Asian Pacific Islanders. AAPIs are at greater risk for diabetes than the non-Hispanic Whites possibly due to genetics and socioeconomic factors." Because there are limited data on AAPIs and diabetes, the BALANCE program also supports the development of comprehensive diabetes research to identify the "true burden" of diabetes among AAPIs.

A key feature of the BALANCE program is to "define and promote excellence in diabetes care and prevention that is community directed and respectful of the individual's cultural practices, languages and beliefs in order to eliminate health disparities and improve the quality of life for AAPIs," says Agbayani. Because mainstream providers and educational materials do not integrate cultural practices and beliefs in their diabetes care, the program targets AAPIs who live in areas where these cultural understandings may not exist. For example, mainstream nutritional guidelines do not consider ethnic foods.

Six project sites are located in California, Hawaii, Massachusetts, and New York. Each program site works to tailor culturally and linguistically sensitive information for its community, serving about 200 patients each year. In their Honolulu, Hawaii, site, the Kalihi-Palama Health Center, diabetes education classes are provided for the local Filipino community in two native Filipino languages, Ilocano and Tagalog. Media campaigns are also conducted to further emphasize the seriousness of diabetes among the AAPI population. The program translated an informational brochure in five languages: Korean, Chinese, Vietnamese, Samoan, and Tagalog.

In addition to reaching out to the AAPI community, BALANCE also serves as an educator and adviser to health care providers and policymakers, Agbayani explains. BALANCE has provided feedback on certain diabetes bills to ensure the inclusion of AAPI information. Also, BALANCE conducted a multilingual and technical review of existing diabetes educational materials, cataloging all available AAPI material. The program continues to translate more materials for the AAPI community. According to Agbayani, BALANCE hopes to extend its message to AAPI youth.

For more information about the BALANCE program and the Association of Asian Pacific Community Health Organizations, log on to *Study Site Chapter 7.*

Voices in the Community:
Dr. Ed Hendrikson

The U.S. Environmental Protection Agency's (2003) Web site provides this profile of a man who provides crucial services.

One man who has made it a lifelong goal to provide migrant workers with basic health care services as a physician assistant and a PhD in environmental health is Ed Hendrikson. Ed is a circuit rider for and director of the Salud Medical Clinic, a nonprofit organization that focuses on providing health care in rural areas of Colorado. Ed has been delivering health care for 15 years by visiting migrant camps throughout Colorado in a converted RV during the growing and harvesting seasons.

While on these visits, Dr. Hendrikson provides basic check ups and does everything from dispensing cold and flu medicine to taking blood samples for white blood cell counts. The problems he treats range from back pains, upset stomachs, fatigue and dehydration, to diabetes, high blood pressure, and exposure to pesticides. He estimates that the mobile clinic will treat about 1,200 patients over the five-month period that makes up the harvest season. Dr. Hendrikson also takes drinking water samples to determine if the water sources that the camps are using are safe. If not, which is often the case, he advises the residents to either boil their water, or in some cases not to drink the water at all. More long-term solutions include drilling deeper wells or finding alternate sources.

The work of the Salud Mobile Clinic staff includes traveling over rough terrain, working long nights, and going to far off locations. But for Ed, getting medical services to the workers isn't the hardest part. What is even more difficult is getting the workers to take advantage of his service. The mobile service is free to the migrants, as funding comes from grants that Dr. Hendrikson secures and from government programs. Nevertheless, out of a camp of 100 or more, Ed and his colleagues may only see a fraction of those needing the medical attention on any given evening. Many fear that they will jeopardize their jobs, while others simply don't have the time or motivation. . . .

While the number of people that Ed and the mobile clinic reach each year is impressive, providing health care is what concerns him most. When asked why he continues to spend long days and evenings year after year doing this work, he explains, "They're the working poor, people who work long, hard days. You feel good just helping them a little, and they are often so appreciative." Ed is quick to add that there are other rewards also. "These folks are interesting people, and I greatly enjoy their company," he says. "I get a lot more from the time I spend with them than they get from my services."

❖ PUTTING IT TOGETHER: Investigate community-based health programs in your city. What programs are available for at-risk groups in your community? For children? For ethnic minorities? For the homeless? For migrant workers?

Community Health Care Management Systems

One approach to reforming health care services is to restructure medical systems. A new approach is called the **community health care management system.** The system's goal is to "maintain and enhance the health of individuals, groups, and the community at large" (Shortell et al. 2000:263) by intentionally linking the medical care and primary health care systems. The medical care system is a response system, treating individuals with illness or disease, whereas the primary health care system uses preventative and health maintenance approaches. The community health care management system links medical care and health care delivery with community health-building assets (e.g., educational, family, religious, employment, and business sectors). The success of the system depends on its ability to integrate providers within and across the medical, health, and community sectors. According to the program, health services should be based on the needs of the community.

Beginning in 1997, the American Hospital Association/Health Research and Educational Trust Community Care Network (CCN) demonstration program funded

25 programs with a community health focus, a seamless continuum of care managing limited resources and remaining accountable to the community (Shortell et al. 2000). The program was created in the late 1980s and early 1990s to address "real world problems" facing hospitals and health care providers (National Community Care Network 2003). The net result of these demonstration programs was an increased capacity to deal with complex health problems within the community, while creating an organizational capacity to adapt to change.

The Northwest Georgia Healthcare Partnership is one CCN site. Serving the city of Dalton, Georgia, and surrounding Whitfield and Murray counties, the partnership was formed by the Hamilton Health Care System and Murray Medical Center in 1992. The partnership identifies several community initiatives targeting families, children, youth, and workers. For example, Growing Healthy, an educational health curriculum for kindergarten through sixth grade, is implemented in all elementary schools in Murray and Whitfield counties. While expanding students' health knowledge, the program encourages healthy attitudes and behaviors. The Working Well program empowers employees to take charge of their health through wellness prevention screenings and healthy lifestyle interventions. The program currently serves six local employers with 3,000 employees. The partnership is expanding its initiatives to serve the area's elderly and indigent populations and to discuss the future of health care and its financing for their community (National Community Care Network 2003).

In Baltimore, Maryland, the Vision for Health Consortium (VFH) serves a community of 10,300 residents in Sandtown-Winchester. VFH is part of a comprehensive neighborhood transformation program, targeting the economically disadvantaged residents. Children's health care has been expanded through school-based efforts. VFH programs provide primary care, referral services, and dental prevention and mental health services. The consortium reports 100 percent compliance for its student immunization program. The consortium also provides outreach programs for adults and substance abusers. In June 2000, VFH, along with the Baltimore City Health Department, opened the nation's first full-time health center for uninsured adult men, the Men's Health Center. At its opening, VFH estimated that 55,000 of its male residents had no health insurance. Since its opening, an average of 30 patients per day are seen; 40 percent of the patients are employed (Matthews 2003). The center's motto is "Building Healthy Families . . . One Man at a Time" (National Community Care Network 2003).

MAIN POINTS

- While medicine can identify the biological pathways to disease, we need a sociological perspective to address the social determinants of health. Research continues to demonstrate the relationship between the individual and society and the structural effects on health: how our health is affected by our social position, work, families, education, and wealth and poverty.

- **Epidemiology** is the study of the patterns in the distribution and frequency of sickness, injury, and death and the social factors that shape them. Epidemiologists focus on communities and populations, addressing how health and illness experiences are based on social factors such as gender, age, race, social class, or behavior.

- According to the functionalist perspective, illness has a legitimate place in society.

- Conflict theorists believe that patterns of health and illness are not accidental or due solely to individuals' actions. They identify how these patterns reflect systematic inequalities based on ethnicity/race or gender and differences in power, values, and interests.

- Although the medicalization of conditions like premenstrual syndrome or menopause may have been effective in treating women, various feminist theorists see this trend as an extension of medicine's control over women.

- From an interactionist's perspective, health, illness, and medical responses are socially constructed and maintained.

- Women live longer than men, but women experience higher rates of nonfatal chronic conditions. Men experience higher rates of fatal illness. These differences in mortality have been attributed to three factors: genetics, risk taking, and health care.

- Data consistently support the notion that those with higher education, income, or occupational prestige have lower rates of morbidity and mortality. No factor has been singled out as the primary link between socioeconomic position and health; however, scholars have offered many factors—standard of living, work conditions, housing conditions, and the social and psychological connections with others at work, home, or the community—to explain the relationship.

- Another problem with health is access to health care and insurance; many groups do not have insurance or access to it, and now the middle class is also experiencing problems in retaining health insurance. Illegal immigrants also do not have insurance and often use the emergency room as their place of primary care.

- The United States spends about 14.1 percent of its gross domestic product (GDP) on health care—the largest expenditure in this category among industrialized countries. The rising cost of health care has been attributed to various factors: increases in the application of high technology for medical treatment and diagnosis, the aging population of the United States, the overall demand for health care, the amount of uncompensated care, and the cost of prescription drugs (the fastest-growing spending category and a particular problem for the elderly).

- Health care reform has been a topic of debate in Congress and the White House for several years. Recent federal health care initiatives include Medicare reform, the State Children's Health Insurance Program, and the Patient's Bill of Rights. But as health care continues to be debated at the federal level, some states are taking action to make reforms. Communities and organizations are also becoming involved.

INTERNET AND COMMUNITY EXERCISES

1. Based on the American Medical Association's Web site, review the organization's mission statement, history, and legislative initiatives. Log on to *Study Site Chapter 7*. Is there evidence to demonstrate how the AMA maintains its power and influence on the medical profession?

2. Select a specific disease or illness that you believe affects college-age men and women. Identify several Internet Web sites and support groups related to the disease or illness. How is the disease defined? Are there objective and subjective aspects of the disease? Does it vary by gender? by ethnicity/race?

3. Select one local hospital or health care system in your area or state. Through the Internet (or by visiting a neighborhood location), identify the organization's mission statement, its patient bill of rights, and community-based programs. How does this

organization define *care*? Does its definition appear to be consistent with the community's population and needs? Why or why not?

4. Children, the poor, and the elderly are three of the most vulnerable populations lacking access to health care and to insurance coverage. Investigate local programs targeting one of these groups. Does your college/university support any of these programs? If yes, identify how. If not, what efforts could be made to link your college/university to at least one of these programs?

5. The United Nations' Human Development Report tracks several health indicators: life expectancy at birth, infant mortality rates, and health expenditure per capita. Log on to *Study Site Chapter 7* for the UN link and compare the United States with Canada, Germany, Mexico, Sweden, and the United Kingdom.

On your own. Log on to *Study Site—Community and Policy Guide* for more information about the social problems, social policies, and community responses discussed in this chapter.

References

Altman, L. 2003. "Lesson of AIDS, Applied to SARS." *The New York Times* May 6, pp. D1, D4.

Altman, S. and U. Reinhardt. 1996. "Where Does Health Care Reform Go From Here? An Unchartered Odyssey." Pp. xxi–xxxii in *Strategic Choices for a Changing Health Care System,* edited by S. Altman and U. Reinhardt. Chicago: Health Administration Press.

American Association of Retired Persons (AARP). 2004. "Medicare Premiums to Increase." Retrieved September 12, 2004 (http://www.aarp.org/bulletin/news/Articles/article.html?SMContentIndex=2&SMContentSet=0).

American Diabetes Association. 2003. "Type 2 Diabetes." Retrieved January 5, 2003 (http://www.diabetes.org/main/application/).

American Medical Association. 2003. "AMA's 2003 Federal Legislative Agenda." Retrieved January 5, 2003 (http://www.ama-assn.org/ama/pub/category/7334.html).

Anderson, R. 2002. "Deaths: Leading Causes for 2000." *National Vital Statistics Reports* 50(16), September 16.

Beatrice, D. 1996. "States and Health Care Reform: The Importance of Program Implementation." Pp. 183–206 in *Strategic Choices for a Changing Health Care System,* edited by S. Altman and U. Reinhardt. Chicago: Health Administration Press.

Begley, C. E., L. A. Aday, D. R. Lairson, and C. H. Slater. 2002. "Expanding the Scope of Health Reform: Application in the United States." *Social Science & Medicine* 55(7):1213–1229.

Bodenheimer, Thomas and Kevin Grumbach. 2001. *Understanding Health Policy* New York: McGraw-Hill/Appleton & Lange.

Brecht, B. 1976. "A Worker's Speech to a Doctor (c. 1938)." Pp. 292–293 in *Poems 1913–1965,* edited by J. Willet and R. Manheim. New York: Methuen.

Broder, J., R. Pear, and M. Freudenheim. 2002. "Problem of Lost Health Benefits Is Reaching into the Middle Class." *The New York Times,* November 25, pp. A1, A17.

Brumberg, J. J. 1988. *Fasting Girls.* Cambridge, MA: Harvard University Press.

Canedy, D. 2002. "Hospitals Feeling Strain from Illegal Immigrants." *The New York Times,* August 25, p. 12.

Centers for Disease Control. 2003. "Diabetes Fact Sheet." Retrieved January 5, 2003 (http://www.cdc.gov/diabetes/pubs/estimates.htm#incidence).

Centers for Disease Control. 2004a. "Basic Information about SARS." Retrieved February 8, 2004 (www.cdc.gov/ncidod/sars/factsheet.htm).

——— . 2004b. "Basic Statistics." Retrieved February 8, 2004 (www.cdc.gov/hiv/stats.htm).

Centers for Medicare and Medicaid Services. 2003. "Medicare Eligibility, Enrollment, and Premiums: Overview." Retrieved March 16, 2003 (www.medicare.gov/Basics/Overview).

Citizens Council on Health Care. 2003. "Summary of Minnesota's 1992 Health Care Reform Law." Retrieved March 11, 2003 (www.cchconline.org/privacy/mncaresumm.php3).

Cockerman, W. and M. Glasser. 2001. "Epidemiology." Pp. 1–2 in *Readings in Medical Sociology,* edited by W. Cockerman and M. Glasser. Upper Saddle River, NJ: Prentice Hall.

Collins, K. S., D. L. Hughes, M. M. Doty, B. L. Ives, J. N. Edwards, and K. Tenney. 2002. *Diverse Communities, Common Concerns: Assessing Health Care Quality for Minority Americans: Findings from the Commonwealth Fund 2001 Health Care Quality Survey.* New York: The Commonwealth Fund.

Commonwealth Fund. 2003a. "Hispanics Face High Rates of Unstable Health Care Coverage, Low Rates of Preventative Care." Retrieved September 12, 2004 (www.cmwf.org/newsroom/newsroom_show.htm?doc_id=223566).

———. 2003b. "Minority Americans Lag Behind Whites on Nearly Every Measure of Health Care Quality." Retrieved July 20, 2004 (http://www.cmwf.org/media/releases/collins523_release03062002.asp).

Conrad, P. 2001a. "General Introduction." Pp. 1–6 in *The Sociology of Health and Illness: Critical Perspectives,* edited by P. Conrad. New York: Worth.

——— . 2001b. "The Social and Cultural Meanings of Illness." Pp. 91–93 in *The Sociology of Health and Illness: Critical Perspectives,* edited by P. Conrad. New York: Worth.

Conrad, P. and V. Leiter. 2003. "Introduction." Pp. 1–6 in *Health and Health Care as Social Problems,* edited by P. Conrad and V. Leiter. Landham, MD: Rowan & Littlefield.

DeNavas-Walt, Carmen, Bernadette Proctor, and Robert Mills. 2004. *Income, Poverty, and Health Insurance Coverage in the United States: 2003* (Current Population Reports, P60–226). Washington, DC: U.S. Census Bureau.

Esmail, N. and M. Walter. 2002. "Executive Summary." *Fraiser Forum,* August, pp. 3–6.

Families USA. 2003. *Going Without Health Insurance: Nearly One in Three Non-Elderly Americans.* Washington, DC: Robert Wood Johnson Foundation.

Federal Interagency Forum on Child and Family Statistics. 2002. *America's Children 2002.* Washington, DC: Government Printing Office.

Freudenheim, M. 2002. "Drug Spending Rises Sharply at Pharmacies and by Mail." *The New York Times,* March 29, p. A18.

——— . 2003. "States Organizing a Nonprofit Group to Cut Drug Costs." *The New York Times,* January 14, pp. A1, A20.

Goffman, E. 1961. *Asylums: Essays on the Social Situation of Mental Health.* New York: Pantheon.

Goodman, J. C. 1998. "Why Your Grandchildren May Pay a 55 Percent Payroll Tax." *Wall Street Journal,* October 7, p. A22.

Hamilton, J. A. 1994. "Feminist Theory and Health Psychology: Tools for an Egalitarian, Women-Centered Approach to Women's Health." Pp. 56–66 in *Reframing Women's Health: Multidisciplinary Research and Practice,* edited by A. Dan. Thousand Oaks, CA: Sage.

Haney, D. 2003. "Big Study Dispels More Myths about Estrogen." *The News Tribune,* March 18, p. A3.

Health Canada. 2003. "About Health Canada." Retrieved March 23, 2004 (www.hc-sc.gc.ca/english/about/about.html).

House Energy and Commerce Subcommittee on Health and Environment. 1993. *Medicaid Sourcebook: Background Data and Analysis.* Washington, DC: Government Printing Office.

Ishida, J. 2003. "Uninsured, Many Seniors Pay 72% More for Drugs, Survey Shows." *The News Tribune,* July 16, p. A11.

Janofsky, M. 2003. "Burden Grows for Southwest Hospitals." *The New York Times,* April 14, p. A14.

Kinsella, W. 2003. "The Racist Face of SARS." *Maclean's* 116(15):60.

Krauss, Clifford. 2003. "Long Lines Mar Canada's Low-Cost Health Care." *The New York Times,* February 13, p. A3.

Krieger, N., D. R. Williams, and N. Moss. 1997. "Measuring Social Class in U.S. Public Health Research: Concepts, Methodologies, and Guidelines." *Annual Review of Public Health* 18:341–378.

Lambert, B. L., R. L. Street, D. J. Cegala, D. H. Smith, S. Kurtz, and T. Schofeld. 1997. "Provider-Patient Communication, Patient-Centered Care, and the Mangle of Practice." *Health Communication* 9(1):27–43.

Link, B. and J. Phelan. 2001. "Social Conditions as Fundamental Causes of Disease." Pp. 3–17 in *Readings in Medical Sociology,* edited by W. Cockerman and M. Glasser. New Jersey: Prentice Hall.

Livingston, M. 1998. "Update on Health Care in Canada: What's Right, What's Wrong, What's Left." *Journal of Public Health Policy* 19(3):267–288.

Lock, M. 1993. *Encounters with Aging: Mythologies of Menopause in Japan and North America.* Berkeley: University of California Press.

Markens, S. 1996. "The Problem of 'Experience': A Political and Cultural Critique of PMS." *Gender and Society* 10:42–58.

Marmor, T. and J. Mashaw. 2001. "Canada's Health Insurance and Ours: The Real Lessons, the Big Choices." Pp. 470–480 in *The Sociology of Health and Illness,* edited by P. Conrad. New York: Worth.

Matthews, J. 2003. "Baltimore Opens Nation's First Men's Health Center." Retrieved March 23, 2004 (www .communityvoices.org/article.aspx?ID=131).

Matthews, T. J., M. F. McDorman, and F. Menacker. 2002. *Infant Mortality Statistics from the 1999 Period Linked Birth/Death Dataset* (National Vital Statistics Report 50[4]). Hyattville, MD: National Center for Health Statistics.

Men's Health Network. 2002. "The Men's Disease Awareness and Prevention Project." Retrieved December 8, 2002 (www.menshealthnetwork.org/ProgramAreas/Prevention).

Mills, R. and S. Bhandari. 2003. *Health Insurance Coverage in the United States: 2002* (Current Population Reports, P60–223). Washington, DC: U.S. Census Bureau.

Moon, M. 1999. "Growth in Medicare Spending: What Will Beneficiaries Pay?" Retrieved March 16, 2003 (www.urban.org/health/medicare_growth).

National Advisory Committee on SARS and Public Health. 2003. *Learning from SARS: Renewal of Public Health in Canada.* Ottawa, Ontario: Health Canada.

National Center for Health Statistics. 2002. *Health, United States, 2002 with Chartbook on Trends in the Health of Americans.* Hyattsville, MD: Author.

———. 2003. "FASTATS:Life Expectancy." Retrieved September 12, 2004 (http://www.cdc.gov/nchs/data/hus/ tables/2003/03hus027.pdf).

National Community Care Network. 2003. "Northwest Georgia Healthcare Partnership." Retrieved March 16, 2003 (www.hospitalconnect.com/communitycare/reports).

National Diabetes Education Program. 2003. "HHS/NDEP Diabetes Prevention Campaign." Retrieved March 18, 2003 (www.ndep.nih.gov/get-info/dpc.htm).

National Institutes of Health. 2003. "HIV Infection and AIDS: An Overview." Retrieved February 8, 2004 (from www.niaid.nih.gov/factsheets/hivinf.html).

National Women's Health Information Center (NWHIC). 2002a. "African American Women's Health." Retrieved December 8, 2002 (www.4woman.gov/faq).

——— . 2002b. "Asian American and Pacific Islander Women's Health." Retrieved December 8, 2002 (www .4woman.gov/faq).

——— . 2002c. "Health Care Access and African American Women." Retrieved December 8, 2002 (www .4woman.gov/faq).

——— . 2002d. "Health Care Access and American Indian/Alaska Native Women." Retrieved December 8, 2002 (www.4woman.gov/faq).

——— . 2002e. " Latina Women's Health." Retrieved December 8, 2002 (www.4woman.gov/faq).

Oberlander, J. 2002. "The U.S. Health Care System: On a Road to Nowhere." *Canadian Medical Association Journal* 167(2):163–168.

Oppel, R. 2003. "With a New Push, Bush Enters Fray over Malpractice." *The New York Times,* January 17, pp. A1, A20.

Parsons, Talcott. 1951. *The Social System.* New York: Free Press.

Pear, Robert. 2002. "Pennsylvania Struggles to Repair Model Prescription Aid Program." *The New York Times,* July 13, pp. A1, A8.

——— . 2003. "Medicare Recipients Face 12.4% Rise in Premiums." *The New York Times,* March 26, p. A12.

Peterson, I. 2002. "New Jersey Doctors Hold Back Services in Insurance Protest." *The New York Times,* February 4, pp. A1, A33

Peterson, S., M. Heesacker, and R. Schwartz. 2001. "Physical Illness: Social Construction or Biological Imperative?" *Journal of Community Health Nursing* 18(4):213-222.

Phalen, K. 2000. "A Community of Men: Project Brotherhood, a Black Men's Clinic." Retrieved March 26, 2003 (www.ama-assn.org/amednews/2000/10/02/hlsa1002.htm).

Richman, J. and L. Jason. 2001. "Gender Biases Underlying the Social Construction of Illness States: The Case of Chronic Fatigue Syndrome." *Current Sociology* 49(3):15–40.

Sacks, H., T. Kutyla, and S. Silow-Carroll. 2002. *Toward Comprehensive Health Coverage for All: Summaries of 20 State Planning Grants* (U.S. Health Resources and Services Administration, Report 577). Washington, DC: The Commonwealth Fund.

Schram, J. 2003. "How Popular Perceptions of Risk from SARS Are Fomenting Discrimination." *British Medical Journal* 326(7395):939.

Seccombe, K. and C. Amey. 2001. "Playing by the Rules and Losing: Health Insurance and the Working Poor." Pp. 323–339 in *Readings in Medical Sociology,* edited by W. Cockerman and M. Glasser. Upper Saddle River, NJ: Prentice Hall.

Sherman, M. 2004. "Health Care Spending Hits Record $1.6 Trillion." *The Maui News,* January 9, p. B12.

Shortell, S., R. Gillies, D. Anderson, K. Erickson, and J. Mitchell. 2000. *Remaking Health Care in America: The Evolution of Organized Delivery Systems.* San Francisco: Jossey-Bass.

Silverstein, K. 1999. "Millions for Viagra, Pennies for Diseases of the Poor." *The Nation,* July 19, pp. 13–19.

Smith, B. 1987. *Digging Our Own Grave: Coal Miners and the Struggle over Black Lung Disease.* Chicago: University of Chicago Press.

Starr, Paul. 1982. *The Social Transformation of American Medicine.* New York: Basic Books.

Street, R. 1991. "Information-Giving in Medical Consultations: The Influence of Patients' Communicative Styles and Personal Characteristics." *Social Science and Medicine* 32:541–548.

Szasz, T. 1960. "The Myth of Mental Illness." *American Psychologist* 15:113–18.

Tanner, L. 2003. "Barbershop/Clinic Serves Black Men in Familiar Setting." *The News Tribune,* November 27, p. A12.

Taylor, M. 1990. *Insuring National Health Care: The Canadian Experience.* Chapel Hill: University of North Carolina Press.

Testa, K. 2003. "More Drug Buyers Turn to Canada." *The News Tribune,* December 10, p. A9.

Toner, R. 2002. "Why the Elderly Wait . . . and Wait." *The New York Times,* June 23, Week in Review, pp. 1, 14.

U.S. Census Bureau. 2002. "Motherhood: The Fertility of American Women, 2000." *Population Profile of the United States: 2000* (Internet Release). Retrieved February 22, 2003 (http://www.census.gov/population/pop-profile/2000/chap04.pdf)

———. 2004. *Current Population Survey, 2004 Annual Social and Economic Supplement, Table H106.* Washington, DC: U.S. Census Bureau.

U.S. Department of Health and Human Services. 2002. "HHS Issues Report Showing Dramatic Improvements in America's Health Over Past 50 Years" (Press Release September 12). Retrieved December 8, 2002 (www.cdc.gov/nchs/releases/02news).

U.S. Environmental Protection Agency. 2003. "Environmental Profile: A circuit Rider for Farm Worker Health." Retrieved March 14, 2003 from www.epg.gov/cgi-bin/epaprintonly.cgi.

U.S. Immigration and Naturalization Service. 2001. "Illegal Alien Resident Population." Retrieved January 10, 2003 (http://www.ins.usdoj.gov/graphics/aboutins/statistics/Illegals.htm).

Waldron, I. 2001. "What Do We Know about Causes of Sex Differences in Mortality? A Review of the Literature." Pp. 37–49 in *The Sociology of Health and Illness: Critical Perspectives,* edited by A. Dan. New York: Worth.

Weitz, R. 2001. *The Sociology of Health, Illness, and Health Care: A Critical Approach.* Belmont, CA: Wadsworth/Thompson Learning.

Wilkinson, R. G. 1996. *Unhealthy Societies: The Afflictions of Inequality.* London: Routledge.

8

Drug Abuse ❖

As a nation, we have been in the War on Drugs for the past 30 years. It has been referred to as a war with "no rules, no boundaries, no end" (PBS 2000). Since the mid 1980s, the United States has adopted a series of aggressive law enforcement strategies and criminal justice policies aimed at reducing and punishing drug abuse (Fellner 2000). Changes in federal law require all sentenced federal offenders to serve at least 87 percent of their court-imposed sentence. Many drug offenders are subject to mandatory minimum sentences based on the type and quantity of drug involved in their arrest (Scalia 2001). According to the Uniform Crime Report, 1,532,000 drug arrests were made in 1999, up from 580,900 in 1980 (Bureau of Justice Statistics 2003). Although some consider the increase in drug arrests a good sign, critics charge that mandatory sentencing denies drug users what they really need, access to treatment. Tougher sentencing has failed to decrease the availability of drugs and has failed to reduce illicit drug use. In addition, some argue that the focus on drug-related crimes has distracted law enforcement from monitoring more serious crimes.

On the prevention front, there was a new in-your-face public service campaign after the September 11, 2001, terrorist attacks. The Office of National Drug Control Policy [ONDCP] released a series of public service commercials linking the sales of illicit drugs with terrorism. One commercial featured a drug user named "Dan." The commercial voice over says, "This is Dan. This is the joint that Dan bought." The ad continues, ending eventually with the terrorist that Dan supported (Teinowitz 2002). Although the drugs and terrorism campaign generated much public attention and debate, the commercials were considered ineffective. The campaign officially ended in May 2003 when the ONDCP decided to switch to a traditional campaign targeting young people already using drugs (Teinowitz 2003).

There seems to be no argument about the seriousness of the drug problem in the United States. According to a 2002 National Survey on Drug Use and Health, 19.5 million Americans ages 12 and older reportedly were current illicit drug users (Substance Abuse and Mental Health Services Administration [SAMHSA] 2003c). It is estimated that 1 in every 13 adults or nearly 14 million people are alcoholics (National Institute on Alcohol Abuse and Alcoholism [NIAAA] 2003d). Although we might focus first on a single drug user and his or her personal trouble with drugs, it doesn't take long to recognize how drug use has impacts on the user's family and friends, workplace or school, and neighbors and community. Throughout this chapter, we will examine the social problem of drug abuse, reviewing its extent, its social consequences, and our solutions. We begin first with a look at how the sociological perspectives address the problem of drug abuse.

Sociological Perspectives on Drug Abuse

Biological and psychological theories attempt to explain how alcohol or drug abuse is based in the individual. Both perspectives assume that there is a little a person can do to escape from their abuse: Their abuse is genetic or inherited. Abuse may emerge from a biological or chemical predisposition or from a personality or behavioral disorder. Such explanations also have consequences for treatment. Programs are directed at the individual, arguing that the abuser needs to be "fixed." Although both perspectives have been important in shaping our understanding of drug abuse, these perspectives cannot explain the social or structural determinants of drug abuse. In this next section, we will examine how sociological perspectives address the problems of alcohol and drug abuse.

Functionalist Perspective

Functionalists argue that society provides us with norms or guidelines on alcohol and drug use. A set of social norms identify the appropriate use of drugs and alcohol. Drugs, prescription drugs in particular, are very functional. They alleviate pain, reduce fevers, and curb infections. Alcohol in moderation may be routinely consumed with meals, for celebration, or for health benefits. At least one glass of red wine a day has been shown to reduce one's risk of heart disease.

In addition, society provides norms regarding the excessive use of drugs. For example, college students share the perception that excessive college drinking is a cultural norm (Butler 1993); this perception is enforced by the media and advertisers (Lederman et al. 2003). Aaron Brower (2002) argues that binge drinking is determined by and is a product of the college environment. Unlike alcoholics, college students are able to turn their willingness to binge-drink on and off depending on their circumstances (e.g., whether they have to study for an exam).

Drug abuse can also occur when society is unable to provide guidelines for our behavior. To explain drug abuse, functionalists rely on Emile Durkheim's theory of **anomie**. Durkheim believed that under conditions of rapid cultural change, there would be an absence of common social norms and controls, a state he called anomie. If people lack norms to control their behavior, they are likely to pursue self-destructive behaviors like alcohol abuse, he thought (Caetano, Clark, and Tam 1998). During periods when individuals are socially isolated (such as moving to a new neighborhood, experiencing a divorce, or starting a new school year), they may experience high levels of stress or anxiety, which may lead to deviant behaviors, including drug abuse.

Conflict Perspective

Although many drugs can be abused, conflict theorists argue that intentional decisions have been made over which drugs are illegal and which ones are not. Powerful political and business interest groups are able to manipulate our images of drugs and their users. Heroin, opium, and marijuana were considered legal substances in the late 18th and early 19th centuries; but public opinion and law changed when their use was linked to ethnic minorities and crime.

Katherine Beckett (1995) and Dorothy Roberts (1991) describe how women of color have been unfairly targeted in the war on drugs. As crack cocaine use spread throughout the inner cities in the 1980s, prosecutors shifted their attention to drug use among pregnant women, making drug and alcohol abuse during pregnancy a crime. The approach treated pregnant drug users as criminals and was "aimed at punishing rather than empowering women who use drugs during their pregnancy" (Beckett, 1995: 589). Beckett (1995) explains, "Prosecutions of women for prenatal conduct thus create a gender specific system of punishment and obscure the fact that male behavior, socio-economic conditions, and environmental pollutants may also affect fetal health" (p. 588).

Roberts (1991) argues that poor Black women were the primary targets for prosecutors. Research indicates that African American women are about 10 times more likely than other women to be reported to civil authorities for drug use. Public health facilities and private doctors are more inclined to turn in pregnant Black women than pregnant White women who use drugs. Are they being prosecuted for their drug use or for something else? Roberts (1991) states, "Society is much more willing to condone the punishment of poor women of color who fail to meet the middle-class ideal of motherhood" (p. 1436).

Feminist Perspective

Theorists and practitioners in the field of alcohol and drug abuse have ignored the experiences unique to women, ethnic groups, gay and lesbian populations, and other marginalized groups. Women face unique social stigmatization as a result of their drug use and may also experience discrimination as they attempt to receive treatment (Drug Policy Alliance 2003b). It wasn't until the 1970s that the scientific literature addressed women's addiction.

Specifically, there has been a lack of sensitivity to the range of drug abuse experiences, beyond the male or White perspective. Early prevention and treatment models treated female abusers no differently than men. However, there is increasing recognition of the importance of gender-specific and gender-sensitive treatment models, including the development of separate women's treatment programs. Female users have a variety of different treatment and psychosocial needs, influenced by their backgrounds, experiences, and drug problems. For example, single career-oriented women without children will have different treatment needs and priorities than single mothers or married mothers (National Clearinghouse for Alcohol and Drug Information [NCADI] 2003b).

Gail Unterberger (1989) offers a feminist revision of the traditional 12-step statement used by Alcoholics Anonymous. As originally written, the 12 steps send a negative message for women, reinforcing feelings of powerlessness and hopelessness during recovery. Unterberger believes that alcoholic women are more likely to suffer from depression than their male counterparts, and unlike men, women alcoholics may turn their anger on themselves rather than others. Unterberger's revised 12-step statement is presented in Table 1.

❖ Table 8.1 The 12 Steps for Women Alcoholics

1. We have a drinking problem that once had us.

2. We realize that we need to turn to others for help.

3. We turn to our community of sisters and our spiritual resources to validate ourselves as worthwhile people, capable of creativity, care, and responsibility.

4. We have taken a hard look at our patriarchal society and acknowledge those ways in which we have participated in our own oppression, particularly the ways we have devalued or escaped from our own feelings and needs for community affirmation.

5. We realize that our high expectations for ourselves have led us either to avoid responsibility and/or to overinvest ourselves in others' needs. We ask our sisters to help us discern how and when this happens.

6. Life can be wondrous or ordinary, enjoyable or traumatic, danced with or fought with, and survived. In our community we seek to live in the present with its wonder and hope.

7. The more we value ourselves, the more we can trust others and accept how that helps us. We are discerning and caring.

8. We affirm our gifts and strengths and acknowledge our weaknesses. We are especially aware of those who depend on us and our influence on them.

9. We will discuss our illness with our children, family, friends and colleagues. We will make it clear to them (particularly our children) that what our alcoholism caused in the past was not their fault.

10. As we are learning to trust our feelings and perceptions, we will continue to check them carefully with our community, which we will ask to help us discern the problems we may not yet be aware of. We celebrate our progress toward wholeness individually and in community.

11. Drawing upon the resources of our faith, we affirm our competence and confidence. We seek to follow through on our positive convictions with the support of our community and the love of God.

12. Having had a spiritual awakening as a result of these steps, we are more able to draw upon the wisdom inherent in us, knowing we are competent women who have much to offer others.

Source: Unterberger 1989.

❖ PUTTING IT TOGETHER: To review the original 12-steps for alcoholics, log on to *Study Site Chapter 8*. In what ways is the original statement different from the woman's statement presented in Table 8.1?

Interactionist Perspective

Sociologists Edwin Sutherland and Howard Becker state that deviant behavior, such as drug abuse, is learned through others. Sutherland (1939) proposed the theory of **differential association** to explain how we learn specific behaviors and norms from the groups we have contact with. Deviance, explained Sutherland, is learned from people who engage in deviant behavior. In his study, "Becoming a Marijuana User," Becker (1963) demonstrated how a novice user is introduced to smoking marijuana by more experienced users. Learning is the key in Becker's study:

> No one becomes a user without (1) learning to smoke the drug in a way which will produce real effects; (2) learning to recognize the effects and connect them with drug use...; and (3) learning to enjoy the sensations he perceives. (P. 58)

This perspective also addresses how individuals or groups are labeled "abusers" and how society responds to them. For example, consider alcohol abuse among the Native American population. Alcohol abuse and alcoholism are leading causes of mortality among American Indians, and there are disproportionately higher rates of alcohol-related crimes among American Indians. Yet, Holmes and Antell (2001) argue that alcohol abuse and its related problems are not entirely objective phenomena; they also involve interpretation and stigmatization of deviant behavior. One persistent societal myth maintains that as a group, American Indians have problems handling alcohol. However, research indicates that factors such as demography (a young population) and geography (rural Western environment) may explain high rates of alcohol-related problems in Indian populations.

The authors highlight the considerable variation in drinking patterns within and between tribal communities; in other words, not all American Indians have drinking problems. The social construction of the "drunken Indian" stereotype links alcohol abuse to the perceived "weaker" cultural and individual characteristics of American Indians. Holmes and Antell (2001) explain, "The persistence of such myths in the symbolic-moral universe of the dominant White culture, despite evidence to the contrary, suggests that alcohol use by American Indians still serves to document allegations of weak will and moral degeneracy" (p. 154). For a summary of the various sociological perspectives, see Table 8.2.

What Is Drug Abuse?

Drug abuse is the use of any drug or medication for a reason other than the one it was intended to serve or in a manner or in quantities other than directed, which can lead to clinically significant impairment or distress. **Drug addiction** refers to physical and/or psychological dependence on the drug or medication. Although many drugs can be abused, five drugs will be reviewed in the following section: alcohol, nicotine, marijuana, methamphetamine, and cocaine. Most of the information presented in this section is based on data from the National Institute on Drug Abuse [NIDA] and the ONDCP. For more information, log on to *Study Site Chapter 8*.

Alcohol

We may not consider it a drug, but alcohol is the most abused drug in the United States. Although the consumption of alcohol by itself is not a social problem, the

❖ Table 8.2   Summary of Sociological Perspectives: Drug Abuse

	Functional	Conflict/Feminist	Interactionist
Explanation of drug abuse	Drug abuse is likely to occur when society is unable to control or regulate our behavior.	Powerful groups decide which drugs are illegal. Certain social groups are singled out for their drug abuse. There has been a lack of sensitivity to the range of drug abuse experiences.	Drug abuse is learned through interaction with others. The perspective also focuses on society's reaction to drug abuse, noting that certain individuals are more likely to be labeled as drug users than others.
Questions asked about drug abuse	What rules exist to control or encourage drug abuse? Are some groups or individuals more vulnerable to drug abuse than others?	What groups are able to enforce their definitions about the legality or illegality of drug use? How are they able to enforce their definitions? How are the experiences of women and minority drug users different from those of White males?	How is drug abuse learned through interaction? How are drug users labeled by society? Why are specific groups targeted?

continuous and excessive use of alcohol can become problematic. Four symptoms are associated with alcohol dependence or **alcoholism:** craving (a strong need to drink), loss of control (not being able to stop drinking once drinking begins), physical dependence (experiencing withdrawal symptoms), and tolerance (the need to drink greater amounts of alcohol to get "high") (NIAAA 2003d).

Current drinking (12 or more drinks in the past year) and heavy drinking (five drinks on a single day at least once a month for adults) among adults is highest for American Indians and Alaska Natives, followed by Native Hawaiians. Prevalence of

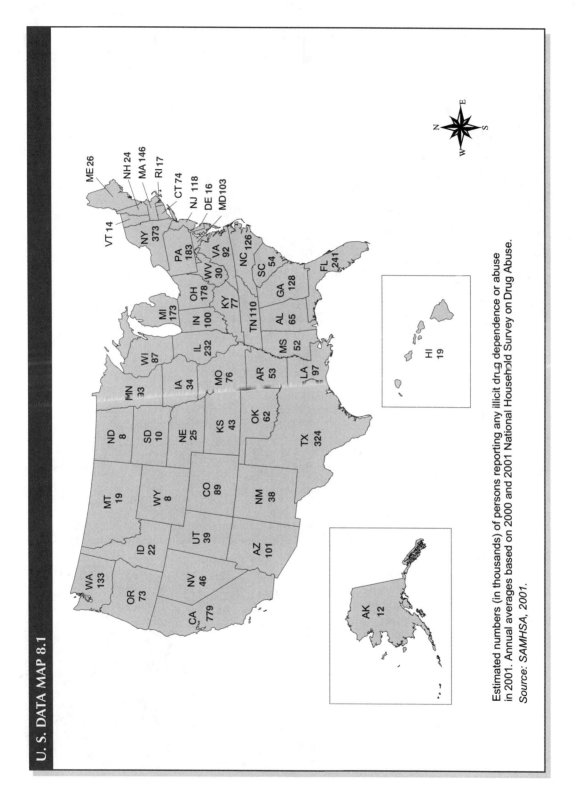

Estimated numbers (in thousands) of persons reporting any illicit drug dependence or abuse in 2001. Annual averages based on 2000 and 2001 National Household Survey on Drug Abuse.

Source: SAMHSA, 2001.

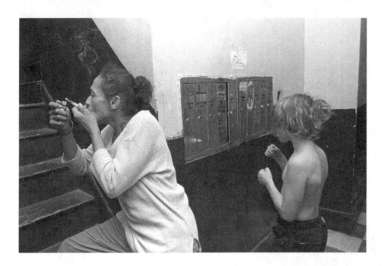

Drug abuse is related to many social factors, including hopelessness, poverty, and violence. In her own Brooklyn neighborhood, photographer Brenda Ann Kenneally documented the legacy of drug abuse passed down from parent to child and its effects on their community. While his mom is taking a hit from her crack pipe, Andy "boxes" with the mailboxes in the hallway. The electricity for the family's apartment has been turned off.

Kenneally also documents common violence and self-destructive behavior in her neighborhood. Fay, a crack dealer and user, tries to avoid being hurt by the man she sells crack for. She has smoked all the profits from her drug sales. She has also left her child with one of her customers, hiding him from authorities who would place him in foster care. Meanwhile, Lisa reveals the injury she inflicts on herself. Lisa has attempted many times, unsuccessfully, to quit using drugs; out of frustration she began cutting her left forearm with a knife.

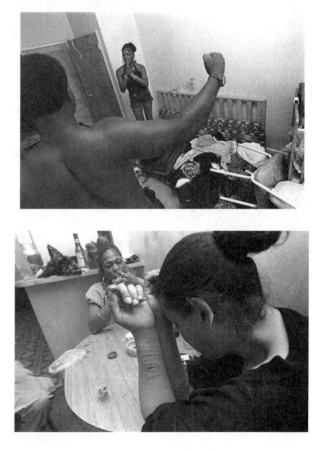

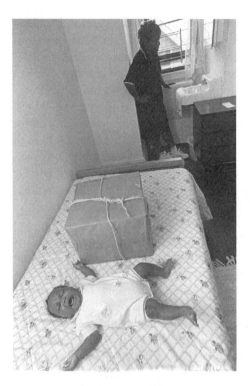

The vicious cycle of drug abuse can be broken, however. One young woman, Moya, learned from her mother, Theresa, to be a cocaine smoker and dealer. Theresa spent eight years in recovery from her own addiction before dying of a weakened heart. At the time, Moya was out of prison on parole. Three weeks after the funeral, Moya was caught dealing again and sent back to prison. She bore a child while in prison but had to find a temporary home for her daughter while she finished her sentence. When released, all the resources Moya had to start over were her baby, named Theresa after her mother, and a single box of belongings.

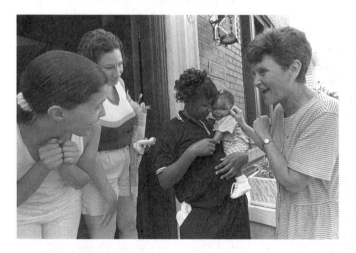

Moya and Theresa found a temporary home in Hour Children, a convent-run support community. Hour Children operates five residences, offering a safe home environment for formerly incarcerated mothers and their children. As a condition of her stay, Moya is required to get a job or attend school. Perhaps baby Theresa's life may turn out differently from Moya's.

Which do you believe is more effective in breaking the cycle of drug abuse—punishment through incarceration or rehabilitation through community programs like Hour Children?

deaths from chronic liver disease and cirrhosis is about four times higher, and fatal car accidents due to alcohol three times higher, among American Indians and Alaska Natives than the rest of the U.S. population. Adult drinking is lowest among Asian Americans and Pacific Islanders, but alcohol use is increasing significantly in this group.

Among adolescent minorities, African Americans have the lowest rates of drinking and the lowest frequency of being drunk. Hispanic adolescents have the highest rates of heavy drinking, followed by White adolescents. Decline in alcohol abuse with increased age is called "aging out" or simply part of the maturation process. Although studies suggest that White adolescents drink alcohol more heavily and frequently than other ethnic/racial groups, White adolescents are also more likely to age out. During early to middle adulthood, the frequency of heavy drinking stabilizes among Whites, increases among African Americans, and declines but remains high for Hispanics (Caetano and Kaskutas 1995; Chen and Kandel 1995).

Alcohol researchers have begun to identify the importance of individual attributes, cultural factors, and structural factors in minority drinking. Studies suggest that ethnic/racial groups have different sets of norms and values regulating drinking. For example, some groups exhibit low rates of problem drinking because their culture associates the use of alcohol primarily with eating, social occasions, or rituals (Herd and Grube 1996). However, other ethnic/racial groups may consider drinking as an activity separate from eating or ritual celebrations, leading to higher rates of problem drinking. Researchers have also attributed alcoholism among ethnic minorities to three stressors: **acculturative stress**, experienced by most immigrants who are faced with leaving their homeland and adapting to a new country; **socioeconomic stress**, experienced by ethnic minorities who feel disempowered because of social and economic inequalities in U.S. society; and **minority stress**, which refers to the tension that minorities encounter due to racism (Caetano et al. 1998).

Research indicates that among all age and ethnic groups, men are more likely to drink than women and are more likely to consume large quantities of alcohol in a single sitting (NIAAA 2002). Although social class, occupational and social roles, and family history of alcohol all play a role in determining the drinking patterns of people in general, specific factors put women particularly at risk (Collins and McNair 2003). Research indicates that a woman's risk for drinking increases with the experience of negative affective states, such as depression (Hesselbrock and Hesselbrock 1997) or loneliness, and negative life events, such as physical or sexual abuse during childhood or adulthood (Wilsnack et al. 1997). Other factors decrease women's chances of developing alcohol problems. Traditionally, women are socialized to abstain from alcohol use or to drink less than men (Filmore et al. 1997). Women who do not participate in the labor force may have less access to alcohol than men (Wilsnack and Wilsnack 1992), and women's roles as wife and mother may also discourage alcohol intake (Leonard and Rothbard 1999).

People who begin drinking before age 15 are four times more likely to develop alcohol dependence at some time in their lives compared to people who have their first drink at age 20 or older (NIAAA 2003c). O'Malley, Johnston, and Bachman (1998) report that adolescents who use alcohol are at higher risk for social, medical, and legal problems, such as poor school performance; interpersonal problems with friends,

❖ TAKING A WORLD VIEW

THE SCOTTISH DRINKING PROBLEM

Some have noted that "Scotland has a special relationship with alcohol" (Ritson 2002). Scotland is known for its Scotch whisky, a national beverage that is more than just a drink or a means of getting drunk. According to Sharon MacDonald (1994), whiskey is "a symbolic distillation of many images of Scottishness, especially hospitality, camaraderie, joviality, and masculinity" (p. 125).

Alcohol abuse in Scotland is increasing because of excessive drinking levels among adults and the frequency and level of drinking among teenagers. In recent studies, a third of Scots men (019,930) and 13 percent of women (394,487) between 16 and 64 years old were drinking more than the recommended weekly limits of less than 21 units for men and 14 units for women (a unit of alcohol is eight grams by weight) (Ritson 2002; Varney and Guest 2002). Younger age groups were more likely to exceed the weekly limits (Ritson 2002). It has been estimated that alcohol misuse costs Scottish society about 1,071 million pounds per year, the majority of the costs due to the criminal justice system, emergency services, losses of workplace productivity, and accidents (Varney and Guest 2002).

Men's and women's drinking are not viewed as equally problematic by Highland residents or the Scottish population in general. According to MacDonald (1994), in the Highlands, although more men abuse alcohol, their drinking is viewed as a lesser problem than that of women who drink. Drunkenness is accepted, even expected, of Scottish males; but a drunken woman is considered unrespectable, slovenly, and loose. The drunk Scottish woman is a pathetic figure rather than the humorous figure of a drunk Scot male. It is likely, says MacDonald, that the number of women who abuse alcohol is underestimated due to the added stigma associated with women's drinking. In her research, MacDonald was told of female alcoholics in hushed, conspiratorial" tones. Women were desperate to conceal their drinking problem. Women's drinking was more likely to be confined to home than men's (MacDonald 1994).

In January 2002, the Scottish Executive launched a "Plan for Action on Alcohol Problems," a national and local program aimed at reducing alcohol-related harm (Ritson 2002). The plan will focus on correcting harmful drinking patterns and influencing the habits of children and young people through prevention and education programs. The plan will also support and improve existing treatment services. The plan promises to achieve a "cultural change by an immediate investment [in] a national communication strategy that will challenge current stereotypes of binge drinking" (Ritson 2002:218).

family, and others; physical and psychological impairment; drunk driving; and death. The rate of fatal crashes related to alcohol among drivers ages 16 to 20 is more than twice the rate among drivers age 21 or older (NIAAA 2003c). The most common alcohol-related problem reported by adolescent drinkers is that alcohol use causes them to behave in ways that they later regret (O'Malley et al. 1998). Underage use of alcohol is more likely to kill young people than all illegal drugs combined (NIAAA, 2003c).

Nicotine

Nicotine is the most frequently used addictive drug in the United States (NCADI 2003a), with cigarette smoking the most prevalent form of nicotine addiction. Nicotine is both a stimulant and a sedative to the central nervous system. An average cigarette contains about 10 milligrams of nicotine. Through inhaling the cigarette smoke, the smoker takes in 1 to 2 milligrams of nicotine per cigarette. Nearly 35 million users try to quit smoking per year, but it is estimated that less than 7 percent are able to achieve more than one year of abstinence (NIDA 1998).

About 66.5 million Americans reported current use of a tobacco product in 2001, about 29.5 percent of the population 12 years or older. The majority of tobacco users, about 56.3 million, reported smoking cigarettes (NCADI 2003a).

The prevalence of smoking is highest among Native Americans/Alaska Natives (40.9 percent), followed by African Americans and Whites (24.3 percent), Hispanics (18.1 percent), and Asians and Pacific Islanders (15.1 percent). It is estimated that 4.5 million teenagers are cigarette smokers; 22.4 percent of high school seniors smoke on a daily basis (American Lung Association 2002b).

Cigarette smoking is the most important preventable cause of cancer in the United States. It has been linked to 90 percent of all lung cancer cases and one third of all cancers. Smoking has also been linked to other lung diseases, such as chronic bronchitis and emphysema, and to cancers of the mouth, stomach, kidney, bladder, cervix, pancreas, and larynx. The overall death rates from cancer are twice as high among smokers as nonsmokers (NIDA 1998). It is estimated that 430,700 annual deaths are attributable to cigarette smoking (American Lung Association 2003b).

Passive or secondhand smoke is a major source of indoor air contaminants. Secondhand smoke is estimated to cause about 3,000 lung cancer deaths per year and may contribute to as many as 40,000 deaths related to cardiovascular disease (NIDA 1998). Exposure to cigarette smoking at home is harmful to children with asthma. The Environmental Protection Agency estimates that exposure to secondhand smoke may worsen the health of about 200,000 to 1 million asthmatic children (American Lung Association 2002a).

Despite the persistent public health message that smoking is bad for your health, smoking among teenagers has been on the rise since 1991 (Lewinsohn et al. 2000). In a study comparing adolescent smokers to nonsmokers, adolescent smokers were found to have more stressful environments, more academic problems, and poorer coping skills than nonsmokers. Adolescent smoking has also been associated with a number of environmental factors, such as disruptive home environment, parental and peer smoking, low social support from family and friends, conflict with parents, and stressful life events (Lewinsohn et al. 2000).

Data indicate that the use of smokeless chewing tobacco products (referred to as "snuff," "dip," or "chew") occurs at a significantly younger age than cigarette smoking. Smokeless tobacco products are consumed orally, with packets of the tobacco tucked in a front lip or cheek. An average size chew kept in the mouth for 30 minutes provides the same amount of nicotine as three cigarettes (National Cancer Institute 2003). Smokeless tobacco may cause permanent gum recession, mouth sores, lesions, and cancers of the mouth and throat. Jones and Moberg (1988) examined smokeless tobacco use among adolescent males and discovered that regular use was related to being White, living in other than a two-parent home, performing poorly in school, smoking cigarettes, consuming alcohol, and engaging in delinquent behavior. Participation in team sports was associated with experimenting with smokeless products but not with regular use.

❖ PUTTING IT TOGETHER:
In your community.

The American Lung Association rates each state on smoke-free air ordinances, state laws limiting youth access to tobacco, state spending on tobacco prevention, and cigarette taxes. To determine your state's rating, go to *Study Site Chapter 8.*

Marijuana

Marijuana is the most commonly used illicit drug, widely used by adolescents and young adults (NIDA 2002a). The major active chemical in marijuana is THC or delta-9-tetrahydrocannainol, which causes the mind-altering effects of the drug. THC is also the main active ingredient in oral medications used to treat nausea in chemotherapy patients and to stimulate appetite in AIDS patients (ONDCP 2003c).

Marijuana was used by 76 percent of the current illicit drug users, according to the National Household Survey on Drug Abuse 2001 (ONDCP 2003c). More than 83 million Americans (or 37 percent) age 12 or older have tried marijuana at least once in their lifetime (NIDA 2002a). According to the Centers for Disease Control, 42.4 percent of surveyed high school students have used marijuana in their lifetime. Male students (46.5 percent) were more likely to report lifetime marijuana use than female students (38.4 percent) (ONDCP 2003c). Longitudinal data show increases in marijuana use during the 1960s and 1970s, declines in the 1980s, with increasing use since the 1990s (NIDA 2002a).

Acute marijuana use can impair short-term memory, judgment, and other cognitive functions as well as a person's coordination and balance, and it can increase heart rate. Chronic abuse of the drug can lead to addiction, as well as increased risk of chronic cough, bronchitis, or emphysema. Addictive use of the drug may interfere with family, school, or work activities. Smoking marijuana increases the risk of lung cancer and cancer in other parts of the respiratory tract more than smoking tobacco does (NIDA 2002a). Marijuana smoke contains 50 percent to 70 percent more carcinogenic hydrocarbons than tobacco smoke (ONDCP 2003c). Because marijuana users inhale more deeply and hold their breath longer than cigarette smokers do, they are exposed to more carcinogenic smoke than cigarette smokers. In 2001, marijuana use was a contributing factor in more than 110,000 emergency room visits. About 15 percent of these patients were between 12 and 17 years of age, and almost two thirds were male (NIDA 2002a).

Methamphetamine

Methamphetamine or "meth" is a highly addictive central nervous system stimulant that can be injected, snorted, smoked, or ingested orally. A derivative of amphetamine, methamphetamine was therapeutically used in the 1930s to treat asthma and narcolepsy (sleeping disorder) (Pennell et al. 1999). It is the most prevalent synthetic drug manufactured in the United States. The increase in methamphetamine use has been attributed to the ease of manufacturing the drug and to its highly addictive nature (ONDCP 2003d). The drug is commonly referred to as "speed," "crystal," "crank," "go," and "ice" (a smokable form).

More than 9 million people have tried methamphetamine at least once in their lifetime (ONDCP 2003d). The highest rate of use is in the 18 to 25 age group. Meth is concentrated in the rural and Western areas of the United States, but it has spread throughout every major metropolitan area, except in the Northeast. Among high school students, male students (10.5 percent) are more likely to report methamphetamine use than female students (9.2 percent). White students (11.4 percent) are more likely than Hispanic (9.1 percent) or Black (2.1 percent) students to have used the drug.

Chronic methamphetamine use can cause violent behavior, anxiety, confusion, and insomnia. Users may also exhibit psychotic delusions, including homicidal or suicidal thoughts. Long-term use of the drug can lead to brain damage, similar to damage associated with Alzheimer's disease, stroke, or epilepsy (ONDCP 2003d).

Cocaine

Cocaine is one of the oldest known drugs, derived from the leaves of the coca bush. Cocaine is listed as a Schedule II drug, a drug with a high potential for abuse. The drug is a strong central nervous system stimulant and can be snorted, smoked, or injected. Crack is the street name for cocaine that has been processed from cocaine hydrochloride into a smokable substance. Because crack is smoked, the user experiences a high in less than 10 seconds.

In 2002, 2 million Americans were current cocaine users. Adults 18 to 25 years old have a higher rate of use than any other age group. Overall, men have higher rates of use than women. Rates of cocaine use are higher for American Indians/Alaska Natives (2.0 percent) and African Americans (1.6 percent) than for Hispanics (0.8 percent) and Whites (0.8 percent). Cocaine initiation is more likely to occur among adults rather than youths under 18. In 1968, the average age of a new user was 18.6 years; it was 23.8 years in 1990 and 21 years from 1995 to 2001 (SAMHSA 2003c).

Some of the most common complications of the drug include cardiovascular disease (disturbances in heart rhythm and heart attacks), respiratory effects (chest pain and respiratory failure), neurological effects (strokes, seizures), and gastrointestinal complications (NIDA 2002b).

The full effect of prenatal drug exposure is not completely known. Babies born to mothers who abuse cocaine are often premature, have low birth weights, and are often shorter in length. It has been predicted that "crack babies" will suffer severe irreversible damage. However, it appears that most crack babies recover, although there is indication of some learning deficits, such as the child's inability to block distractions or to concentrate for long periods of time (NIDA 2002c).

The Problems of Drug Abuse

Drug Abuse and the Relationship with Crime and Violence

Drinking- and alcohol-related problems have been associated with intimate partner violence among White, Black, and Hispanic couples. This does not mean that violence can only occur when drinking is involved or that alcohol is the prime cause of the violence. Rather some people may consciously use alcohol as an excuse for violent behavior. Also, alcohol may be related to violence because heavier drinking and violence have common predictors, such as impulsive personalities (Caetano, Schafer, and Cunradi 2001).

Alcohol use has also been associated with child abuse as both a cause and a consequence (Widom and Hiller-Sturmhofel 2001). Parental alcohol abuse may increase a child's risk of experiencing physical or sexual abuse, either by a family member or another person. Parental alcohol abuse may also lead to child neglect. Studies indicate that girls who were abused or neglected are more likely to have alcohol problems as adults than other women (Widom and Hiller-Sturmhofel 2001).

National Crime Victim Surveys indicate that the rate of alcohol-involved violent crimes (crimes in which the offender has been drinking, as perceived by victims) has decreased 34 percent from 1993 to 1998, a shift from 2.1 million incidents in 1993 to 1.4 million in 1998. Alcohol abuse is more often suspected in crimes than abuse of any other drug. However, the number of violent offenses in which the offender was believed to be using other drugs (illicit drugs) increased 19 percent during the same time period (143,420 in 1993 to 526,522 in 1998). For 1998, 41 percent of probationers, 41 percent of jail inmates, 38 percent of state prisoners, and 20 percent of federal prisoners reported that they were drinking at the time of the offenses for which they were convicted. Nearly one half of the violent victimizations that involved alcohol occurred in a residence, with more than 20 percent occurring in the victim's home. About one third of the alcohol-involved victimizations resulted in an injury to a victim. It has been estimated that the loss per victim of alcohol-involved violence was about $1,016 or an estimated annual loss of $400 million per year (Greenfeld and Henneberg 2001).

Drug Abuse and the Impact on Work

Employers have always been concerned about the impact of substance abuse on their workers and their businesses. According to the U.S. Department of Labor, although the rate of current illicit drug use is higher among unemployed people, about 73 percent of drug users or 8.1 million people are employed, costing businesses billions of dollars annually in lost productivity and health care costs (U.S. Department of Labor 2003). It is estimated that drug abuse cost American businesses $81 billion in lost productivity, $37 billion due to premature death, and $44 billion due to illness in 2002. Alcohol abuse contributed to about 86 percent of the costs (U.S. Department of Labor 2003b).

In their examination of occupational risk factors for drug abuse, MacDonald, Wells, and Wild (1999) found that problem drinking or drug use was linked to the quality and organization of work, drinking subcultures at work, and the safety of the workplace. Respondents reporting alcohol problems were more likely to have jobs involving repetitive tasks and dangerous working conditions. Respondents with alcohol problems were also more likely to drink with coworkers and experience some social pressure to drink. The same pattern was also true for workers with drug problems: They considered their jobs "boring" or repetitive; they identified their job as dangerous; they experienced stress at work; or they were likely to be part of a drinking subculture at work. Among all factors they identified, the presence of a drinking subculture at work was the strongest risk factor for alcohol and drug abuse.

By occupation, the highest rates of current illicit drug use and heavy drinking were reported by food preparation workers, waiters/waitresses, and bartenders (19 percent); construction workers (14 percent); service occupations (13 percent); and transportation and material moving workers (10 percent) (U.S. Department of Labor 2003b).

Among employed adults, White, non-Hispanic males between the ages of 18 and 25 who have less than a high school education are likely to report the highest rates of heavy drinking and illicit drug use (U.S. Department of Labor 2003b).

Problem Drinking among Teens and Young Adults

Binge drinking is defined as drinking five or more drinks within a few hours (or within one sitting). For 2002, the National Survey on Drug Use and Health (NSDUH) reported that about 54 million people (or 22.9 percent) ages 12 to 20 participated in binge drinking at least once in the 30 days prior to the survey. In 2002, the highest prevalence of binge and heavy drinking (five or more drinks on the same occasion on at least five different days in the past 30 days) was for young adults ages 18 to 25, with the peak rate occurring at age 21. Heavy drinking was reported by 14.9 percent of people 18 to 25 and by 20.1 percent of people age 21. Binge and heavy drinking were lowest for people age 65 or older, with reported rates of 7.5 percent and 1.4 percent respectively (SAMHSA 2003c). See Figure 8.1 for a summary of 2002.

Binge drinking among college students has been called a major public health concern (Clapp, Shillington, and Segars 2000). Henry Wechsler (1996) reported results from the 1996 Harvard School of Public Health College Alcohol Study, highlighting how binge drinking has become widespread among college students. In the Wechsler study, binge drinking was defined as five or more drinks in a row one or more times during a two-week period for men and four or more drinks in a row one or more times during a two-week period for women. The author explains how men, students under 24, fraternity and sorority residents, Whites, students in athletics, and students who socialize more are most likely to binge drink. On average, students who engaged in high-risk behaviors such as illicit drug use, unsafe sexual activity, and cigarette smoking were more likely to be binge drinkers. In contrast, students who were involved in community service, the arts, or studying were less likely to be binge drinkers (Wechsler 1996). Access to alcohol is also related to problem drinking. Weitzman et al. (2003) reported a positive relationship between alcohol outlet density (number of bars, liquor stores near campus) and frequent drinking (drinking on 10 or more occasions in the past 30 days), heavy drinking (five or more drinks at an off-campus party) and drinking problems (self-reported).

The Task Force of the National Advisory Council on Alcohol Abuse and Alcoholism (2002) concluded that 1,400 college students between the ages of 18 and

❖ **Figure 8.1** Past Month Alcohol Use by Age: 2002

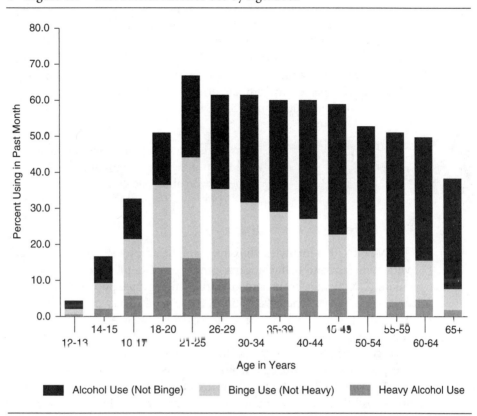

Source: Substance Abuse and Mental Health Services Administration. 2003c.

24 die each year from alcohol-related unintentional injuries, including motor vehicle crashes. About half a million students between the ages of 18 and 24 are unintentionally injured while under the influence of alcohol, and more than 600,000 students are assaulted by another student who has been drinking. In addition the Task Force reports that 25 percent of college students report academic consequences (poor grades, poor performance, missing classes) as a result of their drinking, and more than 150,000 develop an alcohol-related health problem. Based on self-reports about their drinking, 31 percent of college students met the criteria for alcohol abuse, and 6 percent met the criteria for alcohol dependence (Task Force of the National Advisory Council on Alcohol Abuse and Alcoholism 2002).

Brower (2002) explains that there is no evidence that drinking in college leads to later-life alcoholism or long-term alcohol abuse. He writes, "Real life is a strong disincentive for the kind of binge drinking that college students do" (p. 255). He suggests using the term *episodic high-risk drinking* to describe more accurately how college students drink: infrequently drinking a large quantity of alcohol in a short period of time.

By the time they reach the eighth grade, nearly 50 percent of adolescents report having had at least one drink, and more than 20 percent report having been drunk (NIAAA 2003d). Underage drinkers account for nearly 20 percent of the alcohol consumed in the United States (Tanner 2003). In 2001, among youth ages 12 to 17, 17.3 percent used alcohol in the month prior to the National Household Survey on Drug Use, higher than the rate of youth alcohol use reported in 2000, 16.4 percent. Among all youth, 10.6 percent were binge drinkers, and 2.5 percent were heavy drinkers, no increase from the 2000 figures (SAMHSA 2003c).

❖ **PUTTING IT TOGETHER:** **On your campus.** What is the drinking policy on your campus? What educational or service programs are provided for students who abuse alcohol?

The Increase in Club Drugs

MDMA (3–4 methylenedioxymethamphetamine) is a synthetic psychoactive drug with stimulant and hallucinogenic properties. The pill—popularly known as Ecstasy, Adam, X, XTC, hug, beans, and love drug—first gained popularity at dance clubs, raves, and college scenes. The 1998 National Household Survey on Drug Abuse reported that 1.5 percent or 3.4 million Americans have used MDMA at least once during their lifetime. The heaviest use was among 18 to 25 year olds, about 5 percent or 1.4 million in this age group (NIDA 2003c). MDMA is usually taken in pill form at the cost of about $25 per tablet, but the drug can also be snorted, injected, or used in a suppository.

Rohypnol, GHB, and Ketamine are other drugs commonly used in club and rave scenes. All three are also known as "date rape" drugs. Previously confined to club or rave subculture, Ecstasy has become a mainstream drug (NIDA 2003c), second only to marijuana as the most frequently used illicit drug among young adults (Johnston, O'Malley, and Bachman 2001).

From 2002 to 2004, a public service announcement sponsored by the Partnership for a Drug Free America featured Jim and Elsa Heird. The Nevada couple's 21–year-old daughter, Danielle, took Ecstasy on three occasions; the last time it resulted in her death. After taking one or one and a half pills, Danielle began to feel ill and decided to stay home to rest. A few hours later when her friends came home, they found her dead. There were no other controlled substances or alcohol in her body at the time of her death (Vaughn 2002). Ecstasy-related deaths like Danielle Heird's are rare. In 1999, there were 13 Ecstasy-related deaths, 8 in Miami, Florida, and 5 in Minneapolis/St. Paul, Minnesota (NIDA 2003c).

Even when they are not fatal, Ecstasy and other related drugs, known collectively as methylated amphetamines, are not harmless drugs. Ecstasy produces an intense release of serotonin in a user's brain, which can cause irreparable damage to the brain and memory functions. Research indicates that long-term brain damage, especially to the parts of the brain critical to thought and memory, may result from its use. Users may also experience psychological difficulties (such as confusion, depression, and sleeping problems) while using the drug and sometimes for weeks after. As a result of using the drugs, individuals can also experience increases in heart rate and blood pressure and physical symptoms such as nausea, blurred vision, or faintness (NIDA 2003c). When users overdose, they can experience rapid heartbeat, high blood pressure, faintness, panic attacks, and even loss of consciousness (Vaughn 2002).

In a study of undergraduates at a large Midwestern university, Boyd, McCabe, and d'Arcy (2003) found that men and women were equally likely to have used Ecstasy, and several factors predicted its use. White students were more likely to report lifetime Ecstasy use than African American or Asian students. According to the researchers, sexual orientation was also related to Ecstasy use: Those who identified themselves as gay, lesbian, or bisexual were more likely to report lifetime, annual, or past month Ecstasy use than heterosexual students. Students with a GPA of 3.5 or higher were consistently less likely to have used Ecstasy in the past year or their lifetime than students with GPAs below 2.5. Students who reported binge drinking within the past two weeks were also more likely to report past-month Ecstasy use.

Do You Have a Meth Lab Next Door?

In the early 1990s, the primary sources of methamphetamines were super laboratories in California and Mexico. Super labs are able to produce 10 pounds of meth in a 24-hour production cycle. In 2001, 298 super labs were raided by enforcement officials. Authorities seized 1,370 kilograms of meth along the U.S.-Mexico border in 2001, compared with only 6.5 kilograms in 1992. At the same time, there has been an increase in the number of small-scale labs operated by independent "cooks." Meth produced in these labs is primarily for personal use or limited distribution. In 2001, the number of labs with capacities under 10 pounds totaled more than 7,000, by one estimate (Drug Enforcement Administration 2003).

Certain aspects of the manufacturing and use of methamphetamines, compared to other illegal drugs, have different consequences. Unlike other drugs, meth is easy to make with common chemicals that are easy to obtain (Pennell et al. 1999). The drug can be manufactured illicitly in laboratories set up in homes, motels, trailers, cars, or public storage lockers. Of the 32 chemicals that are used to make or "cook" meth, about one third of the chemicals are toxic (Snell 2001). The waste and residue remaining from meth cooking can contaminate water supplies, soil, and air, causing danger to people, animals, and plant life in the area. Many of the chemicals are explosive, flammable, and corrosive. Among the 1,654 labs seized in 1998, nearly one in five were found because of fire or explosion (Snell 2001). Nationally, meth labs caused more than 200 fires and explosions in 2003 (Johnson 2004).

Sandra Rupert, an elementary school counselor in Boone, North Carolina, was worried about two sisters who were second and third graders. The sisters had headaches, colds, and coughs nearly every day. When the Sheriff's Department raided the children's home, a meth lab was discovered in the room next to where the sisters slept. The girls were suffering from toxic fumes emitted by the chemicals. They were removed immediately from the home and the custody of their mother (Butterfield 2004). For every pound of meth that is produced, five to six pounds of highly toxic waste are generated (Pennell et al. 1999; Snell 2001). Cleanup is very dangerous; law enforcement officers must wear hermetically sealed suits and self-contained breathing apparatuses for protection. Cleanup costs of large meth labs can exceed $100,000 (Snell 2001).

Once cooking locations are discovered, they often have to be stripped, fumigated, or destroyed before the site can be safely lived in again, but there is no guarantee that complete cleanup will be possible. The North Carolina sisters had to leave all their belongings, toys, and clothing when they were removed from their mother's home. The consequences of methamphetamine use and production present serious challenges to law enforcement, policymakers, and the public (Pennell et al. 1999). Drug and law enforcement agencies have created public educational materials informing the public of what to look for if a meth lab is suspected in their neighborhood (refer to Table 8.3).

❖ Table 8.3 Is There a Meth Lab in Your Neighborhood?

Meth causes health problems not only for its users, but also for those unintentionally exposed to meth and to the chemicals used to make it. Even brief exposure to high levels of the chemicals found in meth labs may cause shortness of breath, chest pain, lack of coordination, and possibly even death. Illegal meth labs can be set up in homes, rest areas, rental properties, abandoned cars, and vacant buildings.

Here are some things you should look out for in your neighborhood:

- Unusual strong odors (like cat urine, ether, ammonia, acetone, or other chemicals)
- Residences with windows blacked out
- Renters who pay their landlords in cash
- Lots of traffic, with people coming and going at unusual times; little traffic during the day, but dramatically increased activity at night
- Excessive trash including large amounts of items such as antifreeze containers, lantern fuel cans, red chemically stained coffee filters, drain cleaner, and duct tape
- Unusual numbers of clear glass containers being brought into the home

The presence of the following items could also indicate the existence of a meth lab:

- Alcohol
- Paint thinner
- Gasoline/kerosene/camp stove fuel
- Drain cleaner (sulfuric acid)
- Epsom salts
- Batteries/lithium
- Propane cylinders (20 lbs)
- Hot plates
- Cold tablets (Ephedrine or Pseudophedrine)

Do not enter a site or handle materials you think may be used for cooking meth. Immediately contact local law enforcement.

Source: KCI 2003.

Drug Advocacy, Innovation, and Policy

Federal Programs

Throughout the first part of this chapter, I have already referred to three offices: the NIDA, the ONDCP, and the NIAAA. All three programs are federally funded.

The NIAAA was established after the passage of the Comprehensive Alcohol Abuse and Alcoholism Prevention, Treatment, and Rehabilitation Act of 1970. Signed into law by President Richard Nixon, the legislation acknowledged alcohol abuse and alcoholism as major public health concerns. The law instructed the NIAAA to "develop and conduct comprehensive health, education, research, and planning programs for the prevention and treatment of alcohol abuse and alcoholism and for the rehabilitation of alcohol abusers and alcoholics" (NIAAA 2003a). Since then, the NIAAA's mission has been revised to include support and implementation of biomedical and behavioral research, policy studies, and research in a range of scientific areas to address the causes, consequences, treatment, and prevention of alcoholism and alcohol-related problems (NIAAA 2003b).

NIDA was established in 1974 as the federal office for research, treatment, prevention, training services, and data collection on the nature and extent of drug abuse. Like NIAAA, NIDA is part of the National Institutes of Health, the federal biomedical and behavioral research agency. NIDA's stated mission is to bring "the power of science to bear on drug abuse and addiction" (NIDA 2003a). NIDA supports more than 85 percent of the world's research on the health aspects of drug abuse and addiction.

The ONDCP is the newest federal drug program. Established in 1988 through the Anti-Drug Abuse Act, the ONDCP's mission was to set national priorities, design comprehensive research-based strategies, and certify federal drug control budgets. According to the Act, the purpose of the Office was to prevent young people from using illegal drugs, reduce the number of drug users, and decrease the availability of drugs (ONDCP 2003b). Ten years later, ONDCP's mission was expanded under the Reauthorization Act of 1998. Some of the legislative requirements included a commitment to a five-year national drug control program budget, the establishment of a parents' advisory council on drug abuse, development of a long-term national drug strategy, and increased reporting to Congress on drug control activities (ONDCP 2003b). The Act also provided support for the High Intensity Drug Trafficking Areas (HIDTA) program, coordinating local, state, and federal law enforcement drug control efforts.

 ❖ PUTTING IT TOGETHER: On the Web.

You can visit the HIDTA Web site by logging on to the *Study Site Chapter 8*. On the state map, click on the location nearest to your college. Not all states have been identified as including a HIDTA. The link should take you to regional or state HIDTA program information, including a description of the extent of drug trafficking in the area, along with a list of participating agencies and significant achievements in the fight against drug trafficking.

Extensive use of illegal drugs continues despite the efforts of these three lead agencies. The War on Drugs comes with huge economic cost, $19.2 billion in 2003, paid directly to the ONDCP (2003a). Although most advocates support prevention and law enforcement efforts, some have attempted to explore alternative strategies to the problem of drug abuse.

Drug Legalization

The contemporary debate about the legalization of drugs emerged in 1988 during a meeting of the U.S. Conference of Mayors. Baltimore's Kurt L. Schmoke called for a national debate on drug control policies and the potential benefits of legalizing marijuana and other illicit substances (Inciardi 1999). Proponents present several arguments for the legalization of drugs: Current drug laws and law enforcement initiatives have failed to eradicate the drug problem; arresting and incarcerating individuals for drug offenses does nothing to alleviate the drug problem; drug crimes are actually victimless crimes; legalization will lead to a reduction in drug-related crimes and violence and improve the quality of life in inner cities; and legalization will also eliminate serious heath risks by providing clean and high-quality substances (Cussen and Block 2000; Silbering 2001). Many supporters of legalization argue that drugs should be legalized based on the libertarian legal code (Trevino and Richard 2002), namely that the legalization of drugs would give a basic civil liberty back to citizens by granting them control over their own bodies (Cussen and Block 2000).

The term **legalization** is often used interchangeably with another term, **decriminalization**. The terms vary in terms of the extent to which the law can regulate the distribution and consumption of drugs. In general, decriminalization means keeping criminal penalties but reducing their severity or removing some kinds of behavior from inclusion under the law (e.g., eliminating bans on the use of drug paraphernalia). Some would support regulating drugs in the same way alcohol and tobacco are regulated, whereas others would argue for no restrictions at all. Legalization suggests removing drugs from the control of the law entirely (Weisheit and Johnson 1992).

Drug legalization is generally opposed by the medical and public health community (Trevino and Richard 2002). The American Medical Association has consistently opposed the legalization of all illegal drugs, arguing that most research shows drugs, particularly cocaine, heroin, and methamphetamines, are harmful to an individual's health. Opponents charge that drug use is a significant factor in the spread of sexually transmitted diseases such as HIV, and drug users are more likely to engage in risky behaviors and in criminal activity (Trevino and Richard 2002). The Drug Enforcement Administration has also been clear about its opposition to drug legalization, citing concerns over potential increases in drug use and addiction, drug-related crimes, and costs related to drug treatment and criminal justice.

In the 1990s, the drug debate began to change, with legalization proponents advocating a "harm reduction" approach. Many opposed to legalization began to accept aspects of the harm reduction approach. Harm reduction is a principle suggesting that "managing drug misuse is more appropriate than attempting to stop it all together" (Inciardi 1999:3). Proponents acknowledge that current drug polices are not working, but they are still not in favor of full decriminalization (McBride, Terry, and Inciardi

1999). The harm reduction approach emphasizes treatment, rehabilitation, and education (McBride et al. 1999), including advocacy for changes in drug policies (such as legalization), HIV/AIDS-related interventions, broader drug treatment options, counseling and clinical case management for those who wish to continue using drugs, and ancillary interventions (housing, healing centers, advocacy groups) (Inciardi 1999).

❖ **PUTTING IT TOGETHER:**
On the Web.

The Drug Policy Alliance (2003a) is an organization "working to broaden the public debate on drug policy and to promote the realistic alternatives to the war on drugs based on science, compassion, health, and human rights." Since 1996, 40 states have enacted more than 100 drug policy reforms. The reforms usually target drug sentencing and the legalization of medical marijuana. For more information on drug policies in your state, go to *Study Site Chapter 8.*

Punishment or Treatment?

Stricter federal policies have increased the number of men and women serving jail or prison time for drug-related offenses. As conflict and symbolic interaction theories suggest, drug laws are not enforced equally, with certain minority groups being singled out. Although most illicit drug users are White, Blacks constitute about 80 percent to 90 percent of all people sent to prison on drug charges. Nationwide, Black men are sent to state prison on drug charges at 13 times the rate of White men (Fellner 2000). Drug enforcement usually targets urban and poor neighborhoods while ignoring drug use among middle- or upper-class people. Whereas our society treats middle- or upper-class drug use as a personal crisis (consider, for example, that despite talk show host Rush Limbaugh's 2003 rehabilitation for prescription drug addiction, he was never charged for illegal drug use and doctor shopping for painkillers), lower-class drug use is defined as criminal. However, in 2004, John P. Walters, director of the White House's ONDCP, announced the first comprehensive plan to attack prescription drug abuse, "an increasingly widespread and serious problem in this country." The program would monitor patients suspected of doctor shopping, would detect suspicious prescriptions, and would track illegal Internet sales (ONDCP 2004).

Sasha Abramsky (2003) explains that with tougher drug laws, the drug war was taken away from the public health and medical officials and placed into the hands of law enforcement and courts. The notion that drug abuse is a disease was replaced with the idea that drug abuse is a crime. However, as overall crime rates began to decline, public support for the get-tough–on-drugs policy began to wane. Research conducted by the Pew Research Center in 2001 found that 73 percent of Americans favored permitting medical marijuana prescriptions, 47 percent favored rolling back mandatory minimum sentences for nonviolent drug offenders, and 52 percent believed drug use should be treated as a disease rather than as a crime. Although federal policy seems unlikely to change in the near future, several states are reexamining the way they deal with drug offenders.

Abramsky (2003) recognizes key legislative changes in several states. Arizona and California passed recent legislation that diverted thousands of drug offenders into treatment programs instead of prisons. In 1998, Michigan repealed its mandatory life sentence law for those caught in the possession of more than 650 grams of certain narcotics. In 2002, Michigan Governor John Engler signed legislation that rolled back the state's tough mandatory-minimum drug sentences. The Kansas Sentencing Commission proposed reforms of the state's mandatory sentencing codes, along with expansion of treatment programs. The reforms were accepted in March 2003. Abramsky (2003) explains, "Increasingly impatient with the costly combination of policing and prosecution, voters, along with a growing number of state and local elected officials, have abandoned their support for incarceration-based anti-drug strategies and have forced significant policy shifts" (p. 26).

Drug Treatment and Prevention Programs

Individual Approaches

Drug addiction is a "treatable disorder" (NIDA 2003b). Traditional treatment programs focus on treating the individual and his or her addiction. The ultimate goal of treatment is to enable users to achieve lasting abstinence from the drug, but the immediate treatment goals are to reduce drug use, improve the user's ability to function, and minimize their medical and social complications due to drug use.

Treatment may come in two forms: Behavioral treatment includes counseling, support groups, family therapy, or psychotherapy; medication therapy, such as maintenance treatment for heroin addicts, may be used to suppress drug withdrawal symptoms and craving. Short-term treatment programs can include residential treatment, medication therapy, or drug-free outpatient therapy. Long-term programs (longer than six months) may include highly structured residential therapeutic community treatment or, in the case of heroin users, methadone maintenance outpatient treatment. Over the past 25 years, research indicates that treatment does work to reduce drug intake and drug-related crimes. Patients who stay in treatment longer than three months have better outcomes than people who undergo shorter treatment (NIDA 2003b).

Workplace Strategies

Certain employers, such as employers in the transportation industry or organizations with federal contracts in excess of $100,000, are required by law to have drug-free workplace programs. The federal government, through the Drug Free Workplace Program, also encourages private employers to implement such programs in an effort to reduce and eliminate the negative effects of alcohol and drug use at the workplace (SAMHSA 2003b). The American Management Association reported that the percentage of companies that test employees for drugs increased from 22 percent in 1987 to more than 81 percent in 1997 (Hoffman and Larison 1999). After implementing a drug-free workplace program, employers, unions, and employees are likely to see a decrease in administrative work losses (sick leave abuse, health insurance claims, disability payments, and accident costs), hidden losses (poor performance, material waste, turnover, and premature death), legal losses (grievances, threat to public safety, worksite security) and costs of health and mental health care services (SAMHSA 2003a).

Drug-testing programs have been subject to lawsuits over the past decade for challenging the employees' right to privacy and their constitutional freedom from unreasonable searches by the government (SAMHSA 2003b). There have also been challenges to the accuracy of drug tests. Critics have asserted a positive test does not always correlate with poor job performance, a criterion for assessing the adverse effects of drugs (Klingner, Roberts, and Patterson 1998). Consistent with conflict theories on drug use, some have argued that drug testing promotes various political agendas and reflects the manipulation of interest groups that market and sell drug testing and security services (Klingner et al. 1998). Yet, many U.S. companies consider drug-testing programs part of an effective policy against substance abuse among workers (Hoffman and Larison 1999).

Roman and Blum (2002) report that employee assistance programs (or EAPs) are the most common intervention used in the workplace to prevent and treat alcohol and other drug abuse among employees. The primary goal for many of these programs is to ensure that employees maintain their employment, productivity, and careers. These EAPs usually include health promotion, education, and referral to abuse treatment as needed. Most of these programs do not target the general workplace population; rather, services are directed to those already affected by a problem or in the early stages of their abuse. There is some evidence of the effectiveness of these programs, returning substantial proportions of employees with alcohol problems to their jobs (Roman and Blum 2002).

Campus Programs

The U.S. Supreme Court ruled that drug testing in schools is legal for student athletes (1993) and for students in other extracurricular activities (2002). In both rulings, the Court stated that drug screenings play an important role in deterring student drug use.

However, a national study of 76,000 high school students reported no significant difference between drug use among students in schools with testing versus students in schools without testing. Researchers Yamaguchi, Johnston, and O'Malley (2003) reported that 37 percent of 12th graders in schools that test for drugs said that they had smoked marijuana in the previous year, compared to 36 percent of 12th graders in schools that did not test. In addition 21 percent of 12th graders in schools with testing reported that they had used illicit drugs (cocaine or heroin) in the previous year compared with 19 percent of 12th graders in schools without drug screenings. The study found that only 18 percent of schools did any kind of drug screening between 1998 and 2001. Large schools (22.6 percent) reported more testing than smaller schools (14.2 percent). The majority of drug tests were conducted in high schools. The study did not compare schools that conducted intensive regular screenings with those that occasionally tested for drugs. The study indicated that education, not testing, may be the most effective weapon against abuse (Winter 2003).

In their review of 94 college drug prevention programs, Andris Ziemelis, Ronald Buckman, and Abdulaziz Elfessi (2002) identified three prevention models that produced the most favorable outcomes in binge-drinking prevention efforts. The first model includes student participation and involvement, such as volunteer services, advisory boards, or task forces to discourage alcohol or other drug use or abuse. The researchers documented how these activities serve to reinforce students' beliefs that they are in control of the outcomes in their lives and that their efforts and contributions are valued. This model encourages student ownership and development of the program. The second model includes educational and informational processes, such as instruction in classes, bulletin boards and displays, and resource centers. The most effective informational strategies were those that avoided coercive approaches but instead encouraged interactive communication between students and professionals on campus. The last model includes efforts directed at the larger structural environment, changing the campus regulatory environment and developing free alternative programming, such as providing alcohol-free residence halls or mandatory alcohol and drug abuse classes as part of campus intervention. In general, models that discourage or deglamorize alcohol and drug use were associated with better outcomes than those that merely banned or restricted substance use (Ziemelis et al. 2002).

Voices in the Community:
Jill Ingram

This article about Jill Ingram, of the National College Commission of Mothers Against Drunk Driving (MADD), was taken from MADD's Web site (Glenn 2000).

. . . Ingram became involved in underage drinking prevention after her brother was hit by a drunk driver in 1996.

Ingram's brother, Dan, and his date were on their way home from a college sorority formal when the drunk driver—who [was] driving her van, headlights off, on the wrong side of a divided highway—hit their car head-on. Dan sustained multiple injuries to his ankle, knee, and wrist in the crash.

"There were several witnesses who saw [the drunk driver] and honked to get her attention, but she was too drunk to notice," said Ingram. "Later it was determined that her blood alcohol content was two times over the legal limit."

"I can't even bear to think about what my brother must have gone through during and in the moments that followed the crash," Ingram said. "But I do know what my family went through in the aftermath of the crash. It was then that I knew I had to do something to prevent another family from going through that kind of pain."

Ingram responded by taking action. Her first step was to attend the 1997 MADD National Youth Summit to Prevent Underage Drinking as a youth delegate. While Ingram was at the Summit, a cheerleading squad teammate back home nearly lost her life in an impaired-driving crash. This second alcohol-related crash fueled Ingram's fire for preventing the senseless tragedy from happening to anyone else.

Armed with the knowledge and driven by the passion of a true activist, Ingram set out to make a difference. Working in conjunction with the MADD Northern Virginia chapter, she began speaking at high schools and local community colleges to educate students about the dangers of alcohol and impaired driving. She also co-founded the student-led Alcohol and Drug Abuse Prevention Team (ADAPT) on her university's campus.

"Underaged students like myself who choose not to drink didn't seem to have the same options to have fun and get together with friends as the students who do drink," Ingram said of her impression upon arriving at [the University of Virginia] her first year. "The drinkers and partyers at the university had an outlet that was not available to students like me on campus. Students need an outlet for their energies and their leadership abilities," she continued. "Our campus alcohol awareness program is 10 years old, but student involvement this year is the highest it has ever been because we have created new and different options for alcohol-free lifestyles."

Community Approaches

In 1997, the Drug Free Communities Act became law. The Act was intended to increase community participation in substance abuse reduction among youth. The program is directed by the Office of Juvenile Justice and Delinquency and the White House's ONDCP. The program supports coalitions of youth, parents, law enforcement, schools, state, local, and tribal agencies, heath care professionals, faith-based organizations, and other community representatives. The coalitions rely on mentoring, parental involvement, community education, and school-based programs for drug prevention and intervention, much like Project Northland.

Based in northern Minnesota, Project Northland was the largest community trial in the United States to address the prevention of alcohol use and alcohol-related problems among adolescents (Williams and Perry 1998). Adopting a holistic approach, the project assumed that prevention efforts should be directed at adolescents and their immediate social environment (family, peers, friends) and should include larger peer groups (teachers, coaches, religious advisers) as well as the broader community of businesses and political leaders. The project was recognized for its programming by the SAMHSA, U.S. Department of Health and Human Services, and the U.S. Department of Education.

Project Northland included youth participation and leadership, parental involvement and education, community organizing and task forces, media campaigns, and school curriculum as part of its strategies for alcohol prevention. The program included two phases. Phase 1 focused on strategies to encourage adolescents not to use alcohol. Phase 2 emphasized changing community norms about alcohol use, reducing the availability of alcohol among high school students, and adopting a functionalist approach in reinforcing community norms and boundaries. Community strategies included making compliance checks of age-of-sale laws (coordinated through local police departments), holding training sessions for responsible beverage servers at retail outlets and bars, and encouraging businesses to adopt "gold card" programs where discounts are provided to students who pledge to remain free of alcohol. At the end of Phase 1, the intervention group demonstrated significant reductions in the onset and prevalence of drinking. Data are unavailable on the effectiveness of Phase 2 strategies (Williams and Perry 1998).

The Community Anti-Drug Coalitions of America (CADCA) is a nonprofit organization that provides technical assistance and training to community-based coalitions. The organization was established in 1992 by Jim Burke and Alvah Chapman and currently serves more than 5,000 anti-drug coalitions. The program provides community groups with lobbying handbooks, alerts on drug-related legislation, funding information, and coalition training on various drug abuse topics.

One CADCA affiliate is Wilson Families in Action (WFA) of Wilson, North Carolina, incorporated in 1982. Formed by local leaders, agencies, and organizations, WFA attempts to address the growing problem of drug abuse in the community. WFA operates seven programs, including "I'm Special," a science-based program for third and fourth graders, and the Prom "Think Card" campaign, targeting community merchants to discourage high school students from drinking alcohol at their prom.

❖
Voices in the Community:
Linda Elliot

Linda Elliot founded the Parent Party Patrol because of her own teenaged son. After realizing that he was partying every weekend, she tried to find a community program that might provide her with some assistance. She discovered that there were no programs addressing what she calls the core problem—unchaperoned alcohol and drug parties. In an interview, Elliot said,

> There was nothing looking at the core of the problem—where were our children getting the drugs? Where are our children getting the alcohol? I took it upon myself to educate parents about some of the behaviors that go on in unchaperoned parties and the civil and legal liabilities that are attached to parents no matter what their children do. We are all responsible for our children.

Elliot admits that she was seriously concerned for her son's life. There were many weekends where she imagined what it would be like when someone finally called to say that he was dead. But she came to the realization that she didn't have to live this way; Parent Party Patrol was part of her solution. Elliot became concerned not only about the drug and alcohol use, but also about the consequences of these parties: vandalism, alcohol poisoning, violence, rape, and death. "I could not believe that parents were turning a deaf ear and a blind eye to these parties." She says she could not understand why some parents would endorse these teen behaviors. "Why would parents allow their children to party at their home? Why do parents provide the alcohol?"

Parent Party Patrol is funded by Pierce County Human Services and the King County Health Department. Elliot and her volunteer staff provide educational programs for parents, church groups, PTAs, and booster clubs. If Elliot travels outside of these counties, she requests a donation to help with costs. Parent Party Patrol offers a range of information for parents and youth: the manufacturing of fake IDs, types of alcohol consumed by boys versus girls, date rape drugs, rave parties, and the legal impact of unchaperoned parties. She estimates that the program reaches 1,500 to 2,750 parents each year. In addition to local and state honors, Parent Party Patrol was awarded the 1997 National Exemplary Substance Abuse Prevention Program of the Year by the Office of National Drug Control Policy and the Department of Health and Human Services.

After each program visit, Elliot and her staff conduct a follow-up survey with parents. "The intent of our presentation is to make parents more responsible, we have seen the results." Elliot says that there is increased parental awareness about drug and alcohol use and more parents begin monitoring their child's activities and behaviors. Specifically, parents report that they are unlikely to leave their children home alone, are unlikely to allow an unchaperoned party at their home, and are more likely to ask their neighbors or friends to check in with their children if they do have to leave town. In addition, the program also receives telephone calls from parents with questions about drugs found in their child's room or with requests for assistance with their teen's problem behavior(s).

Although Elliot thought that she would stop her work after her children grew up to be "successful good citizens," she discovered that other parents still needed this information. She explains, "The reward is when I have a parent come up to me after two or three years to re-attend a presentation, and she will look at me at say, 'You will never know how many lives you have saved.' That's the reward."

For more information about the Parent Party Patrol, visit *Study Site Chapter 8.*

MAIN POINTS

- There seems to be no argument about the seriousness of the drug problem in the United States. In 2002, 19.5 million Americans age 12 and older reported they were current illicit drug users. It is estimated that 1 in every 13 adults is an alcoholic.

- Functionalists argue that society provides us with norms or guidelines on alcohol and drug use. A set of social norms identifies the appropriate use of drugs and alcohol.

- Conflict theorists argue that intentional decisions by powerful political and business interest groups have been made over which drugs are illegal.

- Feminists argue that theorists and practitioners in the field of alcohol and drug abuse have ignored experiences unique to women and other marginalized groups. However, there is increasing recognition of the importance of gender-sensitive treatment models.

- The interactionist perspective argues that drug abuse is learned from others; it addresses how individuals or groups are labeled abusers and how society responds to them.

- Alcohol is the most abused drug in the United States. Other abused drugs include nicotine, marijuana, methamphetamine, and cocaine. Alcohol problems can be both a cause and an excuse for intimate partner violence and child abuse. Alcohol abuse is more often suspected in crimes than abuse of any other drug.

- Employers have always been concerned about the impact of substance abuse. About 8.1 million drug abusers are employed, costing businesses billions of dollars a year.

- Binge drinking among college students has been called a major public health problem. Some research shows that students who engaged in high-risk behaviors were more likely to be binge drinkers, whereas students who were involved in community service, the arts, or studying were less likely to be binge drinkers. Thousands of college students are injured or die each year from alcohol-related driving or injuries.

- Ecstasy, Rohypnol, GHB, and Ketamine are drugs commonly used in club and rave scenes. Ecstasy has become a mainstream drug and can cause physical problems, irreparable damage to the brain and memory, psychological difficulties long after use, and death.

• In the early 1990s, the primary sources of methamphetamines were super laboratories. More recently, there has been an increase in the number of small-scale labs operated by independent "cooks." The waste and residue remaining from meth cooking can contaminate the surrounding area, and cleanup is very dangerous and costly.

• Three offices—the NIDA, the ONDCP, and the NIAAA—are federally funded agencies that research and educate about drug and alcohol abuse. Extensive use of illegal drugs continues despite the efforts of these three lead agencies and the War on Drugs.

• Some have explored alternatives to the War on Drugs, including legalization (removing drugs from the control of the law). Proponents argue that current laws fail to eradicate the problem; incarceration does not alleviate the drug problem, they say, and drug crimes are victimless. Proponents argue that legalization would reduce drug-related crimes and violence, make drugs cleaner, and return to citizens a basic civil liberty. Legalization is generally opposed by the medical and public health community because research shows that drugs are harmful and cause risky behaviors and criminal activity.

• As conflict and symbolic interaction theories suggest, drug laws are not enforced equally, with certain minority groups (particularly Blacks) and the lower class being singled out. Recently, however, key legislative changes suggest a shift in thinking to treatment rather than incarceration.

• Drug addiction is considered a "treatable disorder." Treatment may be either behavioral or medical and either short or long term. Research in the past 25 years indicates that treatment works to reduce drug intake and drug-related crimes.

• Certain employers are required by law to have drug-free workplace programs. Now, more than 81 percent of companies test employees for drugs. A drug-free workplace program likely decreases administrative work losses, hidden losses, legal losses, and health care services.

• Drug-testing programs have been subject to lawsuits in the past decade over constitutional issues. There have also been challenges to the accuracy of drug tests. Consistent with conflict theories, some have argued that drug testing promotes various political agendas and reflects the manipulation of interest groups. Yet, many U.S. companies consider drug-testing programs part of an effective policy against substance abuse.

• Employee assistance programs are the most common intervention used in the workplace to prevent and treat alcohol and other drug abuse among employees. There is some evidence of the effectiveness of these programs.

• The U.S. Supreme Court ruled that drug testing in schools is legal and an important deterrent to drug use for student athletes (1993) and for students in other extracurricular activities (2002). However, a national study of 76,000 high school students indicated that education, not testing, may be the most effective weapon against abuse.

• In general, prevention models that discourage or deglamorize alcohol and drug use are associated with better outcomes than those that merely ban or restrict substance use.

• Recent acts and initiatives to reduce substance abuse include the Drug Free Communities Act, the Community Anti-Drug Coalitions of America, and Wilson Families in Action.

INTERNET AND COMMUNITY EXERCISES

1. There are several advocacy groups committed to promoting alternative solutions to the drug problem in the United States. Two groups are Students for a Sensible Drug Policy and Stop the Drug War. Log on to *Study Site Chapter 8* for links to their Web site. Examine how both organizations define the drug problem. Are there any differences in their definitions? What solutions does each group support?

2. According to the U.S. Drug Enforcement Administration, the illegal drug market in the United States is one of the most profitable in the world. The DEA posts state fact sheets on its Web site, identifying the drug trafficking situation in each state, along with a list and description of the illicit drugs that are smuggled in the state. For information about drug trafficking in your state, go to *Study Site Chapter 8*. To what extent does drug trafficking occur in your state?

3. According to Maria Alaniz (1998), "alcohol outlet density is an important determinant of the amount of alcohol advertising in a community. Merchants use storefronts and the interiors of alcohol outlets to advertise alcohol products. Therefore, areas with a high density of outlets have a greater number of advertisements" (p. 286). Alaniz cites a study showing that a student walking home from school in a predominately Latino neighborhood in northern California may be exposed to between 10 and 60 storefront alcohol advertisements. The same study found that there are five times more alcohol advertisements in Latino neighborhoods than in predominately White neighborhoods. Count the number of alcohol outlets around your college-university, along with billboard advertising within a five-mile radius. Do these ads target college students? Do you think exposure to alcohol advertising increases alcohol consumption? Why or why not?

4. The Campaign for Tobacco-Free Kids is a national campaign effort to protect children from tobacco addiction and exposure to secondhand smoke. The campaign's Web site includes information on state initiatives, as well as statistics on tobacco use. Log on to *Study Site Chapter 8*.

On your own. Log on to *Study Site—Community and Policy Guide* for more information about the social problems, social policies, and community responses discussed in this chapter.

References

Abramsky, Sasha. 2003. "The Drug War Goes Up in Smoke." *Nation,* 277(5):25–28.

Alaniz, Maria Luisa. 1998. "Alcohol Availability and Targeted Advertising in Racial/Ethnic Minorities Communities." *Alcohol Health and Research World* 22(4):286–289.

American Lung Association. 2002a. "Secondhand Smoke Fact Sheet." Retrieved August 2, 2003 (www.lungusa .org/tobacco/secondhand_factsheet99.html).

————. 2002b. "Smoking Fact Sheet." Retrieved August 2, 2003 (www.lungusa.org/tobacco/smoking_factsheet99 .html).

Becker, Howard. 1963. *Outsiders: Studies in the Sociology of Deviance.* New York: Free Press.

Beckett, Katherine. 1995. "Fetal Rights and "Crack Moms": Pregnant Women in the War on Drugs." *Contemporary Drug Problems* 22:587–612.

Boyd, Carol, Sean Esteban McCabe, and Hannah d'Arcy. 2003. "Ecstasy Use among College Undergraduates: Gender, Race, and Sexual Identity." *Journal of Substance Abuse Treatment* 24:209–215.

Brower, Aaron. 2002. "Are College Students Alcoholics?" *Journal of American College Health* 50:253–255.

Bureau of Justice Statistics. 2003. "Criminal Offenders Statistics." Retrieved July 8, 2003 (www.ojp.usdoj.gov/bjs/ crimoff.htm).

Butler, E. R. 1993. "Alcohol Use by College Students: A Rite of Passage Ritual." *NASPA Journal* 31(1):48–55.

Butterfield, Fox. 2004. "Home Drug-Making Laboratories Expose Children to Toxic Fallout." *The New York Times,* February 23, pp. A1, A15.

Caetano Raul and L. A. Kaskutas, L.A. 1995. "Changes in Drinking Patterns among Whites, Blacks, and Hispanics, 1984–1992." *Journal of Studies on Alcohol* 50:15–23.

Caetano, Raul, Catherine Clark, and Tammy Tam. 1998. "Alcohol Consumption among Racial/Ethnic Minorities: Theory and Research." *Alcohol Health and Research World* 22(4): 233–238.

Caetano, Raul, John Schafer, and Carol Cunradi. 2001. "Alcohol Related Intimate Partner Violence among White, Black, and Hispanic Couples in the United States." *Alcohol Research and Health* 25(1):58–65.

Clapp, John, Audrey Shillington, and Lance Segars. 2000. "Deconstructing Contexts of Binge Drinking among College Students." *American Journal of Drug and Alcohol Abuse* 26(1):139–154.

Chen, K. and D. B. Kandel. 1995. "The Natural History of Drug Use from Adolescence to the Mid-Thirties in a General Population Sample." *American Journal of Public Health* 85:41–47.

Collins, R. Lorraine and Lily McNair. 2003. "Minority Women and Alcohol Use." Retrieved October 5, 2003 (www.niaaa.nih.gov/publications/arh26–4/251–256.htm).

Community Anti-Drug Coalitions of America. 2003. "Beloit's Safe and Drug Free Schools Program." Retrieved August 10, 2003 (www.cadca.org/images/PromPromise.gif).

Cussen, Meaghan and Walter Block. 2000. "Legalize Drugs Now! An Analysis of the Benefits of Legalized Drugs." *American Journal of Economics and Sociology* 59(3):525–536.

Drug Enforcement Administration. 2003. "Drug Trafficking in the United States." Retrieved July 22, 2003 (www.usdoj.gov/dea/concern/drug_traffickingp.html).

Drug Policy Alliance. 2003a. "About the Alliance." Retrieved August 2, 2003 (www.drug policy.org/about/).

———. 2003b. "Women and the War on Drugs." Retrieved August 2, 2003 (www.drug policy.org/communities/women).

Fellner, Jamie. 2000. *Punishment and Prejudice: Racial Disparities in the War on Drugs* (Vol. 2, No. 2). New York: Human Rights Watch.

Filmore, K. M., J. M. Golding, E. V. Leino, et al. 1997. "Patterns and Trends in Women's and Men's Drinking." Pp. 21–48 in *Gender and Alcohol*, edited by R. W. Wilsnack and S. C. Wilsnack. New Brunswick, NJ: Rutgers Center of Alcohol Studies.

Glenn, B. 2000. "A Crusader against Underage Drinking." Retrieved June 9, 2004 (www.madd.org/activism/0,1056,4028_print,00.html).

Greenfeld, Lawrence and Maureen Henneberg. 2001. "Victim and Offender Self Reports of Alcohol Involvement in Crime." *Alcohol Research and Health* 25(1):20–31.

Herd, Denise and Joel Grube. 1996. "Black Identity and Drinking in the U.S.: A National Study." *Addiction* 91(6):845–857.

Hesselbrock, M. N. and V. M. Hesselbrock. 1997. "Gender, Alcoholism, and Psychiatric Comorbidity." Pp. 49–71 in *Gender and Alcohol*, edited by R. W. Wilsnack and S. C. Wilsnack. New Brunswick, NJ: Rutgers Center of Alcohol Studies.

Hoffman, John and Cindy Larison. 1999. "Worker Drug Use and Workplace Drug Testing Programs: Results from the 1994 National Household Survey on Drug Use." *Contemporary Drug Problems* 26:331–354.

Holmes, Malcolm and Judith Antell. 2001. "The Social Construction of American Indian Drinking: Perceptions of American Indian and White Officials." *The Sociological Quarterly* 42(2):151–173.

Inciardi, James. 1999. "American Drug Policy: The Continuing Debate." Pp. 1–8 in *The Drug Legalization Debate*, edited by J. Inciardi. Thousand Oaks, CA: Sage.

Jones, R. B. and D. P. Moberg. 1988. "Correlates of Smokeless Tobacco Use in a Male Adolescent Population." *American Journal of Public Health* 78(1):61–63.

Johnson, Dirk. 2004. "Policing a Rural Plague." *Newsweek*, March 8, p. 41.

Johnston, L. D., P. M. O'Malley, and J G. Bachman. 2001. *Monitoring the future: National Survey Results on Drug Use, 1975–2000* (Vol. II, NIH Publication No. 01–4925). Bethesda, MD: National Institute on Drug Abuse.

KCI. 2003. "Is There a Meth Lab 'Cookin' in Your Neighborhood?" Retrieved August 2, 2003 (www.kci.org/meth_info/neighborhood_lab.htm).

Klingner, Donald, Gary Roberts, and Valerie Patterson. 1998. "The Miami Coalition Surveys of Employee Drug Use and Attitudes: A Five-Year Retrospective." *Public Personnel Management* 27(2):201–222.

Lederman, Linda, Lea Stewart, Fern Goodhart, and Lisa Laitman. 2003. "A Case against 'Binge' as a Term of Choice: Convincing College Students to Personalize Messages about Dangerous Drinking." *Journal of Health Communications* 8:79–91.

Leonard, K. E. and J. C. Rothbard. 1999. "Alcohol and the Marriage Effect." *Journal of Studies on Alcohol* (Suppl. 13):139–146.

Lewinsohn, Peter, Richard Brown, John Seeley, and Susan Ramsey. 2000. "Psychosocial Correlates of Cigarette Smoking Abstinence, Experimentation, Persistence and Frequency during Adolescence." *Nicotine and Tobacco Research* 2:121–131.

MacDonald, Scott, Samantha Wells, and T. Cameron Wild. 1999. "Occupational Risk Factors Associated with Alcohol and Drug Problems." *American Journal of Drug and Alcohol Abuse* 25(2):351–369.

MacDonald, Sharon. 1994. "Whisky, Women, and the Scottish Drink Problem: A View from the Highlands." Pp. 125–144 in *Gender, Drink, and Drugs,* edited by M. McDonald. Oxford, UK: Berg.

McBride, Duane, Yvonne Terry, and James Inciardi. 1999. "Alternative Perspectives on the Drug Policy Debate." Pp. 9–54 in *The Drug Legalization Debate,* edited by J. Inciardi. Thousand Oaks, CA: Sage.

National Cancer Institute. 2003. "Smokeless Tobacco: Health and Other Effects." Retrieved October 5, 2003 (http://dccps.nci.nih.gov/tcrb/less_effects.html).

National Clearinghouse for Alcohol and Drug Information. 2003a. "Cigarettes and Other Nicotine Products." Retrieved August 2, 2003 (http://store.health.org/catalog/facts.aspx?topic=9).

———. 2003b. "Intensive Outpatient Treatment for Alcohol and Other Drug Abuse: The Treatment Needs of Special Groups." Retrieved August 2, 2003 (www.health.org/govpubs/bkd139/8g.aspx).

National Institute on Alcohol Abuse and Alcoholism. 2002. "Alcohol and Minorities: An Update, No. 55." Retrieved July 22, 2003 (www.niaaa.nih.gov/publications/aa55.htm).

———. 2003a. "The Creation of the National Institute on Alcohol Abuse and Alcoholism." Retrieved July 31, 2003 (www.niaaa.nih.gov/about/niaaa-history.htm).

———. 2003b. "NIAAA's Purpose." Retrieved July 31, 2003 (www.niaaa.nih.gov/about/purpose.htm).

———. 2003c. "Underage Drinking: A Major Public Health Challenge." Retrieved July 22, 2003 (www.niaaa.nih.gov/publications/aa59.htm).

———. 2003d. "What Is Alcoholism?" Retrieved July 22, 2003 (www.niaaa.nih.gov/faq/q-a.htm#question1).

National Institute of Drug Abuse (NIDA). 1998. "Nicotine Addiction." Retrieved August 2, 2003 (www.drugabuse.gov/researchreports/nicotine/nicotine.html).

———. 2002a. *Marijuana Abuse* (NIH Publication No. 02–3859, October 2002). Rockville, MD: Author.

———. 2002b. "What Are the Medical Complications of Cocaine Abuse?" Retrieved July 27, 2003 (www.drugabuse.gov/ResearchReports/Cocaine/cocaine3.html#medical).

———. 2002c. "What Is the Effect of Maternal Cocaine Use?" Retrieved July 27, 2003 (www.drugabuse.gov/ResearchReports/Cocaine/cocaine4.html#maternal).

———. 2003a. "About NIDA." Retrieved July 31, 2003 (www.drugabuse.gov/about/AboutNIDA.html).

———. 2003b. "Drug Addiction Treatment Methods." Retrieved August 2, 2003 (www.nida.nih.gov/infofax/treatmeth.html).

———. 2003c. "NIDA Info Facts: MDMA (Ecstasy)." Retrieved July 22, 2003 from www.drugabuse.gov/Infofax/ecstasy.html.

Office of National Drug Control Policy [ONDCP]. 2003a. *Drug Data Summary, March 2003.* Washington, DC: Author.

———. 2003b. "Enabling Legislation." Retrieved July 31, 2003 (www.whitehousedrugpolicy.gov/about/legislation.html).

———. 2003c. "Marijuana." Retrieved July 23, 2003 (www.whitehousedrugpolicy.gov/drugfact/marijuana/index.html).

———. 2003d. "Methamphetamine." Retrieved July 23, 2003 (www.whitehousedrugpolicy.gov/drugfact/methamphetamine/index.html).

———. 2004. "U.S. Drug Prevention, Treatment, Enforcement Agencies Take on "Doctor Shoppers, Pill Mills." Retrieved March 27, 2004 (www.whitehousedrugpolicy.gov/news/press04/0301014.html).

O'Malley, Patrick, Lloyd Johnston, and Jerald Bachman. 1998. "Alcohol Use among Adolescents." *Alcohol Health and Research World* 22(2):85–94.

PBS. 2000. "Frontline: Drug Wars." Retrieved August 2, 2003 (www.pubs.org/wgbh.pages/frontline/shows/drugs/).

Pennell, Susan, Joe Ellett, Cynthia Rienick, and Jackie Grimes. 1999. *Meth Matters: Report on Methamphetamine Users in Five Western Cities.* Washington, DC: U.S. Department of Justice, Office of Justice Programs, National Institute of Justice.

Ritson, Bruce. 2002. "Editorial: Scotland's National Plan on Alcohol Problems." *Drugs: Education, Prevention, and Policy* 9(3):217–220.

Roberts, Dorothy. 1991. "Punishing Drug Addicts Who Have Babies: Women of Color, Equality, and the Right of Privacy." *Harvard Law Review* 104(7):1419–82.

Roman, Paul and Terry Blum. 2002. "The Workplace and Alcohol Problem Prevention." *Alcohol Research and Health* 26(1):49–57.

Scalia, John. 2001. *Federal Drug Offenders, 1999 with Trends 1984–1999* (August 2001, NCJ 187285). Washington, DC: U.S. Department of Justice, Office of Justice Programs.

Silbering, Robert. 2001. "The 'War on Drugs': A View from the Trenches." *Social Research* 68(3):890–896.

Snell, Marilyn Berlin. 2001. "Welcome to Meth Country." Retrieved July 27, 2003 (www.sierraclub.org/sierra/200101/Meth.asp).

Substance Abuse and Mental Health Services Administration (SAMHSA). 2001. "2001 State Estimates of Substance Abuse–Table D.15" Retrieved February 17, 2004 (www.samsha.gov/oas/nhsda/2k1State/v012/appd.htm).

———. 2003a. "Benefits and Costs." Retrieved July 31, 2003 (www.samsha.gov/DrugFreeWP/Benefits.html).

———. 2003b. "Drug Free Workplace Programs." Retrieved July 31, 2003 (www.samhsa.gov/DrugFreeWP/Legal.html).

———. 2003c. *Overview of Findings from the 2002 National Survey on Drug Use and Health* (Office of Applied Statistics, NHSDA Series H-21, DHHS Publication No. SMA 03–3774). Rockville, MD: U.S. Department of Health and Human Services.

Sutherland, Edwin. 1939. *Principles of Criminology*, 3d ed. Philadelphia, PA: J. B. Lippincott.

Tanner, Lindsey. 2003. "Underage Drinkers Consume 20 Percent of Booze, Study Says." *The News Tribune*, February 26, p. A7.

Task Force of the National Advisory Council on Alcohol Abuse and Alcoholism. 2002. *A Call to Action: Changing the Culture of Drinking at U.S. Colleges.* Washington, DC: National Institutes of Health, U.S. Department of Health and Human Services.

Teinowitz, Ira. 2002. "White House Brings Back Ads Linking Drugs to Terrorism." Retrieved July 27, 2003 (www.adage.com/news.cms?newsId=36048).

———. 2003. "White House to End Drugs and Terror Ads." Retrieved July 22, 2003 (www.adage.com/news.cms?newsId=37504).

Trevino, Roberto and Alan Richard. 2002. "Attitudes toward Drug Legalization among Drug Users." *American Journal of Drug and Alcohol Abuse* 28(1):91–108.

Unterberger, Gail. 1989. "Twelve Steps for Women Alcoholics." *The Christian Century* 106 (37):1150–52.

U.S. Department of Labor. 2003a. "Drug Free Workplace Advisor." Retrieved July 31, 2003 (www2.dol.gov/elaws/drugfree.htm).

———. 2003b. "Working Partners: Small Business Workplace Kit: Facts and Figures." Retrieved July 31, 2003 (www.dol.gov/asp/programs/drugs/workingpartners/Screen15.htm).

Varney, Susan and Julian Guest. 2002. "The Annual Societal Cost of Alcohol Misuse in Scotland." *Pharmacoeconomics* 20(13):891–907.

Vaughn, Christy. 2002. "Ecstasy: More Deadly Than Many Young People Know." Retrieved August 2, 2003 (www.health.org/newsroom/rep/182.aspx).

Wechsler, Henry. 1996. "Alcohol and the American College Campus." *Change* 28(4):20–25.

Weisheit, Ralph and Kathrine Johnson. 1992. "Exploring the Dimensions of Support for Decriminalizing Drugs." *Journal of Drug Issues* 92(22):53–75.

Weitzman, Elissa, Alison Folkman, Kerry Folkman, and Henry Wechsler. 2003. "The Relationship of Alcohol Outlet Density to Heavy and Frequent Drinking and Drinking-Related Problems among College Students at Eight Universities." *Health and Place* 9:1–6.

Widom, Cathy Spatz and Susanne Hiller-Sturmhofel. 2001. "Alcohol Abuse as a Risk Factor for and Consequence of Child Abuse." *Alcohol Research and Health* 25(1):52–57.

Williams, Carolyn and Cheryl Perry. 1998. "Lesson from Project Northland: Preventing Alcohol Problems during Adolescence." *Alcohol Health and Research World* 22(2):107–116.

Wilsnack, R. W. and S. C. Wilsnack. 1992. "Women, Work, and Alcohol: Failures of Simple Theories." *Alcoholism: Clinical and Experimental Research.* 16:172–179.

Wilsnack, S. C., N. D. Vogeltanz, A. D. Klassen, and T. R. Harris. 1997. "Childhood Sexual Abuse and Women's Substance Abuse: National Survey Findings." *Journal of Studies on Alcohol* 58:264–271.

Winter, Greg. 2003. "Study Finds No Sign That Testing Deters Student Drug Use." *The New York Times*, May 17, pp. A1, A12.

Yamaguchi, Ryoko, Lloyd Johnston, and Patrick O'Malley. 2003. "Relationship between Student Illicit Drug Use and School Drug-Testing Policies." *Journal of School Health* 73(4):159–164.

Ziemelis, Andris, Ronald Buckman, and Abdulaziz Elfessi. 2002. "Prevention Efforts Underlying Decreases in Binge Drinking at Institutions of Higher Education." *Journal of American College Health* 50(5):238–252.

9

Poverty

hroughout the 20th century, U.S. welfare policy has been caught between two values: the desire to help those who could not help themselves and the concern that assistance could create dependency (Weil and Feingold 2002). The centerpiece of the social welfare system was established by the passage of the Social Security Act of 1935. The Act endorsed a system of assistance programs that would provide for Americans who could not care for themselves: widows, the elderly, the unemployed, and the poor.

Under Franklin D. Roosevelt's New Deal, assistance was provided in four categories: general relief, work relief, social insurance, and categorical assistance. General relief was given to those who were not able to work; most of the people receiving general relief were single men. Work relief programs gave government jobs to those who were unemployed through programs like the Civilian Conservation Corps and the Works Progress Administration. Social insurance programs included social security and unemployment compensation. Categorical assistance was given to poor families with dependent children, to the blind, and to the elderly. To serve this group, the original welfare assistance program, Aid to Dependent Children (later renamed Aid to Families with Dependent Children or AFDC), was created (Cammisa 1998).

Categorical programs became the most controversial, while the social insurance programs were the most popular. It was widely believed that social insurance paid people for working whereas categorical programs paid people for not working. Shortly after these programs were implemented, officials became concerned that individuals might become dependent on government relief (Cammisa 1998). Even President Roosevelt (quoted in Patterson 1981) expressed his doubts about the system he helped create: "Continued dependence upon relief induces a spiritual and moral disintegration fundamentally destructive to the national fibre. To dole out relief in this way is to administer a narcotic, a subtle destroyer of the human spirit" (p. 60).

The next great expansion of the welfare system occurred in the mid 1960s, when President Lyndon Johnson declared a War on Poverty and implemented his plan to create a Great Society. Rehabilitation of the poor was the cornerstone of Johnson's policies, and what followed was an explosion of social programs: Head Start, Upward Bound, Neighborhood Youth Corp, Job Corps, public housing, and affirmative action. Although poverty was not completely eliminated, defenders of the Great Society say that these programs alleviated poverty, reduced racial discrimination, reduced the stigma attached to being poor, and helped standardize government assistance to the poor. On the other hand, opponents claim that these programs coddled the poor and created a generation that expected entitlements from the government (Cammisa 1998).

By the early 1990s, the dominant values of welfare reform focused on decreasing dependency and costs, enforcing responsibility, and empowering welfare recipients (Norris and Thompson 1995). A new era of social welfare began in 1996, when President Bill Clinton signed the Personal Responsibility and Work Opportunity Reconciliation Act (PRWORA) into law (Duncan, Harris, and Boisjoly 2000). PRWORA was a bipartisan welfare reform plan to reduce recipients' dependence on government assistance through strict work requirements and welfare time limits. The Act had an immediate affect on the number of poor. When PRWORA became law, the poverty rate was 13.7 percent; 36.5 million individuals were poor, by the government's definition. A year later, the rate declined to 13.3 percent, 35.6 million were poor. Rates declined to their lowest point in 2000, 11.3 percent or 31.6 million. According to the U.S. Census Bureau, the 2000 poverty rate was the lowest since 1979.

Defining Poverty

Absolute versus Relative Poverty

Sociologists offer two definitions of poverty, absolute and relative poverty. **Absolute poverty** refers to a lack of basic necessities, such as food, shelter, and income. **Relative poverty** refers to a situation in which some people fail to achieve the average income or lifestyle enjoyed by the rest of society. Individuals in this category may be able to afford basic necessities, but they cannot maintain a standard of living comparable to other members of society. Relative poverty emphasizes the inequality of income and the growing gap between the richest and poorest Americans.

Despite the economic growth of the 1980s and 1990s, the gap between the richest and poorest Americans has actually increased. In 2001, the Center on Budget and Policy Priorities and the Economic Policy Institute reported that in most states, the gap between the incomes of the richest 20 percent of families and the incomes of the poorest 20 percent of families is wider than it was two decades ago In the late 1990s, the poorest 20 percent of families had an average income of $14,620 per year whereas the richest 20 percent had about 10 times as much, $145,990. This increasing income gap has been attributed to the growth in wage inequality. Wages at the bottom or middle of the income scale have declined or remained constant over the past two decades. Additional factors include increases in the number of families headed by a single person, specific government policies, declines in investment income, and persistent unemployment.

The Federal Definitions of Poverty

There are two federal policy measures of poverty: the poverty threshold and the poverty guidelines. These measures are important for statistical purposes and for determining eligibility for social service programs.

The **poverty threshold** is the original federal poverty measure developed by the Social Security Administration and updated each year by the U.S. Census Bureau. The threshold is used to estimate the number of people in poverty. Originally developed by Mollie Orshansky for the Social Security Administration in 1964, the original poverty threshold was based on the economy food plan, the least costly of four nutritionally adequate food plans designed by the U.S. Department of Agriculture (USDA). Based on the 1955 House Food Consumption Survey, the USDA determined that families of three or more people spent about one third of their after-tax income on food. The poverty threshold was set at three times the cost of the economy food plan. The definition of the poverty threshold was revised in 1969 and 1981. Since 1969, annual adjustments in the levels have been based on the Consumer Price Index (CPI) instead of changes in the cost of foods in the economy food plan

The poverty threshold considers money income before taxes and excludes capital gains and non-cash benefits (public housing, Medicaid, and food stamps). The poverty threshold does not apply to people residing in military barracks or institutional group quarters or to unrelated individuals under the age of 15 (foster children). In addition, the definition of the poverty threshold does not vary geographically. The poverty threshold for 2003 is presented in Table 9.1.

The **poverty guidelines,** issued each year by the U.S. Department of Health and Human Services, are used to determine family or individual eligibility for federal programs such as Head Start, the National School Lunch Program, or the Low-Income Energy Assistance Program. The poverty guidelines are designated by the year in which they are issued. For example, the guidelines issued in February 2004 are designated as the 2004 poverty guidelines, but the guidelines reflect price changes through the calendar year 2003. There are separate poverty guidelines for Alaska and Hawaii (refer to Table 9.2).

Poverty in the United States

Census data for 2003 indicates that for the third consecutive year, the poverty rate and the number of people in poverty have increased. In 2003, the poverty rate was 12.5 percent or 35.9 million (DeNavas, Proctor, and Mills 2004) compared with the 2002 poverty rate of 12.1 percent or 34.6 million (Proctor and Dalaker 2003), or the 2001 rate of 11.7 percent or 32.9 million (Proctor and Dalaker 2002). (See Table 9.3 for a summary of poverty characteristics for 2003.)

Based on 2003 poverty figures and redefined racial and ethnic categories, Whites (who reported being White and no other race category, along with Whites who reported being White along with another race category) compose the largest group of poor individuals in the United States. About 44 percent of the U.S. poor were non-Hispanic Whites. However, the poverty rate for non-Hispanic Whites was the lowest, at 8.2 percent. Blacks continue to have the highest poverty rate, 24.4 percent, followed by Hispanics with a rate of 22.5 percent (DeNavas et al., 2004). Analysts predict that within a few years, Hispanics will have a higher poverty rate than Blacks. Racial segregation and discrimination have contributed to the high rate of minority poverty in the United States. Minority groups are disadvantaged by their lower levels of education, lower

❖ Table 9.1   Poverty Threshold in 2003 by Size of Family and Number of Related Children Under 18 Years (Dollars)

Size of Family Unit	Related Children Under 18 Years								
	None	1	2	3	4	5	6	7	8+
One person									
under 65	9,573								
65 years or older	8,825								
Two people									
Householder under 65	12,321	12,682							
Householder 65 or older	11,122	12,634							
Three	14,393	14,810	14,824						
Four	18,979	19,289	18,660	18,725					
Five	22,887	23,220	22,509	21,959	21,623				
Six	26,324	26,429	25,884	25,362	24,586	24,126			
Seven	30,289	30,479	29,827	29,372	28,526	27,538	26,454		
Eight	33,876	34,175	33,560	33,021	32,256	31,286	30,275	30,019	
Nine or more	40,751	40,948	40,404	39,947	39,196	38,229	37,229	36,998	35,572

Source: U.S. Census Bureau 2003.

levels of work experience, lower wages, and chronic health problems—all characteristics associated with higher poverty rates (Iceland, 2003).

According to the National Center for Children in Poverty (2001), children are more likely to live in poverty than Americans in any other age group. The poverty rate among children is higher in the United States than in most other major Western industrialized nations. From a peak rate of 22.5 percent in 1993, the poverty rate for children declined to 16.7 percent in 2001 and 2002, but increased to 17.6 percent in 2003 (DeNavas et al. 2004). Although improvements have been made in the poverty rate among children, there remains a wide variation among states. In 2000, New Mexico had the highest rate of child poverty, 23.5 percent, whereas Maryland had the lowest, 6.9 percent (U.S. Census Bureau 2001).

Families with a female householder and no spouse present were more likely to be poor than families with a male householder and no spouse present, 28 percent

❖ Table 9.2   2004 Federal Poverty Guidelines

Size of Family Unit	48 Contiguous States and District of Columbia	Alaska	Hawaii
1	$9,310	$11,630	$10,700
2	12,490	15,610	14,360
3	15,670	19,590	18,020
4	18,850	23,570	21,680
5	22,030	27,550	25,340
6	25,210	31,530	29,000
7	28,390	35,510	33,660
8	31,570	39,490	36,320
For each additional person, add	3,180	3,980	3,660

Source: *Federal Register,* Vol. 69, No, 30, February 13, 2004, pp. 7336–7338.

versus 13.5 percent. In contrast, the poverty rate for married couple families is 5.4 percent (DeNavas et al. 2004). Single-parent families are more vulnerable to poverty because there is only one adult income earner; and female heads of households are disadvantaged even further because women in general make less money than men.

Although the majority of poor women and men live in cities and suburbs within metropolitan areas, poverty was still higher for residents outside metropolitan areas (14.2 percent) than for those living inside metropolitan areas (12.1 percent). Among those living in metropolitan areas, the poverty rate within central cities was 17.5 percent, almost twice as high as the rate in suburbs, 9.1 percent. The South had the highest poverty rate (14.1 percent), followed by the West (12.6 percent), the Northeast (11.3 percent), and the Midwest (10.7 percent). The states with the highest three-year average poverty rate were Arkansas, Mississippi, Louisiana, West Virginia, and New Mexico (see U.S. Data Map 9.1).

Explaining Poverty

Why are some families poor while others prosper? Why does poverty persist in some families, while others are able to improve their economic situation? In the next section, we will review the four sociological perspectives to understand the causes of poverty.

❖ Table 9.3   Selected Poverty Characteristics, 2003 (Numbers in thousands)

	Number	Poverty Rate
Total	35,861	12.5
Race/Ethnicity		
White alone or in combination	24,950	10.6
White alone, non-Hispanic	15,902	8.2
Black alone or in combination	9,108	24.3
Black alone	8,781	24.4
Asian alone or in combination	1,527	11.8
Asian alone	1,401	11.8
Hispanic (of any race)	9,051	22.5
Age		
Under 18 years of age	12,866	17.6
18 to 64 years	19,443	10.8
65 years or older	3,552	10.2
Inside Metropolitan Areas	28,367	12.1
Inside central cities	14,551	17.5
Outside central cities	13,816	9.1
Outside Metropolitan areas	7,495	14.2

Source: DeNavas et al. 2004.

Note: White alone, Black alone, and Asian alone include respondents who indicated only one race. White alone or in combination, Black alone or in combination, and Asian alone or in combination include respondents who indicated one race or a combination of races.

Functionalist Perspective

Functionalists observe that poverty is a product of our social structure. Specifically, rapid economic and technological changes eliminated the need for low-skilled labor, creating a population of workers who were unskilled and untrained for this new economy. In many ways, theorists from this perspective expect this disparity among workers, arguing that only the most qualified should fill the important jobs in society and be rewarded for their talent. Lower wages and poverty are natural consequences of this system of stratification.

It is undeniable that poverty is dysfunctional for the poor and the non-poor in society. In many ways, poverty magnifies many of the social problems discussed in other chapters of this text. Poverty has a serious impact not only on the economic status of women, men, and children but also on their social, psychological, and physical well-being.

Herbert Gans (1971) argued that poverty exists because it is functional for society. Gans explained that the poor serve to uphold the legitimacy of dominant norms. The poor help reinforce cultural ideals of hard work and the notion that anyone can succeed if only they would try (so if you fail, it is your fault). Poverty helps preserve social boundaries. It

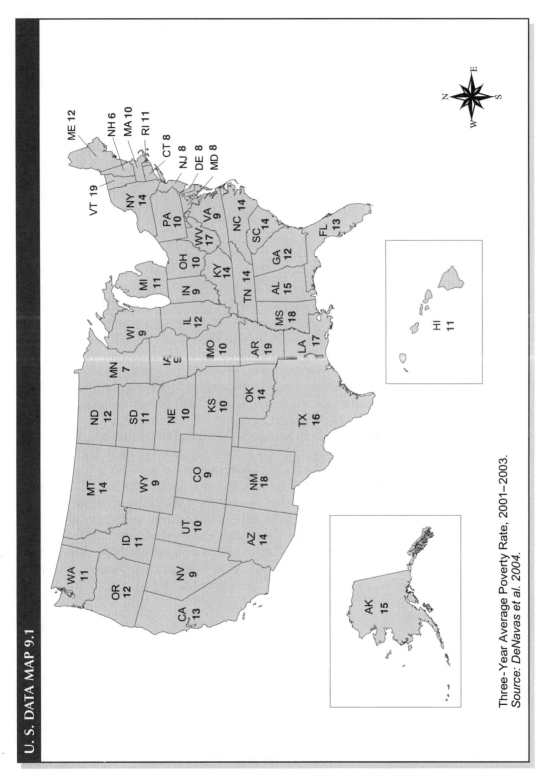

ME 12
NH 6
MA 10
RI 11
CT 8
NJ 8
DE 8
MD 8
VT 19
NY 14
PA 10
VA 9
WV 17
NC 14
SC 14
FL 13
OH 10
KY 14
GA 12
MI 11
IN 9
TN 14
AL 15
IL 12
WI 9
MS 18
MO 10
AR 19
LA 17
MN 7
IA 9
ND 12
SD 11
NE 10
KS 10
OK 14
TX 16
MT 14
WY 9
CO 9
NM 18
UT 10
AZ 14
ID 11
NV 9
WA 11
OR 12
CA 13

HI 11

AK 15

Three-Year Average Poverty Rate, 2001–2003.
Source: DeNavas et al. 2004.

serves to separate the haves from the have-nots not only in terms of their economics but also according to their educational attainment, marriage, and residence. The poor also provide a low-wage labor pool to do the "dirty work" that no one else wants to do.

Poverty helps create jobs for the non-poor, in particular the social welfare system designed to assist the poor. Yet, the social welfare system has been accused of being dysfunctional itself. Critics argue that the welfare bureaucracy is primarily concerned with its own survival. As a result, the bureaucracy will develop programs and structures that will ensure its survival and legitimacy. Based on her personal experience working with and for the system, Theresa Funiciello (1993) observed, "Countless of middle class people were making money, building careers, becoming powerful and otherwise benefiting from poverty. . . . The poverty industry once again substituted its own interests for that of poor people" (p. xix). We will discuss this further in the next perspective.

Conflict Perspective

Inequalities built into our social structure create and maintain poverty. Michael Harrington (1963) argues, "The real explanation of why the poor are where they are is that they made the mistake of being born to the wrong parents, in the wrong section of the country, in the wrong industry, or in the wrong racial or ethnic group" (p. 21).

Conflict theorists assert that poverty exists because those in power wish to maintain and expand their base of power and interests, with little left to share with others. Welfare bureaucracies—local, state, and national—represent important interest groups that influence the creation and implementation of welfare policies. A welfare policy reflects the political economy of the community in which it is implemented (Handler and Hasenfeld 1991).

Francis Fox Piven and Richard A. Cloward (1993) explain that the principal function of welfare is to allow the capitalist class to maintain control over labor. They assert that welfare policy has been used by the state to stifle protest and to enforce submissive work norms. During periods of economic crisis, the state expands welfare rolls to pacify the poor and reduce the likelihood of serious uprising. However, during economic growth or stability, the state attempts to reduce the number of people on welfare, forcing the poor or dislocated workers back into the expanding labor force. Those who remain on welfare are condemned and stigmatized for their dependence on the system. In particular, the welfare state serves capitalist interests by promoting women's roles as reserve labor and as caretakers to reproduce the labor force (Kuhn and Wolpe 1978).

Feminist Perspective

Feminist scholars argue that the welfare state is an arena of political struggle. The drive to maintain male dominance and the patriarchal family is assumed to be the principal force shaping the formation, implementation, and outcomes of U.S. welfare policy (Neubeck and Cazenave 2001).

Social welfare scholar Mimi Abramovitz (1996) notes that welfare has historically served to distinguish between the deserving poor (widows with children) and the undeserving poor (single and divorced mothers). In the 1970s and 1980s, media and politicians created the image of the "Cadillac driving, champagne sipping, penthouse

❖ FOCUS ON: ANOTHER KIND OF WELFARE

Corporate welfare is defined as any government spending program that provides special benefits to individual companies or industries through government subsidies, loans, government service, or tax breaks. According to Bartlett and Steele (1998), the federal government spends roughly $125 billion a year on economic incentives, empowerment zones, or enterprise zone programs, making our federal government America's biggest "sugar daddy." State and local governments offer grants, loans, or other subsidies to attract corporations and industries. For example, in 2003, the state of Washington offered Boeing, an aircraft manufacturer, a subsidy package of $3.2 billion to build its new 7E7 airliner in the state (Uchitelle 2003).

State subsidies have not always been successful. In the early 1990s, the state of Indiana made a deal with United Airlines, offering the company $320 million to build an advanced aircraft maintenance center near the Indianapolis International Airport. The center was successful for several years, but in April 2003, United Airlines closed its doors. The decline in airline travel after September 11, 2001, and conflicts with the mechanics union pushed the company into bankruptcy and into a cost-cutting mode.

Heavy maintenance work was transferred to private contractors in the South, who took longer to complete the job but paid workers a third of the wages and benefits of an Indianapolis mechanic (Uchitelle 2003).

Although some see benefits to corporate welfare, others believe the costs outweigh any benefits. Bartlett and Steele (1998) believe that these incentive packages provide short-, not long-term employment. Also, the system is unfair, as favors seem to be granted to the largest and most politically influential businesses (the ones that can afford to pay taxes or construction costs). In the end, smaller, less influential companies must establish their businesses with little if any government assistance. Critics of corporate welfare argue that these government handouts are stealing funds from programs essential to the health and well-being of the nation, including welfare assistance to individuals and families.

The City of Indianapolis is searching for a new tenant for the United Airlines maintenance center. Meanwhile, the city and state are paying $34 million a year to retire the $320 million bond that helped build the facility. The Airport Authority is paying an additional $6 million a year to maintain the center (Uchitelle 2003).

living welfare queens" (Zucchino 1999), suggesting that women—specifically, single mothers—were abusing welfare assistance. Women were accused of having more children to avoid work and to ensure an increase in welfare benefits. Marriage, hard work, honesty, and abstinence were offered as solutions to their poverty. The negative stereotypes of poor women stigmatized these women but also fueled support for punitive social policies (Abramovitz 1996).

As a group, teenage mothers were targeted during welfare reform in the 1990s. They were blamed for everything, as one journalist wrote: "The fact remains: every threat to the fabric of this country—from poverty to crime to homelessness—is connected to out-of-wedlock teen pregnancy" (Alder 1994). Despite the fact that there is little empirical evidence to support the link between birthrates and welfare benefits, the government seeks to punish these women, making it difficult for them to obtain and retain public assistance and to gain self-sufficiency.

Fraser (1989) argues that there are two types of welfare programs: masculine programs related to the labor market (social security, unemployment compensation) and feminine programs related to the family or household (AFDC, food stamps, and Medicaid). The welfare system is not only separate but also unequal. Fraser believes that masculine programs are rational, generous, and nonintrusive whereas feminine programs are inadequate, intrusive, and humiliating. The quintessential program for women, AFDC, institutionalized the feminization of poverty by failing to provide adequate support, training, and income to ensure self-sufficiency for women (Gordon 1994). As described by Johnnie Tillmon (1972), a welfare recipient and welfare rights organizer:

> The truth is that AFDC is like a super-sexist marriage. You trade in a man for the man. But you can't divorce him if he treats you bad. He can divorce you, of course, cut you off anytime he wants. The man runs everything. In ordinary marriage sex is supposed to be for your husband. On AFDC you're not supposed to have any sex at all. You give [up] control of your own body. . . . You may even have to agree to get your tubes tied so you can never have more children just to avoid being cut off welfare.

The new welfare system, PRWORA, has been criticized for its treatment of women and their families. PRWORA has created a pool of disciplined low-wage laborers: women who must take any job that is available or find themselves and their families penalized by the government (Piven 2002). With its emphasis on work as the path to self sufficiency, PRWORA forces women back to the same low-pay, low-skill jobs that may have led them to their poverty in the first place (Lafer 2002). The new policies fail to address the real barriers facing women: low job skills and educational attainment, racism and discrimination in the labor market, and the competing demands of work and caring for their children.

Interactionist Perspective

Interactionists attempt to explain how poverty is a learned phenomenon. Some sociologists have suggested that poverty is based on a "culture of poverty," a set of norms, values, and beliefs that encourage and perpetuate poverty. In this view, moral deficiencies of individuals or their families lead to a life of poverty. Oscar Lewis (1969) and Edward Banfield (1974) argued that the poor are socialized differently (e.g., living from moment to moment) and are likely to pass these values on to their children. Patterns of generational poverty—poor parents have poor children, who in turn become poor adults, and so on—seem to support this theory. However, the culture of poverty explanation has been widely criticized. Opponents argue that there is no evidence that the poor have a different set of values and beliefs. Poverty data reveal that for most individuals and families, continuous spells of poverty are likely to last less than two years (Harris 1993).

Interactionists also focus on the public's perception of welfare and of welfare recipients. Most Americans do not know any welfare recipients personally or have any direct contact with the welfare system. Their views on welfare are likely to be shaped by what they see on television and what they read in newspapers and magazines (Weaver 2000). As a society we have developed a sense of the "undeserving poor"; dependent mothers and fathers, nonworking recipients, have become powerful negative symbols in society (Norris and Thompson 1995). Martin Gilens, in his 1999 book, *Why Americans Hate Welfare,* explains that *welfare* has become a code word for *race.* Race and racism are important in understanding public and political support for antipoverty programs (Quadagno 1994; Lieberman 1998; Neubeck and Cazenave 2001). Gilens states that Americans perceive welfare as a Black phenomenon, believing that Blacks make up 50 percent of the poor population (compared with an actual 27 percent). This belief is exacerbated by the notion that Blacks are on welfare, not because of blocked opportunities, but largely because of their lack of effort.

Gilens (1999) asserts that the news media are primarily responsible for building this image of Black poverty, for the "racialization of poverty." During the War on Poverty in the early 1960s, the media focused on White rural America, but as the civil rights movement began to build in the mid 1960s, the media turned attention to urban poverty, and the racial character of poverty coverage changed. Between 1965 and 1967, sensationalized portrayals of Black poverty were used to depict the waste, inefficiency, or abuse of the welfare system, whereas positive coverage of poverty was more likely to include pictures and portrayals of Whites. After 1967 and for most of the following three decades, larger proportions of Blacks appeared in news coverage of most poverty topics (see Table 9.4). "Black faces are unlikely to be found in media stories on the most sympathetic subgroups of the poor, just as they are comparatively absent from media coverage of poverty during times of heightened sympathy for the poor" (Gilens 1999:132). According to Gilens, this exaggerated link between Blacks and poverty is a serious obstacle to public support for antipoverty programs.

❖ PUTTING IT TOGETHER:

Note that none of these perspectives (see Table 9.5 for a summary) focus on the role of individual factors in determining poverty. Using our sociological imagination, we begin to recognize the social and institutional conditions that create poverty. Which of these perspectives best explains why poverty exists?

The Consequences of Poverty and Welfare Reform

Welfare Reform or Workfare

During the more than 50 years when the AFDC program operated, welfare rolls were increasing, and even worse, recipients were staying on government assistance for longer periods of time. In a strange irony, welfare, the solution for the problem of poverty, became a problem itself (Norris and Thompson 1995). Between 1986 and

❖ Table 9.4   Percentage of African Americans in News Magazine Pictures of the
              Poor, 1950–1992

Topic	Number of Stories	Number of Poor People Pictured	Percentage African American
Underclass	6	36	100
Urban problems, urban renewal	91	97	84
Poor people, poverty	182	707	59
Unemployment	102	268	59
Legal aid	30	22	56
Welfare, antipoverty programs	399	965	54
Housing, homeless	272	508	52
Children	45	121	51
Employment programs	45	181	50
Education	22	95	43
Medical care	43	36	28
Hunger	52	176	25
Old age assistance	28	12	0

Source: Gilens 1999.

1996, many states began to experiment with welfare reforms. Wisconsin was the first state to implement such a reform with a program that included work requirements, benefit limits, and employment goals.

In 1996, PRWORA was passed with a new focus on helping clients achieve self-sufficiency through employment. Replacing AFDC, the new welfare program is called Temporary Assistance for Needy Families (TANF). Instead of treating assistance as an entitlement, as it was under AFDC, TANF declares that government help is temporary and has to be earned. Under TANF, there is a federal lifetime limit of 60 months of assistance, although states may put shorter limits on benefits. PRWORA also gave states primary responsibility for designing their assistance programs and for determining eligibility and benefits. States are penalized for not meeting caseload targets, either reducing the number of welfare cases to below 1995 levels or increasing the percentage of cases involved in work activities. Refer to Table 9.6 for a summary of

❖ Table 9.5   Summary of Sociological Perspectives: Poverty

	Functional	Conflict/Feminist	Interactionist
Explanation of poverty	Poverty emerges from the social structure. Poverty serves a social function.	Welfare bureaucracies represent important interest groups that influence the creation and implementation of welfare policies.	Poverty is a learned phenomenon based on a "culture of poverty," a set of norms, values, and beliefs that encourage and perpetuate poverty. The public's perception of the welfare system and of welfare recipients is shaped by the media, political groups, and stereotypes.
Questions asked about poverty and income inequality	What are the functions and dysfunctions of poverty? What portions of society benefit from poverty?	What powerful interest groups determine welfare policies? How do our welfare policies reflect political, economic, and social interest groups?	Is poverty learned behavior? How are our perceptions of the poor determined by the media, news reports, and politicians? Has society created two images—the deserving versus the undeserving poor? Are these images accurate?

demographic characteristics and financial circumstances of TANF families for 2000–2001.

Although employment has increased among welfare recipients, many recipients have little education or work experience (Loprest 2002). As a group, welfare recipients are limited to jobs at the lower end of the labor market. In 1999, the median hourly wage of employed former welfare recipients was $7.15. About a quarter of those

❖ Table 9.6   Characteristics and Financial Circumstances of Temporary Assistance
to Needy Families (TANF) Recipients, 2000–2001

- Most TANF adult recipients were women; men represented only 10 percent of adult recipients.
- Average age of TANF adult recipients was 31.3 years.
- Most TANF adult recipients were U.S. citizens; only 8 percent of TANF adults were noncitizens residing legally in the United States.
- Average age of TANF recipient children was 7.8 years. About 13 percent were under two years of age, while 38 percent were under the age of six. Only 8 percent of children were 16 years of age or older.
- Most recipient children were children of the head of the household in TANF families, and 8 percent were grandchildren of the head of household.
- Among TANF families, 99 percent received cash and cash equivalent assistance, with an average monthly amount of $351. Monthly cash benefits to TANF families averaged $288 for one child, $362 for two children, $423 for three children, and $519 for four children or more.
- One in ten TANF families received child support, with an average monthly amount of $179. About 12 percent of TANF families had cash resources (cash on hand, bank accounts, or certificates of deposit), an average of $244 per family.

Source: Office of Family Assistance, Administration for Children and Families 2003.

employed worked night shifts or irregular schedules. In addition, most former recipients have limited employment benefits: About one third of employers offer health insurance, and only one third or one half provide sick leave. Studies indicate that one quarter to one third of those leaving welfare in a given three-month period were receiving benefits again within the next year (Acs and Loprest 2001).

Another issue, which arose again with the reauthorization of PRWORA, is whether child care assistance provisions actually meet the needs of working and poor families. Child care is not just about fostering a child's development; it also supports parents' employment. Child care is essential to promote employment and reduce welfare use among low-income families. Among the working poor, child care arrangements that are difficult to pay for, difficult to access, do not cover parents' work hours, or are unreliable can interfere with parents' employment (Gennetian et al. 2002). In addition, child care policies and funding levels have implications for the development and safety of millions of low-income children and youth (Adams and Rohacek 2002). By 1999, child care represented the largest category of state expenditure of TANF funds after cash assistance. While welfare caseloads fell by half, child care caseloads doubled. By 2000, states were spending $3.96 billion to support child care. However, after 2001–2002, use of TANF funds for child care was likely to decline due to state budget crises, dwindling TANF funding, and declining caseloads (Mezey and Richie 2003).

❖ TAKING A WORLD VIEW

CHILD CARE IN EUROPE

European countries offer comprehensive models of public child care. For example, in Scandinavian countries, there is an integrated system of child care centers and organized family day care serving children from birth till school age and managed by social welfare or educational authorities. Public child care is available to children ages 1 through 12. Nearly all employed parents have access to child care with little or no waiting time. In Sweden and Denmark, one third to one half of children under three years of age are in some form of full-day, publicly supported day care, along with 72 percent to 82 percent of children between the ages of three and five (Waldfogel 2001). Children of unemployed parents are not eligible for day care in about 40 percent of locations (Skolverket 2003). Ken Jaffee, director of the International Child Resource Institute in Sweden, says, "Child care is considered a necessity for the economic and social survival of a country, and there is more universal availability of child care. Every neighborhood has a center" (Polk 1997).

In France and Belgium, there is a two-phase system of child care. For younger children, full-day child care centers are provided under the authority of the social welfare system. Beginning at age two and a half to three, children are enrolled in full-day pre-primary programs within the educational system. Enrollment of younger children in child care is about 30 percent in Belgium and 24 percent in France. Nearly 100 percent of all eligible children are enrolled in pre-primary programs (Gornick and Meyers 2002).

Not only are child care services more available to European families, but child care staff are better trained and paid than they are in the United States. Child care workers and educators in European countries are required to have three to five years of vocational or university training. Funding for these extensive child care programs is provided by local, state, or national governments. Care for very young children is partially funded through parental co-payments that are scaled according to family income. Lower income families generally pay nothing whereas more affluent families pay no more than 10 percent to 15 percent of their income toward child care (Gornick and Meyers 2002).

The United States has never embraced a national system for providing, funding, and regulating early childhood education and care. It is estimated that the U.S. government spends between 25 percent and 30 percent of the cost of child care for children under the age of three and for children age three to six. In contrast, Denmark, Finland, France, Norway, and Sweden pay most of the costs of care, about 68 percent to 100 percent. One study found that the United States spends about $600 per year per preschool-age child, whereas France spends about $3,000 and Sweden spends more than $4,500 (Waldfogel 2001).

Limited Access to Medical Care

Although the poor are eligible for medical care under Medicaid, Medicaid coverage is not comprehensive, forcing most to seek treatment only in cases of medical emergencies. Having a routine physical or a regular family doctor is rare among poor and low-income families. Most of the working poor are not eligible for public assistance medical programs (e.g., Medicaid), even though their employers do not provide health insurance (Seccombe and Amey 1995). In fact, among households with incomes between $25,000 and $49,999 per year, 19.3 percent or 14.6 million did not have health insurance (Mills and Bhandari 2003).

In the past, families were eligible for Medicaid only if they were also receiving government assistance. In 1997, the State Children's Health Insurance program was established to help states expand Medicaid coverage, establish a separate child health insurance program, or combine approaches to cover children with family incomes up to 200 percent of the poverty line or higher. Since 1998, the federal government also provides Transitional Medical Assistance for families leaving welfare for work. The program provides up to 12 months of coverage when families lose regular Medicaid coverage due to an increase in earnings (leaving welfare for work). Despite these medical provisions, a review of data from 25 states where welfare recipients have left welfare for work indicates that there has been a decline in health coverage among eligible low-income families with children.

Jocelyn Guyer (2000) says that in most states, roughly half of parents in families that left welfare and more than one third of children in those families lose Medicaid coverage. In some states, the problem is severe. In New York, 65 percent of children lost Medicaid after they left welfare; in Mississippi, 56 percent of children also lost coverage. Even among families who left welfare for work, fewer than half receive health coverage through their employers. As a result, families are more likely to have unmet medical needs after leaving welfare. Guyer (2000) notes that although little is known about why eligible families lose health coverage, some studies reveal that families were unaware of their eligibility for programs like Medicaid or Transitional Medical Assistance.

Hunger among the Poor

About 10.7 percent of households or 12 million American families were food insecure at least some time during the year (USDA 2003a). **Food insecure** means that these families did not always have access to enough food for all members of the household to enjoy active and healthy lives. In 3.3 percent of households (or 3.5 million), one or more household members were hungry at least some time during the year. The remaining 7.4 percent (or 8 million) avoided hunger by getting emergency food from community food pantries, eating less varied diets, and participating in the federal food assistance programs. Some groups experience higher rates of food insecurity and hunger: single female-headed households with children (31.9 percent), Black households (21.3 percent), Hispanic households (21.8 percent, and households with income below the poverty line (36.5 percent) (USDA 2003b).

The USDA provided food assistance to one in six Americans in 2001 through one of 14 public food assistance programs. Most of us are familiar with the U.S. food stamp program, the nation's largest nutrition program for low-income individuals and families. During 2002, the program served an average of 19 million low-income Americans each month. The average monthly benefit was $79.68 per person, at an annual cost of $20.5 billion. Food stamps cannot be used to buy nonfood items (personal hygiene supplies, paper products), alcoholic beverages, vitamins and medicines, hot food products, or any food that will be eaten in the store. Although the food stamp program and other USDA programs have been shown to be effective in improving the purchasing power and nutritional status of specific populations, a large segment of low-income Americans are not being adequately served or served at all by these programs (Nicholas-Casebolt and McGrath Morris 2001). These families need to rely on private programs, such as food pantries or soup kitchens.

As reported by Briefel et al. (2003), food pantries and emergency kitchens play an important role in the nutritional safety net for America's low-income and needy populations. These organizations are part of the Emergency Food Assistance System, a network of private organizations operating with some federal support. Almost one third of pantry client households and two fifths of kitchen client households are at or below 50 percent of the poverty line. The mean monthly income is $781 for pantry client households and $708 for kitchen client households. Food pantries were likely to serve families with children (45 percent of households included children), whereas emergency kitchens were likely to serve men living alone (38 percent) or single adults living with other adults (18 percent). The U.S. Conference of Mayors (2000) reported that emergency food assistance increased by an average of 19 percent in 25 U.S. cities. Rising hunger was attributed to high housing costs, low-pay jobs, unemployment, and the economic downturn. In 2001, food pantries served about 8.0 million adults and 4.5 million children, and emergency kitchens served about 1.1 million people in a typical month. It is estimated that since the passage of PRWORA, there has been an increase in the number of people who are hungry or at risk of hunger.

Poor households are likely to experience higher food prices than the national average (Kaufman et al. 1997). Poor families are disadvantaged not only because of their low income but also because of their location. Suburban supermarkets are likely to have lower food prices and a wider selection of food, but the poor are likely to reside in central cities and rural areas. Grocery stores in central cities have higher operating costs and tend to be smaller. In rural areas, food prices are also higher because these markets are likely to be smaller and have lower sales volume (Kaufman et al. 1997).

There has also been increasing concern over the number of children served with school meal programs. The National School Lunch Program has existed since 1946, providing free or reduced-price lunches to eligible students. In 2002, the School Breakfast Program served an average of 1.4 billion breakfasts; 83 percent were free or at reduced price for eligible children. Beginning in 1975, the Summer Food Program provided meals for children in low-income areas when school is not in session. In July 2001, the program fed about 2.1 million children per day.

For more information on the Food Stamp Program, go to *Study Site Chapter 9.* The site offers information on the food stamp program and an online eligibility test to determine your eligibility for your state's food stamp program.

Voices of the Community:
Military Families

In her book, *Growing Up Empty,* Loretta Schwartz-Nobel (2002) chronicles the plight of families struggling with hunger. Hunger affects not only the poor but also populations that we least expect: the middle class, the working poor, refugees, and military families.

Military families receive free medical care, dental care, and housing, but some costs are covered while others are not. Housing is free on base only if housing is available, and there is no food allowance for wives or children. In fact, when a soldier is sent away from base, the family paycheck is reduced about $210 a month, based on the cost of the soldier's rations or food money. Shopping on the base or in the commissary does help these families; however, because base outlets routinely have standard markdowns, they rarely have special sales. For some families, it may be cheaper to shop at area Wal-Mart, K-Mart, or other less expensive stores than to shop on base (Schwartz-Nobel 2002).

Under federal poverty guidelines, the first three enlisted ranks, E-1 through E-3, are eligible for food stamps unless they have assets worth more than $4,000. Poverty and hunger are worse in high-cost areas, such as San Diego (California), Norfolk (Virginia), Quantico (Virginia), Washington, D.C., Seattle (Washington), and Honolulu (Hawaii). Schwartz-Nobel (2002) spoke with Marge Johnson, who was stationed in San Diego, California, with her husband, Andy. Ms. Johnson explains:

Everyone thinks when you're in the military you're set for life. They mislead you on purpose and it's a real sin that they commit. They play on your weaknesses and on the injuries you've already suffered . . . . Take today. All I've got in my wallet is the two dollars my aunt sent us to buy ice cream for the kids, and if she hadn't sent it, I wouldn't have anything.

Ms. Johnson explains that her husband is currently an E-5, enlisted for eight years.

He gets $492.70 on the first of the month, and $533.26 on the fifteenth. That's a total of $1,025.96 a month, which is less than $13,000 a year. And, for a family of five with three kids, that's just not enough.

One day, soon after I arrived on this base, my husband was sent away for six months. The kids and I were sleeping on the floor and, as usual at the end of the month, there was no food or money in the house. . . I got so desperate that I just took the kids and got into the car and started driving aimlessly. I had no idea where I was going or what I was looking for. It was a cold, foggy Monday morning. All I knew was that the kids were hungry and I was wondering how on God's earth I would feed them. I was just praying out loud for that I'd find a way. Then out of nowhere, through the rain and fog, I saw this long line of women and children. There must have been a hundred women on that line. I stopped the car and I got out. I walked across the street and I said to a woman who was holding a baby in her arms, "Excuse me, ma'am, by why are all you women standing here in this line in the pouring rain?" She looked at me and said, "Didn't you hear? They're giving away free bread; hamburger buns, hot dog buns, and bakery bread."

So I joined the women and children on that line and I got a loaf of sourdough bread. They could only give me one loaf, I think it was day-old bread but it had gotten wet so I don't really know. Anyhow, I got back in the car and drove home through the rain, holding that bread in my lap. I knew it wouldn't be enough to fill all of us up so I thought I'd feed it to the children first."

Source: Schwartz-Nobel 2002:114, 116–117.

❖ ❖

Lack of Affordable Housing

In the same way that access to child care, medical care, and transportation has been linked to economic self-sufficiency, research has also established the relationship between having affordable housing and leaving welfare. Welfare reform successes are greater among families with assisted housing than among other low-income families (Sard and Waller 2002). Unfortunately, most families who leave welfare for work do not earn enough to afford decent quality housing, and because of their employment status, they are not eligible for housing assistance. The average total monthly income of households that previously received welfare and have at least one working member is $1,261, still below the poverty level for a family of three (Sard and Waller 2002). Families that left welfare between 1997 and 1999 were more likely to report difficulty in paying a mortgage, rent, or utility bill than families leaving welfare between 1995 and 1997. Among the more recent group of people leaving welfare, nearly 1 in 10 reported that they were forced to double up with other family members or friends because they could not afford the cost of housing (Loprest 2001).

Part of the problem can also be attributed to the lack of affordable rental units (defined as requiring the family to pay less than 30 percent of its income for housing costs). In 1987, there were 85 units for every 100 poor families, but the number declined to 75 units for every 100 families by 1999 (Sard and Waller 2002). According to the National Low Income Housing Coalition (Nelson, Treskon, and Pelletiere 2004), there is no state where a low-income worker can reasonably afford a modest one- or two-bedroom rental unit. More than 50 percent of low-income renter households paid more than half their income for gross rent expenses (rent plus utilities). In 40 states, workers needed to earn more than two times the minimum wage to afford basic housing. In some states—California, Connecticut, Maryland, Massachusetts, New Jersey, and New York—workers needed to earn three times the minimum wage to afford housing (Clemetson 2003). Federal housing programs only serve about one quarter of the eligible low-income households, and few states invest in low-income housing programs (Sard and Waller 2002).

In Pierce County, Washington, a strip of 17 motels in the city of Lakewood provides shelter for more than 400 women, men, and children on the brink of homelessness. According to Pierce County's Department of Community Service, the real problem is the shortage of affordable housing for those living on minimum wage. Motel residents are working but cannot afford to pay first and last month's rent. As they live from paycheck to paycheck, the working poor reside in local motels with free furnishings, television, and other utilities. These families are paying as much as $175 to $250 per week for rent (Nguyen 2003).

The combination of low earnings and scarce housing assistance results in serious housing problems for the working poor. Nearly three fifths of working-poor renters with children who do not have housing assistance pay more than 50 percent of their income on housing or live in seriously substandard housing, or both. Among unsubsidized poor renter families with at least full-time year-round minimum-wage earnings, 36 percent spent more than half their income on housing (Sard and Waller 2002).

Voices in the Community:
Richard Saul

In November 1965, Richard Saul was hired for a position as a VISTA project development officer in the Office of Economic Opportunity (OEO). The Economic Opportunity Act of 1964 had just been passed, and President Johnson's War on Poverty was getting under way. That was the beginning of Saul's long career at the U.S. Department of Health and Human Services as an administrator, innovator, and advocate for programs serving the poor. Currently, he serves as a senior program analyst for the Administration for Children and Families in the Office of Community Services. Throughout his career, Saul explains, "I've always been motivated by what I think is right and necessary to accomplish the tasks that I believe we are here to accomplish." I asked him to describe the one program that he knew was a success.

The one program from which I know I've made a difference started back in OEO in the 1970s. In the fall of 1973, the oil embargo wreaked havoc among the poor. Not only did oil and gas prices rise, but for example, in Kentucky the price of coal went overnight from $9.00 per ton to $60.00, so that poor people were walking the railroad tracks to pick up coal that had fallen from hopper cars in passing trains.

With Alvin Arnett's support (OEO director), I organized and brought together a group of colleagues from Community Action Agencies (CAAs) in different parts of the country as an Energy Planning Group to investigate ways we could provide help to the poor in this energy crisis. We came up with a request to Mr. Arnett that he permit CAAs to use some of their existing grant funds to help low-income families pay their energy bills. This was, in effect, the precursor to what is today the Low Income Home Energy Assistance Program administered by the Office of Community Services.

Then, one night when I was lying in bed and wondering what else we could do to help poor people survive the energy crisis, it came to me that OEO could start a program to insulate poor people's houses, which would not only reduce their energy costs, but would also conserve energy and create jobs! The next morning I went to Al Arnett and told him that I had an idea the night before that was one of the best ideas I'd ever had: start a program to insulate poor people's houses. He said, "You're right. Do it." That same morning, I had a phone call from a former colleague who now represented the State of Maine and was looking for ideas that might assure the survival of CAAs in Maine. I told him to get me a proposal to insulate poor people's houses in Maine. The proposal was delivered the next week, and five weeks later, OEO funded its first weatherization program, Project F.U.E.L. in Maine.

When the Economic Opportunity Act was reauthorized the following year, it contained a new section for Emergency Energy Conservation Services and OEO, whose name was by then changed to the Community Services Administrations (CSA), received appropriations for both its new Weatherization Program and for Energy Assistance Payments. At the end of the 1970s, the Weatherization Program was transferred to the Department of Energy, where it remains today.

For more information about the Low Income Home Energy Assistance Program and Weatherization Program, log on to *Study Site Chapter 9.*

When Time Limits Run Out

There is overwhelming evidence that welfare caseloads have declined since the enactment of PRWORA. Two other factors—a strong economy and increased aid to low-income working families—may have also contributed to the early decline (Besharov 2002). Welfare officials often point to how the first to leave welfare were those with the most employable skills. However, research indicates that the early employment success of welfare reform has diminished as the economy faltered. According to the Urban Institute, 32 percent of welfare recipients were in paid jobs in 1999, but the number had fallen to 28 percent by 2002. Employment also declined for those who left welfare, from 50 percent in 1999 to 42 percent in 2002 (Zedlewski and Loprest 2003).

Under PRWORA, adults are limited to five years of federal welfare benefits, although 20 states impose shorter time limits. States are allowed to exempt up to 20 percent of their caseloads from time limits and can provide state assistance to families that have used up their federal assistance. The first set of time limits expired on September 30, 2002. Are those who have left welfare able to sustain themselves? Angie O'Gorman (2002) describes the typical "leaver" as a single woman with two children. She is working full-time on minimum wage and makes about $10,300 annually or $178 per week. (The poverty level for a family of three is $14,824. See Table 9.1.) She continues to receive government assistance—food stamps, Medicaid, health insurance for her children, and other benefits. Is this self-sufficiency?

Studies that have traced people who leave welfare over longer periods of time indicate no significant earnings growth after leaving welfare (O'Gorman 2002). An analysis by the National Campaign for Jobs and Income Support (2001) found that leavers have trouble finding employment; lack child care, transportation, nutrition, and health care assistance; and remain concentrated in the low-wage labor market. It appears that individuals and families are cycling in and out of poverty, working when jobs are available but never achieving complete economic independence. Women who have multiple barriers to obtaining and retaining employment will be least likely to achieve economic self-sufficiency. Barriers may include low-level work experiences, less than a high school education, substance dependence, physical health problems, and other barriers such as domestic violence, transportation issues, or child care problems. Critics argue that welfare reform made little impact on the real barriers to self-sufficiency: the need for a livable wage, employment opportunities, education or technical training, child care, health insurance, transportation, and affordable housing. Sanctioned families, families that will lose their welfare assistance, are seriously at risk. It is likely that the parent in a sanctioned family is unable to comply with TANF requirements due to mental illness, developmental disability, or substance abuse (Blum and Farnsworth Francis 2002).

Problems are compounded for the rural poor, particularly those with little education, no phone, no car, and no jobs. Consider Tulare County, California's top agricultural county, home to Californians with the lowest education level and the highest rate of poverty. By January 2003, when lifetime welfare limits began to run out, Tulare's welfare families were sliding into deeper poverty. On a given day, Tulare County's job center will post 10 new jobs, whereas more than 6,000 new jobs may be posted in Los Angeles County. Realizing that the county cannot provide enough jobs for the poor, the More Opportunity for Viable Employment (MOVE) program paid to move more than 1,000 welfare recipients out of the county. Most of them moved to the Midwest, Las Vegas, or anywhere else jobs were available. Those who stay survive day by day, selling their automobiles for cash, working for minimum wage at fast food places, or attending job training classes. Kelly Young, a mother of two young girls, works two jobs: one for $7.25 an hour afternoons and weekends; the other a graveyard shift for $25 a night caring for an elderly client. Because she has no car, she needs to catch a ride to her workplaces. There is no local bus service in her rural community (Romney 2003).

Poverty Policy, Advocacy, and Innovation

The Reauthorization of Welfare Reform

In 2002, President George W. Bush announced plans for the reauthorization of PRWORA. His plan emphasized four themes: promoting work, increasing resources for welfare families, protecting children and strengthening families, and enhancing state flexibility in welfare funding and programming. Among his proposals was an increase in the number of hours in required work activities from 30 hours to 40 hours a week (24 hours of work or work-related activity and 16 hours of other activities, such as education or counseling). Bush proposed no increased funding for job training, child care, or transportation assistance. Under his proposal, Bush approved up to $300 million per year for marriage promotion programs under the Healthy Marriage and Responsible Fatherhood Community Demonstration Initiative. No change was recommended to the five-year lifetime limit on assistance. PRWORA was extended through 2003 because Congress was unable to pass a reauthorization bill in 2002.

Advocates have asked for a reduction in poverty, not just caseloads, as the primary goal of welfare reform. They argue that by removing current limits on education and training, enhancing support services for families, restoring benefits to legal immigrants, and stopping the time clock penalty, TANF could be transformed into an effective poverty-reducing program (Coalition on Human Needs 2003). Advocacy groups have encouraged federal lawmakers to increase funding for the TANF block grants to states, at a minimum to keep pace with inflation. Critics point to the economic fragility of low-income families and identify the need for sufficient health insurance, child care, and transportation assistance to help low-income families during times of crisis.

Others have argued for the importance of restoring support for postsecondary education as a means to promote self-sufficiency. According to the Center for Women Policy Studies (2003) after PRWORA, college enrollment among low-income women declined. Yet studies indicate that former TANF recipients with a college education are more likely to stay employed and less likely to return to welfare. For example, a study among former welfare recipients in Oregon found that only 52 percent of those with less than a high school diploma were employed after two years. In contrast, 90 percent of former TANF recipients with a bachelor's degree were still employed. Since 1996, 49 states—Oklahoma and the District of Columbia are exceptions—have passed legislation to allow secondary education to count as activity under PRWORA. Georgia is the only state that allows recipients to enroll in graduate programs.

Changing the Definition—Redefining the Poverty Line

In 1995, a panel of the National Academy of Sciences (NAS) called for a new poverty measure to include the three basic categories of food, clothing, and shelter (and utilities) and a small amount to cover other needs such as household supplies, child care, personal care, and non-work related transportation. Because the census measure does not show how taxes, non-cash benefits, and work-related child care and medical expenses affect people's well-being, the NAS panel cautioned that the current poverty measure cannot reflect how policy changes in these areas affect the poor. In addition, the measure does not consider how the cost of basic goods (food and shelter) has changed since the 1960s. As we have already discussed, the federal poverty measurement assumes that costs are the same across most of the states, except Hawaii and Alaska. If you think about it, it does not make sense that a family of four in Manhattan, New York, is expected to spend the same amount of money for food, clothing, and shelter as a family in Manhattan, Kansas (Bhargava and Kuriansky 2002).

The U.S. Census Bureau has been calculating experimental measures of poverty since 1999. For 2001, in measuring the overall poverty rate, the experimental measures report higher levels of poverty, especially when accounting for geographic differences in housing costs and taking into account medical out-of-pocket expenses. Although the official rate is 11.7 percent, experimental measures vary from a low of 12.3 percent to 12.9 percent. When looking at the poverty rate for specific groups, the experimental measures tend to present a poverty population that looks more like the total population in terms of its mix of people: the elderly, White non-Hispanic individuals, and Hispanics (Short 2001).

❖ **FOCUS ON: EARNED INCOME TAX CREDIT**

Enacted in 1975, the Earned Income Tax Credit (EITC) program provides federal tax relief for low-income working families, especially those with children. The credit reduces the amount of federal tax owed and usually results in a tax refund for those who qualify. To qualify for the program, adults must be employed. A single parent with one child who had family income of less than $29,666 (or $30,666 for a married couple with one child) in 2003 could get a credit of up to $2,547 (Center on Budget and Policy Priorities 2004). The EITC can be claimed for children under age 19 or under age 24 if they are still in college.

Expansions of the program in the late 1980s and early 1990s made the credit more generous for families with two or more children. In 1994, a small credit was made available to low-income families without children (Freidman 2000). Receipt of EITC credit does not affect receipt of other programs such as food stamp benefits, Medicaid, or housing subsidies.

Supporters of EITC argue that the program strengthens family self-sufficiency, provides families with more disposable income, and encourages work among welfare recipients. Families can use their credit to reduce debt, purchase a car, or pay for education (Freidman 2000). Almost half of EITC recipients planned to save all or part of their refund (Smeeding, Ross, and O'Conner 1999). The program is credited with lifting more children out of poverty than any other government program (Llobrera and Zahradnik 2004).

Eighteen states offer a state-level earned income credit for residents, usually a percentage of the federal credit. For more information, log on to *Study Site Chapter 9*.

Other alternative measures have been introduced. The Self-Sufficiency Standard developed by Diana Pierce defines the amount of income necessary to meet basic needs without public assistance (public housing, food stamps, etc.) or private/informal subsidies (free baby-sitting by a friend, food provided by churches or local food banks). The Self-Sufficiency Standard determines the level of income necessary to raise a family out of welfare into total independence. The annual standard for a family of four in Alabama is $40,940 (or $3,412 per month), whereas the standard for a family of four in Utah is $45,803 (or $3,817 per month). The Economic Policy Institute offers a basic family budget calculator, a more realistic measure of the income required to support a basic standard of living. The budgets are individualized for 400 U.S. communities and for different family types.

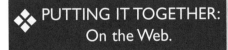
❖ **PUTTING IT TOGETHER:** On the Web.

For more information about alternative poverty measures, visit The Economic Policy Institute and the Self Sufficiency Standard. Log on to *Study Site Chapter 9* for the Web site links.

The Role of Faith-Based Programs

President George W. Bush established the White House Office of Faith-Based and Community Initiatives in 2001 to encourage the development and federal funding of faith-based programs. Acknowledging the role of federal programs in response to welfare, homelessness, substance abusers, ex-offenders, and at-risk youth, Bush also credited faith-based organizations for their community work and support, calling their efforts "indispensable in meeting the needs of poor Americans and distressed neighborhoods. Government cannot be replaced by such organizations, but it can and should welcome them as partners (White House 2001)." The Office has program initiatives in seven federal agencies including Housing and Urban Development, Health and Human Services, and Education.

Opponents of the program, such as the American Civil Liberties Union and Americans United for Separation of Church and State, have argued that this policy violates the constitutional separation of church and state. Faith-based programs would be allowed to discriminate in their hiring practices and also in their service delivery on the basis of religion, gender, race and ethnicity and other factors. Critics were also concerned that program clients would be subject to unwanted proselytizing in the areas where services were provided. President Bush countered by arguing that these programs were not going to preach religion; rather, they were faith-based programs to help people's lives. There has been no comprehensive evaluation of the effectiveness of faith based programs.

In 2002, Secretary of Health and Human Services Tommy Thompson announced $30 million funding for a new initiative, the Compassion Capital Fund. The funds to support research on the effectiveness of faith-based programs were distributed to The National Resource Center and to intermediary organizations that would provide faith-based and community organizations in their target areas with technical assistance and funding. The National Resource Center provides training, tools, and resources for faith-based programs. The Catholic Charities' Stone Soup Collaborative serves as an intermediary organization for rural agency staff throughout New Mexico. In 2003, the Collaborative conducted regional trainings in Las Vegas, Nevada, and Albuquerque, Santa Fe, and Gallup, New Mexico on a variety of topics: grant writing, legal issues for small agencies, board development and training, and working with volunteers.

Community Responses to Poverty

Most community efforts do not address the structural sources of poverty, focusing instead on innovative ways to provide support for poor or low income individuals and families. Community efforts address a wide range of needs: housing, employment, education, and health. Under welfare reform, there has been a renewed emphasis on community building: activities, practices, and policies that support positive connections among individuals, groups, neighborhoods, organizations, and communities (Weil 1996). Programs range in size, serving the needs of an entire community or a select group experiencing poverty.

VISUAL ESSAY: CHARITY AND THE CHURCH ❖

The earliest organized charity programs were organized by religious groups. Well before the birth of Christ, Jews and followers of Confucius believed that they had a responsibility to assist the needy. Several centuries later, Christians and Muslims independently recognized their moral obligation to use their resources to help the poor. However, it was during the 16th century, in England, that the government began taking responsibility for the poor as well.

In the United States, independent secular programs, notably the settlement houses, began supplementing religious and governmental programs in the late 1800s. These "street urchins" represent the typical inhabitants of the best-known U.S. settlement house, Hull House in Chicago, in the 1920s. Hull House was cofounded by social activists Jane Addams and Ellen Gates Starr in 1889.

Social programs got a big boost during the 1960s with the historic passage of civil rights and economic opportunity legislation. One program was the U.S. Department of Agriculture's Child Nutrition Program, which provided cash and food to public and private nonprofit agencies that provided meals for school-age children. The program still operates today.

In the 1980s, the federal government began withdrawing funding from social programs, shifting some of the burden of care for the needy onto not-for-profit agencies. After 2000, the George W. Bush administration went even further and began promoting a "faith-based initiative," enabling religious organizations to compete for federal funding to provide public services, such as welfare programs, child care, and homeless shelters. Federal dollars still cannot be used to support any inherently religious activity, however.

Religious organizations are ambivalent about the new initiative. They want to continue their tradition of services to the needy and could use the additional funding, but they worry about some of the implications of engaging churches and other religious entities in state matters. The National Congress for Community Economic Development published a list of possible reasons not to seek federal funding at its Web site (www.ncced.org/fbi/prosCons.html).

Major Questions and Concerns about the Initiative

The following are among the most frequently raised concerns and criticisms of the Bush faith-based initiatives and the charitable choice concern on which it builds. (Points gleaned from many sources.)

1. Uses a term, "faith-based," that is not defined in law or practice but is usually taken to be a circumlocution for "religious." (The charitable choice statute uses "religious.")

2. May convey the assumption that faith-based or religious organizations have an obligation to perform social services; some claim that role but others do not include such work in their definitions or mission and purpose.

3. May step across the boundary of church-state separation. Concerns of this kind arising from charitable choice include: a) exemption from civil rights laws barring hiring discrimination on religious grounds, b) not requiring separate incorporation of contract holders, c) allow religious symbols to be displayed in service areas, and d) allowing religious content in service programs, even though participation is voluntary.

4. May result in excessive religious reliance on public money, leading to a weakening of the "prophetic role" of religion, particularly as that may involve criticism of government policy; may cause a decrease in giving to religion by members and other private donors.

5. May result in improper religious use of public funds unless each program is closely monitored.

6. May introduce government interference in the internal affairs of religious groups or government scrutiny of religion's financial records—a concern heard across the religious board.

7. May imply that government considers faith-based providers superior to secular ones and result in unequal treatment.

8. May encourage religious groups with insufficient capacity or competence to enter the social service field, especially risky with regard to "performance-based contracts," as is usually the case with government, which requires upfront money. Also introduces burdensome paperwork and the recurring need to reapply since government contracts are often of short duration.

How do the new faith-based initiatives differ from traditional religion-sponsored charity programs and existing social welfare programs sponsored by the government?

❖

One organization with a broad scope is Action for Boston Community Development (ABCD) (2003). ABCD was incorporated in 1962 with a vision to promote self-help for low-income people and neighborhoods. It is the largest independent, private nonprofit human services agency in New England. The agency attempts to provide assistance to clients through decentralized neighborhood-based centers and programs. Neighborhood residents make up the majority of ABCD board members. ABCD offers a wide range of services and programs addressing career development, higher education, health, day care, community development, and youth. ABCD serves more than 100,000 low-income individuals and families annually.

Programs not only provide service but also help welfare recipients make the transition out of welfare by getting jobs or starting their own small businesses. The Cooperative Economics for Women (CEW) began in the mid 1990s with the goal of supplementing welfare recipients' benefits with part-time work. The first women who enrolled in the program identified the greater need for full-time work; thus, the CEW refocused on building cooperative businesses. In 2002, CEW supported three businesses: an Eritrean restaurant, a sewing cooperative of Cambodian worker-members, and a cleaning company owned by Haitian and Cape Verdean women. Profits from each business are reinvested in the business or shared among members. To build the women's economic well-being, CEW focuses on their noneconomic needs, such as education, training, child care, and legal assistance. The businesses provide not only economic support but also emotional support for the women (Guilford 2002).

Community-based kitchens have provided vital assistance for the unemployed and the poor. One such innovative program is the Greyston Bakery based in Yonkers, New York. Greyston Bakery combines community and social action with good business practice. As stated on its Web site, "With each cake, tart and brownie we weave a concern for the community as well as for our employees" (Greyston Bakery 2004). What began in 1982 as a small bakery to employ Zen Buddhist students has grown into a $14 million organization of 180 employees. With more than 50 workers, the bakery makes cakes and sweets, most notably the brownies used in Ben & Jerry's Chocolate Fudge Brownie ice cream and frozen yogurt. The bakery intentionally hires those hard to employ: the homeless, the poor, the chronically unemployed, and recovering drug addicts. Profits from the Greyston Bakery help support the Greyston Foundation, which provides jobs, housing, family services, and health care to low-income residents of southwest Yonkers and surrounding areas (Greyston Bakery 2004; CBS News 2004).

❖ PUTTING IT TOGETHER: On the Web.

For more information on these programs, visit their Web sites at *Study Site Chapter 9.*

MAIN POINTS

- **Absolute poverty** refers to a lack of basic necessities, such as food, shelter, and income. **Relative poverty** refers to a situation where people fail to achieve the average income or lifestyle enjoyed by the rest of society. Relative poverty emphasizes the inequality of income and the growing gap between the richest and poorest Americans.

- The **poverty threshold** is the original federal poverty measure developed by the Social Security Administration and updated each year by the U.S. Census Bureau. The threshold is used for estimating the number of people in poverty. **Poverty guidelines** are issued each year by the U.S. Department of Health and Human Services and are used for determining family or individual eligibility for federal programs. Census data for 2003 indicate that for the third consecutive year, the poverty rate and the number of people in poverty have increased.

- Whites currently compose the largest group of poor individuals in the United States. However, the poverty rate for non-Hispanic Whites is the lowest, and Blacks continue to have the highest poverty rate, followed by Hispanics.

- Functionalists observe that poverty is a product of our social structure. Rapid economic and technological changes eliminated the need for low-skilled labor, creating a population of workers who are unskilled and untrained for this new economy. In many ways, theorists from this perspective expect this disparity among workers. Lower wages and poverty are natural consequences of this system of stratification.

- Conflict theorists assert that poverty exists because those in power wish to maintain and expand their base of power and interests, with little left to share with others. Welfare bureaucracies—local, state, and national—represent important interest groups that influence the creation and implementation of welfare policies. Welfare policies reflect the political economy of the community in which they are implemented

- Feminist scholars argue that the welfare state is an arena of political struggle. The drive to maintain male dominance and the patriarchal family is assumed to be the principal force shaping the formation, implementation, and outcomes of U.S. welfare policy.

- Interactionists attempt to explain how poverty is a learned phenomenon. Some sociologists have suggested that poverty is based on a "culture of poverty" and that moral deficiencies lead to a life of poverty. Opponents argue that there is no evidence that the poor have a different set of values and beliefs. Interactionists also focus on the public's perceptions: Most Americans do not have any direct contact with the welfare system or welfare recipients; thus, their views are likely to be shaped by the media.

- A new era of social welfare began in 1996 with the Personal Responsibility and Work Opportunity Reconciliation Act (PRWORA). PRWORA was a bipartisan welfare reform plan to reduce recipients' dependence on government assistance through strict work requirements and welfare time limits. The Act had an immediate effect on the number of people on welfare. However, although employment has increased among welfare recipients, many recipients have little education or work experience, limited employment benefits (including health care), and continue to struggle with child care.

- About 10.7 percent of households were food insecure (insufficient food for all family members to enjoy active and healthy lives) at least for some time during the year. The U.S. Department of Agriculture provides food assistance programs, but families often need to rely on private programs (food pantries and soup kitchens) as well. For a variety of reasons, poor families encounter higher food prices and a smaller selection of food than other families. Housing is another problem; the combination of low earnings and scarce housing assistance results in serious housing problems for the working poor.

• There is overwhelming evidence that welfare caseloads have declined since the enactment of PRWORA, perhaps helped by a strong economy and increased aid to low-income working families. However, the early employment success of welfare reform diminished as the economy faltered, and time limits to welfare receipt seem to compound problems. It appears that individuals and families, particularly women and the rural poor, are cycling in and out of poverty, working when jobs are available but never achieving complete economic independence.

• More recent policy developments include reauthorizing PRWORA, focusing on areas such as education, devising new measures and standards of poverty, and researching the effectiveness of faith-based programs. Community building has also grown, emphasized by welfare reform.

INTERNET AND COMMUNITY EXERCISES

1. Investigate the welfare assistance or TANF program in your state. First, determine the name and administrative agency for the program in your state. Most TANF programs are administered by the Department of Health and Social Services or Department of Human Services. Determine what time limits and work requirement provisions have been legislated in your state. What educational activities can count toward work requirements? Are family support services (parent skill training, housing assistance) provided? What is your state's record on welfare reform? Has welfare reform made a difference?

2. The United Nations' Human Development Report tracks several poverty indicators: Log on to *Study Site Chapter 9* for the UN link and compare the United States with Canada, Germany, Japan, Spain, Sweden, and the United Kingdom.

3. Visit a local food bank and interview a manager and worker at the site. Who does the food bank serve? How would they characterize food insecurity in your city? Has it increased in recent years or declined? Has the population they serve changed? If yes, in what way?

4. The Bruton Center based at the University of Texas at Dallas supports an Internet site, Windows on Urban Poverty: Describing and Making Concentrated Poverty in the 2000 Census. The director of the project is Paul A. Jargowsky. The Web site allows you to create, print, and copy neighborhood-level maps of any neighborhood in the United States, using several variables: poverty, race/ethnicity, population density, median year built (based on existing housing units), and median housing value. The maps are based on data from the 1970, 1980, 1990, and 2000 Census. Go to *Study Site Chapter 9.*

On your own. Log on to *Study Site—Community and Policy Guide* for more information about the social problems, social policies, and community responses discussed in this chapter.

References

Abramovitz, M. 1996. *Regulating the Lives of Women: Social Welfare Policy from Colonial Times to the Present.* Boston: South End Press.

Acs, G. and P. Loprest. 2001. "Synthesis Report of the Findings from ASPE's 'Leavers' Grants." Washington, DC: U.S. Department of Health and Human Services.

Action for Boston Community Development. 2003. "About ABCD." Retrieved September 17, 2003 (www .bostonabcd.org/about.htm).

Adams, G. and M. Rohace. 2002. "Child Care and Welfare Reform." Pp. 121–142 in *Welfare Reform: The Next Act*, edited by A. Weil and K. Feingold. Washington, DC: The Urban Institute.

Alder, J. 1994. "The Name of the Game Is Shame." *Newsweek* 124(24):41.

Banfield, E. 1974. *The Unheavenly City Revisited*. Boston: Little, Brown.

Bartlett, D. and J. Steele. 1998. "Corporate Welfare." *Time* 152(19):36–39.

Bernstein, J., H. Boushey, E. McNichol, and R. Zahradnik. 2002. *Pulling Apart: A State-by-State Analysis of Income Trends*. Washington, DC: Center on Budget and Policy Priorities and Economic Policy Institute.

Besharov, D. 2002. "Post-Welfare-Reform Welfare." Retrieved August 30, 2003 (www.aei.org/include/news_print.asp? newsID=15142).

Bhargava, D. and J. Kuriansky. 2002. "Defining Who's Poor: Families Suffer as the Government Continues to Rely on the Outdated Measure of the Poverty Line." Retrieved August 30, 2003 (www.sixstrategies.org/files/ Times%20Union%209–22–02.PDF).

Blum, B. and J. Farnsworth Francis. 2002. *Welfare Research Perspectives: Past, Present, and Future*. New York: National Center for Children in Poverty.

Briefel, R., Jonathan Jacobson, Nancy Clusen, Teresa Zavitsky, Miki Satake, Brittany Dawson, and Rhoda Cohen. 2003. *The Emergency Food Assistance System: Findings from the Client Survey: Executive Summary* (Food Assistance and Nutrition Research Report #32). Washington, DC: U.S. Department of Agriculture, Economic Research Service.

Cammisa, A. M. 1998. *From Rhetoric to Reform? Welfare Policy in American Politics*. Boulder, CO: Westview Press.

CBS News. 2004. "Greyston Bakery: Let 'em Eat Cake." Retrieved September 14, 2004 (http://www.cbsnews.com/ stories/2004/01/09/60minutes/main592382.shtml).

Center on Budget and Policy Priorities. 2004. "Facts about the Earned Income Credit." Retrieved July 5, 2004 (www.cbpp.org/eic2004/eic04-factbook.pdf).

Center for Women Policy Studies. 2003. "Fact Sheet: From Poverty to Self-Sufficiency: Role of Postsecondary Education in Welfare Reform." Retrieved September 14, 2004 (http://www.centerwomenpolicy.org/ report.cfm?ReportID=77).

Clemetson, L. 2003. "Poor Workers Finding Modest Housing Unaffordable, Study Says." *The New York Times*, September 9, p. A15.

Coalition on Human Needs. 2003. *Welfare: CHN Issue Brief*. Washington, DC: Author.

DeNavas, Carmen, Bernadette Proctor, and Robert Mills. 2004. *Income, Poverty, and Health Insurance Coverage: 2003* (Current Population Reports, P60–226). Washington, DC: U.S. Census Bureau

Duncan, G., K. Harris, and J. Boisjoly. 2000. "Time Limits and Welfare Reform: New Estimates of the Number and Characteristics of Affected Families." *Social Science Review* 74(1):55–75.

Fraser, N. 1989. *Unruly Practices: Power, Discourse, and Gender in Contemporary Social Theory*. Minneapolis: University of Minnesota Press.

Freidman, P. 2000. *The Earned Income Tax Credit* (Issue Notes, Vol. 4, No. 4, April). Washington, DC: The Welfare Information Network.

Funiciello, Theresa. 1993. *Tyranny of Kindness: Dismantling the Welfare System to End Poverty in America*. New York: The Atlantic Monthly Press.

Gans, H. 1971. "The Uses of Poverty: The Poor Pay All." *Social Policy* 2: 20–24.

Gennetian, L., A. Huston, D. Crosby, Y. Chang, E. Lowe, and T. Weisner. 2002. *Making Child Care Choices*. Washington, DC: Manpower Demonstration Research Corporation.

Gilens, M. 1999. *Why Americans Hate Welfare: Race, Media, and the Politics of Antipoverty Policy*. Chicago: University of Chicago Press.

Gordon, L. 1994. *Pitied But Not Entitled*. New York: Free Press.

Gornick, J. and M. Meyers. 2002. "Support for Working Families: What We Can Learn from Europe about Family Policies" Pp. 90–107 in *Making Welfare Work,* edited by R. Kuttner. New York: New Press.

Greyston Bakery. 2004. "The Greyston Bakery Story." Retrieved September 14, 2004 (www.greystonbakery.com/ bakery.html).

Guilford, M. 2002. "Building Cooperative Businesses." Retrieved March 3, 2004 (www.dollarsandsense.org/archives/ 2002/0902guilford.html).

Guyer, J. 2000. *Health Care after Welfare: An Update on Findings from State-Level Leaver Studies*. Washington, DC: Center on Budget and Policy Priorities.

Hander, J. and Y. Hasenfeld. 1991. *The Moral Construction of Poverty: Welfare Reform in America*. Thousand Oaks, CA: Sage.

Harrington, M. 1963. *The Other America: Poverty in the United States.* Baltimore, MD: Penguin Books.

Harris, K. M. 1993. "Work and Welfare among Single Mothers in Poverty." *American Journal of Sociology* 99:317–352.

Iceland, John. 2003. *Poverty in America.* Berkeley: University of California Press.

Kaufman, P., J. MacDonald, S. Lutz, and D. Smallwood. 1997. *Do the Poor Pay More for Food? Item Selection and Price Differences Affect Low-Income Household Food Costs* (Agricultural Economics Report #759). Washington, DC: U.S. Department of Agriculture, Economic Research Service.

Kuhn, A. and A. Wolpe. 1978. *Feminism and Materialism: Women and Modes of Production.* London: Routledge and Kegan Paul.

Lafer, Gordon. 2002. *Let Them Eat Training: The False Promise of Federal Employment Policy since 1980.* Ithaca, NY: Cornell University Press.

Lewis, O. 1969. *On Understanding Poverty: Perspectives from the Social Sciences.* New York: Basic Books.

Lieberman, R. C. 1998. *Shifting the Color Line: Race and the American Welfare State.* Cambridge, MA: Harvard University Press.

Llobrera, J. and B. Zahradnik. 2004. *A Hand Up: How State Earned Income Tax Credits Help Working Families Escape Poverty in 2004.* Washington, DC: Center on Budget and Policy Priorities.

Loprest, P. 2001. *How Are Families That Left Welfare Doing? A Comparison of Early and Recent Welfare Leavers.* Washington, DC: Urban Institute.

———. 2002. *Families Who Left Welfare: Who Are They and How Are They Doing?* Washington, DC: The Urban Institute.

Mezey, J. and B. Richie. 2003. "Welfare Dollars No Longer an Increasing Source of Child Care Funding." Washington, DC: Center for Law and Social Policy.

Mills, R. J. and S. Bhandari. 2003. *Health Insurance Coverage in the United States: 2002* (Current Population Reports, P60–223). Washington, DC: U.S. Census Bureau.

National Campaign for Jobs and Income Support. 2001. *Leaving Welfare, Left Behind: Employment Status, Income, and Well-Being of Former TANF Recipients.* Washington, DC: Author.

National Center for Children in Poverty. 2001. "Child Poverty Fact Sheet: June 2001." Retrieved September 27, 2003 (http://cpmcent.columbia.edu/dept/nccp/ycpf).

Nelson, K., M. Treskon, and D. Pelletiere. 2004. *Losing Ground in the Best of Times: Low Income Renters in the 1990s.* Washington, DC: National Low Income Housing Coalition.

Neubeck, K. and N. Cazenave. 2001. *Welfare Racism: Playing the Race Card Against America's Poor.* New York: Routledge Press.

Nguyen, C. 2003. "One Stop from the Streets." *The News Tribune,* August 24, pp. A1, A8–A9.

Nicholas-Casebolt, A. and P. McGrath Morris. 2001. "Making Ends Meet: Private Food Assistance and the Working Poor" (Discussion Paper No. 1222–01). Madison, WI: Institute for Research on Poverty.

Norris, D. and L. Thompson. 1995. "Introduction." Pp. 1–18 in *The Politics of Welfare Reform,* edited by D. Norris and L. Thompson. Thousand Oaks, CA: Sage.

Office of Family Assistance, Administration for Children and Families. 2003. *Temporary Assistance for Needy Families Program (TANF): Fifth Annual Report to Congress.* Washington, DC: U.S. Department of Health and Human Services.

O'Gorman, A. 2002. "Playing by the Rules and Still Losing Ground." *America,* July 29–August 5, pp. 12–15.

Patterson, J. T. 1981. *America's Struggle against Poverty, 1900–1980.* Cambridge and London: Harvard University Press.

Piven, F. 2002. "Globalization, American Politics, and Welfare Policy." Pp. 27–42 in *Lost Ground: Welfare Reform and Beyond,* edited by R. Albelda and A. Withorm. Cambridge, MA: South End Press.

Piven, F. and R. Cloward. 1993. *Regulating the Poor: The Functions of Public Welfare.* New York: Vintage Books.

Polk, D. 1997. "Check out the International Neighbors." Retrieved September 1, 2003 (www.4children.org/news/5–97.intl.htm).

Proctor, B. D. and J. Dalaker. 2002. *Poverty in the United States: 2001* (Current Population Reports, P60–219). Washington, DC: U.S. Census Bureau.

———. 2003. *Poverty in the United States: 2002* (Current Population Reports, P60–222). Washington, DC: U.S. Census Bureau.

Quadagno, J. 1994. *The Color of Welfare Reform: How Racism Undermined the War on Poverty.* New York: Basic Books.

Romney, L. 2003. "End of Welfare Leaves Rural Poor in a Bind." *Los Angeles Times,* April 6, pp. B1, B10.

Sard, B. and M. Waller. 2002. *Housing Strategies to Strengthen Welfare Policy and Support Working Families.* Washington, DC: The Brookings Institution and the Center on Budget and Policy Priorities.

Schwartz-Nobel, L. 2002. *Growing Up Empty: The Hunger Epidemic in America*. New York: HarperCollins.

Seccombe, K. and C. Amey. 1995. "Playing by the Rules and Losing: Health Insurance and the Working Poor." *Journal of Health and Social Behavior* 36:168–181.

Short, K. 2001. *Experimental Poverty Measures: 1999* (Current Population Reports Consumer Income, P60–216). Washington, DC: U.S. Census Bureau.

Skolverket/Swedish National Agency for Education. 2003. "Child Care in Sweden." Retrieved September 1, 2003 (www.skolverket.se/english/system/child.shtml).

Smeeding, T., K. Ross, and M. O'Conner, M. 1999. *The Economic Impact of the Earned Income Tax Credit (EITC): Consumption, Savings, and Debt*. Syracuse, NY: Syracuse University, Center for Policy Research.

Tillmon, J. 1972. "Welfare Is a Woman's Issue." Retrieved September 28, 2003 (www.msmagazine.com/spring2002/tillmon.asp).

Uchitelle, L. 2003. "States Pay for Jobs, But It Doesn't Always Pay Off." *The New York Times*, November 10, p. A1.

U.S. Census Bureau. 2001. *Poverty Status by State in 2000, People under 18, Table 25* (Current Population Survey, March 2001). Washington, DC: Author.

———. 2003. "Poverty 2003." Retrieved June 3, 2004 (www.census.gov/hhes/poverty/threshld/thresh03.html).

U.S. Conference of Mayors. 2000. *A Status Report on Hunger and Homelessness in American Cities*. Washington, DC: Author.

U.S. Department of Agriculture. 2003a. "Food Security in the United States." Retrieved August 26, 2003 (www.ers.usda.gov/breifing/FoodSecurity).

———. 2003b. "Food Security in the United States: Conditions and Trends." Retrieved August 27, 2003 (www.ers.usda.gov/breifing/foodsecurity.trends).

Waldfogel, J. 2001. "International Policies toward Parental Leave and Child Care." *The Future of Children* 11(1):99–111.

Weaver, R. K. 2000. *Ending Welfare as We Know It*. Washington, DC: Brookings Institution Press.

Weil, M. 1996. "Community Building: Building Community Practice." *Social Work* 41(5):481–499.

Weil, A. and K. Feingold. 2002. "Introduction." Pp. xi–xxxi in *Welfare Reform: The Next Act*, edited by A. Weil and K. Feingold. Washington, DC: The Urban Institute.

White House. 2001. "Executive Order: Establishment of White House Office of Faith-Based and Community Initiatives." Retrieved August 29, 2003 (www.whitehouse.gov/news/releases/2001/01/20010129–2.html).

Zedlewski, S. and P. Loprest. 2003. "Welfare Reform: One Size Doesn't Fit All." *The Christian Science Monitor, Electronic Edition*, August 25. Retrieved August 27, 2003 (www.urban.org/url.cfm?ID=900648).

Zucchino, D. 1999. *Myth of the Welfare Queen*. New York: Touchstone/Simon and Schuster.

10

Crime

Think of a crime, any crime. Picture the first "crime" that comes into your mind. What do you see? The odds are you are not imagining a mining company executive sitting at his desk, calculating the costs of proper safety precautions and deciding not to invest in them. Probably what you see with your mind's eye is one person physically attacking another or robbing something from another via the threat of a physical attack.

Reiman 1998:57

When we think of crime, we imagine violent or life-threatening acts, not white-collar crimes committed by men and women using accounting ledgers and calculators as deadly weapons. Yet, an act does not have to be violent or bloody to be considered criminal. For our discussion, a **crime** is any behavior that violates criminal law and is punishable by fine, jail, or other negative sanctions. Crime is divided into two legal categories. **Felonies** are serious offenses, including murder, rape, robbery, and aggravated assault; these crimes are punishable by more than a year's imprisonment or death. **Misdemeanors** are minor offenses, such as traffic violations, that are punishable by a fine or less than a year in jail. In this chapter, we will examine crimes as a social problem. We will consider a full range of crimes, not just violent events that make the headlines on your evening news. Before we review the specifics about crime in the United States, let's review sociological explanations on why people commit crime

Sociological Perspectives on Crime

Biological explanations of crime tend to address how criminals are "born that way." Early explanations were intended to classify criminal types by appearance and genetic factors, such as Cesare Lombroso's 19th century theory of "born criminal" types. Lombroso argued that criminals could be easily identified by distinct physical features: a huge forehead, large jaw, and a longer arm span. Contemporary biological explanations focus on biochemical (diet and hormones) and neurophysical (brain lesions, brain dysfunctions) characteristics related to violence and criminality. Like biological theories, psychological perspectives also focus on inherent criminal characteristics.

Researchers link personality development, moral development, or mental disorders to criminal behaviors. Both biological and psychological theories address how crime is determined by individual characteristics or predispositions to crime; but they fail to explain why crime rates vary between urban and rural areas, different neighborhoods, or social or economic groups (Adler, Mueller, and Laufer 1991). Sociological theories attempt to address the reasons for these differences, highlighting how larger social forces contribute to crime.

Functionalist Perspective

Functionalists offer two explanations for criminal behavior. For the first explanation, we return to Robert Merton. Merton argues that we are socialized to attain traditional material and social goals: a good job, a nice home, or a great-looking car. We assume that society is set up in such a way that everyone has the same opportunity or resources to attain these goals. Merton explains that society isn't that fair; some experience blocked opportunities or resources due to discrimination, social position, or talent. People feel strained when they are exposed to these goals but do not have the access or resources to achieve them. When the means are blocked, Merton says that we experience **anomie**, a term that he borrowed from Emile Durkheim (see Chapter 1). Anomie creates an opportunity to create new norms or rules (or break the old ones) in order to attain these goals.

In his theory of anomie, Merton presents five ways in which people adapt to society's goals and means as presented in Table 10.1. Most individuals fit under the first category, conformity. Conformers accept the traditional goals and have the traditional means to achieve them. Attending college is part of the traditional means to attain a job, an income, and a home. Criminal behavior comes under the innovation category. Innovators accept society's goals, but they don't have the legitimate means to achieve them. Individuals in this category innovate by stealing from their boss, cheating on their taxes, or robbing a local store to obtain these goals.

Working from Merton's assumptions, scholars argue that criminal activity would decline if economic conditions improved. Solutions to crime would target strained groups, providing access to traditional methods and resources to attain goals. In fact, several studies have confirmed that when anomie is reduced among the poor, lower crime rates may result. Factors usually associated with anomie—the prevalence of female-headed families, the percentage of the population that is African American, and family poverty rates—are more weakly related to crime in areas with higher levels of welfare support (Hannon and Defronzo 1998).

The second functionalist explanation links social control (or the lack of it) to criminal behavior. Whereas Merton's theory asks why someone does commit a crime, social control theorists ask why someone *doesn't* commit crime. Society functions best when everyone behaves. Society provides us with a set of norms and laws to regulate our behavior. According to sociologist Travis Hirschi, society controls our behavior through four elements: attachments, our personal relationships with others; commitment, our acceptance of conventional goals and means; involvement, our participation in conventional activities; and, beliefs, our acceptance of conventional values and

❖ Table 10.1   Merton's Strain Theory

Mode of Adaptation	Agrees with Cultural Goals	Follows Institutional Means	Method of Adaptation
Conformity	Yes	Yes	Accepts cultural goals and institutional means to achieve them
Innovation	Yes	No	Accepts cultural goals, adopts nontraditional means to achieve them
Ritualism	No	Yes	Rejects cultural goals but continues to conform to approved means
Retreatism	No	No	Rejects cultural goals and the approved means to achieve them
Rebellion	No	No	Challenges cultural goals and the approved means to achieve them

norms. Elliot, Ageton, and Canter (1979) redefined Hirschi's elements as integration (involvement with and emotional ties to external bonds) and commitment (expectations linked with conventional activities and beliefs). They believe that when all these elements are strong, criminal behavior is unlikely to occur.

Conflict Perspective

Sociologist Austin Turk (1969) explains that criminality is not a biological, psychological, or behavioral phenomenon; rather, it is a way to define a person's social status according to how that person is perceived and treated by law enforcement. An act is not inherently criminal; society defines it that way. Theorists from this perspective argue that criminal laws do not exist for our good; rather, they exist to preserve the interests and power of specific groups.

In this view, criminal justice decisions are discriminatory and designed to sanction offenders based on their minority or subordinate group membership (race, class, age, or gender) (Akers 1997). Turk (1969, 1976) states that criminal status is defined by "authorities" or members of the dominant class. Criminal status is imposed on "subjects," members of the subordinate class, regardless of whether a crime has actually been committed. Laws serve as a means for those in power to promote their ideas and interests against others. Law enforcement agents serve to protect the interests and power of the dominant class at the expense of subjects.

From this perspective, problems emerge when particular groups are disadvantaged by the criminal justice system. While the powerful are able to resist criminal labels, the labels seem to stick to those without power: the poor, youth, and minorities. Conflict theorists argue that the criminal justice system is intentionally unequal. We will discuss this further in the section, "The Inequalities of Crime."

Feminist Perspective

For a long time, criminology ignored the experiences of women, choosing to apply theories and models of male criminality to women. Feminist researchers have been credited with making female offenders visible (Naffine 1996) and with documenting the experiences of women as the victims or survivors of violent men and as victims of the criminal justice system (Chesney-Lind and Pasko 2004). Feminist scholarship has attempted to understand how women's criminal experiences are different from those of men, and also how experiences of women differ from each other based on race, ethnicity, class, age, and sexual orientation (Chesney-Lind and Pasko 2004; Flavin 2001).

Freda Adler (1975) was one of the first to explain that women were "liberated" to commit crime when they were no longer restrained by traditional ideals of feminine behavior and could take on more masculine traits including criminal behavior. Called the "liberation approach," the logic of the argument is that as gender equality increases, women are more likely to commit crime. Although the approach was met with wide public acceptance, it has been discredited due to lack of empirical evidence (Chesney-Lind and Pasko 2004).

Recently, gender inequality theories have been presented as explanations of female crime. According to Steffensmeier and Allan (1996), patriarchal power relations shape gender differences in crime, pushing women into criminal behavior through role entrapment, economic marginalization, and victimization or as a survival response. The authors point out that "nowhere is the gender ratio more skewed than in the great disparity of males as offenders and females as victims of sexual and domestic abuse" (p. 470). The logic of the inequality argument is that female crime increases as gender inequality increases.

Women are more likely to kill intimate partners, family members, or acquaintances than men, "so the connection between women's overall homicide offending rates and gender inequality lies largely in the connection between gender stratification and women's domestic lives," explains Vicki Jensen (2001:8). Jensen describes gender inequality as being composed of economic, political-legal, and social inequalities experienced by women. Lower gender equality can negatively impact women's freedom and opportunities; these situations can push women into situations in which lethal violence seems to be the only way out. In the case of women killing abusive intimate partners, low levels of economic security limit women's opportunities to escape abusive situations. Low levels of gender equality can increase the emphasis on traditional gender norms, placing the responsibility on women to please men and requiring that women must be submissive and accepting of whatever their partner does (including violence). Jensen explains that the vast majority of women who kill an intimate partner do so in response to abuse situations, in imminent self-defense, or when all other strategies have failed.

Feminists have also challenged the masculine basis of criminal justice programs. For example, feminist criminologists have been critical of boot camp programs, claiming that these programs embody "a distorted image of masculinity, one that emphasizes aggressiveness, unquestioned authority, and insensitivity to others' pain while deemphasizing 'feminine' characteristics such as group cooperation and empathy" (Flavin 2001:281). Feminist scholarship has also been credited with encouraging the reconsideration of what is known about men's experiences, and it has led to more studies of masculinity and crime (Flavin 2001).

From 1995 to 2002, the number of women in state or federal correctional facilities increased by an average of 5.4 percent (in contrast, the number of men inmates increased 3.6 percent during the same period). In 1995, 60,468 women were in prison facilities; but, by June 2002, the number had increased to 96,099. Research indicates that the surge in women's incarceration has little to do any major change in women's criminal behavior. In fact, the number of women incarcerated since 1999 has increased by 75 percent despite decreases in most violent crime offenses committed by women. However, the differential treatment of women in sentencing and imprisonment is a thing of the past. The public's "get tough with crime" approach, along with a legal system that encourages treating women equally as men, has resulted in the greater use of imprisonment as punishment for female criminal behavior (Chesney-Lind and Pasko 2004).

The increase in the number of women inmates has caused prison officials to reconsider custody procedures for women, especially specific programs and services available to women. Parenting has become a focus of many programs. In 2000, the 80,000 women in prisons and jails were estimated to have about 200,000 children under the age of 18 (Amnesty International 2000).

Voices in the Community:
Barbara Parsons Lane

Barbara Parsons Lane (2003) writes about her time incarcerated and its impact on her children. Lane was sentenced to 25 years on a charge of manslaughter after killing her husband; her defense was emotional duress.

Long-term incarceration is a strange mix of sadness, sameness, and explosiveness. I have now passed my two-thousandth day in prison. There are brighter moments for me now: shared smiles with friends, watching the antics of dogs I train for the prison's Puppy Program. Staff has nicknamed me "the mail lady" because of all the letters and cards I still receive from faithful supporters. For my fifty-second birthday, my best friend, Elle, surprised me with a video she'd worked on for weeks. The tape included a "tour" of our hometown and the good wishes of thirty friends and family members who'd stood before Elle's camera to send me their love. It was one of the best gifts I have ever received.

If life is a puzzle of pieces, my most precious ones remain out of reach. Except for phone calls and visits here at New York, I have been absent from the lives of my children and grandchildren these past two thousand days . . .

Arthur manages a visit once a month, less often when he's swamped with work. Although he never complains, these trips are hard on him. My son's long-term relationships with several wonderful young women have ended in breakups. 'How come you can't make a commitment?' I asked him once. He told me he didn't want to have to go through the things I did. In that response, I heard how deeply his life had been scarred by mine.

. . . . Amanda visits infrequently. She no longer cries during entire visits, but she hardly ever smiles. A chain-smoker, Amanda cites the prison's "no smoking" policy as the reason why she can't stay the two hours we're allotted. My youngest child is floundering, reaching for the wrong things, and I am powerless to do anything but pray for God's mercy. I pray for his forgiveness, too. My failure to escape an abusive marriage, my crime, my incarceration—for all of this I bear the guilt of having let go of my baby. (Pp. 239–240)

Interactionist Perspective

Interactionists examine the process that defines certain individuals and acts as criminal. The theory is called labeling theory, highlighting that it isn't the criminal or his/her act that's important, but it's the audience that labels the person or his/her act as criminal. As Kai Erickson (1964) explains, "Deviance is not a property inherent in certain forms of behavior; it is a property conferred upon these forms by audiences which directly or indirectly witness them" (p. 11).

The basic elements of labeling theory were presented by sociologist Edwin Lemert (1967), who believed that everyone is involved in behavior that could be labeled delinquent or criminal, yet only a few are actually labeled. He explained that deviance is a process, beginning with primary deviation, which arises out of a variety of social, cultural, psychological, and physiological factors. Although most primary acts of deviance go unnoticed, they may lead to a social response in the form of an arrest, punishment, or stigmatization. Secondary deviation includes more serious deviant acts, which follow the social response to the primary deviance. Once a criminal label is attached to a person, a criminal career is set in motion.

❖ FOCUS ON: THE SOCIAL CONSTRUCTION OF HATE CRIMES

Although violence directed at specific groups based solely on racial, religious, or other social characteristics and statuses is not new, only in the last 20 years has this kind of violence been categorized and labeled as hate crime. According to sociologists Valerie Jenness and Ryken Grattet (2001), the problem of hate crime was first socially constructed by the civil rights and victim's rights movements. In their book, *Making Hate a Crime,* they explain that there are three types of anti-hate crime movements: the citizen action model of communities, the victim services movement, and the racial justice movement. Each of these movements is organized around the framework of civil rights and pursues legal reforms and educational awareness.

According to the authors, the victim's rights movement brought attention to crime victims and also brought into the public consciousness an understanding of what it means to be a victim. Beginning in the late 1960s, national, regional, state, and local organizations began to form the anti-hate crime movement. Organizations, such as the Anti-Defamation League of B'Nai B'rith, the Center for Democratic Renewal, and the National Gay and Lesbian Task Force began to monitor, document, and publicize instances of violence directed at members of minority groups. At the same time, these groups also called for changes in public policy and laws covering such violence.

The social construction of hate crimes continued as politicians crafted legislation that defined the parameters of hate crime. In the 1990s, Congress passed three legislative acts that addressed hate crimes. The Hate Crimes Statistics Act of 1990 requires

the Attorney General's office to collect data on hate crime. This was the first federal law to use the term, defining hate crime as "crimes that manifest evidence of prejudice based on race, religion, sexual orientation, or ethnicity." The Violence Against Women Act of 1994 added gender as a hate-crime category. The Hate Crimes Sentences Enhancement Act of 1994 specifies the penalties that should be imposed on hate crimes committed on federal lands and properties or while engaging in federally protected activity. Under this Act, hate crime is defined as any criminal conduct wherein "the defendant intentionally selected any victim or property as the object of the offense because of the actual or perceived race, color, religion, national origin, ethnicity, gender, disability, or sexual orientation of any person." Courts have elaborated on the definition of hate crimes; law enforcement officials classify, investigate, and prosecute such behavior as criminal.

Grattet (2000) explains that despite federal hate-crime legislation, there has been considerable variation in how local law enforcement agencies classify and count hate crime. Questions such as "Are hate crimes increasing?" or "What are the typical scenarios that lead to violence?" are still difficult to answer. At this time, the best information on hate crimes comes from local rather than national sources. Research indicates that most hate-crime perpetrators are not members of organized hate groups; rather, they tend to be young men acting in informal groups (Grattet 2000). Research on hate crime also demonstrates how different groups are victimized (Glaser, Dixit, and Green 2002). For example, gays and

❖ **FOCUS ON (Continued)**

lesbians who are perceived to be a moral and sexual threat are more likely to be physically assaulted. On the other hand, Jews who are stereotyped as affluent are more frequently victims of vandalism than assault. African Americans are attacked in a variety of ways as an attempt to separate them from whites and to confine them to a subordinate status (Glaser et al. 2002).

Data on the number of hate crimes reported to the FBI's Uniform Crime Report are presented here.

Total number of hate crimes reported 2001	9,730
Type of bias motivation	
Race	4,367
Anti-Black	2,899
Anti-White	891
Anti-multiracial	217
Anti-Asian	280
Anti-American Indian	80
Sexual orientation	1,393
Anti-male homosexual	980
Anti-homosexual	173
Anti-female homosexual	205
Anti-bisexual	17
Anti-heterosexual	18
Religion	1,828
Anti-Jewish	1,043
Anti-other religious group	181
Anti-Catholic	38
Anti-Protestant	35
Anti-Islamic	481
Anti-multireligious group	45
Anti-atheist	5

Note: Additional reported categories include crimes motivated against ethnicity and disability.

Source: Federal Bureau of Investigation 2001a.

Yet, some groups may be more resistant to the criminal label. Criminologist William Chambliss in his classic 1973 (reprinted in 1995) study, "The Saints and the Roughnecks," noted the differential treatment given two groups of boys. The Saints, a group of eight boys from White upper-class families, were always engaged in truancy, drinking, theft, and vandalism. Yet, throughout his study, a Saint was never arrested. The local police saw the Saints "as good boys who were among the leaders of the youth in the community" (Chambliss 1973/1995:258). On the other hand, a group of six lower-class White boys, the Roughnecks, were "constantly in trouble with police and community even though their rate of delinquency was about equal with that of the Saints" (Chambliss 1973/1995:254). The community and the police viewed the Roughnecks, who were "not so well dressed, not so well mannered, not so rich boys," as a group of delinquents. According to Chambliss, "from the community's viewpoint, the real indication that these kids were trouble was that they were constantly involved with the police" (1973/1995:259).

Henry Brownstein (2001) argues that race and class matter in our perception of crime. It matters in how we conceptualize victims and offenders, even whether we believe that a person could have been a perpetrator or a victim of violence. When Susan Smith told police that a Black man carjacked her car with her two young sons still buckled in their car seats, no one questioned her story. There was no doubt that this young White mother of two was the victim and that an unknown Black man was the offender. Police in Union, South Carolina, released a composite sketch based on Smith's description of the carjacker. For days, police and community members searched for the man and Smith's two sons. The Fox television program, "America's Most Wanted," came into town to film a segment about Smith and her two sons. But the segment never aired. Nine days after the alleged carjacking, Smith confessed to rolling her car into a local lake, murdering her two sons.

❖ PUTTING IT TOGETHER: What are your perceptions of a typical victim or perpetrator? What role do the media—news, television, and movies—play in creating these perceptions? From what other sources are these perceptions learned?

Interactionists also attempt to explain how deviant or criminal behavior is learned through association with others. Edwin Sutherland's 1939 theory of differential association states that individuals are likely to commit deviant acts if they associate with others who are deviants. This criticism is often raised about our jail and prison systems; instead of rehabilitation, prisoners are able to learn more criminal activity and behavior while serving their sentence. Sutherland's theory does not address how the first criminal learned criminal behavior, but he does highlight how criminal behavior emerges from interaction, association, and socialization.

For a summary of sociological perspectives, see Table 10.2.

Sources of Crime Statistics

We rely on three sources of data to estimate the nature and extent of crime in the United States. The primary source is annual data collected by the Federal Bureau of Investigation (FBI). Since 1930, the FBI has published the Uniform Crime Report

❖ Table 10.2   Summary of Sociological Perspectives: Crime

	Functional	Conflict/Feminist	Interactionist
Explanation of crime	Crime emerges from the social order. People experience "strain" when they are exposed to cultural goals but do not have the access or resources to achieve them. Individuals are likely to make some new rules (or break the old ones) in order to attain these goals. Society also serves to control criminal behavior through four elements: attachments, commitment, involvement, and beliefs.	Criminal justice decisions are discriminatory and designed to sanction offenders based on their minority or subordinate group membership (race, class, age, or gender). Problems emerge when particular groups are disadvantaged more than others by the criminal justice system.	Interactionists examine the process that defines certain individuals and acts as criminal. Interactionists also examine how criminal or deviant behavior is learned through association with others.
Questions asked about crime and criminal behavior	How/why are individuals denied access to resources to achieve their goals? What social controls are in place to reduce criminal behavior?	How do our criminal justice policies reflect political, economic, and social interests? Why/how are particular groups targeted as "criminals"? How are women's experiences as crime victims and offenders different from men's?	Is criminal behavior the result of being labeled a "criminal"? Is criminal behavior learned? How are our perceptions of criminals and victims socially created?

(UCR), data supplied by 17,000 federal, state, and local law enforcement agencies. The UCR reports two categories of crimes: **index crimes** and **nonindex crimes**. Index crimes include murder, rape, robbery, assault, burglary, motor vehicle theft, arson, and larceny (theft of property worth $50 or more). All other crimes except traffic violations are categorized as nonindex crimes. Beginning in 1999, the FBI began to use the National Incident-Based Reporting System (NIBRS), which adds detailed offender and victim information to the UCR data. Currently, only 18 states provide NIBRS information.

The often-cited problem with the UCR and the NIBRS is that the data reflect reported crimes. The FBI cannot collect information on crimes that have not been reported, but it is estimated that only 3 percent to 4 percent of crimes are actually discovered by police (Kappeler, Blumberg, and Potter 2000). Also, being reported doesn't mean that a crime has actually occurred. The FBI does not require that a suspect has been arrested or that a crime is investigated and found to have actually occurred; it only needs to be reported (Kappeler et al. 2000).

In addition to the UCR, the FBI releases the Crime Clock, a graphic display of how often specific offenses are committed. Although it may make for good newspaper copy or give law enforcement and political officials clout (Chambliss 1988), the Crime Clock has been accused of exaggerating the amount of crime, leaving the public with the impression that they are in imminent danger of being victims of violence (Kappeler et al. 2000).

The third data source about crime is the National Crime Victimization Survey (NCVS or NCS), which has been published by the Bureau of Justice Statistics since 1972. Twice a year, the U.S. Census Bureau interviews members of about 42,000 households regarding their experience of crime. The NCVS identifies crime victims whether or not the crime was reported. The survey includes information about victims and crimes but covers only six offenses (compared with the eight index crimes reported by the UCR). Also included is information on the experiences of victims with the criminal justice system, self-protective measures used by victims, and possible substance abuse by offenders. The number of crime victims in the NCVS for 2003 is presented in Table 10.3.

The results of the NCVS are often compared to the UCR to indicate that the number of crimes committed is actually higher than the number of crimes reported, suggesting that the UCR may not be an adequate measure of violent crime. However, "a more thoughtful interpretation of the inconsistency between these statistical reports concludes that while neither the UCR nor the NCVS is by itself an adequate measure of violence, each is an estimate of the scope and nature of violent crime" (Brownstein 2001:8–9). Violent and property crimes dipped in 2003 to their lowest levels since records started being compiled more than 30 years ago, and they have dropped more than 50 percent in the last decade.

Types of Crime

Violent Crime

Violent crime is defined as actions that involve force or the threat of force against others and includes aggravated assault, murder, rape, and robbery. The victimization rate for crimes of violence in 2003 was 22.6 victimizations per 1,000 people age 12 or older, declining from 23.1 for 2002 (Catalano 2004). While the rate of violent crime declined, the number of victimizations increased from 5.3 million in 2002 to 5.4 million in 2003.

❖ Table 10.3   Number of Crime Victims 2003

Type of Crime	Number of Incidents
All crimes	24,212,800
All violent crimes	5,401,720
– Rape/sexual assault	198,850
– Robbery	596,130
– Assault	4,606,740
Aggravated	1,101,110
Simple	3,505,630
All Property crimes	18,626,380
– Household burglary	3,395,620
– Motor vehicle theft	1,032,470
– Theft	14,198,290

Source: Catalano 2004.

Except for rape/sexual assault, males had higher victimization rates than females. The victimization rate was 26 victimizations per 1,000 men and 20 victimizations per 1,000 women (Catalano 2004). Males are more likely to be victimized by a stranger, whereas women are more likely to be violently victimized by a friend, an acquaintance, or an intimate partner (Bureau of Justice Statistics 2003a). In 2001, more than 6 in 10 rape or sexual assault victims reported that they knew the offender.

Intimate violence (violence at the hands of someone known to the victim) is primarily committed against women. In 2001, women experienced 588,490 rape, sexual assault, robbery, aggravated assault, and simple assault victimizations at the hands of an intimate partner, a decrease from 1.1 million incidents in 1993. For men during 2001, 103,220 were victims of violent crimes by an intimate partner, down from 160,000 cases in 1993 (Bureau of Justice Statistics 2003a). About 34 percent of all female murders are committed by an intimate partner compared with only 4 percent of male murders. The number of men and women killed by an intimate partner has declined since 1976. In 1976, 1,600 women and 1,357 men were killed by an intimate partner; in 2000, 1,247 women and 440 men were murdered by an intimate partner (Rennison 2003).

Since 1973, Blacks have had the highest violent crime victimization rates. In 2003, 29 out of 1,000 Black people experienced a violent crime versus 21.5 out of 1,000 Whites (Catalano 2004). Among Hispanics, the rate of violent crime fell from a high of 70 crimes per 1,000 in 1993 to 24.2 violent crimes per 1,000 in 2003. The high rate of minority crime and victimization is often explained by structural factors, such as neighborhood poverty, unemployment, social isolation, and economic disadvantage. Research by Wilson (1996) and Sampson and Wilson (1995) indicates that structural disadvantages, not race, contribute to higher levels of crime and victimization in Black communities (Ackerman 1998).

The younger the person, the more likely that person was to experience a violent crime. In addition, the young had higher rates of injury from crime than older people (Simon, Mercy, and Perkins 2001). People who never married were more likely to be victims of violent crime than those married, widowed, or divorced (Catalano 2004). In general, the number of violent crimes was higher among households with an annual income under $7,500. Victimization rates were lowest among households earning $75,000 or more. Violent crime rates were highest in the West and in urban areas (Catalano 2004). Refer to Table 10.4 for a summary of violent crime rates by selected social characteristics.

❖ Table 10.4　Number of Violent Crimes per 1,000 People Age 12 or Older by Selected Social Characteristics, 2003

	Number of Violent Crimes per 1,000 Persons Age 12 or Older
Income	
Less than $7,500	49.9
$7,500–$14,999	30.8
$15,000–$24,999	26.3
$25,000–$34,999	24.9
$35,000–$49,999	21.4
$50,000–$74,999	22.9
$75,000 or more	17.5
Region	
Northeast	122.1
Midwest	160.2
South	160.5
West	207.4
Urban	216.3
Suburban	144.8
Rural	136.6

Source: Catalano 2004.

PUTTING IT TOGETHER:
In your community.

Crime rates have dropped significantly in most large cities since the 1990s. Take, for example, the homicide rate. The rate peaked in 1980 at 10.2 homicides per 100,000 people (Blumstein and Rosenfeld 1998). For 2003, the homicide rate was 5.6 per 100,000 persons (Catalano 2004). In 1994, about 25.1 million households or household members experienced one or more violent or property crimes (Klaus 2004); by 2003, the number had dropped to 23.6 million households (Catalano 2004). There is less violent crime, but do we still live in fear? Why or why not?

Property Crime

Property crime consists of taking money or property from another without force or the threat of force against the victims. Burglary, larceny, theft, motor vehicle theft, and arson are examples of property crimes. Property crimes make up about three fourths of all crime in the United States (Bureau of Justice Statistics 2003a). In 2003, there were an estimated 18.6 million property crimes, 3.4 million household burglaries, and 1 million motor vehicle thefts (Catalano 2004).

Women were more likely to be victimized by someone they knew; males were more likely to be victimized by a stranger. Blacks experienced higher rates of robbery and personal theft than Whites. Robbery and personal theft were generally higher for Hispanic than non-Hispanic households. Households earning less than $7,500 had a higher rate of property victimization (burglary, motor vehicle theft, and theft) than households with higher income (Catalano 2004).

Juvenile Delinquency

The term *juvenile delinquent* often refers to a youth who is in trouble with the law. Technically, a **juvenile status offender** is a juvenile who has violated a law that only applies to minors 7 to 17 years old, such as cutting school or buying and consuming alcohol (Sanders 1981). In certain cases, minors can also be tried as adults. Crimes committed by juveniles are more likely to be cleared by law enforcement than crimes committed by adults.

The Office of Juvenile Justice and Delinquency Prevention monitors data on rates of juvenile crime. For 2000, the total number of juvenile arrests was 2,369,400. The majority of juveniles were arrested for property crimes: burglary, theft, motor vehicle theft, or arson. Only 98,900 or 4 percent of all juvenile arrests were for violent crimes (Snyder 2002).

The majority of juvenile offenders in 2000 were male; only 28 percent were female. Since 1993, the number of female juvenile offenders has increased 6 percent, while the number of male juvenile offenders has declined by 16 percent. Table 10.5 presents the 10-year difference in arrests of boys and girls for selected offenses (FBI 2003). Although fewer females are processed through the juvenile justice system, research

❖ Table 10.5   Ten-Year Arrest Trends by Sex, 1993–2002

Offense or charge	Males Under Age 18			Females Under Age 18		
	1993	2002	Percent Change	1993	2002	Percent Change
Total	1,186,822	992,153	−16.4	377,504	401,599	+6.4
Murder	2,326	795	−65.8	159	91	−42.8
Robbery	24,263	14,908	−38.6	2,242	1,430	−36.2
Assault	41,055	29,127	−29.1	8,372	8,955	+7.0
Motor vehicle theft	49,534	23,777	−52.0	8,206	4,887	−40.4
Prostitution	39,160	20,123	−48.6	3,370	2,492	−26.1
Drug abuse violations	65,051	98,383	+51.2	8,362	18,398	+120.0
Driving under the influence	7,584	10,416	+37.3	1,294	2,505	+93.6
Disorderly conduct	80,673	79,064	−2.0	23,074	33,780	+46.4
Vagrancy	1,893	1,023	−46.0	361	323	−10.5
Curfew violations	49,007	63,454	+29.5	19,035	28,530	+49.9
Runaways	54,022	32,016	−40.7	73,334	47,720	−34.9

Source: FBI 2003.

suggests that they are at greater risk for alcohol and drug use or mental disorders, are less likely to stop their problem behaviors, and are more likely than males to develop new and more serious mental disorders (Sondheimer 2001).

In 2000, the racial composition of juvenile offenders was 79 percent White (Hispanics are also classified as White), 16 percent Black, 4 percent Asian/Pacific Islander, and 1 percent American Indian. Black youth were overrepresented in juvenile arrests for violent and property crimes. The violent crime index arrest rate (arrests per 100,000 juveniles in the same racial group) for Black juveniles was nearly four times the rate for American Indian juveniles and White juveniles and about seven times the rate for Asian youth. For property crime arrests, the arrest rate for Black juveniles was two thirds greater than the rate for American Indian juveniles, about double the rate for White juveniles, and about four times the rate for Asian juveniles (Snyder 2002).

Delinquency is often explained by the absence of strong bonds to society or the lack of social controls. In studies of serious adolescent crime, research indicates that the economic isolation of inner-city neighborhoods, along with the concentration of poverty and unemployment, leads to an erosion of the formal and informal controls that inhibit delinquent behavior (Laub 1983). Juveniles without any or much social control, when they live in any environment that offers opportunities for illegal activities, are likely to engage in illegal behavior. Youth who are strongly bonded to conventional role models and institutions (parents, teachers, school, community leaders, and law-abiding peers) are least likely to engage in delinquent behaviors.

White-Collar Crime

The term *white collar crime* was first used by sociologist Edwin Sutherland in 1939. He used the term to refer to "a crime committed by a person of respectability and high social status in the course of his occupation" (Sutherland 1949:9). Since then, the term has come to include three categories of crimes: those committed by an offender as described by Sutherland (someone of high social status and respectability), crimes committed for financial or economic gain, and crimes taking place in a particular organization or business (Barnett n.d.).

The FBI has defined white-collar crime by the type of crime:

[White-collar crime includes] illegal acts which are characterized by deceit, concealment, or violation of trust and which are not dependent upon the application or threat of physical force or violence. Individuals or organizations commit these acts to obtain money, property or services; to avoid payment or loss of money or services; or to secure personal and business advantage. (FBI 1989:3).

Such acts include credit card fraud, insurance fraud, mail fraud, tax evasion, money laundering, embezzlement, or theft of trade secrets. Corporate crime may also include illegal acts committed by corporate employees on behalf of the corporation and with its support.

From 1997 through 1999, white-collar crime accounted for 3.8 percent of the incidents reported to the FBI. The majority of the offenses involved fraud, counterfeiting, or forgery (Barnett n.d.). Check fraud and counterfeiting are among the fastest-growing problems affecting our financial system, producing estimated annual losses of about $10 billion (National White Collar Crime Center 2002a). It is estimated that as many as three quarters of all employees steal from their employers at least once, and some may regularly engage in theft at work. Losses due to employee theft can range from $20 billion to $90 billion annually (National Center for White Collar Crime 2002b). It is estimated that white-collar crimes cost taxpayers more than all other types of crime.

One of the most widespread forms of white-collar crime is Internet fraud and abuse, also known as *cybercrime*. In 2002, the Internet Fraud Complaint Center referred more than 48,000 Internet-related fraud complaints to law enforcement. In the same year, 263,000 Internet-related fraud complaints were received by the Federal Trade Commission (Agency Group 07 2003). The crimes include identity theft, online credit card fraud schemes, theft of trade secrets, sales of counterfeit software, and computer intrusions (a hacker breaking into a system). Years ago, when computer systems were relatively self-contained, there was no concern over cybercrime. Committing cybercrime is easier with the growth of the Internet, increasing computer connectivity, and the availability of break-in programs and information. As computer-controlled infrastructure and networks have expanded, many systems—power grids, airports, rail systems, hospitals—are vulnerable (Wolf 2000).

In response to Internet crimes, the FBI and the Department of Justice have established computer crime teams or offices. Some states, like Massachusetts and New York, have created high-technology crime units. Despite the increasing attention to cybercrime, "law enforcement at all levels is losing the battle" (Wolf 2000). Law enforcement does not have enough resources or technical support to detect and prosecute a significant number of cyberthieves. It is estimated that the government catches only 10 percent of those who break into government-controlled computers and fewer who break into computers of private companies (Wolf 2000).

PUTTING IT TOGETHER: Of the crimes that we have just reviewed, which type do you think is more problematic than others? What makes one crime more problematic than others?

The Inequalities of Crime—Offenders and Victims

Offenders

Reports consistently reveal that African American males are overrepresented in incarceration statistics. The majority of jail or prison inmates are male and African American (refer to Tables 10.6 and 10.7). As reported by the Bureau of Justice Statistics (2003b), the lifetime chances of a person going to state or federal prison are higher for men (9 percent) than women (1.1 percent) and higher for Blacks (16.2 percent) and Hispanics (9.4 percent) than Whites (2.5 percent). An estimated 28 percent of Black males will enter prison during their lifetime, compared to just 16 percent of Hispanic males and 4.4 percent of White males (Bureau of Justice 2003b). But the fact that a category of people is overrepresented among violent offenders does not necessarily mean that they are responsible for more violent acts (Brownstein 2001). Keep in mind that these statistics are based only on those who were caught by the criminal justice system.

A number of studies confirm that regardless of the seriousness of the crime, racial and ethnic minorities, particularly African Americans and Hispanics, are more likely to be arrested or incarcerated than their White counterparts. This is also true for minority juvenile delinquents. Minority youth are overrepresented at every stage in the juvenile justice system; they are arrested more often, detained more often, overrepresented in referrals to juvenile court, and institutionalized at a disproportionate rate compared to White youth (Joseph 2000).

VISUAL ESSAY: ENRON'S VICTIMS ❖

In 2001, the giant energy-trading company Enron Corporation unexpectedly filed for bankruptcy protection. It acknowledged losing more than $1 billion in complex trading schemes involving a tangled web of subsidiaries and shell companies. In the months prior to this disclosure, CEO Kenneth Lay kept telling employees and investors that the company was in good shape. Meanwhile, he was selling tens of millions of dollars' worth of his own Enron stock, allegedly to avoid losing money when the stock price collapsed. In 2004, Lay was indicted on 11 criminal charges of fraud, conspiracy, insider trading, and tax avoidance. If convicted of all charges, he faces up to 175 years in prison and $5.75 million in fines. Lay maintains that he did nothing wrong. A host of other top Enron executives have also been charged with similar crimes.

Some may consider these penalties excessive for a nonviolent crime. But consider the many victims. When Enron disintegrated, thousands of employees in Houston, Texas, and elsewhere in the United States and other countries lost their jobs. Shareholders lost about a billion dollars when the price of a share plunged from a high of more than $90 to under a dollar.

Roy Rinard, an employee for Portland General Electric, saw the value of Enron stock in his retirement account drop from $475,000 to $2,800. Sadly, many of Enron's older employees and retirees lost 70 to 90 percent of their retirement assets.

A death has been linked to Enron's collapse as well. A month after the company declared bankruptcy, Cliff Baxter, a former vice chairman of the company, apparently shot himself to death outside his Houston home.

Ripples from Enron's collapse spread far and wide. The investigation and prosecution of the Enron crimes have cost U.S. taxpayers untold millions of dollars. Venerable global accounting firm Arthur Andersen, which as Enron's audit company had a responsibility to uncover and report fraudulent operations, was convicted of obstruction of justice and forced to break up.

Enron's fraudulent ways also seem to have extended to its more conventional business operations. Enron was accused of manipulating California's energy market to create a 2000–2001 crisis of frequent power outages and then profiteering by selling the desperate state energy at vastly inflated prices. The ploy was no small factor in the state's crippling budget deficit. It also affected the health, safety, and financial well-being of California citizens, government entities, and businesses.

Does the Enron story change your opinion about the seriousness of white-collar crime? Does the government have an obligation to try to prevent these types of crimes? What solutions or punishments might be pursued?

❖ FOCUS ON: PROSTITUTION—THE VICTIMLESS CRIME?

There is an additional category of crimes to review: "victimless crimes" or *mala prohibita* crimes. Mala prohibita crimes are those behaviors that are criminalized because of "their perceived threat to society's moral or public safety" (Cosby et al. 1996:371). These crimes include drug abuse, gambling, pornography, and prostitution. Increased attention has focused on the decriminalization of these crimes, arguing that laws making these behaviors criminal are actually regulating personal behavior and dictating morality. Proponents explain that our criminal justice system wastes vital resources on arresting and punishing people for crimes that do not physically harm a person or physical property.

Prostitution is often referred to as a victimless crime or a "consensual crime" because both the prostitute and the client are consenting adults. In the United States, prostitution is legal only in Nevada, although not in every county or city of that state. It is difficult to determine the exact number of prostitutes in the United States. According to the National Taskforce on Prostitution, more than one million people in the United States have worked as prostitutes, or about 1 percent of all American women (Prostitutes' Education Network 2003). In 2001, 67,336 were arrested for prostitution or commercialized vice (FBI 2002). Prostitutes or sex workers can be male or female, although the majority of prostitutes are female. The demand for prostitutes comes primarily from male clients seeking heterosexual sex.

Studies have linked sexual abuse, substance addiction, and low social integration to prostitution. Runaway teens are likely to turn to prostitution because they have no skills and resources to support themselves.

However, a growing number of teen prostitutes come from middle- or upper middle-class homes and have no history of mental, sexual, or physical abuse (Smalley 2003). The FBI reports that the average age of a new prostitute is 13 years. Many are being recruited at local shopping malls, enticed by the offer to make quick easy spending money for food or clothing (Smalley 2003).

Kelly Hill (quoted in Saviano 2001) explains, "A lot of kids think it's glamorous. They see the girls on MTV, the gold jewelry, a lot of flash and cash. . . . The kids talk about 'pimpin' but they put it in a positive light, where it means you're in control" (p. 34). Hill was lured into prostitution at age 16, working in Canada and Hawaii for three years. With the help of her sister and grandmother, she was able to leave prostitution and founded Sisters Offering Support (SOS), a grassroots organization that helps women and children escape prostitution. Based in Hawaii, SOS includes a prevention program for youth, community education, and parent support services. In 2000, SOS helped 500 victims of sexual exploitation. About 85 percent of them found legal employment, went back to school, or returned to their families. Twenty-nine-year-old Hill was named "America's Best Young Community Leader" in 2000 by *Rolling Stone Magazine* and by Do Something, a national organization focusing on young people and activism. As an advocate, she helped create two state laws providing additional rights and protections for victims of commercial sexual exploitation. Hill says, "When you say prostitute, you immediately see a woman in a short skirt, high heels, on a street corner somewhere. What you don't see is your mother, your sister . . . your daughter" (quoted in Saviano 2001:34).

❖ Table 10.6 Percentage of Prisoners under State or Federal Jurisdiction by Race, Based on Inmates with Sentences of More than One Year

	1995	2002
White	33.5	34.2
Black	45.7	45.1
Hispanic	17.6	18.1
Other	3.2	2.6

Source: Harrison and Beck 2003.

❖ Table 10.7 Number of Inmates by Gender for 1995 and 2002

	Men	Women
1995	1,057,406	68,468
2002	1,343,164	97,491

Source: Harrison and Beck 2003.

An early criminological explanation was offered by Marvin Wolfgang and Franco Ferracuti (1967). They argued that Blacks have adopted violent subcultural values, creating a "subculture of violence." Although this is an often-cited theory, there is insufficient empirical evidence to support the idea that Blacks are more likely to embrace a violent value system. In fact, studies have indicated that White males are more likely to express violent beliefs or attitudes than Black males (Cao, Adams, and Jensen 2000).

Criminologists and sociologists have also studied patterns of racial bias or discrimination in the law enforcement and criminal justice system. Research has identified patterns of discrimination by law enforcement officers designed to sanction offenders based on extralegal variables (e.g., race, age, low socioeconomic status, and unemployment) (Cureton 2001). Police in high-crime areas are more likely to be harsh on suspected criminals, to use coercive authority, and to make arrests than they are in lower crime areas (Smith 1986).

In his analysis of criminal sentencing, Darren Warner (2000) explains that despite the public perception that racial bias exists within the criminal sentencing stage, no consistent pattern can be identified from empirical research on sentencing practices in state and federal courts. Warner says that the exception is that Blacks are more likely to receive a death sentence than Whites, especially in cases that involve a White victim. "Public perception has held firm that such discrimination does, in fact, exist and continues to taint criminal justice systems throughout the United States" (Warner 2000:175).

Victims

Early studies on crime victims tend to perpetuate the image that the victim was simply at the "wrong place at the wrong time" (Davis, Taylor, and Titus 1997). Following that reasoning, not being a victim of crime could be explained simply by good luck. However, research indicates that some individuals, by virtue of their social group or social behavior, are more prone than others to become victims (Davis et al. 1997). What people do, where they go, and whom they associate with affect their likelihood of victimization (Laub 1997).

Victimization is distributed across key demographic dimensions (Laub 1997). We reviewed some of the characteristics of crime victims in the section on "Types of Crime." Victimization rates are substantially higher for the poor, the young, males, Blacks, single people, renters, and central city residents (Davis et al. 1997). The likelihood of being injured because of a violent crime is higher among the young, the poor, urban dwellers, Blacks, Hispanics, and American Indians (Simon et al. 2001). Injury rates are lower for the elderly, people with higher income or higher educational attainment, and people who are married or widowed (Simon et al. 2001).

Black males have the highest rate of violent victimization, while White females have the lowest (Laub 1997). Blacks also have the highest rate of overall household victimization. Although rates of violent crimes declined during the 1990s, mortality from homicide among minority groups is still high. Homicide is the leading cause of death among Black males between the ages of 15 and 24, and it is the second leading cause of death for Latino males in the same age group (Rich and Ro 2002). People who have been victims once are at an elevated risk of becoming a victim again. Repeat victimization is likely to occur in poor, predominately Black areas (Davis et al. 1997).

 **PUTTING IT TOGETHER:** In your community.

Have you been a victim of nonviolent or violent crime? Were you victimized because of your social behavior or your membership in a particular social group? Or were you at the wrong place at the wrong time?

Our Current Response to Crime

The Police

As of June 2000, federal agencies employed more than 80,000 full-time personnel authorized to make arrests and carry firearms. Among all federal officers, 30.5 percent were racial or ethnic minorities (Bureau of Justice Statistics 2001). Local police departments had 565,915 full-time employees, including 441,000 sworn personnel.

Among all local police officers, 22.7 percent were racial or ethnic minorities (Bureau of Justice Statistics 2003c). In 1999, federal, state, and local governments spent over $146 billion for civil and criminal justice, about $521 per resident (Bureau of Justice Statistics 2002).

We rely on the police force to serve as the first line of defense against crime, and some officers lose their lives in the line of duty. In 2001, 142 law enforcement officers were feloniously killed in 30 states and Puerto Rico (this includes 72 officers who died as a result of the attacks on September 11, 2001), and 78 were killed in accidents. From 1992 through 2001, 34.4 percent of officers who were killed were involved in arrest situations at the time, 16.2 percent were investigating suspicious people, and 15.6 percent were responding to disturbance calls. About 15 percent were involved in traffic stops or pursuits, 13.7 percent were caught in ambush situations, and 20.4 percent were performing other duties (FBI 2001b).

American policing has gone through substantial changes over the past several decades (MacDonald 2002). Traditional models of policing emphasized high visibility and the use of force and arrests as deterrents to crime. Policing under these models relies on three tactics: police patrols, rapid response to service calls, and retrospective investigations (Moore 1999). These models reinforce an "us" versus "them" division, sometimes pitting the police against the public it was sworn to protect. High-profile incidents of police brutality and violence, such as the cases that involved Rodney King in Los Angeles and Abner Louima and Amadou Diallo in New York City, increased public distrust and tainted the image of policing.

Studies indicate that Whites trust police more and have more positive interactions with them than Blacks and that Hispanics fall between these two groups (Norris et al. 1992). Black youth tend to have the most negative or hostile feelings toward police (Norris et al. 1992). Residents from poor or disadvantaged areas have a much lower regard for the police than the general public. However, research has also indicated that when citizens believe that they are treated fairly, they tend to grant police more legitimacy and are more likely to comply with police (Stoutland 2001).

Police departments are now incorporating new methods of policing based on the community and problem-solving approaches (Goldstein 1990; MacDonald 2002). The community policing approach refers to efforts to increase the interaction between officers and citizens, including the use of foot patrols, community substations, and neighborhood watches (Beckett and Sasson 2000). By 2000, two thirds of all local police departments and 62 percent of sheriff's offices had full-time sworn personnel engaged in community policing activities (Bureau of Justice Statistics 2003c). We will talk more about community policing in the section, "Crime Policy, Advocacy, and Innovation."

Prisons

Despite the decline in crime rates, prison populations are increasing (Anderson 2003). At the end of 2002, the federal and state inmate population was more than 1.4 million (see U.S. Data Map 10.1). Mandatory sentencing, especially for nonviolent drug offenders, is a key reason why inmate populations have increased for 30 years. Drug offenders now make up more than half of all federal prisoners (Anderson 2003).

POLICING IN BRAZIL

Policing in Brazil has a dark and ugly history. The death squads of Brazil began in 1958, when Army General Amury Kruel, chief of the police forces in Rio de Janeiro, handpicked a group of special policemen to combat rising theft and robberies in the city. These "bandit hunters" were given permission to hunt and kill these criminals. In other states and cities, teams of police hunters were formed to pursue *pistoleiros* (armed criminals), undesirables, and gangsters. Each new death squad, whether targeting economic or political criminals, became more distant from the formal criminal justice system (Huggins 1997). Over the course of several political regimes, Brazilian police have never abandoned their practices of violent enforcement and vigilantism.

After 21 years of military dictatorship (1964–1985), the civilian government (inaugurated in 1985) set out to reform Brazil's authoritarian practices. In 1988, armed with a new constitution, the democratic leadership lifted the barriers to political participation and attempted to restore the legal premises of universal citizenship rights (Mitchell and Wood 1999). In 1996, President Fernando Henrique Cardoso released the National Human Rights Plan, a comprehensive set of measures to address human rights violations in Brazil, including cases of police abuses (Human Rights Watch 1997).

Yet, police violence and human rights violations all increased dramatically under democratic rule (Caldeira and Holston 1999). Police are some of the primary agents of violence in Brazil. According to organizations such as Amnesty International and the Human Rights Watch, many citizens continue to suffer systematic abuse and violations at the hands of their own police force. Data from 1986 to 1990 reveals that police committed 10 percent of the killings in Sao Paulo; in 1991, it was 15.9 percent, and in 1992, it was 27.4 percent. By comparison, police only accounted for 1.2 percent of killings in New York City during the 1990s and 2.1 percent of killings in Los Angeles. In 1991, Sao Paulo police killed 1,171 civilians, compared with only 27 people killed by New York police and 23 killed by Los Angeles police (Caldeira and Holston 1999).

While Brazilian law endorses due process, criminal proceedings and police methods subvert this principle (Mitchell and Wood 1999), supporting extralegal conduct in the majority of cases (Huggins 1997; Mitchell and Wood 1999). Government leaders also offer their support of extralegal activities. Three days after state civil police officers killed 13 suspected drug traffickers, Marcello Alencar, governor of Rio de Janeiro, was quoted as saying, "These violent criminals have become animals. . . . They are animals. They can't be understood any other way. . . . These people don't have to be treated in a civilized way. They have to be treated like animals" (Human Rights Watch 1997).

According to Martha Huggins (1997), police violence in Brazil comes in two forms: on-duty police violence and death squads. Highly organized, elite police units carry out extralegal killings while on duty.

The police violence is usually deliberately planned and conducted during routine street sweeps and dragnets, actions justified by the state's war on drugs and crime. There is also death squad violence conducted by a group of murderers, usually off-duty police, who are paid by local businesses or politicians for their services. Huggins calls them privatized security guards serving commercial or political interests.

In 1985, Brazil implemented women's police stations, *Delegacias de Policia dos Dieritos da Mulher* (DPM or *delegacias*). Brazil commonly uses specialized police stations and forces; there are stations devoted to robbery, burglary, theft, drugs, and others. The delegacias were created in response to pressure from feminist groups demanding that violence against women be addressed. The first groups were formed in Rio de Janeiro and San Paulo, where the first DPM was established in 1985 (Hautzinger 1997). The female officers at each station are conventionally trained police, with no specialized training or qualifications for serving at the delegacias except for the fact that they are women. It is estimated that there are more than 250 delegacias in Brazil today (Hautzinger 2002). Although domestic violence complaints were the original mission of the DPMs, these account for only 80 percent of the caseloads (Hautzinger 2002). The Human Rights Watch reports that despite the presence of DPMs, "many rural and urban women have found police to be unresponsive to their claims and have encountered open hostility . . . when they attempted to report domestic violence" (Human Rights Watch 1995).

Along with the increase in the number of prisoners comes an increase in prison budgets. In 1996, the average state inmate cost about $20,100 per year; the average federal inmate about $23,500 (Stephan 1999). Average operating costs per inmate varied by state, indicating differences in costs of living, wage rates, and other related factors. The states with the five highest annual operating costs per inmate were Minnesota ($37,800), Rhode Island ($35,700), Maine ($33,700), Alaska ($32,400), and Utah ($32,400). States with the lowest annual operating costs per inmate included Alabama ($8,000), Oklahoma ($10,600), Mississippi ($11,200), Texas ($12,200), and Missouri ($12,800). Expenditures for state prison activities increased from $9.6 billion in 1985 to $22 billion in 1996, including construction, staffing, and maintenance of prisons. State correctional spending increased an average of 7.2 percent per year, more than the annual increase for education (3.6 percent) and for natural resources (2.9 percent) (Stephan 1999).

Under the Eighth Amendment, prison facilities are required to provide prisoners with adequate medical care. Nearly all state-operated adult confinement facilities screen inmates for mental health problems or provide treatment. On June 2000, more than 150,000 inmates were in mental therapy or counseling programs, about 114,200 inmates were receiving psychotropic medications; and 19,100 were in 24-hour care (Beck and Maruschak 2001). At the end of 1999, correctional authorities reported that 24,607 state inmates (2.3 percent) and 1,150 federal inmates (0.9 percent) were HIV positive, and there were 6,642 confirmed AIDS cases in all U.S. prisons. New York

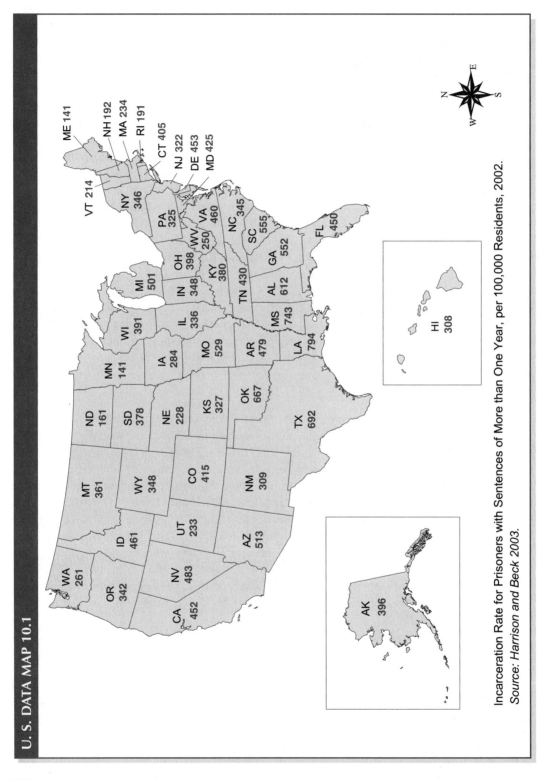

Incarceration Rate for Prisoners with Sentences of More than One Year, per 100,000 Residents, 2002.
Source: Harrison and Beck 2003.

(7,000), Florida (2,633), and Texas (2,520) had the highest number of HIV-positive prison inmates. In 1999, there were 242 AIDS-related deaths among state prisoners (Maruschak 2001). It is estimated that it costs $80,396 per year to care for an HIV-positive inmate and $105,963 per year to care for an inmate with AIDS (AIDS Action 2001).

What is the purpose of the prison system? Some argue that the system is intended to rehabilitate offenders, to prevent them from committing crime again. But rates of recidivism, or repeat offenses, serve as an indicator of how badly the system is working. Data from the Bureau of Justice Statistics revealed that among 300,000 prisoners released in 1993, 67.5 percent were rearrested within three years (Langan and Levin 2002). Among those rearrested, 46.9 percent were reconvicted for a new crime, and 51.8 percent were back in prison for a new sentence or for a technical violation of their release (failing a drug test, missing an appointment with their parole officer). Men, Blacks, non-Hispanics, and prisoners with longer prior records were more likely to be rearrested. Younger prisoners were also more likely to reoffend than older prisoners (Langan and Levin 2002).

❖ PUTTING IT TOGETHER: The latest in American corrections is home detention. Electronic surveillance equipment allows law enforcement to monitor large numbers of offenders through monitors strapped to their legs. Nonviolent offenders can leave for work by 7 a.m. and be home by 6 p.m., continue to follow scheduled appointments and drug tests, and be continuously monitored. Keeping offenders imprisoned but not behind a prison wall, the system is said to be less expensive than prison and more flexible. What do you think about the effectiveness of these surveillance systems? Is this an effective system of punishment or rehabilitation?

The Death Penalty

Since 1979, 869 men and women have been executed in the United States. The majority of executions have occurred in the South, with Texas and Virginia having a total of 398 executions since 1979 (Death Penalty Information Center 2003b). As of April 2003, 3,525 inmates were awaiting execution (Fins 2003). About 43 percent of Death Row inmates are Black; about 2 percent are women. About 2 percent were 17 or younger when they committed the crimes that resulted in the death sentences (Liptak 2003).

The death penalty was instituted as a deterrent to serious crime. However, research indicates that capital punishment has no deterrent effect on committing murder. In fact, states with the death penalty have murder rates significantly higher than states without the death penalty. The death penalty applies only to capital murder cases, where aggravating circumstances are present. Kappeler et al. (2000) explain that only

❖ Table 10.8   Race of Death Row Inmates, as of April 1, 2003

Race	Number	Percentage of Death Row Inmates	Percentage of U.S. Population (2000)
White, not Hispanic	1,610	46	69.1
Black, not Hispanic	1,490	42	12.1
Hispanic	344	10	12.5
Other (Native American, Asian, Iraqi)	81	2	6.3

Source: Death Penalty Information Center 2003a.

a small proportion of people charged with murder can be sentenced to death. For example, between 1980 and 1989, 206,710 murders were reported to the police, but during the same time period, only 117 executions were carried out. This is about one execution for every 1,767 murders committed during the same time frame (Kappeler et al. 2000).

Opponents of the death penalty point out the racial disparities in its application. The most significant studies of racial disparities point to the race of the victims as the critical factor in sentencing. Those convicted of committing a crime against a White person are more often sentenced to death. Since 1976, 82 percent of murder victims in the cases resulting in executions have been White, even though Whites are victims in less than 50 percent of all murders. When figures for race of defendant and victim are analyzed, 84 Black defendants have been executed for the murder of a White person while only four White defendants have been executed for the murder of a Black victim (Dieter 1996). In federal cases, racial minorities are being prosecuted beyond their proportion in the general population or in the population of criminal offenders. In an analysis of prosecutions under the federal death penalty provisions of the Anti-Drug Abuse Act of 1988, 89 percent of defendants were either African American or Mexican American (Subcommittee on Civil and Constitutional Rights 1994). The number of prisoners on Death Row is presented in Table 10.8.

Crime Policy, Advocacy, and Innovation

U.S. Department of Justice

We may perceive our criminal justice system as a single system when, in fact, we have 51 different criminal justice systems, one federal and 50 state systems. The federal system is led by the U.S. Department of Justice. Headed by the Attorney General of the United States, the Department of Justice comprises 39 separate component organizations, including the FBI; Drug Enforcement Administration (DEA); the Bureau of Alcohol, Tobacco, Firearms, and Explosives; the Immigration and Naturalization Service (INS), which controls the border and provides services to lawful immigrants; the Anti-Trust Division, which promotes and protects the competitive process in business and industry; and the Bureau of Prisons, which oversees correctional operations and programs (U.S. Department of Justice 2002).

Funding for the U.S. Department of Justice and its organizations comes from federal legislation. The 1994 Violent Crime Control and Law Enforcement Act was the largest crime bill in history, providing funds for 100,000 new officers, $9.7 billion for prisons, and $6.1 billion for prevention programs. Under the Violence Against Women Acts of 1994 and 2000, the Office on Violence Against Women, administered by the Department of Justice, has awarded more than $1 billion in grant funds to U.S. states and territories. These grants have helped state, tribal, and local governments and community-based agencies to train personnel, establish domestic violence and sexual assault units, assist victims of violence, and hold perpetrators accountable (Office on Violence Against Women 2003).

Juvenile Justice and Delinquency Prevention Programs

The U.S. Department of Justice also supports the Office of Juvenile Justice and Prevention Programs. As its mission, the Office attempts to provide national leadership, coordination, and resources to prevent and respond to juvenile delinquency and victimization. The Office is guided by the Juvenile Justice and Delinquency Prevention Act of 1974. As stated in the 2002 reauthorization bill, "Although the juvenile violent crime arrest rate in 1999 was the lowest in the decade, there remains a consensus that the number of crimes and the rate of offending by juveniles nationwide is still too high" (U.S. Congress 2002).

The Office sponsors more than 15 programs targeting juveniles and their communities. Through the Program of Research on the Causes and Correlates of Delinquency, the Office sponsors three longitudinal programs in Denver, Colorado; Pittsburgh, Pennsylvania; and Rochester, New York, to examine how delinquency, violence, and drug use occur among juveniles. The Tribal Youth Program is part of the Indian Country Law Enforcement Initiative to support tribal efforts to prevent and control juvenile delinquency. The Child Protection Division administers programs related to crimes against children, such as the National Center for Missing and Exploited Children and the Internet Crimes Against Children Task Force.

In one of its ongoing programs, the Juvenile Mentoring Program or JUMP, the Office supports one-to-one mentoring programs for youth at risk of failing in school, dropping out of school, or becoming involved in delinquent behavior. JUMP matches adults 21 years or older with youths age 5 through 17 years. Congress has appropriated more than $56 million to support one-to-one mentoring programs in schools. Since 1994, 204 JUMP sites in 47 states and two territories have been funded, serving 9,200 students.

Preliminary evaluation data suggest significant improvement in peer relationships, aggressive behavior, and delinquency risks in youth who have participated in

JUMP projects (JUMP 2003). Both youth and their mentors were extremely positive when rating aspects of their mentoring experiences, and both had similar perceptions of how the program benefited the youth. Among the most beneficial aspects of the program were helping youths to get better grades, avoid friends who start trouble, and stay out of fights (JUMP 1998).

Faith-based and community organizations have also been involved in delinquency prevention programs. One such program is the Blue Nile Rites of Passage program based in Harlem's Abyssinian Baptist Church (established before President George W. Bush's initiative). Since 1994, the program has relied on a community-based mentoring component to address the spiritual, cultural, and moral character development of African American youth (Harlem Live 1999). In general, the program was designed to have "a positive impact on the family relationships, self-esteem, sexual behaviors, drug use, peer and sibling relationships, and the religious and social values of the youth" (Irwin 2002:30). Irwin (2002) says that faith-based initiatives contain much of what has been found to be valuable in traditional mentoring programs, with the church as a backdrop. In the Harlem program, students were assigned to a mentor, either a church minister or a congregation member. During weekly meetings, mentors worked with their partnered youth, emphasizing problem-solving and decision-making skills. In addition, the mentors introduce the youth to different educational and cultural activities as examples of potential community interactions. The program also includes a media literacy component where students learn how to film, edit, direct, and produce their own videos (Harlem Live 1999).

The New American Prison

In an effort to reduce the costs of incarceration to state and federal correctional agencies, the idea of private correctional institutions has gained momentum. The perception that public prisons are deteriorating and overcrowded helped to encourage the growth of private prisons in the 1980s (Pratt and Maahs 1999). Private prisons incarcerate about 5 percent of the sentenced adult population (Camp and Gaes 2002), usually housing low-risk offenders. It has been argued that private correctional institutions save taxpayers' money, providing more services with fewer resources; studies reveal a slight advantage to private prisons and demonstrate a reduction in per-inmate cost over time (Larason Schneider 1999). Studies have indicated that the savings from private prisons are likely to come from lower wages and benefits, fewer staff, more efficient uses of staff, or a combination of these factors (Camp and Gaes 2002).

Camp and Gaes (2002) found private prisons did not perform better than public ones and in some cases did worse. According to the researchers, one of the most reliable indicators of prison operations is the rate at which inmates test positive for use of drugs or alcohol. If substance abuse is high, it indicates a pattern of poor security practices. For the private institutions, tests showed no drug use in 34 percent of the facilities and low to high drug use in 66 percent of the facilities. Nearly 62 percent of public prisons showed no evidence of drug use. In addition, Camp and Gaes found that 85 percent of private prisons had no escapes, and there were 23 escapes from private prisons. For the same time period, public facilities had only one escape, and 98.5 percent of prisons had no escapes in 1999.

Passed in 1996, the Prison Litigation Reform Act requires prisoners to exhaust all internal and administrative remedies before they can file federal lawsuits to challenge the conditions of their confinement or to report civil rights violations. The Act was intended to prevent frivolous or unfounded lawsuits, but it has made it impossible for prisoners with valid complaints to be heard. Prisoners cannot file lawsuits for mental or emotional injury unless they can also show that physical injury occurred. Prisoners are required to pay for their own court filing fees; monthly installments can be taken out of their prison commissary account (American Civil Liberties Union [ACLU] 1999). The Act also prohibits prison officials from settling lawsuits by agreeing to make changes in unconstitutional prison conditions. The ACLU and its National Prison Project have challenged the constitutionality of the Prison Litigation Reform Act, claiming that it "slams the courthouse door on society's most vulnerable members" (ACLU 1999). Despite its questionable constitutionality, many government leaders and courts have applauded the Act.

Community Approaches to Law Enforcement and Crime Prevention—COPS

Community-Oriented Policing Services or COPS was created in response to the Violent Crime Control and Law Enforcement Act of 1994. The goal of the program is to shift from traditional law enforcement to community-oriented policing services, a change that includes putting law enforcement officers within a community and emphasizing crime prevention rather than law enforcement (COPS 2003). As stated on the COPS Web site: "By earning the trust of the members of their communities and making those individuals stakeholders in their own safety, community policing makes law enforcement easier and more efficient, and makes America safer" (COPS 2003). Researchers found that "police administrators have hailed community oriented policing as the preferred strategy for the delivery of services" (Novak, Alarid, and Lucas 2003:57).

One of the central premises of community policing is the relationships among the police, citizens, and other agencies. Since 1981, the National Night Out program has worked to strengthen police-community partnerships in anti-crime efforts. Usually scheduled in August, National Night Out activities first involved just turning the front lights of houses on but now include block parties, cookouts, parades, and neighborhood walks involving community members and police officers (National Night Out 2003). Indeed, the community plays an important role in ensuring its own safety. In community policing, "problem solving requires that police and the community work together in identifying neighborhood problems, and that the community assumes greater 'guardianship' of the neighborhood" (Greene and Pelfrey 1997:395).

COPS sponsors grants and initiatives in selected communities, offering specialized training and programs to police professionals, such as technological innovations (mobile computing, computer-aided dispatch, automated fingerprint identification systems) or policing methods. In addition, the program supports innovative strategies linking police with their communities. For example, COPS supported community organizations in New York City and Los Angeles as they developed police magnet schools. In New York, the East Brooklyn Congregations/East New York High School of Public Safety and Law was established in 1999 to serve largely Hispanic and African American neighborhoods in East Brooklyn. The college-track high school program, developed in partnership with the John Jay College of Criminal Justice, exposes students to public safety, security, and law courses. COPS reports that the program has been successful in increasing attendance and retention rates, increasing student grades, and helping students exceed the benchmarks set for scores on the state's Regents tests. Graduating students are encouraged to pursue careers in public safety, law, forensics, and corrections (Pressman, Chapman, and Rosen 2002).

It is difficult to assess the effectiveness of community policing methods because many of these community approaches have not been sufficiently implemented (MacDonald 2002). Zhao, Scheider, and Thurman (2002) report that an additional problem is that much of the research designed to assess COPS programs is limited to the individual programs or cities. However, based on their analysis of COPS programs in 6,100 cities, the researchers discovered that COPS hiring and innovative programs resulted in significant reductions in local violent and nonviolent crime rates in cities with populations greater than 10,000. In addition, an increase of $1 in grant funding per resident for hiring contributed to a decline of 5.26 violent crimes and 21.63 property crimes per 100,000 residents. However, COPS grants had no significant impact on violent and property crime rates in cities with less than 10,000 residents.

Prison Advocacy and Death Penalty Reform

Several national, state, and local organizations are committed to reforming our prison system and advocating for prisoner rights. Most of their work comes in the form of advocacy, educational campaigns, and litigation.

Not With Our Money is a network of student and community activists working to end the use of prisons for profit. The group successfully mobilized against Sodexho Marriott, a food service provider that owned more than 10 percent of Corrections Cooperation of America (CCA), one of the largest owners and operators of U.S. private prisons. Efforts to pressure university administrators to end their food service contracts with Sodexho Marriott were successful at several colleges and universities. Since protests against Sodexho Marriott began, its parent company Sodexho Alliance divested all its interest in CCA (Bigda, 2001).

State and local grassroots organizations, such as Coloradans Against the Death Penalty, Mississippians for Alternatives to the Death Penalty, and the Texas Coalition to Abolish the Death Penalty, support prisoners' rights and legislation to abolish the death penalty in their states. Citizens United for Alternatives to the Death Penalty (CUADP) attempts to "end the death penalty through aggressive campaigns of public education and the promotion of tactical grassroots activism" (CUADP 2003a). CUADP is using public education, funding, direct action, and professional media campaigns to send its message to the public. CUADP (2003b) believes that "we as a people, and the media in particular, have a responsibility to the public to expose wrongful convictions." On its Web site, the organization includes a list of cases that the organization believes may merit the attention of investigative reporters.

One organization that has accepted the mission of correcting wrongful convictions is the Innocence Project. Established in 1992 by attorneys Barry Scheck and Peter Neufeld, the Innocence Project is a nonprofit legal clinic at the Benjamin N. Cardozo School of Law at Yeshiva University in New York. The clinic handles only cases "where postconviction DNA testing of evidence can yield conclusive proof on innocence" (Innocence Project 2003). As of August 2, 2003, the project had helped exonerate 131 individuals. These cases highlight the problems of misidentification, corrupt scientists and police, overzealous prosecutors, inept defense attorneys, and the influence of poverty and race in the criminal justice system. The Innocence Project is currently working to establish the Innocence Network, a group of law and journalism schools and public defender offices that assist inmates trying to prove their innocence, even if their cases do not involve biological or DNA evidence. Several states have established their own innocence or justice projects.

The Innocence Project and similar organizations consistently draw the public's attention when an innocent inmate is released. One recent case occurred in New Orleans, Louisiana. Gregory Bright and Earl Truvia were convicted in 1975 for the fatal shooting of a teenager (Innocence Project New Orleans 2003). Their convictions were thrown out in 2002 after their defense team, the Innocence Project New Orleans, showed that the prosecution's lone eyewitness was battling drug addiction and mental illness at the time of her testimony. Her story did not match the coroner's autopsy results regarding the time of death and other matters related to the shooting. The District Attorney's office was accused of hiding important facts from Bright and Truvia's defense team. The men were held for a retrial; but in 2003, District Attorney Eddie Jordan dropped all charges against the two men.

❖ **PUTTING IT TOGETHER:**
In your community.

To learn more about Innocence Projects in your state, log on to *Study Site Chapter 10.*

MAIN POINTS

- A **crime** is any behavior that violates criminal law and is punishable. Crime is divided into two legal categories: **felonies** (serious offenses) and **misdemeanors** (minor offenses).
- Biological and psychological theories of crime address how crime is determined by individual characteristics or predispositions but do

not explain why crime rates vary in certain areas. Sociological theories attempt to address these reasons.

- Functionalists argue that society sets goals and expectations, but people feel strain when they do not have the access or resources to achieve these goals. They then experience anomie and create new norms or rules. Functionalists argue that solutions to crime should target strained groups, providing access to resources to attain goals.

• A second functionalist explanation links social control to criminal behavior. Social control theorists ask why someone *doesn't* commit crime. When societal elements are strong, criminal behavior is unlikely to occur.

• Conflict theorists believe that criminality is a way to define a person's social status according to how that person is perceived and treated by law enforcement. An act is not inherently criminal; society defines it that way. Theorists argue that criminal laws exist to preserve the interests and power of specific groups. Problems emerge when particular groups are disadvantaged by the criminal justice system, which conflict theorists argue is intentionally unequal.

• In feminist scholarship, gender inequality theories have been presented as explanations of female crime. In this view, patriarchal power relations shape gender differences in crime, pushing women into criminal behavior through role entrapment, economic marginalization, and victimization or as a survival response.

• Interactionists examine the process that defines certain individuals and acts as criminal. The theory is called **labeling theory**, highlighting that it isn't the criminal or act that's important but rather the audience that labels the person or act as criminal. Once a criminal label is attached, a criminal career is set in motion.

• There are different types of crime, including **violent crime** and **property crime** (three fourths of all crime in the United States). **Juvenile crime** refers to youths in trouble with the law. **White-collar crime** includes crimes committed by someone of high social status, for financial gain, or in a particular organization.

• Within the prison system, African American males are overrepresented. A number of studies confirm that regardless of the seriousness of the crime, racial and ethnic minorities are more likely to be arrested or incarcerated than their White counterparts. Studies also show that police in high-crime areas are more likely to be harsh on suspected criminals, to use coercive authority, and to make arrests than they are in lower crime areas.

• No consistent pattern can be identified in sentencing practices in state and federal courts. The exception is that Blacks are more likely to receive a death sentence than Whites, especially in cases involving a White victim.

• Research indicates that some individuals are more prone than others to become victims. Victimization rates are substantially higher for the poor, the young, males, Blacks, single people, renters, and central city residents.

• American policing has gone through substantial changes over the past several decades. Traditional models emphasized high visibility and the use of force and arrests as deterrents. These models reinforce an "us" versus "them" division. Police departments are now incorporating new methods based on the community and problem-solving approaches.

• Despite the decline in crime rates, prison populations are increasing. Mandatory sentencing, especially for nonviolent drug offenders, is a key reason why inmate populations have increased for 30 years.

• Some argue that the prison system is intended to rehabilitate offenders. But rates of recidivism, or repeat offenses, serve as an indicator of how badly the system is working.

• The death penalty was instituted as a deterrent to serious crime. However, research indicates that capital punishment has no deterrent effect on committing murder. In fact, states with the death penalty have murder rates significantly higher than states without the death penalty.

• Several national, state, and local organizations are committed to reforming our prison system and advocating for prisoner rights. Most of their work comes in the form of advocacy, educational campaigns, and litigation.

❖

INTERNET AND COMMUNITY EXERCISES

1. Investigate the two official sources of U.S. crime data: the U.S. Department of Justice's Bureau of Justice Statistics and the FBI's Uniform Crime Reports. Search both sites for information on one type of crime (e.g., homicide, property crime, rape). Log on to *Study Site Chapter 10* for the Web links.

2. The debate over gun control has two vocal sides: those advocating for gun control and those supporting the right to own guns. Investigate local or national organizations on both sides of this issue. You can start out by visiting the following sites: Women Against Gun Control, The Brady Campaign to Prevent Gun Violence, and The National Rifle Association (log on to *Study Site Chapter 10* for links). How do these organizations define the problem of handgun violence? How does each side identify the pros and cons of gun control? What solutions does each side offer?

3. Do your local police support the National Night Out program? Contact the local police station to learn more about the program and other community policing efforts in your city. What community programs are implemented? What residents or social groups are police attempting to reach? To learn more about the program, visit the National Association of Town Watch, the sponsor of the program. The Web site includes links to selected city and state programs. Log on to *Study Site Chapter 10*.

4. The largest mentoring program in the United States is Big Brothers Big Sisters of America. In more than 5,000 communities, the organization links adult volunteers with little brothers or little sisters. Contact your local Big Brothers Big Sisters program to find out more about the organization. Are other mentoring programs operating in your neighborhood? based in your school?

On your own. Log on to *Study Site–Community and Policy Guide* for more information about the social problems, social policies, and community responses discussed in this chapter.

References

Ackerman, W. 1998. "Socioeconomic Correlates of Increasing Crime Rates in Smaller Communities." *Professional Geographer* 50(3):372–387.

Adler, F. 1975. *Sisters in Crime*. New York: McGraw-Hill.

Adler, F., Gerhard Mueller, and William Laufer. 1991. *Criminology*. New York: McGraw-Hill.

Agency Group 07. 2003. "Operation E-Con: Cracking Down on Internet Crime." *FDCH Regulatory Intelligence Database*, May 16, 2003. Lanham, MD: Federal Document Clearing House.

AIDS Action. 2001. *Incarcerated Populations and HIV/AIDS*. Washington, DC: Author.

Akers, R. 1997. *Criminological Theories: Introduction and Evaluation*. Los Angeles: Roxbury.

American Civil Liberties Union (ACLU). 1999. "Prisoners' Rights" (ACLU Position Paper). New York: Author.

Amnesty International. 2000. "Pregnant and Imprisoned in the United States." *Birth* 27(4):266–271.

Anderson, C. 2003. "Prison Populations Challenge Already Cash-Strapped States." *The News Tribune*, July 28, p. A7.

Barnett, C. n.d. *The Measurement of White Collar Crime Using Uniform Crime Reporting (UCR) Data*. Washington, DC: Government Printing Office.

Beck, A. and L. Maruschak. 2001. *Mental Health Treatment in State Prisons, 2000* (NCJ 188215). Washington, DC: U.S. Department of Justice, Office of Justice Programs.

Beckett, K. and T. Sasson. 2000. *The Politics of Injustice*. Thousand Oaks, CA: Pine Forge.

Bigda, C. 2001. "College Students Oppose Private Prisons." Retrieved March 20, 2004 (www.dollarsandsense.org/archives/2001/0901bigda.html).

Blumstein, A. and R. Rosenfeld. 1998. "Explaining Recent Trends in U.S. Homicide Rates." *The Journal of Criminal Law and Criminology* 88(4):1175–1216.

Brownstein, H. 2001. *The Social Reality of Violence and Violent Crime.* Boston: Allyn & Bacon.

Bureau of Justice Statistics. 2001. "Federal Law Enforcement Statistics." Retrieved July 14, 2003 (www.ojd.usdoj.gov/bjs/fedle.htm).

———. 2002. "Expenditure and Employment Statistics." Retrieved July 14, 2003 (www.ojd.usdoh.gov/bjs/easnde.htm).

———. 2003a. "Crime Characteristics." Retrieved July 8, 2003 (www.ojp.usdoj.gov/bjs/cvict_c.htm).

———. 2003b. "Criminal Offenders Statistics." Retrieved July 8, 2003 (www.ojp.usdoj.gov/bjs/crimoff.htm).

———. 2003c. "State and Local Law Enforcement Statistics." Retrieved July 14, 2003 (www.ojp.usdoj.gov/bjs/sandlle.htm).

———. 2003d. "Victim Characteristics." Retrieved July 8, 2003 (www.ojp.usdoj.gov/bjs/cvict_v.htm).

Caldeira, T. and J. Holston. 1999. "Democracy and Violence in Brazil." *Society for Comparative Study of Society and History* 41(4): 691–729.

Camp, S. and G. Gaes. 2002. "Growth and Quality of U.S. Private Prisons: Evidence from a National Survey." *Criminology and Public Policy* 1(3):427–450.

Cao, Liqun, Anthony Troy Adams, andVickie Jensen. 2000. "The Empirical Status of the Black-Subculture-of-Violence Thesis." Pp. 47–62 in *The System in Black and White*, edited by M. Markowitz and D. Jones-Brown. Westport, CT: Praeger.

Catalano, Shannan. 2004. *Criminal Victimization, 2003* (NCJ 205455). Washington, DC: U.S. Department of Justice, Office of Justice Programs.

Chambliss, W. 1988. *Exploring Criminology.* New York: Macmillan.

———. 1995. "The Saints and the Roughnecks." Pp. 254–267 in *Down to Earth Sociology,* edited by J. Henslin. New York: Free Press. (Original work published in 1973)

Chesney-Lind, M. and L. Pasko. 2004. *The Female Offender: Girls, Women, and Crime.* Thousand Oaks, CA: Sage.

Citizens United for Alternatives to the Death Penalty. 2003a. "About CUADP." Retrieved August 2, 2003 (www.cuadp.org/about.html).

———. 2003b. "Potential Cases for Wrongful Conviction." Retrieved August 2, 2003 (www.cuadp.org/pris/pot.html).

Community Oriented Policing Services (COPS). 2003. "Who We Are." Retrieved July 22, 2003 from www.cops.usdoh.gov/default.asp?Item=35.

Cosby, A., D. May, W. Frese, and R. G. Dunaway. 1996. "Legalization of Crimes against the Moral Order: Results from the 1995 United States Survey of Gaming and Gambling." *Deviant Behavior* 17:369–389.

Cureton, Steven. 2001. "Determinants of Black-to-White Arrest Differentials: A Review of the Literature." Pp. 65–71 in *The System in Black and White,* edited by M. Markowitz and D. Jones-Brown. Westport, CT: Praeger.

Davis, R., B. Taylor, and R. Titus. 1997. "Implications for Victim Services and Crime Prevention." Pp. 167–182 in *Victims of Crime,* edited by R. Davis, A. Lurigio, and W. Skogan. Thousand Oaks, CA: Sage.

Death Penalty Information Center. 2003a. "Death Row Facts Inmates by Race." Retrieved July 26, 2003 (www.deathpenaltyinfo.org/article.php?scid=5&did=184#inmaterace).

———. 2003b. "Executions by Year." Retrieved July 25, 2003 (www.deathpenaltyinfo.org/article.php?scid=8&did=146).

Dieter, R. 1996. "Twenty Years of Capital Punishment: A Re-evaluation." Retrieved July 26, 2003 (www.deathpenaltyinfo.org/article.php?did=543&scid=45#sxn4).

Elliot, D. S., S. Ageton, and R. Canter. 1979. "An Integrated Perspective on Delinquent Behavior." *Journal of Research in Crime and Delinquency* 16:3–27.

Erickson, Kai. 1964. "Notes on the Sociology of Deviance." Pp. 9–21 in *The Other Side: Perspectives of Deviance,* edited by Howard Becker. New York: Free Press.

Federal Bureau of Investigation. 1989. *White Collar Crime: A Report to the Public.* Washington, DC: Government Printing Office.

———.2001a. *Hate Crime Statistics 2001.* Retrieved July 14, 2003 (www.fbi.gov/ucr/01hate.pdf).

———. 2001b. *Law Enforcement Officers Killed and Assaulted.* Retrieved July 17, 2003 (www.fbi.gov/ucr/killed/2001eoka.pdf).

———. 2002. *Crime in the United States: 2001.* Washington, DC: Government Printing Office.

Federal Bureau of Investigation. 2003. *Crime in the United States: 2002.* Washington, DC: Government Printing Office.

Fins, D. 2003. *Death Row U.S.A. Spring 2003.* Washington, DC: The Criminal Justice Project, NAACP Legal Defense and Educational Fund, Inc.

Flavin, J. 2001. "Feminism for the Mainstream Criminologist: An Invitation." *Journal of Criminal Justice* 29:271–285.

Glaser, J., J. Dixit, and D. Green. 2002. "Studying Hate Crime with the Internet: What Makes Racists Advocate Racial Violence?" *Journal of Social Issues* 58(1):177–193.

Goldstein, H. 1990. *Problem-Oriented Policing.* Boston, MA: McGraw-Hill.

Grattet, Ryken. 2000. "Hate Crimes: Better Data or Increasing Frequency?" *Population Today* 28(5):1, 4.

Greene, J. R. and W. V. Pelfrey. 1997. "Shifting the Balance of Power between Police and Community: Responsibility for Crime Control." Pp. 393–423 in *Critical Issues in Policing: Contemporary Readings,* edited by R. Dunham and G. Alpert. Prospect Heights, IL: Waveland.

Hannon, L. and J. Defronzo. 1998. "The Truly Disadvantaged, Public Assistance, and Crime." *Social Problems* 45(3):383–392.

Harlem Live. 1999. "The Blue Nile Rites of Passage." Retrieved August 7, 2003 (www.harlemlive.org/community/pop/10–18–99).

Harrison, P. and A. Beck. 2003. *Prisoners in 2002* (NCJ 200248). Washington, DC: U.S. Department of Justice, Office of Justice Programs.

Hautzinger, S. 1997. "'Calling a State a State': Feminist Politics and the Policing of Violence against Women in Brazil." *Feminist Issues* 15(1):3–30.

———. 2002. "Criminalizing Male Violence in Brazil's Women's Police Stations: From Flawed Essentialism to Imagined Communities." *Journal of Gender Studies* 11(3):243–251.

Hirschi, T. 1969. *Causes of Delinquency.* Berkeley, CA: University of California Press.

Huggins, M. 1997. "From Bureaucratic Consolidation to Structural Devolution: Police Death Squads in Brazil." *Policing and Society* 7:207–234.

Human Rights Watch. 1995. "Global Report on Women's Human Rights 1990 to 1995." Retrieved July 30, 2003 (www.hrw.org/about/projects/womrep/General-187.htm#P2966_897325).

———. 1997. *Police Brutality in Urban Brazil.* Retrieved July 30, 2003 (www.hrw.org/reports/brazil/).

Innocence Project. 2003. "About This Innocence Project." Retrieved August 6, 2003 (www.innocenceproject about/index.php).

Innocence Project New Orleans. 2003. "Gregory Bright and Earl Truvia." Retrieved August 2, 2003 (www.ip-no.org/brightandtruvia2.html).

Irwin, Darrell. 2002. "Alternatives to Delinquency in Harlem: A Study of Faith-Based Community Mentoring." *The Justice Professional* 15(2):29–36.

Jenness, V. and Ryken Grattet. 2001. *Making Hate A Crime: From Social Movement to Law Enforcement.* New York: Russell Sage Foundation.

Jensen, V. 2001. *Why Women Kill: Homicide and Gender Equality.* Boulder, CO: Lynne Rienner.

Joseph, J. 2000. "Overrepresentation of Minority Youth in the Juvenile Justice System: Discrimination or Disproportionality of Delinquent Acts? Status of the Black-Subculture-of-Violence Thesis." Pp. 227–240 in *The System in Black and White,* edited by M. Markowitz and D. Jones-Brown. Westport, CT: Praeger.

JUMP. 1998. *Juvenile Mentoring Program: 1998 Report to Congress.* Washington, DC: U.S. Department of Justice, Office Justice Programs, Office of Juvenile Justice and Delinquency Programs.

———. 2003. "Overview and Purpose." Retrieved July 27, 2003 (http://ojjdp.ncjrs.org/jump/oview.html).

Kappeler, V., M. Blumberg, and G. Potter. 2000. *The Mythologies of Crime and Criminal Justice.* Prospect Heights, IL: Waveland Press.

Klaus, P. A. 2004. *Crime and the Nation's Households, 2002* (Bureau of Justice Statistics Bulletin, NCJ 201797). Washington, DC: U.S. Department of Justice, Office of Justice Programs.

Lane, Barbara Parsons. 2003. "Puzzle Pieces." Pp. 211–244 in *Couldn't Keep It to Myself,* edited by W. Lamb. New York: Regan Books.

Langan, P. and D. Levin. 2002. *Recidivism of Prisoners Released in 1994* (NCJ 193427). Washington, DC: U.S. Department of Justice, Office of Justice Programs.

Larason Schneider, A. 1999. "Public-Private Partnerships in the U.S. Prison System." *American Behavioral Scientist* 43(1):192–208.

Laub, J. 1983. "Urbanism, Race, and Crime." *Journal of Research of Crime and Delinquency* 20:183–198.

———. 1997. "Patterns of Criminal Victimization in the United States." Pp. 9–26 in *Victims of Crime,* edited by R. Davis, A. Lurigio, and W. Skogan. Thousand Oaks, CA: Sage.

Lemert, E. 1967. *Human Deviance, Social Problems, and Social Control.* Englewood Cliffs, NJ: Prentice Hall.

Liptak, A. 2003. "Death Row Numbers Decline as Challenges to System Rise." *The New York Times,* January 11, pp. A1, A13.

MacDonald, J. 2002. "The Effectiveness of Community Policing in Reducing Urban Violence." *Crime and Delinquency* 48(4):592–618.

Maruschak, L. 2001. *HIV in Prisons and Jails, 1999* (NCJ 187456). Washington, DC: U.S. Department of Justice, Office of Justice Programs.

Merton, R. 1957. *Social Theory and Social Structure.* Glencoe: IL: Free Press.

Mitchell, M. and C. Wood. 1999. "Ironies of Citizenship: Skin Color, Police Brutality, and the Challenge of Democracy in Brazil." *Social Forces* 77(3):1001–1020.

Moore, M. 1999. "Security and Community Development." Pp. 293–337 in *Urban Problems and Community Development,* edited by R. F. Ferguson and W. T. Dickens. Washington, DC: Brookings Institution.

Naffine, N. 1996. *Feminism and Criminology.* Philadelphia: Temple University Press.

National Night Out. 2003. "The History of NATW and National Night Out." Retrieved August 6, 2003 (www.nationaltownwatch.org/nno/history.html).

National White Collar Crime Center. 2002a. *WCC Issue: Check Fraud.* Morgantown, WV: Author.

———. 2002b. *WCC Issue: Embezzlement/Employee Theft.* Morgantown, WV: Author.

Norris, C., N. Fielding, C. Kemp, and J. Fielding. 1992. "Black and Blue: An Analysis of the Influence on Being Stopped by the Police." *British Journal of Sociology* 43(2):207–224.

Novak, K., L. Alarid, and W. Lucas. 2003. "Exploring Officers' Acceptance of Community Policing: Implications for Policy Implementation." *Journal of Criminal Justice* 31:57–71.

Office on Violence Against Women. 2003. "About the Office on Violence Against Women." Retrieved July 27, 2003 (www.ojp.usdoj.gov/vawo/about.htm).

Pratt, T. and J. Maahs. 1999. "Are Private Prisons More Cost-Effective Than Public Prisons? A Meta-Analysis of Evaluation Research Studies." *Crime and Delinquency* 45(3):358–371.

Pressman, D., R. Chapman, and L. Rosen. 2002. "Creative Partnerships: Supporting Youth, Building Communities." Washington, DC: U.S. Department of Justice, Office of Community Oriented Policing Services.

Prostitutes' Education Network. 2003. "Prostitution in the United States—the Statistics." Retrieved August 17, 2003(www.bayswan.rog/stats.html).

Reiman, J. 1998. *The Rich Get Richer and the Poor Get Prison.* Boston: Allyn & Bacon.

Rennison, C. 2002. *Criminal Victimization 2001: Changes 2000–01 with Trends 1993–2001* (NCJ 194610). Washington, DC: U.S. Department of Justice, Office of Justice Programs.

———. 2003. *Intimate Partner Violence, 1993–2001* (NCJ 197838). Washington, DC: U.S. Department of Justice, Office of Justice Programs.

Rich, J. and M. Ro. 2002. *A Poor Man's Plight: Uncovering the Disparity in Men's Health.* Battle Creek, MI: W. K. Kellogg Foundation.

Sampson, R. J. and W. J. Wilson. 1995. "Towards a Theory of Race, Crime, and Urban Inequality." Pp. 37–54 in *Crime and Inequality,* edited by John Hagen and Ruth Peterson. Stanford, CA: Stanford University Press.

Sanders, W. 1981. *Juvenile Delinquency: Causes, Patterns, and Reactions.* New York: Holt, Rinehart and Winston.

Saviano, J. 2001. "Kelly Hill." *Honolulu,* March, p. 34.

Simon, T., J. Mercy, and C. Perkins. 2001. *Injuries from Violent Crime, 1992–1998* (NCJ 168633). Washington, DC: U.S. Department of Justice, Office of Justice Programs.

Smalley, S. 2003. "This Could Be Your Kid." *Newsweek,* August 18, pp. 44–47.

Smith, D. 1986. "The Neighborhood Context of Police Behavior." Pp. 313–341 in *Communities and Crime,* edited by A. J. Reiss and M.Tonry. Chicago: University of Chicago Press.

Snyder, H. 2002. *Juvenile Arrests 2000* (Juvenile Justice Bulletin, November 2002). Washington, DC: Office of Juvenile Justice and Delinquency Prevention.

Sondheimer, D. 2001. "Young Female Offenders: Increasingly Visible Yet Poorly Understood." *Gender Issues* 19(1):79–90.

Steffensmeier, D. and E. Allan. 1996. "Gender and Crime: Toward a Gendered Theory of Female Offending." *Annual Review of Sociology* 22:459–487.

Stephan, James. 1999. *State Prison Expenditures, 1996* (NCJ 172211). Washington, DC: U.S. Department of Justice, Bureau of Justice Statistics.

Stoutland, S. 2001. "The Multiple Dimensions of Trust in Resident/Police Relations in Boston." *Journal of Research in Crime and Delinquency* 38(3):226–256.

Subcommittee on Civil and Constitutional Rights, Committee on the Judiciary. 1994. "Racial Disparities in Federal Death Penalty Prosecutions 1988–1994." Retrieved July 26, 2003 (www.deathpenaltyinfo.org/article.php?scid=45&did=528).

Sutherland, E. 1949. *White Collar Crime*. New York: Dryden Press.

Turk, A. 1969. *Criminality and Legal Order*. Chicago: Rand McNally.

———. 1976. "Law as a Weapon in Social Conflict." *Social Problems*. 23:276–291.

U.S. Congress. 2002. Public Law 107–273, Title II Juvenile Justice. Retrieved August 29, 2003 from ojjdp.ncjrs.org/about/PL_107_273.html.

U.S. Department of Justice. 2002. "DOJ Seal—History and Motto." Retrieved July 22, 2003 from www.usdoh.gov/jmd/ls/dojseal.htm.

Warner, Darren. 2000. "Race and Ethnic Bias in Sentencing Decisions: A Review and Critique of the Literature." Pp. 171–180 in *The System in Black and White*, edited by M. Markowitz and D. Jones-Brown. Westport, CT: Praeger.

Wilson, W. J. 1996. *When Work Disappears: The World of the New Urban Poor*. New York: Knopf.

Wolf, J. 2000. "War Games Meets the Internet: Chasing 21st Century Cybercriminals with Old Laws and Little Money." *American Journal of Criminal Law* 28:95–117.

Wolfgang, M. and F. Ferracuti. 1967. *The Subculture of Violence: Towards an Integrated Theory in Criminology*. New York: Tavistock.

Zhao, J., M. Scheider, and Q. Thurman. 2002. "Funding Community Policing to Reduce Crime: Have Cops Grants Made a Difference?" *Criminology and Public Policy* 2(1):7–32.

11

The Media

Imagine that you wake up tomorrow in a sort of "Twilight Zone" parallel society where everything is the same except that media do not exist: no television, no movies, no radio, no recorded music, no computers, no Internet, no books or magazines or newspapers.

Croteau and Hoynes 2000:5

What would your life be like without the media? Without communication, and the media to communicate with, there would be no society. The term *media* is the plural of *medium,* derived from the Latin word *medius,* which means *middle.* A medium is a method of communication—television, cable, Internet, radio, or print—between (or in the middle of) a sender and a receiver. But taken all together, **the media** are the "different technological processes that facilitate communication between the sender of the message and the receiver of that message," as defined by sociologists David Croteau and William Hoynes (2000:7). According to the sociologists, "Our everyday lives are saturated by radio, television, newspapers, books, the Internet, movies, recorded music, magazines and more. . . . They are like the air we breathe, ever present yet rarely considered" (p. 3).

Communication is a basic social activity (Seymour-Ure 1974). It is impossible not to communicate and not to come in contact with the media. According to the U.S. Census Bureau (2003), in 2001, the average U.S. adult watched 1,661 hours of television, listened to 264 hours of recorded music, and watched 56 hours of original motion pictures. The average U.S. adult also spent 177 hours reading the daily newspaper, 119 hours reading magazines, and 134 hours on the Internet.

 **PUTTING IT TOGETHER:** For at least a week, record your own media usage. How many hours of television do you watch? How many hours do you spend on the Internet? Is it possible to live a day without the media? Why or why not?

The media reflect "the evolution of a nation that has increasingly seized on the need and desire for more leisure time" (Alexander and Hanson 1995:i). Technological developments have increased our range of media choices, from the growing number of broadcast and cable channels to the ever increasing number of Internet Web sites. New technologies have also increased our viewing control over and access to the media. For example, technology allows us to choose where and when we want to see a recent film. Are you taking a long road trip? You can pack your portable DVD player and watch your favorite movie on the way. Need to access your e-mail? You can check e-mail at an airport kiosk, with a wireless connection at your local coffee shop, or with your cell phone from nearly any location. Indeed, as Croteau and Hoynes (2001) point out, "At the dawn of the twenty-first century, we navigate through a vast mass media environment unprecedented in human history" (p. 3).

Yet, the media have been blamed for directing creating and promoting social problems and have been accused of being a problem themselves. The most commonly identified problem is the media's content: controversial programming that features violence, racism, and sexism. In addition, media critics have expressed concern about the highly controlled process by which the images that we see are conceived, produced, and disseminated by media conglomerates. Social researchers and policymakers have identified the unequal advantage some social groups have over others in our increasingly high-tech media environment. Before we review the media and their related social problems, we should first examine the media from a sociological perspective.

Sociological Perspectives on the Media

Functionalist Perspective

Functionalists examine the structural relationship between the media and other social institutions. Even before the content is created, there are political, economic, and social realities that set the stage for media content. The media are shaped by the social and economic conditions of American life and by society's beliefs in the nature of men and women and the nature of society (Peterson 1981). The first American printing press arrived in Boston along with a group of Puritans fleeing England in 1638. The press became an instrument of religion and government, used to print a freeman's oath that presented the conditions of citizenship in this new country, along with an almanac and a book of hymns (Peterson 1981).

Through electronic and print messages, the media continue to frame our understandings about our lives, our nation, and our world. The media serve as a link between individuals, communities, and nations. They help create a *collective consciousness,* a term used by Emile Durkheim to describe the set of shared norms and beliefs in a society. The mass media provide people with a sense of connection that few other institutions can offer. Live media events, such as the Olympics, the Super Bowl, or the Oscars, are set off from other media programs. People gather in groups to watch, they talk about what they see, and they share the sense that they are watching something special (Schudson 1986). News events captured by the media, such as the

1995 Oklahoma City bombing or the terrorist attacks of September 11, 2001, serve to connect a nation and even the world.

In particular, television has contributed to a corresponding nationalization of politics and issues, taking local or regional events and turning them into national debates. Socially and politically, the media make our world smaller. In 1992, when the city of Los Angeles, experienced three days of violence and civil unrest, it made us more aware of the racial tensions and inequalities, not only in Los Angeles, but also in our own cities. In 2004, the entire nation watched as gay and lesbian couples were allowed to marry in San Francisco. Other mayors and cities began to follow their lead, and the number of gay and lesbian wedding ceremonies increased across the country, along with the growing debate about how same-sex marriages would impact the institution of marriage.

The media have been accused of creating serious dysfunctions and social problems in society. Research has documented the link between viewing of media violence and the development of aggression, particularly among children who watch dramatic violence on television and film. Television has been called the "other parent" or the "black box," accused of draining the life and intelligence out of its young viewers. Postman (1989) argued that popular media culture undermines the educational system, subverting traditional literacy. Public health studies have documented the link between television viewing and poor physical health among children and adults. The one thing television viewers seem to do while watching television is eat, and the danger is in what they choose to eat and drink—unhealthy snack foods or high-calorie drinks (Van Den Bulck 2000). We will examine these dysfunctions more closely in the section, "Do the Media Control Our Lives?"

Conflict Perspective

The media, says Noam Chomsky (1989), are like any other businesses. The fundamental principle in American media is to attract an audience to sell to advertisers. Yes, you read that correctly. Commercial television and radio programming depend on advertising revenue, and in turn, the networks promise that you, the consumer audience, will buy the advertisers' products. "The market model of the media is based on the ability of a network to deliver audiences to these advertisers" (Croteau and Hoynes 2001:6).

In the United States, media organizations are likely to be part of larger conglomerates where profit making is the most important goal (Ball-Rokeach and Cantor 1986). Since the very beginning of mass communications, ideas, information, and profit have mixed. The first books printed in the colonies may have been devoted to religion, but the printers made money (Porter 1981). The media, according to conflict theorists, can only be fully understood when we learn who controls them.

One of the clearest and some say most problematic trends in the media is the increasing consolidation of ownership. The corporate media play a major role in managing consumer demand, producing messages that support corporate capitalism, and creating a sense of political events and social issues (Kellner 1995). In 1984,

❖ Table 11.1   Ten Largest Media Companies

1. AOL–Time Warner (U.S.)
2. Disney (U.S.)
3. General Electric (U.S.)
4. News Corporation Limited (Australia)
5. Viacom (U.S.)
6. Vivendi (France)
7. Sony (Japan)
8. Bertelsmann (Germany)
9. AT&T (U.S.)
10. Liberty Media (U.S.)

Note: For more information about these media companies, visit the Web site, "Who Owns What," sponsored by the *Columbia Journalism Review.* Log on to *Study Site Chapter 11* for a link.

more than 50 corporations controlled most of our newspapers, magazines, broadcasting, books, and movies. By 1997, Ben Bagdikian reported that there were 10 media giants. Bagdikian (1997) declared that "media power is political power" (p. xiii). In 2002, media scholar Mark Crispin Miller reported on the new 10 multinational conglomerates controlling the media, listed in Table 11.1. Four of them—Disney, AOL Time Warner, Viacom, and News Corporation Limited—are truly multimedia corporations, producing movies, books, magazines, newspapers, television programming, music, videos, toys, and theme parks.

Miller (2002) warned that the most corrosive influence of these 10 media conglomerates was their impact on journalism. Journalism has traditionally been referred to as the fourth estate, an independent institutional source of political and social power that monitors the actions of other powerful institutions like politics, economics, and religion. However, conflict theorists remind us that someone is in charge of the fourth estate; in fact, those who control the media are able to manipulate what we see, read, and hear. The media, serving the interest of interlocking state and corporate powers, frame messages in a way that supports the ruling elite and limits the variety of messages that we read, see, and hear (Chomsky 1989).

Epstein (1981) reveals that what we consider news is not the product of chance events, "it is the result of decisions made within a news organization" (p. 119). He explains that the crucial decisions on what constitutes news—what will and what won't be covered—are made not by the journalists but by executives of the news organization. (See the Voices in the Community feature on p. 302 for a behind-the-scenes report on how news programming is biased.) While the public expects news reporters to act like independent fair-minded professionals, reporters are employees of corporations that control their hiring, firing, and daily management (Bagdikian 1997). News executives are in control of the selection and deployment of specific reporters, the expenditure of time and resources for gathering the news, and the allocation of space for the presentation of news (Epstein 1981). The news divisions of the media cartel are motivated to work on behalf of their parent companies and

WOMEN'S FEATURE SERVICE, NEW DELHI, INDIA

"In New Delhi, India is the headquarters of Women's Feature Service, an international news organization directed and staffed by women who produced articles reported from 40 countries for newspapers, magazines and Web sites. By gathering and providing access to these stories about women's lives, Women's Feature Service (WFS) seeks to create 'space' for women's voices and experiences in mainstream media, where such topics don't usually receive this same kind of attention. WFS produces and markets women-centric articles. It also lobbies with decision makers in newspapers and magazines about such coverage and trains journalists to be able to recognize stories about women's concerns, to use gender-correct language, and to ask the right questions of appropriate sources.

"WFS exists because of the felt need for a gender balance in news coverage and because of dissatisfaction about the ways in which news organizations—in India and elsewhere—treat news coverage about women. Often, the media either ignore important stories altogether, relegate reporting to obscure places in the newspaper, or sensationalize incidents without examining the underlying context or causes. The media tend to focus on women only when it comes to 'women's issues,' forgetting that women also have an equal stake in so-called 'male concerns' such as the budget, economy, globalization, agriculture, and conflict resolution. . . .

"Despite the presence of women journalists on the crime beat, incidents of rape and dowry deaths (shockingly regular occurrences in the Indian subcontinent) are usually reported in a routine manner, with the police being the sole source of information. Deadline pressure is one reason, but the other is that editors rarely insist that reporters get more information from other sources. Nor is there any follow-up to an incident. When it comes to issues that impact most directly on women, news that should cause concern and lead to analytical articles that examine a particular issue in depth, is often dismissed in a couple of paragraphs on an inside page.

"The other drawback is that there are only a few women writers—and fewer men—who can give a fresh perspective or insights into issues that concern women. Many women journalists have been conditioned (both socially and through the competitiveness of this profession) to adopt masculine attitudes and values. For instance, for a month after the United States declared its 'war on terror' and began bombing Afghanistan, none of the leading newspapers in India wrote on its editorial page about the women in the conflict.

"In India, there is a glass ceiling that women journalists have yet to break. Not a single mainline newspaper in India has a woman chief editor. One reason, of course, is that women joined the profession late—the first batch of women entered the profession in the 1960's—and took to covering politics even later. But it must be pointed out that there are male chief editors who are much younger than many senior women journalists are. Though women journalists have proven as competent, if not more, than men, they still lag behind in the power game. Two women who are at the top—Shobhana Bhartia (managing editor of *The Hindustan Times*) and Malini Parthasarathy (executive editor of *The Hindu*)—both belong to the families that own the newspapers.

They've had to work hard to prove themselves and overcome some amount of intra-office opposition, but the fact remains they would not have risen this far but for their family connections. Interestingly, both do not have brothers, giving rise to the question: Would they have been given these opportunities had there been male siblings?"

Source: Parekh 2001.

their advertisers, even when that means working against the public interest (Miller 2002). Bagdikian (1997) asserts that the integrity of much of the country's professional news has become more ambiguous than ever.

❖ Voices in the Community:
Kimberly Davies

Kimberly Davies (2003) was a summer intern at a popular evening ABC news show. This is not her real name.

In TV news there are executive and senior producers who field story ideas from producers, who in turn go about gathering the important elements of a newsworthy story. The producers usually get their ideas from whatever sources they happen to have access to. If the producers decide what stories are going to be told to the public, it's important to realize that their decisions will be influenced by their background and lifestyle. The ideas that make it to production reflect important elements of any newsworthy story, but also are chosen by "gut instinct," or what the producers subjectively feel are important issues.

When I look around at the show's staff, I realize that this is where the twin specters of race and culture come in. At work, I found that the people who make critical decisions are White and male, with the exception of one senior producer who is White and female. This, perhaps, reflects the state of mainstream media on the whole, where major decision makers—high-level producers and editors—tend to be White, male, middle aged, and middle or upper class. This, of course, doesn't affect one's ability to do a great job, but it does affect the kinds of resources a person can draw upon in order to tell a good story. It can affect what a person considers a good story and it can certainly influence "gut instinct."

This bias towards the familiar can even extend to the guests chosen to appear on the show. Bookers are responsible for booking people to make guest appearances on the show. It is important that the guest have what is popularly considered to be an articulate and adequate television presence. Guest-lists are composed through personal or professional connections and research. In the early 1990s, Fairness and Accuracy in Reporting, a watch group whose objective it is to monitor its namesake, found that of the total number of guests that made up the show's guest-list, 89 percent were male, and 92 percent were White. In my brief time behind the scenes, I would venture to say that the race and gender composition of the guest list has changed very little since this survey.

When I look around the intern cubicle, I see a pointed attempt at racial and cultural diversity. We are Asian, Black, White and ethnic Jewish. Four out of five of us are women. I realize that to have any tangible effect on the state of journalism in this country, we have to move up and beyond our tokenized intern status to a place where we can exert our will. I don't know when that might be or how it will happen—or whether we will ever get to decide "what makes news."

❖ ❖

A 2002 study released by Fairness and Accuracy in Reporting (2004) documented how network news programs rely on White (95 percent), male (85 percent), and Republican (75 percent) sources for their news. Women made up only 15 percent of all news sources and were featured rarely as experts but most often as "ordinary Americans" in news stories (Howard 2002).

Feminist Perspective

Kellner (1995) says that the media represent "a contested terrain, reproducing on the cultural level the fundamental conflicts within society" (p. 101). Feminist theorists attempt to understand how the media represent and devalue women and minorities. This perspective examines how the media either use stereotypes disparaging women and minorities or completely exclude them from media images (Eschholz, Bufkin, and Long 2002).

One of the most important lessons young children learn is expected gender roles, learning masculine versus feminine behaviors. Although these lessons are taught by parents and teachers, a significant source of cultured gendered messages is television programs (Powell and Abels 2002). As VandeBerg (1991) explains, television programs are "designed to . . . evoke, activate, reference, and occasionally challenge mainstream social myths, policies and beliefs, including those concerning gender" (p. 106).

In his analysis of children's programming, Barner (1999) found that women are typically portrayed in passive roles as housewives, waitresses, and secretaries, whereas men are seen in active roles as construction workers or doctors. In their study of children shows *Barney and Friends* and *Teletubbies,* Powell and Abels (2002) reported that neither popular program showed men and women in nonstereotypical roles. The female characters were followers the majority of the time, were underrepresented in a variety of occupations, and played feminine roles. The male characters on these children's programs were leaders or directors of action and were larger and stereotypically male in appearance.

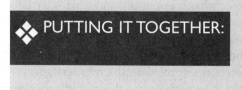

❖ PUTTING IT TOGETHER:

Research suggests that women's magazines also promote a traditional gender ideology. Review four women's magazines, *Ms., More, New Woman,* and *Essence,* and identify the images of women presented. Through the articles and advertisements, how do these magazines promote feminism, independence, beauty, or social class?

In recent years, the media have adopted more feminized forms of pop culture. "Girl power" programming features a female action heroine, as in the UPN program *Buffy the Vampire Slayer* or the WB's *Charmed,* that is both feminist and feminine (Corliss and McDowell 2001). But Durham (2003) points out that while these new "kick ass" heroines are powerful and strong, the girls' bodies "conform to the social ideals of slenderness and voluptuousness that epitomize current dominant definitions of beauty" (p. 26). The new girl heroines meet every standard for conventionally, yet unrealistically defined beauty: they are White, fine-featured, thin, heterosexual, middle class, and usually blonde. Their performances are an important part of the interdependent cycle of media profits, advertising, and girls' purchasing power. These heroines and their beauty images are linked to the advertisers who underwrite their shows, modeling for cosmetics, soft drinks, or clothing. According to Signiorelli (1990), "The majority of women in television have not really changed during the past two decades; society has undergone numerous changes, and while things are not perfect, they are greatly improved" (p. 80).

❖ PUTTING IT TOGETHER: Janet Jackson's "wardrobe malfunction" brought more than a half million complaints to the Federal Communications Commission (FCC) after the 2004 Super Bowl halftime show. Most of the media attention and blame was directed at Janet Jackson. Little criticism was leveled against Justin Timberlake, even though he was the one who ripped off the front of Ms. Jackson's costume, in what he later called a "wardrobe malfunction." Why do you think more criticism was directed to Ms. Jackson and not to Mr. Timberlake?

Interactionist Perspective

In what they tell us and what they choose not to tell us, the media define our social world (McNair 1998). The interactionist perspective focuses on the symbols and messages of the media and how the media come to define our "reality." It might be best to view the media, as Gurevitch and Levy (1985) suggest, as "a site on which various social groups, institutions, and ideologies struggle over the definition and construction of social reality" (p. 9).

The mass media become the authority at any given moment for "what is true and what is false, what is reality and what is fantasy, what is important and what is trivial" (Bagdikian 1997:xliv). The mass media define what events are newsworthy. The first criterion is proximity; events happening close are more newsworthy than those happening at a greater distance. Second, deviation is an important criterion. Events that can be reported as disruptions (natural disasters, unexpected deaths, murders), deviations from cultural or social norms of behavior (especially sexual, e.g., philandering clergy or politicians), and lifestyle deviance (alternative lifestyle report) make the news (Galtung and Ruge 1973).

Sociologist Herbert Gans (1979) explained that the news isn't about just anyone, it is usually about "knowns." Women and men identified by their position in government or their fame and fortune are automatically newsworthy. Knowns are elites in all walks of life, but especially from politics, the entertainment industry, and sports. Incumbent presidents appear in the news most often. The president is the only individual whose routine activities are noteworthy. (When was the last time that a news crew followed your every move?)

One of the biggest news stories of the late 20th century was the death of Princess Diana. The facts and circumstances of her 1997 death and the fairy tale life that preceded it conformed to all the criteria of newsworthiness. Although it occurred in France, her death involved cultural proximity: Princess Diana was a worldwide celebrity. The nonstop coverage of her life and death began as a story of celebrity fascination but ended as an international tragedy (McNair 1998). Shortly after Princess Diana's death, Mother Teresa, a renowned humanitarian, died. Although Mother Teresa's death was a news story, it never got the same attention and coverage as the death of the Princess of Wales. As journalist Daniel Schorr (1998) says, the difference between the two women's lives was "the difference between a noble life well lived and a media image well cultivated. . . . Mother Teresa was celebrated, but was not a celebrity" (p. 15).

The mass media play a large role in shaping public agendas by influencing what people think about (Shaw and McCombs 1997) and, ultimately, what people consider a social problem (Altheide 1997). David Altheide (1997) describes the news media as part of the "problem-generating machine" produced by an entertainment-oriented media industry. The news informs the public, but its message is also intended to serve as entertainment, voyeurism, and a "quick fix" rather than an understanding of the underlying social causes of the problem.

Altheide (1997) argues that the fear pervasive in American society is mostly produced through messages presented by the news media. According to Barry Glassner (1997), the disproportionate coverage of crime and violence in the news media affects readers and viewers. Despite evidence that Americans have a comparative advantage in terms of diseases, accidents, nutrition, medical care, and life expectancy, American women and men perceive themselves to be at greater risk than their counterparts elsewhere and express fears about this (Altheide 1997). In a national poll, respondents were asked why they believe the country has a serious crime problem. About 76 percent said they had seen serious crime in the media whereas only 22 percent said they had a personal experience with crime (Glassner 1997). In a study of 56 local news programs, crime was the most prominently featured subject, accounting for more than 75 percent of all news coverage in some cities (Klite, Bardwell, and Salzman 1997).

For a summary of sociological perspectives, see Table 11.2.

The Media and Social Problems

The Digital Divide

The term *digital divide* was first used in the mid 1990s by policy leaders and social scientists concerned over the emerging split between those with and those without access to the computer and the Internet. The term refers to the gap separating individuals who have access to new forms of technology from those who do not. In

❖ Table 11.2   Summary of Sociological Perspectives: The Media

	Functional	Conflict/Feminist	Interactionist
Explanation of the media and social problems	Functionalists examine the structural relationship between the media and other social institutions. Sociologists using this perspective also examine the functions and dysfunctions of the media.	Conflict theorists focus on the media and how their messages are controlled by an elite group. Feminist theorists address how the media use stereotypes disparaging women and minorities or completely exclude them from media images.	From this perspective, sociologists investigate how the media define our social reality.
Questions asked about the media	How do other institutions affect the media and their content? What functions do the media serve in society? What are their dysfunctions?	Who owns the media? How are the media's messages manipulated? What images of women and minorities are presented by the media?	How do the media define what is newsworthy? How do the media define the public agenda? How do the media define what we believe is a social problem?

addition, others have identified a gap between those who can effectively use new information and communication tools and those who cannot (Gunkel 2003). Despite the increasing diffusion of computers and an overall increase in Internet use, a deep divide remains "between those who possess the resources, education and skills to reap the benefits from the technology and those who do not" (Servon 2002).

The digital divide is a symptom of a larger social problem: social inequality based on income, educational attainment, and ethnicity/race. The digital divide implies a chain of causality: Lack of access to computers and the Internet harms one's life chances. But it is also true that those who are already marginalized will have fewer opportunities to access and use computers and the Internet (Warschauer 2003).

Beginning in 1995, the U.S. Department of Commerce National Telecommunications and Information Administration (NTIA) began to measure the extent of the digital divide in a series of reports called *Falling Through the Net*. Since the study began, certain groups, such as Whites, Asian Americans/Pacific Islanders, and those with higher income and educational levels, have higher than average levels of computer ownership and Internet access. The following data were reported in the recent 2000 NITA study.

- Households with an annual income of $75,000 or more are 20 times as likely to have Internet access as those households with the lowest income levels. Almost 13 percent of households with less than $15,000 in income had Internet access, compared with almost 80 percent of households with incomes over $75,000. The NTIA study concluded that although computers and Internet access are coming down in price, they are still sufficiently expensive that household income remains an important factor in home Internet access.
- Householders with a bachelor's degree or higher were more likely to have access to computers and the Internet. According to the study, better educated adults are more likely to use and become familiar with computers and the Internet at work or school. About 64 percent of householders with bachelor's degrees have Internet access compared with 30 percent of high school or GED graduates. Only 12 percent of those with less than a high school degree had Internet access.
- Households of Asian Americans and Pacific Islanders have the highest rates of Internet access, 56.8 percent in 2000. White households had the second-highest rate of Internet access at 46.1 percent. Blacks and Hispanic households have the lowest rates at 23.5 percent and 23.6 percent, respectively. Between 1998 and 2000, Internet access grew 110 percent in Black households and 87 percent in Hispanic households.
- Internet access among ethnic/racial groups differs by geography and income level. All groups had higher rates of Internet access in urban areas, and all ethnic/racial groups experienced lower access rates in rural areas. The rate of Internet access declines among all groups as household income declines. (See Table 11.3 for a summary of NTIA 2000 results. U.S. Data Map 11.1 reports the percentages of households with Internet access per state.)

❖ Table 11.3   Households with Computers and Internet Access by Selected Characteristics, 2000

Characteristics	Percentage of Households with Computers	Percentage of Households with Internet Access
Householder Race/Ethnicity		
White	55.7	46.1
Black	32.6	23.5
Asian or Pacific Islander	65.6	50.8
Hispanic	33.7	23.6
Education of householder		
Less than high school	12.8	11.7
High school graduate	21.9	29.9
Some college	39.6	49.0
Bachelor's degree	60.3	64.0
Postgraduate	75.7	69.9
Household Income		
Under $15,000	19.2	12.7
$15,000–$24,999	30.1	21.3
$25,000–34,999	44.6	34.0
$35,000–49,999	58.6	46.2
$50,000–74,999	73.2	60.9
$75,000	86.3	77.7

Source: U.S. Department of Commerce, 2000.

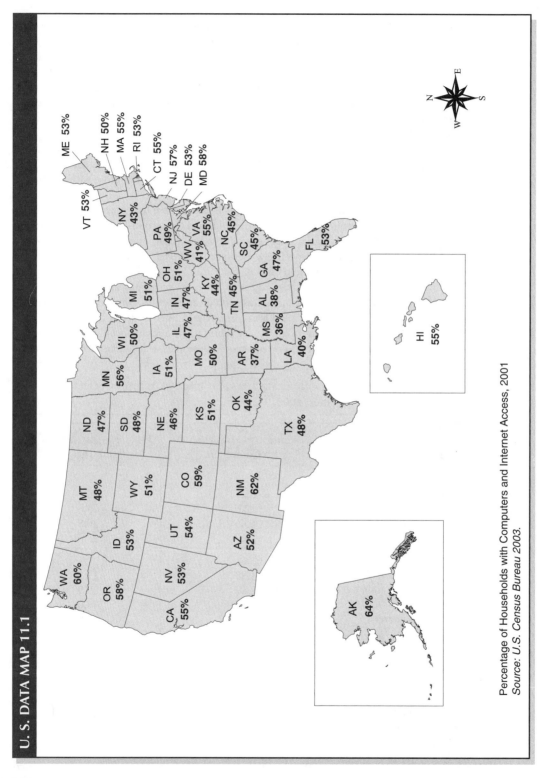

Percentage of Households with Computers and Internet Access, 2001
Source: U.S. Census Bureau 2003.

Internet access is not the only issue facing underserved communities. Lazarus and Mora (2000) identified four online content barriers. The greatest barrier is the lack of locally relevant information. They discovered that low-income users seek practical and relevant information that affects their daily lives, topics such as education (adult high school degree programs), family (low-cost child care), finances (news on public benefits, consumer information), health (local clinics, low-cost insurance resources), and personal enrichment (foreign-language newspapers). In some instances, information may be available in printed documents, but these may be difficult to locate or obtain. General information may exist online, but it might not be suitable to low-income audiences. For example, online housing services might list high-end rental units rather than lower-rent housing.

The second barrier identified by Lazarus and Mora (2000) was the lack of information at a basic literacy level. According to the authors, a number of online tutorials that review computer program and Internet skills are written at a higher level of literacy. The third barrier was the need for content for non-English speakers. For example, there is little government material (for example, on voting, Medicare, or taxes) translated in Spanish. Last, there is a need for more Web sites that reflect diverse cultural heritages and practices.

❖ PUTTING IT TOGETHER:
In your community.

Access the Web site for your city or state government. Determine whether links and information are available in different languages. How many different language translations are provided? For what specific material or information? Are the materials easily accessible?

Media Indecency

Shock jocks, bare bottoms, the F-word, and Janet Jackson's exposed breast led to a period of increased scrutiny of broadcasting in 2004. Although the media are owned and operated by private organizations, their content is regulated by federal standards. The FCC enforces federal law and commission rules regarding indecency, defined as language that depicts or describes sexual or excretory organs or activities in language that is offensive, based on community standards. The FCC regulates program content between 6 a.m. and 10 p.m., when children are most likely to be watching television or listening to the radio (FCC 2004b). After the 2004 Super Bowl incident, the FCC began to impose huge fines on, among others, Viacom and Clear Channel Communications for broadcasting Howard Stern's radio program. In response, Clear Channel Communications declared a zero tolerance policy for indecency and stopped broadcasting Howard Stern's program.

In a study of 400 hours of television programming, the Parents Television Council (2003) found that foul language increased during every time slot between 1998 and 2002. The council reviewed programs for all instances of foul language including curses (*hell* and *damn*), offensive epithets (*bitch, bastard*), scatological language (*ass* or *asshole*), sexually suggestive or indecent language (*screw*), and censored language (*shit* or *fuck*). Foul language during the family hour (8 to 9 p.m. in most areas of the country) increased by 94.8 percent between 1998 and 2002, the council found. A 2003 study by the Kaiser Family Foundation found that 64 percent of all shows and 71 percent of all prime-time shows have at least some sexual content. Only 15 percent of all sexual references or actions were deemed "responsible," suggesting responsibility or consequences (Kunkel et al. 2003).

Although many people were outraged by Janet Jackson's exposed breast during the 2004 Super Bowl halftime show, others suggest that earlier portions of the program were also inappropriate. Commercial advertisements featured during the game included Budweiser ads showing a sleigh ride interrupted by horse flatulence and a dog biting a man's crotch. Comedian Bill Cosby (quoted in Kelly, Clark, and Kulman 2004) explains,

> What needs to be discussed prior to commenting on Miss Jackson's performance is what came before it. Look at the rest of the halftime show and the ads. Didn't I witness a couple of hundred situations where the female was being exploited or her body parts were being exploited? (P. 50)

In 1997, the FCC implemented the television rating system for cable and broadcast television. This system is used with the V-chip control device (the V stands for violence) in your television, which can block programming by age-based categories or content labels. The TV parental guidelines were established by the National Association of Broadcasters, the National Cable Television Association, and the Motion Picture Association of America. The guidelines include seven ratings. TV-Y identifies programming appropriate for all children, including children from ages of two to six. TV-Y7 designates programming for children age seven and above. Programming in this category may include mild fantasy violence or comedic violence. TV-Y7FV identifies programs where fantasy violence may be more intense. TV-G programs are suitable for all ages, containing little or no violence, no strong language, and little or no sexual dialogue or situations. TV-PG programs contain material that parents may find unsuitable for young children, for example, one or more of the following: moderate violence, sexual situations, suggestive dialogue, or infrequent coarse language. TV-14 identifies programming that many parents would find unsuitable for children under 14 years of age because it is likely to contain intense violence, sexual situations, strong language, or suggestive dialogue. The last rating is TV-M designating programming to be viewed by adults and unsuitable for children under 17 because it may contain graphic violence, explicit sexual activity, or crude indecent language (FCC 2004c). All shows except news, commercials, and sports programming (including the Super Bowl) begin with a rating in the upper left-hand corner. Critics argue that the rating system is ineffective because show producers rate their own programs, and many parents remain confused by the rating system.

Do the Media Control Our Lives?

Internet Abuse and Addiction

Researchers define Internet addiction as the excessive use and nonproductive use of the Internet. The literature suggests that addiction does exist but that it affects very few users (Griffiths 2003). Internet addiction is a broad term that covers a variety of behaviors and impulse controls (Griffiths 2002). Five types of addiction have been identified: cybersexual addiction (compulsive use of adult Web sites for cybersex and cyberporn), cyberrelationship addiction (overinvolvement in online relationships), net compulsions (online gambling, shopping, or trading), information overload (compulsive web searching), and computer addiction (computer game playing) (Griffiths 2002).

Internet use, including Web surfing, instant messaging, shopping, and visiting chat rooms can become a problem when it begins to interfere with one's job or social life ("Doctors Diagnose" 2003). Online computer games, such as Sims Online, EverQuest, or Ultima Online, attract an estimated hundreds of thousands of players each day. Aaron Hazell (quoted in Snider 2003) admits to playing Ultima Online for up to 18 hours per day, even skipping his job as a software developer a few times so that he could continue playing the game. According to Hazell, "These games have an amazing amount of depth. You can buy a boat and sail to another continent. Or you can buy a house and then chop wood and make furniture for your home. The possibilities are endless" (p. 23).

Employers have identified Internet abuse as a serious work problem. According to a recent SurfControl study, office workers who spend one hour a day at work on nonwork Internet activities (shopping online, booking vacations) could cost businesses as much as $35 million per year. The study found that 5 percent of the Internet use at the office was not work-related (Griffiths 2003). Unlike Internet addiction, Internet abuse has no negative effects for the user, except for a decrease in work productivity if occurring at the workplace (Griffiths 2003).

A survey of human resource management directors revealed that 83 percent of the companies have Internet access policies regulating how much Internet time employees can have during their workday. Despite the existence of such policies, 64 percent of companies disciplined employees and more than 30 percent terminated employees for inappropriate use of the Internet. The leading causes for disciplinary action or termination included accessing pornography, online chatting, gaming, sports, investing, and shopping at work (Case and Young 2002). For more on Internet pornography, see the Focus On feature on the following page.

The Problem with Television

In his 1932 book, *Brave New World,* Aldous Huxley writes about a society in which the pain of living is eased by the "television box." In Huxley's world, the television was constantly on, like a "running tap." Although TV may not be on 24/7, on average, individuals in the industrialized world devote an average of three hours per day to television viewing. About 40 percent of families always eat dinner while watching television (TV Turnoff Network 2004).

The average child or adolescent watches nearly three hours of television per day, not including time spent watching videotapes or playing video games. A recent study indicated that children spend more than six hours a day with various media combined (American Academy of Pediatrics 2001a). By the time the average young person graduates from high school, he or she will have spent about 12,000 hours in the classroom and about 18,000 hours watching television (Greeson and Williams 1986).

❖ FOCUS ON: CYBERPORN

The Internet has provided us with easy access to a vast amount of information and material. Although most of the information is educational or useful, some material can be categorized as dangerous. For example, on the Web, you can find information posted by hate groups, cults, or terrorist organizations or instructions on how to build your own pipe-bomb. What has particularly alarmed parents and political figures is the possibility that children will look at and download pornographic materials from the Internet. Cyberporn or pornography on the Internet has been called the newest danger to the innocence of childhood (Potter and Potter 2001).

Lo and Wei (2002:13–14) argue that Internet pornography is different from traditional pornography (e.g., magazines and videos). First, it is widely available via the World Wide Web, e-mail, and real-time data feeds. Second, it is both an active and inactive format through digitized moving images, animated sequences, hot chats, and interactive sexual games. Finally, there has been an explosion of cyberporn since consumers have also become producers of their own pornographic material. According to Podlas (2000), "Would-be Larry Flynts now require only a web-cam, video cameras to upload real-time images to a website, maybe a digital camera, and software ranging from shareware to a $100 commercial package" (p. 849).

It is estimated that the number of pornographic Web sites has grown tremendously in the past few years, increasing by nearly 300 sites per day (Chen 1999) and generating more than $700 million per year

(Hapgood 1996). There is no conclusive count on the number of pornographic Web sites. The literature identifies the number of sites as being from 150,000 to one million.

Despite the concern over children's access to pornography on the Internet, little empirical research on children and Internet dangers exists (Potter and Potter 2001). The Henry J. Kaiser Family Foundation (2001) reported that 70 percent of 15- to 17-year-olds accidentally stumbled across pornography online, with 9 percent saying that this happens very often. Among those who were exposed to pornography, 45 percent said they were upset by the experience, but more than half (55 percent) said they were not too upset or not at all upset at viewing this material.

In 1998, the U.S. Congress adopted the Child Online Protection Act (COPA), which makes it a crime for commercial Web site operators to post any material that is harmful to minors. Minors were defined as those 17 years of age or younger. Enacted in 2000, the Child Internet Protection Act (CIPA) requires public libraries that receive federal funds for Internet use to install filtering devices on computers to protect children from cyberporn.

In 2004, the U.S. Supreme Court voted 5–4 to prevent the enforcement of COPA. The American Civil Liberties Union and online publishers challenged COPA, believing that it violates free speech rights. The Supreme Court argued that it would be difficult to enforce COPA restrictions. In the case of protecting minors from pornography, the justices suggested the use of filtering software on home computers.

A large body of scholarly literature has consistently confirmed the negative impact of television on children and adolescents, who are particularly vulnerable to the messages conveyed through television (American Academy of Pediatrics 2001a). Exposure to violence in the media, including television, poses a significant risk to the health of children and adolescents (American Academy of Pediatrics 2001b). It is estimated that by age 18, the average young person will have viewed more than 200,000 acts of violence on television (American Academy of Pediatrics 2001b). Girls and boys who are exposed to violent behavior on film or TV behave more aggressively immediately afterward, are more tolerant of aggressive behavior (Huesmann et al. 2003), and are desensitized to the pain of others (American Academy of Pediatrics 2001b). Researchers have also linked high levels of exposure to violent television programs to aggression in later childhood, adolescence, and young adulthood (Anderson et al. 2003).

Exposure to violent video games has been linked with heightened levels of aggression in young adults and children (Anderson and Bushman 2001). Interactive video games are the preferred leisure activity for children and adolescents, yet about 80 percent of today's most popular games contain violence (Vessey and Lee 2000). Playing violent video games has been found to account for a 13 percent to 22 percent increase in violent adolescent behavior (American Academy of Pediatrics 2001b).

Simply stated, television may be bad for your physical health. Elevated television viewing and physical inactivity have been found to promote obesity in children (Faith et al. 2001). In addition to the unhealthy snacking that may occur while watching television, when people watch television, they burn fewer calories (Van den Bulck 2000). TV watching reduces the amount of time spent on more physical activities (Dietz and Gortmaker 1985). Television viewing by children is also correlated with between-meal snacking, consumption of foods advertised on television, and children's attempts to influence their mother's food purchases (Dietz and Gortmaker 1985).

Do You Trust the News Media?

Whether we are watching CNN, ABC, NBC, or Fox, we rely on reporters for most if not all of our information about our community and our world. According to the Project for Excellence in Journalism (2004), public attitudes about the press have been growing less positive for about 20 years. In its report, *The State of the News Media 2004*, the Project for Excellence in Journalism identified the disconnection between the public and the news media over motive as the fundamental reason for the decline in public support. Whereas journalists believe they are working in the public interest, the public believes that news organizations are working primarily for profit and that journalists are motivated by professional ambition. The public debate over whether media are liberal or conservative also sensitizes the public to how the media could be manipulated or subjective in content. In addition, people are increasingly distrustful of the large multinational corporations that own and control most of the news media (Project for Excellence in Journalism 2004).

Despite the increase in news coverage since September 2001, the public's news habits have been largely unaffected. In 2002, about one third of Americans

VISUAL ESSAY: TV AND CHILDHOOD OBESITY ❖

Obesity among young people is a national epidemic. According to a 2004 report by the Henry J. Kaiser Foundation, *The Role of Media in Childhood Obesity,* research confirms the link between time spent watching TV and children's body weight. Four-year-old Jacqueline once weighed 95 pounds, twice the amount she should have weighed. She spent much of her time watching television instead of exercising and playing outdoors.

The problem with spending excessive time with media is not just the lack of physical activity. It is estimated that children view more than 40,000 TV ads a year. The endless ads for sodas, cereals, candies, and fast foods make it hard for young people even to consider healthier food choices.

Excessive media viewing also affects children's self-esteem. Images of young men and women who are exceptionally slender or fit are everywhere. Young people who don't meet those unrealistic standards often feel inadequate. Their insecurity may contribute to their overeating, which only makes them feel even less confident about themselves.

The Kaiser Foundation recommends several policy options to address the epidemic of obesity among young people. One approach is to educate children and their parents about the benefits of a healthy lifestyle and ways to achieve it.

Programs that attempt to reduce the amount of time that children spend with TV and other media are another recommendation. Electronic media are not the real culprit, however. The Kaiser Foundation study found that time spent in any sedentary activity, even reading books, can be detrimental. The solution is to get children up and out, engaging in any type of physical activity. Improving school physical education programs would be beneficial. But even getting obese young people to take a walk or goof around with friends helps them slim down—and it has the further benefit of providing them with a little social support that might help boost their self-confidence. These two boys are walking as part of the Committed to Kids program, an educational and exercise program based in several states throughout the country.

How could TV and other media help solve the problem of childhood obesity? What could parents do to reduce their children's time with the media?

(32 percent) regularly watched one nightly network news show, compared with 30 percent in 2000 (Pew Research Center for the People and the Press 2002b). Roughly one in four Americans say they believe all or most of what they see on ABC, NBC, and CBS. CNN continues to be rated the most believable news source, with 37 percent saying they believe all or most of what they hear on CNN (Pew Research Center for the People and the Press 2002a).

But should you believe everything you read and hear? During the early months of the 2004 presidential campaign, news reports exposed a manipulated photo featuring presidential candidate Senator John Kerry (D-Massachusetts) with actress and activist Jane Fonda during an anti-Vietnam war rally in 1970. The photo, widely released in the news media, angered veterans, who said Kerry's association with Fonda was a slap in the faces of Vietnam War veterans. Days later, when the photo was exposed as a hoax, its photographer, Ken Light (2004), referred to the doctored photograph as "the troublesome combination of Photoshop and the Internet" and a political "dirty trick" (Cockrell 2004). Light reports that John Kerry never shared the demonstration podium with Fonda during the rally.

Manipulation isn't limited to photos. In 2003, Jayson Blair, a *New York Times* reporter, resigned after a Texas newspaper questioned whether he plagiarized a profile on Juanita Anguiano of Los Frenos, Texas, the mother of a soldier who died in Iraq (Kurtz 2003). Blair never spoke with Anguiano, instead taking quotes and details about her home from another publication. Blair reportedly pretended to be making cross-country trips while writing front-page stories from his Brooklyn apartment. *USA Today* foreign correspondent Jack Kelley was forced to resign in 2004 after admitting that he fabricated a witness for a story he reported in Belgrade in 1999. After the newspaper reviewed a sample of Kelley's work from 1995 to 2001, *USA Today* editors concluded that they will never know whether there were inaccuracies in his stories (Morrison 2004).

The Pew Research Center for the People and the Press examined how Americans regard their news organizations. The Center documents how, after the media's focus shifted away from terrorism, Americans grew increasingly skeptical. In August 2002, 49 percent of respondents thought that news organizations were highly professional, down from 73 percent in November 2001. About 35 percent felt that the news media usually get their facts straight, and 56 percent believed that news organizations usually provide inaccurate reports. And if the news organizations do make a mistake, 67 percent of respondents believed that the news organizations were likely to try to cover up their mistakes; only 23 percent believed that media are willing to admit their mistakes (Pew Research Center for the People and the Press, 2002a).

Media Policy, Advocacy, and Innovations

Federal Communications Commission and the Telecommunications Act of 1996

The FCC was established by the Communications Act of 1934 and is charged with regulating interstate and international communications by radio, television, wire, satellite, and cable. As an independent agency, the FCC oversees violations of federal law and policies and reports directly to the U.S. Congress (FCC 2004a). Under current FCC rules, radio stations and broadcast television channels cannot air indecent language or material that shows or describes sexual or excretory functions between 6 a.m. and 10 p.m., when children may be watching. In response to a violation, the FCC may issue a warning, revoke a station's license, or impose a monetary fine. In the entire history of the FCC, the commission has fined two television stations for indecency (Kelly et al. 2004).

Introduced a week before the Super Bowl in 2004, the Broadcast Decency Enforcement Act was designed to amend the Communications Act of 1934. The bipartisan bill seeks to increase penalties to $500,000 for violating FCC regulations. Broadcasters could also lose their licenses if they violate indecency standards three times. The Act would not apply to cable television programming. In the case of the 2004 Super Bowl halftime show, each CBS station that aired the program could be fined up to $27,500. After the 2004 Super Bowl halftime show, television broadcasters began to police their programming more closely. The 2004 Grammy and Oscar award telecasts each included a broadcast delay (five seconds to five minutes) to ensure that no inappropriate language or situations would be aired.

Through the FCC, the public can file complaints on a range of issues: billing disputes, wireless questions, telephone company advertising practices, telephone slamming (switching a consumer's telephone service without permission), unsolicited telephone marketing calls, and indecency and obscenity complaints. Along with the Federal Trade Commission (FTC), the FCC is enforcing the National Do-Not-Call Registry, which went into effect on October 2002. The FCC and FTC report that more than 55 million people have signed up for the registry. Its success has led lawmakers to consider implementing a do-not-spam list. However, in June 2004, the FTC rejected the idea of a do-not-spam list, arguing that creating such a list would not help decrease the amount of spam. In fact, such lists might be used by spammers to send more unwanted commercial e-mail.

The first major overhaul of the original 1934 act, the Telecommunications Act of 1996, was seen as a way to encourage competition in the communications industry. The law specified how local telephone carriers may compete, how and under what circumstances local exchange carriers can provide long distance services, and ways to deregulate cable television rates. Also included in the Act were provisions to make telecommunications more accessible to disabled Americans; a Decency Act makes it a crime to knowingly convey pornography over the Internet on a Web site accessible to children.

Although the Act was presented as an opportunity to encourage competition and break down media monopolies, industry watchers noted how the 1996 law swept away the minimal consumer and diversity protections of the original 1934 Act. In fact, the 1996 Act reduced competition and allowed more cooperation between media giants. Data we reviewed in an earlier section of this chapter seem to support this. The new law permitted some of the largest industries—those not active in creating media content, like telephone companies—to enter the television, radio, and cable industry. New industries joined older media companies to form interlocking partnerships, rather than become independent competitors as the Act had predicted. For example, U.S. West, one of the largest telephone companies in the country, acquired Continental Cablevision, the third-largest cable system. Sprint, the long-distance telephone company, formed a joint venture with TCI, a cable company. The merger between Disney, ABC Broadcasting, and CAP Cities was made possible only through the passage of the 1996 law (Bagdikian 1997).

Who Is Watching the Media?

Numerous organizations have emerged as watch groups monitoring media accuracy and content. Groups such as Accuracy in the Media (AIM) and Fairness and Accuracy in Reporting (FAIR) are nonprofit, grassroots organizations that attempt to expose biased and inaccurate news coverage, while encouraging members of the media to report the news fairly and objectively. Accuracy in the Media publishes a newsletter and weekly newspaper column, broadcasts a daily radio commentary, and promotes a speaker's bureau to expose faulty reporting. On its Web site, current news stories are posted, along with AIM's analysis of the story's accuracy or inaccuracies, as the case may be. In addition to a weekly program and a magazine, FAIR also operates research and advocacy desks that work with activists and professionals on women's issues; analyze the effects of sexism, racism, and homophobia in the media; and monitor the media's marginalization, misrepresentation, and exclusion of people of color in the news and in the newsroom (FAIR 2004).

Several organizations attempt to improve and protect the integrity of journalists in print, electronic, and internet media. The Project for Excellence in Journalism (2004) began as an initiative by journalists to clarify and raise the standards of American journalism. The project serves as a research organization, conducting an annual review of local television news, producing a series of content studies on press performance, and offering educational programs for journalists. The project also provides information to the public on what to expect from the press, how to write a letter to the editor, and how to talk to the news media. Another organization, the Committee to Protect Journalists, is an independent, nonprofit organization promoting press freedom worldwide by defending the rights of journalists to report the news without fear of reprisal. The organization documents attacks on the press world wide, including the number of journalists killed, missing, or imprisoned. For 2003, the Committee reported that 36 journalists were killed and 136 were imprisoned.

Media Literacy and Awareness

Evidence shows that media education can help mitigate the harmful effects of the media. Parents can mount the most effective intervention to reduce the effects of media violence on children. Nathanson (1999) reports that parental co-viewing of and commenting on the programs seems to reduce the effects of TV violence on the child, probably because it reduces the child's perception that the violence is real and reduces the likelihood that the child will act out the violence. Huesmann et al. (1983) also reported on the effectiveness of a school-based intervention that teaches children violence on television is not real and should not be imitated.

According to the Media Awareness Network (2004), **media literacy** is the ability to sift through and analyze the messages that inform, entertain, and sell to us every day.

❖ FOCUS ON: MEDIA MYTH MAKING—
THE STORY OF PRIVATE JESSICA LYNCH

How the story developed

In the early evening of April 1, the night of the rescue, the 24-hour news networks broke in with a briefing from US CENTCOM in which it was revealed that the military had rescued a "U.S. Army prisoner of war held captive in Iraq." In the days and weeks following Lynch's rescue, stories about how she was captured and what happened after her capture began to circulate. The day after the rescue, April 2, the Associated Press quoted "officials who spoke on the condition of anonymity" who said Lynch has "at least one gun shot wound." That same day the *New York Times* cited "an Army official" as saying that Lynch "had been shot multiple times." On April 3, a front-page story in the *Washington Post* cited unnamed U.S. officials and said that Lynch "fought fiercely" and that she sustained gunshot and stab wounds. "She was fighting to the death," the official was quoted as saying in the story. "She did not want to be taken alive."

That story appears to be the genesis of a spate of stores that accepted that *Post* sequence of events. Many articles focused on the Rambo-like firefight Lynch reportedly engaged in—some even cited her valiant fighting as proof that women belonged in combat zones. Some stories went further saying she had been abused or denied basic care by the Iraqis who captured and tended to her. Several accounts said she had been "saved" by a courageous Iraqi lawyer named Mohammed Rehaief who risked his life to tell U.S. troops where Lynch was.

Within days, conflicting accounts began to appear simultaneously. Some wire and newspaper accounts went with the Post account and alleged Lynch had been shot and stabbed and cited unnamed surgeons who had cared for her or family members. Other stories denied that she had been shot or stabbed. Those stories cited a specific person, the commander of the hospital in Landstuhl, Germany, where Lynch was treated. Interestingly though, given the choice between two stories, many news organizations chose the more theatric of circumstances, even though the other version of events had better sourcing. For instance, the April 14 *Newsweek*, which made Lynch its cover subject, said how Lynch was injured remained a mystery and briefly reported that the hospital said she had not been stabbed or shot. But in the next sentence, the magazine reported that "Later that day, though, surgeons discovered that she had been shot—and according to family spokesperson in West Virginia, Dan Little, her wounds were 'consistent with low-velocity small arms.'" The magazine then went on for two paragraphs outlining what might have happened to her.

On April 15, a *Washington Post* story questioned the paper's own earlier account. On April 27 a *St. Louis Post-Dispatch* story called into question many of the stories from the war, including those around Lynch. Still, despite these two pieces, the early version of the Lynch story dominated until the UK paper *The Guardian* published a lengthy deconstruction of the Lynch story written by a BBC reporter on May 15. On May 18, the BBC aired a documentary on which the Guardian article was based, reviewing the incident in depth. The BBC account began to raise questions in the American press.

On June 17, the *Washington Post* ran a story refuting much of what appeared in its April 3 story. Though the new piece still relied heavily on unnamed U.S. officials, it maintained that [Lynch] was not stabbed or shot, that she had not killed any Iraqis because of a gun jam, and that the hospital U.S. forces raided was unguarded.

Source: Chinni 2003.

It is about shifting from the role of passive receiver of media to an active critical receiver of it. Media literacy includes asking several questions: Who is this media message intended for? Who wants to reach this audience and why? From whose perspective is this story being told? Whose voices are being heard and whose are absent? (Media Awareness Network 2004). The Action Coalition for Media Education offers 10 basic principles for media literacy presented in Table 11.4.

Media awareness organizations seek to increase awareness and control of the media by key groups, often targeting children and youth. MAGIC (Media Activities and Good Ideas by, with, and for Children) is sponsored by the United Nations Children's Fund.

❖ **Table 11.4**   The 10 Basic Principles of Media Literacy Education

1. Medium. The form of communication that transmits messages, tells stories, structures learning, and constructs a "reality" about the world.

2. Media Literacy. An educational approach that seeks to give media users greater freedom and choice by teaching them how to access, analyze, evaluate and produce media.

3. Construction of reality. Media construct our culture which involves trade-offs. Ask yourself: What are the trade-offs in this media experience? Who produced this media? What kind of reality does this media create? How accurate is this "reality"? What stories are NOT being told and why?

4. Production Techniques. Media use identifiable production techniques (camera angles, editing, sound effects, colors and symbols, etc.). Ask: What kinds of production techniques does this media employ?

5. Value Messages. Media contain ideological and value messages. Ask: What kinds of value messages does this media promote?

6. Commercial motives. Media are commercial and business interests. Ask: What are the commercial motives behind this media? Who or what paid for this media and why? Who or what owns this media product?

7. Individual meanings. Individuals construct their own meaning of media. Ask: What meanings do YOU find in this media? What different meanings might other individuals or groups find?

8. Emotional Transfer. Commercials and other multi-media experiences operate primarily at an emotional level and are usually designed to transfer the emotion from one symbol or lifestyle onto another. Ask: What emotions does this media tap? What might we consider if we think more deeply about this media?

9. Pacing. TV runs at 30 frames per second; movies at 24 frames per second. The conscious mind can process about 8 frames per second; hence, television and movies tend to keep us from conscious analysis and reflection about individual messages and larger industry contexts. Ask: What do you observe about this media upon reflection?

10. Symbolic Rhetoric/Techniques of Persuasion. Symbols, flattery, repetition, fear, humor, words, and sexual images are common and effective techniques of media persuasion. Ask: What persuasive techniques is this media using?

Source: Action Coalition for Media Education 2004.

The program "calls on children and young people to learn as much about the media as they can to help them in their choice of media and make sure they benefit from the media" (MAGIC 2004). MAGIC sponsors international conferences and meetings that celebrate children's excellence and creativity in film, video, and Internet programming. Listen Up! Youth Media Network is a coalition of youth media groups, professional media organizations, nonprofit groups, and foundations which help youth to be heard in the mass media. Listen Up! partners with youth, creating media in high schools, media art centers, and nonprofits throughout the country. Partner programs include 911 Media Arts Center (Seattle, Washington), Vid-Kid Productions and Teen Vision Productions (White Sulphur Springs, Montana), Appalshop (Whitesburg, Kentucky), and North East School of the Arts (San Antonio, Texas).

Giving control of the media and their message to youth is part of the mission of Young People's Press and *The Beat Within*. Young People's Press (2004) is a North American online publication featuring nonfiction writing from youth and young adults between 14 and 24 years of age. Young People's Press publishes several online e-zines on domestic violence, anti-racism, and crime prevention. Established in 1996 by David Inocencio and Sandy Close of the Pacific News Service, *The Beat Within* is a bi-weekly publication of writing and art from young women and men in juvenile hall facilities, mainly in the San Francisco Bay area in California. The publication serves as an outlet for young people who are "locked up and want to express themselves" (The Beat Within 2004).

❖ Voices in the Community:
Mervyn Wool

While Mervyn Wool was in the San Francisco juvenile hall, he attended a *The Beat Within* writing workshop. During his time at the California Youth Authority (CYA), Wool continued to write for *The Beat Within*. Upon his release, Wool contacted the magazine and has been working as a part-time associate. Wool is currently a full-time student at San Francisco State University. He wrote the following piece on his release from CYA. In his essay, "Questions," Wool writes about the power he found in his paper and pencil (Wool 2004).

Questions

Questions:
How does it feel to be locked up?
Stressful?
Feeling a little lonely?
Want to be with your family?
How does it feel to be stuck in that little cage they call a cell or "your room"?
What can you do when you are thinking about being free?
Thinking about all the fun you were having when you were out and now you have realized that you messed up?

All those things I have just mentioned, I have been through and was going through for four long years. All the things: the way I was feeling, the loneliness I was experiencing and the feeling of being controlled, I kept all that in me in the beginning of my incarceration. I didn't talk to staff about my problems, I didn't share with them my story and I didn't tell anyone because I was afraid nobody would hear me. I was afraid when I shared my feelings with others that they might laugh at me. That's why I kept it to myself.

When I was introduced to The Beat I found a friend. A friend that gave me a feeling of safety, a friend that was always there to listen to my problems, my thoughts, and my feelings. This friend gave me the freedom I so wanted, the freedom we all cherish when we are behind those metal doors. For those who don't know what I am talking about, my friend is a tool everybody uses. My friend is thin, it can have lines on it and can also have no lines. It comes in all different types of colors and shapes, and it can cut you if you are not careful. Everyone, meet my friend, paper.

Yeah paper. This is what The Beat introduced me to, a piece of paper and a pencil. Then, I soon learned how to introduce the paper and pencil to my thoughts. Writing how I felt and what I thought felt good. Letting that load of stress, pain, fear, and dreams off my shoulder felt good.

You see, a piece of paper doesn't care what you write. And it also can't laugh back at you when you keep it real with other people.

The paper and pencil also helped me figure out how to turn my life around. See, that inspired me to write, plus writing gave me a chance to leave reality and forget about where I was. It allowed me to use my imagination and set myself free. It gave me a chance to share my thoughts and experience with others. It also gave me a chance to look back at my old lifestyle and learn from it. Look at me: I used to write a lot and still do, but I never thought about writing on the streets.

Sometimes people tell me that I am a good writer, and where did I learn to write so well, or where do I get my ideas from. I tell them, do you know where I learned from? Books? That's right books. I never even touched a book on the street (except for those love books called, "How to Make Love All Night," or, "How to Please Your Lady" types).

I tell you when you are in that lonely cell, you can either pick up a book and escape from reality or face reality and stress out. Books, like writing, gave me a way out and a way to escape reality, to be free for awhile. Isn't it funny how there are things that we never even bothered to do when we were out, but once we get locked up, we will do just about anything to escape reality.

So tell me, what has a piece of paper and pencil done for you?

❖ ❖

MAIN POINTS

- **Media** are the technological processes facilitating communication, and they have increased to include more broadcast and cable channels and Internet Web sites. Yet, the media have been blamed for directly creating and promoting social problems and have been accused of being a problem themselves through controversial programming and manipulating how we see events.

- Functionalists examine the structural relationship between the media and other social institutions that affect content, including the social and economic conditions of American life and society's beliefs in the nature of men, women, and society. Research has documented the link between viewing media violence and the development of aggression, particularly among children who watch dramatic violence on television and film.

- Conflict theorists believe that the media can be fully understood only when we learn who controls them. The media, serving the interest of interlocking state and corporate powers, frame messages in a way that supports the ruling elite and limits the variety of messages that we read, see, and hear.

- Feminist theorists attempt to understand how the media represent and devalue women and minorities. They examine how the media either use stereotypes disparaging women and minorities or completely exclude them. One of the most important lessons young children learn is expected gender roles.

- The interactionist perspective focuses on the symbols and messages of the media and how the media come to define our "reality." The mass media define what events are newsworthy, using proximity (nearness of events) and deviation (something different from what we are accustomed to) as criteria. The mass media play a large role in shaping public agendas by influencing what people think about and, ultimately, what people consider a social problem

- The term **digital divide** refers to the gap separating individuals who have access to and understanding of new forms of technology from those who do not. This divide is a symptom of a larger social problem: social inequality based on income, educational attainment, and ethnicity/race. Internet access is not the only issue facing underserved communities. A lack of locally relevant information, a lack of information at a basic literacy level, and English-only content are also barriers.

- Although the media are owned and operated by private organizations, their content is regulated by federal standards enforced by the Federal Communications Commission (FCC). The FCC enforces federal law and commission rules regarding indecency.

- Other social problems include **Internet addiction**, a broad term that covers a variety of behaviors and impulse controls. Internet use can become a problem when it begins to interfere with one's job or social life. Employers have identified Internet abuse as a serious work problem.

- The average child or adolescent watches nearly three hours of television per day. Research confirms the negative impact of television on children and adolescents, including more aggression and physical problems such as health and obesity.

- Public attitudes about the press have been growing less positive for about 20 years. The public believes that news organizations are working primarily for profit and that journalists are motivated by professional ambition; doubts over the political bent of the media and the motives of the multinational corporations that own and control them also lead to distrust.

- Aside from the FCC, numerous organizations have emerged as watch groups monitoring media accuracy and content, including the Project for Excellence in Journalism and the Committee to Protect Journalists.

- Evidence shows that media education can help mitigate the harmful effects of the media. Parents can provide the most effective intervention to reduce the effects of media violence on children, and school-based intervention also seems to help. The goal is media literacy, shifting the viewer from the role of passive receiver to active critical receiver.

INTERNET AND COMMUNITY EXERCISES

1. Interview the editorial staff of your school newspaper. Ask the editor how decisions are made regarding the leading stories in the paper. What qualifies as news? Who makes decisions about the content of the paper? About what appears as the lead story on the front page? Is it done by the entire news staff or by a small group?

2. How many Americans watched television last week, and what were they watching? Go to the Nielsen Media Research Web site (log on to *Study Site Chapter 11*). The site also provides information on the Nielsen "Ethnic TV Audiences" project, tracking television viewing habits for African American and Hispanic American audiences. Is there a difference between the highest-rated programs for these groups and non-African American or non-Hispanic American households?

3. The Ad Factor Web site is sponsored by the Open University U.K. The Web site chronicles the advertising process, from the "pitch," the presentation in which an agency outlines its suggestions for the advertisement, to the "rollout," when the advertisement is presented. The material presents the advertising process from a British perspective, but the process and the issues are the same in U.S. advertising. You can visit the Ad Factor Web site by logging on to *Study Site Chapter 11*.

On your own. Log on to *Study Site—Community and Policy Guide* for more information about the social problems, social policies, and community responses discussed in this chapter.

References

Action Coalition for Media Education. 2004. *Questioning the Media: Ten Basic Principles of Media Literacy Education.* Albuquerque, NM: Author.

Altheide, D. L. 1997. "The News Media, the Problem Frame, and the Production Fear." *The Sociological Quarterly* 38(4):647–668.

Alexander, A. and J. Hanson. 1995. *Taking Sides: Clashing Views on Controversial Issues in Mass Media and Society.* Guilford, CT: Dushkin.

American Academy of Pediatrics, Committee on Public Education. 2001a. "Children, Adolescents, and Television." *Pediatrics 107*(2):423–426.

———. 2001b. "Media Violence." *Pediatrics* 108(5):1222–26.

Anderson, C., L. Berkowitz, E. Donnerstein, L. R. Huesmann, J. Johnson, D. Linz, N. M. Malamuth, and E. Wartella. 2003. "The Influence of Media Violence on Youth." *Psychological Science in the Public Interest* 4(3):81–110.

Anderson, C. and B. Bushman. 2001. "Effects of Violent Video Games on Aggressive Behavior, Aggressive Cognition, Aggressive Affect, Physiological Arousal, and Prosocial Behavior." *Psychological Science* 12(5):353–359.

Bagdikian, B. 1997. *The Media Monopoly.* Boston: Beacon Press.

Ball-Rokeach, S. and Muriel Cantor, eds. 1986. *Media, Audience, and Social Structure.* Newbury Park, CA: Sage.

Barner, M. 1999. "Sex-Role Stereotyping in FCC-Mandated Children's Educational Television." *Journal of Broadcasting and Electronic Media* 43:551–564.

Beat Within. 2004. "About Us." Retrieved March 23, 2004 (http://thebeatwithin.org/news/view_custom.html?cutstom_page_id=54).

Case, C. and K. Young. 2002. "Employee Internet Management: Current Business Practices and Outcomes." *CyberPsychology and Behavior* 5(4):355–361.

Chen, W. 1999. "Web 547 Is Launched to Combat Pornography in Cyberspace." *China Times*, July 22, p. 7.

Chinni, D. 2003. "Jessica Lynch: Media Myth-Making in the Iraq War." Retrieved March 14, 2004 (www.journalism.org/resources/research/reports/war/postwar/lynch/asp).

Chomsky, N. 1989. *Necessary Illusions: Thought Control in Democratic Societies.* Boston: South End Press.

Cockrell, C. 2004. "Photo Fakery 'at Its Worst' Riles Ken Light." Retrieved March 23, 2004 (www.berkeley.edu/news/berkeleyan/2004/02/18_light.stml).

Corliss, R. and J. McDowell. 2001. "Go Ahead, Make Her Day." *Time* 157:64–66.

Croteau, D. and W. Hoynes 2000. *Media Society: Industries, Images, and Audiences.* Thousand Oaks, CA: Pine Forge.

———. 2001. *The Business of Media: Corporate Media and the Public Interest.* Thousand Oaks, CA: Pine Forge.

Davies, K. 2003. "Behind the Scenes." Retrieved March 22, 2004 (www.wiretapmag.org/print.html?Story ID=16633&wiretap=yes).

Dietz, W. and S. Gortmaker. 1985. "Do We Fatten Our Children at the Television Set? Obesity and Television Viewing in Children and Adolescents." *Pediatrics* 75(5):807–812.

"Doctors Diagnose Extreme Internet Use." 2003. *Biotech Week*, August 27, pp. 512–15.

Durham, M. G. 2003. "The Girling of America: Critical Reflections on Gender and Popular Communication." *Popular Communication* 1(1):23–31.

Epstein, E. J. 1981. "The Selection of Reality." Pp. 119–132 in *What's News*, edited by E. Abel. San Francisco: Institute for Contemporary Studies.

Eschholz, S., J. Bufkin, and J. Long. 2002. "Symbolic Reality Bites: Women and Racial/Ethnic Minorities in Modern Film." *Sociological Spectrum* 22:299–334.

Fairness and Accuracy in Reporting (FAIR). 2004. "What's FAIR?" Retrieved March 23, 2004 (www.fair.org/whats-fair.html).

Faith, M. S., N. Berman, M. Heo, A. Pietrobelli, D. Gallagher, L. H. Epstein, M. T. Eiden, and D. B. Allison. 2001. "Effects of Contingent Television on Physical Activity and Television Viewing on Obese Children." *Pediatrics* 107(5):1043–1048.

Federal Communications Commission. 2004a. "About the FCC." Retrieved March 21, 2004 (www.fcc.gov/aboutus.html).

———. 2004b. "Parents' Place: Obscene and Indecent Broadcasts." Retrieved March 23, 2004 (www.fcc.gov/parents/content.html).

———. 2004c. "V-Chip: Viewing Television Responsibly." Retrieved March 21, 2004 (www.fcc.gov/vchip/#guidelines).

Galtung, J. and M. Ruge. 1973. "Structuring and Selecting News." Pp. 67–72 in *The Manufacture of News*, edited by S. Cohen and J. Young. London: Constable.

Gans, H. 1979. *Deciding What's News: A Study of CBS Evening News, NBC Nightly News, Newsweek, and Time.* New York: Pantheon Books.

Glassner, B. 1997. *The Culture of Fear: Why Americans Are Afraid of the Wrong Things.* New York: Basic Books.

Griffiths, M. 2002. "Occupational Health Issues Concerning Internet Use in the Workplace." *Work and Stress* 16(4):283–286.

———. 2003. "Internet Abuse in the Workplace: Issues and Concerns for Employers and Employment Counselors." *Journal of Employment Counseling* 40:87–96.

Greeson, L. and R. Williams. 1986. "Social Implications of Music Videos for Youth: An Analysis of the Content and Effects of MTV." *Youth and Society* 18(2):177–189.

Gunkel, D. J. 2003. "Second Thoughts: Towards a Critique of the Digital Divide." *New Media and Society* 5(4):499–522.

Gurevitch, M. and M. Levy. 1985. *Mass Communication Review Yearbook* (Vol. 5). Beverly Hills, CA: Sage.

The Henry J. Kaiser Family Foundation. 2001. *Generation Rx.com, Young People Use the Internet for Health Information.* Menlo Park, CA: Author.

Hapgood, F. 1996. "Sex Sells." *Inc. Technology* 4:45–51.

Howard, I. 2002. "Power Sources: On Party, Gender, Race and Class, TV News Looks to the Most Powerful Groups." Retrieved March 20, 2003 (www.fair.org/extra/0205/power_sources.html).

Huesmann, L. R., J. Moise-Titus, C. L. Podolski, and L. D. Eron. 2003. "Longitudinal Relations between Children's Exposure to TV Violence and Their Aggressive and Violent Behavior in Young Adulthood: 1977–1992." *Developmental Psychology* 39(2):201–222.

Huesmann, L., L. E. Rowell, R. Klein, P. Brice, and P. Fischer. 1983. "Mitigating the Imitation of Aggressive Behaviors by Children's Attitudes about Media Violence." *Journal of Personality and Social Psychology* 44:899–910.

Kellner, D. M. 1995. *Media Culture: Cultural Studies, Identity, and Politics between the Modern and the Postmodern.* New York: Routledge.

Kelly, K., K. Clark, and L. Kulman. 2004. "Trash TV." *U.S. News and World Report* 136(6):48–51.

Klite, P., R. A. Bardwell, and J. Salzman. 1997. "Local TV News: Getting Away with Murder." *Harvard International Journal of Press/Politics* 2:102–112.

Kunkel, D., E. Biely, K. Eyal, K. Cope-Farrar, E. Donnerstein, and R. Fandrich. 2003. *Sex on TV3.* Washington, DC: The Henry J. Kaiser Family Foundation.

Kurtz, H. 2003. "N.Y. Times Article Bears Similarities to Texas Paper's." *Washington Post,* April 29. Retrieved March 20, 2004 (www.washingtonpost.com/ac2/wp-dyn?pagename=article&contentID=A55132-2003April29&notFound=true).

Lazarus, W. and F. Mora. 2000. *Online Content for Low Income and Underserved Americans: The Digital Divide's New Frontier.* Santa Monica, CA: Children's Partnership.

Light, K. 2004. "Fonda, Kerry, and Photo Fakery." *Washington Post,* February 28, p. A21.

Lo, V. and R. Wei. 2002. "Third-Person Effect, Gender, and Pornography on the Internet." *Journal of Broadcasting & Electronic Media* 46(1):13–33.

MAGIC. 2004. "About Magic." Retrieved March 19, 2004 (www.unicef.org/magic/briefing/about.html).

McNair, B. 1998. *The Sociology of Journalism.* London: Oxford University Press.

Media Awareness Network. 2004. "What Is Media Literacy?" Retrieved March 20, 2004 (www.media-awareness .ca/english/teachers/media_literacy/what_is_media_literacy.cfm).

Miller, Mark Crispin. 2002. "What's Wrong with This Picture?" *The Nation* 274(1):18–22.

Morrison, B. 2004. "USA TODAY Reporter Resigns after Deception." Retrieved March 23, 2004 (www.usatoday.com/news/2004–01–13-reporter_x.htm).

Nathanson, A. I. 1999. "Identifying and Explaining the Relationship between Parental Mediation and Children's Aggression." *Communication Research* 26(2):124–143.

Parekh, Angana. 2001. "Bringing Women's Stories to a Reluctant Mainstream Press." *Nieman Reports* 55(4):90–92.

Parents Television Council. 2003. "The Blue Tube: Foul Language on Prime Time Network TV." Retrieved March 14, 2004 (www.parentstv.org/ptc/publications/reports/stateindustrylanguage/main.asp).

Peterson, T. 1981. "Mass Media and Their Environments: A Journey into the Past." Pp. 13–32 in *What's News,* edited by E. Abel. San Francisco: Institute for Contemporary Studies.

Pew Research Center for the People and the Press. 2002a. "News Media's Improved Image Proves Short-Lived." Retrieved March 7, 2004 (http://people-press.org/reports/display.php3?ReportID=159).

———. 2002b. "Public's News Habits Little Changed by September 11." Retrieved March 7, 2004 (http:// people-press.org/reports/display.php3?PageID=612).

Podlas, K. 2000. "Mistresses of Their Domain: How Female Entrepreneurs in Cyberporn Are Initiating a Gender Power Shift." *CyberPsychology & Behavior* 3(5):847–854.

Porter, William, E. 1981. "The Media Baronies: Bigger, Fewer, More Powerful." Pp. 97–118 in *What's News,* edited by E. Abel. San Francisco: Institute for Contemporary Studies.

Postman, N. 1989. *Amusing Ourselves to Death.* London: Methuen.

Potter, R. H. and L. A. Potter. 2001. "The Internet, Cyberporn, and Sexual Exploitation of Children: Media Moral Panics and Urban Myths for Middle-Class Parents?" *Sexuality and Culture* 5(3):31–51.

Powell, K. and L. Abels. 2002. "Sex Role Stereotypes in TV Programs Aimed at the Preschool Audience: An Analysis of Teletubbies and Barney and Friends." *Women and Language* 25(1):14–22.

Project for Excellence in Journalism. 2004. *The State of the News Media 2004.* Retrieved March 21, 2004 (www .stateofthenewsmedia.org/narrative_overview_publicattitudes.asp?media=1).

Schorr, D. 1998. "Mother Teresa and Diana." *Christian Science Monitor* 90(193):15.

Schudson, M. 1986. "The Menu of Media Research." Pp. 43–48 in *Media, Audience, and Social Structure,* edited by S. Ball-Rokeach and Muriel Cantor. Newbury Park, CA: Sage.

Servon, L. 2002. *Bridging the Digital Divide: Technology, Community, and Public Policy.* Boston: Blackwell.

Seymour-Ure, C. 1974. *The Political Impact of Mass Media.* Beverly Hills, CA: Sage.

Shaw, D. L. and M. E. McCombs. 1997. *The Emergence of American Political Issues: The Agenda Setting Function of the Press.* St. Paul, MN: West.

Signiorelli, N. 1990. *Sourcebook on Children and Television.* New York: Greenwood Press.

Snider, M. 2003. "Wired to Another World." *Maclean's* 116(9):23–24.

TV Turnoff Network. 2004. "TV Facts and Figures." Retrieved March 1, 2004 (www.tvturnoff.org/facts.htm).

U.S. Census Bureau. 2003. *Statistical Abstract of the United States.* Washington, DC: Author.

U.S. Department of Commerce. 2000. *Falling Through the Net: Toward Digital Inclusion.* Washington, DC: National Telecommunications and Information Administration.

VandeBerg, L. R. 1991. "Using Television to Teach Courses in Gender and Communication." *Communication Education* 40(1):105–111.

Van den Bulck, J. 2000. "Is Television Bad for Your Health? Behavior and Body Image of the Adolescent 'Couch Potato.'" *Journal of Youth and Adolescence* 29(3):273–288.

Vessey, J. and J. Lee. 2000. "Violent Video Games Affecting Our Children." *Pediatric Nursing* 26(6):607–610.

Warschauer, M. 2003. *Technology and Social Inclusion.* Cambridge, MA: MIT Press.

Wool, M. 2004. "Testimonials: Questions." Retrieved March 23, 2004 (http://thebeatwithin.org/news/view_ custom.html?custom_page_id=58#).

Young People's Press. 2004. "About Young People's Press." Retrieved March 23, 2004 (www.ypp.net/aboutus.asp).

12

Cities and Suburbs

❖

Columnist Carrie Bradshaw, from HBO's *Sex and the City*, once mused how her city of Manhattan was "for millions of our forefathers the gateway to hope, opportunity, and happiness beyond their wildest dreams." Cities, not just Manhattan, continue to have the allure of better living, work, and wages. But an examination of our cities and their surrounding areas reveals a "profound duality" (Stanback 1991). Although our urban areas are shining examples of economic and social progress, they are also characterized by poverty, crime, crowding, pollution, and collapsing infrastructures. Moreover, opportunities and resources are unevenly distributed: Some neighborhoods have safer streets and better services and offer a better quality of life than others (Massey 2001). Cities may offer a better life, but they also harbor significant social problems.

Before we begin our analysis of urban problems, we should first review two sociological fields of study. Both remind us that cities don't just happen overnight; rather social and demographic factors help shape our urban areas and their problems.

Urban Sociology and Demography

The first field is **urban sociology**. In the 1920s, sociologists from the University of Chicago examined their city and the impact of city life and its problems on its residents. Their research provided the basis for urban study and for understanding the determinants of urbanization. Urban sociology examines the social, political, and economic structures and their impact within an urban setting. There is also rural sociology, the study of the same structures within a rural setting.

The first studies on urbanization or urban sociology adopted a functionalist approach, comparing a city to a biological organism. The growth of a city was likened to the development of a social organism, with each part of the city serving a specific and necessary function. Out of the Chicago School of Sociology came two dominant traditions in urban study, one focusing on **human ecology** (the study of the relationship between individuals and their physical environment) and population dynamics and the second focusing on community studies and ethnographies (Feagin 1998a).

Although this chapter's primary focus is on urban problems, an essential part of urbanization is the number of residents in an area, its population. The second sociological field we will rely on is **demography:** the study of the size, composition, and distribution of human populations. Demography isn't just about counting people. Demographers analyze the changes and trends in the population. Their work begins with two fundamental facts: We are born and then we die. In Chapter 7, "Health and Medicine," we reviewed two basic demographic elements, fertility and mortality, identifying how each is determined by biological and social factors.

❖ PUTTING IT TOGETHER: On the Web.	Based on census data, confirm census figures for the population of your college state and city. Identify the five largest cities in your college state. Log on to *Study Site Chapter 12.*

An additional demographic element is **migration,** the movement of individuals from one area to another. Migration is distinguished by the type of movement: Immigration is the movement of people into a geographic area; emigration is the movement of people out of a geographic area. About 40 million people moved between 2002 and 2003 (Schachter 2004). People migrate to pursue employment opportunities, to move to be closer to family, to find a more temperate climate, and to seek the opportunity of a better life. Most movers have housing-related reasons: They move to a new, better, or more affordable home or apartment (Schachter 2004).

Urbanization, the process by which a population shifts from rural to urban, took off in the later half of the 19th century (Williams 2000). The economy of the United States in the middle of the 19th century was divided: The northern economy was characterized by a mixture of family-based agriculture, commerce, finance, and an increasing industrial base, while the southern economy remained dependent on agriculture (Gordon 2001). But as the industrial economy began to grow in the North and extended into the Midwest, thousands of people were attracted to these emerging urban centers, drawn by the promise of work in factories and mills (Williams 2000). Also contributing to early urban growth was the emigration of Europeans and the migration of rural Blacks and Whites from the South to northern and midwestern urban areas (Dreier 1996).

After World War II, the United States experienced another significant population shift: **suburbanization**. Although suburbanization has come to represent the outward expansion of central cities into suburban areas (Smith 1986), it has also been linked with two additional population shifts: from the Snow Belt (industrial regions of the North and Midwest) to the Sun Belt (South and Southwest) and from rural to metropolitan areas (Dreier 1996). Although many factors contributed to suburbanization, the key players were government leaders and their policies. The U.S. Congress passed the Housing Act of 1949, which encouraged construction outside city boundaries and made home purchasing easier through the Federal Housing Authority (FHA) and Veterans Association home mortgage loan programs. The 1956 Federal Aid Highway Act, which established the modern interstate highway system, made rural areas more accessible. President Dwight Eisenhower, a chief proponent of the Act, believed in the importance of the interstate highway system. Eisenhower (1963) declared,

> More than any single action by the government since the end of the war, this one would change the face of America. . . . Its impact on the American economy—the jobs it would produce in manufacturing and construction, the rural areas it would open up—was beyond calculation. (Pp. 548–49)

Currently, about 46 percent of all housing units are located in the suburban parts of metropolitan areas, while about 30 percent of all housing units are located in central cities (U.S. Census Bureau 2002a). Suburbs attract all types of families, especially in older industrial urban centers of the Northeast and Midwest (Armas 2002). Nonfamily households—those headed by a young, single professional or an elderly woman—now outnumber households of married couples with kids in the suburbs (Armas 2002).

The U.S. Census Bureau defines an **urban population** as an area with 2,500 or more individuals. An **urbanized area** is a densely populated area with 50,000 or more residents, and a **metropolitan statistical area** is a densely populated area with 100,000 or more people. Census data indicate a rapid increase in the urban population, especially after World War II (Table 12.1). For 2000, the five largest metropolitan statistical areas were New York City, Los Angeles, Chicago, Washington, D.C., and San Francisco (U.S. Census Bureau 2002b). The largest area was New York City-northern New Jersey–Long Island with 21,199,865 people. A complete list of the 10 largest cities is presented in Table 12.2.

❖ Table 12.1   U.S. Population, Percentage of Urban Residents

Year	Percentage Urban
1900	40.0
1910	45.8
1920	51.4
1930	56.2
1940	56.5
1950	64.0
1960	69.9
1970	73.5
1980	73.7
1990	75.2

❖ Table 12.2   Ten Largest U.S. Cities in 2000

City in Rank Order	Number
New York, New York	8,008,278
Los Angeles, California	3,694,820
Chicago, Illinois	2,896,016
Houston, Texas	1,953,631
Philadelphia, Pennsylvania	1,517,550
Phoenix, Arizona	1,321,045
San Diego, California	1,223,400
Dallas, Texas	1,188,580
San Antonio, Texas	1,144,646
Detroit, Michigan	951,270

Source: U.S. Census Bureau 2000a.

Changes in the fertility, mortality, and migration rates affect the population composition, the biological and social characteristics of a population. For example, **age distribution**, the distribution of individuals by age, is particularly important as it provides a community with some direction in its social and economic planning, assessing its education, health, housing, and employment needs. Demographers have long predicted the graying of the U.S. population, warning of the growing number of elderly and the increasing demands they will make on health care and social security.

The ethnic composition of communities also has an impact on social and human services. Roberto Suro and Audrey Singer (2002) explain that the Latino population has spread out further and faster across the nation than any previous wave of immigrants. Hispanics are the fastest-growing U.S. minority group as their numbers increased 58 percent during the 1990s, from 22.4 million in 1990 to 35.3 million in 1999. In 2003, the U.S. Census Bureau announced that Hispanics are the largest minority group in the United States, numbering 37 million in 2001 (Ramirez and de la Cruz 2003). Although the number of Latinos remains high in metropolitan areas such as Los Angeles, New York, and Miami, the largest increases of Latinos occurred in smaller metropolitan areas. About 54 percent of all Latinos now live in suburbs.

Housing, education, and public transportation demands will vary with the rate of growth in the Latino community. For instance, communities like Suffolk County, New York, should prepare for a growing Latino population characterized by low-wage workers, large families, and significant numbers of adults with little English proficiency (Suro and Singer 2002). In California, researchers from the UCLA Medical

School recommend shifting health care services, as Hispanic Californians tend to live longer than non-Hispanics and are less likely to die from heart disease or cancer (Murphy 2003).

How would you characterize the age and sex distribution of your college state? How would you characterize the ethnic composition of your state? What is the largest minority group? What is the smallest? Log on to *Study Site Chapter 12* for U.S. Census Bureau links.

Sociological Perspectives on Urbanization

Functionalist Perspective

Early functionalists were critical about the transition from simple to complex social communities. Emile Durkheim described this transition as a movement from **mechanical solidarity** to **organic solidarity**. Living under mechanical solidarity, individuals in small simple societies are united through a set of common values, beliefs, and customs and a simple division of labor. Durkheim argued that organic solidarity was the result of increasing industrialization and the growth of large complex societies, where individuals are linked through a complex division of labor. Under organic solidarity, individuals begin to share the responsibility for the production of goods and services. New relationships are created according to what people can do or provide for each other. Durkheim believed that as a result of industrialization, the social bonds that unite us will eventually weaken, leading to social problems.

Although industrialization and urbanization have been functional, creating a more efficient, interdependent, and productive society, they have also been problematic for society. Due to the weakening of social bonds and an absence of norms, society begins to lose its ability to function effectively. As our social bonds with each other have loosened, our sense of obligation or duty to one another has declined. Urbanization can lead to social problems such as crime, poverty, violence, and deviant behavior. Functional solutions to these problems may encourage reinforcing or re-creating social bonds through existing institutions like churches, families, and schools or instituting societal changes through political or economic initiatives.

Conflict and Feminist Perspectives

Since the late 1960s, a new perspective on urban study has emerged. Referred to as the **critical political-economy** or **socio-spatial perspective**, this approach uses a conflict perspective to focus on how cities are formed on the basis of racial, gender, or class inequalities. From this perspective, cities are shaped by powerful social and political actors from the private and public sectors, working within the modern capitalistic structure (Feagin 1998b). Social problems are natural to the system, rising from the unequal distribution of power between politicians and taxpayers, the rich and the poor, or the home owner and the renter.

Within this tradition, scholars examine the role of capitalism and capitalists in shaping cities (Feagin 1998b). Land use decisions are made by politicians and businesspeople (Gottdiener 1977), real estate developers and financiers (Molotch 1976), or coalitions between public officials and private citizens (Rast 2001). Joe Feagin (1998b) presented a theory of urban ecology that accented the role of class structure and powerful land-oriented capitalist actors in shaping the location, development, and decline of American cities. Land speculators shape the internal structure of cities by identifying and packaging particular parcels of land for business or residential use. As Feagin (1998b) describes it,

> Powerful land-interested capitalists have contributed substantially to the internal physical structure and patterning of cities themselves. The central areas of cities such as San Francisco have been intentionally remade, in the name of private profit, by combinations of speculators and other capitalists, such as developers. (P. 154)

Although women play a pivotal role in urban life, theories about urbanization have taken a gender-blind approach (Women's International Network News 1999). Urban studies have not systematically considered cities as sites of institutionalized patriarchy (Garber and Turner 1994) and have not legitimately considered the role of women in urban development. Feminist urbanists have argued for the development of a comprehensive field of theory and research that acknowledges the role of women in urban structures (Masson 1984).

By incorporating feminist theory in patriarchy and urban studies, we can understand an additional dimension of urban life, namely the complex ways in which cities serve to reproduce and challenge patriarchy (Appleton 1995) and the problems these create. Garber and Turner (1994) explain:

> Urban environments are constructed around the delivery of public services and the development of policies. These shape women's ability to cope with complex urban locations, largely through the responsiveness of public and private organizations to the needs of diverse groups of women and children. (P. xxiii)

Robyne Turner (1994) argues that the living conditions of lower income, inner-city women have been affected by the economic restructuring of cities and the patterns of downtown development. Woman-headed households increasingly make up the majority of inner-city households. Turner explains that although low-income women may find inner-city housing less costly and more accessible than housing in the suburbs, urban living also presents a unique set of challenges in transportation, housing, employment, services, and safety. Inner-city women have less control over their living situation than suburban women. City development decisions are made by those in power, often men, while the recipients of these decisions are female, the young, or the elderly. Turner (1994) concludes, "It is important to recognize the implications for women, as the heads of households, in the debate on economic restructuring, land based economies, and the portrayal of political power" (pp. 287–288).

Interactionist Perspective

Georg Simmel (1903/1997) was the first sociologist to explain how city life is also a state of mind. In his 1903 essay, "The Metropolis and Mental Life," Simmel described how life in a small town is self-contained; interactions with others are routine and rather ordinary. But a city's economic, personal, and intellectual relationships cannot be defined or confined by its physical space; rather, they are as extensive as the number of interactions between its residents. City dwellers must interact with a variety of people for goods and services but also for personal and professional relationships. City living stimulates the intellect and individuality of its residents (Karp, Stone, and Yoels 1991). Within this complex web of city life, Simmel (1903/1997) argued that man would struggle to define his own individuality "in order to preserve his most personal core" (p. 184). A city represents an opportunity for individuals to find self-expression while being connected with fellow city dwellers.

How well are city dwellers connected with their neighbors? The answer is that they may not be as connected as Simmel predicted. The way a city is constructed might actually interfere with social interaction. Our dependency on automobiles compartmentalizes neighborhood relations (we only know those on our block or street) and interferes with street life (no space for ball games, block parties, bike riding, and joggers) (Gottdiener 1977). Home and residential designs limit our face-to-face contact with our neighbors. Without porches, there is no place to sit out front and visit with one's neighbors, without sidewalks or local parks, families find it less appealing to take walks around their neighborhood and less easy to meet with neighbors.

Banerjee and Baer (1984) discovered that how we define our cities is linked to what we value or use within them. What goods and services do people use in their community? Is it the coffee shop, the local dry cleaner, or the neighborhood grocery store? Or is it the local park, the bicycle lanes, or the athletic center down the street? The researchers asked residents of several Southern California cities to draw maps of their residential areas. Banerjee and Baer found that illustrations by middle- and upper-income individuals contained more details and area than illustrations by lower income people. Upper-income groups included amenities such as tree-lined streets, wooded areas, and golf courses, whereas middle- and low-income groups included commercial and retail locations, such as gas stations, discount stores, or drug stores. Corporate symbols were commonly used to define landmarks in middle- and low-income illustrations. Banerjee and Baer concluded that income was the single most important variable in explaining the quality of residential experiences and residents' judgments about what constitutes a "good place" to live.

Urban communities continue to be segregated by income, race/ethnicity, or immigrant status. This contributes to our isolation, not just physically but also through the meanings we attach to these different neighborhoods. In many towns, there is a "bad" neighborhood, a place where only the "rich" people live, or an area where one racial/ethnic group lives. Thinking this way, we define not only what a neighborhood is like but also how its residents and their social problems are different from us and our problems. This social isolation leads us to believe that certain social problems—substandard housing, poverty, crime, or pollution—are unique to someone else's neighborhood. It becomes their problem, not ours.

For a summary of the different sociological perspectives, see Table 12.3.

❖ PUTTING IT TOGETHER:

Can a city person find some personal space? Symbolic interactionists have also noted how urban dwellers are able to create a "public privacy" while living in a demanding urban world (Karp et al. 1991). Using props like the newspaper or a Walkman, individuals send messages that they aren't interested in talking with others. You may bump into people while walking on a busy street but never stop to say "excuse me." The proportion of unlisted phone numbers is greater in the city than in small town or suburban areas (Karp et al. 1991). Your coffee barista may have memorized your morning coffee order, but does she know your name or any other personal information? How do you create and maintain your public privacy?

❖ Table 12.3　Summary of Sociological Perspectives: Cities and Suburbs

	Functional	Conflict/Feminist	Interactionist
Explanation of urbanization and its social problems	This perspective focuses on the weakening of social bonds and the functions and dysfunctions of urbanization.	Both perspectives focus on how cities are formed on the basis of racial, gender, or class inequalities.	City living is a state of mind. Urban living and its related social problems are socially defined.
Questions asked about urbanization and its social problems	How does urbanization enhance or destroy our social bonds? In what ways does urbanization impact existing institutions like churches, families, and schools? How can we strengthen our social bonds?	Does one's race, gender, and social class determine the quality of urban living? How can we address the needs of all urban dwellers? How does one urban group gain power over the others?	How is urban living defined? How can we establish common ideas on urban life and its social problems?

The Consequences of Urbanization

Along with suburbanization came the decentralization, some may even say the demise, of American cities. Inner cities became repositories for low-income individuals and families, as the suburbs enjoyed higher tax bases and fewer social programs (Massey and Eggers 1993). Researchers have suggested that the poor economic outcomes of racial minorities, particularly African Americans, are partly the result of patterns of housing prejudice and discrimination that have prevented minority groups from moving at the same pace as the suburbanization of employment (Massey 2001; Pastor 2001). According to Douglas Massey and Mitchell Eggers (1993),

> The simultaneous proliferation of poverty and affluence created a situation in which social problems among those at the bottom of the income hierarchy multiplied rapidly at a time when more and more people had the means to escape these maladies. (P. 313)

Many of the social problems we discuss in this text seem to be magnified in urban areas. In this next section, we will review several social problems plaguing urban areas: crowding, quality housing, affordable housing, transportation, gentrification, and homelessness.

❖ TAKING A WORLD VIEW

IS THE GRASS GREENER FOR OUR NORTHERN NEIGHBORS?

According to Canadian writer Jeanne Wolfe (1992):

> It sometimes has been noted that the U.S. was founded on the principles of "life, liberty and the pursuit of happiness," while the preamble to Canada's British North American Act calls for "peace, order and good government." Yet it is hard to explain away Canada's more livable cities as simply the result of a more peaceful and less individualistic culture. Conscious policies and traditions have led to the condition of Canada's cities today. As U.S. cities seem to drift toward an increasing sense of crisis, Canadian thinking about cities and

planning may provide a useful point of comparison. (P. 56)

In her article, "Canada's Livable Cities," Wolfe (1992) identifies several characteristics that distinguish Canada's urban reality from our own.

1. *Highways and mass transit.* Unlike the United States, Canada has no interstate highway program. In fact, the United States has four times as many lanes of urban freeways per 100,000 metropolitan residents as Canada has. On the other hand, mass transit systems

receive more support in Canada—2.5 times the revenue miles per capita compared to the United States. Automobiles and car insurance, along with gas, cost more in Canada because of taxation, discouraging the ownership of multiple automobiles.

2. *Urban and suburban policies.* Although suburban growth has been vigorous in Ontario, British Columbia, and Quebec, Canada instituted agricultural zoning laws in the 1970s to prevent the loss of farming land; Ontario introduced a land-speculation tax to control development. Other Canadian provinces have worked with a "land-banking" program, allowing municipalities to hold land in reserve, to be sold off for development only when needed.

Wolfe explains that the policies of Canadian central cities have always aimed to persuade residents to stay. Such programs include: subsidies for property renovation, sites available for residential construction at or below cost, subsidies or tax relief programs for first-time homeowners and the elderly, rent supplements for the poor, and renovation of boarding houses together with the provision of nonprofit subsidized housing. These programs, along with Canada's social and human service programs, have stopped the decline of inner-city Canadian neighborhoods.

3. *Housing policies.* Canada has experimented with public housing projects. Unlike large U.S. housing projects, Canadian projects are smaller in scale and focused on the nonprofit sector. The National Housing Act of 1973 encourages community groups (churches, labor groups, groups of apartment tenants) and municipalities to develop nonprofit housing. Funds were also made available for community resource groups, which employ architects, planners, and accountants, to offer technical expertise to any association developing a project.

Canadian public housing projects, usually low- to mid-rise dwellings averaging 50 units, are located in urban areas, inner cities, and suburbs. The projects do not always involve a new structure; some projects may convert an unused school or warehouse into housing.

The advantages of the Canadian program are many. Residents and community groups have control over their living environment and costs; residents build confidence and management skills; and because low-income housing is integrated into existing communities, Wolfe notes, there is no stigma associated with living there. These units cannot be sold; if a family moves out, another family on the waiting list moves in.

Household Crowding

Interior residential density refers to the number of individuals per room in a dwelling. The criterion for **crowding** is more than one person per room in the household. Household crowding is more likely to be found among poor, immigrant, or urban families. Research indicates that children who live in more crowded homes have greater behavioral problems in the classroom. Crowding also leads to greater conflict between parents and children. In crowded homes, parents have been found to be more critical and less responsive to their children (Evans, Saegert, and Harris 2001).

Clark, Deurloo, and Dieleman (2000) argue that household crowding is linked to inequalities in housing consumption. The researchers explain that the rising income of a large segment of U.S. society has led to increases in the overall quality of housing in the United States. But at the same time, growing income inequalities create affordability and crowding problems for very-low-income households. Affluent households demand better quality and larger housing, increasing their consumption of livable space, pushing housing outside of inner-city boundaries. Clark et al. explain that as middle-class families move to the suburbs, they leave behind inner cities plagued with increased density and housing shortages.

Cities with large numbers of immigrants, such as those in a state like California, Texas, Arizona, and Florida, are especially subject to crowding. A study based in Southern California reveals that households of Hispanics who immigrated in the 1970s are two and half times more likely be overcrowded than those of earlier Hispanic immigrants or White immigrants (Myers and Lee 1996). Clark et al. (2000) also report that in metropolitan areas with high levels of recent immigration, overcrowding is higher than in nonimmigrant areas. Poor immigrant households experience the most crowding and have the most difficulty in transitioning to better, more affordable housing. Studies suggest that competition for housing in cities with many immigrants may increase the cost of housing and can lead to a housing squeeze. Cultural norms may also play a role in crowding among Hispanic immigrant homes.

Substandard Housing

Many aspects of urban life—quality of air and drinking water, sanitation and fire services, and the availability and affordability of health care—have well-established connections to the health of urban dwellers (Cohen and Northridge 2000). One area that is often overlooked is the quality of housing. Substandard housing is a major public health issue (Krieger and Higgins 2002), particularly among urban dwellers. Data indicate that about 7 percent of all housing and 15 percent of all low-income rental housing has severe or moderate structural problems (malfunctioning plumbing, heating, or electrical systems, inadequate maintenance) (Freeman 2002). Housing quality has been associated with morbidity from infectious diseases, chronic illnesses, injuries, poor nutrition, and mental disorders (Krieger and Higgins 2002).

People of color and people with low income are disproportionately exposed to substandard housing (Krieger and Higgins 2002). Data from the American Housing Survey (U.S. Census Bureau 2002a) showed that of those residing in an estimated 13.3 million housing units occupied by Blacks, about 5 percent reported having no working toilets in the previous three months, 10 percent reported being uncomfortably cold for 24 hours or more the previous winter, about 15 percent said they were subjected to bothersome street noise or traffic, and 27 percent reported the presence of neighborhood crime. About 10 percent of Black respondents reported having unsatisfactory police protection. Refer to Table 12.4 for a comparison of findings about Black-occupied and Hispanic-occupied housing units with overall results.

❖ Table 12.4   A Comparison of Housing Quality for Total Housing Units, Black
Housing Units, and Hispanic Housing Units, in Thousands, 2001

	Total	Black-Occupied	Hispanic-Occupied
Number of households	106,261	13,292	9,814
Water supply stoppage within the last three months	4,539	486	448
No working toilets in the last three months	2,828	654	473
Uncomfortably cold for 24 hours or more last winter	6,311	1,362	916
Bothersome street noise or traffic	11,624	1,949	1,224
Neighborhood crime present	14,429	3,556	1,741
Bothersome odors present	2,356	843	575
Unsatisfactory police protection	7,662	1,349	964
Major accumulation of trash, litter, or junk on the street within 300 feet	2,615	733	408

Source: U.S. Census Bureau 2002a.

Affordable Housing

Today, 65.1 percent of Americans own their own home. It was not until the passage of the 1949 Housing Act that the majority of Americans became home owners. In 1940, only 43.6 percent of Americans were home owners; but by 1950, 55 percent were home owners (Bunce et al. 1996). Although the majority of Americans still aspire to own a home, for many poor and working Americans, home ownership is just a dream (Freeman 2002). Central city residents of all income levels are less likely to own a home than suburban residents with the same income (U.S. Department of Housing and Urban Development [HUD] 1999).

As rates of home ownership have increased, the affordability of homes has declined (Savage 1999). The generally accepted definition of affordability is for a family to pay no more than 30 percent of its annual income on housing. Today, it is estimated that 12 million renter and home owner households pay more than 50 percent of their annual incomes for housing (HUD 2004). Lance Freeman (2002) explains that because housing is the single largest expenditure for most households, "housing affordability has the potential to affect all domains of life that are subject to cost constraints, including health" (p. 710). Most families pay their rent first, buying basic needs such as food, clothing, and health care with what they have left.

The National Housing Conference, a nonprofit coalition of industry experts, advocates, and academics, reports that the average janitor earns enough to rent a one-room apartment and pay for other necessities in only 6 of the nation's 60 largest cities (Loven 2001). For instance, in Las Vegas, Nevada, the monthly rent for a one-bedroom apartment was $582, while the median hourly wage for a janitor was $8.92. The wage is below the $11.19-per-hour minimum recommended by the National Housing Conference to comfortably afford an apartment and additional expenses.

It is not just the increasing cost of housing that limits renters; there is also a rental shortage. Higher land prices have made it less profitable to build new low- and moderate-priced housing. The National Low Income Housing Coalition reports that the nation is five million apartments short of meeting the need among people with the lowest incomes (Loven 2001).

Consider the housing situations of Guadalupe Herrera and Rosalba Ceballos, janitors at two Silicon Valley high-tech companies in California (Greenhouse 2000). At the end of their busy workday, the women return home to their husbands and children. But home for Ms. Herrera and Ms. Ceballos and their families may not be what we expect; these women and their families live in converted garages. As the cost of housing has increased in the Silicon Valley, janitors like Ms. Herrera and Ms. Ceballos, who earn $7 to $8 per hour, are reduced to living in trailers, crowded one-bedroom apartments, or garages. Renting a home would cost about $1,300 per month, but illegal garage homes rent for about $750 per month. In 1995, only 10 percent of all renters could afford a modestly priced house in their residential area (Savage 1999). (See U.S. Data Maps 12.1 and 12.2.)

Although economic factors account for much of the disparity in home ownership, discrimination and prejudice also play a role. African Americans and Latinos are more likely than Whites to be turned down for a home loan, even if they have similar financial, employment, and neighborhood backgrounds (Oliver 2003). The U.S. Department of Housing and Urban Development (HUD) estimates that more than two million instances of housing discrimination occur each year. The highest number of complaints comes from African Americans, people with disabilities, and families with children. Hispanic renters experience higher rates of discrimination than African American renters (Turner et al. 2002) and are discriminated against as much as 70 percent of the time in their housing search (Fair Housing Law 2004).

Homelessness

By its very nature, homelessness is impossible to measure with 100 percent accuracy (National Coalition for the Homeless 2002). Most estimates are based on head counts in shelters, on the streets, or at soup kitchens. These estimates do not include

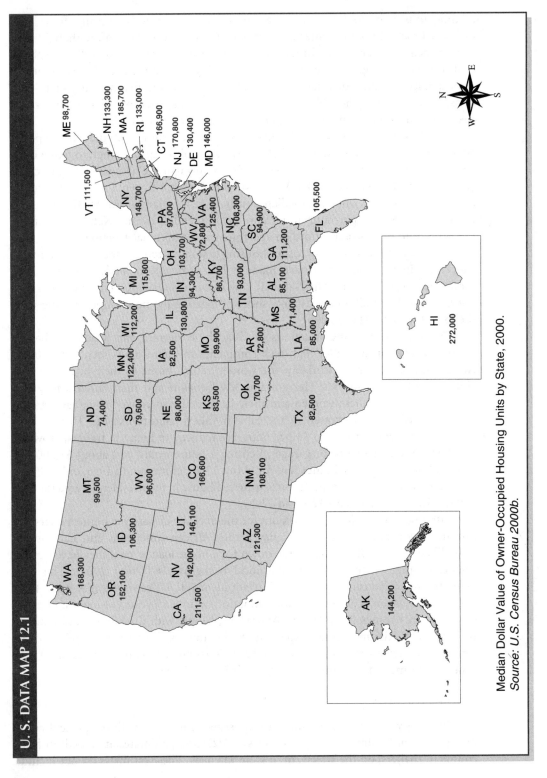

Median Dollar Value of Owner-Occupied Housing Units by State, 2000.
Source: U.S. Census Bureau 2000b.

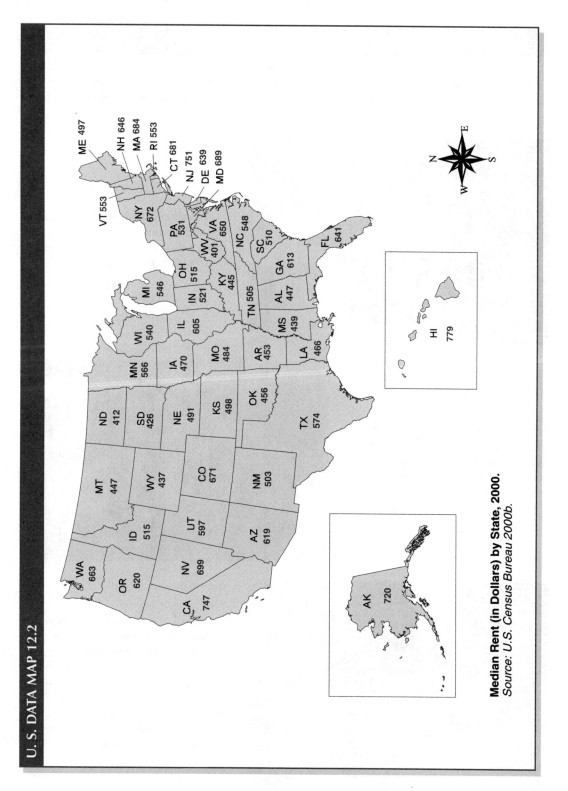

Median Rent (in Dollars) by State, 2000.
Source: U.S. Census Bureau 2000b.

VISUAL ESSAY: HOUSING THE HOMELESS AND POOR ❖

There are many reasons why people become homeless: job loss, chronic substance abuse, mental illness, divorce, lack of a sufficient income to support themselves, or a family or personal disaster. Shelters offer vital services to the homeless. However, they lack permanency and privacy.

This is a traditional shelter for transient homeless men in Denver, Colorado, open only during harsh weather and offering only meager comforts.

This emergency shelter in San Bernardino, California, also lacks privacy, but it has been set up for people like the Demers family, who lost their home in a wildfire. Notice the differences between these accommodations and those for the chronically homeless.

Increasingly, the chronically homeless are families, especially women and their children. Although they are temporary, shelters for families like this one in the Bronx, New York, may offer more privacy and security and a few more of the comforts of home. Laundry facilities, basic health services, and employment assistance may also be offered.

Low-income households that can afford nominal rent may be eligible for public housing, which provides more permanent homes. According to the U.S. Department of Housing and Urban Development, about 1.3 million households are living in government-owned developments. The traditional "project" is a nondescript urban structure, like this huge Harlem apartment complex, built for efficiency and to house as many people as possible.

In rural areas, such as the Pine Ridge Indian reservation in South Dakota, public housing can be more spread out, but it still lacks aesthetic appeal.

Newer public housing projects, like this one in Oakland, California, which was developed through a public/private partnership, are more attractive additions to the neighborhood. They are designed to give people with low incomes a greater sense of security and privacy and more pride in their homes, and they often incorporate spaces for the community to gather, as in the common play area shown here.

Is it society's responsibility to provide housing for those who cannot provide it for themselves? What kind of housing should society provide to the poor and homeless?

those who live in temporary or unstable housing (e.g., those who move in with friends or relatives). There are several national estimates of homelessness. During one week in 1988, 500,000 to 600,000 homeless people were found in shelters, eating in soup kitchens, or congregating on the street (Burt and Cohen 1989). The National Law Center on Homelessness and Poverty (1999) estimates that up to 2 million people experience homelessness during one year, and more than 700,000 people are homeless on any given night. Most public and private sources agree that the number of homeless people is at least in the hundreds of thousands, not counting those who live with relatives or friends (Choi and Snyder 1999).

In their 2000 Status Report on Hunger and Homelessness in the United States, the U.S. Conference of Mayors (2000) reported that on average, single men make up 44 percent of the homeless population, families with children 36 percent, single women 13 percent, and unaccompanied minors 7 percent. Based on a survey of 25 cities, the report noted that the average demand for emergency shelter increased by 15 percent in 1999, the highest one year increase of the 1990s. About 76 percent of the cities, the highest increase since 1994, reported that the demand for shelter had increased. People were homeless for an average of five months in the cities surveyed by the group of mayors. About half of the cities noted that the length of time people are homeless increased in the previous year.

Peter Rossi (1989) maintains that the new homeless are likely to be more visible, female, a member of an ethnic minority, somewhere in their twenties or thirties, and unemployed, with no or low monthly incomes. Prior to the mid 1970s, the majority of the homeless were older single males with substance abuse or physical or mental problems (Choi and Synder 1999). Their individual disabilities or personal pathologies were likely to have caused their homelessness. However, since the mid 1970s, the increasing number of homeless men, women, and families indicates that more than individual disabilities or personal characteristics are causing homelessness (Choi and Snyder 1999). Studies indicate that family homelessness in the 1980s and 1990s was primarily attributable not to individual deficits but to the increased number of the poor, especially minority single female-headed households, and to the lack of affordable low-income housing units (Choi and Snyder 1999). The U.S. Conference of Mayors (2000) identified several causes of homelessness: substance abuse, mental illness, domestic violence, poverty, low-paying jobs. However, in nearly every city surveyed by the U.S. Conference of Mayors, the lack of affordable housing was identified as the primary cause of homelessness.

❖ PUTTING IT TOGETHER: In your community. What is the estimated number of homeless in your community and/or state?

Gentrification

In their report, "Dealing with Neighborhood Change," Maureen Kennedy and Paul Leonard (2001) reveal that "**gentrification**, the process of neighborhood change which results in the replacement of lower income residents with higher income ones, has changed the character of hundreds of urban neighborhoods in America over the last 50 years" (p. 1). Gentrification has occurred in waves: the urban renewal efforts in the 1950s and '60s and the "back-to-the-city" movement of the late 1970s and 1980s. Although a number of U.S. cities are experiencing another round of gentrification, that is not occurring across the country. Gentrification occurs primarily in a select number of neighborhoods in cities with tight housing markets.

Kennedy and Leonard (2001) explain that gentrification is re-emerging for three basic reasons. First, the nation's strong economy creates a greater demand for labor and housing, making housing in central cities and inner suburbs attractive to higher income newcomers. Second, federal, state, and local governments, along with non-profit organizations, have increased their level of motivation, funding, and policy initiatives to revitalize central cities. Under some circumstances, these revitalization efforts may lead to gentrification. Finally, in an effort to reduce the concentration of poverty in inner cities, public officials have attempted to attract higher income families to the area.

Kennedy and Leonard (2001) describe gentrification as a "double edged sword." Officials and developers point to the increasing real estate values, tax revenues, and commercial activity that take place in revitalized communities. But is there a price for these capital and economic improvements? The most contentious by-product of gentrification is the involuntary displacement of a neighborhood's low-income residents. Gentrification is most often associated with the disproportionate pressure it puts on marginalized poor, elderly, or minorities, particularly renters. There are no consistent data on the number of individuals who have been displaced through gentrification; yet the evidence suggests that where housing markets are tight (or limited), the amount of displacement is likely to be greater and the impacts on those displaced more serious.

Urban Sprawl—The Problems of Transportation and Commuting

As urban areas spread out, they create a phenomenon referred to as **urban sprawl.** Urban sprawl began with land development after World War II. Sprawl is defined as the process in which the spread of development across the landscape outpaces population growth (Ewing, Pendall, and Chen 2002). Sprawl creates four conditions for an urban area: a population that is widely dispersed in low-density developments; rigidly separated homes, shops, and workplaces; a network of roads marked by huge blocks and poor access; and a lack of well-defined activity centers, such as downtowns or town centers (Ewing et al. 2002).

As sprawl increases, so do the number of miles traveled, number of vehicles owned per household, traffic fatality rates, air pollution (Corvin 2001; Ewing et al. 2002), and eventually our risk of asthma, obesity, and poor health. On average, an American spends 443 hours per year behind the wheel (Crenson 2003). According to the U.S. Department of Transportation, there are more cars than people per household: the average U.S. household has 1.75 drivers, but 1.90 personal vehicles (Wald 2003).

In areas with high urban sprawl, only 2.3 percent of workers take public transportation to work, whereas in areas that have less urban sprawl, an average of

5.1 percent of workers take public transportation (Ewing et al. 2002). New suburban residential developments don't include sidewalks, and automobiles are needed to get from place to place. The Centers for Disease Control reports how urban sprawl increases our time on the road and decreases our time spent exercising, including walking, jogging, or riding a bike (Corvin 2001). Residents who live in spread-out areas spend fewer minutes each month walking and weigh about six pounds more on average than those who live in densely populated areas (Stein 2003).

Driving safety becomes an additional issue with urban sprawl. Take, for example, the most "savage road in New York City," the Cross Bronx Expressway (Feuer 2002). This major commercial freeway, which carries about 180,000 vehicles per day, should come with a warning label. In 2002, there were 2,622 accidents on the expressway, with five fatalities. The two other major expressways in the Bronx had 858 and 1,827 accidents during the same time period. The narrow, pothole-ridden Cross Bronx Expressway is also plagued with poor lighting, inadequate drainage, and limited lines of sight. As a major route for trucks and automobiles, the Cross Bronx has numerous on- and off-ramps, making it difficult for drivers. Don't even think about getting stalled on the side of the road. It is reported that there are no rules on the Cross Bronx Expressway—dividing lines are ignored, along with the posted speed limit.

❖ PUTTING IT TOGETHER:
In your community.

Examine the public transportation system for your college city. First, is one available? Second, assess its effectiveness. Does the system serve all areas of your community? How much does it cost to use the system? How does the system serve disadvantaged populations—elderly, poor, or disabled residents? Does the system provide discounted fares for students?

Urban and Community Policy, Advocacy, and Innovation

Department of Housing and Urban Development (HUD)

The federal agency responsible for addressing the nation's housing needs and improving and developing the nation's communities is HUD. Created in 1965 as part of Lyndon Johnson's War on Poverty, HUD was given the authority to enforce fair housing laws and to administer a variety of federal programs to provide a decent, safe, and sanitary living environment for every American (HUD 2003b; Martinez 2000).

HUD's history extends back to the National Housing Act of 1934 and to the 1937 amendment that created the United States Housing Authority for low-rent housing. HUD's efforts to encourage home ownership are rooted in the Housing Act of 1949, a declaration that all Americans have the right to become home owners. In spite of its expressed goal of creating "well planned and integrated residential neighborhoods," the Housing Act did not improve housing conditions for nonminority households (Martinez 2000). The goals of the Housing Act of 1949 were reaffirmed in the Fair Housing Act of 1968, authorizing the Federal Housing Administration (FHA) to make sure that home ownership was affordable and accessible for every American family, including minorities and the poor (Martinez 2000). HUD continues its housing mission, expanding services to elderly residents, and also oversees health care facilities and lead hazard control.

In addition, HUD has been a major player in influencing land use decisions in urban areas (Williams 2000), spurring economic growth and development in distressed communities (HUD 2003b). HUD's major urban initiatives have included the Housing and Development Act of 1970, establishing a national growth policy that emphasized new community and inner-city development; the Housing and Development Act of 1974, which established community development block grants; and the Omnibus Budget Reconciliation Act of 1993, which created the first enterprise zones to stimulate economic development in distressed areas. Enacted in 2000, the Community Renewal and New Markets Initiative reinforced HUD's focus on fostering economic opportunity, enhancing the quality of life, and building a stronger sense of community in impoverished inner-city neighborhoods (Williams 2000). Renewal communities, urban empowerment zones, and urban enterprise communities were part of this initiative, and each will be discussed in the following section.

Renewal Communities, Empowerment Zones, and Enterprise Communities

With oversight provided by HUD, the renewal communities, empowerment zones, and enterprise communities program takes an innovative approach to revitalization that targets inner cities and rural areas. The program attempts to bring communities together through public and private partnerships to attract the social and economic investment necessary for sustainable economic and community development (HUD 2003c). Each program integrates four principles: a strategic vision for change, community-based partnerships, economic opportunity, and sustainable community development. The program begins with the assumption that local communities can best identify and develop local solutions to the problems they face (HUD 2003c).

Enterprise communities and empowerment zones rely on local and regional partnerships. Proposed by the Clinton administration, the Economic Empowerment Act of 1993 provided federal support to distressed cities and communities in the form of funding, increased spending on social programs, tax credits or deductions to encourage business growth, and affordable housing production. The resulting empowerment zones have been characterized as urban laboratories where a variety of economic development strategies are tested and where lessons can be applied to future community policies (Butler 1991). Since the program's initiation, 32 empowerment zones have been created, 8 of them in 2001. The selected communities must have census tracts with poverty rates of at least 20 percent of median family income or areas with pervasive poverty, unemployment, and general distress. The only difference between enterprise communities and empowerment zones is the level of support and tax credits. Communities designated as empowerment zones receive larger direct grants, up to $100 million, whereas enterprise communities receive up to $3 million in grant and loan guarantees. Rural empowerment zones may receive up to $40 million. Businesses located in empowerment zones also receive tax credits not available in enterprise communities.

The renewal communities program was created under the Community Renewal Tax Relief Act of 2000, which authorized up to 40 renewal communities. Rather than providing federal funds or grants to support business development and economic growth, the renewal communities program offers federal tax breaks and incentives for local businesses and communities. For example, the program offers a Work Opportunity Tax Credit to businesses, federal tax credits of up to $2,400 for each new hire from groups that have high unemployment rates or other special employment needs, including youth ages 18 to 24 years, and summer hires of teens 16 to 17 years old who live in the renewal community area. To be eligible, each renewal community must meet criteria related to population, unemployment, poverty, and general distress.

❖
Voices in the Community:
Magic Johnson

Since his retirement from the Los Angeles Lakers, Earvin "Magic" Johnson has become a commercial developer opening state of the art multiplex theaters including restaurants, retail, personal service, and Starbucks locations. Johnson's company, Johnson Development Corporation, specifically targets business opportunities in minority inner-city and suburban neighborhoods.

At the opening of the 12-screen multiplex, the Magic Johnson Theaters, in South Central Los Angeles, Johnson was confident that such a business would succeed in inner cities because African Americans make up about 13 percent of the movie-going audience (Dretzka 1995). Johnson said:

> We're the No. 1 movie goers of any (minority) group but you can't find any theaters in your neighborhood. That's why our theaters are doing so much business. We have great numbers, and for everybody in the neighborhood, it means more to them than just a theater. It's a pride situation, bringing the community together. (Dretzka 1995:1)

The Magic Johnson Theaters cost an estimated $11 million and feature an art-deco lobby with a large concession stand and a two-level parking garage. The Johnson Development Corporation has also opened theaters in Atlanta, Houston, Cleveland, and Harlem. It is estimated that the five theater complexes grossed $30 million in revenue in 2002 (Johnson 2003).

Johnson brought his understanding of the inner-city community to the business. In his movie concessions, knowing that inner-city children grew up drinking Kool-Aid, Johnson sells flavored sodas. "Used to be we couldn't afford to go to dinner and the movie afterward. I told Loew's [his theater partner], 'Black people are going to eat dinner at the movies,'" says Johnson (Wilborn 2002). As a result, in addition to hot dogs and popcorn, the concessions sell chicken wings and buffalo shrimp.

At his theaters, no gang colors or hanging out in large groups is allowed. Before each movie, a clip of Johnson is played, reminding his audiences: "So we got a few policies that apply to everyone. They are not meant to disrespect. They're there so we can all have a good time. So if you have a problem, leave it in the street." (Wilborn 2002).

Johnson has joined with Howard Schultz, chief executive officer of Starbucks, in a franchise deal. Their partnership opened 37 locations by the end of 2002, with plans to expand to 125 locations within the next five to seven years. Their first location was in Ladera Center, a few miles away from the Los Angeles International Airport. The location is one of the biggest grossing in the Starbucks chain. Schultz explains that through the partnership, "we could create unique opportunities for the community—employment opportunities, opportunities for vendors—and also some hope and aspiration about a leading consumer brand doing business in underserved communities, and perhaps other companies would follow us in" (Johnson 2003:77).

Johnson's business philosophy is simple, "All of my businesses deal with people, customer service, and entertainment because that's what I'm good at. Everything flows together from that, and all the companies help each other" (Smith 1999:80).

Urban Revitalization Demonstration Program: Hope VI

The HOPE VI program was established by Congress in 1992. Originally called the Urban Revitalization Demonstration Program, HOPE VI spent nearly $4.8 billion to tear down 115,000 public housing facilities and revitalize some 85,000 others into larger modern townhomes and detached homes with the goal of creating mixed-income communities in inner cities (Armas 2003; HUD 2003a). Funding was awarded to 146 housing authorities in 37 states, the District of Columbia, Puerto Rico, and the Virgin Islands (HUD 2003a).

The HOPE VI program was created based on the recommendations from the National Commission on Severely Distressed Public Housing (HUD 2003a). The commission recommended revitalization in three areas: physical improvements, management improvements, and social and community services to address residents' needs. Program grants pay for demolition of distressed public housing and rehabilitation or new construction. The program has been criticized for worsening the local housing situation because not all demolished units are replaced and program data reveal that not all residents return to the redeveloped HOPE VI sites. As of September 2002, the HOPE VI program planned to demolish more than 78,000 public housing units but to replace only 34,000 units (Center for Community Change 2003).

Although the program's primary focus is on the quality of housing units, HUD officials report that the HOPE VI program has made an impact on its residents through community and supportive programs for residents. When the program was honored in 2000 by the Institute for Government Innovation, HOPE VI officials reported that nearly 3,500 public housing residents left welfare and more than 6,500 residents found new jobs as a result of the program (Institute for Government Innovation 2000).

In 1995, the Seattle Housing Authority was one of the first public housing authorities to receive HOPE VI funding (Naparstek et al. 2000). With $48 million, the Authority tore down and replaced Holly Park, one of the most distressed public housing projects in Seattle, Washington. Holly Park, with 893 units, has been replaced with NewHolly, a mixed-income community with 400 public housing units, 400 tax credit rental units for low-income households, and 400 affordable home ownership units. Of the original 893 residents, 393 moved into NewHolly. The majority of residents who did not return moved into other public housing or into Section 8 rental housing. The renovation of Holly Park also involved a collection of supportive service programs and educational initiatives called the Campus of Learners, each program promoting self-sufficiency. The Campus of Learners includes a career development center, the Atlantic Street Family Center, a branch campus of South Seattle Community College, child care resources, and an onsite public library, among other community partners. Through the program, "the housing authority moved to a new kind of partnership—a collaborative, community-resource, community building model" (Naparstek et al. 2000:16). In 2003, the Bush Administration announced plans to end the HOPE VI program. HUD officials say that the program has been plagued by inefficiency and lack of planning at local levels (Armas 2003).

Creating Sustainable Communities

Tyler Norris (2001) chronicled the emergence and importance of the sustainable community movement. Since the early 1960s, Norris explains, thousands of public-private partnerships have been formed to work for economic development, educational improvement, environmental protection, health care, social issues, and other issues critical to communities. An array of private and public community groups form these partnerships. These alliances have been identified by several names and terms: healthy communities, sustainable communities, livable communities, safe communities, whole communities, or smart growth. Much of the improvement in public health, community revitalization, and quality of life can be attributed to these alliances. The best partnerships, explains Norris, bring together traditional leaders and community members often not included in the decision-making process. A summary of best practices from successful sustainable communities is presented in Table 12.5.

Examples of sustainable communities include:

• Urban Resources Initiative, Detroit, Michigan. The initiative is a program of the Department of Forestry, a community forestry program that uses a "bottom up" approach to address community needs (Sustainable Communities 2002). Since 1990, Detroit residents have been reclaiming vacant city land and using it for innovative forestry projects that offer social, economic, and environmental benefits. When a community is ready to start its own project, it contacts the Urban Resources Initiative. The work begins with a community assessment. The Initiative builds on the skills and

❖ Table 12.5   Best Practices for Sustainable Communities

1. Define community broadly, using not only physical space but also community of interest (e.g., youth assets).
2. Make the community's vision reflect the core values of all its members.
3. Define health as the optimum state of well-being—physical, mental, emotional, and spiritual.
4. Address the quality of life as experienced by all residents.
5. Invite diverse participation and promote widespread community ownership.
6. Focus on system change to address how people live and work together.
7. Use local assets and resources to build capacity.
8. Measure and report your progress and outcomes to keep citizens informed and to keep partners accountable.

Source: Adapted from Norris 2001.

materials already available in the community; for example, identifying the resident "gardener" in the community and someone who has a spare lawnmower that could be used. Their Appoline Street project may exemplify the best of their efforts. Appoline community members have worked on a community garden for several years. Block Club President Alice Dye teaches neighborhood children about plants, bugs, and ecology while they work together in the garden. The children sell their produce at a vegetable stand for a nominal fee and use the profits for other community projects. Funding for the program expired in 1996; the organization's primary objective was to provide resources for community sustainability and not rely on the Urban Resources Initiative.

• Highlander Research and Education Center, New Market, Tennessee. The Center was established in 1932, working primarily on social change and education in the areas of labor, civil rights, and Appalachian issues. In the 1990s, the Center expanded its program focus to be a multi-issue, multicultural and intergenerational movement for social and economic change. Current programs include an environmental economic education program, a community environmental health program, a cultural and diversity initiative, a global education project, a residential education program, and the Southern Appalachian Leadership Training program. Each program serves as an invaluable resource to community groups in Appalachia and the South.

❖ PUTTING IT TOGETHER:
On the Web.

Go to *Study Site Chapter 12* to identify the sustainable communities and initiatives in your area. What principles and values does your local group embrace? Is there evidence that their efforts have worked in the community? Why or why not?

❖

Voices in the Community:
Dan Burden

Dan Burden is spreading the message of his Walkable Communities, Inc., a nonprofit Florida business that helps communities become more walkable and livable (Walkable Communities 2003). Established in 1996, the organization—led by Burden and his wife, Lys—provides community presentations, workshops, training, and community dispute mediation. On the Web site for Walkable Communities, Burden describes how promoting a walkable community ensures area sustainability, leads to better social interaction and fitness, and can curb crime and other social problems (Walkable Communities 2003).

Burden has supported nonmotorized transportation for years. In 1971, he and Lys participated in Hemistour, a bicycle expedition from Alaska to Argentina sponsored by National Geographic. In 1975, he and friend Greg Siple participated in a transcontinental ride, the Bikecentennial, to celebrate the bicentennial. Burden worked for the Department of Transportation and then served as Florida's bicycle and pedestrian coordinator.

He started Walkable Communities, Inc., after a vacation to Australia, where he realized that highways and shopping have done more damage to America's communities. "I started to walk the streets and wander through the villages [of Australia]. . . . every town I was in, was the America I remembered as a child," Burden told reporter Matt Crenson (2003) during a recent visit to East Aurora, New York.

> There are the places that were built and intended to be built as bedroom communities, and you can't find a town center, you can't find a real store, you can't find anything. But you have to live there. What I learned is where a lot of America has been destroyed, so much of it is waiting to be recrafted and perfected.

In East Aurora, Burden provided assistance to a community group, Aurora Citizens for Smart Growth. In a few years, the New York State Department of Transportation plans to tear up its main street and the citizen group wants to be prepared. Burden tells residents that they have already made some planning mistakes—building a new high school a mile outside of town and moving their post office out of the town center. But, according to Burden, residents need to persuade officials to keep their main street as a focal point, not as a thoroughfare. Burden explains that "cities work best if we keep them compact" (Crenson 2003).

As reporter Crenson (2003) sees it, "What makes Burden special is how he spreads the word to nonprofessionals who share his vision for a pedestrian-friendly America." At the end of his visit, Burden tells East Aurora residents that if they do nothing now, "then what you get is going to haunt you for years."

❖ ❖

Housing and Homelessness Programs

The one community response to homelessness that most of us are familiar with is the homeless shelter. These shelters have been referred to as "band aid" solutions, helping but not really fixing the problem. However, these emergency programs can provide immediate and necessary assistance and, in particular, security for families with children. If these shelters are to be truly effective, more humane and supportive shelter environments should be promoted to assist families and to better prepare them for independent living (Choi and Snyder 1999). For example, existing social and human services programs will be more effective if the homeless are able to obtain the benefits that they are already eligible for (Rossi 1989), such as social security, disability payments, and food stamps.

❖ PUTTING IT TOGETHER: On the Web.

Access the HUD Web site to locate homeless assistance programs in your state and neighborhood. What volunteer opportunities exist in your area? Are any opportunities sponsored by your university or college?

In 1987, Congress passed the Stuart B. McKinney Homeless Assistance Act, which established assistance programs for homeless individuals and families. Under this Act, 20 programs were authorized to provide emergency food and shelter, transitional and permanent housing, education, mental health care, primary health care, and veteran's assistance services. In an effort to create more affordable housing, under Title II of the 1998 Cranston-Gonzalez National Affordable Housing Act, the HOME Program provides grants to state and local governments to build, buy, or rehabilitate affordable housing for rent or home ownership. Working with community groups, the HOME Program targets low-income families.

Community efforts are important for the homeless. The best-known community-based housing program is Habitat for Humanity International. Habitat serves primarily low- and very-low-income families with support from local volunteers, churches, and businesses, as well as the sweat equity of future home owners. At the time of a 1998 HUD review of the program, 84 percent of Habitat's participants were families with an average family income of $24,251 (Applied Real Estate Analysis 1998). The average sales price for a Habitat home was $37,782. Habitat home buyers reported that the greatest benefit of home ownership was the pride and security they felt. Habitat's U.S. housing production volume puts it in the ranks of the nation's top 20 home builders (Applied Real Estate Analysis 1998). Other community-based initiatives include Trinity Housing Corporation (Columbia, South Carolina), established by the Trinity Episcopal Church in 1989. It relies primarily on volunteers to provide safe, affordable, transition housing for homeless families (Grass-Roots.org 2003b). Another is the Light Street Housing Corporation (Baltimore, Maryland), established in 1985 by a group of local churches. The program purchases and renovates (one at a time) low-cost housing for the homeless (Grass-Roots.org 2003a).

Although supportive services are necessary for the homeless, homelessness cannot be prevented or eliminated without enough housing for the poor. Homelessness cannot be prevented or eliminated without a livable wage, employment opportunities for inner-city residents, more efficient management of public housing projects, emergency rent assistance programs, and the expansion of low-income housing subsidies (Choi and Snyder 1999).

MAIN POINTS

- Although urban areas provide examples of economic and social progress, they also have many social problems, with opportunities and resources distributed unevenly. Urban sociology examines social, political, and economic structures and their impact within an urban setting.

- The first studies in urban sociology adopted a functionalist approach, comparing a city to a biological organism. Out of the Chicago School came two dominant traditions in urban study, one focusing on human ecology (the study of the relationship between individuals and their physical environment) and population dynamics and the second focusing on community studies and ethnographies.

- Demography, an essential part of urban studies, is the study of the size, composition, and distribution of human populations, as well as changes and trends in those areas. An additional demographic element is migration, the movement of individuals from one area to another.

- Urbanization, the process by which a population shifts from rural to urban locales, expanded in the latter half of the 19th century. After World War II, the United States experienced another significant population shift: suburbanization, or the outward expansion of central cities into suburban areas.

- Changes in fertility, mortality, and migration rates affect the population composition. Age distribution, or the distribution of individuals by age, is particularly important as it provides a community with some direction in its social and economic planning. Demographers have predicted the graying of the U.S. population and accompanying problems.

- Functional solutions to urban social problems encourage reinforcing social bonds through existing institutions or instituting societal changes.

- Since the late 1960s, a new approach called the critical political-economy or sociospatial perspective uses a conflict perspective to focus on how cities are formed on the basis of racial, gender, or class inequalities stemming from capitalism. In this view, social problems are natural to the system, arising from the unequal distribution of power among various groups.

- Feminist theorists have argued for the development of a comprehensive field of theory and research that acknowledges the role and experiences of women in urban environments.

- Urban communities continue to be segregated by income, race/ethnicity, or immigrant status. This contributes to isolation, not just physically but also through the meanings attached to different neighborhoods. This social isolation leads us to believe that certain social problems are unique to someone else's neighborhood.

- Along with suburbanization came the decentralization of American cities. Inner cities became repositories for low-income individuals and families.

- Substandard housing and crowding are major public health issues, particularly among urban dwellers. Housing quality has been associated with morbidity from infectious diseases, chronic illnesses, injuries, poor nutrition, and mental disorders. People of color and those with low income are disproportionately exposed to substandard housing.

- The increasing number of homeless people in the 1980s and 1990s was primarily attributable to the increased number of the poor, especially minority single female-headed households, and to the lack of affordable low-income housing units. Substance abuse, mental illness, domestic violence, poverty, and low-paying jobs also have contributed.

- Another problem is gentrification, or the process of neighborhood change that results in the replacement of lower income residents with higher income ones, a process most often associated with the disproportionate pressure it puts on marginalized groups.

- As urban areas spread out, they create urban sprawl, in which development across the landscape outpaces population growth. As sprawl increases, so do the number of miles traveled, number of vehicles owned, traffic fatality rates, air pollution, and eventually the risk of poor health.

- The federal agency responsible for addressing the nation's housing needs and improving and developing the nation's communities is the U.S. Department of Housing and Urban Development (HUD). With HUD oversight, renewal communities, empowerment zones, and enterprise communities have attempted to bring communities together through public and private partnerships to attract necessary social and economic investments.

- Since the early 1960s, a sustainable community movement composed of thousands of public-private partnerships has worked for economic development, educational improvement, environmental protection, health care, social issues, and other issues critical to communities. Much of the improvement in public health, community revitalization, and quality of life can be attributed to these alliances.

❖

INTERNET AND COMMUNITY EXERCISES

1. Assess the growth of your community over the past 50 years. Use U.S. Census (log on to *Study Site Chapter 12*) or local data to determine the population growth or decline for your community. What areas of your community are thriving? What areas are declining? Overall, how would you characterize the state of your community?

2. Investigate the Center for Neighborhood Technology, the Civic Practices Network, and Citistates Web sites. Identify how each defines the problem of urbanization. Based on each definition(s), what solutions are promoted? Log on to *Study Site Chapter 12*.

3. According to the American Public Transportation Association (2002), increasing public transportation is the most effective way to improve air quality and reduce energy consumption without imposing new taxes or regulations on a community. Review the American Public Transportation Association's Web site by logging on to *Study Site Chapter 12*. What national or local transportation initiatives are promoted by the site? Can any be applied to your community?

4. Community interest developments are private subdivisions where residents own their homes and pay an annual or monthly home association fee. For their nominal or sometimes large fee, residents ensure that their "neighborhood" is strictly managed by a residential board backed by a series of covenants, codes, and restrictions dictating the color of one's home, how many cars can be parked in the driveway, or where fences or a garden shed can be built. These communities have also been referred to as "gated communities," reinforcing the notion that their residents are separating themselves physically and psychically from the general population in their city or town. Although the exact number of community interest developments is not known, industry estimates suggest that by the year 2000, some 48 million Americans were living under such agreements (Drew 1998). Determine if there are any community interest developments in your community. If available, interview a member or officer of a development's board. What does the development's codes statement cover? How does the board member describe the quality of life in the development? Would you want to live in this development? Why or why not?

On your own. Log on to *Study Site—Community and Policy Guide* for more information about the social problems, social policies, and community responses discussed in this chapter.

References

American Public Transportation Association. 2002. "Use of Public Transportation by One in Ten Americans Would Lead to Cleaner Air and Reduce U.S. Oil Dependency by 40 Percent." Retrieved February 11, 2003 (www.apta.com/news/releases/energystudy.htm).

Appleton, L. 1995. "The Gender Regimes in American Cities." Pp. 44–59 in *Gender in Urban Research,* edited by Judith A. Garber and Robyne S. Turner. Thousand Oaks, CA: Sage.

Applied Real Estate Analysis. 1998. *Making Home Ownership a Reality: Survey of Habitat for Humanity International (HFHI), Inc. Homeowners and Affiliates, April 1998* (Report prepared for Office of Policy Development and Research). Washington, DC: U.S. Department of Housing and Urban Development.

Armas, G. 2002. "Fewer Families, More Singles Taking Up Residence in Suburbs." *The News Tribune,* February 26, p. A7.

———. 2003. "Public Housing Revitalization Program May Be Scrapped." *The News Tribune,* February 7, p. A9.

Banerjee, T. and W. Baer. 1984. *Beyond the Neighborhood Unit: Residential Environments and Public Policy.* New York: Plenum Press.

Bunce, H., S. G. Neal, W. Reeder, and R. J. Sepanik. 1996. *New Trends in American Homeownership.* Washington, DC: U.S. Department of Housing and Urban Development.

Burt, Martha and B. Cohen. 1989. *America's Homeless: Numbers, Characteristics, and Programs That Serve Them.* Washington, DC: Urban Institute.

Butler, S. M. 1991. "The Conceptualization of Enterprise Zones." Pp. 27–40 in *Enterprise Zones: New Directions in Economic Development,* edited by R. E. Green. Newbury Park, CA: Sage.

Center for Community Change. 2003. *A HOPE Unseen: Voices from the Other Side of HOPE VI.* Washington, DC: Author.

Choi, N. and L. Snyder. 1999. *Homeless Families with Children: A Subjective Experience of Homelessness.* New York: Springer.

Clark, W., M. Deurloo, and F. Dieleman. 2000. "Housing Consumption and Residential Crowding in U.S. Housing Markets." *Journal of Urban Affairs* 22(1):49–64.

Cohen, H. and M. Northridge. 2000. "Getting Political: Racism and Urban Health." *American Journal of Public Health* 90(6):841–843.

Corvin, A. 2001. "Urban Sprawl Creates Belly Sprawl, CDC Suggests." *The News Tribune,* November 2, p. A11.

Crenson, M. 2003. "He Wants to Reclaim Towns for Pedestrians." *The Christian Science Monitor,* October 15. Retrieved March 19, 2004 (www.csmonitor.com/2003/1015/p13s02-lihc.htm).

Dreier, P. 1996. "America's Urban Crisis: Symptoms, Causes, and Solutions." Pp. 79–141 in *Race, Poverty, and American Cities,* edited by J. C. Boger and J. W. Wegner. Chapel Hill: University of North Carolina Press.

Dretzka, G. 1995. "Filling Void, Real and Symbolic Ex-Laker 'Magic,' Sony Bring First-Run Movies, Hope to South-Central L.A." *Chicago Tribune,* July 21, Business section, p. 1.

Drew, B. 1998. *Crossing the Expendable Landscape.* St. Paul, MN: Graywolf Press.

Eisenhower, D. 1963. *Mandate for Change 1953–1956.* Garden City, NY: Doubleday.

Ewing, R., R. Pendall, and D. Chen. 2002. *Measuring Urban Sprawl and Its Impact.* Washington, DC: Smart Growth America.

Evans, G., S. Saegert, and R. Harris, R. 2001. "Residential Density and Psychological Health among Children in Low-Income Families." *Environment and Behavior* 33(2):165–180.

Fair Housing Law. 2004. "About Fair Housing Campaign." Retrieved February 28, 2004 (www.fairhousinglaw.org/about_us/).

Feagin, J. 1998a. "Introduction." Pp. 1–24 in *The New Urban Paradigm,* edited by J. Feagin. Lanham, MD: Rowman and Littlefield.

———. 1998b. "Urban Real Estate Speculation." Pp. 133–58 in *The New Urban Paradigm,* edited by J. Feagin. Lanham, MD: Rowman and Littlefield.

Feuer, A. 2002. "Hell on Wheels, and Nerves." *The New York Times,* September 30, p. A24.

Freeman, L. 2002. "America's Affordable Housing Crisis: A Contract Unfulfilled." *American Journal of Public Health* 92(5):709–713.

Garber, Judith A. and Robyne S. Turner. 1994. "Introduction." Pp. x–xxvi in *Gender in Urban Research,* edited by Judith A. Garber and Robyne S. Turner. Thousand Oaks, CA: Sage.

Gordon, J. S. 2001. "The Business of America." *American Heritage* 52(4):6–59.

Gottdiener, M. 1977. *Planned Sprawl: Private and Public Interests in Suburbia.* Beverly Hills, CA: Sage.

Grass-Roots.org. 2003a. "Groups That Change Communities: Light Street Housing Corp." Retrieved March 24, 2003 (www.grass-roots.org/usa/lightst).

———. 2003b. "Groups That Change Communities: Trinity Housing Corp." Retrieved March 24, 2003 (www.grass-roots.org/usa/trinhous).

Greenhouse, S. 2000. "Janitors Struggle at the Edges of Silicon Valley's Success." *The New York Times,* April 18, p. A12.

Institute for Government Innovation. 2000. "Awards Recipients: Hope VI Mixed Finance Public Housing." Retrieved March 11, 2003 (www.innovations.harvard.edu/).

Johnson, Roy S. 2003. "It Must Be Magic." *Savoy,* February, pp. 70–71, 72–78, 80.

Karp, D., G. Stone, and W. Yoels. 1991. *Being Urban: A Sociology of City Life.* London: Greenwood.

Kennedy, M. and P. Leonard, P. 2001. "Dealing with Neighborhood Change: A Primer on Gentrification and Policy Choices" (Discussion paper). Washington, DC: Brookings Institution Center on Urban and Metropolitan Policy and Policy Link.

Krieger, J. and D. Higgins. 2002. "Housing and Health: Time Again for Public Health Action." *American Journal of Public Health* 92(5):758–768.

Loven, J. 2001. "Affordable Housing Shortage Getting Worse." *The News Tribune,* December 24, p. A4.

Martinez, S. 2000. "The Housing Act of 1949: Its Place in the Realization of the American Dream of Home-ownership." *Housing Policy Debate* 11(2):467–487.

Massey, Douglas. 2001. "Residential Segregation and Neighborhood Conditions on U.S. Metropolitan Areas." Pp. 391–434 in *America Becoming: Racial Trends and Their Consequences, Vol. 1,* edited by N. Smelser, W. J. Wilson, and F. Mitchell. Washington, DC: National Academy Press.

Massey, Douglas and Mitchell Eggers. 1993. "The Spatial Concentration of Affluence and Poverty during the 1970s." *Urban Affairs Quarterly* 29(2):299–315.

Masson. D. 1984. "Les Femmes dans les Structures Urbanies: Apercu d'un Nouveau Champ de Recherché." *Canadian Journal of Political Science* 17:753–782.

Molotch, H. 1976. "The City as a Growth Machine." *American Journal of Sociology* 82:309–332.

Murphy, D. E. 2003. "New Californian Identity Predicted by Researchers." *The New York Times,* February 17, p. A13.

Myers, D. and S. W. Lee. 1996. "Immigration Cohorts and Residential Overcrowding in Southern California." *Demography* 33:51–65.

Naparstek, A., S. Freis, G. T. Kingsley, D. Dooley, and H. Lewis. 2000. *Hope VI: Community Building Makes a Difference.* Washington, DC: U.S. Department of Housing and Urban Development.

National Coalition for the Homeless. 2002. "How Many People Experience Homelessness?" Retrieved June 10, 2003 (http://nch.ari.net/numbers.html).

National Law Center on Homelessness and Poverty. 1999. *Out of Sight–Out of Mind? A Report on Anti-Homeless Laws, Litigation, and Alternatives in 50 United States Cities.* Washington, DC: Author.

Norris, T. 2001. "Civic Gemstones: The Emergent Communities Movement." *National Civic Review* 90(4):307–318.

Oliver, M. 2003. "American Dream? How Government Initiatives Made Blacks House Poor." *The New Crisis* 110(5):17–19.

Pastor, M. 2001. "Geography and Opportunity." Pp. 435–468 in *American Becoming: Racial Trends and Their Consequences, Vol. 1,* edited by N. J. Smelser, W. J. Wilson, and F. Mitchell. Washington, DC: National Academy Press.

Ramirez, R. and G. P. de la Cruz. 2003. *The Hispanic Population in the United States: March 2002* (Current Population Reports, P20–545). Washington, DC: U.S. Census Bureau.

Rast, J. 2001. "Manufacturing Industrial Decline: The Politics of Economic Change in Chicago, 1955–1998." *Journal of Urban Affairs* 23(2):175–190.

Rossi, P. 1989. *Down and Out in America: The Origins of Homelessness.* Chicago: University of Chicago Press.

Savage, H. A. 1999. *Who Could Afford to Buy a House in 1995?* (U.S. Census Bureau Current Housing Reports, H121/99–1). Washington, DC: U.S. Census Bureau.

Schachter, J. 2004. *Geographical Mobility: 2002 to 2003* (Current Population Reports, P20–549). Washington, DC: U.S. Census Bureau.

Simmel, Georg. 1997. "The Metropolis and Mental Life." Pp. 174–186 in *Simmel on Culture: Selected Writings,* edited by D. Frisby and M. Featherstone. London: Sage. (Original work dated 1903)

Smith, Eric L. 1999. "The Magic Touch." *Black Enterprise,* May, pp. 74–82.

Smith, N. 1986. "Gentrification, the Frontier, and the Restructuring of Urban Space." Pp. 15–34 in *Gentrification of the City,* edited by Neil Smith and Peter Williams. Boston: Allen and Unwin.

Stanback, T. M., Jr. 1991. *The New Suburbanization: Challenge to the Central City.* Boulder, CO: Westview Press.

Stein, R. 2003. "Waistlines Sprawl with Suburbs, Study Finds." *The News Tribune* August 29, p. A3.

Suro, R. and A. Singer. 2002. *Latino Growth in Metropolitan America: Changing Patterns, New Locations* (Brookings Institution Center on Urban and Metropolitan Policy and Pew Hispanic Center, Survey Series). Washington, DC: Brookings Institution.

Sustainable Communities. 2002. *Urban Resources Initiative: Detroit, MI.* Retrieved February 27, 2003 (www .sustainable.org/casestudies/SIA_PDFs/SIA_michican.pdf).

Turner, M. A., S. L. Ross, G. Galster, and J. Yinger. 2002. *Discrimination in Metropolitan Housing Markets: National Results from Phase 1 HDS 2000.* Washington, DC: The Urban Institute and U.S. Department of Housing and Urban Development.

Turner, Robyne. 1994. "Concern for Gender in Central-City Development." Pp. 271–288 in *Gender in Urban Research,* edited by Judith A. Garber and Robyne S. Turner. Thousand Oaks, CA: Sage.

U.S. Census Bureau. 2000a. *County and City Data Book: 2000,* Table C-1. Washington, DC: Author.

———. 2000b. "Quick Tables: DP-1 Profile of General Demographic Characteristics, 2000." Retrieved February 6, 2003 (http://factfinder.census.gov).

———. 2002a. "American Housing Survey, 2002. Detailed Tables for Total Occupied Housing Units, Black Occupied Housing Units, and Households of Hispanic Origin." Retrieved March 23, 2003 (www.census .gov/hhes/www/housing/ahs/01ddtchrt).

———. 2002b. *Population Profile of the United States: 2000* (Internet Release). Washington, DC: Author.

U.S. Conference of Mayors. 2000. *A Status Report on Hunger and Homelessness in America's Cities.* Washington, DC: Author.

U.S. Department of Housing and Urban Development. 1999. "The State of Cities, 1999." Retrieved March 25, 2004 (www.huduser.org/publications/polleg/tsoc99/part2–3.html).

———. 2003a. "About HOPE VI." Retrieved March 11, 2003 (www.hud.gov:80/offices/pih/programs/ph/ hope6/about/index.cfm).

———. 2003b. "HUD's History." Retrieved March 11, 2003 (www.hud.gov/library/bookshelf18/hudhistory.cfm).

———. 2003c. "Welcome to the Community Renewal Initiative." Retrieved June 24, 2004 (www.hud.gov/offices/ cpd/economicdevelopment/programs/rc/index.cfm).

———. 2004. "Affordable Housing." Retrieved February 28, 2004 (www.hud/gov/offices/cpd/affordablehousing .index.cfm).

Wald, M. 2003. "One Vehicle on the Road, Two Others in the Garage." *The New York Times,* August 30, p. B2.

Walkable Communities. 2003. Home Page. Retrieved April 1, 2003 (www.walkable.org).

Wilborn, P. 2002. "Magic Johnson Now Winning at Business; Politics Could Be Next." *The Cincinnati Enquirer On Line Edition,* May 26. Retrieved October 8, 2002 (http://enquirer.com/editions/2002/05/26/spt_Magic_ johnson_now.html).

Williams, D. C. 2000. *Urban Sprawl: A Reference Handbook.* Santa Barbara, CA: ABC-CLIO.

Wolfe, J. 1992. "Canada's Livable Cities." *Social Policy* 23(1):56–65.

Women's International Network News. 1999. "Women and the Urban Environment." *Women's International Network News* 25(1):60–61.

13

The Environment

Between September 11 and 14, 2001, there was an unprecedented grounding of all commercial aircraft in the United States because of the attacks on New York and Washington, D.C. This gave scientists David Travis, Andrew Carleton, and Ryan Lauritsen (2002) a unique opportunity to test their theory about the effects of aircraft contrails, the white streams of frozen water emitted from aircraft above 30,000 feet. They suspected that the contrails block the sun during the day and trap the heat at night, reducing the daily range in daytime highs and nighttime lows. With increasing air traffic and contrails, some speculate that regional ecosystems could be disrupted. Certain tree and insect species require specific temperature variation to survive (Stenger 2002).

In their experiment, Travis and his colleagues measured diurnal temperature ranges or the difference between the daytime maximum and nighttime minimum temperatures, looking specifically during the three-day period when air travel was prohibited. Based on temperature readings from about 4,000 weather stations, they discovered that temperatures were hotter during the day and cooler at night during the grounding period. The diurnal temperature ranges were 1.8 Celsius degrees higher than temperatures on equivalent dates of the past 30 years (Travis et al. 2002). Once air travel resumed, daytime temperatures cooled while nighttime temperatures rose. The scientists concluded that the absence of commercial air travel (and the contrails) was responsible for the difference in temperatures.

Environmental Problems Are Human Problems

Travis et al.'s 2002 study, along with many other studies, confirms how our daily activities (yes, even air travel) impact our environment. Humans create environmental problems through intentional efforts to exploit or manage nature. Rivers that are dammed, straightened, or treated as sewers may create unintended downstream environmental problems (Caldwell 1997). The removal of rainforests to harvest wood or to create farmland decreases the number of plants and trees that absorb carbon dioxide, leading to higher amounts of greenhouse gases in the air. But environmental problems don't exist just because of our actions. Our pursuit of economic development, growth, and jobs has also led to the degradation of the environment (Caldwell 1997). The state of the environment is also influenced by our cultural values and attitudes toward the environment, our social class, our technology, and our relationship with others (Cable and Cable 1995).

The field of **environmental sociology** considers the interactions between our physical and natural environment, on the one hand, and our social organization and social behavior on the other (Dunlap and Catton 1994). Human beings are an integral part of the ecosystem (Irwin 2001). When we use a sociological perspective to understand environmental problems, we acknowledge that "human activities are causing the deterioration in the quality of the environment and that environmental deterioration in turn has negative impacts on people" (Dunlap 1997:27).

Paul Hawken (1997) refers to the Biosphere II experiment to demonstrate just how vital and fragile our ecosystem is. The Biosphere II was a three-acre glass-enclosed ecosystem intended to sustain eight people for a two-year experiment, from September 1991 through September 1993. The Biosphere II's $200 million budget was not enough to create a viable ecosystem for eight people. By the time the experiment ended, the Biosphere's air and drinking water were polluted, crops and trees had been killed by other vegetation, and 19 of the 25 small animal species they brought with them had died. The scientists who lived in the biosphere showed signs of oxygen starvation from living at the equivalent of an altitude of 17,500 feet. Even with scientific knowledge and planning, there are no man-made substitutions for essential natural resources. Hawken explains (1997):

> We have not come up with an economical way to manufacture watershed, gene pools, topsoil, wetlands, river systems, pollinators, or fisheries. Technological fixes can't solve problems with soil fertility or guarantee clean air, biological diversity, pure water, and climatic stability; nor can they increase the capacity of the environment to absorb 25 billion tons of waste created annually by America alone. (p. 41)[1]

Sociological Perspectives on Environmental Problems

Functionalist Perspective

Whether they are looking at a social system or an ecosystem, functionalists examine the entire system and its components. Where are environmental problems likely to arise? Functionalists would answer that problems develop from the system itself. Agricultural and industrial modes of production are destabilizing forces in our ecosystem. Agriculture replaces complex natural systems with simpler artificial ones to sustain select highly productive crops. These crops require constant attention in the form of cultivation, fertilizers, and pesticides, all foreign elements to the natural environment (Ehrlich, Ehrlich, and Holdren 1973). When it first began, industrialization entered a society that had fewer people, less material well–being, and a lot of natural resources. But modern industrialization uses "more resources to make few people more productive" and as a result, "more people are chasing fewer natural resources" (Hawken 1997:40). As much as agriculture, industrialization, and related technologies have improved the quality of our lives, we must also deal with the negative consequences of waste, pollution, and the destruction of our natural resources.

Biologists Paul Ehrlich and Anne Ehrlich (1990) contend that the impact of any human group on the environment is the product of three different factors. First is the population; second, the average person's consumption of resources or level of affluence; and third, the amount of damage caused by technology. They present a final formula: Environmental Damage = (Population Growth) × (Level of Affluence) × (Technological Damage). For more on the impact of population on the environment, see the Focus On feature on p. 362.

A high rate of population growth or consumption can lead to a "hasty application" of new technologies in an attempt to meet new and increasing demands. "The larger the absolute size of the population and its level of consumption, the larger the scale of the technology must be, and, hence, the more serious are the mistakes that are made" (Ehrlich et al. 1973:15). There is no simple way to stop the escalation of environmental problems. Halting population growth would be a good start but by itself could not solve the problem. Reducing technology's impact on the environment might be useful, but not if our population and affluence were allowed to grow. According to Ehrlich et al., the only way to address environmental problems is to simultaneously attack all components.

Conflict Perspective

Public discourse on environmental problems is often framed in terms of costs and interests. Do you save the spotted owl habitat or hundreds of logging jobs? Should you close a factory or save the river where its waste is being dumped? From this sociological perspective, environmental problems are created by humans in competing for power, income, and their own interests.

Our capitalist economic system has been identified as a primary source of the conflict over polluting (or conserving) our physical and natural world. J. Clarence Davies (1970) argues that the capitalist system encourages pollution, simply because air and water are treated as infinite and free resources. Polluters don't really consider who or what is being affected by environmental problems. If a paper mill is polluting the river, it doesn't affect the paper mill itself but rather the users of the water or the residents downstream. If a power plant is polluting the air, the plant doesn't pay for the cost of using the air, only the cost of cleaning up a polluted area (Davies 1970).

Environmental problems occasionally make life unpleasant and inconvenient, but most Americans will tolerate this in exchange for the benefits and comforts associated with a developed industrial economy (Tobin 2000). A higher standard of living has been confused with consumption: More is better. Politicians encourage lower taxes so that we have more money to spend. Television and print media overwhelm us with products and services and tell us that we cannot live without them. But increased consumption requires increased production, which in turn leads to environmental damage. David Korten (1995) explains:

> About 70 percent of this productivity growth has been in . . . economic activity accounted for by the petroleum, petrochemical, and metal industries; chemical intensive agriculture; public utilities; road building; transportation; and mining . . . the industries that are most rapidly drawing down natural capital, generating the bulk of our toxic waste, and consuming a substantial portion of our renewable energy. (Pp. 37–38)

❖ FOCUS ON: POPULATION AND THE ENVIRONMENT

As of July 2004, the world's population was estimated at 6,378,375,943. It is predicted that the global population will reach nine billion by 2050 (U.S. Census Bureau 2004a). The total U.S. population was estimated at 253,652,382 in July 2004, with projected growth to 419,854,000 by 2050 (U.S. Census Bureau 2004b).

Whether through pollution or overuse, people have been identified as the source of many problems with our environment. But according to Ehrlich and Ehrlich (1990),

> The assault . . . upon the environment and resources of the planet is not just a matter of brute numbers of people. Rather it is what those people do; it is their impact on the things we care about—on each other, on nonrenewable resources, and above all on the environmental systems that sustain us. (P. 000)

Paul Hawken (1993) says, "Human activity *is* part of the natural world, in the largest sense, but human activity ignores the means-and-ends, give-and-take factors that are inherent in any maturing ecosystem" (p. 26).

Environmentalists have expressed concern about the Earth's carrying capacity, asking how many people can the Earth support consistently (Hawken 1993). The quality of our lives and our continued existence depend on more than just our food and water supply. Due to our complex and highly industrialized lives, our existence depends on biodiversity, cloud formation, genetic preservation, fuel consumption, topsoil stability, and dozens of other environment-related issues (Hawken 1993).

Whether we look at individuals, cities, or nations, everyone and everything has an impact on the Earth because we consume the finite products and services of nature. As a result, we each leave an ecological footprint, some environmental impact on the amount of natural resources we use and waste output we create. Countries with the highest ecological footprint per capita in 2003 are presented in the following table. Footprints were calculated by measuring the amount of resources that a country consumes in a given year. Indicators include data on fossil fuel use, acreage and land use, housing characteristics, and transportation statistics. A higher score indicates a larger ecological footprint (Venetoulis, Chazan, and Gaudet 2004).

United States	9.57
United Arab Emirates	8.97
Canada	8.56
Norway	8.17
New Zealand	8.13
Kuwait	8.01
Sweden	7.95
Australia	7.09
Finland	7.00
France	5.74

❖ FOCUS ON (Continued)

Because fossil fuels (e.g., crude oil) are finite resources, their depletion accelerates as population needs for food, energy, and services increase. Currently, the United States is importing nearly 60 percent of its oil, and the amount is expected to increase to 64 percent by 2020 (American Petroleum Institute 2004). Although the G7 nations (a coalition of the major industrial democracies)—the United States, Canada, Britain, France, Germany, Japan, and Italy—represent only 10 percent of the global population, these nations consume more than 40 percent of the Earth's fossil fuels and forest products. The United States, as it continues to have a higher rate of population growth than most of the other industrial countries, increases its impact on the environment and its limited resources (Union of Concerned Scientists 2004).

To estimate your personal ecological footprint, please visit *Study Site Chapter 13.*

Polluters target those with the least amount of power. Robert Bullard (1994) defines **environmental racism** as "any environmental policy, practice or directive that differentially affects or disadvantages individuals, groups, or communities based on race or color" (p. 98). Research consistently indicates that low-income people and people of color are exposed to greater environmental risks than those who live in White or affluent communities. There is also evidence that members of these groups suffer higher levels of environmentally generated diseases and death as a result of their elevated risk (Ringquist 2000).

Some companies openly disregard citizens and their best interests. In the late 1980s, Chemical Waste Management Incorporated proposed construction of a large commercial toxic waste incinerator in Kettleman City, California (Ringquist 2000). Kettleman City was a tiny farmworker town of 1,100 residents in the San Joaquin Valley. Government officials in Kings County approved the facility, along with related construction permits. Residents of Kettleman City formed a group, *El Pueblo para el Aire y Agua Limipio* (People for Clean Air and Water) and filed a lawsuit to stop construction (Cole and Foster 2001). The lawsuit claimed that the company was practicing environmental racism. The population of Kettleman City was 90 percent Latino, with 40 percent of the population speaking only Spanish. None of the public announcements, technical reports, or any official documents related to the incinerator proposal were written in Spanish. The county refused to provide residents with a Spanish-language interpreter at one public meeting. Chemical Waste Management Incorporated withdrew its application to build the incinerator.

Feminist Perspective

The feminist perspective argues that a masculine worldview is responsible for the domination of nature, the domination of women, and the domination of minorities (Scarce 1990). Ecofeminism may be the dominant feminist perspective for explaining the relationship between humans and the environment (Littig 2001). Ecofeminism was introduced in 1974 in an effort to bring attention to the power of women to bring about an ecological revolution. Ecofeminists argue that "men driven by rationalism, domination, competitiveness, individualism, and a need to control, are most often the culprits in the exploitation of animals and the environment" (Scarce 1990:40). According to ecofeminists, "respect for nature generally promotes human welfare and genuine respect for all human beings tends to protect nature" (Wenz 2001:190). Other feminist approaches include the feminist critique of natural science, feminist analyses of specific environmental issues (work, garbage, consumption), and feminist contributions to sustainable development (Littig 2001).

Cynthia Hamilton (1994) argues that environmental conflicts mirror social injustice struggles in other areas—for women, for people of color, for the poor. In environmental movements, Hamilton explains, what motivates activist women is the need to protect home and children. As the home is defined as the woman's domain, her position places her closest to the dangers of hazardous waste, providing her with an opportunity to monitor illnesses and possible environmental causes within her family and among her neighbors. As Hamilton sees it, these women are not responding to "'nature' in the abstract but to their homes and the health of their children" (p. 210).

The modern environmental justice movement emerged out of citizen protests at Love Canal, near Niagara Falls, New York (Newman 2001). At the center of Love Canal's citizens' protest movement was a group of local women who called themselves "housewives turned activists." Lois Gibbs and Debbie Cerillo formed the Love Canal Homeowners Association in 1978. Concerned about the number of miscarriages, birth defects, illnesses, and rare forms of cancer among their families and neighbors, the women worked along with Beverly Paigen, a research scientist, to document the health problems in their community (Breton 1998). The information they collected became known as "housewife data" (Newman 2001). The women held demonstrations, wrote press releases, distributed petitions, and provided testimony before state and federal officials (Newman 2001). In 1978, Love Canal was declared a disaster area, some 800 residents were evacuated and relocated, and the site was cleaned up. Gibbs went on to form the Center for Health, Environment, and Justice and continues to work on behalf of communities fighting toxic waste problems.

Interactionist Perspective

Theorists working within the interactionist perspective address how environmental problems are created and defined. Dunlap and Catton (1994) explain that "environmental sociologists have a long tradition of highlighting the development of societal recognition and definition of environmental conditions as 'problems'" (p. 20). Environmental problems do not materialize by themselves (Irwin 2001). As John Hannigan (1995:55) describes, the successful construction of an environmental problem requires six factors: the scientific authority for and validation of claims; the existence of "popularisers" (activists, scientists) who can frame and package the "problem" to journalists, political leaders, and other opinion makers; media attention that frames the problem as novel and important (such as the problems of rainforest destruction or ozone depletion); the dramatization of the problem in symbolic or visual terms; visible economic incentives for taking positive action; and the emergence of an institutional sponsor who can ensure legitimacy and continuity of the problem.

Social constructionists do not deny that real environmental problems exist. Rather their interest is "the process through which environmental claims-makers influence those who hold the reins of power to recognize definitions of environmental problems, to implement them and to accept responsibility for their solution" (Hannigan 1995:185). This perspective helps us understand how environmental concerns vary over time and how some problems are given higher priority than others.

PUTTING IT TOGETHER: Which sociological perspective offers the best explanation of environmental problems? Based on your answer, what solution(s) would be appropriate? For a summary of these perspectives, see Table 13.1.

Social Problems and the Environment

Air Quality

Ground-level ozone or smog is causing a public health crisis, impacting people in nearly every state (Clean Air Network 2003). Smog is formed when nitrogen oxides emitted from electric power plants and automobiles react with organic compounds in sunlight and heat. Our reliance on automobiles has been blamed for much of the increase in smog levels. It is estimated that there are more cars in American households than people; the average household has about 1.75 drivers but 1.90 personal vehicles and only .86 adult-size bicycles (Wald 2003).

Scientists report that one out of every three people in the United States is at a higher risk of experiencing ozone-related health effects. Those most vulnerable to the health effects of smoggy air are children, people who work or exercise regularly outdoors, the elderly, and people with respiratory diseases. Short-term effects of smog mostly attack the lung and lung functioning: irritating the lungs, reducing lung function, aggravating asthma, and inflaming and damaging the lining of the lungs (Environmental Protection Agency [EPA] 1999a). The prevalence of asthma has increased in recent years; three times as many people have it as in 1980, pointing to problems of air quality and industrialization. Among children, who tend to be outdoors more than adults, asthma is the most common chronic disorder, the leading cause of missing school, and the leading cause of hospitalization (Eisele 2003). In the same way that the ozone damages human health, it also affects the health of other animals and vegetation and damages buildings (Palmer 1997).

The Environmental Protection Agency (EPA) monitors smog levels throughout the nation. The EPA sets federal eight-hour smog standards and collects data on the number of days that exceed the standard. A day is considered unhealthy if smog levels exceed the eight-hour standard. The EPA reported that 2002 was the worst recorded smog season; the eight-hour health standard was exceeded 8,818 times nationwide. The states with the highest number of unhealthy ozone days were California, Texas, and Tennessee (Clean Air Network 2003). Data for all states are presented in U.S. Data Map 13.1.

❖ Table 13.1 Summary of Sociological Perspectives: The Environment

	Functional	Conflict/Feminist	Interactionist
Explanation of environmental problems	Environmental problems are dysfunctions of modern living; the result of agricultural and industrial modes of production.	Problems are created by humans competing for power, income, and their own interests. Our capitalist economic system has been identified as a primary source of the conflict over polluting (or conserving) our physical and natural worlds. According to the feminist perspective, it is a masculine worldview that is responsible for the domination of nature, the domination of women, and the domination of other minorities.	Theorists from this perspective address how environmental problems are created and defined.
Questions asked about the environment and environmental problems	How are environmental problems related to our modes of production? To our patterns of consumption? Are environmental problems inevitable consequences of modern living?	How do environmental problems emerge from our capitalist economic system? from a patriarchal society? Which particular groups are at risk for experiencing environmental problems or their impacts?	How are environmental problems created? What factors are included in the process? How is a problem legitimized? What individuals or groups play a role in the process?

❖ FOCUS ON: POLITICS AND THE
SOCIAL CONSTRUCTION OF GLOBAL WARMING

According to Aaron McCright and Riley Dunlap (2000), in the past decade, global climate change has been widely accepted as a social problem. However, there has been a green backlash of environmental opposition led by the conservative movement. They say:

> The characterization of global warming as a major problem and the consequent threat of an internationally binding treaty to curb carbon dioxide emissions are seen as a direct threat to sustained economic growth, the free market, national sovereignty and the continued abolition of governmental regulations. (P. 505)

During the 2000 presidential campaign, then-GOP candidate George W. Bush was quoted as saying that although he believed global warming exists, he was not certain about the scientific evidence pointing to the causes and consequences of "this slight warming." On the campaign trail, Bush appeared on "Late Night with David Letterman," where he explained that technology is not available to do anything about global warming (Bryce 2000).

To sustain life on Earth, a certain amount of surface heat is required. Heat becomes trapped through the buildup of greenhouse gases—water vapor, carbon dioxide, and other gases—making the Earth's average temperature a comfortable and sustainable 60 degrees Fahrenheit (EPA 2003b). The term *global warming* refers, literally, to the warming of the Earth's surface. It refers to perceptible climate trends on a time scale of decades or more rather than weather conditions or atmospheric events in a specific area at a particular time. According to the National Academy of Sciences, the surface temperature has risen by about 1 degree Fahrenheit in the past century, with warming accelerating during the last two decades. The problem is the accumulation of specific greenhouse gases—carbon dioxide, methane, and nitrous oxide—primarily attributable to human activity over the past 50 years (EPA 2003b).

Since the Industrial Revolution, concentrations of carbon dioxide have increased nearly 30 percent, methane concentrations have increased by 145 percent, and nitrous oxide concentrations have increased 15% (Ehrlich and Ehrlich 1996). Fossil fuels used to run cars and trucks, heat homes and businesses, and power factories are responsible for about 98 percent of carbon dioxide emissions, 24 percent of methane emissions, and 18 percent of nitrous oxide emissions. Agriculture, deforestation, landfills, and mining also add to the amount of emissions.

The EPA (2003b) asserts that global warming poses real risks. Although scientists are unable to predict specifically what will happen, where it will happen, and when it will happen, scientists have identified how our health, agriculture, resources, forests, and wildlife are vulnerable to the changes brought about by global warming. Soil moisture may decline in many regions; rainstorms may become more frequent. Changing regional climates could alter forests, crop yields, and water supplies. Sea levels could rise two feet along most of the U.S. coast. The Intergovernmental Panel on Climate Change (IPCC) projects that global warming should increase by 2.2 to 10 degrees Fahrenheit by 2100 (EPA 2003b).

❖ **FOCUS ON** (Continued)

Since taking office, President George W. Bush has downplayed the problem of global warming, referring often to the lack of scientific evidence confirming the causes and consequences of global warming. In March 2001, President Bush announced that the United States would not support the Kyoto Treaty, which was drawn up in 1997 to implement the United Nations Framework Convention for Climate Change. The treaty limits the emissions of greenhouse gases by an average of 5.2 percent below 1990 levels. According to President Bush, the Kyoto regulations would have become too burdensome for U.S. industry at a time when U.S. businesses were struggling with a slowing economy. In addition, the president called for more research to understand global warming. Responding to the president's announcement, European Union Environment Commissioner Margot Wallstrom told reporters, "We don't see that it's such a good idea to sort of let the Americans off the hook, those who are among the biggest emitters of greenhouse gases." It is estimated that the United States produces 25 percent of the world's greenhouse gases but includes only 4 percent of its population (NewsMax .com 2001).

In June 2001, after increasing criticism over his failure to confront global warming, President Bush announced two research initiatives: examining the causes of global warming and developing technologies to reduce greenhouse gas emissions (CNN 2001). In February 2002, the president announced the Clear Skies Initiative, a proposal to cut emissions from all power plants by 70 percent over the next 15 years. However, in 2003, during Senate testimony to discuss the Clear Skies Initiative, administration officials backed off the original

plan to cut mercury emissions from 48 tons to 26 tons by 2010. Mercury pollution has been linked to several public health concerns. It was reported that administration officials are divided on whether it is economically or technologically feasible for power plants to achieve these administrative standards (Pianin and Gugliotta 2003). A revised 10-year global warming research plan was released in 2003 with this agenda: Identify natural variability in climate change; find better ways of measuring climate effects from fossil fuels, industrial production of warming gases, and changes in land use; and reduce uncertainty in climate forecasting (Heilprin 2003).

In 2003, the White House was criticized for editing a "State of the Environment" report prepared by the EPA, modifying a discussion on global warming. The first draft of the report included references to studies concluding that global warming was partly caused by increasing concentrations of industrial emissions and that it could threaten health and ecosystems. White House officials deleted these references. For the final version of the report, EPA officials decided to delete the entire discussion on global warming, "to avoid criticism that they were selectively filtering science to suit policy" (Revkin and Seelye 2003:A21). In August 2003, the Bush Administration relaxed Clear Air Act rules, allowing about 17,000 older power plants, oil refineries, and industrial plants to make upgrades without installing current pollution controls (Seelye 2003). However, in a 2004 report to Congress, the Bush administration supported scientific data indicating that carbon dioxide emissions and other heat-trapping gases were the only likely explanations for global warming (Revkin 2004).

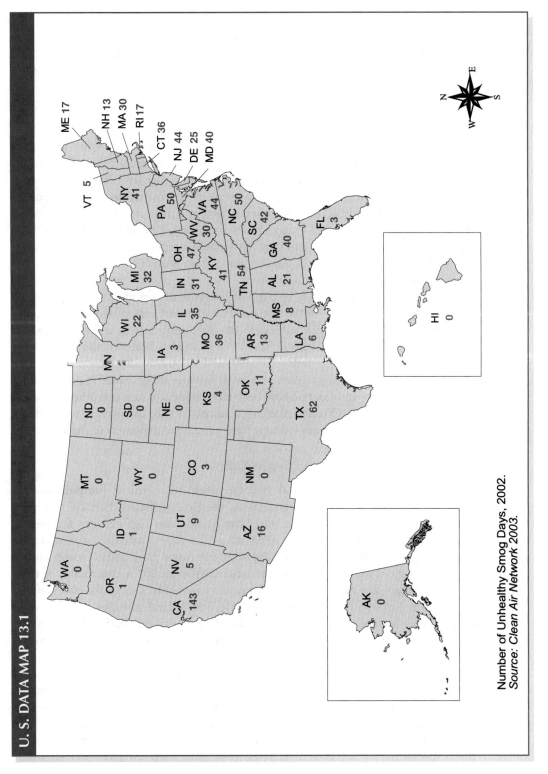

Number of Unhealthy Smog Days, 2002.
Source: Clean Air Network 2003.

You can determine the ozone level in your community through the EPA's Web site. Log on to *Study Site Chapter 13*. Forecasts and ozone maps are listed by city name (not all cities may be listed). The site also provides a list of state and local air quality agencies.

Air pollution from about 80 power plants will cause nearly 6,000 premature deaths in 2007 (Seelye 2002). This was the conclusion made by a technical consultant firm named Abt Associates, contracted by the Rockefeller Family Fund, which supports environmental projects. The power plants are owned by eight companies: American Electric Power (Columbus, Ohio), Cinergy (Cincinnati, Ohio), Duke Power (Charlotte, North Carolina), Dynegy (Houston, Texas), First Energy (Akron, Ohio), Siego (Indiana), Southern Company (Atlanta, Georgia), and Tennessee Valley Authority (Knoxville, Tennessee). All companies have been cited for violations of the Clean Air Act by the Justice Department.

The researchers used existing epidemiological studies to project the mortality and morbidity figures. According to the Abt study (Seelye 2002), in addition to the deaths, the pollutants from the facilities will lead to 140,000 asthma attacks and 14,000 cases of acute bronchitis in 2007. The study indicates that emitted pollutants (sulfur dioxide and nitrogen oxides) can cause respiratory ailments and serious diseases such as lung cancer. The particles are carried across each state with the prevailing winds. Plant emissions from Ohio, Kentucky, and Georgia have been blamed for acid rain and other pollutants in the Northeast, but they are also affecting residents in their own states (Seelye 2002). Representatives from the utilities industry have questioned the results of the study.

Hazardous Waste Sites and Brownfields

The story of Love Canal awakened the world to chemical dumping hazards (Breton 1998). During the 1940s and 1950s, the Hooker Electrochemical Company dumped 20,000 tons of chemicals into Love Canal, New York (Center for Health, Environment, and Justice 2001). In 1953, after filling the canal and covering it with dirt, the company sold the land to the Board of Education for a dollar. Homes and an elementary school were built next to the canal. By the late 1970s, dioxin and benzene chemicals began seeping through backyards and basements. Due to the efforts of the Love Canal Neighborhood Association, state and federal agencies responded by cleaning the area and relocating many residents. In 1995, the Occidental Chemical Company (which bought out the Hooker Electrochemical Company) agreed to pay the government $129 million to cover the costs of the incident.

As a result of the Love Canal incident, the EPA created the Superfund Program to clean hazardous waste sites. Hazardous materials may come from chemical manufacturers, electroplating companies, petroleum refineries, and common businesses such as dry cleaners, auto repair shops, hospitals, and photo processing centers (EPA 2003a). Sites may be placed on the national priority list (NPL) by their state if the site meets specific hazard and cleanup criteria. As of 2003, a total of 1,499 NPL sites were identified. About 93 percent of the sites or 1,394 had completed cleanup or construction, were undergoing cleanup, or were deleted from the NPL list (if no further response is required to protect human health or the environment) (EPA 2003c).

Toxic sites continue to be identified even today. The Child Proofing Our Communities Campaign is a collaboration of groups concerned about children's environmental health. The campaign focuses on where children spend most of their time: in school. In their 2001 report, the campaign identified more than 1,100 public schools within a half-mile radius of known contaminated sites in California, Massachusetts, Michigan, New Jersey, and New York. The campaign estimates that more than 600,000 students attend classes in schools near contaminated land (Center for Health, Environment, and Justice 2001).

One endangered school is Southside High School in Elmira, New York. Elmira supported industry and manufacturing from the Civil War to the 1970s (Archibold 2000). Southside High School was built on a former industrial site that the city purchased for $1. Since the school's 1979 opening, the State Department of Health has received reports of 53 cancer cases among the 7,500 current students and graduates. The most prevalent forms of cancer were leukemia and lymphoma, all at normal levels. However, state officials are concerned with the number of testicular cancer cases (fewer than six cases reported in 2000), checking the medical records of current and former students to assess if there is a pattern of risk factors for this disease (Archibold 2000). The New York State Department of Environmental Conservation confirms that petroleum tanks buried beneath the school are leaking into the soil and a nearby pond. Soil and air tests reveal high levels of volatile organic compounds and other carcinogenic chemicals (Center for Health, Environment, and Justice 2001). Although the Elmira School District reports that Southside High School is not at risk, it admits that it would never buy the land today (Norris 2001). Southside High School remains open.

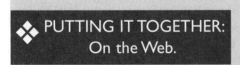

❖ PUTTING IT TOGETHER: ❖ On the Web.

As a result of the cleanup in Love Canal, 239 homes closest to the canal were demolished; in 1988, Love Canal was declared habitable, and more than 200 homes north of the canal were renovated and sold. The area has been renamed Black Creek Village. Are there any Superfund sites in your state? Go to the EPA's Web site—a link is available at *Study Site Chapter 13*—to find out.

In 2002, President George W. Bush signed the Brownfields Economic Revitalization Act into law, which authorized up to $250 million annually for the cleanup of brownfields. **Brownfields** are abandoned or underused industrial or commercial properties where expansion or redevelopment is complicated by the presence or potential presence of hazardous substances, pollutants, or contaminants. It is estimated that there are more than 450,000 sites throughout the United States. Redevelopment efforts have included restoring waterfront parks and converting landfills to golf courses, as well as commercial or business expansion (EPA 2003a).

Water Quality

With the passage of the Water Pollution Control Act or the Clean Water Act in 1972, the federal government declared its commitment to cleaning the nation's waterways, which had become badly polluted from industrial contaminants and untreated sewage (Ehrlich and Ehrlich 1996). Since the passage of both acts, the overall quality of water in U.S. lakes and streams has improved or at least has not significantly deteriorated. Yet, a variety of harmful substances have found their ways into bodies of water, including chemical compounds unknown to nature. A recent study conducted by the Pew Oceans Commission revealed a "crisis" in U.S. waters caused by pollution and fishing practices (Weiss 2003). The commission expressed concern over runoff from agricultural fields, lawns, and roads. Oil from gas stations and nutrients from agricultural fields disrupt the balance of river and ocean ecosystems. A "dead zone" in the Gulf of Mexico near the mouth of the Mississippi River has been attributed to contaminated runoff (Revkin 2003).

Toxic substances are turning up in greater frequency in groundwater, the source of drinking water for one of every two Americans (Ehrlich and Ehrlich 1996). The EPA (1999b) reports that "while tap water that meets federal and state standards generally is safe to drink, threats to water quality and quantity are increasing." Groundwater contaminant problems are being reported throughout the country (Kraft and Vig 2000).

Our drinking water is monitored in more than 55,000 community water systems for more than 80 known contaminants, including arsenic, nitrate, human and animal fecal waste, or legionella (the cause of Legionnaire's Disease). In 1996, 7 percent of water systems reported maximum contaminant levels (EPA 1999b). It is estimated that nearly 1,000 deaths per year and at least 400,000 cases of waterborne illness may be attributed to contaminated water (Kraft and Vig 2000).

Outside the river city of Plaquemine, Louisiana, sits the Myrtle Grove Trailer Park, which is home to some 300 residents (Bragg 2003). From 1997 to 2001, residents used well water that was contaminated with vinyl chloride, a colorless chemical poison that is used to make plastic pipes, furniture, and upholstery. Incidents of contaminated well water are so rare that scientists are unsure about how toxic it is, but animal testing indicates that long-term exposure could cause reproductive problems, such as miscarriages. The Louisiana Department of Health and Hospitals first detected the contamination in 1997 but did not inform the trailer park's residents or the state's Department of Environmental Quality or the EPA. The park was scheduled to close in 2003 (Bragg 2003).

Where Do We Get Our Water?

Fresh water comes from surface water sources (lakes, rivers, and streams) and groundwater sources (wells and underground aquifers). About 66 percent of people get their drinking water from surface water sources. Large metropolitan areas rely on surface water whereas small communities and rural areas depend on groundwater sources. In recent years, there has been growing concern about the availability of fresh water sources. Due to pollution, increasing urbanization, and sprawling development, we may be running out of water.

Fresh water has become a valuable resource. Developers, cities, and states will get it wherever they can. Water from the Colorado River is shared by seven western states for use as drinking water. So much of the river is diverted that by the time it reaches the Sea of Cortez, it isn't much more than a trickle. In 2003, the Interior Department announced that California's share of the Colorado River water would be reduced to ensure allocations for the six other western states. California is expected to lose water supply for roughly 1.4 million people. Some areas will be hit harder than others. In San Diego County, 95 percent of the water used is imported. California is encouraged to develop other water sources ("American Waters" 2003).

Humans have attempted to harness water and its power through the construction of dams. About 75,000 dams in the United States provide water for irrigation, drinking, water control, and hydroelectricity. Once lauded as engineering miracles, dams have been blamed for serious environmental impacts affecting surrounding forests, watershed, beaches, habitat, and life. Former Secretary of Interior Bruce Babbitt (1998) explains:

> The public is now learning that we have paid a steadily accumulating price for these pro-jects in the form of: fish spawning runs destroyed, downstream rivers altered by changes in temperature, unnatural nutrient load and seasonal flows, wedges of sediment piling up behind structures, and delta wetlands degraded by lack of fresh water and saltwater intru-sion. Rivers are always on the move and their inhabitants know no boundaries; salmon and shad do not read maps, only streams.

More than 400 dams have been decommissioned nationwide. In 2002, 63 dams in 15 states were scheduled for removal to respond to growing ecological concerns, as well as to address the aging infrastructures of dams (American Rivers 2002).

Drought and development exacerbate the pressure on water supply. Currently, an intense battle is being waged over the Klamath River in Oregon. As described by Bruce Barcott (2003), the Klamath was born "a cripple." The river begins in Klamath Falls, Oregon, at the southern outlet of Klamath Lake, in "a body of water so shallow that a tall man could nearly cross it without wetting his hat" (Barcott 2003:46). First, water is diverted to irrigate more than 1,400 farms and ranches. Later, some of the water drains back into local lakes and refuges and is eventually pumped back into the Klamath River itself. The area used to be the picture of growth and prosperity, flour-ishing with housing development, farming, ranching, and expanding recreational activities. But in recent years, as the area has suffered severe droughts and with the Klamath water supply dwindling, contentious battle lines have been drawn between the farmers, ranchers, fishermen, native tribes, recreational outfitters, and environ-mental groups. The problem with the Klamath water war, says Barcott (2003:51), is that there are "too many takers, not enough water." Eight major lawsuits have been filed by tribes, commercial fishermen, farmers, and environmental groups (Symmes 2003). Similar battles are likely to be waged over water from the Columbia, the Colorado, and the Rio Grande rivers (Symmes 2003).

Land Conservation and Wilderness Protection

Efforts in land conservation and wilderness protection seem to be successful largely due to federal protection policies. Since adopting the 1964 Wilderness Act, Congress

VISUAL ESSAY: DIVVYING UP THE COLORADO RIVER ❖

In 1922, the big problem with the Colorado River was its tendency to rage like a demon in the spring and slow to a trickle in the hot summer. Disputes over rights to divert its waters had also been building since the 1800s. A commission, chaired by Herbert Hoover, was formed in 1922 to help decide how to control the river and apportion its seemingly ample waters among the seven states sharing its watershed. The Colorado River Compact hammered out by the commission cleared the way for the Hoover Dam, completed in 1935, which began the process of taming the river.

The chief purpose of the compact was to bring some order to competing claims for the water rights. It equally apportioned the river's waters between the Upper Basin states (Wyoming, Colorado, Utah, New Mexico) and the Lower Basin states (Nevada, Arizona, California). It was thought that with a more reliable estimate of the water available to them, public and private entities could plan for the growth of cities such as Salt Lake City, Las Vegas, Phoenix, and San Diego; build dams to produce hydroelectric power; irrigate commercial crops; and even enhance recreational uses of the river, as in the world-class raft trips now available in the Grand Canyon.

Unfortunately, the compact overestimated the river's annual water volume and underestimated the region's growth. It also did not take into account the legitimate claims of various Native American nations within the Colorado River watershed and of Mexico, in which the river's delta lies. Disputes over the pact's provisions began almost immediately. Among the most prolonged and costly disputes was an argument between Arizona and California over just which portion of the Lower Basin allocation each would receive. The case was settled by the U.S. Supreme Court in 1963, after 11 years of litigation.

But that decision still left a number of issues unresolved. Mexico, for instance, had begun to realize that taking water out of the river all along the U.S. stretch would result in increasing concentrations of salt in the water reaching Mexico. In this 1964 march, citizens of Tijuana in Baja California were already drawing attention to the salinity of the Colorado River, which was damaging their crops and tainting their drinking water.

Since then, the problems have only gotten worse as the cities and populations drawing from the Colorado River have grown. In the late 1970s, with the construction of a huge pipeline network, Arizona finally began diverting its legal share of water. Downstream, regions in California joined Mexico in feeling the pinch of a declining share of Colorado River water.

For many years, Imperial Valley farmers in California had access to the water allocations unused by Arizona, Nevada, and the Indian tribes. The network of irrigation canals in the valley have made it a prime source of food crops for the nation and indeed the world. Today, all the state allocations of Colorado River water have been claimed, and there is no real surplus for the Imperial Valley. In addition, the demand for water in fast-growing Southern California cities, most notably San Diego, is further pressuring farmers.

Such intensive use of Colorado River water is having grave environmental effects as well. The river's delta is drying up, affecting birds and other fragile animal and plant life; less and less water is reaching and replenishing the Sea of Cortez and its fisheries. The only good news is that awareness of the problem is growing, and solutions are being discussed by policymakers, scientists, and community groups.

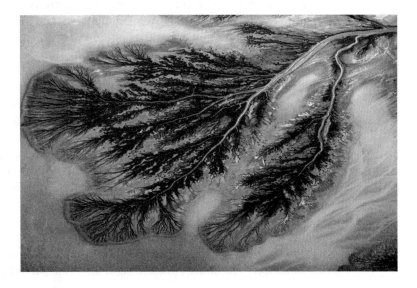

Is there a way for society to balance people's lives and livelihoods with the environment so that both may prosper?

has designated more than 106 million acres as "wilderness areas" through the National Wilderness Preservation System (2004). Under the Act, timber cutting, mechanized vehicles, mining, and grazing activities are restricted. Human activity is limited to primitive recreation activities. The wilderness lands are protected for their ecological, historical, scientific, and experiential resources. The areas range in size from the smallest, Pelican Island, Florida (five acres), to the largest, Wrangell-St. Elias, Alaska (almost 10 million acres of land).

The Endangered Species Act of 1973 attempts to preserve species of fish, wildlife, and plants that are of "aesthetic, ecological, educational, historical, recreational and scientific value to the Nation and its people." The Act has been controversial because it preserves the interests of the species above economic and human interests. For example, if endangered species are present, the Act will restrict what landowners can do on their land (Palmer 1997). Through the Act, 1,263 U.S. species (517 animals, 746 plants) have been listed as endangered or threatened, with recovery plans approved or implemented for 999 species (U.S. Fish and Wildlife Service 2003b). Thirty-four species have been removed from the list, with 14 of the species "recovered" and seven species listed as extinct (U.S. Fish and Wildlife Service 2003a). Although federal funding for the Endangered Species Act expired in October 1992, Congress has appropriated funds in each fiscal year to support the program.

The National Park System includes 384 areas covering more than 83 million acres. Unlike the National Wilderness Preservation System, the National Park System allows and supports recreational activities. However, human activity in the form of motorized access, road and highway developments, logging, and pollution threaten the health of several national parks. For 2003, the National Parks Conservation Association listed 10 parks on its most endangered list: Big Thicket National Preserve (Texas), Denali National Park and Preserve (Alaska), Everglades National Park (Florida), Glacier National Park (Montana), Great Smoky Mountains National Park (North Carolina and Tennessee), Joshua Tree National Park (California), Ocmulgee National Monument (Georgia), Shenandoah National Park (Virginia), Virgin Islands National Park, and Yellowstone National Park (Montana).

The Great Smoky Mountains National Park is the most visited national park, with about 10 million visitors each year (National Parks Conservation Association 2003). The park features an ecosystem of rare plants and wildlife along with historical structures representing southern Appalachian culture, all of which are endangered according to the National Parks Conservation Association. The park has been listed as "endangered" for several years due primarily to chronic air pollution problems. The pollution has been attributed to coal-fired power plants and other industrial sources. Local developers are allowed to build right up to the park's boundaries.

Environmental Policy, Advocacy, and Innovation

Federal Responses

The government's first response to the environment was directed at cleaning the nation's polluted water, air, and land. In 1969, Congress adopted the National

SCHOOL YARD ECOLOGY IN LATIN AMERICA

What kinds of plants grow in the corners and center of the school yard, and how many are there? If I asked this question about your college campus, would you know the answer? Thinking about my own campus, I don't think I could identify more than 10 trees or shrubs. And I don't think I could tell you how many there are in front of my own building.

With funding and organizational support from the Audubon Society, Peter Feinsinger, a tropical ecologist and conservation biologist, created the Schoolyard Ecology Education Initiative. Through the initiative, thousands of teachers in South America and the United States have been trained to incorporate the school yard ecology approach into their basic curriculum. Using the basic learning tenets of questioning, investigating, and reflecting (such as the opening questions), the program encourages teachers and students to use the physical world around them to understand the ecological process and how what they do affects the local environment. It is estimated that 25,000 students are involved in the program from Mexico to Argentina.

School lessons can be based on problems in the students' communities. In Bolivia's northern mountains, residents deal with land erosion, which has been attributed to road construction and to the slash–and-burn techniques farmers use to clear land. Alejandra Roldán, a local conservation biologist (quoted in Markels 2001), explained:

> The kids are naturally curious and concerned about things happening around them. When the mudslides hit the school last year they were very interested in understanding how and why this happened. So we put together a schoolyard-ecology lesson in which the kids went out and investigated the erosion problems. (P. 46)

School yard ecology programs in Bolivia and Peru have also been used with Audubon initiatives to save rare birds. Alejandro Grajal, director of the Latin America and Carribean Program for Audubon (quoted in Markels 2001:44), explains how children thought the puna flamingo was a common bird, since there were so many of them nested near their school. "They were surprised to find out they are actually endangered, and that most of them nest in that one lake," he said. While it may not persuade them to protect the birds, Grajal argues, "It's very hard to ask people to save the local ecosystem if they don't even understand the ecology of their surroundings." According to Grajal, the program "is a crucial step toward raising environmental consciousness in Latin America."

Environmental Policy Act (NEPA), a comprehensive policy statement on our environment. For the first time in our nation's history, the government was committed to maintaining and preserving the environment (Caldwell 1970). The EPA, established in 1970, is charged with providing leadership in the nation's environmental science, research, education, and assessment efforts (EPA 2004). As the chief environmental agency, the EPA sets national standards and delegates to states and tribes the responsibility for issuing permits and monitoring and enforcing compliance. Beginning in the 1980s, the agency shifted its policies from cleanup to pollution management or prevention through market-based and collaborative mechanisms with business and industry and environmental strategic planning (Mazmanian and Kraft 1999). Additional environmental legislation, some of which we have already reviewed, includes:

- The Land and Water Conservation Act and the Wilderness Act of 1964. In our discussion on land conservation, we already reviewed the Wilderness Act. The Land and Water Conservation Act provides the necessary funds and assistance to states in planning, acquiring, and developing recreational lands and natural areas. The Act also regulates admission and special user fees at national recreational areas. These two Acts have been referred to as the "initial building blocks of environmental action" (Caulfield 1989:31).
- The Clean Air Act of 1970 regulates air emissions from area, stationary, and mobile sources. The Act helped establish maximum pollutant standards. In 1990, the Clean Air Act was amended to address acid rain, ground-level ozone, ozone depletion, and air toxics. In 2003, seven state attorney generals filed a lawsuit against the EPA, accusing the agency of neglecting to update air pollution standards. The suit seeks regulations on carbon dioxide emissions, which are not listed under the Clean Air Act (Lee 2003).
- The Clean Water Act followed in 1977. This Act established standards and regulations regarding the discharge of pollutants into the waters of the United States. The EPA was authorized to implement pollution control programs, setting wastewater standards and water quality standards for all contaminants in surface waters.
- The Endangered Species Act of 1973 created a program for the conservation of threatened and endangered plants and animals and their habitats.
- Under the Toxic Substances Control Act of 1976, the EPA has the authority to track 75,000 industrial chemicals being produced or imported into the United States.
- The most recent law is the Food Quality Protection Act of 1996. The law modified earlier statutes creating a single health-based standard for all pesticides in all foods.

In its strategic plan for 2003 to 2008, the EPA identified five long-term goals: Achieve clean air, assure clean and safe water, preserve and restore the land, build healthy communities and ecosystems, and develop a compliance and environmental stewardship.

Over the life of its Superfund program, the EPA has assessed 44,418 sites for hazardous waste (EPA 2003c). In addition to cleanup and construction, the EPA has been awarded more than $16 billion in settlements from private and responsible parties. In cases where hazardous substances cannot be removed from a site, the EPA conducts five-year reviews to determine whether the hazards have been sufficiently contained for the protection of human health and the environment.

One such site is the Whitewood Creek Superfund Site in South Dakota (EPA 2003b). Since the 1870s, mining waste products have been deposited into the creek, which was used for irrigation, livestock watering, and residents' recreation. Area groundwater, surface water, and soils contained arsenic, known to increase the risk of skin cancer, neurological ailments, and vascular disease. In 1994, cleanup activities included the removal and replacement of 4,500 cubic yards of contaminated soil. Development is prohibited in certain areas near the creek, as is the construction of water wells. An educational program was developed to inform local residents about the EPA's actions. The EPA conducted its first five-year review of Whitewood Creek in 2002.

Environmental Interest Groups

Organizations concerned with the protection of the environment have played an important role in American politics since the foundation of the Sierra Club in 1892. The first wave of environmental interest groups included the National Audubon Society (1905), the National Parks and Conservation Association (1919), and the National Wildlife Federation (1935). These groups were concerned with land conservation and the protection of specific sites and wildlife species. These first-wave groups depended on member support and involvement. All these organizations remain among the most influential groups in the environmental movement (Ingram and Mann 1989).

As public attention shifted to the problems of environmental pollution, the second wave of environmental groups emerged during the 1960s and 1970s. These new organizations focused their efforts on fighting pollution. In general, the second wave of environmental groups adopted an ecological approach to our natural environment, recognizing the interrelationship between all living things and using science as a tool for understanding and protecting the environment. The Environmental Defense Fund (1967) and the Natural Resources Defense Council (1970) were started with funding support from the Ford Foundation. Both organizations relied on litigation as their instrument of reform. Other second-wave groups include Friends of the Earth, the Environmental Policy Institute, and Environmental Action. After the 1970s, environmental groups began to direct their appeals to policymakers rather than the general public (Ingram and Mann 1989).

Although each group is committed to the environment, each has adopted its own cause, from broad environmental themes to specific problems like toxic pollution or land conservation. The groups also have different strategies and tactics. Environmental groups may attempt to influence political policy, litigate environmental disputes, form coalitions with other environmental or interest groups, or endorse specific political candidates (Ingram and Mann 1989). Some, like the Sea Shepherd Society, which rams and sinks whaling vessels throughout the word's oceans, adopt "in your face" tactics.

Now almost 70 years old, the National Wildlife Federation has nine field offices and 46 state affiliates. The affiliates operate at the grassroots level by working to educate, encourage, and facilitate conservation efforts at the state level. One such organization is the Arkansas Wildlife Federation, established in 1936 by a group of sportsmen. The federation's goal has been to serve as a leader in educating people about conservation issues and in encouraging responsible stewardship of the state's natural resources. The federation, which represents a variety of constituents—hunters, sportsmen, hikers, anglers, and campers (Arkansas Wildlife Federation 2003a)—sponsors a variety of educational and community activities and projects. Seminars are offered to the public covering issues such as forest management, wet lands and water management, hunting, and fishing. The federation sponsors annual conservation achievement awards to honor citizens and organizations dedicated to natural resource endeavors. The organization also sponsors political candidate forums where citizens can ask candidates about their position on various conservation and environmental issues (Arkansas Wildlife Federation 2003b).

A new environmental interest group is the Earth Island Institute, founded in 1982 by David Brower, who was the first executive director of the Sierra Club and cofounder of Friends of the Earth. The institute supports more than 30 projects worldwide, pledging "to provide activists with the freedom to develop program ideas, supported by services to help them pursue those ideas, with a minimum of bureaucracy" (Earth Island Institute 2003). Among its many projects, the organization also honors youth for their environmental community work. For 2003, the Brower Youth Awards honored Illai Kenney (age 14) from Jonesboro, Georgia, and Thomas Nichols (age 14) from Corrales, New Mexico. Kenney co-founded Georgia Kids Against Pollution, a group that educates citizens and encourages them to work for clean air and water. Nichols created and implemented a program to preserve threatened cottonwood trees along the Rio Grande, using chicken wire to protect them from beavers. Before Nichols's innovative program, the policy was to kill the animals to save the trees.

❖ PUTTING IT TOGETHER:
On the Web.

Find out if there are local affiliates or programs sponsored by the National Wildlife Federation or Earth Island Institute in your area. (Log on to *Study Site Chapter 13*.) If not, what environmental interest groups are active in your community or state?

Radical Environmentalists

Rik Scarce (1990) explains that radical environmentalists wish to preserve our biological diversity. This isn't just a question of preserving the living things in our ecosystem, like plants and animals; nonliving entities such as mountains, rivers, and oceans must also be protected. Radical groups confront problems through direct action, such as picketing an office building, breaking the law, or performing acts of civil disobedience. Other radical environmentalists may destroy machinery, property, or equipment used to build roads, kill animals, or harvest trees. Most "eco-warriors" act on their own and without the leadership of an organizational hierarchy.

Radical environmentalists are poor by choice. Scarce (1990) says they adopt lifestyles that have minimal impact on the environment: not owning cars, adopting vegetarian diets, and avoiding occupations that involve the destruction of the environment. Although they are committed to their issues, radical environmentalists recognize that on their own, they will never be able to end the practices they protest. Their actions usually attract media attention, creating a groundswell of public support for their particular issue. Or their actions are done in concert with mainstream efforts; for example, radicals might stage tree sittings in Oregon to delay the cutting of timber until courts can hear a more mainstream group's request for injunction.

Tree sitting is a form of protest targeting timber companies at the point of production, slowing or even stopping tree cutting. Scarce (1990) explains how tree sitters make their protest in areas with active cutting, finding and choosing trees that will make the right statement. The trees they choose are the tallest, most impressive, and clearly visible from a road, or those that overlook a recently cut area. Although we may think of tree sitting as a lonely activity, tree sitters require a support group for assistance, food, and clothing, including the hauling of waste (including human) from the site. The group will carry about 250 pounds of gear and provisions—food, water, clothing, and platform materials—as far as 10 miles to their intended site. Suspended about 80 to 150 feet off the ground, the 2½ by 6-foot wooden platform becomes the tree sitter's home for days, weeks, or months. Julia "Butterfly" Hill sat in a 600–year-old California redwood tree for 738 days, withstanding eviction threats and legal action from the Pacific Lumber Company, which owned the tree. Tree sitting has been effective in bringing public and media attention to the practices of timber and logging companies and in rallying support for the tree sitter's message. In several cases, agreements have been made with lumber companies to divert logging to other areas or to pursue viable logging programs.

Enviro-Capitalists

Terry Anderson and Don Leal (1997) describe enviro-capitalists as entrepreneurs who use business tools to "preserve open space, develop wildlife habitat, save endangered species, and generally improve environmental quality" (p. 3). To meet the increasing demand for recreational and environmental amenities, enviro-capitalists are practicing a new kind of business. They use economic incentives and market-based approaches, such as buying an endangered species habitat or leasing water to increase in-stream flow, to save the habitat. Although enviro-capitalists have not solved global environmental problems, their entrepreneurial solutions to small local problems can provide a foundation for thinking innovatively about bigger problems (Anderson and Leal 1997).

Developer Peter O'Neill is an enviro-capitalist (Anderson and Leal 1997). His River Run residential development in Boise, Idaho, was the first development in the country to create a viable trout habitat in its waterways. O'Neill recognized the growing demand for and value of natural amenities in an urban setting. Working with the Idaho Department of Fish and Game, Timberline Reclamation, Inc., and other Idaho and federal agencies, O'Neill transformed an ugly flood control channel into a beautiful stream that could sustain trout. It took several years to complete the work, but by 1991, trout were thriving in the channel. In this 650-unit development, O'Neill included a seven-acre lake called Heron Lake and free-flowing streams. The Urban

Land Institute awarded O'Neill the Design Excellence Award for his River Run Development. Since completing River Run, O'Neill has worked on several other development projects, each featuring natural surroundings and enhanced habitat for fish and wildlife.

Other companies have adopted "green" or environmentally responsible and friendly technologies in their business practices. Colorado's New Belgium Brewing (NBB) Company may be better known for its signature "Fat Tire" beer, but the company has also been recognized as an environmental technology innovator. Included in NBB's statement of core beliefs and values is "environmental stewardship; minimizing resource consumption; maximizing energy efficiency and recycling" (NBB 2003). The company practices what it preaches. In 1998, company owners Jeff and Kim Lebesch and their employees agreed to transform their facility into the first wind-powered brewery in America. With their wind-powered technology, NBB eliminates about 1,800 metric tons of carbon dioxide emissions per year. Instead of relying on electricity for artificial lighting, light tubes provide natural lighting in the warehouse. The plant also uses low-energy fluorescent lighting and motion detectors to switch off lights when people leave rooms (NBB 2003). In 2000, the company recycled 96 tons of glass, 31 tons of cardboard, and 9 tons of shrink wrap (NBB 2003). The brewery also recycles its water resources (Colorado Sustainability Project 1998). For its efforts, the company has been awarded the Corporate Energy Management Award 1998 from the Rocky Mountain Chapter of the Association of Energy Engineers (Colorado Sustainability Project 1998), and in 1999, it was named Rocky Mountain Region Entrepreneur of the Year for Manufacturing (NBB 2003).

❖ PUTTING IT TOGETHER:
In your community.

Using the Web or your local phone book, identify two "green" companies in your community. Contact each company and determine what environmentally friendly practices they use.

Grassroots Movements

Sherry and Charles Cable (1995) argue that the grassroots environmental movement has improved the lives of many individuals and has spread environmental awareness among the public. In contrast with national environmental organizations, grassroots organizations usually consist of working-class participants, people of color, and women. Although some groups are led by experienced organizers or community activists, many grassroots groups are led by inexperienced but passionate leaders. In the fight against environmental racism, these grassroots environmental groups have given a voice to communities of color (Epstein 1995).

Cable and Cable (1995) suggest that the motivating factor for most grassroots organizations is a desire to protect the health and safety of families against some immediate environmental threat. Grassroots organizations emphasize environmental justice, acting in the belief that some injustice has been committed by a corporation, business, or industry and that appropriate action should be taken to correct, improve, or remove the injustice(s). These organizations not only have tackled toxic waste issues but have also sought justice on housing, transportation, air quality, and economic development issues (Bullard 1994).

Sociologists Riley Dunlap and Angela Mertig (1992) note that the environmental movement is among the few movements that "significantly changed society" (p. xi). Nicolas Freudenberg and Carol Steinsapir (1992:33–35) identify seven achievements of grassroots organizations.

1. A number of environmentally hazardous facilities have been controlled by cleaning up contaminated sites, blocking the construction of new facilities, and upgrading corporate pollution control equipment.

2. Grassroots organizations have forced businesses to consider the environmental consequences of their actions.

3. These groups encourage preventative approaches to environmental problems such as reducing or limiting the use of environmental contamination.

4. The grassroots movement has expanded citizens' rights to participate in environmental decision making.

5. Grassroots organizations have served as psychological and social support networks for victims and their families.

6. The movement has brought environmental concerns and action to working class and minority Americans.

7. The grassroots movement has influenced how the general public thinks about the environment and public health.

❖
Voices in the Community:
Concerned Citizens of South Central Los Angeles

When the Los Angeles City Council decided to build a 13-acre incinerator in a poor, residential African American and Mexican American community, no one considered the power of a group of local women. Organizing a group called Concerned Citizens of South Central Los Angeles, they opposed the construction of the LANCER (Los Angeles City Energy Recovery) project, a solid waste incinerator that would have burned 2,000 tons of municipal waste per day. At first, the women were not taken seriously, according to Charlotte Bullock, one of the community activists (quoted in Hamilton 1994):

I noticed when we first started fighting the issue how the men would laugh at the women . . . they would say, "Don't pay no attention to them, that's only one or two women . . . they won't make a difference." . . . But now, since we've been fighting for about a year, the smiles have gone. (P. 208)

The California Waste Management Board hired Cerrell Associates, a Los Angeles consulting firm, to determine the best place to locate the incinerator. The firm advised the Board to stay away from middle and higher socioeconomic strata neighborhoods because "members of middle or high socioeconomic [status] are more likely to organize into effective groups to express their political interests and views." (Hamilton 1994:211). Having followed this advice, you can imagine how surprised they were to face the Concerned Citizens of Los Angeles. The organizers had a high school education or less, were middle aged, elderly, and young, nonprofessionals and unemployed, and had low incomes. Writes Hamilton (1994), these were "women with no political experience, who had no history of organizing, [who] responded first as protectors of their children" (p. 211).

Hamilton (1994) reports that for some time, the women and their message were not taken seriously. The women just got tougher and less willing to compromise. Ms. Bullock (quoted in Hamilton) explains,

> In the 1950s, the city banned small incinerators in the yard, and yet they want to build a big incinerator. . . . The council is going to build something in my community which might kill my child. . . . I don't need a scientist to tell me that's wrong. (P. 212)

The organization was able to form alliances with a diverse set of international, national, and grassroots environmental groups: Greenpeace, Citizens for a Better Environment, the National Health Law Program, and the Center for Law in the Public Interest. For a year and half, the group operated without a formal leadership structure, rotating the chair's position at each meeting. When asked by the media for an official spokesperson, they replied that everyone could speak for the neighborhood.

The experience transformed the women and their family relationships. Meetings in individual homes involved children and spouses. Hamilton (1994) describes: "The transformation of relations continued as women spoke up at hearings and demonstrations and husbands transported children, made signs and looked on with pride and support at public forums" (p. 216).

Hamilton (1994) also described how the issue politically transformed the women:

> The coincidence of the principles of feminism and ecology found expression and development in the consciousness of participants; the concern for earth as home; a recognition that all parts of a system have equal value; the acknowledgment of process; and, finally, the awareness that capitalist growth has social costs. (P. 217)

Robin Cannon (quoted in Hamilton 1994), another activist mother, explains:

> This fight has really turned me around; things are intertwined in ways I hadn't realized. . . . All these social issues as well as political and economic issues are really intertwined. Before I was only concerned about health, and then I began to get into politics, decision making and so many things. (P. 212)

Concerned Citizens won their fight. Former Mayor Tom Bradley reversed his position on the project and asked the Los Angeles City Council to cancel the incinerator plan. They agreed to do so.

❖ ❖

❖

Voices in the Community:
Susan Bernstein

Many cities and their communities are returning to their green roots and restoring farming and gardening parcels in urban areas. These urban gardens promote sustainable food production and also enhance the environmental, economic, and social health of a community. The Salishan Family Garden project "grew" out of a vacant ball field in Tacoma, Washington. Based in the Salishan Public Housing Development, the one-acre garden began in May 1991, as part of a Head Start program idea to serve Cambodian refugee parents. (The word *Salishan* is a Native American word meaning "people of many colors coming together.")

Program developers hoped that the garden would serve as a bridge between the refugees and their newly adopted city and as a way to reduce isolation among recent immigrants. In addition, the garden would give refugee adults an opportunity to grow food and work with the land as they did at home. During the first year, there were 12 garden plots. More than 10 years later, the garden has transformed into a lush productive urban farm with 60 garden plots and 200 farmers.

Community support has been invaluable since the beginning of the program. The gardens began with the support of the City of Tacoma's Metro Parks Agency (which allows use of the land), Tacoma Housing Authority (which pays for water expenses), and Pierce County/Washington State University Cooperative Extension Program (which provided leadership in the early years of the garden). Recently, the garden has become an independent operation, with Susan Bernstein serving as volunteer director.

According to Bernstein, who was interviewed for this book, the program currently serves Cambodian, Vietnamese, Russian, and Ukrainian families. Bernstein's nine-year-old "garden helper" is the grandson of a Ukrainian couple who have been farming for several years. Bernstein explains that their son and daughter have their own garden plots, and as part of their Ukrainian culture, their grandchildren are encouraged to garden alongside the adults. "One of the best benefits of the garden," explains Bernstein, "is the cross cultural and intergenerational interaction."

For the gardeners and their families, the garden provides fresh produce, helps extend their summer budgets, and allows them to grow food that they cannot find in local grocery stores. Farmers grow a variety of produce: corn, green beans, tomatoes, beets, cilantro, assorted basil, and Southeast Asian herbs, some started with seeds brought from their homelands. In addition, the ability to connect with others seems to be an important benefit for farmers; the garden has become a vital gathering place. According to Bernstein,

> One gardener told me she loves the garden because during the winter months she doesn't see her friends. During the winter, people from the community are busy working or staying indoors. But during the garden season she is able to reconnect and spend time with her friends in the garden.

When asked how she knows if the program works, Bernstein replies,

I can tell by the smiles on their faces and also by how it has affected the entire neighborhood. It's become a center for recreation and for social life. . . . Over the years, it has been a place where newcomers to America and American urban dwellers have connected with nature and their neighbors through the (literal) common ground of gardening.

The gardeners regularly contribute their time and produce to local food banks, even contributing money when they can.

Similar urban garden programs are based in Chicago, Illinois, Rochester, New York, Kansas City, Kansas, and Virginia Beach, Virginia. To find more about community gardening or gardens sponsored in your own community, go to *Study Site Chapter 13*.

MAIN POINTS

- Daily human activity, economic development, cultural values, social class, and technology all affect the health of the environment. **Environmental sociology** considers the interactions between our physical and natural environments and our social organization and behavior.

- Functionalists believe that environmental problems develop from the system itself. Thus, although agriculture, industrialization, and related technologies have improved quality of life, they have also led to waste, pollution, and the destruction of natural resources. Functionalists believe that the only way to address environmental problems is to simultaneously halt population growth and reduce technology's impact.

- Conflict theorists believe that environmental problems are created by humans competing for power, income, and their own interests in a capitalist system. Those with the least amount of power are targeted in **environmental racism**, in which marginalized groups are disadvantaged. Research indicates that low-income people and people of color are exposed to greater environmental risks than White or affluent people.

- Feminists argue that a masculine worldview is responsible for the domination of nature, women, and minorities. One strand of

thought, ecofeminism, believes that men are the primary culprits in the exploitation of animals and the environment. Other feminist approaches include feminist critiques of natural science, analyses of specific environmental issues, and contributions to sustainable development.

- Interaction theorists believe that environmental problems do not materialize by themselves. Social constructionists focus on the political process affecting the environment rather than on the problems themselves.

- Environmental problems include air pollution, hazardous waste sites, brownfields (abandoned or underused commercial properties with hazardous substances), and polluted and toxic water.

- Because of pollution, increasing urbanization, and sprawling development, we may be running out of water. Human efforts to conserve water, such as building dams, are now recognized as causes of serious and negative environmental problems.

- Efforts in land conservation and wilderness protection seem to be successful largely due to federal protection policies and legislation. Examples, among many, are the Wilderness Act, the Endangered Species Act, and the formation of the Environmental Protection Agency (EPA).

- Established in 1970 as the chief environmental agency, the EPA provides leadership in the nation's environmental science, research, education, and assessment efforts. It sets national standards and delegates certain functions of enforcement to states. The EPA's five long-term goals through 2008 are to achieve clean air, assure clean and safe water, preserve and restore the land, build healthy communities and ecosystems, and develop a compliance and environmental stewardship.

- Environmental organizations have played an important role in American politics since the foundation of the Sierra Club in 1892. Groups include the National Audubon Society and the National Wildlife Federation. These first-wave groups are concerned with land conservation and the protection of specific sites and species, and they rely on member support and involvement.

- A second wave of environmental groups, such as the Environmental Defense Fund and the Natural Resources Defense Council, focus on fighting pollution and emerged during the 1960s and 1970s. They adopt an ecological approach, recognizing the interrelationship between all living things and using science as a tool for understanding and protecting the environment. After the 1970s, environmental groups began to direct their appeals to policymakers rather than the general public.

- Each environmental group has its own cause and strategies. Groups may attempt to influence political policy, litigate disputes, form coalitions with other environmental or interest groups, endorse specific political candidates, or even adopt more radical tactics.

- Radical groups confront problems through direct action, such as breaking the law, destroying property or equipment, or performing acts of civil disobedience. Most "eco-warriors" act on their own and without the leadership of an organizational hierarchy. They recognize that they cannot effect change on their own, but their actions usually draw media attention and thus engender public support. They also work with mainstream groups.

- Enviro-capitalists use economic incentives and market-based approaches to save the habitat.

- Grassroots organizations usually consist of inexperienced but passionate working-class participants, people of color, and women. These groups are motivated by a desire to protect the health and safety of families against some immediate environmental threat. Grassroots organizations emphasize environmental justice.

- The environmental movement has had a significant impact in controlling hazardous facilities, urging businesses to consider environmental impact, encouraging preventative approaches to problems, expanding citizens' rights to participate in decision making, serving as psychological and social support networks for victims and their families, bringing concerns and action to working class and minority Americans, and influencing how the general public thinks about the environment and public health.

INTERNET AND COMMUNITY EXERCISES

1. Access "Envirofacts," a one-stop source for environmental information about your community sponsored by the EPA. Go to *Study Site Chapter 13*. You can use the "Quick Start" on the page and type your area's zipcode, city, county, or state. Or you can select a topic—water, waste, toxics, air, or radiation—to find out if any local emissions, sites, violations, or companies are being monitored by the EPA. Based on the information provided, how would you rate the environmental quality of your community? Of your state?

2. What school programs similar to the Latin American program targeting school-age children exist in your community? Investigate elementary or secondary schools in your area. Ask whether local schools sponsor recycling or environmental student clubs or initiatives. Examine whether these programs have been effective. Each year, the EPA honors K–12 students who develop programs to protect their communities and to address local environmental concerns with the President's Environmental Youth Awards. For more information, go to *Study Site Chapter 13*.

3. Invite a faculty member from the Biology or Natural Sciences Department to talk about the ecosystem of your college campus. How does your campus impact its environmental habitat? How much waste is produced on campus? Does your campus have a recycling program? What environmentally friendly practices are supported on campus?

4. Community sustainable agriculture (CSA) is a partnership between community members and an independent local farm. The CSA movement began in Japan almost 30 years ago with a group of women who were concerned about pesticides, the increase in processed foods, and their country's shrinking rural population. Community members purchase seasonal shares, for about $300 to $400, which entitles them to weekly food allowances throughout the growing season. It is estimated that there are more than 1,200 CSA groups in the United States, some serving more than 1,000 families (Roosevelt 2003). According to FoodRoutes.org, independent local farms encourage biodiversity by diversifying the local landscape and natural environment. The CSA arrangement is beneficial to the farmer and to her customers. Customers receive fresh produce and have the satisfaction of supporting a local business. Customers can help out at the farm and provide input and suggestions to their farmer. Instead of spending time marketing produce, farmers can focus their efforts on growing quality produce and working with their community members. Go to *Study Site Chapter 13* and follow the links to search for a CSA in your community. If one exists in your community, contact the farmer and ask for more information about the CSA program.

On your own. Log on to *Study Site—Community and Policy Guide* for more information about the social problems, social policies, and community responses discussed in this chapter.

Note

1. After a second experiment during 1993–1994, no other human experiments were conducted. In 1996, Columbia University took over the management of the Biosphere and was using the facility as a research and education center. In 2003, Columbia University announced that it would end its relationship with Biosphere II.

References

American Petroleum Institute. 2004. "Energy Policy." Retrieved July 4, 2004 (http://api-ep.org/issues/).

American Rivers. 2002. "63 Dams in 16 States to Be Removed in 2002." Retrieved August 16, 2003 (www.amrivers.org/pressrelease/damremova1071802.htm).

"American Waters: A Resource in Peril." 2003. *Outside* 28(8):59–62.

Anderson, T. and D. Leal. 1997. *Enviro-Capitalists: Doing Good While Doing Well.* Lanham, MD: Rowman and Littlefield.

Archibold, R. 2000. "The Specter of Cancer Haunts a High School." *The New York Times,* December 27, p. A18.

Arkansas Wildlife Federation. 2003a. "About the Arkansas Wildlife Federation." Retrieved June 20, 2003 (www.arkansaswildlifefederation.org/about/html).

Arkansas Wildlife Federation. 2003b. "Educational Projects." Retrieved June 20, 2003 (www.arkansaswildlife federation.org/education.html).

Babbitt, B. 1998. Speech to the Ecological Society of America, August 4, 1998. Retrieved August 16, 2003 (www.hetchhetchy.org/babbitt_on_dams_9_4–98.html).

Barcott, B. 2003. "What's a River for?" *Mother Jones* 28(3):44–51.

Bragg, R. 2003. "Toxic Water Numbers Days of a Trailer Park." *The New York Times,* May 5, pp. A1, A18.

Breton, M. J. 1998. *Women Pioneers for the Environment.* Boston, MA: Northeastern University Press.

Bryce, R. 2000. "It's the Planet, Stupid." Retrieved June 20, 2003 (www.austinchronicle.com/issues/dispatch/2000–10–27/pols_feature.html).

Bullard, R. 1994. *Dumping in Dixie: Race, Class, and Environmental Quality.* Boulder, CO: Westview Press.

Cable, Sherry and Charles Cable. 1995. *Environmental Problems, Grassroots Solutions: The Politics of Grassroots Environmental Conflict.* New York: St. Martin's Press.

Caldwell, L. 1970. *Environment: Challenge to Modern Society.* Garden City, NY: Natural History Press.

———. 1997. "Environment as a Problem for Policy." P. 118 in *Environmental Policy: Transnational Issues and National Trends,* edited by L. Caldwell and R. Bartlett. Westport, CT: Quorum Books.

Caulfield, H. 1989. "The Conservation and Environmental Movements: A Historical Analysis." Pp. 13–56 in *Environmental Politics and Policy,* edited by J. Lester. Durham, NC: Duke University Press.

Center for Health, Environment, and Justice. 2001. *Poisoned Schools: Invisible Threats, Visible Actions.* Fall Church, VA: Child Proofing Our Communities Campaign.

Clean Air Network. 2003. *Danger in the Air: Unhealthy Levels of Smog in 2002.* Washington, DC: U.S. Public Interest Research Group Education Fund.

CNN. 2001. "Bush to Unveil Global Warming Plan." Retrieved June 25, 2003 (www.cnn.com/2001/ALLPOLITICS/06/01/bush.global.warming).

Cole, L. and S. Foster. 2001. *From the Ground Up: Environmental Racism and the Rise of the Environmental Justice Movement.* New York: New York University Press.

Colorado Sustainability Project. 1998. "New Belgium Brewing Company Focuses on Efficiency." Retrieved June 25, 2003 (www.sustainablecolorado.org/Best_Practices/New_Belgium/).

Davies, J. C. 1970. *The Politics of Pollution.* New York: Pegasus.

Dunlap, R. 1997. "The Evolution of Environmental Sociology: A Brief History and Assessment of the American Experience." Pp. 21–39 in *The International Handbook of Environmental Sociology,* edited by M. R. Redclift and G. Woodgate. Cheltenham, UK: Edward Elgar.

Dunlap, R. and W. Catton. 1994. "Struggling with Human Exemptionalism: The Rise, Decline, and Revitalization of Environmental Sociology." *The American Sociologist* 25(1):5–30.

Dunlap, Riley and Angela Mertig. 1992. *American Environmentalism: The U.S. Environmental Movement, 1970–1990.* Washington, DC: Taylor & Francis.

Earth Island Institute. 2003. "About EII: Origins and Purpose." Retrieved July 27, 2003 (www.earthisland.org/abouteii/abouteii.html).

Ehrlich, Paul and Anne Ehrlich. 1990. *The Population Explosion.* New York: Touchstone/Simon & Schuster.

———. 1996. *Betrayal of Science and Reason: How Anti-Environmental Rhetoric Threatens Our Future.* Washington, DC: Island Press.

Ehrlich, Paul, Anne Ehrlich, and John Holdren. 1973. *Human Ecology: Problems and Solutions.* San Francisco: W. H. Freeman.

Eisele, K. 2003. "With Every Breath You Take." Retrieved March 2, 3003 (www.nrdc.org/onearth/03win/asthma1.asp).

Environmental Protection Agency (EPA). 1999a. *Smog—Who Does It Hurt? What You Need to Know about Ozone and Your Health* (EPA-452/K-99–001). Washington, DC: Author.

———. 1999b. "Water on Tap: A Consumer's Guide to the Nation's Drinking Water." Retrieved June 27, 2003 (www.epa.gov/safewater/wot/introtap.html).

———. 2003a. "EPA Announces $73.1 Million in National Brownfields Grants in 37 States and Seven Tribal Communities." Retrieved August 26, 2003 (www.epa.gov/brownfields/news/pr062003.htm).

———. 2003b. "Region 8—Whitewood Creek." Retrieved June 22, 2003 (www.epa.gov/region8/superfund/sites/sd/witwdck.html).

———. 2003c. "Superfund Accomplishment Figures, Summary Fiscal year (FY) (2003)." Retrieved June 22, 2003 (www.epa.gov/superfund/action/process/numbers.htm).

———. 2004. "About EPA." Retrieved June 28, 2004 (www.epa.gov/epahome/aboutepa.htm).

Epstein, B. 1995. "Grassroots Environmentalism and Strategies for Social Change." *New Political Science* 32(Summer):1–24.

Freudenberg, N. and C. Steinsapir. 1992. "Not in Our Backyard: The Grassroots Environmental Movement." Pp. 27–35 in *American Environmentalism: The U.S. Environmental Movement, 1970–1990,* edited by R. Dunlap and A. Mertig. Washington, DC: Taylor & Francis.

Hamilton, C. 1994. "Concerned Citizens of South Central L.A." Pp. 207–219 in *Unequal Protection,* edited by Robert Bullard. San Francisco: Sierra Club Books.

Hannigan, J. 1995. *Environmental Sociology: A Social Constructionist Perspective.* London and New York: Routledge.

Hawken, P. 1993. *The Ecology of Commerce: A Declaration of Sustainability.* New York: Harper Collins.

———. 1997. "Natural Capitalism." *Mother Jones* 22(2):40–58.

Heilprin, J. 2003. "Bush Take on Global Warming Due Today." *The News Tribune* July 24, p. A9.

Ingram, H. and D. Mann. 1989. "Interest Groups and Environmental Policy." Pp. 135–157 in *Environmental Politics and Policy,* edited by J. Lester. Durham, NC: Duke University Press.

Irwin, A. 2001. *Sociology and the Environment.* Cambridge, U.K.: Polity Press.

Korten, David. 1995. *When Corporations Rule the World.* West Hartford, CT: Kumarian Press.

Kraft, M. and N. Vig. 2000. "Environmental Policy from the 1970s to 2000: An Overview." Pp. 1–31 in *Environmental Policy,* edited by N. Vig and M. Kraft. Washington, DC: Congressional Quarterly Press.

Lee, J. 2003. "7 States to Sue EPA over Standards on Air Pollution." *The New York Times,* February 21, p. A24.

Littig, B. 2001. *Feminist Perspectives on Environment and Society.* Harlow, UK: Prentice Education Limited.

Markels, Alex. 2001. "The Sky's the Limit." *Audubon* 103(6):40–46.

Mazmanian, D. and M. Kraft. 1999. "The Three Epochs of the Environmental Movement." Pp. 3–42 in *Toward Sustainable Communities: Transition and Transformations in Environmental Policy,* edited by D. Mazmanian and M. Kraft. Cambridge, MA: MIT Press.

McCright, A. and R. Dunlap. 2000. "Challenging Global Warming as a Social Problem: An Analysis of the Conservative Movement's Counter-Claims." *Social Problems* 47(4):499–522.

National Parks Conservation Association. 2003. "Ten Most Endangered." Retrieved June 27, 2003 (www.npca .org/across_the_nation/ten_most_endangered/).

National Wilderness Preservation System. 2004. "Fast Facts." Retrieved June 28, 2004 (www.wilderness.net/index .cfm?fuse=NWPS&sec=fastFacts).

Naples, N. 1998. *Grassroots Warriors: Activist Mothering, Community Work, and the War on Poverty.* New York: Routledge.

New Belgium Brewing Company. 2003. "Our Story" and "The Vibe." Retrieved June 25, 2003 (www.newbelgium .com/).

Newman, R. 2001. "Making Environmental Politics: Women and Love Canal Activism." *Women's Studies Quarterly* 1–2:65–84.

NewsMax.com. 2001. "Bush Defends Rejection of Kyoto Treaty." Retrieved June 25, 2003 (www.newsmax.com/ archives/articles/2001/3/29/164418.shtml).

Norris, M. 2001. "Poisoned Schools? Schools near Toxic Waste Sites Are Making Children Sick." Retrieved March 2, 2003 (www.abcnews.go.com/sections/wnt/WorldNewsTonight/wnt010319_sickschools_feature)

Palmer, C. 1997. *Environmental Ethics.* Santa Barbara, CA: ABC-CLIO.

Pianin, E. and G. Gugliotta. 2003. "White House Backing Off Key Environmental Promise." *The News Tribune,* June 30, p. A8.

Revkin, A. 2003. "U.S. Is Urged to Overhaul Its Approach to Protecting Oceans." *The New York Times,* June 5, p. A32.

———. 2004. "U.S. Report, in Shift, Turns Focus to Greenhouse Gases." *The New York Times,* August 6, p. A16.

Revkin, A. and K. Seelye. 2003. "White House Cuts Data on Warming in an E.P.A. Report: Some at Agency Protest." *The New York Times,* June 19, pp. A1, A21.

Ringquist, E. J. 2000. "Environmental Justice: Normative Concerns and Empirical Evidence." Pp. 232–256 in *Environmental Policy,* edited by N. Vig and M. Kraft. Washington, DC: Congressional Quarterly Press.

Roosevelt, M. 2003. "Fresh off the Farm." *Time,* November 3, pp. 60–61.

Scarce, Rik. 1990. *Eco-Warriors: Understanding the Radical Environmental Movement.* Chicago: Noble Press.

Seelye, K. 2002. "Study Sees 6,000 Deaths from Power Plants." *The New York Times,* April 18, p. A19.

———. 2003. "Clean Air Rules Eased for Plants, Utilities." *The News Tribune,* August 28, p. A3.

Stenger, R. 2002. "9/11 Study: Air Traffic Affects Climate." Retrieved March 2, 2003 (www.cnn.com/2002/tech/ science/08/07/contrails.climate/).

Symmes, P. 2003. "River Impossible." *Outside* 28(8):64–68, 108–111.

Tobin, R. 2000. "Environment, Population, and the Developing World." Pp. 326–349 in *Environmental Policy,* edited by N. Vig and M. Kraft. Washington, DC: Congressional Quarterly Press.

Travis, D., A. Carleton, and R. Lauritsen. 2002. "Contrails Reduce Daily Temperature Range." *Nature,* 418 (August 8):601.

Union of Concerned Scientists. 2004. "Global Environment." Retrieved June 28, 2004 (www.ucsuca.org/global_environment/archive/page.cfm?pageID=548#3).

U.S. Census Bureau. 2004a. "Total Midyear Population for the World: 1950–2050." Retrieved July 4, 2004 (www.census.gov/ipc/www/worldpop.html).

———. 2004b. "U.S. Interim Projections by Age, Sex, Race, and Hispanic Origin." Retrieved July 4, 2004 (www.census.gov/ipc/www/usinterimproj/).

U.S. Fish and Wildlife Service. 2003a. "Delisted Species Report as of 07/01/2003." Retrieved July 1, 2003 (http://ecos.fws.gov/tess_public/TESSSWebPageDeslisted?listings=0).

———. 2003b. "Threatened and Endangered Species System." Retrieved July 1, 2003 (http://ecos.fws.gov/tess_public/html/boxscore.html).

Venetoulis, J., D. Chazan, and C. Gaudet. 2004. *Ecological Footprint of Nations, 2004.* Washington, DC: Redefining Progress.

Wald, M. 2003. "One Vehicle on the Road, Two Others in the Garage." *The New York Times,* August 30, p. B2.

Weiss, K. 2003. "Life in U.S. Ocean Waters in Death Spiral, Study Says." *The News Tribune,* June 5, p. A3.

Wenz, P. 2001. *Environmental Ethics Today.* New York: Oxford University Press.

14

War and Terrorism

R esponding to the August 1998 U.S. embassy bombings in Nairobi, Kenya, and Tanzania, President Bill Clinton (1998) warned the General Assembly of the United Nations about the unending dangers of terrorism:

> We still are bedeviled by ethnic, racial, religious and tribal hatreds; by the spread of weapons of mass destruction; by the almost frantic effort of too many states to acquire such weapons; and despite all efforts to contain it, terrorism is not fading away at the end of the 20th century.

According to Clinton (1998), the problem of terrorism was not just an American problem: "It is a clear and present danger to tolerant and open societies and innocent people everywhere," he said. Later that year, a U.S. federal court indicted Osama bin Laden and Muhhamed Atef for the embassy bombings and for conspiring to kill Americans outside of the United States. It was not the last time we would hear of bin Laden's terrorist acts.

The secure life many Americans took for granted changed on the morning of September 11, 2001 (Hoge and Rose 2001). For the first time since the attack on Pearl Harbor in 1941, U.S. citizens were under attack on our nation's soil (although some historians and social commentators refer further back to the War of 1812, noting that the Pearl Harbor attack should not count since Hawaii was not a state at the time.) In New York City, 2,752 were killed at the World Trade Center; at the Pentagon, 189 were killed; and in Pennsylvania, 44 were killed when their hijacked plane crashed into an open field.

In his address before the nation that evening, President George W. Bush (2001) stated, "Today, our fellow citizens, our way of life, our very freedom came under attack in a series of deliberate and deadly terrorist acts." The Bush Administration vowed to bring those responsible to justice. The events of September 11th brought home the need for the cooperation and support of U.S. allies (Booth and Dunne 2002; Hoge and Rose 2001). According to Britain's Prime Minister Tony Blair (2001):

Around the world, 11 September is bringing governments and people to reflect, consider, and change. . . . There is a coming together. The power of the community is asserting itself. We are realizing how fragile our frontiers are in the face of the world's new challenges.

Defining Terrorism and War

Terrorism

According to the FBI, terrorism is "the unlawful use of force or violence against persons or property to intimidate or coerce a government, the civilian population, or any segment thereof, in furtherance of political or social objectives" (28 C.F.R. Section 0.85). **Domestic terrorism** is defined as terrorism supported or coordinated by groups or individuals based in the United States. **Foreign or international terrorism** is defined as terrorism supported or coordinated by foreign groups threatening the security of U.S. nationals or the national security of the United States. International terrorism can occur outside of the United States, but it must be directed at U.S. targets. The secretary of state authorizes a list of foreign terrorist organizations in consultation with the attorney general and secretary of the Treasury. The first list of 30 groups was designated by Secretary of State Madeline Albright in 1997. The 2003 list certified by her successor, Colin Powell, includes 37 known groups (see Table 14.1). Acts of terrorism have occurred on every continent, and perpetrators come from diverse religious and ethnic groups; however, Islamic governments and networks have committed the most extreme acts of terror (Booth and Dunne 2002).

Pillar (2001) explains that there are five elements of terrorism. First, terrorism is a premeditated act. It requires intent and prior decision to commit an act of terrorism. Terrorism doesn't happen by accident; rather, it is the result of an individual's or group's policy or decision. Second, terrorism is purposeful; it is political in its motive to change or challenge the status quo. Religiously oriented or national terrorists are driven by social forces or shaped by circumstances specific to their particular religious or nationalistic experiences (Reich 1998). Third, terrorism is not like a war, in which both sides can shoot at one another. Terrorism targets noncombatants, those who cannot defend themselves against the violence. The direct targets of terrorist activity are not the main targets. Fourth, terrorism is usually carried out by subnational groups or clandestine agents. If uniformed military soldiers attack a group, it is considered an act of war; an attack conducted by nongovernmental perpetrators is considered terrorism. Individuals acting alone may also commit terrorism. Finally, terrorism includes the threat of violence. It does not involve only terrorist acts that may have occurred; it also involves the potential for future attacks.

Terrorist activity has changed little over the years. Six basic tactics account for 95 percent of all incidents: bombings, assassinations, armed assaults, kidnappings, hijackings, and other kinds of hostage seizures. As Brian Jenkins (1988) explains, "Terrorists blow up things, kill people, or seize hostages. Every terrorist attack is merely a variation on these three activities" (p. 257).

❖ Table 14.1 Designated Foreign Terrorist Organizations (as of January 30, 2003)

1. Abu Nidal Organization (ANO)
2. Abu Sayyaf Group
3. Al-Aqsa Martyrs Brigade
4. Ansa al-Islam
5. Armed Islamic Group
6. Asbat al-Ansar
7. Aum Shinrikyo
8. Basque Fatherland and Liberty
9. Communist Party of the Phillippines/New People's Army
10. Gama'a al-Islamiyya
11. HAMAS
12. Harakut ul-Mujahidin
13. Hizballah
14. Islamic Movement of Uzbekistan
15. Jaish-e-Mohammed
16. Jemaah Islamiya Organization
17. al-Jihad
18. Kahane Cahi
19. Kurdish Workers' Party
20. Lashkar-e Tayyiba
21. Laskar I Jhangvi
22. Liberation Tigers of Tamil Eelam
23. Mujahedin-e Kalq Organization
24. National Liberation Army
25. Palestinian Islamic Jihad
26. Palestinian Liberation Front
27. Popular Front for the Liberation of Palestine
28. PFLP-General Command
29. al-'Qai'da
30. Real IRA
31. Revolutionary Armed Forces of Colombia
32. Revolutionary Nuclei
33. Revolutionary Organization 17 November
34. Revolutionary People's Liberation Army/Front
35. Salafist Group for Call and Combat
36. Shining Path
37. United Self-Defense Forces of Colombia

Source: U.S. Department of State 2004.

❖ PUTTING IT TOGETHER:
In your community.

Which tactic do you think is most effective? Is fear of potential attack sufficient to produce political or social results? Why or why not?

A Brief History of U.S. Conflicts

War is a violent political instrument (Walter 1964). It is a legitimate violent activity between armed combatants, one side hoping to impose its will on the other. Our nation's birth was marked by a war, the American Revolution of 1775–1783. In 1776, the Declaration of Independence was adopted, a public statement of a new nation's independence from Great Britain and its rights to "life, liberty, and the pursuit of happiness." The British were defeated in 1783. It is estimated that more than 4,000 lives were lost in the Revolution against the British.

The American Revolution was followed by the War of 1812 (1812–1815) and the Mexican War (1846–1848), both part of the economic and continental expansion of the United States. The effort was justified under the principle of manifest destiny. U.S. leaders felt it was their mission to extend freedom and democracy to others. At the end of the war, the United States acquired the northern part of Mexico, later dividing the area into Arizona, California, Nevada, New Mexico, and Utah.

The Civil War (1861–1865) between northern and southern states has been referred to as the bloodiest battle on U.S. soil. Although we tend to think that the war was waged solely over the issue of slavery, it was also based on deep economic, political, and social differences between the two groups of states. During his second inaugural address in 1865, President Abraham Lincoln said, "One of them would make war rather than let the nation survive, and the other would accept war rather than let it perish, and the war came." It is estimated that more than 600,000 died.

Beginning with the Spanish American War (1898), U.S. troops and soldiers began to wage war in other countries, mostly responding to tyranny, oppression, and communism. The Spanish American War was fought to liberate Cuba from Spain and to protect U.S. interests in Cuban sugar, tobacco, and iron industries. U.S. participation during World War I (1914–1918) and World War II (1939–1945) helped establish its dominance as a worldwide military force. That accomplishment, however, came with great cost: the United States had heavy losses, 53,000 deaths in World War I and 400,000 deaths in World War II. In the latter war, the United States and its allies claimed victory against Germany, Japan, and Italy. After the North Korean People's Army invaded the Republic of Korea, the United States joined United Nations forces in the Korean War (1950–1953). No winner of the war has ever been declared. An armistice was agreed upon in 1953, forever separating North and South Korea. Fifty years after the invasion, Communist and UN soldiers still guard their sides of the demilitarized zone in Panmunjom. The United States fought against North Vietnamese communists in the jungles of South Vietnam from 1961 to 1973. Although U.S. troops had begun withdrawing from Vietnam in 1969, the formal ceasefire was declared in January 1973.

Our engagement in Middle East wars began with the Persian Gulf War of 1990–1991. The United States was joined by U.N. forces to liberate Kuwait from Iraqi forces. Operations Desert Shield and Desert Storm were the first display of high tech warfare: cruise missiles, stealth fighters, and precision guided munitions (it was also the first time that the Pentagon began to name our wars.). Iraq accepted the terms for the cease fire in April 1991. After September 11, 2001, U.S. forces attacked Afghanistan in an effort to destroy al-Qaeda forces and to locate their leader, Osama bin Laden. The first war of the 21st century was the U.S. war against Iraq (2003–) or Operation Iraqi Freedom. On May 1, 2003, President George W. Bush declared that the period of major combat was over. At this writing, U.S. troops still occupy Iraq. A listing of U.S. wars and casualties is presented in Table 14.2.

❖ Table 14.2   America's Wars and Casualties

War	Participants	Deaths in Service
American Revolution 1775–1784	Unknown	4,435
War of 1812 1812–1815	286,730	2,260
Mexican War 1846–1848	78,718	13,283
Civil War, Union Only	2,213,363	364,511
Spanish-American War 1898–1902	306,760	2,446
World War I 1917–1918	4,734,991	116,516
World War II 1940–1946	16,112,566	405,399
Korean War 1950–1953	5,720,000	36,576
Vietnam Era 1964–1973	8,744,000	58,200
Persian Gulf War 1990–1991	2,225,000	392

Source: U.S. Department of Defense 2003b.

Sociological Perspectives on Terrorism and War

Functionalist Perspective

Functionalists examine how war and terrorism help maintain the social order, serving to create and reinforce social, religious, or national boundaries. War creates social stability by letting everyone know what side they are on: the good guys versus the bad guys or us versus them. There are norms and boundaries in war: Individuals will know what their roles are, what they should believe in, how they should respond in case of an attack, and how they should interact with members of the other side. But unlike war, the social boundaries in terrorist activities are less certain. In some cases, the identity of terrorists and their goals may never be known.

Second, war and terrorism provide a "safety valve" function, giving marginalized or oppressed groups a means to express their discontent or anger. Acts of terrorism, according to Crenshaw (1990), are selected as a course of action from a range of alternatives. Groups may choose terrorism because the other methods may be expected not to work or may be too time consuming for the group. Radical groups choose terrorism when they want immediate action and when they want their message to be heard. As they act, they also spread their group's message and recruit others for their cause.

Third, warfare serves to establish power and domination. It assumes that the victor is able to acquire the "spoils of war"—a country's land, people, and resources. Beyond those tangible fruits of victory, the winning side also gets to make new rules or impose its rules about appropriate political, social, and economic structures.

Conflict and Feminist Perspectives

War and terrorism are forms of conflict. Conflict may be based on disputes over resources or land. Modern conflict theorists have focused on how war is used to promote economic and political interests. In 1961, Dwight D. Eisenhower cautioned the nation about the **military-industrial complex**, the growing collaboration of the government, the military, and the armament industry. Years earlier, Eisenhower (1953) warned:

> Every gun that is made, every warship launched, every rocket fired, signifies in the final sense a theft of those who hunger and are not fed, those who are cold and are not clothed. The world in arms is not spending money alone. It is spending the sweat of its laborers, the genius of its scientists, the hopes of its children.

He explained that the complex had a corrupting influence—economic, political, and spiritual—in every city, state, and federal office of government. A decision to go to war could be motivated not to preserve or promote freedom or to fight for what is right, but to ensure the economic well-being of the defense contractor.

Although the United States now has a smaller army and is using technologies that are less human-intensive, military expenditures have been increasing, and with those increases comes the greater likelihood of waste, inefficiency, and "good old fashioned pork," according to opponents (Knickerbocker 2002). For fiscal year 2004, the U.S. Department of Defense (2003a) requested a $379.9 billion budget, $15.3 billion above the previous year. As it released the 2004 budget figures, the Department explained that the budget would provide strong support for winning the global war on terrorism, sustaining high-quality people and forces, and transforming the U.S. military and defense establishment. Although some believe that these additional defense expenses are necessary to win the war on terrorism, others have been critical of the escalation in military expenditures. They also point out that although the amount of direct funding going to weapons development and construction has increased, the salaries of soldiers have not (refer to Chapter 9 for a discussion on poverty among military families).

From the feminist perspective, "war is a patriarchal tool always used by men to create new structures of dominance and to subjugate a large mass of people" ("The Events" 2002:96). War is considered a primarily male activity that enhances the position of males in society. In our military system, decision making and economic power are held primarily by men; as a result, international relations and politics are played out on women's bodies (Cuomo 1996). According to Cynthia Enloe (1990), local and global sexual politics shape and are shaped through the presence of national and international U.S. military bases—through the symbolism of the U.S. soldier, the reproduction of family structures on bases, and systems of prostitution that coexist alongside bases. She explains, "Bases are artificial societies created out of unequal relations between men and women of different races and classes" (p. 2).

Men reserve the right to make war themselves and claim that they fight wars to protect vulnerable people, such as women and children, who are viewed as not being able to protect themselves (Tickner 2002). During wars, women are charged with caring for their husbands, sons, and the victims of war. The ideal of the "caretaking woman" helps exclude women from public and political institutions by reminding women that their first responsibility is to the family. According to Kaplan (1994), this ideal "helps co-opt women's resistance to the war by convincing women that their immediate responsibility to ameliorate the effects of war takes precedence over organized public action against war" (p. 131). Yet, wartime can also change the material role of women in society, especially the specific assignment of tasks (Higonnet et al. 1987). During World War II, women working in military plants and bases helped to redefine and promote women's participation in the workforce. American women in combat help reshape our definitions of bravery, heroism, and the "typical" American soldier.

Feminist theorists focus on the gender rhetoric used in war. Consider how the heroic images of September 11 focused on male firefighters and police officers. What were the images of women? As Judith Lorber (2002) explains, "The gender rhetoric heard over and over portrayed our men as heroes and theirs as terrorists, our women as sad widows and theirs as equally sad oppressed wives" (p. 379). Most of the images represented men "acting" while women were "reacting" to the events of September 11. The one exception was First Lady Laura Bush, who after maintaining a low profile before September 11, became highly visible in the archetypal role of nurturer for the nation (Jansen 2002). Instead of focusing on the female soldiers deployed against Afghanistan, the media chose to focus on faceless, helpless Afghan women in blue burqas (Tickner 2002).

Interactionist Perspective

Interactionists focus on the social messages and meaning of war and terrorism. *Terrorism* is a word with intrinsically negative connotations. According to political scientist Martha Crenshaw (1995), the word "projects images, communicates messages, and creates myths that transcend historical circumstances and motivate future generations" (p. 12). In addition, the concept serves as an "an organizing concept that both describes the phenomenon as it exists and offers a moral judgment" (p. 9). Brian Jenkins (1980) explains,

> What is called terrorism thus seems to be dependent on one's point of view. Use of the term implies a moral judgment; and if one party can successfully attach the label terrorist to its opponent, then it has indirectly persuaded others to adopt its moral viewpoint. (P. 10)

Crenshaw (1995) cautions that once political concepts like terrorism are constructed, "they take on a certain autonomy, especially when they are adopted by news media, disseminated to the public, and integrated into a general context of norms and values" (p. 9). Use of the word *terrorism* promotes condemnation of the actors and may reflect an ideological or political bias (Gibbs 1989).

Terrorism is particularly useful for agenda-setting (Crenshaw 1990) by the terrorist group and its target. If the reasons behind the violence are articulated clearly, terrorists can put their issues on the public agenda. Instantly, the public is aware of the group and its cause. The act may make some sympathetic to the group or could elicit anger and calls for retaliation. But the target—let's say the U.S. government—can also use terrorism to set its own agenda. According to Crenshaw (1990), "conceptions of terrorism affect the ways in which governments define their interests, and also determine reliance on labels or their abandonment when politically convenient" (p. 10). When the problem is labeled *terrorism* or a group *terrorists,* a set of predetermined preferred solutions begins to emerge. When these terms depict the group as "fanatical and irrational," making attempts at diplomacy or compromise seems impossible (Crenshaw 1990); the inference is that the U.S. government has nothing left to do but retaliate with force. But the labeling doesn't stop: Such defensive actions are often "appropriate" and "legitimate" expressions of "self-defense," but not "terrorism."

For a summary of sociological perspectives, see Table 14.3.

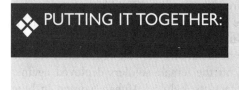

❖ PUTTING IT TOGETHER:

The rhetoric of September 11 also highlighted social differences based on social class and ethnicity/race. Media stories focused on the heroism of White firefighters and financial brokers, not on the victims and heroes who were busboys, maintenance employees, or mailroom workers who were poor, non White, working class, immigrant men (Lorber 2002). Why do you think the public and media ignored their stories?

❖ Table 14.3 Summary of Sociological Perspectives: War and Terrorism

	Functional	Conflict/Feminist	Interactionist
Explanation of war and terrorism	Functionalists examine how war and terrorism help maintain the social order.	War and terrorism may be based on conflict over resources, territory, and power. From a feminist perspective, war is considered a primarily male activity that enhances the position of males in society.	An interactionist focuses on the social messages and meaning of war and terrorism.
Questions asked about war and terrorism	What functions do war and terrorism serve? For terrorist groups? For the targets of terrorism? For groups in conflict?	What groups are in conflict and why?	How do our conceptions of war and terrorism shape political and diplomatic responses? How do they shape our own behavior?

The Problems of War and Terrorism

Fighting Terrorism at Home

Although the United States has shifted its focus to the threat of international terrorism, domestic terrorist groups continue to pose a threat. Between 1980 and 1999, the FBI recorded 327 incidents or suspected incidents of terrorism in the United States. Eighty-eight were attributed to international terrorists, while the remaining 239 were attributed to domestic terrorists. These acts resulted in the deaths of 205 people and the injury of 2,037 (FBI Counterterrorism Unit 1999).

On April 19, 1995, the worst domestic terrorism attack occurred around 9:03 a.m. in Oklahoma City, Oklahoma. A Ryder truck loaded with a mixture of fertilizer and fuel oil exploded in front of the Alfred P. Murrah Federal Building. The blast blew off the front side of the nine-story building, killing 169 and injuring hundreds more. The attack was conducted by Timothy McVeigh and Terry Nichols, motivated by anti-government sentiment over the failed 1993 federal raid on the Branch Davidians

❖ FOCUS ON: THE CULTURE OF WAR

In the following essay, Paul Fussell (1999) describes the culture of war and its impact on American society.

The culture of war . . . is not like the culture of ordinary peace-time life. It is a culture dominated by fear, blood and sadism, by irrational actions and preposterous (and often ironic) results. . . .

If the culture of war solidifies those who fight, it alienates them from those who do not. It has other regrettable aspects, one of which is censorship. War kills people; the culture of war does not, but the culture of war kills something precious and indispensable in a civilized society: freedom of utterance, freedom of curiosity, freedom of knowledge. Recently, an official of the Pentagon explained why the military had censored some TV footage depicting Iraqi soldiers cut in half by automatic fire from U.S. helicopters. He explained, "If we let people see that kind of thing there would never again be any war."

. . . It is obvious that censorship of this type is a necessity in any modern war. It is usually rationalized by the need to keep the enemy in the dark about our plans; it is also valuable to conceal military blunders and war crimes from a public that, in the absence of censorship, might learn to be critical of the military's actions.

The culture of war is the only culture where the concept of morale is crucial, and that is a significant point. Morale is crucial in the culture of war because at all times the troops are engaging in activities sure to undermine cheerfulness and hope. They are either being bored by picking up cigarette butts, or they are being dehumanized by killing their fellow creatures who, like

them, are for the most part helpless conscripts who have done nothing for which they deserve to be blown to bits. In a war-time culture, censorship has the assistance of general euphemism and programmatically inaccurate language. Before long we are calling war "peace keeping." What used to be designated aerial bombing has been euphemized into air strikes and even surgical strikes, dishonestly implying a degree of accuracy which would make combat veterans laugh out loud. Originally, artillery or mortar shells fired by mistake at our own troops were called terrible mistakes, or tragic errors. Then the euphemism of "incontinent ordinance" was devised, and finally some Pentagon genius hit upon the warmer and cozier term "friendly fire."

Earlier in our history, invasion [and] physical pressure against American territory were provocations leading to war. During the Nixon era, the U.S. became "Kissingerized." No longer requiring threats to American territory, threats to American "national interests" became a sufficient reason for sending the troops into action. National interest is an interesting term because it is legally meaningless and constitutionally undefinable, hence popular. The term "national interest" is the best gift ever awarded to those Americans who are neurotically bellicose, but . . . always seem to avoid being on the frontline, preferring to serve their country by getting others to drop bombs on people. Of course, the people they drop bombs on, and this is notable, are always more primitive and unfortunate than themselves. They are always smaller in stature. They usually have darker skins. That is what the current culture of war seems to amount to. Clearly, we should abhor it.

Source: Fussell 1999:420, 421-422.

compound in Texas. The bombing occurred on the second anniversary of the Branch Davidian incident. At the time, it was called the worst terrorist attack on U.S. soil. McVeigh was executed for his crime; Nichols is serving a life sentence.

According to Louis J. Freeh (2001), former FBI director, three types of domestic groups operate in the United States: right-wing extremists, left-wing and Puerto Rican extremists, and special-interest extremists. Right-wing groups, such as the World Church of the Creator, Aryan Nations, and the Southeastern States Alliance, advocate for the principles of racial supremacy and tend to embrace antigovernment or antiregulatory beliefs. They have also been characterized as hate groups. The Southern Poverty Law Center (2004) counted 751 active hate groups in the United States in 2003. According to the Southern Poverty Law Center, "all hate groups have beliefs or practices that attack or malign an entire class of people, typically for their immutable characteristics." (See U.S. Data Map 14.1 for the distribution of known hate groups by state.)

Left-wing groups wish to bring about revolutionary change, adopting a socialist doctrine, and see themselves as protectors of the people. Groups in this category include terrorist or separatist groups seeking Puerto Rico's independence from the United States and anarchists and extremist socialist groups such as the Workers' World Party, Reclaim the Streets, and Carnival against Capitalism. Many of these anarchist groups were blamed for the damage caused at the 1999 World Trade Organization meeting in Seattle, Washington. A comparison of left-wing and right-wing groups is presented in Table 14.4.

Special interest groups wish to resolve specific issues, rather than effect political change. These groups are at the fringes of animal rights, pro-life, environmental, antinuclear, and other political and social movements. Animal rights and environmental groups, such as the Animal Liberation Front (ALF) and the Earth Liberation Front (ELF), have recently increased their activities. Eight terrorist incidents in 1999 have been attributed to either the ALF or the ELF. According to the National Abortion Federation, there were approximately 12,000 attacks against and harassment of abortion service providers from 1984 to 2000, with the highest number of attacks during 1988–1989 (Doyle 2001). In 2003, ELF took credit for vandalism and arson attacks targeting SUV dealerships in California, causing $2.5 million in damages. SUVs were sprayed painted with the words "terrorist" and "gross polluter."

The Impact of War and Terrorism

Psychological Impact

According to Martha Crenshaw (1983), there are small incremental societal changes in terms of trust, social cohesion, and integration as a result of terrorism. Terrorism has a particular impact in small or homogenous societies. Research on the long-term impact of terrorism is limited, although some case studies have been conducted in Northern Ireland, where residents have lived with domestic terrorism since the late 1960s. (See p. 406 for more about the IRA.)

War takes a psychological toll, particularly for soldiers involved in battle. Mental health experts have identified posttraumatic stress disorder (PTSD) as a common aftereffect of battle. Those suffering from PTSD feel depressed and detached and have

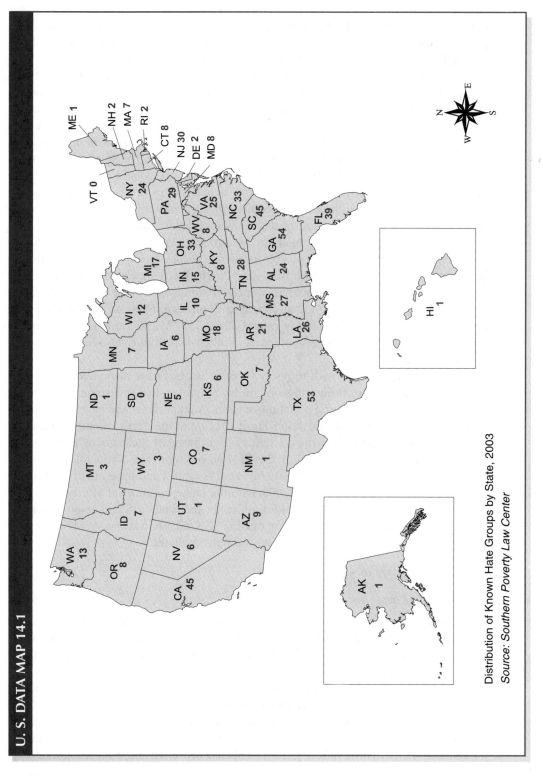

Distribution of Known Hate Groups by State, 2003
Source: Southern Poverty Law Center

❖ Table 14.4   Characteristics of Left-Wing and Right-Wing Terrorist Groups in the United States

Characteristics	Left Wing	Right Wing
Ideology	Political focus, primarily Marxism	Religious focus, ties to Christian Identity Movement (belief that Aryans are God's chosen people)
Economic views	Pro-communist/socialist; belief in Marxist maxim "receive according to one's needs"	Strongly anti-communist; belief in Protestant work ethic, distributive justice
Base of operations	Urban areas	Rural areas
Tactical approach	Cellular structure; use of safehouses	National networking; camps and compounds
Targets for funding	Armored trucks	Armored trucks
Targets for terrorism	Seats of capitalism/government buildings	Federal law enforcement agencies, opposing racial or religious groups
Average age at indictment	35; only 18 percent were over age 40	39; 36 percent over age 40
Gender	73 percent male	93 percent male
Race	29 percent White 71 percent minority	97 percent White 3 percent American Indian

Source: Smith 1994.

nightmares and flashbacks of their war experience. The disorder may also occur with related issues, such as depression, substance abuse, cognition problems, and other problems of physical or mental health (National Center for PTSD 2003b).

Vietnam veterans were particularly hard-hit due to extensive war-related trauma: serving hazardous duty, witnessing death and harm to self or others, and being on frequent or prolonged combat missions. The estimated lifetime prevalence of PTSD among Vietnam veterans is 30.9 percent for men and 26.9 percent for women. An additional 22.5 percent of men and 21.2 percent of women have had partial PTSD sometime in their lives (National Center for PTSD 2003a). In a study of postservice mortality comparing more than 9,000 U.S. Army veterans who served in Vietnam to more than 8,000 veterans who served in Korea, Germany, or the United States during the same time period, it was reported that the total mortality of those who served in

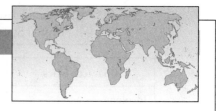

THE DECOMMISSIONING OF THE IRA

"The trouble with the Irish is the English."

A line from a popular Irish song (quoted in Whittaker 2002)

Since 1969, Northern Ireland has experienced violence and bloodshed as a result of confrontations between Nationalist and Unionist (or Loyalist) forces. The Nationalist or Catholic groups are led by the Irish Republican Army (IRA) and its splinter groups. In 1970, the Provisional IRA was created (*provisional* to honor the provisional government declared by the leaders of the 1916 Easter Rising in Dublin). The Provisional IRA was formed to defend the Catholic community and to throw out the British army and police (Wilkinson 1993). The Unionist or Protestant forces are the Ulster Defence Association and its splinter groups: the Ulster Volunteer Force, the Red Hand Commandos, and the Ulster Freedom Fighters. Ulster Protestants see themselves as Britons, loyal to the Protestant crown. These groups represent "Orange Extremism" as described by Wilkinson (1993). Orange extremism has also been blamed for provoking the open conflict in the late 1960s and for creating the conditions in which the Provisional IRA could grow. The division between the groups emphasizes their polarization in religion, politics, and economics (Whittaker 2002).

Between them, both sides amassed an impressive armory of rifles, homemade machine guns, grenade throwers, anti-tank weapons, and explosives. Bombing seemed to be a favorite tactic of both sides. It is estimated that in 30 years of conflict, 3,500 civilians have been killed, some 30,000 have been injured, and there has been a loss of property amounting to millions of pounds (Whittaker 2002).

IRA terrorists also have taken their own lives without attempting to harm others. There was a chain suicide of 11 IRA members who starved themselves to death in a Belfast prison in 1981. The IRA used the hunger strikes and deaths to their organizational advantage, "to reap emotive propaganda, to restore the flow of cash and weapons from the previously dwindling U.S. sources, and to regroup and rearm" (Wilkinson 1993). Many Irish Americans embraced the IRA as freedom fighters and supported their cause politically and financially.

In 1998, both sides agreed to the Good Friday Agreement, a 65-page document that sought to define relationships within Northern Ireland, between Northern Ireland and the Republic, and between Ireland, England, Scotland, and Wales. The agreement acknowledges that the people of Northern and Southern Ireland are the only ones with the power to bring about a united Ireland. Through the agreement, new government institutions were set in place. A cabinet-style Executive of Ministers, with members in proportion to party support, allows for the participation of all groups (Ahern 2003). The new government composed of unionists and nationalists was established with the first elections for the new Assembly for Northern Ireland in June 1998. Since the Good Friday Agreement, many IRA and loyalist prisoners have been released and the number of deployed troops reduced.

However, a number of problems have slowed down the implementation of the agreement, including difficulties over the total disarmament of the Provisional IRA and the dismantling of British military installations in Nationalist areas (Ahern 2003). As of September 2004, shared Protestant and Catholic rule had not been established.

Vietnam was 17 percent higher than other veteran groups. The excess mortality occurred primarily in the first five years after discharge, due to motor vehicle accidents, suicide, homicide, and accidental poisonings. Drug related deaths among Vietnam vets were also higher than other veteran groups (Centers for Disease Control 2003b).

Economic Impact

In April 2003, it was estimated that the U.S. war with Iraq had already cost about $20 billion, but the figure was growing about $2 billion per month for military operations (Mount 2003). In a supplemental budget for 2003, President George W. Bush requested $87 billion for war operations in Iraq and Afghanistan, with $20.3 billion for rebuilding Iraq. President Bush pledged that the United States would win the fight against terrorism, "whatever it takes, whatever it costs." At the beginning of the war, it was projected that the war would cost a half-trillion dollars a year (Knickerbocker 2002).

Do you recall Eisenhower's warning? Billions of dollars spent on the war means that other programs are not receiving any funding. While the war budget increased, proposed cuts in several social programs (such as AmeriCorp, Low Income Home Energy Assistance Program, and Title I education programs for low-income and disadvantaged children) were also being announced.

Political Impact

Terrorism can effect change in two political areas: the overall distribution of political power and government policies (Crenshaw 1983). Terrorism may result in radical changes in the power relationships within a state, involving shifts in who governs and under what rules. As a target of terrorism, the U.S. government has also experienced a redistribution of power as federal and state agencies sought to improve intelligence gathering and security procedures. Institutional changes have occurred, with each major intelligence agency improving its anti-terrorism activities, culminating in the creation of the Department of Homeland Security. In extreme cases, terrorism may lead to the replacement of one government by another.

Government policies usually have two goals: to destroy the terrorist group and to protect potential targets from attack. Policies may include foreign policy efforts seeking the cooperation and support of international allies. After September 11, through a series of executive orders, regulations, and laws, the U.S. government attempted to destroy terrorist groups and to ensure our security. In 2001, Congress passed the Patriot Act, which established a separate counterterrorism fund, expanded government authority to gather and share evidence with wire and electronic communications, allowed agencies to detain suspected foreign terrorists, and provided for victims of terrorism.

Constitutional and civil rights attorneys have been critical of the Patriot Act, alarmed that it would erode individual liberties and increase law enforcement abuses. Often cited is the Act's disregard for the principles of political freedom, due process, and the protections of privacy, principles at the core of a democratic society (Cole and

VISUAL ESSAY: RITUALS OF PUBLIC HEALING ❖

Overcoming trauma in the aftermath of terror is a matter not only of healing people's bodies and psychological wounds but also of helping to repair the sense of community that the terrorists have sought to destroy. Certain rituals of public healing have evolved to restore collective trust and purpose when disaster strikes. We saw many of these rituals following the terrorist attacks of September 11, 2001. Think of the images you saw then, and compare them with these photos taken in the wake of the bombing of the federal building in Oklahoma City on April 19, 1995, which killed 169 and left hundreds more injured and grieving.

Families and friends of the victims, along with first responders such as police and paramedics, gather at the site to grieve for those who were lost as well as for the loss of their own peace of mind.

Spontaneous memorials consisting of photos of the victims, flowers, and other artifacts symbolizing the victims' personalities and interests are assembled by family members, friends, and anonymous donors on the perimeter of the Alfred P. Murrah building, bearing witness to their memory and their loss.

Formal religious services are a comforting and familiar ritual that help members of the local community begin to accept their loss. They are often joined by state or national officials and by celebrities, whose presence symbolizes how the larger community shares the local community's pain.

As the ripples of concern spread nationally, the American flag and other patriotic symbols are prominently displayed on buildings, homes, and cars and as part of personal clothing.

Ultimately, a formal memorial may be constructed. Common features include symbolic representations of the individuals who were lost (in Oklahoma City, an array of stylized chairs, each bearing a victim's name); a pool or fountain accented with plantings, which seem to symbolize a renewal of spirit and the inevitable cycle of life and death; and a structure representing strength and stability while recalling the nature of the particular disaster.

At a dedication ceremony for an Oklahoma City memorial museum in February 2001, almost six years after the bombing, these women appear to have made a sort of peace with the event that so abruptly changed their lives. A few months later, after September 11, a contingent of survivors from Oklahoma City traveled to New York City to offer their deep understanding and support to a new set of terror's victims—yet another way of repairing the social fabric.

What rituals of public healing did you observe or participate in after the tragedy of September 11, 2001? How effective did these rituals seem to be in bringing peace to you and to others and in helping to heal the community's wounds?

❖

Dempsey 2002). More than 330 cities, towns, and counties, as well as four states, have passed resolutions critical of the federal anti-terrorism law (Egan 2004). Two provisions of the Act have caused particular concern among citizens. One is the provision that empowers authorities to search people's homes without notification. The provision may have been used by federal agents to search the home of Brandon Mayfield, a lawyer from Oregon who was suspected, but later cleared, in connection with the 2004 bombings in Madrid, Spain. A second clause allows government officials the right to review a person's library, business, and medical records.

How Did This Happen? The Role of Intelligence and Security

In the aftermath of September 11, serious questions were asked about how teams of hijackers could coordinate and carry out the hijacking of four domestic aircraft. After all, no U.S. plane had been bombed in 13 years, and none had been successfully hijacked since 1987 (Easterbrook 2001). What was airport security doing? What did our intelligence sources indicate? Except for the events of September 11, U.S. intelligence and services have generally done very well in protecting the country; there is no evidence that spending more money would have prevented the September 11 attacks (Betts 2001).

Before September 11, the airline industry was designed to maximize passenger miles and minimize costs (Easterbrook 2001). The industry's imperatives were to attract more passengers, to reduce prices, and to get more flights in the air. Airport security cost money and created hassles that passengers and the industry did not want to deal with. Sewing scissors, fingernail clippers, and tweezers may be everyday items, but they have been considered potential weapons since September 11. Airport security is tighter and more thorough—and also slower. In addition, airplane cockpit doors have been reinforced, sky marshals have been deployed, and there has been some discussion of arming airline pilots.

Before September 11, the Bush Administration was preoccupied with establishing a national missile defense system (Flynn 2001), also known as "Star Wars" missile technology. Did no one imagine that terrorist attacks were possible? Convened in 1998, the bipartisan Hart-Rudman Commission on National Security in the 21st Century (2000, 2001) reported that "mass-casualty terrorism directed against the U.S. homeland [is] of serious and growing concern" (p. 6), predicting that "a direct attack against American citizens on American soil is likely over the next quarter century" (p. 8). The commission suggested that America's first priority should be to "defend the United States and ensure that it is safe from the dangers of a new era" (p. 8).

Immediately after September 11, 2001, weaknesses in U.S. intelligence and security were revealed. Land and sea borders were relatively unprotected, it was found. On September 10, 2001, about 300 border agents and one single analyst were responsible for patrolling the 4,000-mile land and water border we share with Canada. The U.S. Coast Guard, which is charged with maintaining port security and patrolling 95,000 miles of shoreline, had been forced to reduce its ranks to the lowest since 1964 (Flynn 2001). One highly publicized intelligence failure was FBI Agent Colleen Rowley's request to investigate Zacarias Moussaoui under the Foreign Intelligence

Surveillance Act. Moussaoui had been detained in Minneapolis, Minnesota, for a violation of his immigration status. FBI headquarters denied Rowley's request, saying that there was insufficient evidence that Moussaoui was connected to a foreign terrorist organization. He was later charged as a co-conspirator in the September 11 suicide hijackings.

The National Commission on the Terrorist Attacks upon the United States, also known as the 9/11 Commission, was an independent bipartisan commission created by congressional legislation. The 9/11 Commission was charged with documenting and preparing a full account of the 9/11 terrorists attacks. Throughout 2003 and 2004, hearings were held investigating Osama bin Laden's network, the performance of the intelligence community, emergency preparedness and response, and national policy coordination. The commission concluded that U.S. intelligence gathering by the FBI and CIA was inadequate, fragmented, and poorly coordinated.

In 2002, President George W. Bush established the Department of Homeland Security. (Before September 11, the U.S. Commission on National Security in the 21st Century [2001] had recommended the creation of a National Homeland Security Agency, responsible for planning, coordinating, and integrating all U.S. agencies responsible for security.) The primary mission of the department is to prevent terrorist attacks and reduce the vulnerability of the United States to terrorism through coordination with component agencies: Secret Service, Coast Guard, Immigration and Naturalization Service, U.S. Customs Service, Federal Emergency Management Agency, and the Transportation Security Administration. The Department of Homeland Security is also responsible for the Homeland Security Advisory System, which informs the public of the current level of terrorist threat. Table 14.5 identifies all threat levels.

Where Will the Next Attack Come From?

Anthrax

Chemical, biological, and radiological weapons have the potential to kill and injure large numbers of people. Use of these weapons or threat of their use has steadily increased since 1995. Just 24 days after September 11, the Florida Department of Health and the Centers for Disease Control confirmed the first case of inhalation anthrax in more than 25 years (Perkins, Popovic, and Yeskey 2002). Anthrax is a disease caused by a bacterium that forms spores. There are three types of anthrax: skin (cutaneous), lung (inhalation), and digestive (gastrointestinal). The Centers for Disease Control classifies anthrax as a Category A agent: It can spread across a large area, poses the greatest possible threat to public health, and requires a great deal of planning to protect the public. In 2001, anthrax was deliberately spread through the U.S. postal system by someone sending letters with powder containing anthrax (Centers for Disease Control 2003a) Twenty-two cases of anthrax infection were reported in seven East Coast states: Connecticut (1), Florida (2), Maryland (3), New Jersey (5), New York (8), Pennsylvania (1), and Virginia (2). Five people died as a result of their exposure. No one has been charged with these crimes.

❖ Table 14.5   Current Threat Levels

Since September 11, 2001, we've become familiar with the Homeland Security Advisory System. There are five threat conditions, each with a color code and a corresponding description. From lowest to highest, the levels are:

Low	Green
Guarded	Blue
Elevated	Yellow
High	Orange
Severe	Red

The higher the threat condition, the greater the risk of a terrorist attack. Risk is assessed based on the probability of an attack and its potential seriousness. Levels may be set for the entire nation or for specific regions. Threat conditions are assigned by the Attorney General and the Assistant to the President for Homeland Security (Office of Homeland Security 2002).

Nuclear Weapons

The nuclear weapons age began on July 16, 1945, when the United States exploded the first nuclear bomb in Alamogordo, New Mexico. Three weeks later, an atomic bomb was used on the city of Hiroshima, Japan, killing about 100,000 residents. Three days later, an atomic bomb was used on the city of Nagasaki, Japan, killing about 74,000 and injuring 75,000. During the 1950s and 1960s, the United States was engaged in a Cold War with Russia and other nuclear countries, locked in a stalemate over who would be the first to launch a nuclear attack. In 1963, the countries agreed to sign a partial test ban treaty, banning nuclear tests in the atmosphere, under water, and in space, and a nonproliferation treaty was signed in 1968, prohibiting non-nuclear countries from possessing or developing nuclear weapons. In 1996, President Bill Clinton was the first world leader to sign the Comprehensive Nuclear Test Ban Treaty, which prohibits all nuclear test explosions in all environments. However, the treaty has yet to be ratified by the U.S. Senate. All NATO members, except for the United States, have ratified the treaty.

Nuclear weapons are still held by more than eight nations in the world. Suspected weapons have been identified in China (400), France (35), India (60), Pakistan (24 to 48) Russia (about 10,000), United Kingdom (185), and United States (10,656) (Center for Defense Information 2003). It has been estimated that Iran could produce a nuclear weapon before 2010; in 2003, North Korean officials informed the Bush Administration that they had enough plutonium to create six nuclear devices (Sanger 2003).

Internet Threats

According to the FBI Counterterrorism Unit (1999), electronic information-based attacks constitute a relatively new and growing terrorism threat. In some cases, terrorist groups have used the Internet to damage their enemies' information systems, but the Internet has also been used for the organization, recruitment, and dissemination of terrorist information. The FBI reported an increase in "hacktivism," politically motivated attacks on publicly accessible Web pages or e-mail services. Hackers overload e-mail servers or hack into Web sites to send a political message.

War and Terrorism Policy, Advocacy, and Innovation

Grant Wardlaw (1988) states, "Terrorism is a phenomenon that is increasingly coming to dominate our lives." The effects of terrorism are widespread.

> It influences the way governments conduct their foreign policy and corporations transact their business. It causes changes to the structure and role of our security forces and necessitates huge expenditures on measures to protect public figures, vital installations, citizens and perhaps in the final analysis, our system of government. It affects the way we travel, the places we visit and the manner in which we live our daily lives. (P. 206)

Although terrorism is a worldwide growth industry, modes of counterterrorism are piecemeal and ineffective (Whittaker 2002). The current counterterrorist policy includes several tenets: make no concessions and deals with terrorists; bring terrorists to justice for their crimes; isolate and apply pressure on states that sponsor terrorism; and improve the counterterrorist capabilities of countries that work with the United States (Pillar 2001). As a nation, we have used several approaches to combat terrorism and to reduce the risk of warfare: diplomacy, sanctions, and military force. Usually, war is justified as being the last resort in circumstances where there are severe domestic rights violations or international aggression by an offending state (Garfield 2002).

Political Diplomacy

According to Christopher Harmon (2000), "political will, more than new laws or new direction[s] in international politics, is the most important component of an enhanced effort against foreign supported terrorism" (p. 236). Political diplomacy includes articulating policy to foreign leaders, persuading them, and reaching agreements with them (Pillar 2001). Wars reshape diplomacy; victory becomes the goal of foreign policy, and diplomatic relationships are adjusted to achieve it (Mandelbaum 2003).

Relationship building and persuasion are at the heart of U.S. diplomatic efforts. As the lead foreign affairs agency, the Department of State attempts to formulate, represent, and implement the president's foreign policy (U.S. Department of State 2003). The secretary of state is the president's principal adviser on foreign policy and represents the United States abroad in foreign affairs. Primarily, the department manages diplomatic relations with other countries and international institutions (such as the United Nations, the North Atlantic Treaty Organization [NATO], the World Bank, and the International Monetary Fund [IMF]). The Department of State conducts negotiations and concludes agreements and treaties with other countries on issues ranging from trade to nuclear weapons. The United States maintains diplomatic relations with more than 180 countries (U.S. Department of State 2003). Diplomacy is conducted not only by the secretary of state but also by foreign service officers, immigration officers, FBI special agents, intelligence officers, transportation specialists, defense attachés, and other officials (Pillar 2001).

The Use of Economic Sanctions

For many years, the United States and the United Nations have used nonviolent approaches in the form of economic sanctions to punish or pressure countries that have violated U.S. laws or values. Sanctions are considered an alternative to diplomacy or military force. As of July 1999, the United States had imposed sanctions on no fewer than 28 countries. From World War I to 1990, the U.S. imposed sanctions 77 times. The United Nations has imposed economic sanctions 13 times (Marks 1999).

Economic sanctions, in the form of trade embargoes and the termination of development assistance, are the most commonly applied form of sanctions, and they have the most significant public health consequences. U.S. sanctions were used against Iraq in 1990 to force its withdrawal from Kuwait and against Yugoslavia (1991–1996) and Serbia and Montenegro (1992–1996) during the Serbian war (Marks 1999). According to Richard Haas (1997), "economic sanctions are popular because they offer what appears to be a proportional response to challenges in which the interests at stake are less than vital" (p. 75). Sanctions can also serve as a signal of official displeasure with a country's behavior or action.

Many attempts have focused on cutting aid to countries sponsoring or supporting terrorism. The problem is that most terrorist states do not receive significant aid from the United States, and based on past experience, sanctions have only made target countries and nations more angry and impassioned against the United States (Flores 1981). Ayubi et al. (1982) concluded that economic sanctions in U.S. foreign policy may not be effective in their objectives and have often failed to achieve their political purposes. For example, sanctions applied against Cuba since 1960 have failed to destabilize the Castro regime.

Sanctions may not hurt dictators and terrorists, but they may increase suffering and death among civilians (Garfield 2002). A report issued in 1993 by the Harvard Center for Population and Development Studies maintained that sanctions exacerbated malnutrition in Haiti and increased child deaths caused by misgovernment (Neier 1993). One approach has been to freeze only economic assets while continuing to provide food and medical aid through private agencies (Neier 1993). However, although only economic sanctions were directed against Iraq in the early 1990s, the Harvard Study Team (1991) reported that essential goods—food, medicine, infrastructure support—were not reaching those in need. All health facilities surveyed reported major drug shortages. Children were most vulnerable, dying of preventable diseases and starvation. The chance of dying before age five in Iraq more than doubled, from 54 per 1,000 between 1984 and 1989 to 131 per 1,000 between 1995 and 1999 (Ali and Shah 2000).

Military Response

Military action is based on the idea that the most effective way to defeat an enemy is by inflicting destruction of the enemy's armies, equipment, transport systems, industrial centers, and cities. Jenkins (1988) identifies four types of military response to terrorism. First, preemptive operations range from evacuation of U.S. citizens or interests to invasion of a location. Most preemptive operations are based on credible and accurate intelligence. Second, search and recovery operations recover stolen weapons or nuclear material that might have fallen into terrorist hands. Third, rescue operations deploy specially trained units to extract hostages taken by terrorists. Finally, the military may use retaliatory or punitive raids to attack terrorist bases or targets.

Retaliation has been the most important counterterrorist use of U.S. military force. The United States first used it against Libya in 1986, responding to the April 4 bombing of a nightclub in Berlin where two Americans were killed and 71 were wounded. One hundred military aircraft were used to attack military targets in and around Tripoli and Benghazi (Pillar 2001). After September 11, U.S. troops were deployed to destroy Taliban operations based in Afghanistan.

According to Pillar (2001), evidence suggests that military retaliation does not serve as an effective deterrent to terrorism. First, terrorists who threaten the United States present few suitable military targets. It is tough to attack an enemy that can't be located. Many terrorists groups lack any high-value targets, whose destruction would be costly to their organization. Second, a military attack against a terrorist group may serve political and organizational goals of the terrorist leaders. Such attacks may increase recruiting, sympathy, and resources for terrorist groups. And finally, there is no evidence that terrorists will respond peacefully after a retaliatory attack. Terrorists may also respond by fighting back.

Is there a way to end the war on terrorism? Michael Mandelbaum (2003) says that the war on terrorism will not end so neatly.

> Success in this conflict will be measured not, as in other wars, by what American military forces do, but rather by what terrorists do not do. In this new war, a day when nothing happens will be a good day for the United States. (P. 267)

❖ ─────────────────────

Voices in the Community:
Greg Mortensen

> *If we try to resolve terrorism with military might and nothing else, then we will be no safer than we were before 9/11. In the long term, we have to help feed and clothe people where terrorists are recruiting volunteers. And we have to educate them—especially the girls. We have to prove to them that the world can be a better place. If we truly want a legacy of peace for our children, we need to understand that this is a war that will ultimately be won with books, not with bombs.*

Greg Mortenson, cofounder and executive director,
Central Asia Institute (quoted in Fedarko *2003:5*)

In 1993, Greg Mortenson climbed K2, the world's second-highest mountain. Stricken by illness on the mountain, he was forced to return to a base camp. Two porters took him to their homes in Korphe, an isolated northern village in Pakistan. While recovering in Korphe, Mortenson was impressed by the sight of 84 village children sitting outside and scratching their school lessons in the dirt with sticks. The students were working alone; the village was unable to afford the $1-a-day salary to hire a teacher (Fedarko 2003).

When he returned to his home in Montana, Mortenson decided to pay back the villagers for their kindness by building them a school and providing money for a teacher's salary. He was able to raise $12,000 and kept his promise (Fedarko 2003). Mortenson met Jean Hoerni, who helped established the Central Asia Institute (CAI) in 1996 with a donation of $1 million. After Hoerni died in 1997, Mortenson continued his work through the institute. Since then, the CAI completed 34 primary schools, 2 school libraries, 18 water projects, and 8 women's vocational centers, providing more than 10,000 students (including 4,200 girls) with an education (CAI 2004).

Mortenson's program focuses on girls' education and women's empowerment. CAI requires that each village must agree to increase the enrollment of girls by 10 percent each year. He explains,

> You can hand out condoms, build roads, put in electricity, but nothing will change until the girls are educated. They are the ones who remain at home. They are the ones who instill values. Educating the girls is a long-term solution to the war on poverty, and will have a big impact on the war on terrorism. (Fedarko 2003:5)

According to a 2003 CAI press release, students in CAI schools scored higher than the national average on the Pakistan national exams in 2002, 74 percent versus the national average of 46 percent (CAI 2004).

Jahan, a 17-year-old girl from Korphe, is the first girl from her village who has learned to read and write. Mortenson provided her with the tuition to attend a maternal health-care program.

> Jahan is special not just because she was in the first graduating class of my school but also because her mother died while giving birth to her. When Jahan finishes her course in maternal health care, she will have broken the cycle of ignorance. She'll also have an immense impact on the future of the place. What could be more incredible than that? (Mortenson, quoted in Fedarko 2003:6)

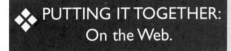 **PUTTING IT TOGETHER: On the Web.** For more information about Mortenson and his Central Asia Institute, visit *Study Site Chapter 14.*

Antiwar and Peace Movements

Antiwar movements have been characterized as reactive, occurring only in response to specific wars or the threat of war. Every 20th-century war conducted by the United States elicited organized protest and opposition (Chatfield 1992). On the other hand, peace movements represent organized coalitions that are "fundamentally concerned with the problems of war, militarism, conscription, and mass violence, and the ideals of internationalism, globalism and non-violent relations between people" (Young 1999:227). According to Young (1999), there are different peace traditions: groups that provide ideas and initiatives for the entire peace movement. For example, the tradition of liberalism and internationalism attempts to prevent war through reformed behavior of states: peace plans, treaties, international law, and arbitration between all groups. Another tradition, anticonscriptionism, linked the peace movement with individual civil rights.

Women as Peacemakers

Another peace tradition is feminist antimilitarism. Peace movements within this tradition are united by the ideal of a distinctive role for women on the issue of peace and female unity across national boundaries (Young 1999). Feminist antimilitary groups first began in the early 1900s. In 1914, Jane Addams, founder of Hull House, led a women's peace parade in New York to protest World War I. Addams, along with Carrie Chapman Catt, the main strategist and leader for the women's suffrage movement, and other women activists formed the Women's Peace Party in 1915. Later that year, the party was renamed the Women's International League for Peace and Freedom. The organization exists today, with chapters in Africa, Asia, South Asia, the Middle East, Europe, and the Americas. Its current global mission includes building a "culture of peace" as opposed to a "culture of war."

College Activists

Knott (1971) explains that college students prior to World War II were mainly upper-middle-class students who treated their education as a privilege. Except for a few campuses, the majority of undergraduates showed little social consciousness and were unwilling to challenge or question the status quo. But increasing diversity on college campuses, in terms of student's age, gender, or ethnic background, helped increase social awareness and infused students with a greater sense of empowerment. Student activism was at its peak in the 1960s and 1970s, supporting the civil rights movement and later protesting the Vietnam War. During the late 1970s, campuses institutionalized many of the gains made in the previous decade: establishing women's centers, Black student unions, and gay and lesbian organizations and ensuring that student government had a greater role in university operations (Vellela 1988).

The college student population is less politicized as a whole than it was 40 years ago. According to UCLA's Annual Freshmen Survey, more than 60 percent of students viewed "keeping up with politics" as "very important" or "essential" in 1966 compared with only 32.9 percent in 2002 (Hamilton 2003). Some argue, however, that progressive student activism didn't stop after the Vietnam War era (Vellela 1988). Student activism is on the rise, but it doesn't reproduce the civil rights and war protests of the 1960s and 1970s. Students are engaged in a broad range of issues: women's rights, discrimination, homophobia, the homeless, labor unions, and political action groups.

The new wave of peace activism builds on existing networks established by the student anticorporate movement, which focused on economic justice related to sweatshop labor and unionization on campuses (refer to Chapter 6, The Workplace). The current wave of peace activism includes a diverse set of schools: rural southern schools (Appalachian State University, North Carolina, University of Southern Mississippi), historically Black colleges (Morehouse College, Georgia), community colleges from Hawaii to Massachusetts, and urban public universities (City University of New York and University of Illinois, Chicago), as well as high schools and middle schools. Student groups have held teach-ins, vigils, and fasts to call attention to a variety of issues (Featherstone 2003).

Although most recent peace activism has protested against the war in Iraq, this sentiment has not been universal. Student peace groups have been sensitive to the message that they send (Featherstone 2003). Peace groups are linking their opposition to war to the campaign for social justice, dealing with racism, economic inequality, and sexism at home. Student protesters seem to have learned from the protests of the 1960s, wanting to prevent the kind of alienation experienced by Vietnam War veterans (Rhoads 1991).

Voices in the Community:
Tracy DiMambro

Established in 1995, SPAN (Student Peace Action Network) was created by student activists who felt that the student peace and justice movement needed a "cohesive unified front, a systematic communication tool under which all students could communicate and organize more effectively," according to Tracy DiMambro, who was interviewed for this book. SPAN serves as a national facilitator to network and organize student activities but remains a grassroots organization. "All of our campaigns come from the students' votes and suggestions. We aren't the directors. We don't decide on the activities, we really respond to what the students ask for," says DiMambro, SPAN's national coordinator. SPAN is a permanent program of the Peace Action Education Fund.

Working with high school and college groups, SPAN is an organization for students and by students. It is difficult to estimate the number of students who participate, but SPAN serves more than 200 student groups across the country. Campus Peace Action, based at the University of Central Florida, is a SPAN member. The chapter has more than 250 members and held the Florida Activist Coalition Conference during summer 2003. SPAN's Web site offers a members' message board, where events or organizing ideas are posted and shared with other student groups. SPAN provides organizing materials and fact sheets for their member groups and their activities.

Their 2003 campaign is the "Flunk the War Machine." In the past, SPAN has focused on disarmament issues or Pentagon pork, but right now, DiMambro says,

> We're focusing on the military's infiltration of high schools and universities. There are three initiatives—we are challenging the No Child Left Behind Act, which contains a military recruitment provision, the Patriot Act's assault on civil liberties and weapons contractors' ties to college campuses. We're trying to make the connection between the lack of social services and exorbitant military spending.

For DiMambro, a recent college graduate, her work with SPAN fits her personal mission to "reach students who are hungry for change and who don't really have the avenues or outlets in their hometowns or schools. Together we can come up with some viable possibilities to make change for the better."

❖ ❖

MAIN POINTS

- September 11, 2001, brought terrorism directly to American soil. Terrorism is the unlawful use of force to intimidate or coerce compliance with a particular set of beliefs and can be either domestic (based in the United States) or foreign (supported by foreign groups threatening the security of U.S. nationals or U.S. national security).

- Terrorism is a premeditated, purposeful, political act targeting noncombatants to force the main target to change course, and it is usually carried out by subnational groups or clandestine agents.

- Terrorist activity has changed little over the years. Six basic tactics account for 95 percent of all incidents: bombings, assassinations, armed assaults, kidnappings, hijackings, and other hostage seizures.

- In contrast to terrorism, war is a violent but legitimate political instrument between armed combatants. From the American Revolution to the 21st-century war in Iraq, American history is replete with war.

- Functionalists examine how war and terrorism help maintain the social order, serving to create and reinforce boundaries. War creates social stability by letting everyone know what side they are on; there are norms and boundaries in war. But unlike war, the social boundaries in terrorist activities are less certain.

- War and terrorism are forms of conflict that may be based on disputes over resources or land. Modern conflict theorists have focused on how war is used to promote economic and political interests, such as replacing social program funding with military expenditures.

- From the feminist perspective, war is considered a primarily male activity that enhances the position of males in society. Women are expected either to be caretakers or to take over certain jobs vacated by men, as occurred in World War II. More recently, women combatants have redefined notions of courage. Feminist theorists focus on the gender rhetoric used in war.

- Interactionists focus on the social messages and meaning of war and terrorism, believing that *terrorism* is a word with intrinsically negative connotations. Use of the word promotes condemnation of the actors and may reflect an ideological or political bias.

- Although the United States has shifted its focus to the threat of international terrorism, domestic terrorist groups continue to pose a threat. The worst domestic terrorist act was the 1995 Oklahoma City bombing.

- Three types of domestic groups operate in the United States. Right-wing ("hate") groups are antigovernment and advocate for the principles of racial supremacy. Left-wing groups wish to bring about socialist revolutionary change. Special-interest groups focus on resolving specific issues rather than bringing about political change.

- Terrorism can effect change in two political areas: the overall distribution of political power and government policies. In extreme cases, terrorism may lead to the replacement of one government by another.

- Government policies usually have two goals: to destroy the terrorist group and to protect potential targets from attack. One recent policy is the 2001 Patriot Act, which has brought criticism from constitutional and civil liberty groups.

- After September 11, a significant question was how it could have happened. The 9/11 Commission is an independent bipartisan commission created to document and prepare a full account of the attacks. It concluded that U.S. intelligence gathering by the FBI and CIA was inadequate, fragmented, and poorly coordinated.

- In 2002, President George W. Bush established the Department of Homeland Security to prevent terrorist attacks and reduce vulnerability to terrorism. Fears of terrorist tactics include the use of chemicals such as anthrax, the proliferation of nuclear weapons, and electronic information attacks.

- Modes of counterterrorism appear piecemeal and ineffective. The current counterterrorist policy includes several tenets: Make no deals with terrorists, bring terrorists to justice, isolate and apply pressure to states sponsoring terrorism, and improve the counterterrorist capabilities of U.S. allies.

- Political diplomacy includes articulating policy to foreign leaders, persuading them, and reaching agreements with them. Wars reshape diplomacy; victory becomes the goal of foreign policy. As the lead foreign affairs agency, the Department of State attempts to formulate, represent, and implement the president's foreign policy.

- For many years, the United States and the United Nations have used nonviolent approaches, in the form of economic sanctions, to punish or pressure countries that have violated U.S. laws or values. Sanctions are considered an alternative to diplomacy or military force. Economic sanctions such as trade embargoes, which are the most commonly applied form, can significantly affect the health of the targeted country's citizens.

- Many counterterrorism attempts have focused on cutting off aid to countries sponsoring or supporting terrorism. However, most such states do not receive significant aid from the United States, and sanctions may have only made targets angrier with the United States.

- There are four types of military response to terrorism: preemptive operations, search and recovery operations, rescue operations, and retaliatory or punitive raids. Retaliation has been the most important counterterrorist use of U.S. military force, but evidence suggests that military retaliation does not serve as an effective deterrent to terrorism because terrorists present few suitable military targets, military attacks may actually help the goals of terrorist leaders, and terrorists may respond violently.

- Every 20th-century war conducted by the United States elicited organized antiwar movements. At the college level, student activism was at its peak in the 1960s and 1970s. Now, the student population is less politicized than it was 40 years ago. Activism is on the rise, but not as much as in the 1960s and 1970s. Students now are engaged in a broad range of issues: women's rights, discrimination, homophobia, the homeless, labor unions, and political action groups.

INTERNET AND COMMUNITY EXERCISES

1. Investigate the history of women's peace movements through the Swarthmore College Peace Collection, established in 1930 by Jane Addams of Hull House, Chicago, Illinois. Current women's peace organizations include Women Waging Peace and the

Women's International League for Peace and Freedom. The site for the Women's International League for Peace and Freedom also lists state branches. Log on to *Study Site Chapter 14* for more information.

2. Investigate peace and/or social justice organizations on your campus. What is the mission of the organization? How many student and/or faculty members? What activities does the organization sponsor? For more information about SPAN, *visit Study Site Chapter 14.*

On your own. Log on to *Study Site—Community and Policy Guide* for more information about the social problems, social policies, and community responses discussed in this chapter.

References

Ahern, B. 2003. "In Search of Peace: The Fate and Legacy of the Good Friday Agreement." *Harvard International Review,* Winter, pp. 26–31.

Ali, M. and I. Shah. 2000. "Sanctions and Childhood Mortality in Iraq." *The Lancet* 355(9218):1851–1857.

Ayubi, S., R. E. Bissell, N. Korsah, and L. Lerner. 1982. *Economic Sanctions in U.S. Foreign Policy.* Philadelphia: Foreign Policy Research Institute.

Betts, R. 2001. "Intelligence Test." Pp. 145–162 in *How Did This Happen? Terrorism and the New War,* edited by J. Hoge, Jr., and G. Rose. New York: Public Affairs.

Blair, T. 2001. Speech to the Labour Party Conference, October 2001. Retrieved November 3, 2003 (http://politics .guardian.co.uk/labour2001/story/0,1414,562006,00.htm).

Booth, K. and T. Dunne. 2002. *Worlds in Collision: Terror and the Future of Global Order.* New York: Palgrave Macmillian.

Bush, G. W. 2001. Statement by the President in His Address to the Nation. September 11, 2001. Retrieved September 17, 2003 (www.whitehouse.gov/news/releases/2001/09/20010911–16.html).

Central Asia Institute. 2003. "When Is a Book More Powerful Than a Bomb?" (Press Release, July). Retrieved November 9, 2003 (www.ikat.org/pressrelease.html).

Center for Defense Information. 2003. "The World's Nuclear Arsenals." Retrieved August 17, 2003 (www.cdi .org/issues/nukef&f/database/nukearsenals.cfm).

Centers for Disease Control. 2003a. "Anthrax: What You Need to Know." Retrieved August 13, 2003 (www.bt.cdc .gov/agent/anthrax/needtoknow.asp).

———. 2003b. *Veterans' Health Activities.* Retrieved August 15, 2003 (www.cdc.gov/nceh/veterans/vet_hlth_ actvy.pdf).

Chatfield, C. 1992. *The American Peace Movement.* New York: Twayne.

Clinton, W. J. 1998. Remarks to the 53rd United Nations Assembly, New York, September 21, 1998. Retrieved August 15, 2003 (www.un.int/usa/98_154.htm).

Cole, D. 2003. "Let's Fight Terrorism, Not the Constitution." Pp. 35–42 in *Rights vs. Public Safety after 9/11: America in the Age of terrorism,* edited by A. Etizioni and J. Marsh. Landham, MD: Rowan & Littlefield.

Cole, D. and J. Dempsey. 2002. *Terrorism and the Constitution.* New York: The New Press.

Crenshaw, M. 1983. "Introduction: Reflections on the Effects of Terrorism" Pp. 1–37 in *Terrorism, Legitimacy, and Power,* edited by M. Crenshaw. Middletown, CT: Wesleyan University Press.

———. 1998. "The Logic of Terrorism: Terrorist Behavior as a Product of Strategic Choice." Pp. 7–24 in *Origins of Terrorism: Psychologies, Ideologies, States of Mind,* edited by W. Reich. Washington, DC: Woodrow Wilson International Center for Scholars and Cambridge University Press.

Crenshaw, M. 1995. *Terrorism in Context.* University Park: Pennsylvania State University Press.

Cuomo, C. 1996. "War Is Not Just an Event: Reflections on the Significance of Everyday Violence." *Hypatia* 11(4):30–45.

Doyle, R. 2001. "The American Terrorist: A Pinch of Politics, a Pound of Hate." *Scientific American* 284(6):28.

Easterbrook, G. 2001. "The All Too Friendly Skies: Security as an Afterthought." Pp. 163–182 in *How Did This Happen? Terrorism and the New War,* edited by J. Hoge, Jr., and G. Rose. New York: Public Affairs.

Egan, T. 2004."Sensing the Eyes of Big Brother, and Pushing Back." *The New York Times,* August 8, 2004, p. 16.

Eisenhower, D. 1953. Speech to the American Society of Newspaper Editors, April 16, 1953, Washington, DC. Retrieved August 14, 2003 (http://www.eisenhower.utexas.edu/chance.htm).

Enloe, C. 1990. *Bananas, Beaches, and Bases: Making Feminist Sense of International Politics.* Berkeley: University of California Press.

"The Events of 11 September (2001) and Beyond." 2002. *International Feminist Journal of Politics* 4(1):95–113.

FBI Counterterrorism Unit, Counterterrorism Threat Assessment and Warning Unit. 1999. *Terrorism in the United States: 1999.* Washington, DC: U.S. Department of Justice, Federal Bureau of Investigation.

Featherstone, L. 2003. "Students Wrestle with War." *Nation* 273(20):18–20.

Fedarko, K. 2003. "He Fights Terror with Books." *Parade,* April 6, pp. 4–6.

Flores, D. A. 1981. "Note: Export Controls and the US Effort to Combat International Terrorism." *Law and Policy in International Business* 13(2):521–590.

Flynn, S. 2001. "The Unguarded Homeland: A Study in Benign Neglect." Pp. 183–198 in *How Did This Happen? Terrorism and the New War,* edited by J. Hoge, Jr., and G. Rose. New York: Public Affairs.

Freeh, L. 2001. "Threat of Terrorism to the United States." Testimony before the U.S. Senate Committees on Appropriations, Armed Services, and Select Committee on Intelligence, May 10, 2001. Retrieved August 14, 2003 (http://www.fbi.gov/congress/congress01/freeh051001.htm).

Fussell, P. 1999. "The Culture of War." Pp. 417–425 in *The Costs of War: America's Pyrrhic Victories,* edited by J. Denzin. New Brunswick, NJ: Transaction.

Garfield, R. 2002. "Economic Sanctions, Humanitarianism, and Conflict after the Cold War." *Social Justice* 29(3):94–107.

Gibbs, J. 1989. "Conceptualization of Terrorism." *American Sociological Review* 54:329–340.

Haas, R. 1997. "Sanctioning Madness." *Foreign Affairs,* November/December, pp. 74–85.

Hamilton, K. 2003. "Activists for the New Millenium." *Black Issues in Higher Education* 20(5):16–21.

Harmon, C. 2000. *Terrorism Today.* London: Frank Cass.

Harvard Study Team. 1991. "The Effect of the Gulf Crisis on the Children of Iraq." *The New England Journal of Medicine* 325(13):977–980.

Hoge, J. F. and G. Rose. 2001. "Introduction." Pp. ix–xiv in *How Did This Happen? Terrorism and the New War,* edited by J. Hoge and G. Rose. New York: Public Affairs.

Higonnet, M. R., J. Jensen, S. Michel, and C. Weitz. 1987. *Behind the Lines: Gender and the Two World Wars.* New Haven, CT: Yale University Press.

Jansen, S. C. 2002. "Media in Crisis: Gender and Terror, September 2001." *Feminist Media Studies* 2(1):139–41.

Jenkins, B. 1980. *The Study of Terrorism: Definitional Problems* (P-6563). Santa Monica: CA: RAND Corporation.

———. 1988. "Future Trends in International Terrorism." Pp. 246–266 in *Current Perspectives on International Terrorism,* edited by R. Slater and M. Stohl. New York: St. Martin's Press.

Kaplan, L. D. 1994. "Women as Caretaker: An Archetype That Supports Patriarchal Militarism." *Hypatia* 9(2): 123–133.

Knickerbocker, B. 2002. "Return of the Military-Industrial Complex?" *Christian Science Monitor* 94(52):2.

Knott, P. 1971. *Student Activism.* Dubuque, IA: William C. Brown.

Lorber, J. 2002. "Heroes, Warriors, and Burquas: A Feminist Sociologist's Reflections on September 11." *Sociological Forum* 17(3):377–396.

Mandelbaum, M. 2003. "Diplomacy in War Time." Pp. 255–268 in *How Did This Happen? Terrorism and the New War,* edited by J. Hoge and G. Rose. New York: Public Affairs.

Marks, S. 1999. "Economic Sanctions as Human Rights Violations: Reconciling Political and Public Health Imperatives." *American Journal of Public Health* 89(10):1509–1513.

Mount, M. 2003. "Pentagon Estimates Cost of War: $20 Billion and Running." Retrieved August 13, 2003 (www.cnn.com/2003/US/04/16/sprj.irq.war.cost).

National Center for PTSD. 2003a. "Epidemiological Facts about PTSD." Retrieved August 15, 2003 (www.ncptsd .org/facts/general/fs_epidemiological.html).

National Center for PTSD. 2003b. "What Is Posttraumatic Stress Disorder?" Retrieved August 15, 2003 (www.ncptsd.org/facts/general/fs_what_is_ptsd.html).

Neier, A. 1993. "Watching Rights." *Nation* 257(19):683.

Office of Homeland Security. 2002. "Homeland Security Presidential Directive-3." Retrieved August 9, 2003 (www.whitehouse.gov/news/releases/2002/03/spring/20020312-5html).

Perkins, B., T. Popovic, and K. Yeskey. 2002. "Public Health at a Time of Bioterrorism." *Emerging Infectious Diseases* (serial online) 8(10). Retrieved August 13, 2003 (www.cdc.gov/ncidod/EID/v018n010/02-0444.htm).

Pillar, P. 2001. *Terrorism and U.S. Foreign Policy.* Washington, DC: Brookings Institution Press.

Reich, W. 1998. "Understanding Terrorist Behavior: The Limits and Opportunities of Psychological Inquiry." Pp. 261–280 in *Origins of Terrorism: Psychologies, Ideologies, States of Mind,* edited by W. Reich. Cambridge, MA: Woodrow Wilson International Center for Scholars and Cambridge University Press.

Rhoads, H. 1991. "Activism Revives on Campus." *The Progressive* 55(3):15–17.

Sanger, D. 2003. "N. Korea Says It Has Material for Nukes." *The News Tribune.* July 15, pp. A1–A9.

Smith, Brent. 1994. *Terrorism in America: Pipe Bombs and Pipe Dreams.* New York: State University of New York Press.

Southern Poverty Law Center. 2004. "Active Hate Groups in 2003." Retrieved July 5, 2004 (www.splcenter .org/intel/map/hate.jsp).

Tickner, J. A. 2002. "Feminist Perspectives on 9/11." *International Studies Perspectives* 3:333–350.

U.S. Commission on National Security in the 21st Century. 2000. *Seeking a National Strategy: A Concept for Preserving Security and Promoting Freedom.* Retrieved August 17, 2003 (www.nssg.gov/PhaseII.pdf).

———. 2001. "Road Map for National Security: Imperative for Change." Retrieved August 17, 2003 (www.nssg .gov/PhaseIIIFR.pdf).

U.S. Department of Defense. 2003a. "Fiscal 2004 Department of Defense Budget Release, February 3, 2003." Retrieved August 15, 2003 (www.defenselink.mil/news/Feb2003/b0232003_bt044–03.html).

———. 2003b. "U.S. Military Personnel Serving and Casualties." Retrieved August 13, 2003 (http://web1 .whs.osd.mil/mmid/casualty/castop.htm).

U.S. Department of State. 2003. "Diplomacy: The State Department at Work." Retrieved October 31, 2003 (www.state.gov/r/pa/ei/rls/dos/4078.htm).

———. 2004. "Foreign Terrorist Organizations: Fact Sheet." Retrieved July 5, 2004 (www.state.gov/s/ ct/rls/fs/2003/12389.htm).

Vellela, T. 1988. *New Voices: Student Activism in the 80's and 90's.* Boston: South End Press.

Walter, E. V. 1964. "Violence and the Process of Terror." *American Sociological Review* 29(2):248–257.

Wardlaw, G. 1988. "State Response to International Terrorism." Pp. 206–245 in *Current Perspectives on International Terrorism,* edited by R. Slater and M. Stohl. New York: St. Martin's Press.

Whittaker, D. 2002. *Terrorism: Understanding the Global Threat.* London: Longman.

Wilkinson, P. 1993. "The Orange and the Green: Extremism in Northern Ireland." Pp. 105–123 in *Terrorism, Legitimacy and Power,* edited by M. Crenshaw. Middleton, CT: Wesleyan University Press.

Young, N. 1999. "Peace Movements in History." Pp. 228–236 in *Approaches to Peace,* edited by D. Barash. New York: Oxford University Press.

15

Social Problems and Social Action

❖

In our first chapter, I introduced you to three connections that would be made throughout this text. The first was the connection between sociology and social problems. We began with two concepts offered by C. Wright Mills: personal troubles and public issues. Mills explained that personal troubles transform into public issues when we recognize that troubles exist not because of individual characteristics or traits but because of social forces. This book has not focused on "nuts, sluts, and perverts" (Liazos 1972) as the source of our social problems. Rather, using our sociological imagination, we've examined how social forces shape social problems in U.S. society. We have relied on four sociological perspectives—functionalist, conflict, feminist, and interactionist—to guide us through each chapter. Each perspective provides a unique look at social problems and, as a consequence, offers suggestions about how we may solve them.

According to a functionalist, all society's needs are met by its social institutions (family, education, politics, religion, and economics). Working interdependently, these institutions ensure social order. When society experiences significant social change (e.g., Industrial Revolution, war), the social order is particularly susceptible to social problems (e.g., crime, poverty, or violence). Social problems do not emerge from individuals; rather problems emerge when the order is disrupted or tested. Functionalist solutions focus on restoring the social order, repairing the broken institutions, and avoiding dramatic social change.

Like the functionalists, conflict and feminist theorists examine social problems at the macro or societal level. For conflict theorists, social problems are the result of social, economic, or political inequalities inherent in our society. Feminist perspectives consider how gender inequalities lead to social problems. Whereas functionalists assume that order is normal for society, the conflict and feminist theorists argue that conflict over resources and power is the status quo. From this perspective, how does one eliminate social problems? The existing social order needs to be replaced with a more equitable society. Midrange solutions attempt to redefine opportunity and power structures to include the participation of marginalized individuals or groups.

The interactionist perspective focuses on social problems at the micro or individual level. According to this perspective, we create our reality through social interaction. Social problems are created by the labels we attach to individuals and their situation (e.g., the "welfare mom" or a "crack addict"). Problematic behavior is also learned from others; interactionists believe that criminal behavior is learned from other criminals. Social problems are not objective realities. Rather, they are subjectively constructed by religious, political, and social leaders who influence our opinions and conceptions of what is a social problem. This perspective leads us to many different solutions: changing the labeling process (being careful of who is being labeled and what the label is), resocialization for deviant or inappropriate behavior (if the behavior was learned, it can be unlearned), and recognizing the social construction of social problems (acknowledging that it is a subjective process).

❖ PUTTING IT TOGETHER: Throughout this text, you have been introduced to four sociological perspectives. Now that we are at the end, which sociological perspective do you agree with most? Which perspective best explains the reasons and solutions for social problems?

Social Problems and Their Solutions

Since its inception, sociology has been considered a means to understand and improve what is wrong with the world. Early sociological thinking emerged out of the late 18th and early 19th centuries during periods of dramatic social, economic, and political change, such as the Industrial Revolution, the French Revolution, and the Enlightenment period. The first sociological thinkers, Karl Marx, Emile Durkheim, and Max Weber, were preoccupied with these social changes and the problems they created for society. They spent their lives studying these problems and attempted to develop programs that would help solve them (Ritzer 2000).

Sociology provides us with the means to examine the social structure or "machinery" that runs our lives. In his book, *Invitation to Sociology,* sociologist Peter Berger (1963) likens our human experience to that of puppets on a stage:

> We located ourselves in society and thus recognize our own position as we hang from subtle strings. For a moment we see ourselves as puppets. . . . Unlike the puppets, we have the possibility of stopping in our movements, looking up and perceiving the machinery by which we have been moved. In this act lies the first step towards freedom. (P. 176)

Freedom comes first in identifying the social "machinery" that controls us and, second, in recognizing that the way society controls individuals is fundamentally different from the strings that control puppets. We have the power to transform or alter that machinery; we have the power to create social change.

The past 14 chapters reveal how we continue to experience many social problems—and, imagine, not every social problem could be addressed in the pages of this text. Yet, over the past decade, there is strong evidence to suggest that problems such as crime, drug abuse, and poverty have been minimized due to effective social policies and solutions. We tend to think of the government as the only effective agent of social change because it is the politicians who pass new laws and policies. But the government is not the only agent of social change. In each chapter, I introduced you to individuals, groups, and communities that have attempted to address a particular social problem. Each in their own way is making the second connection, the one between social problems and their solutions.

Our nation's history is filled with groups of people who attempt to promote or prevent change from taking place (Harper and Leicht 2002). **Social movements** are defined as conscious, collective, organized attempts to bring about or resist large-scale change in the social order (Wilson 1973). In today's society, almost every critical public issue leads to a social movement supporting change (and an opposing countermovement to discourage it) (Meyer and Staggenbord 1996). Social movements are the most potent forces of social change in our society (Sztompka 1994). Social movements lead the way for social reform and policies by first identifying and calling attention to social problems.

Understanding Social Movements

Social movements are classified by two factors. First, what is the scope of the intended change: Is it a group of people or entire society? And second, how much change is intended by the social movement: Is it limited or radical change? Based on these factors, sociologists Charles Harper and Kevin Leicht (2000) distinguish between two types of social movements in their book, *Exploring Social Change: America and the World*. The first distinction is between reform and revolutionary movements. According to Harper and Leicht, **reform movements** try to bring about limited social change by working within the existing system, usually targeting social structures such as education or medicine and directly targeting policymakers. Examples of reform movements are pro- or anti-abortion groups. On the other hand, **revolutionary social movements** seek fundamental changes of the system itself. These types of social movements, such as the U.S. civil rights movement or the anti-apartheid movement in South Africa, consider the political system the key to system change.

The second dimension of social movements identified by Harper and Leicht (2002) is instrumental versus expressive. **Instrumental movements** seek to change the structure of society; examples are the civil rights movement and the environmental movement. **Expressive movements** attempt to change individuals and individual behavior. Based on these dimensions, John Wilson (1973) specified four types of social movements: reformative, transformative, alternative, and redemptive (see Figure 15.1).

❖ **Table 15.1** Types of Social Movements

	Instrumental	Expressive
Reform	Reformative: Partial change within the social structure via policy reform Examples: labor movement, NAACP, antiabortion	Alternative: Partial change in individuals via individual reform Examples: Christian evangelicalism, temperance movement
Revolutionary	Transformative: Total change of the social structure Examples: Bolsheviks, Islamic fundamentalism	Redemptive: Total change in the individuals Examples: millenarian movements, cults, the People's Temple

Source: Adapted from Wilson (1973) and Harper and Leicht (2002).

New social movements theory emphasizes the distinctive features of recent social movements. New social movements first appeared in cultural and radical feminist movements in the late 1960s, in some radical sections of the environmental movement in the 1970s, in parts of the peace movement of the late 1970s through the mid 1980s, and in radical sections of the gay rights movement since the 1980s (Plotke 1995).

Hannigan (1991) and Plotke (1995) distinguish between new social movements and early social movements. First, new movements have different ideologies than earlier movements. Instead of fighting for human rights, such as voting or freedom of speech, new movements are framed around concerns about cultural and community rights, such as the right to be different, to choose one's lifestyle, and to be protected from particular risks like nuclear or environmental hazards (Hannigan 1991). Second, new social movements are distrustful of formal organizations. Consequently, they tend to be small-scale, informal organizations. Finally, whereas previous movements were identified with the economic oppression of workers or minorities, new social movements are associated with a new middle class of "younger, social and cultural specialists" (Plotke 1995). Instead of acting on behalf of their own interests, this new middle class acts on behalf of groups who cannot act on their own (Plotke 1995).

How Do Social Movements Begin?

Social scientists offer several explanations of how social movements emerge. Individual explanations focus on the psychological dispositions or motivations of those drawn to social movements. Women and men are depicted as either frustrated or calculating actors in political or social movements. Empirical studies have

❖ FOCUS ON: THE GAY RIGHTS MOVEMENT

Many attribute the modern gay rights movement to an incident that occurred at the Stonewall Inn in 1969. For decades, police would routinely harass patrons at this New York City gay bar. Individuals were occasionally arrested for "degenerate disorderly conduct," which included same-sex dancing. However, on June 27, during a routine police raid, gay patrons fought back. Police gained control of the unruly crowd a day later, and 13 persons were arrested, but the event served to galvanize the gay community. According to Silver (1997), "Stonewall helped many realize that they could fight back, and sometimes they could even win" (p. 31).

At the time of the Stonewall riot, there were 50 gay and lesbian organizations world-wide; by 1973, there were 800; by 1989, more than 3,000 (Barron 1989). The first legal successes of the lesbian and gay movement began in the 1970s. One of the earliest occurred in December 1973, when the American Psychiatric Association Board of Trustees voted 13–0 to remove homosexuality from its list of mental illnesses. That same year, the American Bar Association adopted a resolution urging states to repeal all anti-gay sex laws. Lesbian and gay activists also won passage of the first laws protecting lesbian and gay citizens from discrimination. In 1982, Wisconsin was the first state to pass an antidiscrimination law (Silver 1997).

It wasn't until the 1980s that the presence of lesbian and gay activists in mainstream politics increased at the national level. The focus on Washington, D.C., increased during the 12-year Republican administration (Presidents Ronald Reagan and George H. W. Bush), which advocates felt could threaten any gains made up to that point. The AIDS epidemic also drew more gays and lesbians to consider the importance of federal intervention on gay-related issues. Gay activists directed their energies to multiple fronts: legal challenges through courts, the lobbying of legislators and officials, promotion of gay and lesbian electoral candidates, and participation in partisan networks (Rayside 1998).

According to Hans Johnson (2000), local activists have played an important role in the gay rights movement.

> Even as gay politics at the national level become more polished and professional, local activists still come up with creative, unpredictable project[s] to promote gay rights. These headline grabbing and sometimes over the top expressions—often involving a lone activist—can pay unexpected dividends and win new allies in the unlikeliest places. (P. 24)

One such activist was Cleve Jones, creator of the Names Project AIDS Memorial Quilt. The moment that inspired Jones to create the quilt happened in November 1985.

> He and a group of protesters marking the seven-year anniversary of the assassination of gay political pioneer Harvey Milk and upset over the federal inaction on AIDS "plaster[ed] a façade" of the San Francisco federal building with "posters inscribed with our dead." As the light drizzle began to fall, Jones surveyed the image, which for him conjured up an enormous quilt that would memorialize those lost to AIDS. (Johnson 2000:25)

Jones, HIV positive himself, was concerned that those with AIDS would die without anyone noticing. The sight of the placards bearing the names of those dead from AIDS reminded him of "a quilt handed down within his family and used to comfort those who were ill or housebound" (Hawkins 1993:757). Jones made the first panel in February 1987, in memory of his best friend, Marvin Feldman. He spray-painted Feldman's name on a 3 by 6-foot white sheet including five stars of David, each one with a pink-red triangle. "When it started, it was very much a cathartic expression of loss and gay community solidarity.

But today, it is really a very important educational tool that reaches across cultures," explains Jones (Johnson 2000:24).

The NAMES Project was officially formed in June 1987. During San Francisco's Lesbian and Gay Freedom Day Parade in 1987, the first 40 quilt panels were displayed. As of October 2003, the AIDS Memorial Quilt included more than 45,000 panels, the equivalent of 47 football fields. It is estimated that more than $3 million has been raised as a result of the NAMES project, money that supports direct services for people with AIDS. Go to www.aidsquilt.org for more information about the NAMES project.

not consistently supported these explanations, demonstrating that individual predispositions are insufficient to account for collective action in social movements. In addition, such theories tend to deflect attention from the real causes of discontent and injustice in our social and political structures (Wilson and Orum 1976).

Social movements do not generally arise from a stable social context; rather, they arise out of a changing social order (Lauer 1976). Social movements arise from the structure itself, primarily the result of social and economic deprivation. People aren't acting just because of their suffering. They are likely to act when they experience **relative deprivation**, a perceived gap between what people expect and what they actually get. James Davies (1974) argued that social movements were likely to occur when a long period of economic and social improvement is followed by a period of decline. Relative deprivation theory has been used to explain the development of urban protests among African Americans during the 1960s, which were initiated by middle-class African Americans who perceived social and economic gaps between Black and White Americans (Harper and Leicht 2002). But relative deprivation alone isn't enough to create a social movement.

Neil Smelser (1963) explains that six structural conditions are necessary for the development of collective behaviors and social movements. These conditions operate in an additive fashion. First, particular structures in society are more likely to generate certain kinds of social movements than others. For example, societies with racial divisions are more likely to develop racial movements. Second, people will become dissatisfied with the current structure only if the structure is perceived as oppressive or illegitimate. Third, there must be growth of a generalized belief system. People need to share an ideology, a set of ideas, which defines the sources of the structural problems or strains and the solutions necessary to alleviate them. The civil rights movement was based on the ideology that racism was the source of restricted opportunities for minorities (Harper and Leicht 2002). Fourth, dramatic events sharpen and concretize issues. These events may initiate or exaggerate people's dissatisfaction with the current structure or redefine their beliefs about the sources of the structural problems. Examples of dramatic or precipitating events include the 1968 Watts riots in relation to the Black Power phase of the civil rights movement and the 1979 Three Mile Island nuclear disaster in relation to the anti-nuclear power movement (Harper and Leicht 2002). Fifth, the movement gains momentum with the mobilization of leaders and members for the movement. At this time, the social movement also begins to take the shape of a formal organization. Finally, forces in society (the existing political structure and/or countermovements) respond to the social movement either by accepting or suppressing it. One of the important features of Smelser's theory is his emphasis on the relationship between the social movement and society itself, a powerful force in shaping the development, direction, and ultimately the success of the movement (Harper and Leicht 2002).

According to **resource mobilization theory**, no social movement can succeed without resources. McCarthy and Zald (1977) argue that human and organizational resources must be mobilized to create a social movement. A social movement requires human skills in the form of leadership, talent, and knowledge, as well as an organizational infrastructure to support its work. On the other hand, the **political process** model emphasizes the relationship between a mobilized social movement and a favorable structure of political opportunities. Social movements are political phenomena, attempting to change social policy and political coalitions, in this view. Political structures enhance the likelihood of a successful social movement by being receptive to change or by being more or less vulnerable at different points in time. For example, McAdam (1982) noted that the efforts of the civil rights movement were enhanced by the expansion of the Black vote and the shift of Black voters to the Democratic Party. Without favorable support from the political structure, the civil rights movement might not have succeeded.

❖ PUTTING IT TOGETHER: In your community.

According to Pippa Norris (2002), the Internet has altered traditional modes of communication for social movements by promoting the diffusion of ideas and tactics quickly and efficiently across local, state, and national borders. The Internet serves multiple functions: lobbying elected officials and policy analysts, networking between related associations and organizations, mobilizing organizers and members, and raising funds. Can you think of other functions the Internet may serve in social movements? Are there any dysfunctions in using the Internet?

Social movements gain strength when they develop symbols and a sense of community, which generates strong feelings and helps direct this energy into organized action. People will form a social movement when they develop "a shared understanding of the world and of themselves that legitimate and motivate collective action" (McAdam, McCarthy, and Zald 1996:6). Doug McAdam (1982) explains that resource mobilization must also include **cognitive liberation**. Much like Karl Marx's concept of class consciousness, cognitive liberation begins when members of an aggrieved group begin to consider their situation as unjust. They must recognize the situation they are in. The second part of cognitive liberation is the group's sense that its situation can be changed. Finally, those who considered themselves powerless begin to believe that they can make a difference (Piven and Cloward 1979). Individuals must move through all three stages to become cognitively liberated. They must organize, act on political opportunities, and instigate change; "in the absence of these necessary attributions, oppressive conditions are likely, even in the face of increased resources, to go unchallenged" (McAdam 1982:34).

How Have Reform Movements Made a Difference?

"The interest of many scholars in social movements stems from their belief that movements represent an important force for social change" (McAdam, McCarthy, and Zald 1988:727); yet "the study of the consequences of social movements is one of the most neglected topics in literature" (Giugni 1999:xiv-xv). Early in human history, most social change was the result of chance or trial and error (Mannheim 1940), but in modern history, social movements have been the basic avenues by which social change takes place (Harper and Leicht 2002).

According to Harper and Leicht (2002), the most dramatic social, cultural, economic, and political transformations come from revolutions. Successful revolutions are rare and dramatic events, such as the early revolutions in France (1789), Russia (1917), and China (1949), and also include the political transformations in South America, Eastern Europe, and the former Soviet Union during the 1980s.

The majority of social movements that we're familiar with are reform movements that focus on either broad or narrow social reforms. They produce significant change, but in gradual or piecemeal ways (Harper and Leicht 2002). The most important reform movements in the first half of the 20th century focused on grievances related to social class, such as the labor movements of the early 1900s, which helped ensure safer working conditions, eliminated child labor, and provided substantial increases in wages and benefits. After World War II, a new type of reform movement, which included the civil rights movement, student movement, feminist movement, gay liberation movement, and ethnic/racial movements, addressed inequalities based on social status rather than social class (Harper and Leicht 2002). Successful reform movements generate change in three areas.

1. **Culture.** Reform movements educate people and change beliefs and behaviors. Change can occur in our culture, identity, and everyday life (Taylor and Whittier 1995). By changing the ways individuals live, movements may effect long-term

❖ FOCUS ON: THE SOCIAL CONSTRUCTION OF AN ALCOHOL PROBLEM

In the following, Craig Reinarman (1988:91, 98–100, 104–105) describes how Mothers Against Drunk Driving (MADD) instigated a redefinition of what constituted alcohol abuse and a change in social rules around the drinking of alcohol.

The anti-drunk driving movement did not spring from any rise in the incidence or prevalence of drinking-driving and in accidents thought to be related to it. In fact, the rate of road accidents in the United States remains lower than in most other Western industrial democracies. . . . None of the organizations or leaders of the movement against drinking-driving have even suggested that their efforts were prompted by some sudden rash of drinking-driving accidents. On the contrary, all claim that their work arose from the fact that the injustices attributed to drinking-driving have long been a problem and have never been treated seriously by legislatures and courts. . . . It was not until 1981 that a movement against drunk driving arose and succeeded in putting the issue in the public policy spotlight.

From the beginning MADD billed itself as the "Voice of the Victim," a victim's rights organization concerned with advocating for and counseling bereaved relatives, preparing them for a trying adjudication process in which "the rights are with the defendant" and ostentatiously monitoring courtrooms in the hope of insuring more convictions and stiffer sentencing [of] drinking-drivers. Although the victim remained the focus at local chapters, the strategy of the national organization grew increasingly media oriented. . . . Unlike some other groups such as the Center for Science in the Public Interest, whose strategy was to work against the alcohol industry's massive promotion of drinking in general, MADD focused exclusively on the sins of the drinking driver.

MADD's [founder and leader Candy] Lightner chose an organization's name that ends with "drunk drivers" rather than "driving"

and yields an acronym symbolizing moral anger; MADD members repeatedly rail against the "Killer Drunk"; they complain of the neglect of drinking driving as "America's most frequently committed violent crime" and the "only socially acceptable form of homicide." MADD's organizing strategy is explicitly one of personal vilification, and it assiduously avoids attention to corporate interests and structural sources of alcohol problems in favor of a rhetoric of individual responsibility.

The efforts of Lightner (MADD's founder) and the national MADD led to the explosive growth of the organization. Only a year after it began, the organization had generated income of nearly a half-million dollars and sprouted eleven new chapters in four states. A year later, in 1982, seventy chapters were in operation. By 1985 MADD had over 600,000 members and donors, 360 chapters in all fifty states, and a budget approaching $10 million administered by a full-time professional staff of at least twenty.

Perhaps the most substantive impact of the movement was on law and public policy. Under pressure from MADD, Reagan appointed a Presidential Commission on drunk driving. It recommended legislation to force states to raise the minimum drinking age to 21. . . . In what seemed to be a well-crafted piece of ideological work, the President turned to smile at Candy Lightner, pen in hand, and announced to an assembled press, "The [drunk driving] problem is bigger than the states . . . [so] we have no misgivings about this judicious use of federal power."

Less noticed [but] equally striking was the passage of more than 230 new anti-drunk driving laws at the local level. In virtually every state and city, MADD was acknowledged as the leading force behind the new statutes. All fifty states toughened their laws against drinking and driving between 1981 and 1985, and the number of states requiring mandatory jail sentences for first offenders convicted of DUI doubled in the same period.

Source: Reinarman 1988.

VISUAL ESSAY: THANKS TO STUDENT ACTIVISTS . . . ❖

Student activists have had considerable impact on social movements, past and present. Consider their role in some of the past century's expressive movements, which aim to change individuals and individual behavior in matters both small and large.

Thanks to these 1946 high school students and many others like them, young women are no longer required to wear skirts and hosiery in school and other public places.

Due, in part, to the voices of students after the terrorist attacks of September 11, 2001, many Americans understood that the majority of Muslims and people who look Middle Eastern were not to blame.

Thanks in part to the environmental concerns expressed by students in the 1970s, a majority of Americans now support environmental causes and try to recycle and conserve the earth's resources.

Students have also been major players in instrumental movements meant to change the structure of society, institutions, and organizations. Although some of these movements have not yet achieved all their goals, they have made a noticeable difference in people's lives.

Thanks to the dedication of students like these NAACP members working on a 1942 campaign for the equal treatment of African American teachers in Norfolk, Virginia, the movement for civil rights gathered strength and stayed on the path that led to far-reaching legislation during Lyndon Johnson's presidency.

Amid massive antiwar protests in the late 1960s and early 1970s, students learned how powerful their voices could be, extended the civil rights movement, and helped to end the Vietnam War.

Thanks to students joining protests against the 1999 World Trade Organization meetings in Seattle, we have all become more sensitive to the inequities of globalization.

What other student movements—expressive and instrumental, local or global in scope—do you believe have made a difference? Have you participated in a social movement?

changes in society (Meyer 2000). The women's movement has established a clear record of cultural change. The women's movement not only changed the way women viewed themselves but also altered our language, our schools, the workplace, politics, the military, and the media.

2. **New organizations or institutions.** Movements lead to the creation of new organizations that continue to generate change. Through these new organizations, social movements may influence ongoing and future initiatives by altering the structure of political support, limiting resources to challengers, and changing the values and symbols used by supporters and challengers. Meyer (2000) argues that by changing participants' lives, "movements alter the personnel available for subsequent challenges" (p. 51).

Out of the women's movement, the National Organization for Women (NOW) was created in 1966, along with the Women's Equity Action League (1968), National Women's Political Caucus (1971), National Women's Law Center (1972), and the Feminist Majority Foundation (1987). NOW is the largest organization of feminist activists in the United States, with more than 500,000 members and 550 chapters in all 50 states. The organization continues its advocacy and legislative efforts in guaranteeing equal rights for women, ensuring abortion rights and reproductive freedom, opposing racism, and ending violence against women.

3. **Social policy and legislation.** Successful social policies have been nurtured by partnerships between the government and social movements (Skocpol 2000). Movements generally organize and mobilize themselves around specific policy demands (Meyer 2000), attempting to minimize or eliminate social problems. Public policy can do many things: New laws can be enacted, or old ones may be struck down; social service programs can be created or ended; taxes can be used to discourage bad behaviors (cigarette or alcohol taxes) or encourage other behaviors (tax breaks to build enterprise zones) (Loseke 2003).

For reform movements, the relationship between desired and actual change varies (Lauer 1976). So far, the women's movement has not achieved the passage of the Equal Rights Amendment, first proposed in 1923. As of 2003, 35 out of the necessary 38 states had ratified the ERA. However, the women's movement has made progress in revising laws pertaining to violence against women, creating family-friendly business practices, and enhancing women's roles in the military, clergy, sports, and politics.

Making the Last Connection

It was a Sunday evening, 31 January 1960, when four freshmen at North Carolina Agriculture and Technical College stayed up late talking about ending segregation in the South. They were extraordinarily poorly positioned to effect political or social change on campus, much less in the United States: young, Black, by no means affluent, and generally disconnected from the major centers of power in America. On Monday morning Ezell Blair, Jr., Franklin McCain, Joseph McNeill, and David Richmond dressed in their best clothes to visit the Woolworth's in downtown Greensboro. After buying some school supplies, they sat at the lunch counter and waited for service. They spent the rest of their day there.

The following day twenty seven other Black students joined them and on Wednesday twice as many. By Thursday, a few sympathetic White students from nearby schools had enlisted and, with the lunch counter at Woolworth's filled, a few started a sit-in at another lunch counter down the street. By the end of the week, city officials offered to negotiate a settlement and, on Saturday night, 1,600 students rallied to celebrate this victory. News of the sit-in campaigns spread throughout the South and then elsewhere across the United States, spurring other activists to emulate their efforts. Sit-ins to desegregate lunch counters and restaurants, stores and libraries, and even buses swept the South. A new organization, the Student Non-Violent Coordinating Committee (SNCC) was formed in April 1960. SNCC would become a leading force in the civil rights movement, setting much of the agenda for liberal politics in the United States during the early 1960s, precipitating the passage of the Voting Rights Act of 1965 and politicizing student activists across the United States. (Meyer 2000:33)

❖❖ **PUTTING IT TOGETHER: On the Web.**

To learn more about the Woolworth's Greensboro sit-ins go to *Study Site Chapter 15*, which includes recordings with sit-in participants, along with related stories and photos and links to other civil rights sites.

Yes, solutions to social problems are complex and, as C. Wright Mills advised, require attention to large social forces, such as those advocated by social movements. But social movements don't appear overnight. Social movements begin with individual efforts such as those taken by college students Blair, McCain, McNeill, and Richmond. Grassroots organizations with strong community and local leadership, such as those on the frontline of the modern environmental movement, have also proven effective in addressing social problems. College and university students have always played an important role in addressing social problems. According to longtime social activist Ralph Nader (1972), it is up to students "to prod and to provoke, to research and to act" (p. 23). What can a student accomplish? Nader thinks the answer is quite a lot:

Take the corporate polluter. Sit-ins and marches will not clean up rivers and the air that he fouls. He is too powerful and there are too many like him. Yet the student has unique access to resources that can be effective in confronting the polluter. University and college campuses have the means for detecting the precise nature of the industrial effluent, through chemical and biological research. Through research such as they perform every day in the classroom, students can show the effect of the effluent on an entire watershed, and thus alert the community to real and demonstrable dangers to public health—a far more powerful way to arouse public support for a clean environment than a sit-in. Using the expertise of the campus, students can also demonstrate the technological means available for abating the discharge, and thus meet the polluter's argument that he can do nothing to control his pollution. By drawing on the knowledge of economists, students can counter arguments that an industry will go bankrupt or close down if forced to install pollution controls. Law and political science students can investigate the local, state, or federal regulations that may apply to the case, and publicly challenge the responsible agencies to fulfill their legal duties. (P. 21)

Some may believe that individual efforts don't amount to much, leading only to short-term solutions or effectively helping one person or one family at a time. But according to David Rayside (1998), the impact of any social movement should be measured over the long term. He writes:

> Much of the change [a social movement] provokes depends on the often isolated effort of thousands of individuals and groups, some working inside the political process, others in the workplace, still others convincing friends and family members of the worthiness of their cause. This localized and varied activity creates changes in social and political climates, which then enable particular groups to make more specific inroads into public policy and institutional practice. (P. 390)

❖
_____

Voices in the Community:
Barbara Smith

Barbara Smith (quoted in Bell-Scott 1995:60–61) talks to an interviewer about the changes she's seen as an activist over the course of a lifetime.

I'm kind of a natural activist. It's a tendency or capacity that probably would have found an outlet eventually—but because I came of age in the civil rights era, I had a vehicle for channeling my justifiable anger at the circumstances under which I saw my community living. By the time I was eight I noticed things that were not fair—that mostly Brown people lived in tenements and only White people lived in mansions. I also had an endless list of questions like, Why were there Black people and why were there White people? Why didn't any White people live in our neighborhood? Why were there only White people on television? Why were all of our teachers White [but] all of the children Black? Why, when a White person knocked on our door—though this almost never happened and then it was an insurance salesman or someone like that—was there anxiety in the air that my sister and I would grasp? Why was the tension so strong when my aunt went into a department store to buy stockings? And why did the clerks ignore her? I wanted to know why about all of this.

I began my activism early, and eventually I came to identify as a Black feminist, a lesbian, and a Socialist. I also believe that the Combahee Collective—of which I was a cofounder and which functioned from 1974 to 1981 in Boston—was one of the most significant groups to come out of any movement. The collective had a series of retreats that brought together Black women artists and activists who were committed to feminism and political organizing. We made a conscious effort to look at how systems of oppression were connected to each other. We understood that dealing with race politics didn't mean that you weren't a race woman, and that speaking out about homophobia didn't mean that you didn't want to end poverty.

There are tangible rewards to the activist life. I've seen a lot of change in my lifetime. When I was born into segregation in 1946, most Black people in this country could not vote; those who did or tried to vote did so on the pain of death. And the women in my family could not try on a hat in a southern department store—and that included Washington, D.C. I never bend over a public water fountain without realizing that once this would have been a revolutionary act. I know these things seem small, particularly to young people who have never lived the other way. We still have a long way to go, but I know that it took revolutionary commitment to get to this point.

_____ ❖ ❖

Student action may lead to significant social change. For example, voting drives led by 17- and 18-year-olds produced the 26th Amendment of the U.S. Constitution, granting voting rights to those 18 years of age and older (Nader 1972). The driving force behind the 26th Amendment came from youth who raised questions about the legitimacy of a representative government that asked 18- to 20-year-olds to fight in the Vietnam War but denied them the right to vote on war-related issues (Close Up Foundation 2004). In another example, Norvald Fimreite, a graduate student at the University of Western Ontario, was the first to report unusual levels of mercury residues in fish caught in the Great Lakes (Nader 1972). Tests conducted by Fimreite indicated mercury levels up to 50 times the accepted level. Fimreite's data led to a worldwide alert about the problems of mercury and other chemicals in the fish we eat.

The last connection presented in this text is the connection between social problems and your community. Throughout the country, college students have affirmed their commitment to community service. According to Levine and Cureton (1998), based on data collected in their 1993 undergraduate survey, nearly two thirds of all undergraduates are involved in varied volunteer activities: food and clothing drives, afterschool mentoring, Habitat for Humanity, and election campaigns. High school students are also involved in community service. School districts in every state except Wyoming, North Dakota, and South Dakota require community service.

The AmeriCorp program uses the slogan, "Your World. Your chance to make it better." AmeriCorp volunteers are involved in numerous activities: mentoring youth, assisting with food bank operations, running afterschool programs, and supporting literacy programs—all community based. The program was created in 1993, and since then, more than 250,000 women and men, usually recent college graduates, have served in more than 2,100 nonprofit public agencies and faith-based organizations. Rhonda Schwinabart (2004) from Cumberland, Maryland, was an AmeriCorp volunteer after her college graduation. According to Schwinabart, "The idea of learning about myself and developing new skills while serving the community was very appealing."

❖
Voices in the Community:
Rhonda Schwinabart

Rhonda Schwinabart (2004) was assigned as a program coordinator for K–8 literacy programs in Frostburg, Maryland. Here she shares her AmeriCorp challenges.

My biggest challenge was balancing theory with practicality. I came to AmeriCorps with very idealistic notions of "giving back to my community" and addressing the literacy needs of the community. The reality of dealing with people who held very different opinions about the values of education was an eye-opener for me. I had to look at the issues affecting those communities in a different way—through the community's eyes. It forced me to develop a more understanding and diplomatic approach to the work I was doing, while also helping parents see the many opportunities that are available to those with solid academic backgrounds.

I gained perspective through my service and realized that, although I couldn't expect to single handedly solve such pressing social problems as illiteracy, I could provide needed support to those who asked. While it may sound trite, I learned that I didn't have all the answers.

College taught me a concern for social problems. AmeriCorps taught me the practical skills of community partnership development, conflict resolution, and problem solving needed to address these social problems. I learned that it takes a community to change a community.

If you think there is nothing that you can do to effect change, you've not been paying attention. The first step is to recognize that you can make a difference. You do not have to believe in quick fixes, universal solutions, or changing the entire world in order to solve social problems. You do not have to join a national organization. To begin, you can join other college and university students who have chosen to become personally involved in their local community. Most efforts are small and practical, but as one college student says, "I can't do anything about the theft of nuclear-grade weapons materials in Azerbaijan, but I can clean up the local pond, help tutor a troubled kid, or work at a homeless shelter" (Levine and Cureton 1998:36).

What does it take to start making that connection with your community? The second step is to explore opportunities for service on your campus and your community. Take the chapters in this text or the material presented by your instructor to consider what social problems you are passionate about. Determine what issues you'd like to address and determine what individuals or groups you would like to serve. Even though you may be in your college community for only four or five years, act as if you're there for life: Take an interest in what happens in your community (Hollender and Catling 1996). Whatever your interests are, you can be sure that there are people and programs in your community who share them. And if they don't exist, what would it take to create such a program?

Step 3, do what you enjoy doing. When you know what you like, when you know what you can contribute, you will find the right connection. Whatever your talent, your community program will appreciate your contribution. It could be that you are an excellent writer; if so, you could help out with a program's monthly newsletter, develop an informational brochure, or design the program's Web site. Do you enjoy working with others? Volunteer to work with clients, to answer phones, or to help out at a rally. In addition to providing invaluable service to the program, recognize the experience and skills that you will gain from your efforts.

And the final step? Go out and do it. It doesn't have to last an entire semester or school year, you could just volunteer for a weekend or a day. Change doesn't happen automatically, it begins with individual action. As Paul Rogat Loeb (1994) explains:

> We need to ask what we want in this nation and why; how should we run our economy, meet human needs, protect the Earth, achieve greater justice? Real answers to these questions won't be spearheaded by the President, though he might follow [if] others lead. They have to come from us, as we reach out to listen and learn, engage fellow citizens who aren't currently involved, and spur debate in environments that are habitually silent.

Put your sociological imagination to work to see where change is possible. According to sociologist Charles Lemert (1997):

> Sociology . . . is different for all because each [must] find a way to live in a world that threatens even while it provides. Grace is never cheap. In the end, what remains is that we all have a stake in the world. Like it or not, life is always life together. Social living is the courage to accept what we cannot change in order to do what can be done about the rest. (P. 191)

❖

MAIN POINTS

- In this book, we have reviewed several social problems; the theoretical perspectives that examine them; and the policies, organizations, and individuals that affect them.

- To functionalists, all of society's needs are met by its social institutions, which ensure social order. When there is significant social change, the social order is particularly susceptible to social problems. In this view, social problems stem from the disruption or testing of social order, and solutions focus on restoring the social order, repairing the broken institutions, and avoiding dramatic social change.

- For conflict theorists, social problems are the result of social, economic, or political inequalities inherent in our society. Feminist perspectives specifically consider how gender inequalities lead to social problems. As opposed to functionalists, conflict and feminist theorists argue that conflict over resources and power is the status quo and that the existing social order needs to be replaced with a more equitable society offering more opportunity to marginalized individuals or groups.

- Interactionists focus on social problems at the individual level, contending that we create our own reality through social interaction. Social problems are subjectively constructed by societal leaders who label people and influence our opinions of what is a social problem. Problematic behavior is also learned from others. This perspective leads us to many different solutions: changing the labeling process, resocializing people who exhibit deviant or inappropriate behavior, and recognizing the social construction of social problems.

- Sociology provides us with the means to examine the social structure or "machinery" that runs our lives. Evidence from the past decade suggests that some social problems have been minimized because of effective social policies and solutions. But the government is not the only source of change; individuals, groups, and communities also make the difference.

- Throughout American history, groups have acted to promote change. **Social movements** are conscious, collective, organized attempts to bring about or resist large-scale change in the social order. They are the most potent forces of social change in our society.

- Social movements are classified by two factors: the scope and the depth of change. **Instrumental movements** seek to change the structure of society itself, whereas **expressive movements** attempt to change individuals. And while **reform movements** try to bring about limited social change by working within the existing system, **revolutionary social movements** seek fundamental changes of the system itself.

- **New social movements theory** emphasizes the distinctive features of recent social movements. Instead of fighting for human rights, new movements focus on cultural and community rights. New social movements are also distrustful of formal organizations and thus tend to be small-scale, informal organizations. Also, new social movements are associated with a new middle class that acts on behalf of groups that cannot act on their own.

- People are more likely to act when they experience **relative deprivation**, a perceived gap between what people expect and what they actually get. Relative deprivation, in conjunction with six necessary conditions surrounding social structure, works to produce social movements.

- In **resource mobilization theory**, no social movement can succeed without human and organizational resources. In contrast, the **political process** model presents social movements as political phenomena, attempting to change social policy and political coalitions.

- Social movements gain strength when they develop symbols and a sense of community, which helps direct energy into organized action. Resource mobilization must also include **cognitive liberation**, which begins only when members of an aggrieved group start to consider their situation unjust, to believe the situation can be changed, and to believe they can make a difference.

- Revolutions produce the most dramatic social, cultural, economic, and political transformations. However, most movements center on gradual but significant reforms. Successful reform movements generate change in three areas: culture, new organizations or institutions, and social policy and legislation.

- You also can make a difference by taking four steps. First, recognize that you can make a difference. Second, explore opportunities for service on your campus and in your community. Third, do what you enjoy doing. And finally, go out and do it. Change doesn't happen automatically; it begins with individual action. Put your sociological imagination to work to see where change is possible.

INTERNET AND COMMUNITY EXERCISES

1. Soundout.Org is a program of the Freechild Project. The Freechild Project attempts to build active democracy by involving young people, especially those who have been historically denied participation, in social change. Soundout.Org is a national online resource center, providing resources and community connections for meaningful student involvement through education. Soundout.Org features a state map with information about student groups and community organizations. Go to *Study Site Chapter 15* for more information.

2. The Corporation for National and Community Service is part of the USA Freedom Corps, a White House initiative to "foster a culture of citizenship, service, and responsibility." The organization includes three programs: AmeriCorp, Senior Corps, and Learn and Serve. The Senior Corp includes volunteers over the age of 55 serving local nonprofits and public agencies. Learn and Serve supports service-learning programs, kindergarten through 12th-grade students combining community service with student learning. For more information on local initiatives and volunteer opportunities in your community, go to *Study Site Chapter 15*.

3. If you do nothing else, make sure to show up on election day to support candidates who support your views (Hollender and Catling 1996). Tracking presidential election years, research indicates that electoral participation of Americans under 25 years of age has declined since 1972. In 2000, 42 percent of 18- to 24–year-olds voted, compared to 70 percent of citizens 25 years or older (Levine and Lopez 2002). Rock the Vote is a nonprofit, nonpartisan organization that attempts to mobilize youth to create positive social and political change in their lives and communities (Rock the Vote 2004). The

organization works year round, encouraging youth to become involved in a range of issues: education, economy, environment, violence, and national and personal debt. You may have seen a Rock the Vote Community Street Team register voters at a local concert or event. Go to *Study Site Chapter 15* for more information.

On your own. Log on to *Study Site—Community and Policy Guide* for more information about the social problems, social policies, and community responses discussed in this chapter.

References

Barron, J. 1989. "Homosexuals See Two Decades of Gains, but Fear Setbacks." Pp. 148–150 in *The Gay Rights Movement*, edited by V. Samar. Chicago: Fitzroy Dearborn.

Bell-Scott, P. 1995. "Reflections with a Home Girl: An Interview with Barbara Smith." *MS. Magazine*, January/February, pp. 59–63.

Berger, P. 1963. *Invitation to Sociology.* New York: Doubleday.

Close Up Foundation. 2004. *The 26th Amendment: Pathway to Participation.* Alexandria, VA: Author.

Davies, J. 1974. "The J-curve and Power Struggle Theories of Collective Violence." *American Sociological Review* 87:363–387.

Giugni, M. 1999. "Introduction." Pp. xiii–xxxiii in *How Social Movements Matter*, edited by M. Giugni, D. McAdam, and C. Tilly. Minnesota: University of Minnesota Press.

Hannigan, J. 1991. "Social Movement Theory and the Sociology of Religion: Toward a New Synthesis." *Sociological Analysis* 52(4):311–331.

Harper, Charles and Kevin Leicht. 2002. *Exploring Social Change: America and the World.* Upper Saddle River, NJ: Prentice Hall.

Hawkins, P. 1993. "Naming Names: The Art of Memory and the NAMES Project AIDS Quilt." *Critical Inquiry* 19:752–779.

Hollender, J. and L. Catling. 1996. *How to Make the World a Better Place.* New York: Norton.

Johnson, H. 2000. "Creative Protests." *The Advocate* 811:24–26.

Lauer, R. H. 1976. "Introduction: Social Movements and Social Change: The Interrelationships." Pp. xi–xxviii in *Social Movements and Social Change*, edited by R. Lauer. Carbondale: Southern Illinois University

Lemert, Charles. 1997. *Social Things: An Introduction to the Sociological Life.* Lanham, MD: Rowan & Littlefield.

Levine, A. and J. Cureton. 1998. *When Hope and Fear Collide: A Portrait of Today's College Student.* San Francisco: Jossey-Bass.

Levine, P. and M. Lopez. 2002. *Voter Turnout Has Declined, by Any Measure.* College Park, MD: Center for Information and Research on Civic Learning and Engagement.

Liazos, A. 1972. "Nuts, Sluts, and Perverts: The Sociology of Deviance." *Social Problems* 20:103–120.

Loeb, Paul Rogat. 1994. *Generation at the Crossroads.* New Brunswick, NJ: Rutgers University Press.

Loseke, D. 2003. *Thinking about Social Problems.* New York: Aldine de Gruyter.

Mannheim, K. 1940. *Man and Society in an Age of Reconstruction.* New York: Harcourt Brace.

McAdam, D. 1982. *Political Process and the Development of Black Insurgency.* Chicago, IL: University of Chicago Press.

McAdam, D., J. McCarthy, and M. Zald. 1996. *Comparative Perspectives on Social Movement: Political Opportunities, Mobilizing Structures, and Cultural Framings.* Thousand Oaks, CA: Sage.

McAdam, D., J. McCarthy, and M. Zald. 1988. "Social Movements." Pp. 695–737 in *Handbook of Sociology*, edited by N. Smelser. Newbury Park, CA: Sage.

McCarthy, J. and M. Zald. 1977. "Resource Mobilization and Social Movements: A Partial Theory." *American Journal of Sociology* 82:1212–1241.

Meyer, D. 2000. "Social Movements: Creating Communities of Change." Pp. 33–55 in *Feminist Approaches to Social Movements, Community, and Power, Vol. 1*, edited by R. Teske and M. A. Tetreault. Columbia: University of South Carolina Press.

Meyer, D. and S. Staggenbord. 1996. "Movements, Countermovements, and the Structure of Political Opportunity." *American Journal of Sociology* 101(6):1628–1660.

Nader, R. 1972. *Action for a Change.* New York: Grossman.

Norris, P. 2002. *Democratic Phoenix: Reinventing Political Activism.* New York: Cambridge University Press.

Piven, F. and R. Cloward. 1979. *Poor People's Movements: Why They Succeed, How They Fail.* New York: Vintage Books.

Plotke, D. 1995. "What's So New about New Social Movements?" Pp. 113–136 in *Social Movements: Critique, Concepts, Case-studies,* edited by S. Lyman. New York: New York University Press.

Rayside, D. 1998. *On the Fringe: Gays and Lesbians in Politics.* Ithaca, NY: Cornell University.

Reinarman, Craig. 1988. "The Social Construction of an Alcohol Problem: The Case of Mothers Against Drunk Drivers and Social Control in the 1980s." *Theory and Society* 17:91–120.

Ritzer, G. 2000. *Sociological Theory.* New York: McGraw-Hill.

Rock the Vote. 2004. "About Us." Retrieved February 29, 2004 (www.rockthevote.org/rtv_about.php).

Schwinabart, R. 2004. "Member Stories." Retrieved February 1, 2004 (www.americorps.org/joining/memberstories/member_rhondaswchwinabart.html).

Skocpol, T. 2000. *The Missing Middle.* New York: Norton.

Silver, D. 1997. *The New Civil War: The Lesbian and Gay Struggle for Civil Rights.* New York: Franklin Watts.

Smelser, N. 1963. *Theory of Collective Behavior.* New York: Free Press.

Sztompka, Piotr. 1994. *The Sociology of Social Change.* Cambridge, MA: Blackwell.

Taylor, V. and N. Whittier. 1995. "Analytical Approaches to Social Movement Culture: The Culture of the Women's Movement." Pp. 163–187 in *Social Movements and Culture,* edited by H. Johnson and B. Klandermans. Minneapolis: University of Minnesota Press.

Wilson, J. 1973. *Introduction to Social Movements.* New York: Basic Books.

Wilson, K. and A. Orum. 1976. "Mobilizing People for Collective Political Action." *Journal of Political and Military Sociology* 4:187–202.

Credits

Chapter 2

Figure 2.1. The Diversity Wheel. From Loden, M. and Rosener, J.B., *Workforce America: Managing Employee Diversity as a Vital Resource.* Copyright © 1991. Reprinted with permission of The McGraw-Hill Companies.

Voices in the Community: Sherri Muzher. Reprinted with permission of Media Monitors Network. www.mediamonitors.net.

Chapter 3

Voices in the Community: Bernice R. Sandler. Reprinted with permission from Bernice Resnick Sandler, Senior Scholar, Women's Research and Education Institute, Washington DC. E-mail: sandler@bernicesandler.com; web site: www.bernicesandler.com.

Chapter 4

Taking a World View: The Study of Families in Israel. From Shamgar-Handelman, Lea, "Family Sociology in a Small Academic Community: Family Research and Theory in Israel," in M. Sussman & R. Hanks (eds.) *Intercultural Variation in Family Research and Theory: Implications for Cross-National Studies.* Copyright © 1996. Reprinted with permission of Haworth Press.

Voices in the Community: Megan McGuire. From *Newsweek*, 11/4/96. Newsweek, Inc. All rights reserved. Reprinted by permission.

Chapter 5

Voices in the Community: Alix M. Reprinted with permission. Copyright © Human Rights Watch.

Chapter 6

Voices in the Community: Barbara Ehrenreich. Reprinted from *Nickel and Dimed: On (Not) Getting By In America* by Barbara Ehrenreich, copyright © 2001 by Barbara Ehrenreich. Reprinted by permission of Henry Holt and Company, L.L.C.

Voices in the Community: Judy Wicks. Reprinted from YES! Magazine, PO Box 10818, Bainbridge Island, WA. www.yesmagazine.org.

Chapter 7

Voices in the Community: Nina Agbayani. Reprinted with permission.

Chapter 8

Table 8.1. Twelve Steps for Women Alcoholics. Copyright © 1989 Christian Century. Reprinted with permission from the December 6, 1989 issue of the Christian Century.

Voices in the Community: Jill Ingram. From Glenn, B., "A Crusader against Underage Drinking," in *Driven*, MADD, Fall 2000. Reprinted with permission.

Voices in the Community: Linda Elliott. Reprinted with permission.

Chapter 9

Voices in the Community: Military Families. From Schwartz-Nobel, *Growing Up Empty*. Copyright © 2002 by Loretta Schwartz-Nobel. Reprinted by permission of HarperCollins Publishere, Inc.

Table 9.4. Percentage of African Americans in News Magazine Pictures of the Poor, 1950–1992. From Gilens, M., *Why Americans Hate Welfare*, copyright © 1999. Reprinted with permission of the University of Chicago Press.

Voices in the Community: Richard Saul. Reprinted with permission.

Chapter 10

Voices in the Community: Barbara Parsons Lane. From "Puzzle Pieces" by Barbara Parsons Lane (pp. 239-240) from *Couldn't Keep it to Myself* by Wally Lamb. Copyright © Wally Lamb. Reprinted by permission of HarperCollins Publishers, Inc.

Chapter 11

Voices in the Community: Kimberly Davies. Reprinted with permission of Wiretap.

Taking a World View: Women's Feature Service, New Delhi, India. Reprinted with permission of the Nieman Reports.

Focus On: Media Myth Making—The Story of Private Jessica Lynch. From D. Chinni (2003) *Jessica Lynch: Media Myth-Making in the Iraq War*, downloaded from http://www.journalism.org/resources/research/reports/war/postwar/lynch.asp. Copyright © Project for Excellence in Journalism. Reprinted with permission.

Table 11.4. The 10 Basic Principles of Media Literacy Education. Reprinted with permission of ACME. The Action Coalition for Media Education (ACME) is an independently-funded coalition that champions critical media literacy education, independent media production, and democratic media reform and justice initiatives. Find out more at http://www.acmecoalition.org.

Voices in the Community: Mervyn Wool. Reprinted with permission from *The Beat Within*. *The Beat Within* is a weekly publication of writings and art from incarcerated youth and adults. www.thebeatwithin.org.

Chapter 14

Focus On: The Culture of War. From Fussell, P., "The Culture of War," in J. Denzin (ed) *The Costs of War: America's Pyrrhic Victories*, copyright © 1999. Reprinted with permission of Transaction Publishers.

U.S. Data Map 14.1. Distribution of Known Hate Groups by State. Reprinted with permission of the Southern Poverty Law Center. www.tolerance.org.

Table 14.4 Characteristics of Left-Wing and Right-Wing Terrorist Groups in the United States. Source: Smith 1994.

Voices in the Community: Greg Mortensen. From Fedarko, K. "He Fights Terror with Books," in *Parade*, April 6, 20003. Reprinted with permission from *Parade*, copyright © 2003.

Voices in the Community: Tracy DiMambro. Reprinted with permission.

Chapter 15

Focus On: The Social Construction of an Alcohol Problem. Source: Reinarman 1988. From Reinarman, C., "The Social construction of an alcohol problem: The case of Mothers Against Drunk Drivers and social control in the 1980s," in *Theory and Society, 17,* copyright © 1988. Reprinted with permission of Kluwer Publications.

Voices in the Community: Barbara Smith. Reprinted by permission of Ms. Magazine. © 1995.

Voices in the Community: Rhonda Schwinabart. Reprinted with permission.

Index

Note: Page references to figures, maps, or tables are followed by an "f," "m," or "t," respectively.

About the Author

Anna Leon-Guerrero received her Ph.D. in sociology from the University of California, Los Angeles. She is Associate Professor of Sociology at Pacific Lutheran University and was honored with the university's Faculty Excellence Award. She teaches courses in statistics, social theory, and social problems. Her areas of research and publications include family business, job retention and social welfare policy, and social service program evaluation.